Reading Revolutions

Consiliarij Mei

Reading Revolutions

The Politics of Reading in Early Modern England

KEVIN SHARPE

YALE UNIVERSITY PRESS

NEW HAVEN AND LONDON

For family and friends

Set in Bembo by Best-set Typesetter Ltd, Hong Kong
Printed in Great Britain by Biddles Ltd, Guildford and Kings Lynn

Library of Congress Cataloging-in-Publication Data

Sharpe, Kevin (Kevin M.)
Reading revolutions: the politics of reading in early modern England/Kevin Sharpe.
Includes bibliographical references and index.
ISBN 0-300-08152-9 (alk. paper)
1. Great Britain – Politics and government – 1603–1714. 2. Politics and literature –
Great Britain – History – 17th century. 3. Books and reading – Great Britain –
History – 17th century. 4. Great Britain – History – Puritan Revolution,
1649–1660. 5. Books and reading – Political aspects – Great Britain. I. Title.
DA375, S55 2000   941.06'3 – dc21   99–089405

A catalogue record for this book is available from the British Library.

10 9 8 7 6 5 4 3 2 1

Contents

List of Illustrations

Preface to the Reader

In some ways this book had its origins in chance. In 1993 I was working at the Huntington Library in California on a study of *Representations of Rule: The Culture of Authority in Early Modern England*. While I was there the library purchased a manuscript diary of the 1630s kept by William Drake of Shardeloes, Buckinghamshire, and the archivist, Mary Robertson, with typical generosity and thoughtfulness, offered me first sight of it before I left. Having just published a study of the 1630s, I was intrigued to read what a Buckinghamshire gentleman, from a puritan family, who served in the Long Parliament, felt about that controversial decade. What, however, struck me when I read the manuscript were the numerous references to Drake's own reading, and the role of reading in shaping his experience and perception of those years. I determined to pursue him further on my return to England. The Phillips sale catalogue, from which the Huntington had made its purchase, led me to a series of commonplace books of Sir William Drake, now in the Ogden manuscripts at University College London and listed twenty years ago by Dr Stuart Clark. Thirty-seven of these consisted of reading notes interspersed with personal and political reflections. In addition, there are among the Ogden collection manuscript and printed books annotated in Drake's hand. Further research led me to still more Drake commonplace books, to his parliamentary diary, and to family papers, among them Drake's will.

My interest in the collection and decision to pursue it were not a matter of chance. Nor were they excited simply by my continuing fascination with the origins of the English Civil War. Work on representations of authority had already made me appreciate that the exercise of government in early modern England involved a reciprocity between rulers and ruled; and that I would therefore have to study the reception as well as production and dissemination of the texts of state. For some years now it has been my belief – some colleagues would say a mistaken belief – that many of the most interesting questions about early modern England, and some of the richest approaches to its study, have been asked and advanced by scholars in other disciplines. In particular, in the 1980s I was stimulated by the New Historicism in literary studies to urge a broadening of the texts studied by hist-

orians of politics and to attempt an argument that the literature of love should
be read as a discourse of politics. For an understanding of how to think about
the reception of texts, therefore, I turned to some of the theoretical and critical studies of reader response, and to the recent work on the history of the
book and of reading, where questions of reception are most obviously being
addressed.

It was in this context that the importance of the Drake commonplace
books struck me. On the one hand, theories and questions posed by historians of reading about how readers constitute meaning made me sense the
potential of this material for a better understanding of how ideology performed in the political culture of early modern England. On the other hand,
the survival, unique to date, of so many volumes of reading notes, annotated
printed books and diaries by one man clearly offered an opportunity to reconsider theories and large narratives of reading habits from a detailed case.

The material, it seemed to me, was also relevant to a number of larger
issues. First, over the last twenty years historians of seventeenth-century
England have lined up in revisionist and anti- or post-revisionist camps,
divided by whether the political culture was characterised by 'consensus' or
'conflict'. Yet few who have cited either elite texts or popular ballads to
support one view or the other have investigated how texts were distributed,
read and deployed. Secondly, there has been some concern recently about the
way history itself is written. Some scholars bemoan the fragmentation of the
big picture and call for a return to grand narrative; others applaud the microhistories that explore the texture of a specific event or moment. Lastly, a battle
about theory has begun to be waged in historical journals, with the protagonists of empiricism standing ground against the advocates of theory in, and
theorising of, historical writing. A study in the history of reading may have
something to contribute to each of these debates. It complicates any simple
choice between revisionist and post-revisionist arguments and opens new perspectives on how society and state were perceived. Because reading is an individual experience, its history has in part to be written from case studies, but
those case studies can and should, as it is hoped this does, help to reconstitute a larger picture – not just of reading but of the political culture more
broadly. And, I would suggest, the history of reading demonstrates the fruits
of a marriage between theory and empirical research, indeed the need both
to ask more of the questions theory has posed and to go to the archives to
help answer them.

Most of all, I would argue that this history of reading further demonstrates
how anachronistic and attenuated are the conceptions of politics that still
prevail in the historiography of early modern England. As well as factional
manoeuvres, parliamentary debates or village squabbles, politics involved, at all
levels, negotiations with texts and the processes of interpreting and consti-
tuting meanings from texts. A full history of the politics of the English Renaissance state therefore must address how such texts were produced, disseminated
and received, how they were written and read.

Acknowledgements

This book, like so many, began its life at the Huntington Library in San Marino, California where Mary Robertson kindly introduced me to the diary of Sir William Drake, and where I began to think about the history and politics of reading in one of the most stimulating and delightful communities in the scholarly world. I would especially like to thank Mary Robertson and Martin Ridge, Roy Ritchie and all the staff of the research division, the library and reader services for making my time so productive and enjoyable. Sir William Drake thence led me to University College London, Buckinghamshire Record Office, to the House of Lords and to the Folger Shakespeare Library. I would like to thank the archivist at Aylesbury, and David Prior of the House of Lords Record Office for all their assistance. At the Folger I was able to extend my researches on Drake while participating in a lively seminar on Habits of Reading in Early Modern England. I owe warm thanks to Barbara Mowat, Kathleen Lynch, Letitia Yendle, Marion Payne, Martha Fay and all the Folger staff; and thanks also to Steven Zwicker, the convenor, and to all the participants in the seminar who contributed so much expertise and so many perspectives and insights to the discussions. Most of all, I record warm thanks to Gill Furlong, Susan Stead and Kate Manners, the librarian and staff of the manuscripts room at University College, where I have been a regular visitor for the last five years. Not only were they unfailingly helpful in promptly providing the materials, they also offered guidance to the collection, and a friendly atmosphere in which to try and keep pace with the languages Drake read. The Drake manuscripts are cited with the kind permission of University College London, the Huntington Library, the Folger Library, the House of Lords and Buckinghamshire Record Office. In addition to these archives, I made extensive use of the Bodleian Library and warmly thank all the staff of the upper reading room and Duke Humphrey's who provide kind help and a welcome on my visits each summer. At Southampton, I would like to thank Nick Graffy for whom no request seems too much, and who patiently guided a technophobe into the mysteries of online resources.

The funds needed to work on these dispersed collections were generously provided by the Huntington Library, the Folger Institute, the National

Endowment for the Humanities, the British Academy and the University of Southampton. Even more important than financial support has been the gift of time that allowed me to pursue this book without abandoning my work on images of authority in early modern England. For that I have to thank a former dean, Professor Peter Ucko, who generously seconded me for a period from undergraduate teaching to concentrate on research and graduate studies and who, more generally, had the vision to promote, one might say create, a research environment at Southampton which encouraged dialogue across disciplinary boundaries.

There are many colleagues and friends, old and new, whose help and advice I would like to acknowledge. Some of my longstanding friends and advisers reacted with incredulity when I announced, shortly after my return from the Huntington Library, that I was going to pursue the history of reading: one even claimed that he thought I had meant the history of his home town. But, whatever their original (or even persistent) scepticism, they generously provided counsel, criticism and encouragement. For all these I would like to thank George Bernard, Glenn Burgess, Peter Lake, John Morrill and Mark Stoyle. Among literary scholars I have greatly benefited from discussions with Sharon Achinstein, Tom Corns, David Norbrook, Annabel Patterson, Joad Raymond, Jonathan Sawday, Nigel Smith and, as always, Greg Walker.

My interest in the subject of reading was, of course, stimulated by the work on the history of the book, and I would like to thank Tony Grafton for illuminating discussion and Robert Darnton for advice and encouragement. I was fortunate in 1992–3 at the Huntington to have the company of two young scholars, Bill Sherman and Heidi Brayman (now Hackel), whose own work on reading so much excited my interest in this field. Most of all my greatest debt is to Steve Zwicker who not only, typically, welcomed me into a field which he is making his own, but shared his knowledge and insights and generously took time to read the whole book in draft. I am enormously grateful to him for his incisive comments, ready advice and for a myriad of suggestions which have improved this study. I also thank the press readers for all their helpful suggestions.

Though during the preparation of this book I was led, under protest, to the world of the computer, I am grateful to Claire Parry who saved me from typing it at my usual speed of an hour a page. Once again those who ensured that a typescript turned into a book were my agent and my publisher, who have also become friends. I thank Peter Robinson of Curtis Brown for all his continued support of an author who seems at times determined not to write a book that makes money, and Robert Baldock who remained, as ever, enthusiastic about an unusual project which has delayed another book I promised to write. At Yale University Press I would also like to thank Candida Brazil for all her careful attention and assistance with the process of publication.

Writing *Reading Revolutions* has given me a heightened sense of the power of readers and the devices used by authors to try and win the reader's con-currence and approval. I must, therefore, close with my warm gratitude to all the readers (especially purchasers) of this book, who, in various different ways I am sure, will manifest the reader's freedom of interpretation and judgement.

List of Abbreviations

Amer. Hist. Rev.	*American Historical Review*
Austral. J. French Studies	*Australian Journal of French Studies*
BL	British Library
Bodleian Lib. Record	*Bodleian Library Record*
Bucks R.O.	Buckinghamshire Record Office
Bull. Inst. Hist. Res.	Bulletin of the Institute of Historical Research
Bull. John Rylands Lib.	Bulletin of the John Rylands Library
C.J.	*Commons Journals*
Cal. S. P. Dom.	*Calendar of State Papers Domestic*
Cal. S. P. Venet.	*Calendar of State Papers Venetian*
Camden Soc.	Camden Society
Clarendon MS	Clarendon MSS Bodleian Library
DNB	*Dictionary of National Biography*
Eng. Lang. Notes	*English Language Notes*
Eng. Lit. Ren.	*English Literary Renaissance*
Europ. Studies Rev.	*European Studies Review*
Folger MS	Folger Shakespeare Library MS v.a 263
Harvard Lib. Bull	*Harvard Library Bulletin*
H. Lords MS 49	House of Lords Record Office, Historical Collections MS 49
Hist. MSS Comm.	*Historical Manuscripts Commission*
Hunt Lib. Quart.	*Huntington Library Quarterly*
Hunt MS	Huntington Library MS HM 55603
H. Lords MS	House of Lords Manuscript
J. Brit. Studies	*Journal of British Studies*
J. Chester Arch. Soc.	*Journal of Chester Archaeological Society*
J. Early Mod. Hist.	*Journal of Early Modern History*
J. Eng. & Germ. Philol.	*Journal of English and Germanic Philology*
J. Eng. Studies	*Journal of English Studies*
J. Hist. Ideas	*Journal of the History of Ideas*
J. Hist. Philos.	*Journal of the History of Philosopy*
J. Inst. Romance Studies	*Journal of the Institute of Romance Studies*
J. Lib. Hist.	*Journal of Library History*
J. Med. & Ren. Studies	*Journal of Medieval and Renaissance Studies*
J. Mod. Hist.	*Journal of Modern History*
L.J.	*Lords Journals*
Mod. Lang. Rev.	*Modern Language Review*
OED	*Oxford English Dictionary*
Ogden MSS	Ogden MSS, University College, London
Parl. Hist.	*Parliamentary History*

Philol. Quart.	*Philological Quarterly*
Philos. Quart.	*Philosophical Quarterly*
Proc. Amer. Philos. Soc.	*Proceedings of the American Philosophical Society*
Pub. Hist.	*Publishing History*
Ren. Forum	*Renaissance Forum*
Ren. Quart.	*Renaissance Quarterly*
Ren. Studies	*Renaissance Studies*
R.O.	Record Office
Scottish Hist. Soc.	*Scottish History Society*
Social Hist.	*Social History*
Times Lit. Supp.	*Times Literary Supplement*
Trans. Bibliog. Soc.	*Transactions of the Bibliographical Society*
Trans. Camb. Bibliog. Soc.	*Transactions of the Cambridge Bibliographical Society*
V. C. H.	*Victoria County History*

Part One
LEARNING TO READ

I

Reading in Early Modern England

Returning to the Renaissance

The study of early modern England has, ever since Clarendon wrote his famous *History of the Rebellion*, produced some of the finest work of historical scholarship. Debates about the rise of the gentry, the crisis of the aristocracy, puritanism and its role in revolution have drawn audiences from outside their narrow fields of specialisms, and even attracted general readers to a lively interest in our sixteenth- and seventeenth-century past. Christopher Hill, Lawrence Stone, Keith Thomas, to cite but three, are names known to all historians, and to most readers of history, or of literary magazines and review pages.[1] Over the last twenty years the historiographical debates about seventeenth-century England, and in particular about the causes of the Civil War, have been even more heated and lively than before. The so-called revisionists of the 1970s questioned nearly all the received wisdom about the period and, even more daringly, challenged the most reputed scholars. Not only did they overturn the traditional narrative of an escalating constitutional crisis, a struggle for liberty and property against absolute monarchy; the revisionists also exposed problems in the methods and sources deployed to write the traditional narrative. Revisionist history denounced teleology and urged the close study of archives – manuscript parliamentary diaries and local records rather than the familiar printed speeches, pamphlets and collections.[2]

1. C. Hill, *Puritanism and Revolution* (1965), L. Stone, *The Crisis of the Aristocracy* (Oxford, 1965) and K. Thomas, *Religion and the Decline of Magic* (1971) are three of the most influential books on early modern England. Hill and Stone have written influential surveys of the period, Hill's and Thomas's books are published as Penguin paperbacks, and all are cited frequently by literary scholars and sociologists as well as historians in other fields.
2. See K. Sharpe, ed., *Faction and Parliament* (Oxford, 1978); C. Russell, *Parliaments and English Politics 1621–1629* (Oxford, 1979); J. C. D. Clark, *Revolution and Rebellion: State and Society in England in the Seventeenth and Eighteenth Centuries* (Cambridge, 1986); G. Burgess, 'Revisionism: An Analysis of Early Stuart Historiography in the 1970s and 1980s', *Hist. J.* 33, (1990), pp. 609–27; A. Maclachlan, *The Rise and Fall of Revolutionary England* (Basingstoke, 1996).

Predictably, revisionism provoked noisy debate and sharp controversy. The old guard, led by Lawrence Stone and Christopher Hill, reiterated the familiar interpretation and denounced their critics as 'narrow antiquarian empiricists' who threatened to fragment the story of English history and to rob history itself of all meaning.[3] Later, a younger generation of critics raised more powerful and interesting objections to the revisionists' conclusions and approaches: they questioned the revisionist emphasis on consensus in seventeenth-century political culture; they decried the marginalisation in revisionist scholarship of issues of ideology; and they pointed up the problems involved in the revisionist obsession with manuscripts and their distrust of the printed documents that circulated in a broader public sphere. Acknowledging and accepting the revisionists' critique of teleology, and imitating their methods – the close study of specific historical moments – the anti- or post-revisionists (the latter is a better term) rejected the revisionists' picture of contending factions in a world of shared values and urged a more nuanced address to conflict – religious and political – and to the relationships of conflicts of values to civil war and revolution.[4]

It is not my purpose here to rehearse and review the debates over revisionism,[5] but rather to draw brief attention to the specific questions those debates have not pursued, and to the broader approaches to history they have discouraged and occluded. To begin with those pertinent to the seventeenth century itself: neither the revisionists nor their critics have discussed what 'ideology' or 'conflict' meant to the men and women of early modern England; how a language of difference related to division; or indeed how values were constituted, validated, appropriated – and contested.[6] To observe that is, I fear, to come close to saying that neither revisionists nor post-revisionists have really understood the nature of early modern politics. Indeed they may – ironically – have committed the sin that it was the revisionist project to expiate: the sin of anachronism. Conrad Russell writes of seventeenth-century ministries and parliaments very much in nineteenth-century terms, and, as has been observed, devotes much of his scholarly attention to the very parliaments whose importance in early modern government he seems to question.[7]

3. L. Stone, 'The Revival of Narrative: Reflections on a New Old History', *Past & Present* 85 (1979), pp. 3–24; C. Hill, 'Parliament and People in Seventeenth-Century England', *Past & Present* 92 (1981), pp. 100–24; C. Hill, *The Century of Revolution, 1603–1714*, 2nd edn (1980), preface.

4. See D. Hirst, 'The Place of Principle', *Past & Present* 92 (1981), pp. 79–99, and most importantly R. Cust and A. Hughes, eds, *Conflict in Early Stuart England* (1989). In methodology Cust and other post-revisionists such as Cogswell and Reeve follow the revisionists. See R. Cust, *The Forced Loan and English Politics 1626–28* (Oxford, 1987); T. Cogswell, *The Blessed Revolution: English Politics and the Coming of War 1621–1624* (Cambridge, 1989); J. Reeve, *Charles I and the Road to Personal Rule* (Cambridge, 1989).

5. See Burgess, 'Revisionism', and Maclachlan, *The Rise and Fall of Revolutionary England*, ch. 6.

6. This lack is especially evident in Cust and Hughes, *Conflict in Early Stuart England*.

7. See C. Russell, *Parliaments and English Politics 1621–1629* (Oxford, 1979); P. Lake, 'Retrospective: Wentworth's Political World in Revisionist and Post-revisionist Perspective',

As his critics have argued, Russell ignores the wider political sphere and community of news, scurrilous pamphlet, squib, ballad and gossip that formed political opinion and shaped political behaviour.[8]

But if post-revisionist social and political historians have valuably drawn attention to those omissions, they have done little to address them. Much recent work on pamphlets, news and ballads has, as I shall argue, too simply read such complex texts as straightforward documents.[9] More seriously, post-revisionist scholarship too has been marked by an attenuated and anachronistic view of politics. As well as disputes about foreign policy, theological wrangles, gentry quarrels or popular squibs against corrupt favourites, the politics of the English Renaissance state was a matter of rhetoric, display and representation. And yet historians, revisionist and post-revisionist alike, fail to analyse the rhetoric of parliamentary speeches and pamphlets and pay scant attention to how power and authority were acquired and demonstrated through display and representation. For all that the incident is well known, historians have never grasped the significance of the fact that George Villiers attracted royal favour by rescuing a dull entertainment by a brilliant display of dancing.[10] He did so because from the monarch down to the JP, even to the constable, authority was won and lost through careful performance on what contemporaries frequently called the stage of the theatre of state. It is ironic that as our own age of the spin doctor and photo opportunity transforms the politics of democratic elections, parliamentary process and party manoeuvre, we as historians continue to impose an earlier, narrower notion of politics on the past. Until historians refigure – in all the word's senses of redrawing, reimagining, of opening study of the trope and the image – texts of politics, an understanding of early modern political culture will continue to elude us.[11] Though we begin to discern the first signs of a new address to these issues, much of the most interesting work has been published not by historians but by scholars from other disciplines who, it is often charged, fall short of those virtues practised by revisionist and post-revisionist historians: the close situating and historicising of texts and events.

in J. F. Merritt, ed., *The Political World of Thomas Wentworth Earl of Strafford, 1621–1641* (Cambridge, 1996), p. 272 and passim; cf. P. Lake, 'The Causes of the English Civil War', *Hunt. Lib. Quart.* 57 (1994), pp. 167–97.

8. Cust and Hughes, *Conflict in Early Stuart England*, pp. 13–15, 18–19; K. Sharpe and P. Lake, eds, *Culture and Politics in Early Stuart England* (Basingstoke, 1994), introduction; see T. Cogswell, 'Underground Verse and the Transformation of Early Stuart Political Culture', in S. D. Amussen and M. A. Kishlansky, eds, *Political Culture and Cultural Politics in Early Modern England* (Manchester, 1995), pp. 277–300; A. Bellany, 'The Poisoning of Legitimacy? Court Scandal, News, Culture and Politics in England in 1603–1660', Ph.D. diss., Princeton University, 1995.

9. Cf. K. Sharpe, 'Political Culture and Cultural Politics in Early Modern England', *J. Early Mod. Hist.* 1 (1998), pp. 344–68. Below, pp. 25–6.

10. R. Lockyer, *Buckingham: The Life and Political Career of George Villiers* (1981), p. 33.

11. Sharpe and Lake, *Culture and Politics*, introduction and passim; cf. K. Sharpe and S. Zwicker, eds, *Refiguring Revolutions: Aesthetics and Politics from the English Revolution to the Romantic Revolution* (Berkeley and London, 1998), introduction.

As well as attenuating the study of early modern politics, the debate prompted by revisionism has also curiously ignored the wider methodological and theoretical issues that underlay several of the exchanges. The revisionist attack on 'teleology', and the charge that revisionists took the 'meaning' out of history passed without any full consideration of the assumptions they expressed about the methodology and philosophy of history.[12] When philosophers of history have examined these debates, their work has been ignored by the participants in them.[13] Revisionists and anti-revisionists have wilfully avoided discussion of hindsight, the nature of historical method or the construction of historical narrative; even those deploying 'empiricist' as a charge have adhered resolutely to the traditional empiricism of the historical discipline.[14] If matters more fundamental than differences about the seventeenth-century divided revisionists and their critics, neither wished to draw attention to them. And while there has been much vague talk about revisionism being the historiographical manifestation of a neoconservatism, neither the politics nor the ideology of revisionist writings has been properly pursued.[15] Talk of a generation disenchanted by Britain's loss of empire not only fails to explain the revisionists of different countries and generations, it provides no substitute for examination of a fascinating scholarly moment and phenomenon.[16]

The lack – or refusal – of self-consciousness among the historians involved in the revisionist controversy extended to their perception as well as their practice of history. Those revisionists for instance who condemned Whig history as teleological paid little attention to the political culture in which it was born, or the later conditions in which it has flourished. In brief, Whig history was the polemical response to a need and a moment: the need to render the violent break with hereditary kingship perpetrated in 1688 as a natural course of events, part of a national English narrative that seamlessly connected past and present. The Whig party and cause triumphed in and after 1688 because, more successfully than the republicans of the 1650s, they established a cultural dominance which helped to secure political hegemony. The representations of William III as the Protestant Hercules, the recruitment of literary champions of the Whig cause, the canonisation of Milton and Marvell were all part of that cultural underpinning of what might have been a short-

12. Cf. Lake, 'Retrospective', p. 264.
13. Historians, for instance, seldom cite the work of W. Dray who has taken the debates over early modern England as the locus for an examination of historical method and philosophy. See W. Dray, 'J. H. Hexter, Neo-Whiggism and Early Stuart Historiography', *History & Theory* 26 (1987), pp. 133–49.
14. Lawrence Stone, for instance, has excoriated New Historicist critics and postmodern theory. See Stone, 'History and Postmodernism', *Past & Present* 131 (1991), pp. 217–18; cf. below, pp. 24–5.
15. D. Cannadine, 'British History: Past, Present and Future?' *Past & Present* 116 (1987), pp. 169–91; cf. J. Raven, 'British History and the Enterprise Culture', *Past & Present* 123 (1989), pp. 178–204; and P. Hutber, ed., *What's Wrong with Britain?* (1978).
16. See K. Sharpe, *Remapping Early Modern England* (Cambridge, 2000), introduction.

lived dynastic coup.[17] And the editions of historical documents and texts – by the Whig historiographer royal Thomas Rymer – constructed a Whig view of the past, enshrined in histories like those of Thomas Petyt, White Kennet, John Oldmixon and Paul Rapin.

Whig history, in other words, was a central component of the Whig political culture that was essential to the Whig ascendancy.[18] No one grasped that better than Macaulay, when he became part of a Whig government returned to power after decades in the wilderness. Macaulay sought to construct a continuous historical narrative of England's progress to parliamentary government and indelibly to associate the English story with the Whig party and cause.[19] He succeeded so well that a Whig view of history became part of the English national identity – and through Macaulay's nephew G. M. Trevelyan, and his *History of the American Revolution*, part of an American identity too.[20] While the polemics and politics of Macaulay's history are familiar to students of the nineteenth century, they have been insufficiently pondered by historians of the seventeenth century. Rather than the narrow vision of politics evident in modern revisionism, Macaulay understood that the political history of seventeenth-century England had to be a history of its political culture broadly considered.[21] And he recognised that the histories written during the first Whig ascendancy, and the *History* he wrote himself, were both part of a broader political culture – and instruments of its creation and survival. Whatever they may reject of his interpretation, revisionist and post-revisionist scholars of seventeenth-century England would do well to follow Macaulay's sense of the polemics and rhetoricity, the political freight of history in the past, and of our own historical narrations in the present.

Any future historian of revisionism's own historical and ideological moment will be struck by another story: the contemporaneous history of other humanities disciplines and the relationship of revisionism to them – or rather its distance from them. During the 1970s other disciplines – social sciences,

17. See, for example, S. Baxter, 'William III as Hercules: The Political Implications of Court Culture', in L. G. Schwoerer, ed., *The Revolution of 1688–89: Changing Perspectives* (Cambridge, 1992); T. Claydon, *William III and the Godly Revolution* (Cambridge, 1996); K. Sharpe and S. Zwicker, eds, *Politics of Discourse* (Berkeley and London, 1987), pp. 12–13.

18. J. G. A. Pocock, *The Ancient Constitution and the Feudal Law*, 2nd edn (Cambridge, 1987), part 2, pp. 364ff.; see A. B. Worden, ed., *Edmund Ludlow: A Voyce from the Watch Tower*, Camden Soc. 21 (1978), introduction. We await a good study of histories written after 1688, but see L. Okie, *Augustan Historical Writing: Histories of England in the English Enlightenment* (New York, 1991).

19. J. Clive, *Macaulay: The Shaping of the Historian* (New York, 1975); H. R. Trevor-Roper, ed., *Lord Macaulay: The History of England* (Harmondsworth, 1968); and J. P. Kenyon, *The History Men: The Historical Profession in England since the Renaissance* (1983), pp. 214–21.

20. Trevor-Roper, *Lord Macaulay*, introduction; D. Cannadine, *G. M. Trevelyan* (1992).

21. Macaulay's famous chapter 3 of *The History of England*, for example, discusses coffee houses, newspapers, books, literacy and education, literature and fine arts as essential for comprehending the political culture.

language studies, most of all literary criticism – were transformed by a number of theoretical perspectives and a self-reflexivity that were part of the academic manifestation of postmodernism. Theoretical and polemical approaches – pyschological, linguistic and epistemological – not only questioned what was studied and taught, but the fundamentals of critical practice, the nature of interpretation itself, in a variety of fields. Though by no means all scholars applauded the theoretical turn, all were led to ask what constituted the 'meaning' of an event, performance or text in the past, and what is involved in the exegesis of the 'meaning' by and for us. As we shall see, such reflections led to changed habits of thinking and working, often removing rigid subject boundaries to advocate a more interdisciplinary approach to the humanities. Historians, perhaps especially early modern historians, showed little or no interest in the dialogue that these developments invited.[22] Indeed the revisionists' preference for arcane manuscript and fine detail, their rigid separation of the realities of the past from its representations, amounted to a claim for the uniqueness of the historian's craft.[23] And for all their differences on smaller issues, the anti- and post-revisionists shared with the revisionists a confidence in the traditional historical practices – common sense, the study of 'documents', and the construction of narratives or case studies.[24] In one interesting case, a historian who earlier trumpeted the value of interdisciplinary methods and new models and techniques for research transmuted into an enemy of theoretical reflections and new critical approaches, condemning literary scholars and postmodernists as subversives to be barred from the historical academy.[25]

What I wish to suggest is that the early modern historian's refusal to enter into debate with new critical questions and approaches has been, in several senses, a lost opportunity. While excessive self-analysis, in any area of human behaviour, can be dangerously destabilising or aridly self-indulgent, some reflection periodically on what one is doing and how one goes about it seems worthy in itself. More particularly, it seems to me that the consequences of the revisionist debate have led us to an unsatisfying impasse, from which some engagement with the questions being asked in other disciplines might rescue us. For to all historians of seventeenth-century England a central question remains: how a society and culture that appeared to speak the language of harmony divided in violent conflict. For those who stress consensus, the

22. Cf. Q. Skinner, ed., *The Return of Grand Theory in the Human Sciences* (Cambridge, 1985), introduction and passim; R. D. Hume, 'Texts within Contexts: Notes towards a Historical Method', *Philol. Quart.* 71 (1992), pp. 69–100, esp. pp. 69, 96–8.
23. See Sharpe and Lake, *Culture and Politics*, pp. 4–5.
24. Cf. J. H. Hexter, 'The Rhetoric of History', *History & Theory* 6 (1967), pp. 1–12; G. McLennan, 'History and Theory', *Literature & History* 10 (1984), pp. 139–64.
25. Stone, 'History and Postmodernism'. Stone had earlier been an advocate of interdisciplinary engagement with sociology and anthropology and with quantitative methods. See 'History and the Social Sciences in the Twentieth Century', in his *The Past and the Present Revisited* (1981), pp. 3–44, and the chapter on 'Theories of Revolution' in the influential *The Causes of the English Revolution* (1972, 1986).

problem is that of explaining the – to them – sudden eruption of conflict; for those to whom early modern England appears ideologically riven, the conundrum is how it escaped civil war for so long.[26] As has recently been recognised, the choice we are asked to make between two such historical readings may be a false one. In a complex political culture, unity and division may coexist, and a shared language may convey, or be interpreted as conveying, different, even contested, meanings.[27] Actions, pronouncements, 'documents' may be multivalent. It may be that the traditional unspoken historical approach does not easily accommodate the fluidity of meanings possible and/or 'intended' in the production and perception of an action or text. For where the historian has adhered for the most part to the unarticulated assumption that *actors or authors intended meanings that contemporaries usually understood as they were intended*, other critics have challenged every one of the links in the chain of 'meaning'.

From different viewpoints the post-Freudian psychoanalyst Jacques Lacan and the critic Michel Foucault have questioned the subject/author as a timeless essence, and argued that the construction of the autonomous self as subject and author is a historical process and ideological move that took place towards the end of the seventeenth century.[28]

Language theorists and postmodern philosophers have similarly contested our very notions of intentionality and meaning, Jacques Derrida most radically going so far as to deny any quest to determine meaning outside the endless play of words or signs.[29] And reception theorists have complicated the relationship between the production and reception of 'meanings' and considered whether and how we can recapture them.[30] To most early modern historians, Lacan, Foucault, Derrida, together with Bakhtin, Bourdieu or Barthes, form a gallery of unknowns or a litany of anathemas and demons who have subverted scholarship by ideology and replaced lucid exposition by jargon.[31] As the editorial of a new journal recently put it, 'Central to historians' sense of what they are doing are such things as the documentary record, evidence, verification, falsification . . . and a scepticism concerning the value of theory.'[32]

26. Revisionists have rightly been criticised for virtually arguing that the civil war could not happen. Post-revisionists, however, seldom discussed how the ideologically riven society they depict avoided civil conflict for so long.
27. Cf. Sharpe and Lake, *Culture and Politics*, pp. 13–20.
28. For J. Lacan see *Écrits* (1977) and *The Four Fundamental Concepts of Psychoanalysis* (1977); M. Foucault, *The Order of Things* (1970); *Madness and Civilisation* (1967). See M. Philip's essay on Foucault in Skinner, *Return of Grand Theory*, pp. 65–82.
29. See J. Derrida, *Of Grammatology* (Baltimore, 1976), and his 'Structure, Sign and Play in the Discourse of the Human Sciences', in *Writing and Difference* (Chicago, 1978), pp. 278–94. See too J. Culler, *On Deconstruction* (1983); I. Hassan, *The Postmodern Turn* (Ohio, 1987); D. Hoy, 'Jacques Derrida', in Skinner, *Return of Grand Theory*, pp. 41–64.
30. See below, pp. 15–16.
31. For a literal demonisation see G. R. Elton, *Return to Essentials* (Cambridge, 1991). For a critique, see K. Jenkins, *On What Is History* (1995), ch. 3.
32. G. Burgess, 'Renaissance Texts and Renaissance Republicanism', *Ren. Forum* 1 (1996), p. 4.

Scepticism is healthy, but only when it is applied to our own assumptions and practices as well as to those of others. Being asked to reflect on our own practices as historians, the processes of evidence and verification, reminds us of the history of those practices – in the rise of positivism – and of how different they are to the working methods of a Renaissance historian, for whom invented speeches and political agendas were very much the matter and purpose of a historical story.[33] It reminds us too that in the early modern period which we study, history was not a separate discipline, scarcely an academic subject at all, and that it was read as part of the training in logic, rhetoric and style that were the goals of a classical education. To recognise that, I would argue, is to acknowledge that rather than offering 'an occasional and supplementary approach to the Renaissance', interdisciplinary and critical approaches are essential to understanding a Renaissance culture in which epistemology, interpretation, the exegesis of meaning had not fragmented into discrete disciplinary practices.[34]

It has perhaps not been sufficiently observed that much of the theoretical and interdisciplinary work of the last two decades has been concerned with the Renaissance. Language theorists and semioticians have undoubtedly been drawn to the contemporary debates about the rhetoricity of Renaissance culture, and its own concerns about the instabilities of meaning and the misuse and misunderstanding of language that were consequent on the fall and the loss of the divine word and the shared language of Adam.[35] Scholars such as the anthropologist Clifford Geertz and the formalist critic Bakhtin viewed the Renaissance state as a 'theatre state', a social theatre of roles and performances with, as Bakhtin studying Rabelais would have it, behind the arras of order, a carnivalesque element always staging other pageants, some subversive of the authorised performance.[36] For Foucault, the seventeenth century was a crucial period in which the discourse of power constructed the individual subject as a creature of its ideology, as one who interiorised its discourse and order – in what, in a different reading, might be called the 'civilising process'.[37]

33. P. Burke, *The Renaissance Sense of the Past* (1969); E. Cochrane, *Historians and Historiography in the Italian Renaissance* (Chicago, 1981); D. Woolf, *The Idea of History in Early Stuart England* (Toronto, 1990), pp. 11–12.

34. Burgess, 'Renaissance Texts', p. 2. See W. J. Costello, *The Scholastic Curriculum at Early Seventeenth Century Cambridge* (Cambridge, Mass., 1958); M. H. Curtis, *Oxford and Cambridge in Transition* (Oxford, 1959); J. McConica, *The History of the University of Oxford*, vol. 3 (Oxford, 1986), ch. 4, esp. p. 173.

35. J. H. Seigel, *Rhetoric and Philosophy in Renaissance Humanism* (Princeton, 1968); W. S. Howell, *Logic and Rhetoric in England 1500–1700* (1961). On the contemporary concern with dissimulation, see P. Zagorin, *Ways of Lying* (Cambridge, Mass., 1990); D. S. Katz, 'The Language of Adam in Seventeenth-Century England', in H. Lloyd Jones, V. Pearl and B. Worden, eds, *History and Imagination* (1981), pp. 132–45.

36. C. Geertz, 'Centres, Kings and Charisma: Reflections on the Symbolics of Power', in J. Ben David and T. N. Clark, eds, *Culture and its Creators* (Chicago, 1977), pp. 150–71; M. Bakhtin, *Rabelais and his World* (Cambridge, Mass., 1968).

37. M. Foucault, *Discipline and Punish* (1991 edn), part 3; see N. Elias, *The Civilising Process* (Oxford, 1983).

While we may not be persuaded by their histories, still less by their questioning of history itself, what such critics have demonstrated is that a positivist epistemology and the assumption that text and meaning have organic integrity and coherence may lead us to misrepresent Renaissance culture, to delimit its own multiple and conflicting histories. If the culture of our own discipline restricts us from our proud claim that we just get on with the job of understanding the past, then it is surely time to ask some new questions. It may even be that some of the theoretical perspectives and approaches, rather than being irrelevant or a threat to history, can lead us as historians to a richer understanding of the past.

Representations and Texts

Common to most theoretical investigations has been an interest in representation, the means by which societies and cultures constitute and convey meaning for and within themselves. The study of *representations*, the title of one of the most important disciplinary journals to emerge from the turn to theory in the humanities, is founded on the principle, central to Nietzsche, that humans do not have access to truth or reality; they construct it.[38] The texts, discourses and performances by which a culture structures the chaos of experience are the representations of the world that become the only reality that human beings can know. Since the distinction between the represented and the 'real' is a false one, all the texts and performances, the myths and stories, the fables and fictions of a society, its histories, become 'evidence' for the historian who, of course, operates within another set of discursive practices that alone give meaning to his activity and being.[39]

To view the past (and to write about the past)[40] as a series of shifting representations is also to recognise that all social organisations, the structures of power, are themselves constructs, endowed with authority by the discourses and signs that in turn they, and the culture, authorise. Representation uses not the language of facts and events, a language that implies an escape from culture, but the vocabulary of texts and performances, with all their implications that the discursive and theatrical constitute society and

38. See the first issue of *Representations*; R. Chartier, *Cultural History: Between Practices and Representations* (Cambridge, 1988). A major influence is C. Geertz, *The Interpretation of Cultures* (1973). See too R. Chartier, *On the Edge of the Cliff: History, Language and Practices* (Baltimore, 1997), ch. 7 and passim.

39. Chartier defines the 'world as representation' as 'a world fashioned by means of the series of discourses that apprehend and structure experience', *Cultural History*, p. 11; cf. R. Chartier, *The Cultural Uses of Print in Early Modern France* (Princeton, 1978), pp. 10–12.

40. See H. Kellner, *Language and Historical Representation* (Madison, 1989).

culture.[41] History as the study of representations collapses the boundaries
traditionally placed between rhetoric and truth, play and politics; it makes
all accounts of the past a cultural history, and politics itself a set of discourses and performances in the process of construction, deconstruction
and reconstitution.[42] If such an approach to the past appears at first sight
alien to our traditional historical practices, second thoughts remind us that
'not only was the notion [of representation] known to the ancient regime
societies' but it held a central place in them.[43] The sense of artful self-con-
struction in courtesy literature, the politics of elite and popular festival, the
popularity of fables and emblems, the preoccupation with display all underline the omnipresence of representation in Renaissance culture and the
Renaissance state.

Representations are constructed across all social performances and media:
the game or procession, the image as well as the word. And social theorists
and cultural critics have advanced a number of methodologies for 'deconstructing' all these texts – that is for examining the processes of their production, and the processes through which they circulate meaning.[44] Cultural
criticism and media studies were born of the interest, excited by postmodernism and deconstruction, in the processes of signification. Yet while they
have succeeded in particular areas – such as film studies – they have hitherto
developed no satisfactory theory or methodology for the study of how meanings are constructed, disseminated and validated across various media. Nor has
media studies exhibited a historical dimension, failing both to deal with the
history of important media developments and to historicise our contemporary media.[45] As Steven Zwicker and I have argued elsewhere, 'what in reality
has driven Cultural Studies has been neither history nor theory, but contemporary political commitments.'[46]

More important for the historian of culture, construed as the systems by
which a society structures meaning for itself, has been the work of symbolic
anthropologists, especially Clifford Geertz. Geertz posited it as the goal of
anthropology to decode the meanings a society makes through the study of
its cultural practices, in particular by a method of contextualisation he called
'thick description'.[47] From a famous study of *Negara: The Theatre State in Nineteenth Century Bali*, Geertz deployed his method to demonstrate how study of
state ceremonies opened on to the structures of hierarchy and power in Bali-

---

41. Chartier observes that 'the fundamental distinctions between representation and the
    represented . . . are distorted by the theatricality of social life in ancien regime society',
    Cultural History, p. 8.
42. Ibid., pp. 11–12.
43. Ibid., p. 7.
44. See C. Belsey, *Critical Practice* (1980), pp. 104ff.; this is a helpful and famous introduc-
    tion to poststructuralist criticism.
45. R. Giddings, *The Author, the Book and the Reader* (1991), pp. 8–9.
46. Sharpe and Zwicker, *Refiguring Revolutions*, pp. 1–2.
47. See C. Geertz, 'Thick Description: Toward an Interpretative Theory of Culture', in
    Geertz, *Interpretation of Cultures*, pp. 3–31.

nese society.[48] Closer to home, Geertz has also turned his attention to the relationship of procession and display to the exercise of rule in Elizabethan England, arguing the utility of thick description for a historical anthropology.[49] Though Geertz has been criticised for his method and his history, his interpretation of culture as 'a set of control mechanisms' 'for the governing of behaviour' invaluably directs the historian of politics to the history of culture from which it was for so long artificially separated.[50] Curiously, however, with few exceptions, early modern historians have not followed Geertz in studying procession, festival and play as texts of politics and power.[51] Nor, as I argued nearly a decade ago, have they discussed the potential for a broader understanding of politics in a variety of cultural practices that encoded contemporary notions of order: namely music, chess, dancing, horse-riding, the discourses of which explicitly announced the politics they represented.[52]

As far as early modern England is concerned, the theoretical questions about meaning and the processes of signification have not, as they have in other fields, produced a new art historicism (to coin a term) concerned with situating the object, artefact or image in the moment and conditions of its cultural production, and in elucidating how it performed in that culture, structuring, circulating and questioning its values and beliefs. These are the questions – along with questions about art and gender, the placement of works of art and their organisation in different spaces, the position and manipulation of the viewer's gaze, the commercialisation and commodification of the aesthetic – that have transformed our understanding of image, society and politics in other fields, notably in eighteenth-century England.[53] Similar questions, about the relationships of word and image in Tudor painting, the iconicity of portraits of Elizabeth, the Elizabethan vogue for the miniature and its revival in the 1650s, the creation of a courtly community by Van Dyck, the role of the print in Royalist, then in 1688 in Williamite propaganda: these are the questions that would enable a cultural *history* of art, a study of the image not as an aesthetic object outside history, but as a text encoding social

---

48. C. Geertz, *Negara: The Theatre State in Nineteenth Century Bali* (Princeton, 1980).

49. Geertz, 'Centres, Kings and Charisma'.

50. Geertz, *Interpretation of Cultures*, p. 49. For critique of Geertz, see G. Levi 'On Microhistory', in P. Burke, ed., *New Perspectives on Historical Writing* (Cambridge, 1991), pp. 96–104, and V. Crapanzano, 'The Hermes Dilemma: The Masking of Subversion in Ethnographic Description', in J. Clifford and G. Marcus, eds, *Writing Culture: The Poetics and Politics of Ethnography* (Berkeley, 1986), pp. 57–76; and V. P. Pecora, 'The Limits of Local Knowledge', in H. A. Veeser, *The New Historicism* (1989), pp. 243–76.

51. And those historians of early modern England who have studied ritual, charivari and festival seldom theorise or cite Geertz. See e.g. D. Underdown, *Revel, Riot and Rebellion: Popular Politics and Culture in England* (Oxford, 1985).

52. K. Sharpe, 'A Commonwealth of Meanings: Languages, Analogues, Ideas and Politics', in Sharpe, *Politics and Ideas in Early Stuart England* (1989), pp. 3–71.

53. See, for example, on the eighteenth century, M. Pointon, *Hanging the Head* (1993); J. Barrell, ed., *Painting and the Politics of Culture* (Oxford, 1992); and now J. Brewer, *The Pleasures of the Imagination* (1997).

meanings at the moment of its creation, circulation and viewings.[54] Before
the current wave of theory, at a time when intellectual history reified 'ideas'
as autonomous forces, from the Warburg Institute came some scholars who
studied to write a genuine history of art, and an analysis of art *in* history. Sir
Roy Strong's studies *The Elizabethan Image, Art and Power* and *The Renaissance
Garden* were among the most important works on the cultural politics of the
early modern state; his book on a single portrait, Van Dyck's *Charles I on
Horseback*, is, in some ways, a magnificent demonstration of the method of
'thick description' of the image.[55]

More recently, early modern art history appears to have returned to the
traditions of formalism and connoisseurship, the close study of technique
and the appreciation of a timeless aesthetic, approaches that (like the New
Criticism in literary studies) enclose the image from its histories.[56] The rich
questions that Strong asked and began to answer might fruitfully be re-posed
in the context of the theorising of text and context and the renewed concern
with representation, with the consequent focus on symbol as social reality,
and visual culture as power.[57] As we shall have cause to remark, some theoretical initiatives might also add a crucial history to our understanding of art
and society: that of how the image was perceived in different times and contexts, by various audiences. Until we have such histories informed by the basic
questions of what works of art 'meant' and how their meanings performed,
we shall never understand a Renaissance culture in which those were, for sovereigns and subjects too, the arts of state.

It is vital to remind ourselves, albeit surprising to need to remind ourselves,
that for the early modern age, as for our own, the performance (be it coro-
nation, charivari or beach wedding) and the image (royal portrait, scatalogical
woodcut or computer graphic) were and are ways in which we structure,
communicate and interrogate our systems of values and meanings. One of
those values – and one with its own history and politics to be explicated –
is the attribution of greater seriousness and importance as a conveyor of
meaning to the word, spoken and written. Language we hold as the principal
agent of our identity, the repository of our values and the essential medium
of their communication and circulation. Postmodern theories more than anything else share an address to theories of language and discourse, and to a
greater or lesser extent have questioned all the assumptions about language
that have underlain (some would prefer to say underpinned) the humanist

54. See, for example, J. Peacock, 'The Politics of Portraiture', in Sharpe and Lake, *Culture
and Politics*, pp. 199–228.
55. R. Strong, *The Elizabethan Image* (1969); *Art and Power* (Woodbridge, 1984); *The Renaissance Garden in England* (1979); *The English Renaissance Miniature* (1983); *Van Dyck:
Charles I on Horseback* (1972).
56. I was struck by this when reading books on Van Dyck. See, for example, C. Brown,
Van Dyck (Oxford, 1982).
57. John Peacock is working on such a study of Van Dyck. Cf. D. Howarth, *Images of
Rule: Art and Politics in the English Renaissance* (Houndmills, 1997).

culture of modernism. The origin of nearly all such questions lay in the argument at the beginning of the century, by Ferdinand de Saussure, that language, rather than coming after and reflecting some anterior truth, actually constituted it; rather than things giving birth to words, words created things.[58] Such a radically different thesis about the relationship of language to the world carried even more radical implications, many of which have been pursued only more recently. If language is not fixed to 'reality', but is a cultural system for its representation, then language can function only relatively: to a cultural system specific in place and in time. Secondly, if language is socially and culturally constructed, it is itself part of the process through which the society and culture are themselves formed, that is part of the structures and systems of power and control: language is *politics*, not the means of articulating *Politics*. Thirdly, if there is no anterior, external, transcendent truth to which 'I' have access outside of language, then the 'I' itself must be constituted by and through language; or as critics put it, language speaks through the subject rather than the subject through the language.[59]

Theorists and critics have developed these perspectives to argue different cases, or to press different agendas. Structuralist critics study the deep levels of language and signification in society, how communities share a consensus about meaning and how texts 'express the values of the system out of which they emerge'.[60] Others take further Saussure's arguments about the relativism, the arbitrariness of language, to deny that any utterance or text can have a fixed meaning, even within a cultural system, let alone across different linguistic communities. Derrida posits that no meanings can be fixed because all systems of signification are subject to changing contexts, and language continues in infinite play with, and within, itself. Some have taken Derrida as a nihilist denying the possibility of any/all meaning(s).[61] Yet, as has been observed, there is a diachronic and historical dimension to Derrida's arguments, despite his scepticism about history itself, and the possibility for historical questions in the theory or method associated with him: deconstruction.[62]

Derrida is interested in how writing can generate meaning in a number of contexts. Because language is not 'fixed', he posits, the meaning of a text

58. See F. de Saussure, ed., *Course in General Linguistics* (New York, 1959).
59. See C. Belsey, 'Addressing the Subject' in Belsey, *Critical Practice*, ch. 3.
60. L. H. Lefkowitz, 'Creating the World: Structuralism and Semiotics', in G. D. Atkins and L. Morrow, eds, *Contemporary Literary Theory* (Houndmills, 1989), p. 67.
61. See J. Appleby, L. Hunt and M. Jacob, *Telling the Truth about History* (New York, 1995), pp. 206, 224. Even this excellent introduction and open-minded review of postmodern critics regards Derrida as 'nihilist'. See too C. McCullagh, 'Can our Understanding of Old Texts be Objective?' *History & Theory* 30 (1991), pp. 302–23.
62. See D. LaCapra, *Soundings in Critical Theory* (Ithaca, 1989); LaCapra, *Rethinking Intellectual History* (Ithaca, 1983); H. White, *Topics of Discourse* (Baltimore, 1978); White, *The Content of the Form: Narrative Discourse and Historical Representation* (Baltimore, 1987). See too P. Joyce, *Democratic Subjects* (Cambridge, 1994) and J. Scott, *Gender and the Politics of History* (New York, 1988).

cannot be fixed – either in time, or even within a culture. For words structure cultures, as well as taking their authority from them; and words carry
traces from different contexts, temporal as well as geographic. The meaning
of any utterance or writing, therefore, will always be plural, performing and
being read in a multiplicity of ways. For Derrida and his disciples, the purpose
of deconstructing any text is to open up the text to all its possible meanings
and to investigate what and how meanings arise from each reader's encounter
with the text.[63] As we shall see, Derrida's deconstruction has been one of the
most important dimensions of a move, common to several critical perspectives, from a concern only with the text and the production of the text to
the reception of the text: to what meanings auditors, readers and observers
took away from the multiple meanings that all texts carried and permitted.[64]

It is not my purpose, nor do I have the necessary skills, to review critically
the history of those philosophical, semiotic and literary theories that are often
herded into the corral of 'postmodernism'.[65] Still less do I seek, nor is there
a need, to 'defend' theorists or critics from the charge, often levelled by historians, that they undermine 'scholarship' (not least because they intend to:
to force a recognition that 'scholarship' too is an ideological discourse and
historical process, with multiple not fixed meanings). My project is to suggest
that for Renaissance scholars, for early modern historians, the issues and questions raised and some of the methods advocated by theory may help us to
reimagine a Renaissance culture that did not share the positivism or 'the
organicist ideology of modernism', but which was concerned with many of
the questions and topics re-posed by postmodernism: issues of identity and
subjectivity, questions of language and sign, relations of text and meaning,
ideology and power.[66]

It is not the least of ironies that for all that the revisionist movement in
historical studies ran simultaneously and in seeming contradiction to the
theoretical turn, they shared *some* objectives and conclusions. Most obviously,
both revisionists and postmodernists have called into question what the first
would call a Whig, teleological history, and the other a master narrative of
progress or modernism.[67] And while revisionist historians are less self-
conscious about their own ideological practices than critics, both have
exposed those modernising narratives as not simple representations of historical truth (about the developments of liberty, parliaments and democracy) but
as polemical and partisan accounts, even 'misreadings' of a past that did not

---

63. Hoy, 'Jacques Derrida', pp. 51–4; cf. K. M. Newton, *Interpreting the Text* (Hemel
    Hempstead, 1990), ch. 4, esp. pp. 70–2.
64. Cf. Belsey's comment that in poststructuralist criticism 'meanings circulate between
    text, ideology and reader and the work of criticism is to release possible meanings',
    Critical Practice, p. 144.
65. For historians, excellent introductions are Appleby, Hunt and Jacob, *Telling the Truth
    about History*, and Richard J. Evans, *In Defence of History* (1997).
66. R. Wilson, *Will Power: Essays on Shakespearian Authority* (1993), p. 7. See Hume, 'Texts
    within Contexts: Notes towards a Historical Method'.
67. Peter Lake uses almost this language in 'Retrospective', pp. 253–4.

share those values. In that sense, for all that theory is often demonised as the opposite to history, postmodernism has itself historicised the modern perspective, and by returning it (ourselves) to history has enabled us to see that historical meaning resides in particulars not in universals, and helped to free the past from being judged or evaluated by anachronistic, even trans-historical, criteria.[68]

And there is more of benefit that a conversation with theory could bring to early modern historical studies. A greater willingness by historians – not one that should present difficulties to a historian of the Tudor and Stuart court or of the fabrication of Louis XIV's kingship – to see systems of authority and order as culturally constructed rather than, as it were, outside culture would surely facilitate a more nuanced history of the performance of power: how the relations between sovereigns and subjects functioned and shifted in the early modern state.[69] Once we take on board something of the argument that authority and meaning are constituted through language and texts, we are led to consider authority itself as more indeterminate, more open to multiple meanings and interpretations than our traditional concept of the sovereign utterance (commanding, as well as issued by one in command) usually implies. A notion of language, meaning and authority as multivalent in their construction and reception renders, for example, the current choice early modernists are asked to make, between 'consensus' and 'conflict', a simplistic dichotomy that flattens the many textures of a complex culture.[70] And some adoption of the deconstructive opening of texts may replace an obsession – one that characterised Hobbes studies for years – with finding organic coherence and consistency with a more historical recognition of the traces of many and variant meanings in the language of texts that were seeking to order meanings and give new meaning to order.[71] Some synthesis of theory's questions and techniques with the historian's contextualisation in particular moments might assist us better to perceive contemporaries' own negotiations between indeterminacy and desire for order, as well as to understand better the nature of our own differences as historians writing about them.

68. That is to say that postmodernism challenges Enlightenment rationalism and historical positivism, both of which belong to a historical moment rather than standing 'outside' history and culture.

69. See e.g. S. Orgel, *The Illusion of Power* (Berkeley, 1975); P. Burke, *The Fabrication of Louis XIV* (1992); and see the recent interesting collection, P. Griffiths, A. Fox and S. Hindle, eds, *The Experience of Authority in Early Modern England* (Houndmills, 1996).

70. Indeed Derrida's remarks on the multiple and conflicting meanings of texts seem helpful for a historiography which has powerfully argued from contemporary sources both conflict and consensus. LaCapra comments on Derrida's rejection of binary oppositions, *Rethinking Intellectual History*, p. 251.

71. Some still cling to such coherence: see J. Somerville, *Thomas Hobbes: Political Ideas in Historical Context* (Houndmills, 1992). Quentin Skinner's latest book demonstrates the ways in which older tropes performed even in texts that sought a radical new politics, and even a new philosophy of language and rhetoric: Q. Skinner, *Reason and Rhetoric in the Philosophy of Hobbes* (Cambridge, 1996).

There will already have been a rush to dismiss any intimacy between history and theory as a fantasy. A young and open-minded historian recently aired his doubt whether 'many of the dominant theoretical and methodological predilections' of critics 'actually *permit* . . . an open engagement with revisionist historical research'.[72] (We note the formulation.) And critics sympathetic to theory acknowledge the difficulty when structuralists, poststructuralists and deconstructionists 'all share the same scepticism about recovering the past'.[73] After all it is difficult for historians to face the erasure of 'authors' and 'actors' from their sense of and writing about the past. And it is easy to read Derrida as denying the historian any access to meanings in the past. But this is by no means the necessary or only way of reading Derrida, let alone theory in general. Derrida's own arguments about changing meanings, as opposed to structuralism's more anthropological synchronicity, imply that the elucidation of any meaning(s) is an act of historical interpretation. A leading intellectual historian, who regards Derrida as inspiring important thinking about history and historical methods, also points out that 'Derrida's enterprise requires genuine respect for tradition' and that he contributed much himself to an understanding of 'the transferences of the metaphysical tradition in the course of history'.[74] And critics of Derrida have suggested that our capacity to reconstruct the languages and contexts of past texts enables historians to be 'objective' within the rules and established practices of their discipline.[75]

Indeed the claim that history and theory can fruitfully coexist is one that can be argued historically as well as theoretically. While the rhetoric of 'antitheory' has been loud in the historical profession, it has not been the only voice. One of the most important developments in historical writing over the last two or three decades has been a move which had its origins in theoretical questions and which has transformed the history of political ideas: what is now referred to as the 'linguistic turn' advocated and practised by John Pocock and Quentin Skinner.[76] In commencing their work Pocock and

---

72. G. Burgess, 'Revisionist History and Shakespeare's Political Context', *The Shakespeare Yearbook* 6 (1996), pp. 3–35, at p. 5.Contrast D. Simpson, 'Literary Criticism and the Return to "History"', *Critical Inquiry* 14 (1988), pp. 721–47.
73. D. F. McKenzie, *Bibliography and the Sociology of Texts* (1986), p. 19.
74. McCullagh, 'Can our Understanding of Old Texts be Objective?'; Simpson, 'Literary Criticism'; Appleby, Hunt and Jacob, *Telling the Truth about History*, ch. 7, esp. pp. 261ff.; Evans, *In Defence of History*, ch. 8, esp. pp. 231–3, 249–53.
75. LaCapra, *Rethinking Intellectual History*, pp. 253, 336.
76. See J. G. A. Pocock, *Politics, Language and Time* (1972); Pocock, 'Verbalising a Political Act: Towards a Politics of Language', *Political Theory* 1 (1973), pp. 27–45; Q. Skinner, 'Meaning and Understanding in the History of Ideas', *History & Theory* 8 (1969), pp. 3–53; 'On Performing and Explaining Linguistic Actions', *Philos. Quart.* 21 (1971), pp. 1–21. See J. H. Tully, *Meaning and Context: Quentin Skinner and his Critics* (Cambridge, 1988), and J. E. Toews, 'Intellectual History after the Linguistic Turn: The Autonomy of Meaning and the Irreducibility of Experience', *Amer. Hist. Rev.* 92 (1987), pp. 879–907.

Skinner owed much to linguistic analysis and speech act theories, and they have continued to be influenced by theories of discourse, and of the production, performance and reception of texts and utterances in the past. Moving from the traditional intellectual history of political thought – analytical and formalist narrative of the great texts, driven by ideas of 'influence' – Pocock and Skinner sought to write a history of political thinking through a history of the paradigmatic shifts in language, the processes through which discourses faded and became accredited. Where Skinner early on concentrated on the question of what authors intended, he now has a greater interest in how texts perform, and, most recently demonstrated in a brilliant study of Hobbes, in the rhetoric and form as vital constituents of the meaning and performance of texts.[77] Implicit in the notion of performance – of what texts *do*, as well as what authors intend – and evident in Skinner's account of Hobbes's readoption of humanist rhetoric, is a concern, both of the historian and the contemporary thinker, with audience. In his later work, Pocock too takes up the dimension of the reception as well as production of texts. Not only does he urge that, in order to know what the author was doing, we 'move from author to reader': Pocock goes so far as to say that 'we cannot absolutely distinguish the author's performance from the reader's response.'[78] This is to follow postmodern theory in the direction of claiming that language structures the intended meanings of authors, rather than being the tool of an autonomous actor operating on and outside language. Pocock complicates the traditional historical notion of intention and meaning, and comes close to representing discourse as unstable and free when he writes: 'any text or simple utterance in a sophisticated political discourse is by its nature polyvalent: it consists in the employment of a texture of language capable of saying different things.'[79] Yet Pocock seems anxious to hold on to the notion that the author may have intended to perform in more than one language at a time, 'to move among these patterns of polyvalence, employing and recombining them'.[80] And he appears to wish, despite the acknowledgement of polyvalency, to retain the notion of coherence: within the text, between authors and readers, and within the culture.

A fuller engagement with some theoretical challenge may here be enriching rather than destructive. Derrida's claim that all language resists the delimitations of any authorial intention or social code, that words carry traces of meaning from other times and contexts, complicates any narrative of paradigmatic shifts in discourse. And it moves, more radically than Pocock or Skinner have done, the study of performance and the process by which

---

77. J. G. A. Pocock, *Virtue, Commerce and History* (Cambridge, 1985), p. 5; Skinner, *Reason and Rhetoric*, passim.
78. Pocock, *Virtue, Commerce and History*, pp. 13–18. Pocock acknowledges his debt to *Rezeptionsgeschichte* and to reader response theory. See below pp. 34–7. It is readers as well as writers that make languages 'accredited'.
79. Pocock, *Virtue, Commerce and History*, p. 9.
80. Ibid.

languages become accredited towards the history of the *receptions* of texts.[81]
Moreover Skinner's *Reason and Rhetoric* raises the fact that in Hobbes's case a
language of classical humanism is being deployed to persuade readers to an
epistemology and politics that are not conventionally humanist, opening dis-
junctures between language, intention and reception that the Pocock–Skinner
method may need to readdress. Hobbes's use of rhetoric in *Leviathan* also
prompts the larger question about the relationship within the texts of art,
play, polemic, and what Roger Chartier has called the 'emotive charge' of language, to the meanings intended and performed.[82] Even after the linguistic
turn, an adherence to and a predisposed belief in textual coherence may have
repressed much of the work that Renaissance texts were doing, whether
'intended' or not. And more deconstructive readings – of Hobbes not least –
may return texts of 'political thought' to other contexts, communities and histories than those that have been the historian's traditional concern.

   Here, on a larger frame, we might note that the Pocock–Skinner approach
to the history of political thought has for long suggested possibilities for other
histories that have not been pursued; and this is true both for the histories
of other discourses and for other media. Despite the work done on sexual
slander, for example, no social historian has pursued the paradigmatic shifts
in the discourses of defamation, sexual and other, as charting the shifting
attitudes to rhetoric, honour, gender, the boundaries of private and public,
and politics itself.[83] Nor have historians attempted a history of the changing
images of women and female sexuality on canvas contextualised by the other
modes of their representation – on the stage, in verse, or in medical or household treatises. Once again theoretical refigurations of the role of language in
effecting historical meaning and in (re)constituting the self and the subject
offer new approaches to, say, the history of class, gender, party or nation that
early modern scholars have little pursued.[84] How did languages perform to
construct, reconstitute and define gentry elites in a society in flux; and what
did the power and status of aristocracy owe to the traces of feudal values
encoded in the language and genres used long after the demise of feudal relations and abolition of feudal tenure?[85] Did the discourse of social order and

---

81. As Burgess points out, Skinner and (to a lesser extent) Pocock 'remain strongly inclined
     to a perspective that rests on intentional explanation', 'Renaissance Texts', p. 3.
82. Chartier, *Cultural History*, p. 29, a conscious echo of Roland Barthes, *The Pleasure of
     the Text* (1976).
83. J. A. Sharpe's *Defamation and Sexual Slander in Early Modern England*, Borthwick Papers
     no. 58 (York, 1980) is based on evidence from church courts which needs to be read
     alongside ballads, verse and popular manuals.
84. For successful studies in other fields see P. Joyce, *Democratic Subjects: The Self and the
     Social in Nineteenth Century England* (Cambridge, 1994); G. Stedman Jones, *Languages
     of Class* (New York, 1983).
85. Here an example of the sort of work that would have benefited from a more
     theoretical approach is R. Cust, 'Honour, Rhetoric and Political Culture: The Earl of
     Huntingdon and his Enemies', in Amussen and Kishlansky, *Political Culture*, pp. 84–
     111.

the mystification of authority in early modern England repress (to take a term from Derrida) the powerful aspirations and ambitions of subjects, or open themselves to the deconstructive readings of a Machiavelli, Marlowe or Milton?[86] Was the imagining of and debate about republics recently discovered in Elizabethan England submerged in its very texts of royal power that intended to inhibit them, so enabling at least some (and why *then these some*) to 'think the unthought'?[87] How did those languages of authority perform in different communities both to sustain and critique the institutions they structured – and deconstructed? The questions of language and meaning revised by theory invite a myriad of histories, firmly anchored in the historian's traditional methods of research and critical evaluation of evidence. Undertaken, they might even effect a happy miscegenation of history and theory, and produce that fertile offspring – a historicised theory and theorised history.

As well as the linguistic turn, another school of Renaissance scholars has claimed to conjoin theoretical and historical approaches: that generation of literary critics who sprang into print (and highly paid professorial chairs) in the 1980s, known as the 'New Historicists'.[88] New Historicist criticism was in part a reaction against the New Criticism which had dominated literary studies since the 1930s. (The New Critics advocated the formalist analysis of literary texts as aesthetic objects enshrining universal values rather than as products of their culture and moment.) Some have argued too that New Historicist critics represented, as J. Hillis Miller put it, a 'turn away from theory toward history'; and at times the founder of New Historicism, Stephen Greenblatt, appears to accept such a characterisation.[89] As he put it in an autobiographical moment, 'my own work has always been done with a sense of just having to go about and do it.'[90] The denial of theory is, however, in the end disingenuous. 'The New Historicism distinguishes itself from the old in that it has engaged poststructuralist theory';[91] and, as Greenblatt acknowledges, 'methodological self-consciousness is one of the distinguishing marks of the New Historicism' – certainly one that sets it apart from an old historical

86. See A. D'Andrea, 'Aspiring Minds: A Machiavellian Motif from Marlowe to Milton', in B. Kunze and F. Brautigam, eds, *Court, Country and Culture* (Rochester, N.Y., 1992), pp. 211–22.
87. See P. Collinson, 'The Monarchical Republic of Queen Elizabeth I', *Bull. John Rylands Lib.* 69 (1987), pp. 394–424; cf. B. Worden, *The Sound of Virtue: Philip Sydney's Arcadia and Elizabethan Politics* (1997). Quotation from Heidegger, cited in LaCapra, *Rethinking Intellectual History*, p. 29.
88. The founding text was S. Greenblatt's *Renaissance Self-Fashioning* (Chicago, 1980). For a selection of seminal essays, see H. A. Veeser, ed., *The New Historicism Reader* (1994).
89. H. A. Veeser, ed., *The New Historicism* (1989), introduction, p. x.
90. S. Greenblatt, 'Towards a Poetics of Culture', in M. Kreiger, ed., *The Aims of Representation* (New York, 1987), rev. and repr. in Veeser, *New Historicism*, pp. 1–14, quotation p. 1.
91. B. Thomas, 'The New Historicism and Other Old-Fashioned Topics', in Veeser, *New Historicism*, p. 183.

criticism 'based upon faith in the transparency of signs and interpretative procedures'.[92]

New Historicism as a critical school or method is an amalgam of a number of theories and approaches: the work on discourse and power by Foucault, something of Derrida's claims for the instabilities of meaning in texts and languages, Geertz's symbolic anthropology with its method of thick description, and traditional practices of formal literary analysis and old historical situation of texts in context. New Historicists seek to reconfigure the issue of text and context, to deconstruct the category of literature which has separated the imagined and fictive from other social discourses, and to reread literary works as cultural texts encoding the structures of meaning, and especially the arrangements of power, in the society and state that produced them. The new historicist programme for which Greenblatt prefers the term he earlier used, 'cultural poetics', seeks to return texts to their historical culture, but to a 'culture', a 'history' that itself is now read as a text, or series of texts and stories: cultural poetics is, to use Louis Montrose's neat formulation, 'a reciprocal concern with the historicity of texts and the textuality of history'.[93] Like 'revisionism', 'New Historicism' is an oversimplified term to describe the practices of many scholars. Moreover, like revisionism, it has not remained static. In his earlier work, Greenblatt appeared wedded to Foucauldian arguments about discourse, power and the containment of subversion, and read Renaissance literature as the hegemonic texts of an authoritarian culture which appeared to tolerate dissent and difference only to neutralise them for enhanced power.[94] In *Shakespearean Negotiations*, the title itself signalled his shift from the totalising notion of power, and Greenblatt accepted that 'even those literary texts that sought most ardently to speak for a monolithic power could be shown to be the sites of institutional and ideological contestation.'[95] New Historicist critics, as well as Greenblatt and Montrose, Goldberg, Fineman and Marcus, have written excellent analyses of Renaissance plays and poems as sites of the tensions in all the structures and arrangements of hierarchy and authority in early modern England: kingship, degree, imperial authority, gender, the rule of fathers.[96]

New Historicism has faced challenges from a number of critical perspec-

92. Greenblatt, 'Towards a Poetics of Culture', p. 12.

93. L. Montrose, 'Professing the Renaissance: The Poetics and Politics of Culture', in Veeser, *New Historicism*, pp. 15–36, quotation p. 20.

94. Cf. D. Shuger, *Habits of Thought in the English Renaissance: Religion, Politics and the Dominant Culture* (Berkeley, 1990), pp. 1–16; J. Dollimore and A. Sinfield, eds, *Political Shakespeare*, 2nd edn (Manchester, 1994), pp. 2–17.

95. S. Greenblatt, *Shakespearean Negotiations* (Berkeley, 1988), pp. 1–20, at p. 3.

96. J. Goldberg, *James I and the Politics of Literature* (Baltimore, 1983); Goldberg, 'Fatherly Authority: The Politics of Stuart Family Images', in M. W. Ferguson, M. Quilligan and N. Vickers, eds, *Rewriting the Renaissance: The Discourses of Sexual Difference in Early Modern Europe* (Chicago, 1986), pp. 3–32; J. Fineman, *Shakespeare's Perjured Eye: The Invention of Poetic Subjectivity in the Sonnets* (Berkeley, 1986); L. Marcus, *The Politics of Mirth* (Chicago, 1986).

tives. It has been accused of being too theoretical and not theoretical enough, a threat to traditional literary values and as construing all culture as the property of literary critics.[97] My concern has been and is here with the importance of New Historicism for historians and particularly the history of the English Renaissance. To take the more general question, historians such as E. P. Thompson and Elizabeth Fox-Genovese have sharply condemned the New Historicist preoccupation with discourse and texts as a retreat from ideology, an aestheticising of history, a distraction from history as social struggle, to play textual games: a 'radical opposition to history'.[98] There is as much the politics of Marxist ideology as critique of method in such objections, and something of an irony in a Marxist call for a history that happened outside of ideological structures and narratives. But all traditional historians may hear alarm bells when New Historicists talk of the historical 'discipline' as a rhetorical practice or text.[99] If so, it is probably a false alarm. For as Hayden White reminds us, in a lucid and sensible essay, there is nothing intrinsically threatening in such an approach:

> every approach to the study of the past presupposes or entails some version of a textualist theory of historical record. That is because, primarily, the historical past is . . . accessible to study 'only by way of its prior textualisations', whether these be in the form of the documentary record or in the form of accounts of what happened in the past written up by historians.[100]

In many senses, as Stanley Fish comfortingly puts it, New Historicism is not all that new, but rather 'another move in the practice of history as it has always been done'.[101] A practitioner of the art bears him out: 'writing and reading are always historically and socially determinate events. . . . We may simultaneously acknowledge the theoretical indeterminacy of the signifying process and the historical specificity of discursive practices – acts of speaking, writing and interpreting.'[102]

If, then, there is nothing intrinsically ahistorical in New Historicism, what of its importance in elucidating early modern politics and culture, the principal fields of its practice? Certainly there has been a vast industry of New Historicist readings of Renaissance texts and history which have claimed to

---

97. See Montrose, 'Professing the Renaissance', p. 19.
98. E. P. Thompson, *The Poverty of Theory and Other Essays* (1978); E. Fox-Genovese, 'Literary Criticism and the Politics of the New Historicism', in Veeser, *New Historicism*, pp. 213–30, quotation p. 222. Cf. E. Said, *The World, the Text and the Critic* (Cambridge, Mass., 1983).
99. See Evans, *In Defence of History*, pp. 252–3 and ch. 4; Appleby, Hunt and Jacob, *Telling the Truth about History*, ch. 8.
100. H. White, 'New Historicism: A Comment', in Veeser, *New Historicism*, p. 297; cf. White, *Content of the Form*, pp. 187–8.
101. S. Fish, 'Commentary: The Young and the Restless', in Veeser, *New Historicism*, p. 313.
102. Montrose, 'Professing the Renaissance', p. 23.

revise our understanding of the past and of the sources and methods we use
to study it. Literature has been presented as a rich, and neglected, body of
historical material. In the words of Harold Love (not himself a New
Historicist):

> The special value of literary texts to ... historical enquiry is that writers,
> as specialists in the use of figurative language, will often possess a privi-
> leged understanding of the figurative nature of belief systems, and be able
> to engage in a very direct and revealing way with the master narrative of
> their culture.[103]

With few exceptions, however, historians of early modern England have either
not read or have not been persuaded by New Historicist studies;[104] nor, a
separate but related point to which I shall return, have they been drawn to
admit literature into the privileged enclosure of historical evidence.[105] As has
been observed, revisionism and New Historicism, the two contemporary
innovations in the study of early modern England, took place largely sepa-
rately and, when they did encounter each other, reacted with mutual suspicion.[106] In many ways this is surprising as well as regrettable. Like revisionism,
New Historicism was concerned to question and displace 'all defenders of
linear chronology and progressive history, whether Marxist or Whig opti-
mists'.[107] Like revisionists, New Historicists advocated a return to politics,
to issues of power, authority and government. Along with revisionists' rejection of grand theories, be they J curves or Annaliste, Greenblatt, as we
have seen, preferred to pragmatically 'just ... go about and do it'.[108] And
together with revisionists, New Historicists spoke of elucidating meaning in
specific moments thickly contextualised rather than in an overarching long
narrative.

   Why then did not more of a dialogue, even an alliance between the two
take place? Historians have often objected that the New Historicism is not
truly historical: that New Historicist critics do not adequately conduct
research, that their use of evidence is arbitrary and anecdotal, and that the
history they take from other scholars is often 'ludicrously out of date'.[109] One
instance of this, it is argued, is the uncritical acceptance of Christopher Hill

---

103. H. Love, *Scribal Publication in Seventeenth-Century England* (Oxford, 1993), p. 165;
     cf. L. Jardine, 'Companionate Marriage versus Male Friendship', in Amussen and
     Kishlansky, *Political Culture*, p. 236.
104. Blair Worden, one of the historians most engaged in interdisciplinary studies, dis-
     misses New Historicist critics and theorists.
105. LaCapra, *Rethinking Intellectual History*, p. 33.
106. Sharpe and Lake, *Culture and Politics*, pp. 1–7.
107. Veeser, *New Historicism*, p. xv.
108. Above, p. 21.
109. Burgess, 'Revisionist History', p. 6; see too J. H. Zammito, 'Are We Being Theoretical
     Yet? The New Historicism, the New Philosophy of History and Practising Histori-
     ans', *J. Mod. Hist.* 65 (1993), pp. 783–814.

and Lawrence Stone and the apparent ignorance of much revisionist scholarship, the emphasis of which on consensus and stability sits uneasily with New Historicist concerns with contest and subversion.[110] Some of the objections are fair, though they risk caricaturing. But the best critical scholarship in New Historicist vein, books by Goldberg, Patterson and Schoenfeldt, is often well researched in contemporary records and historiography.[111] Besides, the drive for a more historicised New Historicism should motivate historians to cooperate in the enterprise, so as to add the benefits of revisionism to the new critical investigation of history. As Sharon Achinstein generously puts it, 'this revisionist movement in history could give new clarity, accuracy and purpose to the return to history promoted by the so-called new historicism.'[112] This is in part what critics such as Michael Schoenfeldt, Tom Corns and Steve Zwicker and historians like Derek Hirst, Blair Worden and myself have attempted;[113] and there are some signs, principally in volumes of essays, that younger historians are showing interest in a more interdisciplinary history and praxis.[114]

But what, I suspect, continues to inhibit historians is what might most enrich historical method: the New Historicist talk of text and textuality. We have already remarked how postmodern theory, with its questioning of authors making meanings that audiences receive, disturbed traditional historical assumptions.[115] Joel Fineman attributes the hostility to New Historicism to what it shares with such criticism: 'As with deconstruction, New Historicist criticism is regularly concerned with the textuality of its texts, something very foreign to the practical liberalism of UK materialism.'[116] There is an interesting history to be written about the relationship of historical revisionism, the suspicion of theory and 'UK' (should it be English?) liberalism. What instead I want to suggest here is that an address to 'the textuality of its

110. Burgess, 'Revisionist History'; D. Cressy, 'Foucault, Stone, Shakespeare and Social History', *Eng. Lit. Ren.* 21 (1991), pp. 121–33.
111. Goldberg, *James I*; A. Patterson, *Censorship and Interpretation* (Madison, 1984); M. Schoenfeldt, *Prayer and Power: George Herbert and Renaissance Courtship* (Chicago, 1991).
112. S. Achinstein, *Milton and the Revolutionary Reader* (Princeton, 1994), p. 21.
113. S. Zwicker's *Lines of Authority: Politics and English Literary Culture 1649–1689* (Ithaca, N.Y., 1993) offers richly historically contextualised readings of literary texts; cf. T. Corns, *Uncloistered Virtue: English Political Literature, 1640–1660* (Oxford, 1992); D. Hirst, 'The Politics of Literature in the English Republic', *Seventeenth Century* 5 (1991), pp. 135–55; Worden, *Sound of Virtue*; K. Sharpe, *Criticism and Compliment: The Politics of Literature in the England of Charles I* (Cambridge, 1987). For an earlier period, see the work of Greg Walker, *Plays of Persuasion: Drama and Politics at the Court of Henry VIII* (Cambridge, 1991).
114. See D. L. Smith, R. Strier and D. Bevington, *The Theatrical City: Culture, Theatre and Politics in London 1576–1649* (Cambridge, 1995), and S. Pincus's forthcoming volume on Restoration culture.
115. LaCapra criticises historians, including Skinner, for this, *Rethinking Intellectual History*, p. 36; Hume, 'Texts within Contexts'.
116. J. Fineman, 'The History of the Anecdote: Fiction and Fiction', in Veeser, *New Historicism*, p. 65.

texts' could sharpen revisionist history, no less than revisionism could aid New
Historicism. Healthily distrustful of jargon by nature, historians have tended
to regard the use of the word 'text' as a modish term deployed by critics who
take delight in obfuscation. At several conferences I have heard historians, with
more or less of resignation or sarcasm, speak of 'documents, or texts as we
are now taught to call them'.[117] What, I fear, we have not learned is that the
difference is not merely one of synonym. The different language historians
and critics use reveals (and represses) very fundamental differences about the
records of our past (and present) and about how we should interpret them.
The word 'document', for example, owes its origins to that which instructs,
teaches, 'furnishes evidence', as if demanding no action from its historical pupil
but to listen.[118] Similarly our other favourite term 'evidence' has as its first
meaning 'clearness', 'obviousness', and derives from the Latin *videre*, a word
which means to see, to perceive. What both terms *imply* is the availability of
the past to communicate to and be seen by the historian as a clear object or
lesson unmediated by representations – or time. And what they both express
is a positivism, a scientific approach to the past and its facts to which by
instinct historians (we) are prone to cling.

Yet neither 'document' nor 'evidence' are familiar, or essential, terms in
medieval or Renaissance historical writing, and it would be interesting to
chart their emerging use in the historian's lexicon, to trace their history as
part of the history of the historical discipline and historical thought.[119]
The term 'text', though it has come to mean something original or authoritative, literally meant something woven, artfully compiled. If evidence implies
a fixed object, text evokes that which is constructed (as is a textile) of many
strands that can equally be unwoven – or deconstructed. How a text, an object
that is artfully made, becomes a text, an authority or gospel, lies in those
strands – of rhetoric, form, language, tone, genre, voice, typography, punc-
tuation, material (parchment, paper, stone) – which constitute it. To think
of documents and evidence as texts is to open them to fruitful historical
questions that remain unasked. How and why did that speech persuade?
What gave proclamations their authority? How did this work of political
theory, that novel, reconstitute words, language? These were questions
familiar to a Renaissance society in which all who were educated were trained
in oratory, rhetoric, translation, language; in which writers and readers of literature (a literature which included what we would separate as philosophy,
history and fiction) were sensitive to the genre, form and materiality of their
texts.

Historians, in our age, however, pass over such matters or confine them to
their own separate histories – of education, paper and print. None comment

117. Note, for example, the revealing slippage in L. Stone: 'documents – we did not call
     them texts in those days . . .', 'History and Postmodernism', *Past & Present* 135 (1992),
     pp. 189–93; cf. G. Spiegel, in the same issue, pp. 194–208.
118. *OED* 'document'; cf. LaCapra, *Rethinking Intellectual History*, pp. 14, 30, 32–3.
119. *OED* 'discipline'.

on the politics of the continued use of gothic type in proclamations.[120] Conrad Russell writes pages about parliamentary speeches, without stopping to penetrate (let us spare him 'deconstruct') the rhetorical or formal strategies, some intended, some received, that constituted utterance in not only a specific moment and context but an established genre and form.[121] The analysis of texts has always been a skill of critics, one exemplified by 'New' and formalist criticism, one not lost but historicized by the best New Historicists.[122] A huge understatement characterises Glenn Burgess's recent observation that 'there is much that historians have to learn from literary scholars about the reading of past texts.'[123] I would assert that the 'have' should now be mandatory as well as opportunistic: that we leave behind documents – not to float without meaning in the rarefied atmosphere of nihilistic theory, but to explore the rich layers of meanings in texts, and in their writings and readings.

Writing and Authority

A close examination of texts could reveal one of the curiously neglected strands of the political tapestry: the relationship between the word and the exercise of power. From the beginning in Christian belief, the word was the source of authority. Like God, kings gave name to things; the royal voice expressed 'the ability of the royal person to generate new meanings' and 'the royal utterance was seen as the source . . . of all meaning.'[124] The king's word, spoken or written, expressed in person or representation (by a signet or seal), authorised all actions; others derived their authority from that authorisation – the authorisation to speak on the king's behalf.

In many ways the development of print extended that authority. Print was public and it publicised. Through the printed proclamation, the king could reach to all corners of his realm, at a time when the breakdown of feudal tenurial relations severed the links that joined his person to the meanest vassal. The proclamation spoke to and commanded even the illiterate. Pinned to the market cross, its typography and form announcing it to be the royal word, it was the medium through which subjects most frequently experienced royal authority directly. But, of course, it was not, strictly speaking, 'direct'. Print

---

120. See below, p. 51.
121. Searching his footnotes over all his oeuvres I found no reference to Skinner for example.
122. Schoenfeldt urges New Historicists to incorporate the 'close textual analysis pioneered by New Criticism', *Prayer and Power*, p. 13.
123. Burgess, 'Revisionist History', p. 22.
124. Love, *Scribal Publication*, p. 162. See J. Goody, *The Logic of Writing and the Organisation of Society* (Cambridge, 1986), pp. 119–22.

extended royal authority, but it also mediated it; just as it has been argued that printed books distanced the author from the reader, imposing the printer and binder between the producer and consumer of script, so print, while extending, assisted in the process of depersonalising authority.[125] As authority was increasingly conveyed via the printed proclamation, or statute, or Council order, so it was that the text, rather than being merely the medium of that remote authority, became *identified* with authority. Print gave that authority also to others. Where it was nigh impossible, as well as treasonable, to counterfeit the king's signature, the authority expressed in and through print could be appropriated in the same medium. Not long after the impact on Europe of print, the Reformation powerfully demonstrated the simultaneous capacity of print to disseminate and to challenge and ultimately destroy 'authorities' – both textual and political. The Lutheran Bible literally translated authority – both from the Vulgate and from the Vatican. The outpouring of Protestant pamphlets, illustrated with polemical woodcuts, denigrating popes and cardinals, reached deep into popular culture and communities.[126] Almost from its invention, print presented itself as the medium through which authority would be represented and communicated, denigrated and contested.

The ambivalence of print was not lost on a Tudor dynasty that was founded on the precarious authority of victory in battle. Henry VII's naming of his son Arthur was only the most personal expression of a concern with what Harold Love has called ' "fictions of state", those figurative constructs that were invoked to legitimise the exercise of political authority'.[127] Henry VIII and his ministers employed a whole team of pamphleteers to disseminate values that would constitute a Tudor commonweal, in which royal authority was to be safely protected from dynastic or religious challenge.[128] Initially, not least as a consequence of events in Germany, Henry was reluctant to permit an English Bible; when he did, it was very much the king's book, the engraved frontispiece representing Henry presenting the Word to his bishops and his kingdom. Through the King's Bible, Henry underlined the connection between text and his authority, his possession of the power of the word,

125. See E. Eisenstein, *The Printing Press as an Agent of Change: Communications and Cultural Transformations in Early Modern Europe* (Cambridge, 1979), p. 132. See W. Ong, *Orality and Literacy* (Ithaca, N.Y., 1981). For an interesting critique of Eisenstein see A. Johns, *The Nature of the Book: Print and Knowledge in the Making* (Chicago, 1998). Adrian Johns' book appeared after mine was written and has useful perspectives on the relationship of print to credibility and authority.

126. D. R. Olson, *The World on Paper: The Conceptual and Cognitive Implications of Writing and Reading* (Cambridge, 1994), pp. 53–60; see R. W. Scribner, *For the Sake of Simple Folk* (Cambridge, 1988); T. Watt, *Cheap Print and Popular Piety 1550–1640* (Cambridge, 1991).

127. Love, *Scribal Publication*, p. 141.

128. See G. R. Elton, *Reform and Renewal: Thomas Cromwell and the Common Weal* (Cambridge, 1973).

as well as the voice of power.[129] The king's book was not the work of Henry VIII's own mind and pen. He did not 'author' but 'authorised' the work, a distinction that, as we shall see, had neither the clarity nor meaning in the sixteenth century that it has for us.[130] Henry, however, may have had at least a hand in authoring as well as authorising the polemical pamphlets defending the Roman Catholic sacraments and attacking Luther.[131] Even more than the canvases on which Holbein constructed Tudor dynastic authority, writing and print were, in many ways, the foundation of Henry VIII's rule.

Not least of the difficulties facing the last two Tudors was the gendering of speaking and writing in sixteenth-century England. Women were enjoined to be silent; writing remained a male preserve until at least the Civil War or Restoration, when actresses took speaking parts for the first time on the stage and Aphra Benn claimed as a female a place in the world of both print and politics.[132] But whatever these proscriptions, it was Elizabeth I's success in transgressing them that was important to the success of her rule. Indeed, the Queen managed the clever art of speaking, writing and ruling while appearing not to subvert the values that privileged these as masculine prerogatives. Nevertheless, as I have argued, Elizabeth's prayers and translations were texts of power, the acts of a monarch who knew, no less than Shakespeare's Richard II, that her authority was of one with her word.[133]

Elizabeth's successor not only practised but epitomised that belief. Though they await proper study as 'texts' – and as texts of power – James I's polemical writings and paraphrases of scripture are well known. Moreover, as king of Scotland, James VI wrote poetry, and a critical treatise on writing poetry, which were published before he acceded to the English throne. As numerous panegyrical verses to him testify, James was seen as a writer as well as a ruler. Nor could the two be separated: James himself had come close to saying that the 'best of poets', as Ben Jonson put it, might be the 'best of kings'.[134] His *Workes*, a large folio, as the engraved title page and preface make obvious, was the royal word and a royal act – an act of government.[135] What

---

129. See *The Bible in English* (1539); J. N. King, *Tudor Royal Iconography* (Princeton, 1989), pp. 32–3; G. Walker, *Persuasive Fictions: Faction, Faith and Political Culture in the Reign of Henry VIII* (Aldershot, 1996), pp. 92–3.

130. See *OED* 'author' and cf. T. Hobbes, *Leviathan*, ed. R. Tuck (Cambridge, 1991), ch. 16.

131. Henry VIII, *The Glasse of Truth* (1532); *Assertio Septem Sacramentorum* (1521). See J. J. Scarisbrick, *Henry VIII* (Harmondsworth, 1971), pp. 152–8

132. See S. Hull, *Chaste, Silent and Obedient: English Books for Women 1475–1640* (San Marino, 1988); I. Grundy and S. Wiseman, *Women, Writing, History, 1640–1740* (1992).

133. K. Sharpe, 'The King's Writ: Royal Authors and Royal Authority in Early Modern England', in Sharpe and Lake, *Culture and Politics*, pp. 119–23.

134. Ben Jonson, *Ben Jonson Poems*, ed. I. Donaldson (Oxford, 1985), p. 223.

135. See *The Workes of the Most High and Mighty Prince James* (1616), preface to the reader; and for a discussion of the title page, M. Corbett and R. Lightbown, *The Comely Frontispiece: The Emblematic Title Page in England* (1979), pp. 137–44.

James authored, his word, complemented that other folio graced with his image, the Word he *authorised*, the translation of the English Bible published in 1611 as the 'Authorised King James Version'.[136]

If James VI and I displayed confidence in the capacity of his word and authority to stand unanswered, he was to be disappointed. Not only did other institutions – notably Parliament – claim their authority through published speeches and Protestations, the first newspapers and corantos published their own version of events abroad to a public thirsty for information.[137] Far from commanding the field of writing and print, the king faced a 'country oppo- sition' that was in part constructed and sustained through the publication of pamphlets and news.[138] Royal authority was contested not least because the royal utterance and text met with response, riposte and challenge.

The belief that the king could control the word and that his uncontested word was the fount of his power was never more than a fiction, a rewriting of the 'fiction' of the divine logos that wrote the first sentence of St John's gospel: 'in the beginning was the word.' For long, however, the fiction remained unexposed. But it was eroding through a number of cultural changes the effects of which await proper study. For one, the revival of the classics and the teaching of classical oratory reinforced the close asso- ciation between rhetoric and power, but simultaneously exposed the pos- sibility of a gap between language and truth, the capacity of words (and their authors) to mis-represent as well as to represent. Similarly the flourish- ing of the drama in Elizabethan and Jacobean London made the dialogue a familiar form to audiences, lowly and elite. On the stage too, boys person- ated the king – spoke the 'royal' word. We must pause to remind ourselves that when 'Richard II' delivered his famous speech about the royal word and the royal office, a boy spoke Shakespeare's words, themselves partially borrowed from the playwright's sources.[139] Appropriately the theatre exem- plified the way in which the 'fictions of state' could be authored by others; and, with that, the legitimisation or interrogation of authority passed to others too.

One narrative that undoubtedly forms part of this history is the changing attitude to authorship. Critics have begun to study this subject as part of the history of the literary profession – of copyright and 'royalty' (sic) – or as a chapter in the story of the emergent self and subjectivity.[140] What we as his-

---

136. Herbert praised the royal/divine word and a king who might be 'gazed upon on paper'. Schoenfeldt, *Prayer and Power*, p. 29. In the dedication to James of the Autho- rised Version, the translators described him as 'the principal mover and *author* of the work' (my italics).

137. J. Frank, *The Beginnings of the English Newspaper: 1620–1660* (Cambridge, Mass., 1961).

138. See R. Cust, 'News and Politics in Seventeenth Century England', *Past & Present* 112 (1986), pp. 60–90.

139. For a startling contemporary perception of such fictions, see below, p. 222.

140. See R. Chartier, 'Figures of the Author', in Chartier, *The Order of Books* (Cambridge, 1994), ch. 2; M. Rose, *Authors and Owners: The Invention of Copyright* (Cambridge, Mass., 1993); M. Woodmansee and P. Jazzi, eds, *The Construction of Authorship: Textual*

torians need to appreciate is that the history of authorship and intellectual property are political narratives, the debates about literary property being no less important for the struggles over authority than the resistance to taxation, imposts or seizure of 'real' estate.[141] The Renaissance period broadly conceived witnessed a change from valuing a text for its authorised origin to 'granting its author creative autonomy' and valorising 'originality'.[142] As so often, Montaigne articulates the change. Though like others he plundered the established 'auctores' of his day for sententiae, adages and information, he claimed the work as his own (and himself as the matter of his book).[143] These claims did not only – though that was a revolution of itself – appropriate authority from the source to the author. They also elevated the *actual* author of a text over the figure or institution that authorised it. Those, like Thomas Starkey and Richard Morison in Henry VIII's reign, or Thomas Nashe in Elizabeth's, hired as spin doctors to present a view of authority or (in Nashe's case) to counter attacks on it, would emerge over the course of the seventeenth century to become public figures whose name and authority kings and governments were as anxious to secure for their service as writers were to enjoy official patronage and imprimatur. By the end of the seventeenth century, as the career of Dryden manifests, authors had their own authority to sell to a king – or a party cause.[144]

The consequences of these developments for authority are not yet clear and were not at the time fully realised or acknowledged. The fiction that the king's word was the source of authority survived far beyond events such as the publication of the Petition of Right, or the appropriation by critics of Charles I's rule of the 'official' genres of trial report, to make martyrs of Prynne, Burton and Bastwick.[145] But the blatant attacks by the Scots on a text the king authorised, the Prayer Book, could not disguise its assault on his authority, for all the loyal rhetoric deployed by the Kirk.[146] The Civil War, as we know, was preceded by a print war, a war of words – and one that the king lost until other 'authors', chiefly Edward Hyde, were recruited to rescript and rewrite his authority.[147] During the 1640s, it was not only Royalists and Parliamentarians who contended for victory. The word and the sword, legitimisation and conquest, were in contention for the validation of

Appropriation in Law and Literature (Durham, N.C., 1994); Johns, *Nature of the Book*, pp. 246–8, 365–6.

141. A connection made by Milton in *Eikonoklastes*, see below, p. 32.
142. D. Quint, *Origin and Originality in Renaissance Literature* (New Haven, 1983), p. 219.
143. D. Losse, 'From Auctor to Auteur: Authorisation and Appropriation in the Renaissance', *Medievala et Humanistica* 16 (1988), pp. 153–63; cf. A. Ophir, 'A Place of Knowledge Re-created: The Library of Michel de Montaigne', *Science in Context* 4 (1991), pp. 163–89, esp. pp. 180–2.
144. Sharpe and Zwicker, *Refiguring Revolutions*, p. 9; Love, *Scribal Publication*, pp. 173–6.
145. See K. Sharpe, *The Personal Rule of Charles I* (1992), pp. 758–65.
146. Ibid., pp. 813–22.
147. J. E. Hartman, 'Restyling the King: Clarendon writes Charles I', in J. Holstun, ed., *Pamphlet Wars: Prose in the English Revolution* (1992), pp. 45–59.

authority. Charles I's troops lost the military battle; but the king set out to win the war – of words and for words – so as to deny his enemies the fruit of their victory. Such an objective seemed no more attainable than success at arms. Throughout the 1640s every word of the king's had been answered, scrutinised, published and exposed as deceit: the royal word had lost any remnant of the authority to secure trust or determine meaning or values.[148] Yet in the *Eikon Basilike*, the book published in his name the day after his execution, Charles I claimed for the royal word or text a position above the pamphlet fray: he reappropriated for monarchy divine right, the divine logos, the Word.[149]

The civil war and regicide were critical moments in the relationship between text and authority. As Love argues incisively (if not elegantly): 'The rejection of the royal authority by the parliament disposed . . . of the fiction of a single signification – conferring voice as the source of political authority, and initially must have seemed to open the way to a babble of mutually competing voices.'[150] To this crisis, parliamentary regimes reacted by demanding subscription to a number of texts claiming authority for themselves: the vow and covenant of 1643, the Solemn League of 1644. Royalists, by contrast, reasserted that 'where the word of a King is there is Power.'[151] So powerfully persistent was the identity of king as author and authority that the 'royal' text of the *Eikon* seemed set to deny validity or authority to the new republic.[152] Because he sensed and feared that very threat, Milton brought to bear against it all the challenges that could be mustered against the authority of that text – against the textuality of monarchy itself. In *Eikonoklastes*, Milton tried to break the link between text and power.[153] Returning to the old (but still potent) view that the authority of a text depended on its *auctores*, he accused Charles I of plundering other texts without acknowledging his 'authorities'.[154] Secondly, he denied the king's 'authorship', on grounds of style, circumstance and personality, so robbing the words of the authority of a royal author.[155] Finally – as we shall have cause to remark – in deconstructing the king's book, he opened up text and authority to other

---

148. Though it is worth remembering that the most devastating attack on Charles I was seen to be the publication of his own words: his letters to Henrietta Maria, published in *The King's Cabinet Opened* (1645). See J. Raymond, 'Popular Representations of Charles I', in T. Corns, ed., *The Royal Image: Representations of Charles I* (Cambridge, 1999), pp. 47–73.

149. Sharpe, 'King's Writ', pp. 135–8.

150. Love, *Scribal Publication*, p. 163.

151. *The Rebels Looking Glasse* (1649), Thomason E554/23, p. 1.

152. See K. Sharpe, '"An Image Doting Rabble": The Failure of Republican Culture in Seventeenth Century England', in Sharpe and Zwicker, *Refiguring Revolutions*, pp. 33–5.

153. John Milton, *Eikonoklastes*, in *The Works of John Milton*, vol. 5, ed. W. H. Haller (New York, 1932); R. Helgerson, 'Milton Reads the King's Book: Print, Performance, and the Making of a Bourgeois Idol', *Criticism* 29 (1987), pp. 1–25.

154. Milton, *Eikonoklastes*, pp. 83–9.

155. Ibid., pp. 64–8, 72, 104, 258–9, 264.

and different readings, and in the process made claims for the authority of (all) readers as well as writers of text.[156]

It is not clear how far Milton effected a breach between royal author and authority, let alone created a revolutionary reader. The *Eikon* remained popular as the authentic word of a martyred king and the republic never established its legitimacy.[157] Those like Sir Thomas Browne who had branded the printing of royal speeches, no less than counterfeiting the king's coin, as an act of treason, evidently believed that any authority depended on a single 'author' of meaning.[158] Hobbes regarded it as essential that his sovereign should control all language, and have the sovereign right to all signification.[159] Those many who referred to the Civil War and republic, with its outpouring of pamphlets, as a Babel desired the return of a royal author as well as royal rule. As David Lloyd, the author of a tract also entitled *Eikon Basilike*, put it on the eve of the Restoration: 'I wish our Sovereign would exercise a pen as imperial as his sceptre and write himself with the same royalty that he lives.'[160]

The desire may have been conservative, but Lloyd's language was novel, even startlingly postmodern. The reference to the king 'writing' himself explicitly acknowledged that the 'fiction of state' reconstituted at the Restoration differed from earlier regimes and from that of the royal work from which Lloyd took his title. The Restoration 'fiction of state' 'made little attempt to disguise its fictive nature'.[161] Charles II himself not only told the narrative of his escape from Cromwell's forces as a story; as he retold it he openly deployed the devices of fiction – suspense, plot and 'character'.[162] And though the story was the king's, the 'authors' of *Boscabel* and *The Royal Oak* were others, bit part actors who told their own stories and published them under their own names, and wrote the king and his part in their own ways. In the changed world of Restoration, the ultimate 'responsibility for sustaining fictions of authority had been passed to the professional makers of fiction' – to authors.[163]

A simple narrative then of the relationship between text and authority in early modern England might outline the move from the authority of sources

---

156. Below pp. 291–2.
157. Sharpe, '"An Image Doting Rabble"'; cf. now S. Kelsey, *Inventing a Republic: The Political Culture of the English Commonwealth, 1649–53* (Manchester, 1997) for a different view which I find unpersuasive.
158. Holstun, *Pamphlet Wars*, p. 25.
159. Hobbes, *Leviathan*, ch. 6; cf. S. Achinstein, 'The Politics of Babel in the English Revolution', in Holstun, *Pamphlet Wars*, pp. 14–44, esp. p. 31 on Cleveland's argument that 'only the king has authority to validate language.'
160. D. Lloyd, *Eikon Basilike or The True Portraiture of His Sacred Majesty Charles II* (1660) E1922/2, p. 3.
161. Love, *Scribal Publication*, p. 164.
162. W. Matthews, ed., *Charles II's Escape from Worcester: A Collection of Narratives Assembled by Samuel Pepys* (Berkeley, 1966).
163. *Boscobel or The History of His Sacred Majesties Most Miraculous Preservation . . .* (1660), E1838/2; *The Royal Oak* (1660), E1023/15; Love, *Scribal Publication*, p. 173.

('authorities') and authorisers to the growing independence and claims of
authors, who by the end of the seventeenth century had become figures of
political as well as cultural import. Such a narrative is open not only to the
charge of being Whig; it is also oversimplified. Authors and texts inhabit as
well as fabricate a culture, and wider commercial and social changes – urban
growth, the development of a consumer culture, the loosening of ties of
patronage – all altered the place of authors and texts, as did changes in the
print trade, the production, price and distribution of books.[164] But what the
author/authoriser/authority axis crucially omits – and what we must now
bring into focus – is the audience for and of these texts: the reader, or the
'subjects' (that is the matter, the person, those owing obedience) of the text.
If we are to understand how authority was exercised and experienced in early
modern England, we need to understand how the texts of authority were
read.

Pursuing the Reader

The most important move in hermeneutic and critical theory has been to a
concern with the reading and consumption of texts. Where 'until recently the
reader was perhaps the most neglected element in the framework of literary
communication,' the shift from concentration on authors' intentions to the
performances of texts led obviously to readers.[165] Any attempt to understand
how texts structure and make meaning translates at some point into the question of how meaning arises from the reader's 'encounter with these words on
the page'.[166] For, whatever the intentions of authors (or authorisers) of texts,
readers bring their experiences (not least of other texts) to any reading.
Reading indeed becomes a process in which we translate into our own words,
symbols and mental contexts the marks and signs on the page.

   If critics have concurred about the importance of the reader in the process
of construing and constructing meaning, they have differed greatly about what
that place might be and how we might study the reader or the experience
of the text. And where for some the reader comes in at the end of a process

164. W. A. Speck, *Society and Literature in England 1700–1760* (Dublin, 1963); J. Brewer and
     R. Porter, eds, *Consumption and the World of Goods* (1993); P. Rogers, *Grub Street* (1972).
165. Ian Maclean, 'Reading and Interpretation', in A. Jefferson and D. Robey, eds, *Modern
     Literary Theory*, 2nd edn (1986), p. 122. For other introductory guides to reader
     response criticism, see E. Freund, *The Return of the Reader* (1987); S. Suleiman and I.
     Crosman, eds, *The Reader in the Text: Essays on Audience and Reception* (Princeton,
     1980); P. J. Rabinowitz, 'Whirl without End: Audience Orientated Criticism', in
     G. D. Atkins and L. Morrow, eds, *Contemporary Literary Theory* (Houndmills, 1989),
     pp. 81–100; Newton, *Interpreting the Text*, ch. 7; J. P. Tompkins, ed., *Reader Response
     Criticism: From Formalism to Post Structuralism* (Baltimore, 1980).
166. Newton, *Interpreting the Text*, p. 85.

of authors making meanings which the reader modifies, radical theorists like Roland Barthes posit the reader as the maker of texts, the 'producer of the text',[167] very much in the spirit of Nietzsche's assertion that 'ultimately man finds in things nothing but what he himself has imported into them.'[168] The disputes, of course, about whether texts control readers or readers write texts is inextricably bound up with the discussions of the stability or indeterminacy of meanings that we have seen as the subject of poststructuralist criticisms. And, like all criticism (and history), they are part of large ideological issues about coherence or multiplicity, unity or plurality of meanings and values, in the critics' own culture. Not surprisingly therefore, even in its relatively brief history the study of readers and reception has manifested itself very differently from critic to critic, and over place and time. Despite their own differences the so-called Konstanz theorists of *Rezeptionsästhetik*, Hans Robert Jauss and Wolfgang Iser, still accord to the text (if not the author) and its formal properties a major role in its own reception.[169] Though Jauss, for instance, argues that 'the oppositions between fiction and reality, between the poetic and practical functions of language' were available as choices to the reader of a work, that 'potential for meaning' was and is 'embedded in a work' and readers came to texts with a 'horizon of expectations'.[170] Such a 'fusion of horizons' connects readers to texts and authors via a set of shared conventions which do not finally determine but which delimit both writing and reading at specific moments in time. Iser places more emphasis on the indeterminacy of the text, but still in his notion of (and title of his major work) *The Implied Reader* suggests a text's foresight and control of the reading process and the guiding devices operative in it. Though critical of earlier Marxist[171] or formalist assumptions that readings were determined by social position or by authors' intentions and text's formal properties, reception theory tends still to situate reading within the structure of society and literary culture, 'the system of relationships in the literature', as Jauss puts it.[172]

Other critics have approached reading from more personal (liberal humanist, sociological, psychoanalytical) perspectives. Norman Holland, expounding his own theory of reading as a 'personal transaction', argues for the extraliterary facts that shape reading by a powerful recalling of his own reading in puberty of Poe's *The Purloined Letter*.[173] Holland questions the

---

167. Ibid., p. 81. See R. Barthes, *S/Z* (1975).
168. Newton, *Interpreting the Text*, p. 87.
169. H. R. Jauss, *Toward an Aesthetic of Reception* (Minnesota, 1982); W. Iser, *The Act of Reading: A Theory of Aesthetic Response* (1978); Iser, *The Implied Reader: Patterns of Communication in Prose Fiction from Bunyan to Beckett* (Baltimore, 1980).
170. Jauss, *Toward an Aesthetic of Reception*, p. 30; I. Suleiman, 'Varieties of Audience-Orientated Criticism', in Suleiman and Crosman, *Reader in the Text*, p. 36.
171. Iser, *Implied Reader*; cf. Iser, 'Interaction between Text and Reader', in Suleiman and Crosman, *Reader in the Text*, pp. 106–19.
172. Jauss, *Toward an Aesthetic of Reception*, pp. 12–18, 36.
173. N. Holland, 'Recovering "The Purloined Letter": Reading as a Personal Transaction',

notion of a shared response implicit in Jauss and Iser, and insists on the 'unique identity' of the reader in a way that echoes the old emphasis on the individuality of the author – as a coherent self outside of cultural and social relations. Jacques Leenhardt posits a more cultural approach to reading in demonstrating how very different societies, those of France and Hungary, respond to the same novels.[174]

Albeit in less specialised language, everyday experience confirms that the process of reading is something more complex than a simple acceptance or rejection of a unified meaning produced by an author or text, and that reading is a cultural as well as personal action, and indeed that, even in our own lives, it is specific to moments and places. We know that formal novels (even departures from form of the sort practised say by Sterne in *Tristram Shandy*) shape as well as license our imaginative response; that an American reads the irony of an Austen novel rather differently from an English reader; that to read D. H. Lawrence at sixteen and sixty are very different experiences; and that to read in the Library of Congress and on the beach conditions what meaning we take from even the same text – though in this case the place is also likely to influence the text being read. All this is a valuable – and essential – reminder that we read, make meaning of the world, differently in different circumstances. But what it does not do is address the vital question, how. As Robert Darnton recently put it, for all the value of reception theory in turning attention from the authors and texts to the activity of readers, it 'has yet to prove itself because we do not know what reading is even when it takes place under our own noses'.[175] Indeed educational theorists are as divided as critical theorists when it comes to explaining how a child comes to read and whether the one verb accommodates the many (different) practices that are involved in making meaning of signs on the page.[176] Nor, though the subject is understandably now a prominent one, is there any developed understanding of the relationship of the medium of a text – in books, tape, microfilm or computer screen – to the ways we make sense of it for ourselves. Does the poem on the underground train, 'read' as we jostle next to fellow passengers, alert to the pickpocket and our next station, have a meaning different from when read alone in the light of a drawing room fire? Does the scrolled screen render differently from the turned page the unfolding suspense of a thriller novel? How does the removal of the touch on the page affect the pleasures of the text, and is its consequence greater, say, for the reading of erotic fiction than for the economic report?

What such questions do, even when they remain unanswered, is point to the specificity – that is to say to the historicity – of all acts of reading, even

in Suleiman and Crosman, *Reader in the Text*, pp. 350–70; cf. Holland, *5 Readers Reading* (New Haven and London, 1975).

174. J. Leenhardt, 'Toward a Sociology of Reading', in Suleiman and Crosman, *Reader in the Text*, pp. 205–24.
175. R. Darnton, 'How to Read a Book', *New York Review of Books*, 6 June 1996, p. 52.
176. See J. A. Langer, ed., *Reader Meets Author: Bridging the Gap* (Newark, Del., 1982).

if it is the history of the moment of reading this last sentence. Here, as in other respects, theories of reading have not contributed neatly to any history of reading. Theory, however, need not be a rival to history when it comes to understanding how people have read. Jauss and still more Iser urge a diachronic, historical approach to reading as a process of 'successive unfolding' of meanings of a text, 'actualised in the stages of its historical reception', and stress the relationship of literary history to the other histories in which a text is situated and performs.[177] More particularly, the critic Stanley Fish offers a theory of reading or a reader-response criticism that is intrinsically historical. For though he argues that the readers make meanings of texts in the process of reading, Fish delimits the indeterminacy and individuality that implies by arguing that readers (and writers) both act in a context and partake of an 'interpretive community' that determines what is read.[178] 'It is interpretive communities', Fish wrote, 'rather than either the text or the reader that produce meanings. . . . Interpretive communities are made up of those who share interpretive strategies.'[179] Such strategies are historically specific: to write their history is to get to the heart of 'understanding how people construe the symbolic systems made available to them by their culture'.[180]

Along with the New Historicism, many theorists and critics are now calling for a turn to a history of reading as the only means of passing 'beyond the *supposed* experience of a generalised reader' to 'focus on the actual reading experiences and responses of specific individuals to specific works'.[181] As one put it recently, 'literary theorists have debated endlessly whether the reader writes the text or the text manipulates the reader. A history of audiences could lead us out of this deadlock by revealing the interactions of specific readers and texts.'[182] Despite this comforting talk of history and specificity, even Fish's comment (with echoes familiar to seventeenth-century historians) that reading, the structuring of meaning, is 'an event rather than an entity', historians have not for the most part been attracted to the programme of a historicised reception theory or historical reader-response criticism.[183] Indeed the leading historian of print has voiced her scepticism about whether one

177. Jauss, *Toward an Aesthetic of Reception*, p. 30.
178. S. Fish, *Is There a Text in this Class? The Authority of Interpretive Communities* (Cambridge, Mass., 1980).
179. S. Fish, *Is There a Text?* p. 14; cf. Fish, 'Is There a Text in this Class?' in D. H. Richter, *Falling into Theory* (New York, 1994), pp. 226–37.
180. Darnton, 'How to Read a Book', p. 52.
181. Suleiman, 'Varieties of Audience-Orientated Criticism', p. 26.
182. J. Rose, 'Re-reading the English Common Reader: A Preface to a History of Audience', *J. Hist. Ideas* 53 (1992), pp. 47–70, at p. 65.
183. Fish, *Is There a Text in this Class?* p. 3. Conrad Russell spoke of parliaments as events rather than institutions, see his 'The Nature of a Parliament in Early Stuart England', in H. Tomlinson, *Before the English Civil War* (1983), p. 125. Hume writes: 'The paucity of work to date in linking historical particulars with the implications of reader response theory is startling', 'Texts within Contexts', p. 83.

can recover 'what really went on in the minds of silent, solitary readers'.[184] However, just as since Plato there have been theories of reading, so there have been histories of reading, albeit often written before the questions critical theory has raised. Conventional literary histories, after all, based on ideas of influence and pedigree, chart a history of readings, albeit those enacted by a special category of readers – other writers of 'literature'.[185] And books like Richard Hoggart's classic *The Uses of Literacy* presented some startling findings about what and how working-class readers in the Britain of the 1950s read, showing them extracting what they wanted from books on their own terms.[186] More recent work has unearthed equally striking examples of working-class readers of the *Iliad*, but has also sounded a note of caution to politicising critics in revealing how readers can pass over what the critic identifies as ideological freight, ignoring the 'imperialism' in Kipling's novels for example.[187]

If the reader in our own time confounds assumptions and expectations, what possibility is there for understanding the process of reading in the past? Statistical studies of books published and purchased have plotted large narratives of overall reading patterns: the decline of the classics and religious literature, the rise in the eighteenth century of novels, natural histories and travel literature, the shift to extensive from intensive reading.[188] An early adventurous attempt to pursue *The English Common Reader* over four centuries presented valuable information about the printing, sales, distribution and prices of books.[189] Specialised monographs have debated the degree and extent of literacy in premodern times and researched student notebooks as well as official curricula to determine what was studied at school and university.[190] Such studies throw essential light needed to comprehend reading but somehow do not bring the subject itself under the lamp. As Roger Chartier argues, 'the intellectual use to which readers put their reading is a decisive question that cannot be answered either by thematic analyses of the printed works pro-

184. Eisenstein, *Printing Press*, p. 149.
185. J. Culler, 'Prolegomena to a Theory of Reading', in Suleiman and Crosman, *Reader in the Text*, pp. 50ff.
186. R. Hoggart, *The Uses of Literacy: Aspects of Working Class Life with Special Reference to Publications and Entertainments* (1957).
187. Rose, 'Re-reading the English Common Reader', pp. 49ff., 68.
188. See, for example, H. J. Martin, *Livre, pouvoir et société à Paris au XVII siècle* (2 vols, Geneva, 1969); R. Estivals, *Le Statistique bibliographique de la France sous la monarchie au XVIII siècle* (Paris, 1965); L. Febvre and J. Martin, *The Coming of the Book: The Impact of Printing, 1450–1800* (1958, 1971); F. Furet and J. Ozouf, *Reading and Writing: Literacy in France from Calvin to Jules Ferry* (Cambridge, 1982); Chartier, *Cultural Uses of Print*; H. S. Bennet, *English Books and Readers, 1475–1557* (Cambridge, 1952); Bennet, *English Books and Readers, 1603–1640* (Cambridge, 1970).
189. R. Altick, *The English Common Reader* (Chicago, 1957).
190. For example D. Cressy, *Literacy and the Social Order: Reading and Writing in Tudor and Stuart England* (Cambridge, 1980); M. Todd, *Christian Humanism and the Puritan Social Order* (Cambridge, 1987), ch. 3.

duced or by an analysis of the social diffusion of the various categories of works' – be it through bookseller or school.[191]

Recently the response to this problem of how to study 'the intellectual use to which readers put their reading' has led to the creation of a new discipline: that of the history of the book. As Robert Darnton (with Chartier one of its best known founders) argues, the discipline emerged from a convergence of several scholars – critics, sociologists, bibliographers, librarians and historians – all concerned with 'the social and cultural history of communication by print'.[192] The history of the book recognises that certain types of historical enquiry, the ways in which questions are asked as well as answered, need to be an interdisciplinary endeavour. And this, alas, is the problem as well as the promise of the history of the book. With some notable exceptions, there is always the danger that the history of the book fragments back into the smaller identity groups from which it was created. Traditional biographers and librarians do not always feel at home with sociologists and Annaliste historians, let alone critical theorists. Significantly this new discipline has so far done little to incorporate reception theory into a historical and material study of books and their readers. Moreover there is an equal danger that the history of the book is itself becoming a specialism, with its own conferences, journals and programmes (if not departments) – and a specialism that other 'mainstream' historians feel no guilt about ignoring or marginalising.[193] This is perhaps a particular danger in England where intellectual history of a traditional stripe has shown itself disinclined to study what we might call the material culture of ideas: books, bindings, library furniture, leaving such subjects to more artisanal colleagues, less at home in the rarefied world of Platonic philosophy or natural rights theory. It may be no accident that the continental, German and French, inclination to theory and an American comfort with (what the English still regard as vulgar) consumerism, along with a more democratic even populist ideology, have combined to produce the best scholarship so far in the history of reading.

Yet while there are now signs that English historians – especially of the Middle Ages and the eighteenth century – discern that the history of reading may be central to the understanding of the 'master narratives' of society and politics, English historians of the seventeenth century have largely ignored these developments.[194] This is much more serious than contempt for some

191. Chartier, *Cultural History*, p. 35.

192. R. Darnton, 'What is the History of Books?' *Daedalus* 3 (1982), pp. 65–83; cf. Darnton, 'First Steps toward a History of Reading', *Austral. J. French Studies* 23 (1986), pp. 5–30. See too J. P. Feather, 'The Book in History and the History of the Book', *J. Lib. Hist.* 21 (1986), pp. 12–26 and cf. R. Chartier, *Lectures et lecteurs dans la France d'ancien régime* (Paris, 1982).

193. Darnton, 'What is the History of Books?' pp. 65–6.

194. M. B. Parkes, *Scribes, Scripts and Readers: Studies in the Communication, Presentation and Dissemination of Medieval Texts* (1991); M. T. Clanchy, *From Memory to Written Record*, 2nd edn (Oxford, 1993); J. Raven, *Judging New Wealth: Popular Publishing and Responses*

modish new field of enquiry, or lack of interest in some exotic or marginal area of study. For the historian of the Renaissance to ignore the theoretical and historical questions about reading, as well as writing, texts is to be guilty of anachronism. For as Darnton acknowledges, 'to be sure the history of the book did not begin yesterday. It stretches back to the Renaissance if not beyond.'[195] Victoria Khan nicely historicises what at times appears to be a new methodology: 'reader response criticism could only be seen as new and fashionable when the assumptions of a humanist rhetorical tradition had been forgotten.'[196] That rhetorical tradition was throughout as concerned with readers and auditors as with orators and writers: rhetoric presumes readers who may be persuaded or not persuaded, able to 'read' as they decided. And, as Erasmus clearly discerned, 'right reading' was as much an ethical practice, an inculcation and practice of virtue and prudence, as learning to write, speak and act. Reading was an action, an activity, through which people learned to be good citizens in a Christian commonweal.[197]

There can be no doubt that Renaissance educational theory placed great emphasis on the arts of reading. What we must also appreciate is the humanist recognition of the independence and power of readers, as well as authors, to construct their own meanings. This recognition stemmed in part from the nature and conditions of Renaissance authorship and writing. Patronage, for example, the tradition not only of dedicating to patrons but writing as if for them primarily, implicitly placed the reader in a position of greater authority (as he or she usually was) than the author. The dedicatee not only provided the livelihood that was the most basic precondition of writing, but also facilitated publication, authorised the work and at times used influence to bypass the censor.[198] The patronage system placed the reader, chronologically and hierarchically, before the author of the text; and arguably the decline of aristocratic patronage was necessary for the emerging prominence of the author by the early eighteenth century. Secondly, since much of humanist writing involved a rewriting of classical texts and arguments, often the Renaissance writer was a reader (in the technical pedagogic sense of exegete, as well as the wider more common meaning) of those texts.[199] In Terence Cave's words, in the Renaissance theory of 'imitatio', 'the

to Commerce in England, 1750–1800 (Oxford, 1992); J. Brewer, The Pleasures of the Imagination (1997), ch. 4.

195. Darnton, 'What is the History of Books?' p. 65.
196. V. Khan, Rhetoric, Prudence and Scepticism in the Renaissance (Ithaca, N.Y., 1985), p. 19.
197. T. Cave, The Cornucopian Text: Problems of Writing in the French Renaissance (Oxford, 1979), ch. 3; Cave, 'The Mimesis of Reading in the Renaissance', in J. D. Lyons and S. G. Nichols, eds, Mimesis: From Mirror to Method, Augustine to Descartes (1982), pp. 150–65; A. Grafton and L. Jardine, From Humanism to the Humanities: Education and the Liberal Arts in Fifteenth and Sixteenth Century Europe (1986).
198. On the title page of Spenser's Shepherd's Calendar it is the name of Sidney as dedicatee that appears, not Spenser. See A. Marotti, Manuscript, Print and the English Renaissance Lyric (Ithaca, N.Y., 1995), p. 310
199. H. O. White, Plagiarism and Imitation during the English Renaissance (New York, 1965).

activities of reading and writing become virtually identified.'[200] As Nicholas Faret confessed in the aptly titled *The Honest Man* (1632), he had so mingled the views of the ancients with his own that he no longer knew how to unravel them.[201]

As Faret's comment makes clear, this rewriting was never a simple, unmediated rehearsal of classical ideas and texts. Translation was interpretation, an act which translated not only the words from one language to another, but authority over meaning from the original to the new edition and its author/translator.[202] Indeed, the vogue for translations and editions of the classics, far from elevating their authority, appropriated it and opened these texts – as much as the vernacular Bible exposed the scriptures – to interrogation and reinterpretation. 'If venerable texts are to be fragmented and eventually transformed by the process of rewriting, it becomes visibly less necessary to regard them as closed and authoritative wholes.'[203] 'Fragmentation' and 'rewriting' virtually describe the humanist educational programme – especially the practice recommended by Erasmus and all leading educational theorists of keeping a commonplace book in which notes from original texts were reconstituted under subject headings chosen by the note-taker. As we shall see graphically and in detail, the commonplace method made every educated Englishman or woman into a reader who very much made his or her own meaning.[204] From the social system of patronage through to the pedagogic instruction of grammar school education, Renaissance culture foregrounded the reader as a forceful presence in the republic of letters.

Writers themselves were the first to credit the reader's independence and authority. They knew that certain genres virtually demanded readers to make their own meanings and that the habit and freedom so called up were redeployed as common practice. Bacon, for example, regarded fable, a genre that crossed elite and popular culture, as 'pliant stuff': 'how freely it will follow any way you please to draw it, and how easily with a little dexterity and discourse of wit meanings which it was never meant to have may be plausibly put upon it.'[205] Histories too left space for the interpretation of the reader. In the *Advancement of Learning* Bacon described it as 'the true office of history to represent the events themselves together with the counsels and to leave the observations and conclusions thereupon to the liberty and faculty of every man's judgement'.[206] John Hayward, author of the *Lives of the III Normans*, seemed resigned to the fact that 'men will be not readers only but

200. Cave, *Cornucopian Text*, p. 35.
201. N. Faret, *The Honest Man or The Art to Please in Court* (1632), pp. 404–5.
202. R. Crosman compares translation and reading in 'Do Readers Make Meaning?' in Suleiman and Crosman, *Reader in the Text*, pp. 152–4.
203. Cave, 'Mimesis of Reading', p. 155.
204. See below, pp. 277–83.
205. Quoted by J. Wallace, '"Examples Are Best Precepts": Readers and Meaning in Seventeenth-Century Poetry', *Critical Inquiry* 1 (1974), pp. 273–90, at p. 277.
206. F. Bacon, *The Advancement of Learning and New Atlantis*, ed. A. Johnston (Oxford, 1974), p. 77.

interpreters, but wresters, but corrupters and depravers of that which they read.'[207] Experience, not least the bitter quarrels over the interpretation of biblical passages during the English Reformation, had instructed that, like it or not, textual meaning was not absolute, that individuals read – and even chose to read – differently.[208] When John Chamberlain sent Dudley Carleton a copy of the controversial preface to Hayward's *Historie . . . of Henry IV* he invited his friend to proffer a different reading to his own: 'I have just got you a transcript of it that you may pick out the offence if you can; for my part I can find no such bug words but that everything is as it is taken.'[209] Writers like Bacon and Montaigne could not but be aware of the potential freedom of the reader, given their own often audaciously independent rereadings of the classical texts they revered. Montaigne boasted that 'I have read in Livy a hundred things that another man has not read in him';[210] and Bacon regarded the practices of commonplacing of most 'profit and use; because they have in turn a kind of observation'.[211]

In a brilliant thesis Terence Cave has suggested that such a recognition of, even some applause for, the openness of texts to variant readings refashioned the act of writing in the Renaissance. In particular he finds in Ronsard, Rabelais and Montaigne a creative tension between a persistent quest for integrity and coherence and a new desire to open their own writings, as well as those they imitated. 'Plural texts like those of Rabelais and Montaigne by drawing the attention to the problem of how they should be read give licence to an interpretative approach.'[212] Annabel Patterson has made a similar argument for Holinshed leaving the interpretation of his multivocal chronicles to 'each man's judgement', so as to foster an independent, critical spirit.[213] It would be fruitful to pursue this thesis for other early modern English texts, though at first reading Jonson's plays suggest a rather different cultural desire to foreclose and control – a difference that invites its own history. Yet whether they welcomed it or not, English writers by the end of the sixteenth century knew that the fate of their texts/selves lay with their readers. In *A Free and Offenceless Justification of Andromeda Liberata*, George Chapman articulated the falsity of any claim to be 'offenceless' by an author, and his fear 'that let the

---

207. Bennet, *English Books and Readers, 1603–1640*, p. 177.
208. For an example, see B. Crockett, *The Play of Paradox: Stage and Sermon in Renaissance England* (Philadelphia, 1995), pp. 97–8.
209. D. Womersley, 'Sir John Hayward's Tacitism', *Ren. Studies* 6 (1991), pp. 46–59, at p. 46.
210. Khan, *Rhetoric, Prudence and Scepticism*, p. 133.
211. V. F. Snow, 'Francis Bacon's Advice to Fulke Greville on Research Techniques', *Hunt. Lib. Quart.* 23 (1960), p. 372.
212. Cave, *Cornucopian Text*, p. 327. Cf. M. Ferguson, *Trials of Desire: Renaissance Defenses of Poetry* (New Haven, 1983), p. 158.
213. A. Patterson, *Reading Holinshed's Chronicles* (Chicago, 1994). Though the attempt to claim Holinshed as a protoliberal ancient constitutionalist is unpersuasive, the case for the openness of the text is interesting and well made. For a case study in readers' appropriations of a text see A. Beer, *Sir Walter Ralegh and his Readers in the Seventeenth Century* (Houndmills, 1997).

writer mean what he list, his writing notwithstanding must be construed in *mentem legentis* . . . to the intendment of the Reader'.[214]

In the freedom taken by or permitted to readers in early modern England much was at stake. Fable and history may have been open to interpretation but they were also genres in which political allegories were frequently encoded. Chamberlain was predisposed to expect (in this case subversive) politics in a work of history, and the controversies over Hayward's *First Part of the Life and Reign of Henrie IIII* (1599) encouraged him to do so.[215] And, as Chapman protested, it was not readers but authors who were held responsible for subversive 'meanings': 'if a troublesome meaning is brought to the text by a reader, what blame should the author bear,' he asked, knowing that in practice the force of state power fell upon writers, even when their claims to innocence were genuine.[216] Though proclamations called in books, and made an offence of their possession, quite simply it was – and remains – impossible for censorship to police the way texts are read.[217] Such a realisation may even, it has been argued, have helped to forge an acceptance by authorities of a 'functional ambiguity' in texts, of their capacity for multiple and oppositionist readings provided that, to quote Quintilian, they 'can be understood differently'.[218]

When, however, the state functioned as a reader of texts, and the penalties for libel or sedition were mutilation and even death, authors who desired to open their texts to readers had to tread a careful line. And not all desired or applauded the freedoms taken by the reader, for a number of reasons. In the first place, though Montaigne and Machiavelli struck at its core, many still held to a notion of truth and right that they wished to represent and teach. Hayward, we recall, while admitting that readers would be interpreters, pejoratively spoke of them as potential 'wresters', and 'corrupters' and 'depravers' of what they read.[219] Bacon too felt some readings of a text claimed to discover 'meanings which it was never *meant* to have' and accused Machiavelli of expounding the fable of Achilles 'corruptly'.[220] Ben Jonson famously endeavoured to control the interpretations of his works by extensive marginalia and close supervision of publication.[221] In *Bartholomew Fair* he mocked

214. J. Kerrigan, 'The Editor as Reader: Constructing Renaissance Texts', in J. Raven, H. Small and N. Tadmor, eds, *The Practice and Representation of Reading in England* (Cambridge, 1996), pp. 102–24, at p. 114.
215. Woolf, *Idea of History*, pp. 107–8.
216. Kerrigan, 'Editor as Reader', p. 114.
217. See in general Patterson, *Censorship and Interpretation*. There were attempts to prove treason by imagining the king's death and in the case of Algernon Sydney this was 'proved' from his reading of the classics. See S. Zwicker, 'Reading the Margins: Politics and the Habits of Appropriation', in Sharpe and Zwicker, *Refiguring Revolutions*, pp. 102–3.
218. Patterson, *Censorship and Interpretation*, p. 14.
219. Above, p. 41.
220. Bacon, *Advancement of Learning*, p. 82; above, p. 41.
221. See D. Riggs, *Ben Jonson: A Life* (Cambridge, Mass., 1989), pp. 220–6; R. C. Newton,

the judgement of readers and a world in which wealth and status were believed to bequeath understanding and discrimination.[222] Authors therefore developed strategies to contain the hermeneutic liberties of readers. As well as the content and language of their texts they deployed the material features of writing – the size, format and typography of the book – its genre and form, to exercise some measure of control.[223] As readers in turn became more sophisticated in 'reading' and seeing beyond those gestures, so authors adopted different and more sophisticated techniques, in the way they used prefaces, dedications and title pages – ultimately in the way they claimed cultural authority as authors. In some ways the devices (as with the modern dust-jacket with its promises of titillation or scholarly weight – seldom both!) became a game among writers, printers and publishers, and readers – and the state as official reader. But like all games it also had a serious dimension: a desire to win, to gain control of the processes of constructing values. For the historian, observing what Montaigne represented as a tennis match between writers and readers helps us to grasp the rules of the game and the techniques of play: how meanings circulated between author, text and reader in early modern England.[224]

The ways in which a book is read begin to be determined before the reader has passed beyond a sentence. As one critic reminds us, we know quite a bit about the post we receive before we read it: whether it has a logo, the quality of paper, the nature of the letterhead, whether it is laser-printed, typed or handwritten, and the typography give clues (and directions) to how the missive is to be read and pointers (quite literally with modern graphics) on how it is to be interpreted.[225] Some of the best work in the history of the book has been similarly directed to such issues of its material condition and the material circumstances of its distribution and circulation. We know that when we go to the new history books table in an academic bookshop we are expecting something different from that in a popular chain, and both publishers and booksellers respond to and manipulate our expectations. The size and binding of a book, its publisher, price, jacket (illustration and blurb), the

'Jonson and the (Re)Invention of the Book', in C. J. Summers and T. L. Pebworth, eds, *Classic and Cavalier: Essays on Jonson and the Sons of Ben* (Pittsburgh, 1982), pp. 31–58.

222. *Bartholomew Fair*, 'The Induction on the Stage'.

223. Jonson's folio works, published the same year as James I's, makes the point. See also the engraved title page, discussed in Corbett and Lightbown, *Comely Frontispiece*, pp. 149–51; see below, p. 46, on Congreve.

224. C. M. Baushatz, 'Montaigne's Conception of Reading in the Context of Renaissance Poetics and Modern Criticism', in Suleiman and Crosman, *Reader in the Text*, p. 265. Olson points out that sixteenth-century composers added notations to scores to restrict the performer's freedom of interpretation, *World on Paper*, p. 88.

225. M. Nystrand, *The Structure of Written Communication: Studies in Reciprocity between Writers and Readers* (Orlando, 1986), pp. 56–7. Nystrand talks of 'pretextual clues' (p. 60). See too A. Manguel, *A History of Reading* (1996), pp. 13–14. Ben Jonson offers a contemporary case, see Epigrams 2, 3 in C. H. Herford and P. Simpson, *Ben Jonson*, VIII, p. 27.

positioning of scholarly apparatus (or its absence), the size of the index, the length of the chapters all predispose us to a view of the book's contents – usually one that is fairly accurate. Moreover such factors all affect where and when we read (one reviewer of my last book indicated that its weight – I think he meant physical – precluded holiday reading), whether in public or, as some academics with more 'popular' works, in private, alone. Books do not just reflect a market, an interpretive community, of readers, but help to construct it: and so help to fashion the way we classify social groups, and concepts like 'serious' and 'popular', that is to say cultural authority.[226]

The history of the book, rescuing the study of bindings, paper, typeface, etc. from the antiquarianism that characterised some earlier studies, has demonstrated beyond question the relation of the material conditions of the book to its 'meanings' in the past, and especially the era of the Renaissance. We would still like to know more about how readers heard about books, since in England catalogues were rare before the second half of the seventeenth century, when advertisements for books as well as other 'commodities' also became more common.[227] It would be interesting too to learn more about how booksellers displayed and categorised their stock, the way in which they began to specialise in types of material. Did the 200 booksellers estimated to be plying their trade in Paul's Yard serve only the capital, or was there an organised informal delivery service through middlemen to the provinces, as well as the established book fairs?[228] Evidently a Cambridge student in the 1620s could hire books he could not afford to buy, and, at least in Kent, there is evidence of a secondhand market, though we know little of how it worked.[229] Was the bookseller's 'hire shop' a place of congress before the Civil War, a place where recommendations about reading and opinions on current issues were offered and exchanged? All such questions relate to the efforts made by readers to acquire books in general and particular titles – efforts which evidence the value placed on reading in early modern

226. Today, of course, one of the most common questions on consumer surveys is which newspapers one reads; and newspapers are categorised according to A-B etc. readership.
227. *A Catalogue of the Most Vendible Books in England* (1658), Thomason E9551/1, with only slight exaggeration, claims in its title 'the like work never yet performed by any'. After the Restoration such catalogues were regular publications. Advertisements in books from the 1640s and 1650s on await study as an aspect of the commodification of print and political culture.
228. Bennet, *English Books and Readers, 1603–40*, p. 1; cf. G. Pollard, 'The English Market for Printed Books', *Pub. Hist.* 4 (1978), pp. 7–48; D. Stoker, 'The Regulation of the Book Trade in Norwich 1500–1800', *Pub. Hist.* 8 (1980), pp. 127–41; and Altick, *English Common Reader*; R. Myers and M. Harris, *Spreading the Word: The Distribution Networks of Print, 1550–1850* (Detroit, 1990).
229. M. Spufford, 'First Steps in Literacy: The Reading and Writing Experience of the Humblest Seventeenth-Century Spiritual Autobiographers', *Social Hist.* 4 (1979), p. 433; P. Clark, 'The Ownership of Books in England, 1560–1640: The Example of Some Kentish Townfolk', in L. Stone, ed., *Schooling and Society: Studies in the History of Education* (Baltimore, 1976), pp. 95–115.

England. Darnton also reflects on the importance of other changes – from
rag to wood pulp in papermaking, for example – in the reception of books.[230]
Whether a book was purchased bound (in what material) or, as commonly,
in loose leaf for personal binding – perhaps with one's own stamp or arms
– reflected and conditioned the relationship between the book and reader.[231]
The many paintings and engravings of Renaissance figures holding books,
their fingers marking a page, suggest that what Darnton calls the 'corporeal
element in reading' opens into the history of the body and the self as well
as of the book.[232] Books in this culture could be treasured personal posses-
sions; they could also be, as John Lyly complained, the fashion of the day: 'we
commonly see the book that at Christmas hath appeared bound at the Sta-
tioners Hall at Easter to be broken in the Haberdashers Shop.'[233] What determined which books met that fate, or which remained largely fashionable, or
cherished by a few, is part of the history of ideology and values.

The size of books, then as today, conveyed messages. Price was of course
the obvious one. Given that print runs were usually restricted to 1,250–1,500
copies, whatever the anticipated market, a larger folio book tended to be con-
siderably more expensive, and therefore associated with elites, cultural and
social.[234] Ben Jonson's choice of a folio edition for his collected *Works*, coming
hard on the heels of James I's own volume (ill. 1), laid a claim to authority
that was not lost on his contemporaries or successors. As D. F. McKenzie
showed, the 'unruly Congreve of the early quarto editions settled down into
the decorous neo-classicist of the *Works* of 1709' – a stately folio.[235] John
Ogilby himself used explicitly political language when he boasted that
from his first 'mean octavo' edition of Virgil, 'a royal folio flourished'.[236] Big
did not always mean better, nor fit all occasions. The brevity and plainness of

230. Darnton, 'How to Read a Book'; cf. Marotti, *Manuscript, Print*, p. 252.
231. Readers often described their books in terms of physical features: see K. Sharpe,
     'Rewriting Sir Robert Cotton', in C. Wright, ed., *Sir Robert Cotton as Collector* (1997),
     pp. 7–8; cf. Jean Ranson's concern with the 'physical aspects of books', in R. Darnton,
     'Readers Respond to Rousseau: The Fabrication of Romantic Sensitivity', in
     Darnton, *The Great Cat Massacre* (Harmondsworth, 1985), p. 216.
232. Cf. R. Helgerson, 'Soldiers and Enigmatic Girls: The Politics of Dutch Domestic
     Realism, 1560–1672', *Representations* 58 (1997), pp. 49–87, esp. pp. 77–82. I am also
     grateful to Richard Helgerson for his presentation on representations of reading at
     the Folger National Endowment for the Humanities Seminar in July 1997. See Johns,
     Nature of the Book, ch. 6, 'The Physiology of Reading', and Manguel, *History of
     Reading*, pp. 151–4.
233. C. Gebert, ed., *An Anthology of Elizabethan Dedications and Prefaces* (New York, 1966),
     p. 50.
234. Altick, *English Common Reader*, p. 19.
235. Darnton, 'What is the History of Books?' p. 79. See D. F. McKenzie, 'Typography and
     Meaning: The Case of William Congreve', *Wolfenbütteler Schriften zur Geschichte der
     Buchwesen*, vol. 4 (Hamburg, 1981), pp. 81–125; Chartier, *On the Edge of the Cliff*,
     ch. 6.
236. J. Ogilby, *Africa: Being an Accurate Description of the Regions of Aegypt, Barbary Lybia . . .*
     (1670), preface.

1. Title page of James I's
Workes (1616).

the Civil War pamphlets were not just a matter of cheapness, but also of style
– a suspicion, as the author of *The Great Assizes Holden at Parnassus* (1645)
put it, of 'fine attire'.[237] And the decision to issue the early editions of *Eikon
Basilike* as a pocket duodecimo, as well as reflecting the need for secrecy, may
have been intended to invoke intimacy and to make of the book a token,
the form of which allied the work with chivalric ideals.[238]

When books were sold bound, works were sometimes bound together –
whether by decision of author or publisher. This was commonly the case with
poetry and our own experience of compilations or student texts confirms
that 'the larger context of the miscellanies may have influenced the writing

237. *The Great Assizes Holden at Parnassus* (1645), Thomason E269/11, p. 34; cf. pp. 2,
    20–3.
238. Achinstein, *Milton*, p. 134; L. Potter, *Secret Rites and Secret Writing: Royalist Literature,
    1641–1660* (Cambridge, 1989). Marotti compares *Eikon Basilike* to Herbert's duo-
    decimo *The Temple* which, as he says, resembles a prayer-book, *Manuscript, Print*, p.
    289.

48

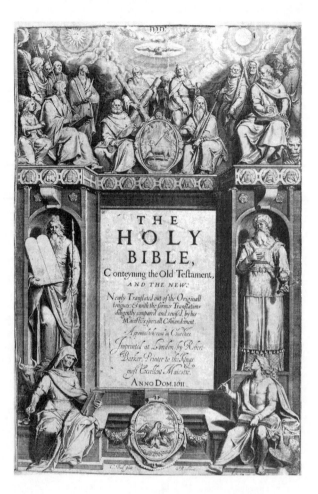

2. Title page of the
Authorised Version of the
Bible (1611).

or reading of the individual poem.'[239] At times the compilation appears obviously ideological. The 1580 Basel Latin edition of Machiavelli's *Prince* was printed with the Calvinist pamphlet now attributed to Philippe du Plessis de Mornay, the *Vindiciae Contra Tyrannos*, a conjunction that would have directed a rather different reading of both texts, as well as demanding the reader's own judgement about issues of power, its limits and resistance.[240] We need a full study of composite editions, and in which libraries they appear, written with the readers as well as the printers in mind. To trace the company that Machiavelli, or Bodin, or Montaigne, kept in composite editions in different countries over two centuries would be a revealing chapter in their shifting reputations and the reception of controversial ideas.[241]

239. Love, *Scribal Publication*, p. 5. See Marotti, *Manuscript, Print*, esp. p. 243. See too J. Gaisser, *Catullus and his Renaissance Readers* (Oxford, 1993), p. 26.
240. D. Womersley, 'Sir Henry Savile's Translation of Tacitus and the Political Interpretation of Elizabethan Texts', *J. Eng. Studies* 42 (1991), pp. 313–42, at p. 326.
241. For an example see Gaisser, *Catullus*, p. 26; Marotti, *Manuscript, Print*, p. 258.

The frontispiece was often the reader's first encounter with the contents of a book, and contemporary writers, publishers and readers had a keen sense of its importance. Like the proscenium arch on the perspective stage of the court theatre, the frontispiece provided a frame for the text, one that endeavoured to contain its meaning. Contemporaries described it indeed as an arch or a door which determined one's angle of vision – and the arch, with all its connotations of authority, triumph and monument as well as entrance, was a common motif of the frontispiece.[242] The arch was not the only association the frontispiece made with authority: apart from portraits of authors and translators of a work, 'the only other portraits that are found on English title pages of our period are those of royal personages.'[243] As the growing practice of a second separate title page released the engraved page to more elaboration, complex pictorial and emblematic devices were adopted to 'epitomise' the book, to direct the reader. Other illustrations served the same function. Maps of the Holy Land, for example, in the Authorised Version of the Bible served to inscribe scriptural stories on the land, and perhaps also to associate the King James whose own name dominated the title page with the promised land, as well as the kingdom of Britain (ill. 2).[244] During the 1630s, a woodcut of Gustavus Adolfus over Psalm 45 not only cast the Swedish king (whose foreign policy goals were very much a matter of interest) as Protestant champion; it pointed the contrast with a Charles I whose inactivity was subtly represented as ungodly.[245]

During the Civil War, engraved and woodcut illustrations were used explicitly to make political arguments: an engraving of Charles I on *The Manner of Holding Parliaments* was a not very subtle reminder in whose power their calling lay.[246] An upside down engraving of a lay preacher in a pulpit signified the world itself turned upside down.[247] *The Great Assizes Holden at Parnassus* criticised pamphleteers for misleading frontispieces and illustrations, but during the years of the republic, the Royalists used visual propaganda to devastating effect, to undermine the new regime.[248] The omnipresence of images of Charles I and Charles II did much to keep the memory – and reality – of monarchy alive during the Commonwealth and Protectorate. Though none would have foreseen it, the Reformation and Civil War deployment of images for political signification paved the way for the cartoon which to this day helps determine our 'reading' of news and our attitude to figures of authority.[249]

242. Corbett and Lightbown, *Comely Frontispiece*, introduction, esp. pp. 7–9.
243. Ibid., p. 43.
244. Bennet, *English Books and Readers, 1603–1640*, p. 95. On the ideology of maps see R. Helgerson, *Forms of Nationhood: The Elizabethan Writing of England* (Chicago, 1992), ch. 3, esp. pp. 105–8.
245. *The Swedish Intelligencer* (1632).
246. *The Manner of Holding Parliaments* (1641), Thomason E157/11.
247. *The Parliament Routed*, Thomason tract 669 f17/12.
248. *The Great Assizes*, pp. 20–3; Sharpe, '"An Image Doting Rabble"', pp. 39–41.
249. It has been suggested that the television depiction in *Spitting Image* of David Steel as a puppet held under David Owen's arm damaged his political credibility.

The authors' and publishers' deployment of the aesthetics of the book was not confined to size, binding or illustration. The page itself *was* an illustration, a visual device of layout, margin and typography.[250] Renaissance writers and readers were used to a relationship between words and the shapes they formed on the page, as evidenced in acrostic verse, and the shapes – like those of Herbert's 'The Altar' – were an important aspect of, indeed a representation of the meaning of the lines. Spenser's neat stanzas, it has been observed, progress in 'magisterial succession . . . with the air of a fleet in full sail', in contrast to Donne's 'bizarrely shaped and constantly varied stanzas', a vehicle for thinking as 'invariably knotty and intricate'.[251] Margins, as our own vocabulary of marginal and marginalise reminds us, were always ideological spaces. Printed marginal notes could flag, cross-reference, interpret or undermine a passage in the text – at precisely the point the reader first encountered it.[252] Unlike the footnote (which did not develop until the late seventeenth and eighteenth centuries) the marginal gloss enjoyed equal status on the page, rather than serving at its feet.[253] Ben Jonson littered his texts with marginalia – to display his learning and to determine their reading, both gestures of authority and control.[254] The 1568 Bishops Bible, along with engraved portraits of Elizabeth I and Cecil was printed with marginal instructions for ministers.[255] James I sought a new edition of the Bible not least to supplant the Geneva Bible which contained subversive marginal notes pointing to the fates of sinful kings.[256] The version he authorised in 1611 was as political in its removal of marginalia, as was the Geneva Bible's publication with them. Printed marginalia, whether as prompts for preachers, directions for readers or the parading of 'authorities', shaped how the reader construed meaning: what was dwelt on, prioritised or passed over.[257]

The reader's own manuscript marginalia, a personal act of interpretation and judgement, were another matter and one (as we shall see) that it was nigh impossible to police. Despite the 1538 proclamation against making margin

---

250. D. R. Carlson, *English Humanist Books: Writers and Patrons, Manuscript and Print, 1475–1525* (Toronto, 1993), e.g. p. 164. R. Hirsch, *Printing, Selling and Reading, 1450–1550* (Weisbaden, 1967), pp. 25–6.
251. Love, *Scribal Publication*, pp. 145–6.
252. See M. Tribble, *Margins and Marginality: The Printed Page in Early Modern England* (Charlottesville, 1993); S. Zwicker, 'Reading the Margins'.
253. A. Grafton, 'The Footnote from De Thou to Ranke', *History & Theory* 33 (1994), pp. 53–76; see now Grafton, *The Footnote: A Curious History* (1997) which appeared after this chapter was written.
254. Ben Jonson added extensive notes to his *Sejanus* to create a frame of reference for the reader that was classical rather than contemporary: Tribble, *Margins and Marginality*, p. 152; but cf. B. Worden, 'Ben Jonson among the Historians', in Sharpe and Lake, *Culture and Politics*, pp. 69–70, 79–80.
255. Tribble, *Margins and Marginality*, p. 36.
256. Ibid., pp. 32, 52; see also W. Allen, *Translating for King James* (1970), p. 33.
257. Tribble points out that the Martin Marprelate tracts also occupied the margin, erasing the bishops from the page, *Margins and Marginality*, pp. 110–11.

notes,[258] surviving Bibles were littered with marks – of mementoes and family records, as well as engagement with the text. Once again, however, the layout of the page could inhibit or invite such textual appropriation and engagement by graphically granting or denying readers their own 'space' of inscription. Those of us who still write in (our) books, and sense the difference when reading a library book, let alone a microfilm, will have no doubt about the significance of that licence or prohibition.

The very material of the word itself, typography, was also a medium of direction and control. England was relatively late in converting to Roman type from gothic or black letter, and it may well have been the association with antiquity which led to the decision to print the Authorised Version in gothic type.[259] Archbishop Laud insisted on it for the controversial Scots Prayer Book which he authorised in 1637.[260] Gothic type remained the norm for proclamations and ordinances through the Commonwealth and Protectorate, significantly the association between gothic and texts of authority ending only after the Restoration.[261] Typography, as the new history of the book and our era of the desktop publisher have made us aware, was always ideological. It could also function directly politically. During the 1630s one of William Prynne's printers was famous for a letter 'C' in his press: turned on one side there 'appeared a pope's head, and then turn it another way and there appeared an army of men and soldiers'.[262] And during the Civil War Royalists practised similar tricks, John Ogilby's 1649 translation of the *Aeneid* hiding within its lines a poem on the regicide.[263]

As well as ciphers and numerology, forms of typography could conceal and reveal, become a code that communicated to those in the know and in sympathy 'meanings' not in the ordinary readings of the words.[264] Contemporary readers evidently became quite sophisticated at reading such codes, still more in retaining a memory for typography and its politics. We know that the Leveller William Walwyn consciously imitated the typography of Prynne's earlier *Independency Examined* – to gain Prynne's supporters for views not entirely in accordance with Prynne's rejection of religious toleration.[265] And the newswriter *Mercurius AntiBritannicus* noted how the typography and capitals of *The King's Cabinet Opened* had been carefully used to 'call and

258. 16 November 1538, P. L. Hughes and J. F. Larkin, eds, *Tudor Royal Proclamations I: The Early Tudors* (New Haven, 1964), pp. 270–6; cf. pp. 284–7.
259. M. Elsky, *Authorising Words: Speech, Writing and Print in the English Renaissance* (Ithaca, N.Y., 1989), p. 131. Cf. S. Morison, *Politics and Script* (1972); Carlson, *English Humanist Books*, p. 164.
260. Elsky, *Authorising Words*, pp. 131–2.
261. See Sharpe, '"An Image Doting Rabble"', p. 42; S. Kelsey, *Inventing a Republic*, p. 172. Olson points out that the comic character Pogo speaks in Gothic script to make him sound ponderous, *World on Paper*, p. 95.
262. *Cal. S.P. Dom. 1635–6*, p. 75.
263. I owe this information to the kindness of Nigel Smith.
264. Potter, *Secret Rites*, ch. 2.
265. Achinstein, *Milton*, p. 143.

beckon readers to it', so as to damage the king's cause.[266] The bare-breasted mermaid that decorated the initial letter of the proclamation for a day of thanksgiving for Charles II underlined the politics of typography.[267] When contemporaries exhibited such a clear sense of the relation of typography to the audiences and meanings of texts, it is time for the historian to return to examine the 'materials' of Renaissance print – quite literally from a different perspective.

Turning to the 'body' of the book, a Renaissance reader would have come first to the dedication, which, unlike our simple and unexplained citation of a name, often consisted of a page or pages. The most common dedications were those to a patron or to one whose patronage the author sought. This was not simply, or even primarily, a matter of financial support. A powerful supporter protected writers – from aesthetic criticism as well as from official disapproval. The playwright Thomas Shirley, dedicating his appropriately titled play, *The Grateful Servant*, to the Earl of Rutland, claimed that it had not been safe to publish without such protection;[268] William Davenant, dedicating *The Just Italian* to Dorset on its publication after an unhappy reception on the stage, confessed: 'the uncivil ignorance of the people had deprived this humble work of life but that your lordship's approbation stepped in to succour it.'[269] As well as honesty and flattery, such a dedication boasted the appreciation for Davenant of a discerning figure who was also Queen Henrietta Maria's chamberlain, and so invited the reader not to share in the ignorant condemnation of the play but to echo the taste of a learned superior. Critical judgement may now grant Davenant worthy of such a reception, but aristocratic patronage was often claimed in less deserving cases, falsely endowing light and worthless works with 'reputation'. As Cornelius Burges protested – in a dedication to the Earl of Bedford – 'tis a practise too common in this scribbling age under pretence of respect to send worthless empty pamphlets abroad in great men's liveries.'[270] Dedications did not always present to the reader the conventional relation of writer and patron as client and lord. Sometimes, as a gesture of vaunting the independence of the writer and the text, they inverted the hierarchical relationship, deploying the acceptable language of counsel to instruct rather than thank dedicatees. Thomas Chaffinge in the *Just Man's Memorial* (1630) reminded the Earl of Pembroke that 'men are big with expectation of you' and that it was his responsibility not to render their hopes stillborn.[271]

Almost the ultimate claim to authority was the dedication of a book to a member of the royal family or the monarch himself – and in the period 1500–1640 over a thousand works were dedicated to the king, queen or

---

266. *Mercurius AntiBritannicus* (1645), E295/9, p. 9.
267. *Proclamation for a Day of Thanksgiving August 1660*, Thomason 669 f25/33.
268. T. Shirley, *The Grateful Servant* (1630), epistle dedicatory.
269. W. Davenant, *The Just Italian* (1630), epistle dedicatory.
270. C. Burgess, *Baptismal Regeneration of Elect Infants* (1629), epistle dedicatory.
271. T. Chaffinge, *The Just Man's Memorial* (1630), epistle dedicatory.

princes, most by authors who had no personal converse with royalty.[272] Not surprisingly the desire for royal association often carried specific as well as general political freight. When in his dedication to Prince Charles of his *Aphorisms* Robert Dallington coupled the maxims of Guicciardini with those of Charles's father, James I, he clearly mollified the controversial reputation of Guicciardini, and appropriated for the Italian and himself the authorities of a writer and king who had based his own representation on his word.[273] Not least for those reasons, to Dallington's readers Guicciardini became an English, even an official, text and Dallington all but a royal spokesman, rather than a schoolmaster struggling for patronage.[274] Dedication to the king could also shape the political reception of a book. When George Wither dedicated his *Britain's Remembrancer* to Charles I in 1628, he informed the king that he had intended no offence, that 'My lines are loyal though they bold appeare.'[275] How did such a dedication, and an accompanying request for the king to remain open to all, influence the way Wither's poem was read? To us, or at least to this reader, a text hard to pin down, full of criticism of the state of affairs, yet conservative and loyal too, appears less as opposition and more as counsel, when introduced by such a dedication. But whether the royal reader of Wither, or for that matter of Prynne, who dedicated several books to Charles I, so took them is another matter and a pointer to the ways in which dedications performed multivalently.

The decision *not* to dedicate a book to the king, especially by an author who often did so, also sent directions to the readers, royal and common. When Prynne dedicated his *Briefe Survey and Censure of Mr Cozens* to the senators of Parliament, he made his larger point in epitome. Against the Arminian bishop, championed by the king, Prynne asserted, in language that, like the dedication, translated authority from the king, 'the parliament hath an . . . lawful prerogative to establish true religion in our church.'[276] The author of *Christ's Confession*, J.P., made a similar point more audaciously. Placing before his dedication to the king a dedication 'to the Honour of Almighty God', J.P. condemned the rebels against God's doctrine on grace and authority, some of whom claimed the – lesser – warrant of the king.[277]

Multiple dedications presented authors and publishers with many opportunities. They represented a hierarchy of authority and obedience and positioned the text within that order. They also enabled the writer to identify

272. F. B. Williams, *Index of Dedications and Commendatory Verses in English Books before 1641* (1962).
273. R. Dallington, *Aphorisms Civill and Militarie*, 2nd edn (1629), epistle 'to the High and Mighty Charles Prince of Great Britaine'.
274. On Dallington's earlier dedications and quests for patronage see R. Strong, *Henry Prince of Wales and England's Lost Renaissance* (1986), pp. 30–1.
275. G. Wither, *Britain's Remembrancer* (1628), 'To the King', p. 8.
276. W. Prynne, *A Briefe Survey and Censure of Mr Cozens His Couzening Devotions* (1628), epistle dedicatory. In *Healthes Sicknesse* (1628), by contrast, he described the king as the state physician to purge disease (dedication to Charles I).
277. J.P., *Christ's Confession* (1629).

and construct a community of readers. In descending from dedications to God, the king and then 'to the Christian Reader', J.P. cleverly sustained the chains of unity and degree that some accused the puritans of breaking; but he also reminded the *Christian* reader, who was to define his Christianity by accepting the premise, that first duty was owed to Christ, whose 'kingdom' it was a king's responsibility to defend.[278] The multiple dedication at least raised the potential need to choose between God and Caesar, and invited the Christian reader to follow Christ and His word: 'to be of truth is to continue in the Word.'[279] In his 1628 *Sion's Plea Against the Prelacie*, Alexander Leighton dedicated his attack on the bishops both to the 'High Court of Parliament', that 'cure-all court of Parliament', and to the reader who was joined with the 'senators' in a secular republic united in defence against the oppression of the subject by canons and ceremonies.[280] Dedications to authority, or authorities, the authority selected as dedicatee, were not mere claims to textual authority: they constituted the 'subjects' of the book and the 'reception' of its embassy by readers outside what Montaigne called the 'kingdom' of the author's study.[281]

The growing number of dedications to readers, however, implies a reciprocal recognition of their growing authority, indeed a nervousness about their independence. It is tempting to see all dedications to the Christian reader, at a time when what constituted Christian worship was contested, as an attempt to define a sympathetic audience; and the language of dedications such as that 'to all the elect children of God' in 1629 increases that temptation.[282] In more secular works, we increasingly encounter dedications to 'understanding' readers – who presumably discover that quality in so far as they concur with the arguments proffered.[283] The author of *The Swedish Intelligencer* may have hoped, as he claimed, that 'if a man of judgement reads, he shall find [it] . . . very true', but the hope only thinly veils the corresponding fear about readers, a fear that necessitated a 'caveatory epistle' even 'to the understanding reader'.[284] Faced with the signs of readerly independence, dedications adopted a number of 'responses': a word that reminds us that their authors were themselves readers – of other works and of other readers. Robert Harris knew that his *Way to True Happiness* would not win all and could only urge dissenters: 'if thou be a Questionist, spare they pains'; but his desire to avoid 'brawls and disputes' was compromised by his own tone of engagement with his critical readers.[285] John Taylor tried a different tack, dedicating his

278. Cf. I.R., *The Spy*, (1628), dedication to 'true hearted patriots'.
279. J.P., *Christ's Confession*, pp. 70, 94.
280. A. Leighton, *An Appeal to the Parliament: or Sion's Plea Against the Prelacie* (1628).
281. Below, pp. 312–13.
282. J. Andrewes, *The Converted Man's New Birth* (1629).
283. E.g. M.R., *Micrologia: Characters or Essays . . .* (1629), 'Caveatory epistle to the understanding reader'.
284. *The Swedish Intelligencer* (1632); above, n. 283.
285. R. Harris, *The Way to True Happiness* (1632), epistle to the reader.

works 'to the most high, most mighty, and most ancient producer, seducer and abuser of mankind, the World' – casting himself upon the common humanity of anonymous readers who, of course, both made (and might abuse) the author.[286] The author's 'dedication' speaks for both his power and his pains.

Because dedications were part of the structures of the control and interpretation of meaning, the Civil War brought about changes in their authority as well as in the structures of authority itself. To whom did one dedicate a book during civil war – or after regicide? Which patrons lent authority to a work when allegiances based on ideological commitments cut across the lines of hierarchy and degree? Attempts to dedicate treatises both to the Parliament and the king echo the behaviour of those in the provinces who pledged their military services to both.[287] The explosion of print during the 1640s created an audience more remote and anonymous, as well as numerous, than any before; an audience harder to read and define or to address from the pulpit of dedication. Moreover, the speed with which claims to truth were exposed by events or other publications undermined the rhetoric of dedications to the reader. *The Love of Truth and Peace* put it well: 'in the variety of opinions and distractions of sides, every one challenging truth to be in their party, how shall we know what is the truth? . . .'[288] And the uncertainty and pace of political change often suggested that, if they did not remain silent, authors addressed all the different sorts of readers, even those who 'art of an opinion contrary to what is here written'.[289] During the Civil War the dedication was poised between the old world with its claims to truth and unity and a new culture of civilised political division and party in which books and their dedications would become the sites of contest.[290] It was of no surprise that for a time dedications declined and that some wondered whether they were needed at all. The author of *Mysteries of Love* (1658) decided that since dedications misled, and clear books had no need of them, he would intend his own 'to the youthful gentry' as but a 'landskip to the work'.[291] For all his denial, his language calls his young gentry readers to a way of seeing the world – through the artist's frame – be it on canvas or in print.[292]

As well as dedications, and sometimes adopting the form of them, prefaces gave authors and publishers another opportunity to address the reader, as if in the prologue of a play. Writers who chose not to dedicate their books to readers still spoke here, usually in the first person, across the gulf of anonymity

286. J. Taylor, *All the Workes of John Taylor the Water Poet* (1630).
287. See for example [M. Quintyne], *A Brief Treatise* (1641), Thomason E163/7, which has epistles to each. And see J. S. Morrill, *The Revolt of the Provinces* (1976), introduction.
288. J. Gauden, *The Love of Truth and Peace* (1640), E204/10, p. 27. Cf. *The Liar or A Contradiciton to Those who in the Titles of their Books Affirmed them to be True* (1640), E169/8.
289. [M. Needham], *The Case of the Commonwealth* (1650), E600/7, to the reader.
290. Cf. Sharpe and Zwicker, *Politics of Discourse*, introduction; Zwicker, 'Lines of Authority', in ibid., pp. 230–70.
291. *The Mysteries of Love and Eloquence* (1658), E1735.
292. On the ideology of landscape in the seventeenth century, see S. Alpers, *The Art of Describing: Dutch Art in the Seventeenth Century* (Chicago, 1984).

that print erected between them and readers. Some tried to bridge it by intimate words, Robert Jones addressing his 'censurers' as 'Dear Friends';[293] others
acknowledged their strangeness: 'what you are I know not,' Nicholas Bacon
wrote nervously; yet others transmuted the fear of the unknown into a stance
of aggression.[294] 'In troth you are a stranger to me,' Nathaniel Field told his
readers, 'why should I write to you? You never writ to me . . .'[295] In asking
his question, Field accepted the need to speak to the audience and expressed
a desire, a need, to be heard. Indeed prefaces in general reveal a mounting
concern about readers, and readers' capacity to determine the fortunes of
authors. This was true at the most basic level of livelihood for those who
depended on the market, but, at some level, all writers, no less than amateur
actors, required the support of an audience and strove to win its applause. So
William Byrd offered his readers psalms for serious moods, and sonnets 'if
thou be disposed . . . to be merry';[296] Breton, hoping the reader might be
content with his tracts, promised 'ere long I will send you something more
to your liking.'[297] Other writers were more concerned to safeguard their stock
of ideas in an ignorant and disputatious world. After a dedication in which
he cautioned against misunderstanding his work, Meric Casaubon wrote a
'Discourse by Way of Preface Concerning the Use and Subject of this Book'
– the *Meditations* of Marcus Aurelius Antoninus.[298]

A growing sense of the need to explain to readers and the fear they would
misunderstand is distinctly audible in the prefaces of later sixteenth- and
seventeenth-century England, leading authors at times to stances of humility,
apology and subservience. 'How hard an enterprise it is,' wrote John Dowland,
'in this skilful and curious age to commit our private labours to the public
view.'[299] What 'many terrible encounters', what 'executioners and tormentors'
Dekker knew his paper would face.[300] While John Day pleaded in the person
of his own book, 'pick no more out of me than he that writ put into me',
others followed Nashe in resignation: 'buy who list, condemn who list, I leave
every reader his free liberty.'[301] Yet if the presence and force of the reader
began to 'mark' the writing of prefaces, we should not take the gestures of
apparent humility and surrender at face value. Though authors felt the need
to write them, prefaces were so popular with the reading public that, it was
said, books sold less well without them.[302] Like dedications, prefaces and

---

293. R. Jones, *The Muses Garden for Delights* (1610), quoted in C. Gebert, ed., *An
    Anthology of Elizabethan Dedications and Prefaces* (New York, 1966), p. 190.
294. Gebert, *Anthology*, p. 145.
295. Ibid., p. 205.
296. Ibid., p. 63.
297. Ibid., p. 122.
298. M. Casaubon, *Marcus Aurelius Antoninus His Meditations* (1634).
299. Gebert, *Anthology*, p. 125.
300. Ibid., p. 163; Tribble, *Margins and Marginality*, p. 8.
301. Gebert, *Anthology*, pp. 168, 101.
302. See the preface to Nathaniel Field, *A Woman in a Weathercock* (1612): 'Reader the sale-
    man swears you take it very ill if I say not somewhat to you too,' quoted in Gebert,

changes in prefaces functioned like the prologue to *Bartholomew Fair*. They established an exchange, a transaction between author and reader – and perhaps evidenced another cultural negotiation between authority and individual judgement.[303]

Central to that exchange was the last of the material conditions of writing and reading that I shall discuss: the nature of genre and form. Classical literary theory bequeathed to the Renaissance distinct genres of writing – tragicomedy, epic, comedy, pastoral – and of rhetoric and oratory: epideictic, forensic and deliberative. Indeed, as Rosalie Colie has argued, 'the transfer of ancient values was largely in generic terms,' with the consequence that the election of a literary or oratorical genre by the author evoked, and also responded to, expectations in the reader.[304] Meaning was encoded in a genre system, 'a body of almost unexpressed assumptions', assumptions which framed how meaning was constructed, conveyed and interpreted.[305] 'Poetry', Richard Loveday could still write in the 1650s, 'is for men of leisure'; romances were 'political stratagems . . . to elevate our thoughts'; and every reader of the *Georgics* or *Aeneid* understood the negotiation with power and retreat in pastoral.[306] Library lists and booksellers' catalogues often followed generic classifications, rather than 'subjects'; and even new modes of speaking and writing – the parliamentary speech or sermon – imitated genres and were assigned to a generic system.[307] Renaissance genre, however, was not a rigid system. Some writers, not least Shakespeare in his sonnets, mixed genres; some, Rabelais for one, drew on generic resources outside the classical canon; others – Bacon and Montaigne in their essays are obvious examples – struggled to create new genres.[308] But throughout early modern society, as well as literary culture, we encounter an addiction to genres and forms – under the heading of which we might usefully study the state trial, the scaffold speech, or the addresses to the Assize judges.[309] It was not least because he possessed such an acute

Anthology, p. 205; and cf. J. Wells, *Poems upon Divers Occasions* (1667): 'The stationer fears nobody will look into the book unless courted by a preface' (epistle to the reader).

303. Marotti, *Manuscript, Print*, p. 222; see too D. Bruster, *Drama and the Market in the Age of Shakespeare* (Cambridge, 1992); and White, *Content of the Form*, p. 201.

304. R. Colie, *The Resources of Kind: Genre Theory in the Renaissance* (Berkeley, 1973), quotation p. 17; Olson, *World on Paper*, pp. 134–5; A. Fowler, *Kinds of Literature: An Introduction to the Theory of Genres and Modes* (Cambridge, Mass., 1982); W. S. Howell, *Logic and Rhetoric in England, 1500–1700* (Princeton, 1956).

305. Colie, *Resources of Kind*, p. 165.

306. R. Loveday, *Haemen's Praeludia* (1655), E1459/2, 'to his esteemed friend Mr Robert Loveday'; see P. Alpers, *The Singer of The Eclogues: A Study of Virgilian Pastoral* (Berkeley, 1979); A. Patterson, *Pastoral and Ideology: Virgil to Valéry* (Berkeley, 1987); and M. McKeon, 'The Pastoral Revolution', in Sharpe and Zwicker, eds, *Refiguring Revolutions*, pp. 267–87.

307. See, for example, *A Catalogue of the Most Vendible Books* (1658).

308. Colie, *Resources of Kind*, pp. 74–9, 89.

309. Achinstein (*Milton*, p. 23) rightly criticises New Historicist critics for inadequate attention to genre and form; historians hardly even think in these terms. Nystrand

sense of these genres and forms that Charles I could manipulate them to such effect at the block and in the *Eikon Basilike*.[310]

To see that is to recognise that genres were political as well as aesthetic categories: they ordered society's values as well as its 'literature'. Epic addressed the loftiest themes and elite audiences, for example, and the selection of a rhetorical genre was seen to determine the audience addressed; masque, we know, was a specifically and exclusively courtly genre. The association of genres with themes and readers meant that genres were implicated in the ideological and political disputes of the seventeenth century, and shifted with the turn of events. The Cavalier love lyric of the 1620s and 1630s still awaits full critical situation in the political discourse as well as events of the Caroline period if we are to understand the values it encoded. Certainly once civil war broke out the association of genres with values and positions made them a political medium, no less than the more studied political pamphlets.[311] As Tom Corns has demonstrated, Lovelace, in writing chivalric romance, wrote to the Royalists within their own value system of loyalty and honour; and in the 1640s the writing and publishing of erotic verse was defiantly 'not ideologically neutral'.[312] Political division politicised all literary genres and forms, and defined audiences more rigidly.[313] By the 1650s romance, once a genre for all, became a Royalist discourse and one that often encrypted its meanings, to be determined only by a coterie familiar in reading its codes.[314]

At the other end of the political spectrum, the pamphlet emerged as a new genre for a new politics and readerships, and the most radical voices, the Ranters and the sects, challenged the systems of genre, form and even language that, they perceived, occluded the voice of the spirit.[315] As with other traditional forms, proclamations or letters patent, established genres were retained because they conveyed authority. And because they conveyed authority they could not be surrendered by any party, but, like the validating language of Scripture and law, were appropriated by all groups for political ends. Just as Cromwell took on much of the king's image and style as Protector, so in the 'Horatian Ode' to Cromwell, Marvell, in Steven Zwicker's words, 'draped royalist forms over republican facts'.[316] Similarly the emergent republican opposition to Cromwell in the later 1650s took up the titles and dialogic style of the old 'country' pamphlets that had criticised Stuart government, *An Appeal from the Court to the Country* and *The Picture of a New*

argues the close link between genre and interpretation in all writing (*Structure of Written Communication*, p. 76).

310. Potter, *Secret Rites*, ch. 3 and pp. 170ff.
311. See E. Skerpan, *The Rhetoric of Politics in the English Revolution* (Columbia, Miss., 1992).
312. Corns, *Uncloistered Virtue*, pp. 70–5, at p. 75.
313. Zwicker, *Lines of Authority*.
314. Potter, *Secret Rites*, ch. 3.
315. See N. Smith, *Perfection Proclaimed: Language and Literature in English Radical Religion* (Oxford, 1989).
316. S. Zwicker, 'Passions of Occasion: Milton, Marvell and the Politics of Reading', paper.

Courtier with its dialogue between Mr Plain Truth and Mr Time Server graphically reinvoking a former genre associated with honesty, simplicity and patriotism.[317]

During the 1640s and 1650s, as the aesthetic in all its forms was indelibly politicised, genres were contested for and waged their own wars against each other. As far as Henry Oxenden was concerned, only the Restoration, *Charles Triumphant*, as he titled his own panegyric, revived poetry; and historians need to appreciate that the reverse was no less true.[318] The Restoration settlement was reconstituted, that is, through aesthetic as well as political genres and forms: through poetry, masque, opera and the theatre, as well as the theatre of state.[319] And, as Nancy Maguire has suggestively argued, the Restoration vogue for the mixed genre of tragicomedy not only mirrored the Restoration's ambiguity but helped to enable the political accommodation of multiple perspectives.[320]

Genres functioned as systems of values because they were understood by readers as well as writers. The 'new' ballad to the tune of 'The Clean Contrary Way' presumed a familiarity with the earlier texts accompanying the tune, as well as the genre of ballad itself; and was able to deploy complex ironies and 'in-jokes' because readers were well experienced in reading that genre.[321] Authors have perhaps always sought to persuade, educate, shock – to change their readers: never more so than in times of political crisis and division. John Milton, it has been argued, endeavoured to create a revolutionary reader who would always critically scrutinise the mystical and rhetorical forms through which power represented itself in an effort to evade the scrutiny of reason.[322] But authors too always imagine the reader, perhaps before any other act of the creative imagination; and writing is conditioned by the readers' expectations and desires. Genres and forms, continuing yet changing, were (and are) forms of negotiation between writers and readers that are essential to the ways in which meaning is communicated and to whom. They form part of those 'interpretive communities' which, Stanley Fish has argued, in any period determine how texts are written and read.[323]

'It is interpretive communities . . . that produce meanings. . . . Interpretive communities are made up of those who share interpretive strategies.'[324] Fish's

---

317. *An Appeal from the Court to the Country* (1656), E891/3; *The Picture of a New Courtier* (1656), E875/6.
318. H. Oxenden, *Charles Triumphant* (1660), the author to the reader. We need a study of the panegyrics that accompanied the Restoration.
319. See G. Maclean, ed., *Culture and Society in the Stuart Restoration* (Cambridge, 1995), esp. chs 1, 2, 3, 7.
320. N. Maguire, *Regicide and Restoration: English Tragicomedy, 1660–1671* (Cambridge, 1992), pp. 35, 42 and passim.
321. The tune of 'The Clean Contrary Way', a ballad circulating in the 1620s, was still used in the Exclusion Crisis.
322. Achinstein, *Milton*; see below, pp. 291–2.
323. Above, p. 37.
324. Above, p. 37.

model of the relation between authors, texts and readers has largely been ignored by historians, but it offers a valuable perspective for the historian of Renaissance England. As Harold Love has pointed out, the notion of a group or network in which manuscripts circulated describes the reading circles that formed around courtly figures, such as Essex, Sidney or Ralegh.[325] And such names underline the relation of shared literary tastes to other identities and sympathies, such circulations 'bonding groups of like minded individuals into a community, sect or political faction with the exchange of text in manuscript seeming to nourish a shared set of values'.[326]

Knowledge about manuscript circulation among court coteries, of course, informs us only about a rather restricted group of readers. But the concept of interpretive communities need not be so confined – either socially, or to the manuscript. During the early seventeenth century, historians and antiquaries such as John Selden, Sir Robert Cotton and Sir Simonds D'Ewes copied and circulated 'scribally published documents', some manuscript, some print; and Sir Edward Dering swapped books with fellow scholars Sir William Dugdale and Christopher Hatton.[327] These circles were rightly seen to share values as well as texts – both the Society of Antiquaries and Sir Robert Cotton's library were closed by the government – and remind us of the role of the book or manuscript in forging and confirming friendships and sympathies.[328] Circulation of books among friends was the most common mode of distributing unorthodox or controversial literature, such as the works of Machiavelli, and the circles that read and discussed *The Prince* could not but be, in the broadest sense, political communities. Lower down the social scale, among the illiterate, the same was true of the scatalogical or seditious squib which was shared cautiously and selectively, creating a community within the larger local society which heard the Sunday sermon and homily on obedience. A history of early modern interpretive communities would open to us the many groups and texts, ideas and beliefs that made up the commonwealth which authority endeavoured to construct as a unified whole. It would render nonsensical the choice we are asked to make between consensus and conflict.

Though the concept of an interpretive community is valuable, it assumes a formalism, for which Fish has been criticised, and ultimately makes the act of reading comprehensible only as a group activity, rather than an individual act.[329] We are left asking how meaning was constituted by the individual

325. Love, *Scribal Publication*, p. 44; Tribble, *Margins and Marginality*, p. 72.
326. Love, *Scribal Publication*, p. 177.
327. K. Sharpe, *Sir Robert Cotton: History and Politics in Early Modern England* (Oxford, 1979); R. J. Fehrenbach and E. S. Leedham-Green, eds, *Private Libraries in Renaissance England: A Collection and Catalogue of Tudor and Early Stuart Book Lists*, vol. 1 (Marlborough, 1992), ch. 4, p. 139; Love, *Scribal Publication*, pp. 70–1.
328. J. Boyarin, *The Ethnography of Reading* (Berkeley, 1992), p. 194: 'Reading groups often form because of a subtext of shared values.'
329. Newton, *Interpreting the Text*, p. 147.

reader engaging with a particular text at a particular moment. To what extent did shared interpretive strategies condition that reading? How did individual readers – Montaigne or Machiavelli – produce such strikingly different readings and writings of the texts of their age, even of the 'interpretive communities' of which they were a part? If, as Robert Darnton put it, teasing reader response theorists, we need to remember that 'a seventeenth century London burgher inhabited a different mental universe from that of a twentieth century American professor', it is as important to acknowledge that not all seventeenth-century London burghers thought (or read) alike.[330] Carlo Ginzburg's celebrated study of Menocchio the Friulese miller gives powerful evidence of how radically individual even a humble reader could be.[331] While, then, postmodern theory and reader-response criticism pose vital questions the historian has not asked, and while the concept of interpretive communities has begun to historicise the question of how readers read, if we are to understand the performance of ideology and politics in early modern England, we still need to know more about the experience of actual readers.[332] As well as some acquaintance with theory and criticism, that is, we need too that traditional skill of the historian: the capacity for scholarly empirical research.

To appeal for a more interdisciplinary praxis, to urge an address to text, to advocate engagement with some of the questions raised by critical theory, and to insist that a history of politics must incorporate the history of reading may seem to ask too much. To add the desire for detailed archival research may confirm a sense of the impossibility of such a project, of a properly documented history of reading, and incline scholars to return to their own specialisations, comforted by the realisation that there is not a practical alternative. As even a historian sympathetic to interdisciplinary questions put it, 'it is hard enough keeping up to date with the flood of new work and debate in one discipline, let alone in several.'[333]

One can, however, concur with such sentiments without pursuing them to the conclusion that a broader study of politics remains an elusive ideal; and here, somewhat ironically, revisionism may have contributed to a more positive possibility. For, as Peter Lake recently argued, revisionism disrupted the old master narrative of modernisation and never really replaced it. Instead the fallout from revisionist and post-revisionist debates has been a series of detailed and specialised histories – of an individual, a parliamentary session or a local factional dispute. Lake urges that such narrowness, often criticised as

330. Darnton, 'What is the History of Books?' p. 78.
331. C. Ginzburg, *The Cheese and the Worms: The Cosmos of a Sixteenth Century Miller* (1980); see below, pp. 269–70.
332. I owe this phrase to Heidi Brayman, 'Impressions from a Scribbling Age: Recovering the Reading Practises of Renaissance England', Ph.D. diss., Columbia University, 1995, p. vii.
333. Burgess, 'Renaissance Texts', p. 1.

'antiquarian empiricism', should not be lamented but 'vindicated', especially if what it surrenders in chronological breadth it makes up for by new approaches of broad cultural contextualisation – a form of thick description in fact.[334] This may sound like nothing more than the old familiar 'case studies' or the more recently modish microhistories – such as *The Cheese and the Worms*, or Natalie Davies's *Martin Guerre*.[335] And it may be akin to what the best case studies have always done: study an episode in detail as a means of interrogating the broad historical narrative, and of revealing what it occludes as well as plots. But what Lake also seeks is the interrogation into the political story of a multiplicity of narratives and contexts, religious, social and cultural, so as to change the way political history is written. While we do not share his optimism that early modern history has already taken this road, Steven Zwicker and I have recently argued for a refiguring of political history and of the way it is researched and written; and have pressed for new case studies in which, say, 1649 is studied for its psychological and aesthetic reverberations, as well as its political tremors.[336] We need to see an episode or moment as a point on a number of contours, a point which constitutes different meanings according to the territory or relief under study – or as a result of the critic's own mappings. In the richly textured case study, we may in fact discern not only the opportunity but the need to combine the questions of theory and techniques of textual criticism with empirical research and close historical situation.[337]

Can there be such a case study for the history of reading? Does the evidence survive to permit answers to the questions about the freedom of readers, the interpretive communities they inhabited, their response to 'authorities', how they discerned and reconstituted the meaning of the texts they read – over changed circumstances and in different personal, social and political conditions? We have portraits of early modern men and women with their books; we have copies of books with marginalia and other marks of reading; we have correspondence about manuscripts and books; we have commonplace books; we know how writers, especially famous, canonical writers, read and rewrote the text that shaped them. Usually, alas, only pieces of this jigsaw survive for any individual, and the picture of their reading remains fragmented in consequence. The study that follows is based upon an unusually rich and varied collection of the reading notes, journal and parliamentary diary of a Buckinghamshire gentleman: some sixty volumes in all, spanning over thirty years of turbulent history from the late 1620s to the early 1660s. For all their lacunae and the difficulties we will face, they present the best opportunity to address all the questions about how seventeenth-century readers read. Whether they resolve them is, of course . . . well, for the reader to determine.

334. Lake, 'Retrospective', esp. pp. 270–8.
335. N. Davis, *The Return of Martin Guerre* (Harmondsworth, 1985).
336. Sharpe and Zwicker, *Refiguring Revolutions*, introduction, esp. pp. 2–3, 20–1.
337. Cf. Wilson, *Will Power*, pp. 15–16.

Part Two
READING EARLY STUART ENGLAND

2

Reading and Politics in Early Stuart England: The Mental World of Sir William Drake

Starting to Read

Historians of early modern England paid little or no attention to the history of reading until in 1990 the leading scholars of humanism, Anthony Grafton and Lisa Jardine, published their article on how Gabriel Harvey, a minor court figure, secretary to the Earl of Leicester and Doctor of Civil Law, 'read his Livy'. Closely examining the marginalia to Harvey's copy of Livy's *History of Rome* they charted Harvey's readings over the period 1568–90, as he returned to the text again and again through changed circumstances. Harvey, they argued, did not read for himself or to enhance his own learning; he read to perform a service for his patrons or would-be patrons. Not only did Harvey read to extract what was useful to patrons at specific moments, he used his reading as a resource to secure advancement in a political culture in which classical learning and precedents possessed authority and were cultural capital. Grafton and Jardine intended primarily that this important study should 'significantly enrich' the history of reading. But they noted too the contribution such an approach might make to elucidating the 'interaction between politics and scholarship' in Elizabethan England.[1]

Very much in the spirit of this seminal essay, Malcolm Smuts and David Norbrook examined how the publication, translation and application of the texts of Tacitus and Lucan helped to articulate and formulate political values in early Stuart England.[2] A reading of Tacitus, Smuts argues, encouraged a 'Machiavellian ethic' at odds with the values of Christian humanism and commonweal; while, as Norbrook shows, Thomas May found in Lucan's *Pharsalia*

---

1. See A. Grafton and L. Jardine, '"Studied for Action": How Gabriel Harvey Read his Livy', *Past & Present* 129 (1990), pp. 30–78; cf. A. Grafton, 'Discitur ut agitur: How Gabriel Harvey Read his Livy', in S. A. Barney, ed., *Annotation and its Texts* (Oxford, 1991), pp. 108–29; and see below, pp. 293–5.
2. M. Smuts, 'Court-Centred Politics and the Uses of Roman Historians c.1590–1630' and D. Norbrook, 'Lucan, Thomas May and the Creation of a Republican Literary Culture', in K. Sharpe and P. Lake, eds, *Culture and Politics in Early Stuart England* (Houndmills, 1994), pp. 21–44, 45–66.

an apologia for republicanism which the official texts of monarchical culture proscribed – but which contemporaries were clearly capable of reading, at times between the lines.[3] Such readings and rewritings, these scholars demonstrate, were not only directed by contemporary moments and events; they scripted a language (a dialogue between past and present) through which contemporary events were in turn perceived and discussed. Translations, marginal notes to classical texts, epistles dedicatory and prefaces were not only marks of the editor's scholarly reading; they were pointers and directions to the application of the text, written to influence the performance of the text in the public sphere, written, that is, as political acts and ideas.[4]

Gabriel Harvey, Henry Savile, the first translator of Tacitus into English, and Tom May, translator of Lucan's *Pharsalia*, were established academics, scholars with powerful patrons, who moved in the circles of the court. We also have abundant evidence of the reading and mental world of some leading Jacobean magnates, such as the Earls of Northampton and Arundel.[5] Northampton's manuscripts in particular reveal not only how classical learning shaped Howard's speeches, papers and political vision, but also (though they await study from this perspective) how his personal and political experiences and concerns shaped what he read of the classical and recent past, and how he deployed that reading.[6] At the English Renaissance court, especially that of James I, learning conveyed authority, and the monarch was anxious to be perceived as learned and served by men well read. Outside the court too the connection between reading and authority was everywhere apparent. Senior teachers at the universities and the Inns of Court held (as they still do) the title of Readers, and in the parishes the local offices, of constable or headborough, often went to the figure who could read – and so interpret the texts of authority for the local community.[7] Reading, the act of interpreting, mediating and personalising texts, cannot be, and in early modern England was not, separated from the structures of hierarchy and authority.[8] The study of how people – not just courtly scholars or magistrates – read is an essential component of how they experienced and perceived society and politics.

3. For a different view see P. Collinson, 'The Monarchical Republic of Queen Elizabeth I', *Bull. John Rylands Lib.* 69 (1987), pp. 394–424.
4. See above, pp. 45ff.
5. For Northampton's commonplace book see BL Cotton MS Titus CVI; for a brief discussion see L. Peck, ed., *The Mental World of the Jacobean Court* (Cambridge, 1991), pp. 148–68. On Arundel, see K. Sharpe, 'The Earl of Arundel, his Circle, and the Opposition to the Duke of Buckingham 1621–1628', in K. Sharpe ed., *Faction and Parliament* (Oxford, 1978), pp. 209–44 and D. Howarth, *Lord Arundel and his Circle* (1985). Linda Peck is preparing an edition of the catalogue of Arundel's books; see BL Sloane MS 862 and *Bibliotheca Norfolciana* (1681).
6. See Cotton MS Titus CVI, ff. 213ff.
7. See Joan Kent, *The English Village Constable, 1580–1642* (Oxford, 1986), ch. 4.
8. Cf. K. Thomas, 'The Meaning of Literacy in Early Modern England', in G. Baumann, ed., *The Written Word: Literacy in Transition* (Oxford, 1986), pp. 97–131.

Once, however, we move from the circles of the elite, the evidence for individuals' reading, how they responded to texts and formed their own values, is hard to find. There are, of course, quite a few diaries and commonplace books from the early Stuart years, some kept by men outside the upper echelons of the nobility and gentry and outside the inner circles of political influence. But in many of those richest in political comments – the diaries, for example, of Sir Humphrey Mildmay, William Whiteway, Bulstrode Whitelocke or Walter Yonge – there are only occasional references to the diarists' reading.[9] The diary of John Rous, a generic mix of personal record and commonplace book, offers some insight into how contemporary texts – speeches, tracts or ballads – melded with his observations of events, but few clues to the other reading of this Suffolk cleric, or indeed to how he read.[10] Scholars' diaries – those of John Shaw or Thomas Crosfield for example – offer only minimal political comment, surprisingly little evidence of their reading habits and practices and, in consequence, almost no clues as to how reading forged with experience to form a view of events.[11] The cases where a dialectic between reading and a view of the world may most readily be discerned are almost all puritan – and exceptional. In the case of Archibald Johnston of Wariston, the movement between his reading of radical Protestant literature (English and continental as well as Scottish), the course of events leading to and after the Prayer Book rebellion and the formation of a revolutionary consciousness appears clear and rapid.[12] Though more muted in tone, the diaries of the puritans Nehemiah Wallington and Robert Woodforde disclose the importance of sermons and puritan polemic in strengthening godly commitments and sharpening opposition to the established church and state.[13]

In a world in which plays and histories were more popular than sermons, the godly, though important in the rise of opposition to the crown, were a small and idiosyncratic section of the literate public.[14] Antiquarian scholars such as Sir Robert Cotton, Sir Roger Twysden, Sir Simonds D'Ewes and Sir William Dugdale open windows into other circles. The interaction in early Stuart England between study of the past and political attitudes awaits a full investigation, but the diaries and papers of antiquarian and historical scholars

9. BL Harleian MS 454 (Mildmay); William Whiteway's diary is BL Egerton MS 784; on Bulstrode Whitelocke see his *Memorials of English Affairs* (1682) and R. Spalding, ed., *The Diary of Bulstrode Whitelocke 1605–1675* (British Academy, Oxford, 1990); Walter Yonge's diary is BL Add. MS 35331.

10. M. A. E. Green, ed., *The Diary of John Rous, Incumbent of Santon Downham, Suffolk, 1625–1642*, Camden Soc. (1856); see below, pp. 296–7.

11. F. S. Boas, ed., *The Diary of Thomas Crosfield* (1935); see too E. Boucier, *Les Journaux privés en Angleterre de 1600 à 1660* (Paris, 1976), and below, pp. 283–5.

12. G. M. Paul, ed., *The Diary of Archibald Johnston of Wariston 1632–1639*, Scottish Hist. Soc. 61 (1911). See K. Sharpe, *The Personal Rule of Charles I* (1992), pp. 818–19.

13. N. Wallington, *Historical Notices of the Reign of Charles I*, ed. R. Webb (2 vols, 1869); Woodforde's diary is in New College, Oxford MS 9502.

14. The historiography of the period pays them disproportionate attention.

such as these give some idea of the ways in which study of the past shaped, and was in turn directed by, political perceptions and values.[15] Much more work could be done on D'Ewes's diaries and Cotton's manuscripts to elucidate how they read the records of the past in the changing circumstances of Jacobean and Caroline England, and how they interpreted contemporary events from the perspective of their historical learning. But it is likely to remain the case that we do not know enough about what such men read, especially in printed books, how they read, or, beyond generalities and occasional instances, what they extracted from their reading or how they applied it to particular circumstances. Neither Cotton's nor D'Ewes's printed books survive so most of what we know of their reading is of medieval manuscripts and Tower records to which few others had such access.

For most gentlemen, education and learning involved reading and hearing expounded scriptural and classical texts – of philosophy and physics, ethics and politics, rhetoric and poetry. For years scholars have emphasised the importance of the revival of classical studies in the humanist curriculum of the Renaissance grammar schools and universities, and have hinted at how such learning impinged on the social and political roles of the young gentry who attended university and the Inns of Court in ever increasing numbers in sixteenth-century England.[16] Yet, for all that, concentration on the official programmes, on university statutes and curricula has left in the shade the consumer of the new learning, the student, and how his engagement with the new editions and exegeses of the classics formed critical skills and broader values.[17] Precisely how a student hears a lecture or interprets texts is a subject difficult to determine in our own time, let alone for the Renaissance past. What took place in the study, in the mind, is something usually beyond the knowledge of the historian. On several counts, then, the existence of a large cache of papers, notes of reading and annotated printed books, with political observations and comments, by a member of the provincial gentry, is a rare and rich source. As we turn to examine these papers, we shall see that they not only offer the best material we have to date for how an early Stuart gentleman read, but also provide a striking and surprising case study of the relationship of individual reading and hermeneutics to political perceptions and ideas. We shall see, indeed, that the history of reading is not only an aspect of the history of politics, but that it may cause us to question and revise some

---

15. See D. Woolf, *The Idea of History in Early Stuart England* (Toronto, 1990); K. Sharpe, *Sir Robert Cotton: History and Politics in Early Modern England* (Oxford, 1979). I intend a study of attitudes to the past and politics from the Reformation to the 1688 Revolution.

16. See, for example, K. Charlton, *Education in Renaissance England* (1965); J. Simon, *Education and Society in Tudor England* (Oxford, 1959); W. Costello, *The Scholastic Curriculum at Early Seventeenth-Century Cambridge* (Cambridge, Mass., 1958). W. R. Prest, *The Inns of Court under Elizabeth I and the Early Stuarts* (1972), chs 6, 7. See below, pp. 307–8.

17. Study of student commonplace books needs to be extended. See, for example, M. Todd, *Christian Humanism and the Puritan Social Order* (Cambridge, 1987), esp. ch. 3; and below, pp. 277–82.

of our assumptions about authority and subjectivity – that is about politics itself.

The Commonplace Books of Sir William Drake

The discovery of the collection was first made in 1943 by Alan Keen, who announced it in *The Times Literary Supplement* on 13 February of that year.[18] Keen found at Shardeloes near Amersham, Buckinghamshire (ill. 3), a large collection of commonplace books, consisting of reading notes and occasional personal entries concerning estates and finances. Shardeloes was an estate acquired in 1595 by William Tothill, steward to Francis Bacon; and, on the basis of this connection and references to 'Lord Bacon's money' in one of the volumes, Keen concluded that Tothill had written the notebooks of commonplaces and adages for Bacon who, he claimed, used and marked them, 'reading each attentively'. The collection was advertised in a sale catalogue as 'The private manuscript library of Francis Bacon, Lord Verulam and of his law clerk and servant William Tothill', and was sold to C. K. Ogden, who in turn bequeathed the 'Bacon Tothill [or Tottel] Collection', as it was described, to University College London, where it has remained since.

In 1976 the collection was examined by Dr Stuart Clark who discovered that the claims that the notebooks were prepared by Tothill for Bacon were erroneous.[19] As Clark argued, there was no sound evidence that Bacon had perused the volumes, many of which excerpted or referred to his own works. Moreover most of the notebooks could be dated to after 1626, when William Tothill died, and several to the Commonwealth or Restoration periods. Clark instead demonstrated that the notebooks belonged to Tothill's grandson William Drake who inherited Shardeloes on his grandfather's death, and posited that fifteen of the fifty-four items were written in Drake's own hand.

William Drake was born in 1606, the only son of Francis Drake of Esher and Joan Tothill (or Tottel), William's daughter, both of whom 'seem to have been puritans'.[20] After being educated at Amersham by Dr Charles Croke, William Drake went up to Christ Church, Oxford in 1624 where, according to Wood, he befriended John Gregory who fostered in him a love of books and learning, and where he was a pupil of George Morley, future bishop of Worcester.[21] In 1626, Drake went on to the Middle Temple where he was

18. See 'Bacon MSS', *Times Lit. Supp.*, 13 Feb. 1943, p. 79.
19. S. Clark, 'Wisdom Literature of the Seventeenth Century: A Guide to the Contents of the "Bacon–Tottel" Commonplace Books. Part I', *Trans. Camb. Bibliog. Soc.* 6 (1976), pp. 291–305.
20. M. F. Keeler, *The Long Parliament, 1640–41* (Philadelphia, 1954), 'Drake', p. 159.
21. Ibid.; A. Wood, *Athenae Oxonienses* (4 vols, Oxford, 1817), vol. 3, p. 205. The Dean's Register at Christ Church, DP i a 2, shows a Drake 'gentleman' at the House in 1623,

3. Drake's manor house, Shardeloes House, Buckinghamshire.

bound with Simonds D'Ewes and the puritan lawyer John White, his cousin; and in the same year he inherited most of the wealth and estates of his maternal grandfather.[22] In 1629 he transferred to Gray's Inn and evidently lived for some time in London, but Shardeloes remained his home throughout his life.[23] On the death of his father in 1633, William inherited Esher in Surrey but sold it – probably to consolidate his Buckinghamshire estate, which he did in 1637 with the purchase of the manor of Amersham from the Earl of Bedford.[24]

Drake was for long an aspirant for some office and in the late 1630s purchased from Sir David Cunningham the reversion to a post in the Fine office in the Court of Common Pleas.[25] William's father, Francis, had sat for every

but Drake neither matriculated nor took a degree. I am grateful to Judith Curthoys, the Christ Church archivist, for her assistance in pursuing Drake's student record. Gregory was born at Amersham, became prebendary of Chichester cathedral and died in 1646.

22. C. T. Martin, ed., *Middle Temple Records, 1501–1703* (4 vols, 1904–5), vol. 2, pp. 703, 733. William Tothill left his estate to William Drake and Catherine Tothill, who renounced her right in Shardeloes to her nephew William. See *V.C.H. Buckinghamshire* (4 vols, 1905–28), vol. 3, p. 149.

23. J. Foster, ed., *The Register of Admissions to Gray's Inn, 1521–1889* (1889), p. 188.

24. *V.C.H. Surrey* (4 vols, 1902–12), vol. 3, pp. 447–50; *V.C.H. Bucks*, vol. 3, p. 149.

25. In November 1635, Cunningham had the reversion after William and Robert Blake, the holders, *Cal. S.P. Dom. 1635–6*, p. 226. He sold it to Drake the following May, G. Aylmer, *The King's Servants: The Civil Service of Charles I, 1625–1642* (1961), p. 97.

parliament between 1621 and 1628 for Amersham, and in April 1640 William followed in his footsteps, being chosen for the borough. Though he spoke only occasionally in the Long Parliament, one of his speeches dated November 1641 was printed and Drake was appointed to several committees, including the Committee for Privileges.[26] In 1641 he was also made a knight and baronet – perhaps in the hope of winning him to the king's service. In 1642 he subscribed to maintain horse for both the king and parliament, evidently reluctant, as were many, to separate, or make the choice between, them.[27] During the Civil War, Drake was one of the members of the parliamentary association for Buckinghamshire.[28] However, he left England in February 1643 and spent most of the next seventeen years abroad, supposedly 'for his health'.[29] Drake was excluded from parliament in Pride's Purge, but evidently remained unmolested by the republican regime.[30] During the 1650s he continued to consolidate his Buckinghamshire landholdings, and in 1652 took office as Chirographer of the Court of Common Pleas when his old acquaintance Oliver St John became Chief Justice.[31] At the Restoration, Drake again took up his seat for Amersham, which he held until his death in 1669.

Drake was a substantial and wealthy landowner, committed to his family seat and devoted to his country.[32] In 1657 William built six almshouses on the south side of the market hall in Amersham and at St Mary's church he is commemorated by a large marble monument (ill. 4).[33] The monument represents him in a shroud with one hand raised in adulation, his statue flanked by Corinthian columns supporting a broken pediment with arms above. On the base were inscriptions to William's mother Joan and grandfather William Tothill. But Sir William, though a Buckinghamshire figure, was by no means enclosed by provincial horizons or concerns. His monument manifests that he was a scholar, 'a promoter and patron of letters'. In particular, his epitaph

26. Keeler, *The Long Parliament*, 'Drake'. See W. Drake, *Sir William Drake, His Speech in Parliament . . . Nov 10th 1641* (1641). It is not certain whether the speech was delivered. See *The Journal of Sir Simonds D'Ewes*, ed. W. H. Coates (1942), pp. 117–18; *C.J.* II, 1640–2, pp. 21, 239, 288, 496.
27. See C. Woodman, 'List of the Names of the Members . . . that Advanced Horse, Money and Plate. . . .', *Notes & Queries* 12 (1855), pp. 337, 338, 358; cf. below, p. 168.
28. *V.C.H. Bucks*, vol. 4, p. 356.
29. Drake received a warrant from the Commons to travel to the Low Countries on 4 Feb. 1643, *C.J.* II, p. 956. He also journeyed to France; but though it has been suggested that he went to Italy (G. Eland, *Shardeloes Papers*, Oxford, 1947, p. 55), I have found no firm evidence.
30. D. Underdown, *Pride's Purge: Politics in the Puritan Revolution* (Oxford, 1971), p. 209; see *Calendar of the Proceedings of the Committee for Compounding, 1643–1660*, part 3, p. 2236.
31. *V.C.H. Bucks*, vol. 3, p. 152; *Hist. MSS Comm., Tenth Report*, Appendix Part IV (1885), p. 217, 'copy of a memorandum 7th June AD 1652', by Oliver St John and Drake.
32. Keeler points out that Drake's father settled only part of his estate on his son because he had been so well provided for by his grandfather. See also below, p. 91.
33. *V.C.H. Bucks*, vol. 3, pp. 141, 153.

4. Monument to Sir William
Drake, St Mary's Church,
Amersham, Buckinghamshire.

states, 'he collected from every quarter the best editions, he sought especially
Latin writers who taught true wisdom and common sense.' It is an epitaph
that hints at a life of collecting and reading directed to an end. Fortunately
that epitaph is far from the last word on Drake's reading or the works he
regarded as the sources of wisdom and sense.

When he listed the Drake manuscripts, Stuart Clark arranged them in three
groups.[34] In the first group he placed the fifteen commonplace books all
written in William's hand, which from notes and internal evidence can be
dated from about 1627 to the mid-1640s.[35] These contain, as well as extensive notes from classical and humanist texts, references to Drake's family, estates
and personal affairs and observations on contemporary figures and events. The
second group of twenty-two volumes continues the series of commonplace

34. See Clark, 'Wisdom Literature I' and also 'Wisdom Literature of the Seventeenth
Century. Part II', *Trans. Camb. Bibliog. Soc.* 7 (1977), pp. 46–73.
35. Clark, 'Wisdom Literature II'. Most of the volumes contain *some* dated notes and references to published works, enabling us to situate others.

books and appears to belong to the mid to late 1640s and the 1650s, with some material from the early years of Restoration. What differentiates these from group one is that they are written, for the most part, in a different hand, and contain fewer references to personal affairs. However, in their common-place headings, authors annotated and favoured, and style they are remarkably consistent with those in Drake's own hand, which also appears here and there in some of the volumes. The continuities and consistencies suggest that Drake's was still the organising mind behind the annotations, and that he had employed an amanuensis to assist him, while occasionally making entries himself. The hypothesis is supported by Drake's expressed intention in one of the earlier notebooks: 'to have a scholar to read my ordinary printed books and still to be discoursing at meals with him or walking in the garden, to reserve the strength of my own mind for things material and most impor-tant'.[36] In early modern England 'reading' consisted of a variety of practices other than the silent and personal activity we take for granted. Having a servant 'read' to auditors was common in aristocratic circles and Francis Bacon advocated the practice and recommended it to Fulke Greville.[37] In Drake's case it may also have been a necessity. For his notebooks contain several notes of remedies for the eyes and his epitaph links his employment of a reader to declining eyesight in middle age, while making it clear that Drake continued his studies, by means of this help, throughout his life.[38] The final group of seventeen volumes is more miscellaneous. None is a commonplace book. Rather they are printed books and manuscripts, some annotated in Drake's hand, compilations of treaties, legal cases, parliamentary speeches and letters which evidently formed part of Drake's library.[39] All in all the fifty-four volumes constitute the greatest archival resource we have to chart how an early modern English gentleman read, and how reading shaped his mental universe.

But rich repository though they are, the Ogden manuscripts catalogued by Stuart Clark are not the only materials we have of Sir William Drake's. In addition to his parliamentary notebooks in that collection, Drake compiled in about 1632 a holograph commonplace book of legal cases and parliamen-tary speeches for the parliaments of James I and Charles I, which is now in the House of Lords Record Office.[40] More importantly, I have identified in the Folger Shakespeare Library in Washington a commonplace book of 307

---

36. University College London Ogden MSS (Bacon–Tottell MSS) 7/7 f. 164v.
37. Bacon, 'Of Studies', in *Francis Bacon: The Essays*, ed. J. Pitcher (Harmondsworth, 1985), p. 209; and V. F. Snow, 'Francis Bacon's Advice to Fulke Greville on Research Tech-niques', *Hunt. Lib. Quart.* 23 (1960) pp. 369–78.
38. Clark, 'Wisdom Literature I', p. 297; concerning Drake's sight see below, p. 173.
39. Drake's hand is found on the front leaf of a volume containing part of William West's *Symboleography*; and he extensively annotates *Francisci Guicciardini . . . Hypomneses Politicae* (1597). See below, pp. 261–2.
40. House of Lords R.O., Historical Collections MS 49, wrongly described as the 'Commonplace Book of Francis Drake'.

pages, there catalogued as anonymous, as another of Drake's books of reading notes, in his own hand.[41] And in Buckinghamshire Record Office, a manuscript listed as 'Latin maxims and epigrams' turned out to be some leaves of a Drake notebook, with annotations in his holograph.[42] Together with internal references to other volumes not identified hitherto, what these discoveries suggest is that the Drake archive, extensive though it is, is far from complete, and that in all likelihood more of his commonplace books may lie under the veil of anonymity in archive offices in England, in America or on the continent where he travelled in the 1630s, 1640s and 1650s.[43]

Such a possibility is rendered all the more probable by the recent emergence of another Drake manuscript, rather different from those we have hitherto encountered. On 18 March 1993, there appeared for sale at Phillips of London a manuscript described in the sale catalogue as the 'autograph journal of Sir William Drake'.[44] The 160-page volume, which, like other Drake manuscripts, was unpaginated and written from both ends, was purchased by the Huntington Library. As the sale catalogue claimed, this was a manuscript rather different from the commonplace books. For where they consisted of reading notes and only occasional observations on public matters, the Huntington volume, while still evidencing Drake's reading, is more of a personal and political diary, chronologically charting events from 30 November 1631 to the outbreak of civil war. In the Huntington manuscript we see Drake as a man of affairs, pursuing and advancing his own ambitions, moving on the public stage with lawyers, MPs, London aldermen and courtiers, and committing to paper his thoughts about the course of events and the developing crisis in church and state. The autograph journal in fact provides a helpful bridge between Drake's commonplace books of reading notes, in group one of the Ogden manuscripts, and his journal of and speech to the Long Parliament in 1641.[45] It also opens new insights into how Drake's reading and note taking not only formed his general worldview, but also helped to script his specific responses to particular contemporary issues and events.

Another important source is Drake's printed books. Five of these are found in group three of the Bacon–Tottel collection at University College, and one, *Francisci Guicciardini . . . Hypomneses Politicae*, is extensively annotated in the margins and borders by Drake. The richness of this single volume led me to wonder whether more of Drake's printed books might not be sitting among the books bequeathed to University College by C. K. Ogden, separated from the Drake notebooks by the modern library's differentiation of manuscript and print. Sure enough, a search of all the printed books still identified as

41. Folger MS v. a. 263. The manuscript is catalogued as 'Proverbs, Wise Sayings and Quotations . . .' It covers a period before and after 1645, and therefore constitutes a full notebook for the later period in Drake's own hand.
42. Bucks R.O., D/DR/10/56. Listed as 'Latin maxims and epigrams'.
43. See below, pp. 171–2.
44. Phillips sale catalogue 18 Mar. 1993, item 23.
45. See below, pp. 121–3.

Ogden bequests (some duplicates were sold off) turned up several that might have been marked or annotated by Drake or his amanuensis and one that almost certainly was.[46] As we shall see, another book in the Folger Library, the Duc de Rohan's *Treatise of the Interest of the Princes and States of Christendom*, is clearly and extensively annotated by Drake, enabling us to discuss his first engagement with a text and the process that preceded the entering of extracts and commonplaces in his notebooks.[47]

Commonplace books, a journal, and annotated manuscripts and printed texts, along with further clues provided by Drake's will and other biographical information: together the various pieces of the Drake collection offer the historian a unique opportunity to observe an early Stuart gentleman reading, reflecting, and organising a programme of study to equip himself for personal gain and considered action in the public sphere.[48] We shall pursue Drake through these various different records and across the years from the late 1620s to the early 1660s, in an endeavour to trace how what he read, his habits of reading and the values he expressed, developed and changed. We shall observe how he read the personal rule of Charles I, civil war, revolution and republic and, in fine, Restoration, and how those cataclysmic events marked his reading. And we shall assess what such a detailed study does to revise both our sense of other readers and our understanding of those events.

Though Drake's notebooks invite another study in the history of humanist editions, translations and commentaries,[49] our focus and emphasis will be on the interaction between scholarship and values, reading and politics. As Stuart Clark observed, above all the manuscript notes from a large corpus of Renaissance literature make it clear that 'William Drake set out to acquire an arsenal of sententious materials' for use.[50] In his list of the Ogden volumes Clark drew attention to some sources of those maxims. In particular, he noted, Drake's repeated annotation of, and admiration for Tacitus, Machiavelli and Guicciardini suggested a strong affinity with 'writers who challenged . . . the assumptions governing traditional views of political life'.[51] Dr Clark did not pursue those suggestions. Having performed a splendid service to scholarship in listing the collection, Clark left Drake and his manuscripts to other scholars. Now, in the light of the other manuscripts that have been discovered, and with some of the questions and approaches pioneered by reading theorists and historians of the book, we may explore just how reading shaped his view of the world, even a radical political philosophy.

46. Below, pp. 260–2.
47. Duc de Rohan, *A Treatise of the Interests of the Princes and States of Christendom* (1641, Folger Library R1868); see below, pp. 262–6.
48. On Drake's will, see below, pp. 273–4.
49. In several cases Drake had more than one edition of a text, used translations as well as originals, and manuscripts as well as printed translations.
50. Clark, 'Wisdom Literature I', p. 298.
51. Ibid., p. 299.

Records of Reading

Together with the notebooks listed by Clark as group 1, written in Drake's own hand and covering the years 1627 to 1645, we may place the leaves from Buckinghamshire, the Lords manuscript and part of the substantial holograph volume in the Folger which continues into the 1650s. The notebooks are not standardised. Two quarters, eight octavos and seven sextodecimos, they are of greatly uneven length with varying numbers of blank folios, not only in the middle. None is continuously foliated by Drake (though certain sections are paginated by him) or any other contemporary.[52] All are used from both ends, with in a few cases some appearances that the back of a book was employed for personal or estate matters, or at least started out that way.[53] In two volumes (Ogden MSS 7 and 8) the same printed passage from Francis Bacon's *Advancement of Learning* is bound in, with interlinings and annotations in Drake's hand (ill. 5).[54] Otherwise the volumes consist of manuscript notes from reading, conversation and reflection, and of reminders, prompts and self-instructions. Some are loosely organised around a theme: volume 11 is dominated by legal notes and cases, volume 33 by 'characters', short lives of classical and more recent statesmen and men of letters;[55] volume 7 is the only manuscript to contain extensive personal memoranda. All the volumes contain detailed, careful, sometimes crowded notes, in several languages, from Drake's reading, alongside copies of correspondence, advice given in conversation, comments on personalities and observations of times past and present. Sometimes the order and conjunctions are striking: Drake moves in two folios (of volume 8) from thoughts on the Irish rebellion to notes for a speech in parliament, to general axioms about flattery and astrological predictions.[56] In volume 26 notes about personal negotiations and deals appear to lead him to Sir Henry Vane's negotiations with the Scots.[57] There are only occasional dates entered in the books, and it is not clear that the notebooks were used sequentially.

52. I have foliated most of the volumes myself, continually through (at the request of the archivist) even when they start from each end. This means that notes from the back will have folio references in declining order.

53. Volume 7 starts at the back with notes on leases; volume 23 begins at the back with entries about Amersham estates; volume 38 has notes about building at the back; volume 48 begins from the back with notes on finances. However, volume 52 begins from the back with notes from Machiavelli.

54. The pagination (pp. 70–104) is haphazard in these printed pages which are bound into volume 7 ff. 3–40, after two folios of manuscript notes from Sir George Carew, Machiavelli, Guicciardini and others. In volume 8 the printed pages 82–105 are bound in after f. 13.

55. Volume 33 opens with 'Some Observations out of Plutarch's *Lives*' and proceeds to lives of recent rulers and politicians, extracted from histories by De Thou, Ralegh, Paulo Jovio, Guicciardini and others.

56. Ogden MS 7/8 ff. 72–3.

57. Ogden MS 7/26 f. 179v, 'Of Negotiating'.

Of the Advancement of Learning.

intention: but *Tanquam aliud agendo*, because of the Naturall hatred of the minde against necessity and Constraint. Many other Axiomes there are touching the Managing of *Exercise* and *custome*: which being so Conducted, doth proue indeed another nature: but being gouerned by chance, doth comonly proue but an ape of nature, & bringeth forth that which is lame and Counterfeite.

So if wee shoulde handle *bookes* and *studies* and what influence and operation they haue vpon manners, are there not diuers precepts of greate caution and direction appartaining thereunto? did not one of the fathers in greate indignation call *Poesy vinum Demonum*, because it increaseth temptations, perturbations and vaine opinions? Is not the opinion of *Aristotle* worthy to be regarded wherein he faith, That yong men are no fitte auditors of Morall Philosophy, because they are not setled from the boyling heate of their affections, nor attempered with *Time* and *Experience*? and doth it not hereof come that those excellent books and discourses of the auncient writers, (whereby they haue persuaded vnto vertue most effectually, by representing her in *state* and *Maiesty*, and popular opinions against vertue in their *Parasites Coates*, fitt to be scorned and derided,) are so little effect towards honesty of life, because they are not red & reuolued by men in their mature and setled yeares, but confined almost to boyes & beginners? but is it not true also that much lesse, young men are fit auditors of Matters of Policy, till they haue beene throughly

The second booke 69

throughly seasoned in religion & Morality, least their Iudgementes be corrupted, and made apt to thinke that there are no true Differences of things, but according to vtility and fortune, as the verse describes it-
Prosperum et Felix scelus virtus vocatur: And Againe
Ille crucem pretium sceleris tulit, Hic diadema: which the
Poets do speak satyrically and in indignation on verities behalfe: But bookes of pollicie do speake it seriously, and positiuely: for so it pleaseth *Machiauell* to
say *That if Caesar had bene ouerthrowne he woulde haue
bene more odious then euer was Catiline*; as if there had
bene noe difference but in fortune, betweene a very
fury of lust & bloud, and the most excellisst spirit (his ambitio relieued) of the world? Againe is there not a Caution likewise to be giuen of the doctrines of Moralities themselues (some kindes of the) leaste they make
men too precise, arrogate, incompatible, as *Cicero* faith
of *Cato* in *Marco Cato*: *Haec bona quae videmus diuina et
egregia ipsius naturae esse propria quae nonnumquam requirunt, si sunt omnia, non aratura sed a Magistro*: Many
other Axiomes & aduises there are touching those
proprieties & effects, which studies doe insuse & instil
into maners: And so likewise (is there touchinge the
vse of all those other pointes of Company, fame, lawes
and the rest, which we recited in the beginning in
the doctrine of Morality.
But there is a kind of CVLTVRE of the MINDE that
semeth yet more accurate & elaborate the the rest &
is built vpon this ground: That the minds of all men
are at some times in a state more perfite, and at o-
ther

Fig. 5. Annotated pages of Francis Bacon's *Of the Advancement of Learning*.

But internal evidence often enables us to date notes at least approximately, and at times fairly precisely.[58] Though we are able here and there to detect some changes in the material read, what is most striking is the return over folios and years to the same authors, still more to the same books and passages. Like Gabriel Harvey, Drake returned to reread and reconsider his favourite authors as circumstances changed.

The range of Drake's reading is awe-inspiring. The list of classical philosophers, historians and rhetoricians whom he excerpts include Plato and Aristotle, Aesop, Plutarch, Thucydides, Isocrates, Strabo, Seneca, Demosthenes, Herodotus, Polybius, Homer, Pindar, Lucian, Cicero, the younger Pliny, Virgil, Martial, Catullus, Terence, Ovid, Petronius, Quintilian, Florus, Sallust, Cato, Dion and Tacitus. In addition to numerous editions of classical texts, Drake's notes show him very well read in humanist commentaries on the classics such as Michael Piccartus on Aristotle's *Politics*,[59] probably Justus Lipsius[60] and Sir William Cornwallis on Seneca,[61] and Sir Richard Baker on Cato,[62] and a host of commentators on Tacitus including Virgilio Malvezzi, Justus Lipsius, Matthias Bernegerus, Strada the Jesuit and Sir Henry Savile.[63]

Indeed the notebooks read like a compendium of Renaissance humanist learning, incorporating nearly all the famous scholars of early modern Europe and some less well known. Drake had read Erasmus, Vives, and Comines, Pascal, Montaigne and Balzac's *The Prince*;[64] Pierre Charron's *Of Wisdom*, Jean Hotman's treatise *The Ambassador*, Pierre Matthieu's *History of Henri IV*, Jacques Auguste de Thou's *History* and Bodin's *Six Livres de la Republique*.[65] Of the leading Dutch humanists he annotated the works of Joseph Scaliger,

58. See for example Ogden MSS 7/7 ff. 117v, 122v, 135, 171v, 164, 162v, 159v, 158v, 146v, 141v, 140; 7/8 f. 198v; 7/11 ff. 1, 13, 18; 7/23 ff. 15, 39, 53, 143v; 7/26 ff. 49, 180; 7/29 ff. 20, 20v, 21, 25, 130, 139, 147; 7/34 ff. 11, 12, 93v; 7/36 ff. 1, 93; 7/38 f. 11; 7/48 ff. 3v, 43, 173v; 7/52 f. 16. Often passages taken from books we can identify and date or references to figures recently promoted or deceased date the entries.

59. Ogden MS 7/7 f. 103v; Folger MS f. 100v; Piccartus (1574–1620), a German historian, poet and philosopher, published *In Politicos Libros Aristotelis* at Leipzig in 1615 (*Biographie Universelle*).

60. Justus Lipsius, the celebrated Netherlands philologian, published an annotated edition of Seneca at Antwerp in 1605.

61. W. Cornwallis, *Discourses upon Seneca the Tragœdian* (1601).

62. Ogden MS 7/45 ff. 23v–24; R. Baker (translator) *Cato Variegatus or Catoes Morall Distichs* (1636).

63. See for example Ogden MSS 7/7 f. 74; 7/8 ff. 177, 153v; 7/29 f. 16; 7/52 f. 120v; 7/21 f. 79; Folger MS f. 131. V. Malvezzi's *Discorsi sopra Cornelio Tacito* (Venice, 1635) was translated into English in 1642; Lipsius published an annotated works of Tacitus in 1574, which went into several editions; M. Bernegerus, professor of history at Strasbourg, published his edition of Tacitus in 1638; the reference to Famianus Strada is to *De Bello Belgico* (see also P. Gaudenzio, *De Candore Politicum in Tacitum Diatribae XIX . . . Praemittitur Exercitio ad Famianiam Historiam Defenditurque idem Tacitus* (Pisa, 1646); H. Savile's *The Ende of Nero and Beginning of Galba* (1591) went into six editions by 1640.

64. Ogden MSS 7/7 ff. 103, 48, 87v, 146; 7/8 ff. 62, 173v, 7/23 f. 1; 7/38 f. 25v; Folger MS ff. 46, 64v, 126v, 118v.

65. Ogden MSS 7/7 ff. 50v, 84, 94v; 7/8 ff. 62, 173v; 7/23 f. 53; 7/48 f. 48.

Janus Gruter, Daniel Heinsius, the history professor at Leiden, Justus Lipsius, the Leiden professor and political theorist, and Hugo Grotius the jurist.[66] Among the Italians we find extracts from Savonarola, Peter Aretine, Girolamo Cardano, author of De Subtilitate, Paolo Sarpi's History of the Council of Trent, Paulus Jovius's history of his own time, Enrico Davila's history of the civil wars in France, and Cardinal Bentivoglio's history of the wars in Flanders, as well as the works of the authors Drake most admired: Machiavelli, Guicciardini and Botero.[67]

To take familiar names we can add Drake's references to Eustache du Refuge's Traité de la Cour, Philippe de Bethune's Councellor of Estate, Philippe Garnier's book of proverbs and grammar, Jacobus Bornitius, the author of Discursus Politicus de Prudentia Politica (1602), Jean Loccenius, historiographer to the Swedish court and epigramist, Peter Cunaeus, historian of the Jews, Christopher Besoldus's De Aerario Publico Discursus, and Lorenzo Valla, the translator of Thucydides, and commentator on Herodotus and Quintilian.[68] As well as the more famous Italians, Drake annotated Paolo Paruta, the historian of Venice and author of political discourses, Stefano Guazzo, author of La Civil Conversatione, Malvezzi on the Spanish monarchy, Agostino Mascardi who penned moral discourses and a treatise Dell'arte historica, and Jovius Pontanus, the fifteenth-century servant of the king of Naples who wrote historical and philosophical works, poetry and dialogues on morality and religion.[69]

As well as the luminaries of continental humanism, Drake was well read in English humanist scholarship and literature: besides Savile, Ascham's Schoolmaster, John Barclay, poet and author of Argenis, Cavendish's life of Wolsey, Clement Edmondes, military writer and author of observations on Caesar, John Robinson's Observations Divine and Moral, Ben Jonson's Sejanus and the verse of Sir John Suckling, and, most of all, the works of Francis Bacon.[70] The English legal learning of this age of advances in legal scholarship is well represented in Drake's notes from William Tothill's (Drake's grandfather's) treatise on the Court of Chancery, William Staunford, William Lambard's Archion, John Rastell's Exposition of the Terms of the Law (1567), Cowell's legal dictionary, The Interpreter (1607), the works of Sir Edward Coke and Sir John Davies, and notes from legal manuscripts, including Sir Roger Owen's discourse on impositions.[71]

---

66. Ogden MSS 7/7 ff. 56, 74; 7/8 ff. 201v, 197v, 153; 7/26 f. 88; 7/29 f. 35; 7/38 ff. 38, 19; 7/45 f. 2; Folger MS ff. 49, 106, 118.
67. Ogden MSS 7/8 ff. 22v, 27, 48, 52v, 64; 7/23 ff. 67, 68v; 7/26 ff. 39, 54; 7/33 f. 27; Folger MS ff. 54v, 90v, 119v, 124v, 66.
68. Ogden MSS 7/7 ff. 46, 70v, 139v, 112; 7/8 f. 69; 7/29 ff. 3, 29, 34v.
69. Ogden MSS 7/7 ff. 48; 7/8 f. 2, 177, 147; 7/23 f. 57; 7/26 ff. 75, 134v. Malvezzi's Successi Principali della Monarchia di Spagna nell'anno 1639 was published in 1641.
70. Ogden MSS 7/7 ff. 53, 88, 104; 7/8 f. 176; 7/11 f. 31; 7/23 f. 34; 7/26 ff. 141, 143; 7/34 f. 1; 7/35 f. 15; 7/38 ff. 116v, 112v; 7/45 f. 23; 7/48 ff. 12, 134v, 125v; Folger MS ff. 49v, 129v.
71. Ogden MSS 7/11 ff. 3–4, 115v; 7/23 ff. 12v, 125v; 7/45 f. 185v; 7/52 ff. 136v onwards.

Religious works are not absent from the list. Drake read the Bible, includ-
ing the Apocrypha, the Koran, Aquinas and other Fathers, Florentius Volusen-
sus's *De Animi Tranquilitate Dialogus* (1543), Gulielmus Bucanus's *Institutions of
Christian Religion* (1606), Nicholas Caussin's *The Holy Court*, John Preston's
The New Covenant, sermons by John Howson, Isaac Bargrave, Samuel Ward
and Dr Andrew Willet, antipapal polemicist, the puritan John Robinson's
Observations, John Salkeld's *Treatise of Angels* (1613), John Durie's *Motives to
Induce the Protestants to Mind the Work of Peace Ecclesiastical among Themselves*
(1639), Thomas Fuller's *History of the Holy Warre*, and the Jesuit Thomas
Fitzherbert's *Treatise Concerning Policy and Religion* (Douai, 1606–10).[72] This
selective gathering of Anglicans, Jesuits, Catholics and Puritans, together with
treatises on religion and politics, suggests a man reading to distil wisdom from
all religions rather than to sustain or reinforce a religious faith, position or
programme. Certainly, whatever his own faith or views (which we shall
examine), Drake did not shy away from writers like Savonarola, Campanella,
Pascal, Charron, La Valla or Ralegh, men deemed heretical or irreligious.[73]
And those authors he most often cites and constantly urges himself to reread
were, by his own admission, 'mere politicians, without religion'.[74]

For whichever of Drake's notebooks we take up, there can be no doubt
that at the top of his own reading list were works of policy and politic historians, full of observations and axioms of an intensely pragmatic and amoral
colour. Drake's heroes were Machiavelli (he read the *History of Florence* as well
as the *Discourses* and *The Prince*, the last in manuscript as well as printed editions)[75] and Guicciardini, their classical antecedents Polybius, Livy and Tacitus,
and their humanist heirs and disciples Botero, Cardan, Lipsius, Montaigne,
Dallington, and the other Tacitean translators and commentators. Among the
English 'Machiavellians' Drake was drawn first and foremost to Francis Bacon
– especially to his discussion of the active life in the passage 'Of Negotiation'
from *The Advancement of Learning*.[76] But Drake conjoined with Bacon, as
authors and works in the same vein, the histories of Sir Thomas More and
Sir Robert Cotton, and works on religion and policy by Martin Fotherby
and John Saltmarsh.[77] For all its apparent eclecticism, Drake's reading is that
of a man preoccupied with the *vita civili*, with advancement in the world,
with the attainment and loss of greatness, with the contests for place and
power, in short with – a word still not respectable in early seventeenth-
century England – politics.[78]

72. Ogden MSS 7/7 f. 131; 7/8 ff. 65v, 187v; 7/23 ff. 34, 37; 7/26 f. 88; 7/29 ff. 147, 192v,
    191v; 7/34 ff. 1–3, 91, 92v, 96v, 107v; 7/38 ff. 36, 107v; 7/45 f. 172v; 7/48 f. 117v;
    Folger MS f. 1; Bucks R.O. D/DR/10/56 f. 27. Clark, 'Wisdom Literature II', passim.
73. On Drake's religious views, see below, pp. 108–11.
74. Ogden MS 7/8 f. 161v.
75. Ogden MSS 7/7 ff. 2, 52, 148v; 7/11 f. 34v; 7/8 f. 14; Folger MS ff. 79v, 90, ★5, ★16v.
76. Pages of this essay are pasted into notebooks Ogden MSS 7 and 8.
77. Clark, 'Wisdom Literature I', p. 300.
78. See K. Sharpe and S. Zwicker, *Politics of Discourse: The Literature and History of Seven-
    teenth Century England* (Berkeley, 1987), introduction, pp. 5–7.

As with his reading of religion, it is politics in the broadest sense. Drake's list of readings indicates no clear constitutional or political sympathies. Bodin is famous (perhaps wrongly) as the theorist of sovereignty; Balzac's *Prince* is often read as an apologia for absolutism; Bargrave delivered a famous sermon in defence of the king's untrammelled power to exact forced loans;[79] Matthieu was a panegyrist of Henri IV.[80] On the other hand, La Valla was infamous as a critic of orthodoxy and authority.[81] Savonarola was renowned for his opposition to tyrannical rulers and his establishment of a republic in Florence, and Peter Aretino was called by Ariosto 'il flagello de principi'.[82] Drake read his common lawyers as well as monarchical apologists, Owen's treatise against impositions as well as Bargrave's defence of loans.[83] And the figure he most admired, Machiavelli, was, and is, read as the defender of virtuous republics and unscrupulous princes. William Drake's reading undoubtedly equipped him to tackle the issues involved in the contemporary debates about the conflict of interest between 'policy' and 'piety', and between the authority of rulers and the liberty of subjects. But to understand further how he tackled them, we shall need to proceed beyond the bare list of what Drake read – extensive and revealing as it is.

One approach to determining the importance Drake attached to particular works might be his efforts to obtain and read books in foreign languages. His French and Italian were clearly not initially perfect for he records his intention to learn these languages and leaves evidence of his continuing efforts to improve his grammar and vocabulary in each language by self-teaching.[84] We can be fairly certain that he read Paolo Parota, Mascardi, Bentivoglio and Malvezzi in the original Italian because there was no known translation in English, or Latin, at the time.[85] But in other cases, where an English edition exists, it is not always obvious whether Drake used it or read the original (in a few cases we know he did both).[86] Nor do we have much information

79. I. Bargrave, *A Sermon Preached before King Charles* (1627); see R. Cust, *The Forced Loan and English Politics, 1626–1628* (Oxford, 1987), pp. 65–7.

80. Pierre Matthieu, poet and historian, was commissioned by Henri IV to write his history which was published in 1612 and translated into English as *The Heroyk Life and Deplorable Death of Henry the Fourth* (1612).

81. Lorenzo La Valla, the leading fifteenth-century philologian who exposed the Donation of Constantine as a forgery, aroused the ire of the papacy. He defended the philosophy of Epicurus in *De Voluptate* (1431) which Drake read (Ogden MS 7/7 f. 70v).

82. *Biographie Universelle*, 'Aretine'.

83. Ogden MS 7/11 f. 115v.

84. See Ogden MS 7/7 f. 148: 'get to have a good skill in the French tongue'; f. 118v: 'Mr. Hague said that in a month after a man had French he might learn Italian'. Grammar exercises and vocabulary lists are found in 7/29 ff. 36, 109–10, 114, 177, 186v; 7/35 f. 50v (French); 7/48 ff. 22v, 119v (Italian).

85. That is up to *c*.1645. Malvezzi's Tacitus was translated into English in 1642, but judging by internal evidence of dates, Drake read it earlier in Italian. See Ogden MSS 7/8 f. 177; 7/52 f. 120v.

86. E.g. Bacon (Ogden MS 7/7 f. 80); Folger MS f. 104 refers to 'Guicc Angl', that is in an English edition.

about where Drake acquired books or what lengths he went to to get them. He had evidently built a considerable collection before he travelled to the Low Countries, and we occasionally get hints of what might be holdings or recent acquisitions. In volume 29, for example, he lists as 'Things of Policy which I have', Lipsius's letters to a nobleman, Campanella, Cardinal Granvelle's Demonstration against the Hollanders, Sir Robert Cotton's account of England's relations with Spain and works by Cardan, Guicciardini and Machiavelli.[87] But the list is undated and unlikely to be complete.

Drake was certainly wealthy enough to buy books, and was prepared to spend quite large sums: he paid his cousin three shillings for buying on his behalf a life of Erasmus and for his copy of the Koran, for example, he laid out twenty shillings.[88] In addition to purchase, he acquired or borrowed books and manuscripts from scholars and antiquaries such as D'Ewes and Cotton and other bibliophiles of his acquaintance.[89] He acquired a manuscript English translation of Machiavelli's *Prince* long before the published edition of 1640 by Edward Dacres.[90] While the source of most of his acquisitions remains unknown, scattered notes throughout the volumes do point to works Drake was keen to buy or read. His list of 'works to be gotten' in Ogden MS volume 35 included Ramus on Aristotle's *Physics* and *Metaphysics*, Bartholomaeus' *De Proprietatibus Rerum* (1472), Thomas Clay's discourse of the well ordering of an honourable estate, William Bradshaw's *English Puritanism* (1605), *Purchas His Pilgrim* and Ralegh's *History*.[91] From Paris he sought out Charron's *Trois Veritez*, Cardano's 'De Arcanis', Casaubon's commentary on Polybius, Josias Mercerus on Tacitus, Battista's Life of Cosimo de Medici, works by Amyot, Du Bellay, Brissonius, 'anything' of Comines, Du Refuge, and Guicciardini and 'what have you of Thuanus', the historian of his own times, Jacques Auguste de Thou.[92] To these he added the best books he could find of French

---

87. Ogden MS 7/29 f. 34v. The brief references are presumably to J. Lipsius, *Epistolae* (Antwerp, 1607; Paris, 1610); T. Campanella, *De Monarchia Hispanica Discursus* (1640); A. P. de Granvelle, *Letters Containing Sundry Devices Touching the State of Flanders . . .* (1582). The reference to Cotton is presumably to the 'A Remonstrance of the Treaties of Amitie and Marriage', which was not published before 1651 (J. Howell, *Cottoni Posthuma* (1657), pp. 93–107) but which circulated in manuscript. See Sharpe, *Sir Robert Cotton*, ch. 4.

88. Ogden MS 7/7 ff. 131, 141v.

89. Ogden MSS 7/11 f. 118v; 7/23 ff. 15, 34, 142v; Clark, 'Wisdom Literature II', p. 49.

90. Clark, 'Wisdom Literature I', p. 300; Ogden MS 7/7 f. 2.

91. Ogden MS 7/35 f. 15; A. Bartholomaeus, *Incipit Prolemium de Proprietatibus Rerum* was published in 1472; there were English editions in 1495 and 1582; T. Clay, *A Chronological Discourse of the Well Ordering of an Honourable Estate* (1618).

92. P. Charron, *Les Trois Veritez contre les athées, idolatres, iuifs . . .* (1593); G. Cardano, *Heironymi Cardini Arcana Politica* (Lyons, 1635); Casaubon's annotated edition of Polybius was published in 1619; J. Mercerus's *Taciti Opera* was published in 1606; Giovanni Battista Adriani's *Orazione . . . fatta all esseguie del Sereniss. Cosimo de Medici* was published at Florence in 1534; Jacques Amyot, bishop, classical scholar and confidant of Charles IX, published editions and translations of classical texts, notably Plutarch's *Lives*. Martin Du Bellay published *Memoires historiques*, covering the years 1513 to 1547. Pierre Brisson wrote a history of the civil wars in France (1569), published in 1578.

proverbs. In England one list of books 'to be got' catalogues Fletcher's work on Scripture and policy, Sir Henry Wotton's treatise on education and comparison of the lives of Essex and Buckingham, Sir Robert Cecil's negotiations in France, Lord Digby's negotiations in Spain, 'Lord Brooke's Justice of the Peace' and the resolutions of the judges, probably those of 1633, the law reports of Lord Husbbard and Sir Francis More, an abridgement of Coke, and Justice Whitelocke's readings at the Inns of Court – many of which, though listed as 'books', were unpublished manuscripts.[93]

Drake's lists themselves suggest that these were not the desiderata of a bibliophile with an obsession for indiscriminate collecting. In one note Drake counsels himself to 'buy not too many books in France' and repeats the self-admonition, adding 'for I have more excellent ones already'.[94] In places he airs his anxiety that if he studies too much it will impede the advancement of his estate: reading too many books was, he feared, a great enemy to 'that audacity . . . I want'.[95] The studies he permitted himself, then, we can be sure, were always directed to use. 'To read' and 'to do' lists scattered through the commonplace books give insights into how he directed his readings to these ends. Sometimes a bare comment – 'Read Camden's Britannia' or 'read Sir Edwin Sandys' – points to the topical reading of a typical English gentleman.[96] In Drake's case, however, they formed part of a more systematic programme. In one volume he informs us that he set himself three major tasks, to acquire a competent knowledge in the law, an understanding of trade and customs and a facility for eloquence in speech.[97]

With each objective he knew how to proceed. Drake reminded himself to 'be well read in parliament journals [and] Star Chamber which are the most useful histories of all, as likewise letters of state'.[98] When abroad he made a mental note to get in England 'the choicest things out of Sir Thomas Cotton's study', adding elsewhere: 'Get as many choice things concerning law and business and employment in the general as you may and study them, Mr. Cotton for journals of parliaments and Sir Simonds D'Ewes'.[99] As well as borrowing Cotton's manuscripts, Drake admired his writings: 'Read often Sir Francis Bacon's, Sir Robert Cotton's works,' he advised himself, making a connection the significance of which has escaped modern scholars.[100] Perhaps to further his plan to understand finance, Drake referred himself to Cotton's advice to James I on ways of raising money and the infamous treatise penned by Sir Robert Dudley, found in Cotton's library.[101] To improve his own management of affairs Drake projected to learn more about law courts, procedure and

93. Ogden MS 7/7 f. 159v; cf. f. 167v.
94. Ogden MS 7/7 ff. 92, 154.
95. Ogden MS 7/7 f. 92.
96. Ogden MS 7/7 f. 99.
97. Ogden MS 7/45 f. 2.
98. Ogden MS 7/7 f. 112v.
99. Ogden MS 7/7 f. 113v; 7/11 f. 118v.
100. Ogden MS 7/7 f. 112v.
101. Ogden MS 7/7 f. 100v; Sharpe, *Sir Robert Cotton*, pp. 121–3, 143–6.

drawing leases.[102] For speech and writing he resolved to take Sir Robert Cecil as a pattern, and extracted too the 'elegant forms of speech' from various writers.[103]

In most matters Drake turned to the study of history as his guide. 'To learn to write a good style,' he set out to 'study chiefly history, politics and the nature of our times and country.'[104] To inform himself of the kingdom, he planned to meditate on histories, and to 'get all matters of public nature whether printed or divulged by pen'.[105] Even for codes of personal conduct in the world he thought it best to 'read seriously Guicciardini's history, and passages of Sir Nicholas Bacon to make sagax, and Tacitus, Machiavel, Sir F. Bacon for acumen'.[106] The plan of historical study was ambitious and organised. Drake set out to read thematically as well as chronologically – to study, for example, plots in classical Rome, papal times, and medieval and Elizabethan England.[107] He drew up a reading programme beginning with Guicciardini's *History of Florence*, moving to histories of France and Spain, then to Polybius and Tacitus, before returning to Machiavelli and Comines, Conestaggio's history of Portugal and Sleidanus's history of Germany.[108] Similarly 'for the grounds and principles of policy' he thought there 'none fitter to be very well read in than Aristotle', read together with Machiavelli and Justus Lipsius.[109] These personal study plans appear to be very much Drake's own, and the reading programme of a man who set out to study for action.

So much for what William Drake read and what he set himself to read. What we now need to examine is what literary theorists and historians of the book have directed attention to: how he read, his reading practice, or rather practices – since readers do not read alike in all works or on all occasions. The rules Drake set himself to govern his reading make it clear that reading was never for him a passive process. He reminded himself on the cover of one of his notebooks to repeat every night what he had learned that day, to study only on an empty stomach in order to sharpen concentration, and to meditate often on what he had read until it was thoroughly digested. 'When you read,' he instructed himself, 'do it earnestly gathering together all the power of your mind to the study thereof, neither let your mind wander.'[110] As an aid to study, and as revealing of his purposes, Drake recommended to

102. Ogden MS 7/7 f. 164v.
103. Ogden MS 7/7 f. 148; 7/38 f. 2.
104. Ogden MS 7/7 f. 113.
105. Ogden MS 7/7 f. 167v.
106. Ogden MS 7/7 f. 91v.
107. See Ogden MS 7/7 f. 111.
108. Ogden MS 7/7 f. 113v. See I. Conestaggio, *The Historie of The Uniting of the Kingdom of Portugal to the Crowne of Castill* (1600); J. Philippson (Sleidanus), *A Famous Chronicle of our Time called Sleidane's Commentaries, Concerning the Reign of the Emperor Charles V* (1560). Cf. Ogden MS 7/7 f. 86: 'Polybius, Tacitus, Guicciardini, Machiavelli, Cardan lege hos authores acumine perspicacis . . .'
109. Ogden MS 7/7 f. 121v.
110. Ogden MS 7/38, cover and f. 1.

himself the breaking of a body of text into its members – chapters – and the epitomizing of chapters into their 'conclusions'. The absence of very long passages of quotation in the notebooks is explained by his observation that 'a wary reader will not endeavour to remember the mass and whole bulk of books but only to extract the spirit and quintessence thereof and what is most applicable to business.'[111]

The distilling of the quintessence did not mean reading quickly or casually – or 'gutting' books, to use a contemporary term. Not least because he sometimes had more than one edition of a work, Drake was sensitive to the status of texts and their historical evolution and conditioning. Interestingly he had a strong sense of the books which had been lost and the relationship of texts that survived to a vanished corpus of learning. 'Christian religion', the scholar in him observed with scarcely veiled contempt, 'has sought to extinguish ancient record'; Pope Gregory, for example, had burnt history books – 'a world of historians and Tacitus the best historian we have, had they been left alone, had never come to our reading.' Even Tacitus, he knew, had survived 'miserably mangled'.[112] But for all their deficiencies as exact records of classical times, it was for what they distilled of ancient wisdom and how it could be applied that Drake read them. And so Tacitus became for him a base text to be read alongside other commentators and historians, and reread in the light of their histories and experiences:

> Gather out and observe how they are applied all Tacitus his sayings, out of Lipsius Civili Doctrina, Clapmarius De Arcanis et Juro publico, Michael Piccartus Hist. Pol. Obser and his comment on Aristotle's Politics; to these join Machiavelli's works and gather the marrow out of what he hath written in this kind, but above all study Guicciardini's history which I esteem the best that ever was written, likewise be frequent in reading Tacitus and noting him as I read him.[113]

Such a passage reminds us of Gabriel Harvey sitting, at least as Grafton and Jardine imagined him, at a book wheel, moving from one text to another.[114] There is no evidence that Drake (or Harvey) used such a device, but it is obvious that he moved from text to text and back again, reading each in the light of the other.

This was not Drake's only negotiation between past texts and times and present discourses and circumstances. His reading was informed not only by other books but by other practices – speaking, listening, meditating and

111. Ogden MS 7/45 f. 166.
112. Ogden MS 7/7 f. 153v.
113. Ogden MS 7/7 f. 148v. The references are to *Iusti Lipsii Politicorum sive Civilis Doctrina Libri Sex* (1590), also in English; Arnoldus Clapmarius, *De Arcanis Rerumpublicarum Libri Sex* (Amsterdam, 1641); M. Piccartus, *In Politicos Libros Aristotelis; Observationes Historico-Politicorum* (Nuremberg, 1621).
114. Grafton and Jardine, '"Studied for Action"', pp. 46–51.

writing. Sir William probably would not even have separated these activities. Reading he regarded as 'a converse with the wise', and there were wise men among his contemporaries as well as in the past.[115] While at Leyden, he evidently attended Daniel Heinsius's lectures on Tacitus, which sent him back once again to reflection on his favourite ancient historian. Once again, unlike many, Drake was no passive student: he heads his lecture notes 'Historical meditations out of the 4th book of Tacitus f. 189, upon my hearing Heinsius lectures 17th of November 1634'.[116] Either Heinsius or Drake himself moved easily in his reading from the subtle practices of Roman politicians to the dissimulation at the Council of Trent of Pope Paul III, who masked his intentions under the specious claim to be acting for Christendom. It was precisely such dialogues – between past and present, between commentators and readers, between men of learning and men of affairs – that Drake esteemed as the most valuable study practices. Reading, converse and thought he held to be inextricably interrelated and of necessary benefit to each other. 'Reading sets the other two awork,' he noted, because it helped to frame the questions to discuss and ponder.[117] But mere reading had limited benefits:

> In books we learn general rules of direction, but that still is unperfect and must have joined with it a piercing discourse of the mind; who by comparing things past and present with due respect to singular circumstances incident is able [sic] probably things to come in which the life of counsel consists.[118]

Accordingly, Drake advised himself to look out for all occasions on which he could 'discourse' with others about what he had been reading. When his eyes failed him, we recall, he decided 'to have a scholar to read my ordinary printed books and still to be discoursing at meals with him or walking in the garden' – a course taken not only to preserve his sight but 'to reserve the strength of my own mind'.[119] For it is clear from the above extract that the conversation with books, the 'piercing discourse of the mind . . . comparing things past and present' could go on alone in the study as well as in company. And it is quite obvious that even in the privacy of his study, Drake had a conversation with his books, and one in which he was very much an equal. For all his admiration for the ancients, Sir William was no uncritical recipient of their wisdom. He criticised and praised passages – 'I like the definition of Aristotle that calls justice the good of another' he wrote, as if grading a paper.[120] Similarly, though he thought highly of the Earl of Salisbury as a rhetorician, he thought it necessary to 'supply his defect' by reading more of

115. Ogden MS 7/8 f. 46.
116. Ogden MS 7/7 f. 146v.
117. Ogden MS 7/8 f. 181v.
118. Ogden MS 7/34 f. 9v.
119. Ogden MS 7/7 f. 164; cf. 7/31 f. 1.
120. Ogden MS 7/8 f. 3v.

Bacon and Sir Robert Cotton.[121] The very practice of comparative reading fostered a critical spirit and attitude to text. Even his hero Machiavelli Drake supplemented and refined by cross-reference to Bodin and others.[122]

Evidently too he was confident that in many cases he could surpass those he read. In the case of a set of projects he was acquiring, he determined to 'let my fancy work upon the reading of them', for, he said confidently, 'I find an inclination to project and fall upon things not thought of by others.'[123] Drake had a sense, akin to some modern theorists of reading, that each act of reading was a reinterpretation of a text – and a reapplication of it to and in the individual's learning and experience. Each text spoke directly and personally to him. Aesop's fable of the two frogs he understood, not least in the context of his other reading, as an admonition to look beyond the apparent good of things.[124] Letters written by and to others, by George Leicester to Alderman Spencer or the Earl of Essex to the Earl of Rutland, he mined for what they might yield him.[125] Even the parliament journals were read as a source to 'observe the carriage of some men'.[126]

The alertness of his mind as he read texts of the past and pondered other works and historical occasions is at times remarkable. As he copied out the axiom that blood relatives were not the best carers of children, he immediately thought of Richard III and the princes in the Tower.[127] As he pondered Machiavelli's advice to the prince to feed man's hopes, the letters the Earl of Somerset penned to Sir Thomas Overbury sprang to his mind.[128] Alongside the adage that it was acceptable to gain one's ends by whatever means, he wrote – quite probably with Strafford's trial as the occasion – 'Sir Henry Vane in Parl[iament]'.[129] This was a man for whom, whatever his admiration for the past, all history was a mirror of human nature and all private and public texts the potential source of advice for 'profit' and self-advancement. And here was a reader who had a vocabulary and an ideological context for placing and reflecting on contemporary figures and events.[130]

Throughout the notebooks we find passages illuminating how Drake read and annotated a wide range of books and manuscripts. On two occasions, however, he extracted printed passages from Bacon's *Advancement of Learning* as the core of a set of observations and other readings; and these offer us a detailed study of Drake's mind at work. The pages from Bacon's second book

121. Ogden MS 7/7 ff. 148–147v.
122. For example, 7/8 ff. 76ff.; cf. Folger MS ff. 16v–17.
123. Ogden MS 7/7 f. 161.
124. Ogden MS 7/8 f. 144v.
125. Ogden MS 7/8 f. 163v.
126. Ogden MS 7/11 f. 32.
127. Ogden MS 7/8 f. 59.
128. Ogden MS 7/8 f. 160v.
129. Ogden MS 7/8 f. 160. There is a reference to Sir John Coke's 'distrust' of proceedings on f. 159v. See *Hist. Mss Comm., Cowper*, II, pp. 278–9.
130. Cf. Sharpe and Lake, *Culture and Politics*, introduction, and Smuts, 'Court-Centred Politics'.

start, with rather odd pagination following, at Bacon's page 72 in volume 7, and at page 82 in volume 8 of the Ogden manuscripts.[131] In both cases the printed text is interlined and bears marginal annotation. On the printed page 77, for example, Drake underlines Bacon's famous comment 'that we are much beholden to Machiavelli and others that write what men do and not what they ought to do'. He is often reading closely, correcting misprints in the text – changing 'visit' to 'insist' on p. 74v or 'inutile' to 'missile' in a passage of Latin verse. The marginal notes serve a variety of purposes. Drake uses them to create his own index. Where Bacon refers generally to another writer – Machiavelli, or Tacitus – Drake provides the exact page reference, suggesting that, again, he is reading Bacon with these other texts on his table. His knowledge and memory are especially tested when Bacon refers only to Duke Valentine, but Drake is able to find the relevant passage in Guicciardini ('l: 4, 157').[132]

Often, however, the marginal references to other writers were not directed by Bacon's text but prompted in Drake's mind as he read it. And he was prompted to a wide range of other authors: Cardan, Balzac, Carew's *Relation of the State of France,* Cicero and Horace, Savonarola, and scripture.[133] Moreover, such comparative readings led Drake to judge and interpret and to amplify and gloss the Baconian passages on which he dwelt. Alongside Bacon's metaphor about the sculptor, he writes 'a very apt comparison'.[134] Many of the marginal notes are Drake's own, or at least are axioms not belonging to Bacon's text. Against p. 77 of the *Advancement,* he writes: 'persuasion of books . . . civilise the rough nature of men'. At p. 87 he adds: 'A man may spoil his words with an uncomely countenance'; at p. 93 he appears to lament as he asks 'men wise for their private and weak for the public like ants and why?' Drake was clearly thinking as he read – and reflecting upon other books and his own experience, making observations and posing questions. He even cross-refers to a compilation of his own maxims.[135] At the foot of several pages he adds to Bacon's text thoughts for which the margin afforded him no room. At the bottom of p. 77, for example, he adds: 'worldly wise men's speeches are seldom heart deep but civil and plausible only and they speak well to practice ill.'

The purpose of all these activities – close reading, comparative reading and gloss – was to make Drake a wiser man in his world and to apply the lessons he culled from Bacon and developed. Here his central goal, as he describes it in the margin to p. 97, was 'to labour to have a true understanding of man's own nature and genius and to consider how it suits with the present times'. The present times spilled into Drake's margins and onto, as well as from,

131. In volume 7 they start after f. 2; in volume 8 after f. 13.
132. Ogden MS 7/7 f. 31v at Bacon p. 97v.
133. Ogden MS 7/7 ff. 3, 18, 27v, 35v, 37, at pp. 69, 70, 93v, 101v, 103.
134. Ogden MS 7/7 f. 19 at p. 69.
135. Ogden MS 7/8 f. 22v at p. 97v. 'See Max 24' probably refers to Drake's own collection. See below, pp. 264–5.

Bacon's pages. Where Bacon warned to avoid friends who espoused too many factions, Drake recalled an acquaintance – 'Park'.[136] Where Bacon urged men always to retain an exit route before embarking upon any enterprise, Drake remembered: 'Mr Chute told me that Alderman Craven was a quiet still man and my Lord Lovelace will be very wary and seldom put his hand to country business but put it upon others.'[137]

It would be hard to find better cases of a reader in constant conversation with his text or between his text and his world.

Reading and Character

At this point therefore, we should now shift our attention to the other side of that dialogue: from Drake as a reader to the man and his world, as written in his commonplace books. This is not, as some historians would still naively maintain, to turn from representation to the real world. The commonplace books do not offer a clear window onto the reality of Drake's life. As he read and conversed for profit, so he wrote down what he read, heard or thought. He did so to advance and improve himself, to write himself, we might say, as a successful actor in the world, a man as much fashioned (the word is Drake's own) and scripted by texts as a reader who reinterpreted and refashioned them.[138] Drake's notes on his financial and personal affairs, local matters or the people he encountered are scattered between and around his notes from books, and his attitudes to them owed much to observations of men and affairs derived from reading, as well as from social intercourse.

Though he spent much time away from Buckinghamshire and several years abroad, Drake never ceased to consider his finances and estates, or how to improve them. His notebooks are full of occasional jottings about buying and selling leases, drainage, tenants, debts owed to him, monies received, bills pending and paid, woods sold, pigs bought and so on.[139] More interesting are the measures he pursued to improve his holdings. For one, he took advice from men he knew and whose judgement he valued; Mr Stiles advised him how to deal with a difficult tenant at Amersham and also passed on advice he had given to Walter Long about how to negotiate the purchase of a lordship.[140] In this latter case, Drake wrote down a formula for calculating the value of a lordship as a guide to future transactions.[141] He was certainly not

136. Ogden MS 7/7 f. 24v at p. 90.
137. Ogden MS 7/7 f. 38 at p. 103.
138. Ogden MS 7/7 f. 93: 'fashion a man's self to humours and times.'
139. See, for example, Ogden MSS 7/7 f. 131; 7/26 f. 180; 7/34 ff. 93v–94v; 7/48 ff. 43, 142v, 137v. See also H. Lords MS 49 ff. 149, 155–8.
140. Ogden MSS 7/23 f. 145v; 7/36 f. 93.
141. Ogden MS 7/45 f. 26.

too proud to take others as a pattern: 'Imitate' appears as a heading in one notebook, with Sir William Slingsby's gardens as one of the list to pursue.[142] The Earl of Bedford was one of the principal speculators of the early seventeenth century, developing Covent Garden and draining the Fens, and Drake avidly sought information about his dealings.[143] He noted how Bedford took two years' rent according to the yearly rent received upon any copyhold in his manors and determined to discuss with him.[144] For, like Bedford, Drake was keen to 'get all projects' for profit.[145] Observation at home and in the Low Countries convinced him that, as he put it in notes 'concerning matters of husbandry and commerce', three-quarters of the wastes and commons of England were lost for want of improving.[146]

Drake evidently pursued his 'serious intention' to examine projects in the Low Countries and inquired of a Dutch surveyor how his country reclaimed land.[147] In Spain, he recorded with approval, the law determined that any who cut down a tree must plant three for future growth.[148] In general, however, to remedy waste, reading and observation taught him 'there is no means but to enclose the said commons.'[149] Drake accordingly planned to buy a large piece of unimproved ground to develop: he considered land in Norfolk, Essex or Kent where the sea had 'newly broken in', assuring himself, not unreasonably given the promises speculators were making in the 1620s and 1630s, that great fortunes had sprung from small beginnings.[150] Then he decided to buy a large unimproved plot near the Thames and to cooperate with the tenants to develop a site where he could take advantage of the ebb and flow.[151] The odds were carefully weighed. Baron Denham told him how many in Devon had improved estates by coming to an agreement with tenants to enclose the commons, so Drake commented:

> If the Commons were laid by equal proportions to the farmers' houses that are bordering and adjoining, then would the gentry gain by improvement of their rents and the clergy by increase of their tithe and the poor may gain by their employment in the said improvements, yet it might be con-

142. Ogden MS 7/7 f. 129v. This may be the Sir William Slingsby J. P. who was living in the Strand (*Cal. S.P. Dom. 1635–6*, p. 315).
143. Ogden MS 7/7 ff. 69, 166v. On Bedford's projects in Covent Garden and the Fens, see H. C. Darby, *The Draining of The Fens* (Cambridge, 1940), pp. 38–48; and L. Stone, 'The Residential Development of the West End of London in the Seventeenth Century', in B. Malament, ed., *After the Reformation* (Manchester, 1980), pp. 167–212.
144. Ogden MS 7/36 f. 94v.
145. Ogden MS 7/7 f. 170.
146. Ogden MS 7/8 f. 190v.
147. Ogden MS 7/7 ff. 123, 128v.
148. Ogden MS 7/8 f. 190v.
149. Ibid.; cf. 7/7 ff. 160, 158.
150. Ogden MS 7/7 f. 157.
151. Ogden MS 7/7 f. 158.

trived that the poor men's cottages might have some small proportion allowed them.[152]

In buying leases, he set out to purchase them from public men, or deans and chapters, 'for these hath not that feeling sense of what they grant as private persons hath'.[153] Here we witness a combination of some of the idealism that underlay the schemes for improvement, a sense of the commonweal, and a gentleman's responsibility to the poor, together with a strong sense of self-interest and skill in cutting a deal – a microcosm in fact of the tensions between the old ethics and Machiavellian practices found in Drake's broader reading. We do not know which won out, or even how Drake's scheme for enclosing and draining fared. But Sir William was worth the very large sum of £8,300 in 1634 and raised his family to the baronetcy.[154] Given his thorough research, wide advice and a view of the world in which all were out for gain, and that fortunes were made by dissembling, it is not likely that he entered into unsuccessful negotiations.[155] For even where his family was concerned, interest appears to have outweighed any affection in Drake's chilling self-counsel: 'Ingratiate myself with my chiefest kindred and wait patiently for the event' – that is for death and inheritance.[156]

William handled his most personal affairs with no less care or consideration. We have heard his prescriptions for the preservation and improvement of his mind; the notebooks reveal him collecting and recording advice for the preservation of the health of his body. Drake was a patient of the greatest physician of his day, Theodore de Mayerne, who prepared purges and broth for him, and counselled bleeding with leeches.[157] True to his philosophy, however, William also endeavoured to prevent as well as cure disease by keeping notes of his condition: 'much sitting breeds the stone,' he observed on one occasion.[158] Accordingly, 'Things good for my accident which I have had experience in' included fortnightly purging, abstention from 'windy meats', drinking no beer above a month old, eating no new bread, and periodically taking a 'vomit', or emetic.[159] In terms both of mind and body, the prospect and choice of a partner exercised him as he weighed on paper the desiderata and anathema of a wife. In principle he attributed great importance to marriage, considering it conventionally 'an invention of almighty God to produce men on earth and to make elect for heaven'.[160] He thought it

152. Ogden MS 7/8 f. 190v; 7/7 f. 171v. Cf. Sharpe, *Personal Rule*, pp. 253–6.
153. Ogden MS 7/7 f. 128.
154. Ogden MS 7/7 f. 164.
155. Ogden MS 7/7 f. 93; below, pp. 93–4.
156. Ogden MS 7/7 f. 148.
157. Ogden MS 7/7 f. 122v.
158. Ogden MS f. 92. Drake evidently suffered from the 'stone' for he notes a remedy prescribed by an Amersham doctor, Ogden MS 7/7 f. 122v.
159. Ogden MS 7/7 f. 126.
160. Ogden MS 7/8 f. 185.

best to marry in youth, and for love – 'I think it unfit to wrench and force inclination for the accommodation of interest.'[161] Not surprisingly, beyond such ideals and generalities, the choice and decision in practice were rather more difficult. Drake warned himself against marrying just for beauty, observing (presumably from others) that lust faded once satisfied and that comeliness was more important than beauty.[162] But in matters of character as well as appearances, all his reading had taught him that, like men, women could be deceptive. Even the best women, he realised, could dissemble before marriage and show their true (and less appealing) disposition afterwards.[163] As usual, he sought wisdom in the writers of policy he most admired. He took notes 'de uxore ducenda' from Cardan's *De Prudentia*; he referred himself on the subject of marriage to Sir Walter Ralegh's advice to his son; he reflected on the role of a wife as governess of the household.[164] But in this most difficult of all human transactions, the best advice Drake could find was in the proverb: 'Choose a horse made and a wife to make.'[165] Perhaps not surprisingly, he did not marry.

Whatever his criteria in a wife, we know that in general Drake regarded people in so far as they were useful to him and sought out those most able to assist his advancement. He believed in extracting every ounce of benefit from converse with his fellows, prepared himself (by reading) to take advantage of men of knowledge and was ever inquisitive on his travels to glean local learning and expertise. In the Netherlands he resolved to learn all he could about Dutch commerce and inventions.[166] His social philosophy was frank in its selfishness: he set out to 'catch at all persons where advantage may be got' and to consider the 'several uses I may make of each acquaintance' or, as he put it even more bluntly: 'make acquaintance with all the able instruments that tend to my ends and suck out of them what may be useful'.[167] And, having a low opinion of others as selfish, deceitful and corrupt, he thought first of how to advance by their example. 'Observe', he counselled himself, 'who are the activest stirring men, both courtiers and others, in raising their estates, and get some interest into their acquaintance . . .'[168] Drake sought out only acquaintances who could help him and drew up a list of those who had got patents granted by Charles I.[169] Then he plotted 'to consider who are

161. Ogden MS 7/8 f. 185.
162. Ogden MS 7/7 f. 54.
163. Ogden MS 7/8 f. 180.
164. Ogden MS 7/7 ff. 55, 114v; 7/8 f. 53v.
165. Ogden MS 7/8 f. 171. Drake repeats this adage in several notebooks.
166. Ogden MS 7/7 ff. 81v, 123. Drake noted, with respect to learning from strangers, that a fool knew more in his own house than a wise man in another's (7/38 f. 36) and that Lord Bristol had built a stock of knowledge from travel that he had drawn advantage from ever since (7/23 f. 71v).
167. Ogden MS 7/7 ff. 95–95v, 133.
168. Ogden MS 7/7 f. 102. Note too 7/7 f. 65v: 'Doctor Gifford hath £2,000 p.a. a meek still man not giving distaste to any party . . . such another Sir Rob Heath.'
169. Ogden MS 7/7 f. 102 and cf. Hunt. MS f. 27.

they that can prefer their friends with public benefits as the Treasurer, Attorney and to get to have dependence upon them'. Once such contacts were made, he had no doubt that it was bribery that oiled the wheels to promotion – 'when once footing is gotten, money may be bestowed with most advantage of all.'[170]

We do not know if all Drake's friends and acquaintances served his ends as he desired, but in some way most appear to have been of assistance to him. Thomas Cotton and a Mr Stansby and Mr Stratton frequently lent him books and manuscripts; William Slingsby and a Mr Barrell kept him informed of affairs while he was abroad.[171] Mr Henley he admired and took as a pattern of audacity and resolution;[172] and he sought out the acquaintance of Peter Heylyn because he esteemed him a great historian and admired his 'seconding the humour of the time' by his publications on the Sabbath and St George.[173] Desire to meet Sir Nathaniel Brent may well have been motivated by the same aim to enter the ranks of the high church party in favour at the Caroline court, albeit (as we shall see) Drake had little sympathy with their brand of churchmanship.[174]

For projects he laboured to get to know a lawyer of the Middle Temple, Mr Joiner, who lived under Mr Potts's chamber and was also known to Stratton.[175] Sir Thomas Aylesbury, he noted, also had acquaintance with projects and from Oliver St John he could learn all about the Earl of Bedford's courses.[176] Gilbert Barrell he singled out as a man who could get him access to the patentees;[177] Mr Barnard told him about a project for drying malt with any fuel,[178] while Jack Cockshutt, who may have been employed as Drake's lawyer and who worked for Attorney-General Bankes, he valued as a contact with the 'most active' – including Mr Dell and Mr Warwick,

170. Ogden MS 7/7 f. 102.
171. Ogden MSS 7/23 ff. 15, 34, 142v; 7/29 ff. 20, 36.
172. Ogden MS 7/7 ff. 133, 135v; 7/8 f. 12v. Mr Henley may be George Henley, the London merchant, who was involved in a long drawn out Admiralty case against the United Provinces after a Dutch man-of-war seized his goods (*Cals. S.P. Dom. 1629–38*, via index).
173. Ogden MS 7/7 f. 156v. The references are to P. Heylyn, *The History of the Sabbath* (1636) and Heylyn, *The Historie of . . . St. George* (1630).
174. Ogden MS 7/7 f. 88v: 'Be acquainted with Nath. Brent.' Brent was Archbishop Laud's Vicar-General. See below, pp. 134–5, 161.
175. Ogden MS 7/7 f. 160v. This was probably Charles Potts (Drake names him in 7/7 f. 73) who became one of the benchers of the Middle Temple, or his brother Sir John Potts who appears frequently in the notebooks and was knighted, at the same time as Drake, in 1641. He was also friendly with D'Ewes (see Keeler, *The Long Parliament*, pp. 312–13).
176. Ogden MS 7/7 f. 160v. Thomas Aylesbury, the Duke of Buckingham's secretary, was one of the Masters of Requests, Surveyor of the Navy and, after 1635, Co-Master of the Mint (Aylmer, *King's Servants*, pp. 77–8); St John served Bedford as a lawyer and became Solicitor-General in 1641. He probably helped Drake to office in 1652.
177. Ogden MS 7/7 f. 102.
178. Ogden MS 7/7 f. 135v. This may be Edward Barnard who was petitioning for the patent for a water engine to dredge the Thames (*Cal. S.P. Dom. 1635*, p. 55).

perhaps William Dell, Laud's secretary, and Philip Warwick, a bedchamber-man.[179] He also knew Walter Tichborne, and Mr Potts, who was a source of knowledge about several leading courtiers.[180] All these contacts were assiduously cultivated and, as we shall see, Drake's efforts paid off. He evidently did get access to the court and secured office and a baronetcy, which suggests that some acquaintance and perhaps too some gift to a great man had served their purpose.

If Drake's attitude to others appears ruthlessly utilitarian, it is only fair to acknowledge that he was, as it were, equally ruthless with himself. Throughout the commonplace books he writes self-counsel in injunctions that appear to be scripting less a life of happiness than a programme of disciplined self-fashioning to an end. 'Confine your mind', he ordered himself, 'to be generally intent upon necessary thoughts.'[181] As he travelled abroad or moved in society at home, he resolved to 'never hear, think or read anything conducing to my end but write it down.'[182] At the end of each day, almost like a religious rite, he examined himself to ascertain what lessons he had learned, and what he needed to act upon. 'I think that day lost in which I have not learned somewhat.'[183] There is no hint here of a meeting or conversation for pleasure, or a social drink that even the puritan Woodforde was inclined to (over)indulge in.[184] Social interaction was also for Drake governed by a set of rules or strategies. As we saw, he sought out the company of those most useful to him. And, observing them to be the 'parts of a politic nature', he studied patience, flattery, eloquence, audacity, resolution and secrecy to extract the maximum benefit from such social encounters.[185] The intimacy of friendship finds little place here. Drake advised himself to listen but not to speak; civil prudence, he believed, dictated courtesy to all (even the wicked), while masking one's real feelings and intents.[186] Recalling, as he understood it, Aristotle's axiom that there was no such thing as a friend, regarding all as out to deceive him in pursuit of their own ends, he resolved to remain on his guard.[187] Because men only advantaged him, he learned from Tacitus, if they

179. Ogden MS 7/7 ff. 133, 135v. John Cockshutt, of Drake's old Inn, Gray's, was in the service of Attorney Bankes, became Clerk of the Council in Star Chamber, and, in 1641, Exigenter of Common Pleas (Aylmer, *King's Servants*, pp. 98–9; *Cal. S.P. Dom. 1635*, pp. 260, 281; *Cal S.P. Dom. 1638–9*, p. 228).

180. Ogden MS 7/7 f. 130; see 7/7 f. 166v; Sir Walter Tichborne of Hampshire described himself as a 'servant' of the king but I have not identified his office (*Cal. S.P. Dom. 1637*, p. 278).

181. Ogden MS 7/7 f. 3.

182. Ogden MS f. 95v; the identical injunction is on f. 170v. See f. 82v: 'What I observed from Dr. Durie's converse'.

183. Ogden MSS 7/8 f. 173; 7/7 f. 129. Cf. 7/7 f. 117: 'Never to speak or hear or do but to have advantage . . .'

184. Drake even regarded the company of 'witty men' as a means to 'quicken and enlarge fancy' (Ogden MS 7/7 f. 155). On Woodforde, see New College, Oxford MS 9502.

185. Ogden MS 7/7 ff. 102, 85v.

186. Ogden MSS 7/7 ff. 78, 129, 167v; 7/8 f. 205v.

187. Ogden MS 7/8 f. 33v.

were forced or deceived into it, he approached each encounter with his fellows as a contest.[188] 'Consider exactly when plain dealing and when dissimulation is necessary, likewise when virtue when vice,' he wrote, making it clear that these were strategic elections rather than moral choices.[189] Men sought not virtue, he concluded, only the appearance of it.[190] At Leyden a Mr Hage told him how Sir Henry Wotton rose, and confirmed his sense that it was appearance rather than depth of knowledge that advanced a man. Accordingly, Drake was anxious to develop his rhetorical skills,[191] not least so that in negotiating he could lead those with whom he treated to open themselves up, in order to take the advantage.[192] When Drake described the strength of the mind as the most precious thing man had, we cannot but suspect that his use of 'strength' had significantly military connotations.[193] Learning to deceive and put others at ease was the social equivalent of drawing advantage from the disorders of enemies. Drake's self-counsel amounted to a battle plan drawn up to emerge victorious from engagement with his fellows and in the human conflict.

Reading before the Storm

In early modern England, as we know, the personal and the public were not as delineated or distinct as we today try (increasingly unsuccessfully) to make them. Ideally, in the sixteenth and seventeenth centuries, the commonweal bound all individuals in a shared ethical community and Christian polity, with subjects and ruler united in the pursuit of virtue. Drake's personal and social world was far removed from such an ideal, for all that it was still the official theory of the state. We shall not then be surprised to find that his perception of public events and personalities, his observations on government and political life, also ill accorded with the contemporary ideal of the commonweal; or that the synthesis of his reading in civil policy and his experience of Stuart politics combined to produce a very different set of values and even a quite radical theory of state.

Drake strongly believed that in order to be a shrewd observer of, and a successful actor in, the affairs of his own age, a man needed to study and heed the lessons of history. Quoting Machiavelli, he noted: 'The heavens have the same influence upon this age as they had in former times; therefore he that

---

188. Ogden MS 7/8 f. 91.
189. Ogden MS 7/7 f. 89.
190. Ogden MS 7/8 f. 150v.
191. Ogden MS 7/7 ff. 2, 113v, 155. Drake recommended himself to see plays for this purpose (f. 113v).
192. Ogden MSS 7/7 f. 2; 7/8 ff. 33v, 194v–194.
193. Ogden MS 7/38 f. 117v.

would see what will be let him consider what hath been for things have one and the same motion in all ages.'[194] 'Dead men', Drake put it succinctly, 'open living men's eyes.'[195] Specifically history was, he believed, the key to an understanding of politics, for 'he that is well read in history seems to be of every country and to have assisted at all councils and public assemblies.'[196] Since 'like enterprises produce like events,' the historian could be the best counsellor to statesmen.[197] And the discerning reader recognised that 'history hath the power to recover the sick' and guide men to advancement in a perilously competitive world.[198] What lessons, then, did Drake learn and where did he derive them from? 'In the primitive and heroical times of the old Romans', Drake found the state maintained by 'pure virtues'.[199] And the past of imperial and republican Rome yielded, he conceived, the best lessons for social and political life. Drake noted that where Caesar pardoned his enemies, Cicero did not – and was banished as a consequence; he admired the art of Augustus in dividing Mark Antony's faction. He recognised that the ancient world was not free of flattery and dissimulation, observing that Cato ill deserved his reputation as a great 'commonwealthsman'.[200]

Such language underlines how Drake studied the ancients always with a mind turned to the present. When, then, he reflected that, moving from Livy to Tacitus, the reader of the history of Rome witnessed a decline in manners from justice, fortitude and temperance to dissimulation and luxury, one suspects that he felt or feared a corresponding decline in his own age.[201] In their heyday, he reflected, the Romans had foreseen potential mischiefs and provided remedies against them. One of the chief causes of their ruin, he noted from Guicciardini, was the change of their ancient manners and customs.[202] Acting on Machiavelli's lament that 'we endeavour not to reduce to the practice of these modern times the valiant acts of foregoing ages', as he read in the humanist histories of almost all the countries of early modern Europe, Drake reinforced and supplemented these lessons taught by Greece and Rome.[203] The reign of Louis XI, for example, showed that foreign enemies were ever ready to make profit of civil dissensions – a point that Drake himself was to make in a speech in the Long Parliament.[204] Recent French history also demonstrated Richelieu's shrewdness in having the soldiers dependent upon him, and his skill in employing the Duc de Rohan and

194. Ogden MS 7/8 f. 43.
195. Folger MS f. 6v.
196. Ogden MS 7/23 f. 23.
197. Ibid.
198. Ogden MS 7/45 f. 166.
199. Folger MS f. *2v.
200. Folger MS f. 20v; Ogden MSS 7/7 f. 79; 7/8 f. 74v.
201. Ogden MS 7/7 f. 57; cf. Smuts, 'Court-Centred Politics' and Sharpe, *Sir Robert Cotton*, pp. 232 onwards.
202. Ogden MS 7/38 f. 11; Bucks R.O. D/DR/10/56 f. 52.
203. Ogden MS 7/52 f. 152v.
204. Ogden MS 7/38 f. 36; below, p. 154.

other Huguenots so as to divert their thoughts from insurrection.[205] The history of the Italian city-states was another rich seam for the miner of lessons of the past. Drake, fascinated by Cesare Borgia, noted how, to prevent the inconveniences that might ensue on his father's death, he endeavoured to win over the nobility and secure the favour of the cardinals. Unhampered by conventional morality, Borgia drew on all means to secure his ends: 'industry, secrecy, celerity, audacity, dissimulation were the means that advanced Caesar Borgia.'[206]

Drake reflected on the great characters of all historical ages, how they had secured their power and fame, and the lessons they taught: Lysander, Demosthenes, Demetrius, Cato, Augustus, Tiberius, Innocent VIII, Julius II, Leo X, Ferdinand of Aragon, Maurice of Saxony, Spinola, the Duke of Savoy.[207] Sweeping over the centuries and specific circumstances that separated them, Drake drew up lists and an index of all the qualities that made up their greatness: a gait, a voice, shrewd frugality, a refusal to credit idle news, a willingness to follow wise courses, most of all deep insight into worldly affairs.[208] So, like Themistocles, Bishop Jewel demonstrated the importance of delaying what one sought to obstruct; like Tiberius, Borgia knew how to feign a desire for reconciliation and, also like Tiberius, Louis XI varied his habits to confound his enemies.[209] And Louis XI, with his appreciation of good intelligence, ever suspicious acuity, command of his passions and singular wisdom, re-embodied many of the skills of the great rulers of antiquity.[210]

Drake pondered all the world's great empires, their origins and the causes of their greatness and fall, following Justus Lipsius's premise that a history of events without causes was 'a tale indeed but no instruction'.[211] From the first rise of the Persian monarchy he learned the importance of careful education of children; the rise of Rome taught the value of discipline, good laws, the maintenance of customs, the right religion and the role of fortune.[212] More recent history revealed Ferdinand of Aragon and Isabella of Castile uniting to drive France out of Naples and laying the foundation of a mighty Spanish empire that brought a link with Austria and the Holy Roman Empire.[213] Drake even seemed persuaded by the Machiavellian suggestion that the Spanish crown fostered Luther's revolt against the papacy so as to divide the Holy See and the German empire. Spain, Drake concluded, made promises only for her own gain; deception was a principal cause of her greatness.[214]

205. Ogden MS 7/23 f. 62.
206. Ogden MS 7/38 f. 12; 7/7 f. 2v.
207. See 'A Discovery of the Worldly Wise Men's Practices drawn from the best historians', Ogden MS 7/23 f. 117v; Folger MS ff. *16v–*26.
208. Ogden MS 7/23 f. 97v.
209. Folger MS ff. *20v, *22, *23v.
210. Folger MS f. *31v.
211. Ogden MS 7/48 f. 118v.
212. Ogden MS 7/29 ff. 4–6, 12–18.
213. Ogden MS 7/7 f. 88v.
214. Ogden MS 7/23 ff. 25v–6.

The English past offered equally important and often similar lessons for 'the worldly wise men'. Henry VII exemplified many of the qualities Drake admired: he was ever alert, kept spies at home and abroad, observed the outward forms while keeping his counsel, and took advantage of other men's passions. Most of all he displayed the virtues praised by Machiavelli – seizing occasions.[215] He strove, Drake noted from Bacon's history, 'to draw all advantage possible from persons, times and accidents', by any expediency.[216] To Drake, the Duke of Somerset's rule as Protector during the minority of Edward VI offered clear demonstration that those designing to advance their fortune, whatever their rhetoric, were ready to sacrifice the public good.[217] The Marquis of Winchester, he observed, served four monarchs, surviving difficult changes in circumstances by bending with the times rather than taking a stand on principles; and Cecil, cunning and malleable, was, no less, a figure 'matched for his ends'.[218] Rising by the help of Sir Anthony Coke, Cecil turned on his old master Somerset in order to attach himself to the ascending star, Dudley. Then, during Mary's reign, he played the skilful double game of securing the favour of Cardinal Pole while courting the favour of Princess Elizabeth. When Elizabeth became queen, Cecil, seeing her unwilling to alter her religion, persuaded her to a temporary change so as not to support a pope who had declared her mother's marriage invalid and herself illegitimate. Thereby Cecil served his own aim, and, having done so, used Arundel and Norfolk, Drake believed, to discredit the Catholics. Witty and charming on the outside, Cecil, as Drake read him, was a brilliant rhetorician and schemer who showed how a consummate politician 'generally pretends short of his ends he aims at', and how he manipulated and deceived men to rise to greatness.[219]

Drake clearly admired Burghley precisely for those skills and qualities, as he also lauded Cecil's mistress Queen Elizabeth for her political acumen and cunning. The queen, Drake copied from a book lent to him, on succeeding to the throne shrewdly retained the body of her sister's Privy Council so as not to alienate powerful figures.[220] Following skilfully the lesson taught by history that in any reform of state some of the old should be retained, Elizabeth altered the religion of the realm almost stealthily, 'step by step', so that change was 'quietly endured by all'. Making use of others' fear as well as subtly winning her subjects' love, 'the wise queen Elizabeth' listened and took counsel but 'would always keep the interest of things in her own power'.[221]

---

215. Folger MS f. *26vff., quotation f. 27. Drake similarly praised Borgia and Louis XI for taking advantage of occasion and often cited the adage 'Sappi cognoscer il tempo' (ibid., f. 134). See below, pp. 214–17, 236–7.
216. Folger MS f. 27.
217. Ogden MS 7/7 f. 121.
218. Ogden MSS 7/45 f. 182v; 7/33 f. 46v.
219. Ogden MS 7/33 ff. 46v–51v.
220. Ogden MS 7/45 f. 182v.
221. Ogden MS 7/8 ff. 87, 145, 141.

Like so many of his Caroline contemporaries, Drake clearly praised Elizabeth – but not like them as a model of virtuous government and champion of Protestantism; rather as a skilful player in the political game of intrigue, the rules of which were cunning, dissimulation and, if need be, ruthless determination.[222] And the lesson she taught was one for all rulers and subjects. Following Machiavelli, Drake believed that every active man should apply the 'wise and valiant acts of foregoing ages' to 'the practice of these modern times'.[223] As the examples of his 'discovery of the worldly wise men's practices drawn from the best historians' make clear, Drake did not equate wise with traditionally virtuous practices, nor view the world as a stage for the performance of good acts.[224]

As he looked up from his books and around him, William Drake, deploying the familiar metaphor of the stage, for quite unconventional observations, saw 'the world is become a theatre of fictions';[225] in that social theatre, men represented flattery and dissimulation as unworthy but daily practised them.[226] A good name or reputation was, he felt, more often than not unrelated to virtue; oaths and promises were subordinated to ambition and profit; 'men are pious or impious', he wrote, 'according to interest.'[227] In an age in which 'religion and the fear of God is in every man extinguished', what marked the difference between men was not virtue and vice but wealth and poverty.[228] Indeed in a world of lies and uncertainty all that seemed evident and predictable was that it was the audacious and crafty who succeeded and those who took advantage of any means or occasion who prospered.[229] All social relationships were pursued for gain: 'there is no union or friendship but what is grounded upon profit.'[230] Government, rather than setting higher standards of virtue and common good, as it was meant to, exemplified the same ruthless pursuit of interest. Enemies to the commonwealth masqueraded as champions of the public interest; the essence of the politician's art was plotting; the court was not the seat of virtue outlined by Castiglione but 'the forge where fortunes are made or at least the shop where they are sold'.[231] So it was the world over. Reviewing the governments of Europe, Drake observed the dexterity of the Dutch state in advancing their wealth, the dubious means used by the Emperor of Russia to bring money into his Exchequer, the use of religion by the Spanish who pretended to fight for God but sought only

222. Cf. C. V. Wedgwood, *Oliver Cromwell and the Elizabethan Inheritance* (1970). Drake described the court of Elizabeth and Cecil as the 'academy of art and cunning', Ogden MS 7/45 f. 174v.
223. Ogden MS 7/52 f. 152v, from Machiavelli's *Discourses*.
224. Ogden MS 7/23 f. 117v.
225. Ogden MS 7/8 f. 186; the phrase is repeated in several notebooks.
226. Ogden MS 7/8 f. 177.
227. Ogden MS 7/8 ff. 71v, 134v; Bucks R.O. D/DR/10/56 f. 32.
228. Ogden MS 7/7 f. 52 (from Machiavelli's *History of Florence*); 7/8 f. 2.
229. Ogden MS 7/8 f. 2.
230. Ibid.
231. Ogden MS 7/7 ff. 85v, 125, 71v.

advantage for themselves, and the stratagems of the pope who maintained his authority only by cunning.[232] 'The most tyrannical and unjust men', Drake concluded, 'rule the world.'[233]

Observations of such a world taught him and others how one had to behave. It was well enough for Walter Tichborne to place conscience above reputation and profit; but Drake sensed that such ideals could not safely be followed when others ignored them.[234] 'The rule of justice', Drake knew, as a central tenet of Christian ethics and the commonwealth, 'is do as you would be done by'; but he knew more realistically, 'the practice of the world is do what possibly you can for your advantage.'[235] In the 'theatre of fictions', the real world, the wise man had to feign in order to survive. 'The better we can speak the language of the stage, the better we can speak to the world in its own tongue for all men . . . utter not themselves but as it were in a play . . . or in a way of fiction or disguise.'[236] Accordingly each man had to 'consider exactly when plain dealing and when dissimulation is necessary, likewise when virtue when vice'.[237] Dissimulation indeed began literally at home, where servants were quick to take advantage of an unwary master. To combat their deceit, 'a man may often feign an ignorance in domestic affairs in things he is notoriously known to be well seen in to give ground to his servants to think that his true ignorance is but art and dissimulation.'[238] In general, the way for each man to make his way and fortune was by keeping his counsel, and by courage, constant distrust and dissembling, by force and fraud, to capitalise on every opportunity that presented itself.[239]

For rulers the message was the same. 'A politician should be so great an architect as to be able to make use of all sorts of spirits and conditions in the building of the fabric of his fortunes, gentlemen, citizens, papist, puritan, Arminian . . .' He should use 'moderation and temper to all factions his end being to make use of all'.[240] Consistent with this vision, Drake judged the nations and rulers of Europe by their wealth, might and success rather than their faith, principles or values. Criticising the French for vain ostentation and the English for lack of judgement, he expressed most admiration for the Italians who knew how to seize advantage by stealth and the Spaniards who used underhand means skilfully to rise from a small kingdom to a mighty empire.[241] Gustavus Adolphus, King of Sweden, whom many heralded as the

---

232. Ogden MS 7/7 ff. 109v–110v.
233. Ogden MS 7/8 f. 2.
234. Ogden MS 7/7 f. 130. Cf. K. Sharpe, 'Private Conscience and Public Duty in the Writings of James VI and I', in J. Morrill, P. Slack and D. Woolf, eds, *Public Duty and Private Conscience in Seventeenth-Century England* (Oxford, 1993), pp. 77–100.
235. Ogden MS 7/7 f. 60.
236. Ogden MS 7/8 f. 164.
237. Ogden MS 7/7 f. 89.
238. Ogden MS 7/8 f. 54v.
239. Ogden MS 7/7 f. 93. Cf. Folger MS f. 134: 'There is not a thing of greater moment than a certain point of time which is called opportunity.'
240. Ogden MS 7/7 f. 71v.
241. Ogden MS 7/7 ff. 105–10.

champion of European Protestantism, Drake praised rather for those qualities Machiavelli summarised in the word 'virtu'. The King of Sweden, Drake wrote, 'knows how to make war with understanding and leaves few things to the discretion of fortune. He hath a great spirit which is conducted by a judgement far greater; he possesseth necessary virtues and wants not those that are agreeable and pleasing.'[242] In the real world princes and commoners alike needed guides to how to behave, taking men as they were, not as they should be. History was the best tutor and the best historians (Polybius, Livy, Tacitus, Guicciardini and Machiavelli) were those from whom the sagacious reader could extract lessons and distil precepts as rules of use in his own time.[243] Drake always compiled precepts and adages as he read, copied them to other notebooks, supplemented them by further reading and observations, and adapted them to the experience and circumstances of his own age. Like Sir Francis Bacon, Sir Walter Ralegh and Sir Robert Cotton, all of whom he admired much, William Drake copied, rewrote and devised adages, and reread and organised a corpus of maxims as his rules for all spheres of life.[244]

Stuart Clark describes these axioms in appropriately military terms: 'William Drake set out to acquire an arsenal of sententious materials from the approved sources.'[245] Certainly the gathering of such intelligence and the arrangement and systematizing of their stock of wisdom for deployment in the battle of life read like a strategic plan. Drake drew on the known classical and humanist sources that distilled knowledge and experience into aphorisms. He cites adages from Isocrates, Seneca, Demosthenes, Polybius, Plutarch, Alexander the Great, Herodotus, Phaedrus, Plautus, Lactantius, Cicero, Lucian, Curtius, Terence, Martial, Livy and Tacitus, and from St Ambrose, St Chrysostom, and others. In addition to the ancients, he copied, or distilled, proverbs from French, Italian and Spanish sources, and he owned and sought to acquire compilations of proverbs: Erasmus's *Adages*, Janus Gruter's *Florilegium Ethicopoliticum Jani Gruteri Sententiae, Proverbi Estratti della Civili Conversatione di Guazzo* and Garnier's French proverbs, for example, are specifically referred to.[246] Predictably Machiavelli, Guicciardini and Cardano are frequently cited as sources. But often Drake merely lists 'proverbs out of various languages' which he has copied and gleaned from a wide variety of sources and, in some cases, translated.[247]

---

242. Ogden MS 7/23 f. 35.
243. Ogden MS 7/23 f. 57.
244. For Bacon, see *Apophthegmes New and Old* (1625) and the *Essays*; 'The Cabinet Council Containing the Chief Arts of Empire . . . In Political and Polemical Aphorisms', in W. Oldys and T. Birch, eds, *The Works of Sir Walter Ralegh* (8 vols, Oxford, 1829), vol. 8; Cotton's maxims are in Bodleian Tanner MS 103 ff. 196–198v. See Sharpe, *Sir Robert Cotton*, pp. 235–40.
245. Clark, 'Wisdom Literature I', p. 298.
246. See, for example, Ogden MSS 7/26 ff. 88, 139; 7/29 f. 29; 7/8 f. 201v; Folger MS ff. 26v, 108v.
247. Ogden MS 7/8 f. 172v; cf. 7/48 passim.

Yet though his range of sources for axioms seems eclectic, there was nothing casual about Drake's purposes or methods in gathering them. In the Folger commonplace book he instructs himself:

> Dispose proverbs in this order: first things of wisdom, next proverbs out of Botero cap de Prudenza with those in Guicc[iardini] Avertimenti. Next those of Seneca. After these ex Martiano Gregor Tholaz[ain], Justo Lipsio De Civile Doctrina, Scip[io] Amirato, L[or]d Bacon and above all the learned adages of Erasmus furnished in this kind & sparsim Polyb[ius] and other historians . . .[248]

The list concludes 'see Toriano with other Italian books of proverbs.'[249] In another notebook an entry headed 'Method' lays out a different but no less careful programme of organisation: 'Proverbs in this order, first such as are confirmed with reasons, 2ndly such as are proved by fables, 3rdly such as are backed with examples or illustrat[ed] by emblems – after those Historical precepts which we can add Discourses to.'[250] The commonplace books give fascinating insights into how such injunctions were translated into Drake's working methods. Though some axioms are listed generally as 'proverbs', many are arranged under specific headings: proverbs tending to profit or frugality, 'practical rules of daily use'; Garnier's French proverbs he indexes under subjects – 'Amor', 'Argent', 'Court', etc.; proverbs out of various languages are arranged similarly under 'Contention', 'Counsel' and indexed in the margin.[251] Drake often numbered maxims and it would seem that he kept a numbered book of his most important adages.[252] Though he frequently cites the source of an adage, we then find it repeated, with no attribution, in other notebooks (or later in the same book) as though it has become his own, just as those he translated into English from Latin, Italian or French became personalised in the act of translation.

Indeed Drake often stamps his very personal interpretation on an adage at the time he copies it. Under the Italian proverb 'Con poco cervello il governe il mondo',[253] Drake writes 'This proverb censureth those who out of over conceitedness of their own wit seek to reduce things to a greater certainty and perfection than their nature will bear.' Similarly 'sappi cognosser il tempo' is glossed: 'the reason is because what is attempted with advantage of time

248. Folger MS f. ★6; cf. front board. The references are evidently to G. Botero, *Della Ragion di Stato* (Venice, 1589); F. Guicciardini, *Avertimenti Politici* (1583); P. Martianus, *In Hippocratis Aphorismum . . . Exposito* (Rome, 1617); P. G. Tholossain, *De Republica* (Frankfurt, 1609); S. Ammirato, *Dell' Istorie Fiorentine* (Florence, 1600) or *Discorsi . . . sopra Cornelio Tacito* (Florence, 1594).
249. Giovanni Torriano whose *Select Italian Proverbs* appeared in English in 1642.
250. Clark, 'Wisdom Literature I', p. 298; cf. below, pp. 192–205.
251. Ogden MSS 7/8 ff. 7, 209; 7/26 f. 1v; 7/29 ff. 29ff.
252. Folger MS f. 131; Ogden MS 7/8 f. 12.
253. Folger MS f. 61: 'With a little wit, or cunning, he ruled the world.'

and occasion is easy to compass.'[254] Such glosses at times amount to readings that seem to go well beyond the obvious meaning of an adage. So Drake does not merely render 'Spero poco e tene assai' as advice to be cautious about excessive hope, but adds 'the last words tene assai counsels us to be fearful and suspicious of all power.'[255] In the case of the axiom 'homo homini lupus', Drake moves from the 'mischiefs' of men concealing their designs, through specific examples, to consideration of the prince 'palliating his most odious actions with the cloak of religion and liberty'.[256] Not only did proverbs form Drake's worldview and values, they were also read through them.

Though we may think it the essence of the proverb that it is timeless, in Drake's case adages were very much connected to circumstances. Most of the proverbs he copies he illustrates by or cross-refers to a historical episode from antiquity or the recent past. So reading the Italian proverb 'Chi non sa adulare non sa regnare', he recalls Homer's account of Agamemnon praising famous men;[257] the adage that one should not embark without biscuit led him both to Pope Julius II who improved his revenues before entering on an enter-prise and to Charles VIII who foolishly invaded Italy without treasure.[258] The axiom that a small fortune with a great mind bred disquiet he thought well 'seen in Bristol', that is John Digby, Earl of Bristol.[259] In many cases a char-acter not only glossed or illustrated but epitomised an adage, and Drake's thumbnail sketches of great men from the past transmuted into historical pre-cepts. As he read Bacon's *Henry VII*, he added Italian and Latin proverbs to the margin.[260]

The care in arrangement, selection and translation, the gloss and illustra-tion, repetition and cross-reference indicates that the adages Drake collected and annotated were carefully weighed and gathered to an end. At times he enthusiastically commends an adage: 'the proverb seems wise'; 'it is well observed by Guicciardini that insolency and timidity are never found asunder.'[261] Clearly Drake copied what he endorsed and found most useful from the wisdom literature he read. And he was ever thinking of the appli-cation of a proverb. Copying the adage that 'by gifts and presents a man attains his ends', he remembered that Mr Henley sent pheasants to ingratiate himself with the Duchess of Buckingham.[262] 'The cat that sets upon the forbidden meat receives a blow at last' was a proverb he felt could be 'applied to those

254. Folger MS f. 33 (repeated f. 43): 'wise men know the [right] moment.'
255. Folger MS f. 29. Literally 'Hope for a little and hold on to much.'
256. Folger MS f. 74. The sense is 'man is a wolf to other men.'
257. Folger MS f. 11 (and frequently in the Ogden notebooks). 'He who knows not how to flatter knows not how to rule.'
258. Folger MS f. 28. 'Il savio non simbarca sempra biscotto' – 'the wise man doth not embark on his ship without biscuit'.
259. Folger MS f. 90v. Drake took an interest in Bristol and his relationship with Buck-ingham. See below, p. 117.
260. Folger MS f. *28.
261. Folger MS f. 54v; Ogden MS 7/48 f. 131v.
262. Ogden MS 7/8 f. 7.

that frequent unlawful sports'.[263] From the Spanish proverb that a fool knew more in his own house than a wise man in another's, he drew the very practical lesson, perhaps as he was about to travel overseas, that he should always learn from strangers.[264] Doubtless, as he copied other axioms, Drake had in mind their application both to his own conduct and the course of public affairs. Notes on the causes of the English Civil War amid a list of general adages suggests a mind that was ever moving from texts to circumstances, and vice versa.[265] We cannot know Drake's mind as he penned each one of his proverbs, but we know that he gathered them all in the belief that 'when a man is deliberate and governed by order, rules and principles no difficulty he meets with faints or abates his courage.'[266]

Which, then, were the 'rules and principles' Drake selected to counter the difficulties of the world? From the Earl of Salisbury he took the rule that 'frugality is better than purchase', from the Earl of Hertford the adage: 'he that would creep cheaply into an inheritance let him first take hold of a lease.'[267] In the witticisms of various countries he discerned wise counsel: 'Think of ease but work on'; 'a man should never commend his wife, wine or horse, for it tempts borrowing'![268] Some of Drake's selections reflected the conventional values, we might even say the social theory, of the early modern commonweal: the wise man mastered his passions; praise to great persons might be counsel as well as compliment, 'praising to instruct them, their praises being but disguised exhortations'.[269] In the main, however, the rules Drake determined to follow were far removed from the prescriptions of a Christian commonwealth. Rather than a community of virtues, justice and good fellowship, Drake wrote of a treacherous world in which the first rule was always to suspect all and be on guard.[270] On his estate, a landlord should never tell his agent his mind.[271] In the wider world, he took it as a guiding principle that those who do not follow their own interest are subject to those that do.[272] To advance one's interest, he thought the height of human wisdom was dissimulation: 'Dissimulation is no less profitable . . . than preservatives in physic.'[273] Feigning gave men the advantage in a world where all converse was a contest for supremacy: 'worldly wise men's speeches', he observed, 'are seldom heart deep but civil and plausible only , and they speak well to prac-

---

263. Ogden MS 7/26 f. 79v. Such topical reading of sources offers clues too to the issues that concerned Drake at the time.
264. Ogden MS 7/38 f. 26.
265. Ogden MS 7/8 f. 39v.
266. Ogden MS 7/8 f. 87.
267. Ogden MS 7/8 ff. 4, 7.
268. Ogden MSS 7/8 f. 172v; 7/26 f. 4. This latter proverb is repeated several times.
269. Ogden MSS 7/8 f. 164; 7/26 f. 24.
270. Ogden MSS 7/7 f. 2v; 7/8 f. 68v.
271. Ogden MS 7/8 f. 71v.
272. Ogden MS 7/8 f. 86v.
273. Ogden MS 7/7 f. 3.

tise ill.'[274] The wise man pursued whatever means were necessary to his ends: 'where the lion's skin will not serve, we must help it with the fox's.'[275] The way to rise was not by talent or virtuous qualities but through connections and bribes: flattery was, Drake agreed with Carpenter, the best policy and 'by gifts and presents a man attains his ends.'[276] For all the talk of justice, 'the stronger gives what law he likes to the weaker'; at law 'as a man is befriended so his cause is ended.'[277] As for the court itself, it was the microcosm and epitome of a treacherous world: 'the court, a whore and a haven', he wrote, echoing country disenchantment with government, 'will make a man wary.'[278] For 'at court, one moment of good fortune is worth more than a hundred years' study.'[279]

Unlike other critics, Drake does not pause for regret or prescribe loftier principles. His advice to princes is as pragmatic as his counsel to himself. The ruler should maintain good order, remember that new favours never made men forget old injuries, be wary of the counsel he received and ever distrustful, remembering William of Nassau's adage that no lie was as dangerous as that which came dressed like the truth.[280] Like all men the ruler was to use whatever means were needed to attain his ends and to recognise that appearance often mattered more than substance. Not least, ceremonies should be carefully orchestrated because 'ceremony suffices to breed opinion and opinion draws on substance.'[281] Most of all, the wise ruler kept his own counsel, proceeded stealthily, dissimulated and played the lion and the fox, as Machiavelli advised in *The Prince*.[282] Guile and force were the arts of government. Glossing the proverb 'oderint dum metuant', Drake observed that 'it keeps states and kingdoms in obedience whereas love without mixture of some awful fear will not keep [even] private families in union.'[283] For kings, as for common subjects, Drake's axioms provided rules for survival, principles quite at odds with the prevailing paradigms for personal, social and public life. William Drake's reading notes suggest that a Buckinghamshire gentleman developed a system of values, a philosophy of life, that we would have expected to encounter, if at all, only among the more radical thinkers in the capital or on the fringes of the universities.

When we look more closely at Drake's notes and observations, however, we see that his was a revealingly complex and ambiguous set of values that

274. Ogden MS 7/7 f. 11v, in the bottom margin to printed page of Bacon, p. 77v.
275. Ogden MS 7/7 f. 77.
276. Ogden MS 7/8 ff. 7, 74.
277. Ogden MSS 7/8 f. 7v; 7/48 f. 133.
278. Ogden MS 7/26 f. 4. This adage is repeated in every notebook. The combination of sexual immorality and corruption is interesting.
279. Ogden MS 7/26 f. 4.
280. Ogden MSS 7/38 f. 11v; 7/8 ff. 68v, 82.
281. Ogden MS 7/26 f. 31v. The adage is from Bacon's essay 'Of Vainglory'.
282. Ogden MSS 7/7 ff. 2v, 77; 7/8 f. 161v.
283. Folger MS f. 104. 'Let them hate, so long as they fear.'

reflected a range of influences and experiences. Traditional ideas and codes are not entirely absent from his notes. Drake was critical of the gallants who were too much captivated by pleasure, believing 'the philosophy of a gentleman ought to be practic and fitted for action.'[284] In one notebook he wrote that active men were most useful to the commonweal when they were virtuous; as well as frequent injunctions to self-regulation, he copied from the puritan John Robinson's *Observations* the exhortation that 'we should aim at the perfection that the law of God requires.'[285] Clearly William appreciated that Machiavelli's dicta were totally at odds with such injunctions, that the Florentine, as he put it, made virtues mere 'arts of life'.[286] But what appears to have won Drake to the Machiavellian worldview was a sense that when others did not behave as they should, it disadvantaged any man to pursue virtue before profit, or to place honesty above dissimulation. Drake regarded his fellows as malicious and cunning, never willing to do good unless force compelled or guile seduced them. He that 'truly understands the world knows it to be but a theatre of . . . disguise', a 'composition of fraud and violence' which necessitated an equal cunning and preparedness to be wicked in order to survive.[287] A man, he wrote in his Folger notebook, is 'less disordered in his affairs who presupposeth the ingratitude and faithlessness of friends, the envy of neighbours, the fraud and force of enemies'.[288]

At times, the ideal and the ruthlessly pragmatic are joined together in a curious and revealing tension. Conventionally enough, Drake writes that 'a wise man must sometimes answer pleasantly such as are choleric and passionate', only to add the Machiavellian twist that it was best to conceal his own and 'turn the others' passion to his end'.[289] While it appears that he could acknowledge that fathers could bear true, selfless love for their children, implicitly rejecting the notion that the commonwealth is the family writ large, he held that 'all love but that . . . is but wind and air.'[290] Even kindred, he observed, 'are not always friends and when not are the worst of enemies'.[291] Rather than love and gratitude it was fear and hope, Drake concluded, that most motivated men, and the wise citizen and wise ruler manipulated both.[292]

'Vita hominis est militia' was a Machiavellian doctrine.[293] But it also pointed to Thomas Hobbes's state of nature, and when Drake developed his belief that 'there is a secret intestine war between man and man', he deployed not only

284. Ogden MSS 7/8 ff. 1, 189v; 7/23 f. 21v.
285. Ogden MSS 7/8 f. 1v; 7/34 f. 1. See J. Robinson, *Observations Divine and Moral for the Furthering of Knowledge and Virtue* (1625).
286. Ogden MS 7/8 f. 41v.
287. Ogden MS 7/8 ff. 52, 137.
288. Folger MS f. 75v.
289. Ogden MS 7/7 f. 47: Drake writes of 'beautiful cunning' . . .
290. Ogden MS 7/26 f. 26.
291. Bucks R.O. D/DR/10/56 f. 33.
292. Ibid., f. 48; Folger MS ff. 98v, 127.
293. Folger MS f. 59; he repeats the axiom as 'vita nostra est militia' (f. 2); cf. 'I live in the world as though I am in an enemy's country', Ogden MS 7/8 f. 162v.

Hobbesian conceits but a recognisably Hobbesian language. The condition of war, he asserted, was natural to men:

> man is created with those desires that are infinite and insatiable to desire all things but is so limited that he can attain but few things, so that there being no proportion between the power of getting and the will and desire of getting, there grows a secret dislike of what a man enjoys; hence proceeds a change of a man's condition, for desiring other men's estates and endeavouring to get them and others loathe to lose what they have already, they proceed to quarrels and divisions . . .[294]

We cannot be certain when Drake penned these lines: in his notebooks they follow comments on the Earl of Strafford in the past tense, but there are no other indications as to their date. It was in 1642 that Hobbes first published his political philosophy in *De Cive*, printed at Paris. Drake may have read it, or had access to a manuscript of *The Elements of Law* which was circulating in the summer of 1640.[295] Whenever he read Hobbes – and we shall see that at some point he did – what is as important is that some of the ideas Hobbes systematised into a philosophy Drake had already begun to formulate and structure into a vision of society.[296] They may lead us to question the extent to which Hobbes revolutionised political thought by rejecting the premises of the Christian commonweal and positing a state of nature in which, to use Drake's gloss on Machiavelli, 'freed from fighting for necessity', men 'presently fall a quarrelling for ambition'.[297]

In another important respect, Drake echoed or pre-empted Hobbes. In *Leviathan*, published in 1651, Hobbes argued that it was reading the classics and the Scriptures that had destabilised society by leading men to question authority.[298] Drake, though he shared the conventional humanist optimism that 'persuasion of books of sermons, of speeches civilize the rough nature of men and dispose them to society and friendship', also became aware of the potential dangers of uncontrolled reading.[299] Recalling Herodotus' report that when Clisthenes, King of the Sicyonians, planned war against the Arguri he banned the verses of Homer 'because they contained commendation of Argus', Drake praised the king for 'wisely foreseeing what alteration a poem so sweetly indicted might work in the minds of his subjects even against the good of the state'.[300] For similar reasons, Drake added with approval, the

294. Ogden MS 7/8 ff. 37v, 43v; cf. T. Hobbes, *Leviathan*, ed. R. Tuck (Cambridge, 1991), ch. 13, pp. 86–90, at p. 70.
295. Hobbes, *Leviathan*, p. xiv.
296. See below, pp. 237–8.
297. Folger MS f. 59.
298. Hobbes, *Leviathan*, p. 150; see too L. Potter, *Secret Rites and Secret Writing: Royalist Literature 1641–1660* (Cambridge, 1989), p. 54; G. Shapiro, 'Reading and Writing in the Text of Hobbes's *Leviathan*', *J. Hist. Philos.* 18 (1980), pp. 147–57.
299. Ogden MS 7/7 f. 11v, in the margin to Bacon p. 77v.
300. Ogden MS 7/29 f. 18.

Romans had triumvirs to check on books.[301] Reading opened up a hermeneutic freedom that compromised authority.[302] Glossing the proverb 'I like not a door that hath many keys', William reflected on how 'laws or religion [are] subjected to diverse interpretations'. And 'when there is differing opinions there is disorder.'[303] Perhaps, then, as England plunged towards civil war, though a highly individual interpreter of his texts, Drake, like Hobbes, came to see the need for authority to determine meaning and to establish itself if need be by force.[304]

Drake's religious views were also to a surprising degree for the 1630s shaped by realpolitik. As we have seen, Drake was well read in religious works, he identified biblical passages easily, quoted Aquinas and the Fathers, and annotated 'the chief heads of divinity gathered out of the best modern writers'.[305] In addition, he attended or read sermons by the champions of the godly – John Preston and Samuel Ward – copying from the former arguments about God's all-sufficiency and from the latter the point that there was no quality God valued in man if he did not take Christ to his bosom and glory in the wisdom of the Lord.[306] Evidently Drake believed in direct divine inspiration and intervention: 'sometimes', he wrote, 'there descendeth into human actions a beam of divinity which draws after them the astonishment and admiration of the people.'[307] On matters of faith the few passages we find in the notebooks in group 1 (we shall have more to say about the later volumes) suggest that Drake was orthodox enough. A section in Ogden MS volume 29, headed 'How faith justifieth', was followed by notes on justification without any human merit: 'the efficient cause of our justification is the free mercy and grace of God.'[308] On the other hand, Drake specifically copied the sentence 'secta lutherana negantes libertatem arbitrii humani perturbant gubernationem', and the gist is repeated in Drake's Folger notebook where he wrote that states where men neither believed in God nor had free will were like to be ruined.[309] If the statements indicate a tension in Drake's religious views, it was one that would intensify over time.

Whatever his private faith, Drake seems to have had little regard for the clergy. 'The kingdom of the clergy', he wrote, in appropriately political language, 'had been long before at an end' had the charitable deeds of some of the inferior churchmen not 'borne out the scandals of the superfluity and

---

301. Ibid.
302. See Ogden MS 7/35 f. 3: 'The pen is the sceptre that rules over the memory of kings.'
303. Folger MS ff. 5v–6v.
304. Cf. below, pp. 246–7.
305. Ogden MS 7/34 f. 113.
306. Ogden MS 7/34 f. 96v; Folger MS f. 1.
307. Ogden MS 7/23 f. 20v.
308. Ogden MS 7/29 f. 191.
309. Ogden MS 7/8 f. 49v: 'Denying free will the Lutheran sect disturb government.' Cf. Folger MS f. ★5.

excesses of bishops and prelates'.[310] He clearly disliked Archbishop Laud whom he blamed for 'troubling men's consciences' and for enhancing clerical wealth and power.[311] High church ceremonialism did not attract him: 'superstition', he believed, 'is always more ceremonious than true religion.'[312] Though he voices none of the anti-papist vitriol of the godly, Drake noted Secretary Winwood's claim, in a letter to Fulke Greville, that all Roman Catholics were traitors at heart.[313] On the other hand, he had no time at all for puritans. For one he regarded them as hypocritical. Following the stereotypes of the early Stuart stage, Drake mocked puritan cant and behaviour. In the 'character of a person vainly precise', he copied the sketch of a figure who imagined that there could be no holiness but in a person pale and lean; a man who defamed all and measured others by his own 'idle dispositions' rather than their virtues; who was so credulous in his own case that he regarded a pinprick as a mark of sainthood; men whose devotion consisted in 'circumcising their hair but not their hearts'.[314] Worse, Drake suspected puritans to be subversives. 'Puritans', he feared, 'would have their fancies and humours give a form to the whole world.'[315] Whilst 'the puritan opinions have little motion in the elder and wiser sort', they took hold of women and the young with ambitions to be popular.[316] Out of love of innovation and pride in their opinions they engendered heresies and 'the sad effects' of 'individual zeal'.[317] They needed to be checked by authority, for 'if men be suffered to hold what opinions they list in matters of religion you shall have a thousand sects.'[318]

Not least because individual opinion was dangerous, and weak individuals could be misled 'under a veil of piety', Drake supported the authority of the church.[319] 'There is a very great danger', he felt, 'in a sect or party if it hath an aim to supplant or oppose what hath been long established by law or authority.'[320] 'Single opinions', he affirmed, 'cannot be so solid as general tenets of the church.'[321] Drake annotated the Earl of Manchester's letter to his son Walter Montagu, a convert to Rome, arguing that the Church of England continued to be the true Catholic church, and copied with approval the

310. Ogden MS 7/8 f. 76; cf. f. 158. See too H. Lords MS 49 f. 34.
311. Ogden MS 7/8 f. 42; cf. below, pp. 140–1.
312. Ogden MS 7/8 f. 203.
313. Ogden MS 7/23 f. 35.
314. Ogden MS 7/8 f. 195. The reference to circumcision points up the familiar comparison (made for one by James I) of puritans with Jews. Cf. Ben Jonson, *Bartholomew Fair*, Act I, on the characterisation of Zeal of The Land Busy as judaical.
315. Ogden MS 7/7 f. 2.
316. Ogden MS 7/7 f. 60.
317. Ogden MS 7/7 f. 105; Folger MS f. 71.
318. Ogden MS 7/7 f. 106.
319. Ogden MS 7/8 f. 68.
320. Ogden MS 7/8 f. 39v.
321. Ogden MS 7/8 f. 179v.

archbishop's denial that the Catholic church was the church of Rome: 'Rome is a particular church and Catholic signifies universal.'[322] It was this unity that Drake seems to have hankered after. Instead, as he scanned the world, he observed that of thirty parts, nineteen were idolatrous or Muslem 'and the other eleven parts serving Christ in so different a manner as if there were not one but many Christs'.[323] Sects had proliferated and fragmented to the point that in Poland some argued Moses was an imposter and denied the creation![324] Even in England, 'in the worship of God, what religions so ever Englishmen choose to themselves they run ever into extremes.' Under popery they gave too much power to religious organisations, later too little, and sects quarrelled with each other rather than joined in one church and common-wealth.[325]

Drake did not think such religious opinions 'worth falling out for'.[326] For all his conventional Anglican Protestantism, his attitude to religion was essentially and strikingly rational, pragmatic and political. His notes on divinity are concerned less with theological controversies than with the philosophical reasons for belief in God based on theories of motion, primary cause and the 'summum bonum', all nations believing in some good.[327] His age, he held, had not 'been subject to that heat for matters of religion' as former times; indeed men had 'lost the fear of God', which was no longer a force for cohesion and obedience.[328] If, however, the power of religion remained to any extent in the minds of the multitude, it was for princes to harness it to their rule rather than concern themselves with doctrine. 'The politician says matters of faith are invisible and uncertain; give him things that are visible and present.'[329] What was sacred to the ruler was interest, and he cared not what was the religion of his state as long as it served him and kept the people in obedience.[330] Drake came close to sharing such sentiments: he confessed an admiration for pagan faiths designed to make men courageous (where Christianity lauded the meek); he observed the shrewdness of Mahomet who, in order to draw to his empire all nations, contrived his Koran so that it might 'participate somewhat of all religions'.[331] Perhaps Drake similarly admired Queen Elizabeth for her politic sense of the need for a comprehensive religious settlement and valued the Church of England for its political as well as religious role. Evidently he regretted its fragmentation and the divisive acts

322. Ogden MS 7/29 f. 68; this appears to be the letter Manchester wrote to his son on 20 May 1636. See *Hist. Mss Comm., De Lisle and Dudley*, VI, p. 44. Ogden MS 7/11 f. 2.
323. Ogden MS 7/7 f. 104.
324. Ogden MS 7/7 f. 106.
325. Ogden MS 7/7 f. 107.
326. Ogden MS 7/8 f. 179v.
327. See the notes in Ogden MS 7/34 ff. 112v onwards.
328. Ogden MS 7/8 ff. 179v, 177v.
329. Ogden MS 7/8 f. 187v.
330. Folger MS f. ★4; cf. Ogden MS 7/7 f. 152v.
331. Ogden MS 7/7 f. 114v; 7/8 ff. 86, 165; 7/23 f. 73v.

of puritans, Laud and other bishops who, he felt, might have retained their positions had they preached and practised charity.[332] But, whatever the cause, religion was no longer the cement of the state, nor the key to how to live in it. Accordingly, as he sought counsel in his reading, Drake returned to Machiavelli, Guicciardini, Cardan (and perhaps Hobbes) – men, as he owned, 'mere politicians without religion'.[333]

Before we at last turn to how Drake's reading and values shaped his attitudes to specific contemporary events, personalities and policies, we must look at another area of his learning and experience: in the law. Along with religion, the law was held to be a unifying bond of the body politic, a shared discourse for the settling of disputes, the very essence of government. In early Stuart England, of course, the law, like religion, had in practice been the site of some of the fundamental tensions, indeed conflicts, within the body politic – over the nature of power and rights, liberty and property; as Drake had observed, 'laws [were] subject to diverse interpretations.'[334] Drake's interest in the law was personal and public. He believed a legal knowledge would aid his advancement; he was involved in some legal practice; he sought and obtained a position in the Court of Common Pleas. Beyond that, following his grandfather, William Tothill, who had written a treatise on the course and proceedings of Chancery, Drake appears to have been fascinated by the processes of the law across a broad spectrum of courts and cases.[335] He borrowed and read reports of cases; he owned works by Stanford, Lambard, Hubbard, Sir Francis More, Sir Edward Coke and Whitelocke; he took notes from legal manuscripts as well as printed books.[336]

As a gentleman ambitious to augment his estate, Drake, not untypically, copied notes on land law: on abatement, disseising, bargains and contract, executors, uses, rents and fines, copyhold, fee simple, conveyance, feoffment, endowment, device, bonds and trespass.[337] His interest, however, went far beyond that. William copied passages on the types of bills and hearings in Chancery, on actions on the case and actions on the statute and out of Rastell's *Terms of the Law* and Cowell's law dictionary, *The Interpreter*.[338] He took notes on murder, manslaughter and high treason, and on the courts of Star Chamber, the Exchequer and the Court of Wards.[339] Drake had full notes of Star Chamber cases from James I's reign and was evidently fascinated by

---

332. Ogden MS 7/8 f. 76; on Elizabeth, see above p. 98 and cf. below, pp. 117, 236.
333. Ogden MS 7/8 f. 161v.
334. Folger MS f. 5v.
335. Ogden MS 7/23 f. 125v; W. Tothill's *The Transactions of the High Court of Chancery* was not published until 1649. Drake had a manuscript.
336. See for example Ogden MSS 7/23 ff. 5, 131v, 127v, 125v; 7/36 f. 1; 7/45 ff. 2, 185. See too H. Lords MS 49 ff. 185v–185.
337. Ogden MSS 7/23 f. 131v; 7/35 f. 41v; 7/52 f. 143v.
338. Ogden MS 7/52 f. 143v. See John Rastell, *The Exposicions of the Termes of the Lawes* (1567); J. Cowell, *The Interpreter or Booke Containing the Signification of Words* (Cambridge, 1607).
339. Ogden MSS 7/23 ff. 5, 10v, 131; 7/11 ff. 34–5, 96v–50 passim.

some of the famous cases of his youth – he obtained copies of the indictments of Mrs Turner and the Earl of Somerset, the censure of the Earl of Suffolk, and copies of Bacon's notes and Lord Egerton's pleadings.[340]

As usual, he was a close and active reader of these texts. He made observations on decisions of the courts and cross-references to other texts, writing alongside his notes on the case of Sir Richard Tracy, 'vide Coke's 5 Rep. 72'.[341] Important legal opinions, such as Doderidge's that an infant might submit himself to a beneficial arbitrament, he recorded as important precedents.[342] Drake went to some lengths to acquire the contemporary proceedings of the prerogative courts of Star Chamber and High Commission. He annotated Star Chamber cases against Theodore Kelley for his challenge to Sir Arthur Gorges, against James Cason and others for forgery and opprobrious words to a JP of Suffolk, against Samuel Travers for scandalous words used to the dean of Exeter, and against Thomas Broughton for a disturbance in church.[343] He took notes too of the Earl of Huntington's suit against Sir William Faunt for challenging his authority as Lord Lieutenant, from the case against Sir Richard Wiseman for his false complaint against Lord Keeper Coventry and from Lambard Osbaston's trial for libel against Laud.[344] From a collection of one 'Lashford', he extracted proceedings in the Court of High Commission in 1632, against Paul Pole for simony, one Amy for serving a subpoena in church, against George Long for stealing church stones and money for the poor, and against conventiclers in Blackfriars.[345]

As well as reading the reports, Drake evidently attended several cases in person. He went to Alcock's case and other cases in the Court of Wards, and attended Star Chamber, Exchequer and possibly King's Bench.[346] Drake was especially interested in and informed about the causes célèbres of his day: he heard or read of Attorney Heath's case against the MPs Sir John Eliot, Denzil Holles and Benjamin Valentine, and against Sir Walter Long.[347] In 1628 he appears to have attended the Star Chamber for the trial of a group of fiddlers and balladeers who had libelled the Duke of Buckingham; and he heard the debate about the prosecution of libel and Coventry's suggestion that there were 'more speedy cures of the malady than censures in the Star Chamber'.[348]

340. Ogden MSS 7/11 ff. 27–8; 7/52 ff. 2, 143v; H. Lords MS 49 ff. 158–146.
341. Ogden MS 7/11 ff. 50v, 49v–40.
342. Ogden MS 7/11 f. 45.
343. Ogden MS 7/11 ff. 13–17. These cases were all in 1632, so Drake may have attended in person. See H. E. Phillips, 'The Court of Star Chamber, 1630–1641', M.A. thesis, London University, 1939, app.
344. H. Lords MS 49 ff. 35, 139–138, 135v.
345. Ogden MS 7/11 ff. 22–6. See S. R. Gardiner, ed., *Reports of Cases in the Courts of Star Chamber and High Commission*, Camden Soc. (1886), pp. 277, 286, 321.
346. Ogden MSS 7/11 ff. 26, 34–5; 7/45 f. 23.
347. Ogden MS 7/11 f. 36. See S. R. Gardiner, *History of England from the Accession of James I to the Outbreak of the Civil War* (10 vols, 1883–4), vol. 7, ch. 68; J. Reeve, *Charles I and the Road to Personal Rule* (Cambridge, 1989), ch. 4.
348. Ogden MS 7/11 f. 75v–74. See BL Lansdowne MS 620 ff. 50v–51.

In Lord Vaux's case he heard a plea of parliamentary privilege rejected on Coventry's argument that 'this court is a limb of parliament, for this court is called the Great Council and the judges are lords of the parliament.'[349]

There is a hint that such claims met with his disapproval. For in November 1632, in the case of Elwood against Sir Edward Dering for criticising the authority of Star Chamber, Drake noted that 'Much was spoken against clashing of the one court with another' and continued, 'I observed an inclination of the great ones to advance the authority of arbitrary jurisdictions.'[350] We do not know whether such observation caused him concern, but Drake certainly had the legal and historical framework which would have enabled him to discern wider and more sinister developments. He knew from his reading that the will of kings had once been the law and that then it came to pass that laws were established to restrain power: 'and that government which had the mixture of equality (holding in an equal balance supreme power and common right) were called legal, the other which had it not was called tyrannical.'[351] But in his brief notes on the infamous cases of the 1630s – against the feoffees for impropriations, or against Prynne for example – Drake makes no comment on the judgment or proceedings.[352]

If anything, rather than regarding the law (and desiring the law) to be above politics, Drake took it for granted that the law and the courts were immersed in political life. We recall his cynical axiom that powerful friends rather than justice often advanced a man's cause.[353] In his detailed notes on the trial of Sir Henry Sherfield (for smashing a coloured glass window in a Salisbury church), he observed and admired political manoeuvring at the highest levels of justice. Drake may have been in the Star Chamber on 6 February 1632 when the case was heard. Whether there or not, he noted the evidence and arguments of all the witnesses and the opinions and sentences of the judges: as well as Laud's and Cottington's defence of church and state, Coke's condemnation of images, Dorset's rejection of 'papist testimonies' and Manchester's desire not to 'uphold superstition'.[354] What most fascinated Drake, however, was Lord Keeper Coventry's balanced and moderate judgment – rejecting images of the deity but requiring Sherfield to make acknowledgement to the bishop for breach of his authority. For he regarded it as not a straightforward legal opinion but a subtle political ruse:

The wise Lord Keeper saw that in joining with the rest in censure [he] could not any way prejudice Sherfield's cause, the general bent to censure

349. Ogden MS 7/11 f. 84v.
350. Ogden MS 7/11 f. 26.
351. Ogden MS 7/45 f. 185.
352. Ogden MS 7/11 ff. 38, 43v. The notes on Prynne's trial for *Histriomastix* are quite detailed. Cf. S. R. Gardiner, ed., *Documents Relating to the Proceedings against William Prynne in 1634 and 1637*, Camden Soc. (1877).
353. Above, p. 105.
354. Ogden MS 7/11 ff. 66v–58v. See T. Hargrave, *A Complete Collection of State Trials* (11 vols, 1767–81), vol. 1, pp. 399–418.

him, and thereby he should uphold his credit with the king thereby to do his party service and so increase his own popularity.[355]

And he added that Coventry, for such reasons, 'would give his sentence oftentimes against that side that he had secretly wrought the court to favour'. Here was no conventional notion of justice – speaking one's mind on the basis of evidence and learning, regardless of any interest or faction. Rather Drake praised what he believed was a Machiavellian strategy to gain an end and advance a party. It was not only the church but the law that had fallen to the practices of 'mere politicians'.

Drake's immersion in the works of Tacitus, Machiavelli and Guicciardini led him like them to question the very assumptions about political life, and to develop 'an essentially amoral view of political activity'.[356] This was by no means a rejection of authority and government: Drake shared with Cicero the conviction that without government nothing could continue; with Seneca he believed authority the essential chain which linked all together.[357] But unlike conventional Christian moralists and traditional political thinkers he did not expect government to be a condition of perfection or means to the attainment of the moral good. 'It is', he opined, 'with states as tis with more sensible creatures which the more they haste to arrive at the perfection of their being, the sooner they fail and perish.'[358] Kings were, like ordinary subjects, a mixture of evil and good; and against Christian humanist thinking, Drake noted that a 'bad man may make a good king'.[359] Rulers and statesmen, he accepted, sought power for the greatness it brought and therefore deployed all means to attain and retain it. If princes sought to rule with the love of their subjects, that was as much an expedient as a right course: because 'it is always necessary for a prince to have the good will of the people; otherwise in adversity he shall find no certain refuge.'[360] More often they deployed deception and force to secure their ends. Promises made kept the people in hope and obedience. 'It is a usual art with princes to confess the evil and to promise the amendment thereof without any thought to effect anything but only lull asleep those that are not wary to enjoy the benefit of time.'[361] From Ralegh Drake learned that princes had always been prepared to be authoritarian and even cruel to make themselves masters of the world, and from Balzac he took it for a norm that 'our statesmen would have us resign our religion and liberty into their hands to mould them to what forms took best with their designs and interests.'[362]

355. Ogden MS 7/11 f. 59v.
356. Clark, 'Wisdom Literature I', p. 302.
357. Ogden MS 7/38 f. 19.
358. Ogden MS 7/35 f. 40.
359. Ogden MS 7/23 f. 27; Folger MS f. 12.
360. Ogden MS 7/38 f. 11v.
361. Ogden MS 7/38 f. 27v.
362. Ogden MSS 7/38 f. 116v; 7/8 f. 173v.

Such a Machiavellian view did not lead Drake to opposition, but rather to the Hobbesian notion that, however selfish the ruler, any order he provided was better than none. 'I have no mind', he noted, 'to murmer against present government, nor to find fault with that which is above me. I never dispute against the pilot that carries me though he sometimes varies the course to decline tempests.'[363] What was settled, he was inclined to think, whether originally or intrinsically good or not, ultimately became so on account of the stability it provided.[364] And even if the ruler tended to overstrain his authority, he was to be borne with patience as preferable to the excesses of a multitude which had always to be restrained.[365] In a state of nature in which all men pursued self-interest by guile and force, it was necessary at times for the ruler to deploy them with greater skill and ruthlessness, to preserve some order for the good of all.

These were not the abstract musings of a thinker detached from the realities of contemporary problems and politics. Drake's reading in what we would call political theory was matched by an extensive knowledge of contemporary tracts and politics. He took notes on the Powder treason and the censure of the Earl of Northumberland; he copied Cardinal Wolsey's correspondence and letters such as Secretary Winwood's to Greville or John Durie's from Elbing about relations between Calvinists and Lutherans;[366] he transcribed speeches delivered in Elizabethan and early Stuart parliaments and annotated the journals of parliament from 1604 and 1628; he summarised contemporary debates about 'the king's estate' – royal lands and royal finances.[367] In some cases the notes are full enough for us to hear Drake weighing all the contemporary arguments. For example, he summarises Roger Owen's arguments against the king's right to levy impositions outside of parliament on the ground that otherwise subjects would be left mere tenants of their own goods. But alongside Owen's distinction between the king's powers in and out of parliament, he placed extracts from Sir John Davies 'in defence of the king's prerogative', in which Davies outlined the absolute and ordinary powers of the king and drew up precedents 'as may be of use in the building of a fortress in defence of the king's prerogative'.[368] Similarly from notes of the 1628 parliament he underlined speeches both critical and supportive of the royal prerogative, and Wentworth's injunction to his fellow MPs: 'let us proceed equally between King and people.'[369]

We can be sure that Drake was always concerned with the immediate and

363. Ogden MS 7/23 f. 16v.
364. Ogden MSS 7/8 f. 133v; 7/38 f. 115v.
365. Ogden MS 7/38 ff. 28–26.
366. Ogden MSS 7/23 ff. 35, 37, 118v; 7/11 f. 97v.
367. Ogden MSS 7/11 ff. 32, 68; 7/23 f. 42.
368. Ogden MS 7/11 f. 115v–106. See M. Jannson, *Proceedings in Parliament, 1614.* (Philadelphia, 1988), p. 154 n46; cf. S. R. Gardiner, ed., *Parliamentary Debates in 1610*, Camden Soc. (1862), pp. 112–15.
369. H. Lords MS 49 ff. 2–12.

personal applications of his reading and reflections. Francis Bacon's advice that statesmen should leave a window through which to escape led him to note: 'Mr. Chute told me that alderman Craven was a quiet, still man and my Lord Lovelace will be very wary . . .'[370] Charron's passages about pliability clearly made him think of 'Suckling', whose poetry he read.[371] Alongside one of a series of proverbs, 'The king subsists by the field that is tilled', he writes 'Pim 4 Earl of Strafford'.[372] The adage that it was acceptable to gain ends by any means he applies to 'Sir Henry Vane in Parl'.[373] Occasionally a date renders the context and application of reading to politics clear. It was in 1635, for example, against the background of ship money and other Caroline fiscal expedients, that Drake took an interest in Elizabethan debates about monopolies and impositions, observing that 'to stretch authority too far cracks it.'[374] Notes on sedition follow shortly after others dated March 1638, and the period of the Scottish troubles.[375] In other cases we are left to make an informed guess. Notes from Jonson, Donne and others on libels may have been prompted by the Star Chamber case or the attacks on Buckingham.[376] 'Notes taken from a book which seemed to censure the rashness of later parliaments' seem to have been taken in the aftermath of the dissolution in 1629.[377] Bodin's maxim that he who was master of the militia was master of the state may belong to the debates of 1641–2 over the control of the nation's forces.[378] Finally the observation that it was easier to oppose than limit the demands of a multitude may reflect the experience of mob politics in the 1640s.[379]

In general, we can be confident that contemporary personalities and events were always in Drake's mind as he read. Notes on Machiavelli and Guicciardini found between comments on Strafford's trial indicate how momentous events pushed him back to his core texts and forwards to further reading and reflection.[380] As well as his intimate acquaintance with politic histories and advice books, Drake, in order to understand the affairs of state, set himself the task of reading arraignments, legal proceedings, letters of state, patents, proclamations, acts of Council and diplomatic negotiations.[381] His knowledge of both the theorists of politics and the daily affairs of early Stuart government not only equipped Drake to understand and participate in contemporary political discussion; they led him, as the commonwealth fragmented, to

370. Ogden MS 7/7 f. 38, note on Bacon p. 103.
371. Ogden MS 7/7 f. 50v; 7/29 f. 143; 7/45 f. 23v.
372. Ogden MS 7/26 f. 24v.
373. Ogden MS 7/8 f. 160.
374. Ogden MS 7/23 ff. 39–41.
375. Ogden MS 7/8 ff. 198v–197v.
376. Folger MS ff. 20–1.
377. Ogden MS 7/45 f. 22.
378. Ogden MS 7/8 f. 81v (cf. 7/26 f. 1). The notes follow material on Strafford, ff. 42–3.
379. Ogden MS 7/38 f. 28.
380. Ogden MS 7/8 ff. 161v–159.
381. Ogden MS 7/29 f. 132.

the conviction that a man who had studied for action should bring his learning to active use on the public stage.

The contemporary figures Drake admired were those who had pursued the
agenda he set himself or exemplified the Machiavellian values he celebrated.
We have remarked on his praise of Cecil's strategies of advancement.[382]
He also noted how the Earl of Somerset, James I's favourite, had employed
teachers to instruct him in history and policy, 'mixing study and the ways and
practices of court together'.[383] Evidently Drake hoped to add to his own
studies experience of the 'practices of court', to participate in public life. He
took a keen interest in the means by which men rose to place – through
patronage and contacts; he followed the marriages that joined men to powerful families; his observation convinced him that the Treasurer, the Lord
Keeper, the Attorney, the Secretaries and the bedchambermen 'are the most
potent to pleasure or to stand to a man' and resolved to 'get their acquaintance'.[384] He noted the skills of the Elizabethan and Jacobean Councillors:
Burghley for his dexterity, Cecil for sage advice to Essex, Elizabeth herself for
balancing factions, Pembroke for eschewing controversy, Somerset for shield-
ing James from suitors and his refusal to sell honours.[385] Though he criticised
Buckingham for making titles 'common' and so debasing their value, and
appears to have disliked him, he noted his skill in dispensing favours and political strategy over his clash with Bristol, keeping him from access to the king
while he played him in a Machiavellian manner keeping him between fear
and hope of return to favour.[386]

On the politics of the 1630s, Drake's commonplace books are largely silent.
While he was abroad, he was kept informed by friends of the (often controversial) news at home. In 1634, Sir William Slingsby sent him news of the
Treasury Commission and the king's finances, about ship money and foreign
affairs; Mr Barrell, in February 1635, passed on gossip about court appointments, the deaths of leading figures, news about forest fines, the Book of
Sports, and the report that 'the money towards setting forth the fleet comes
but heavily.'[387] Such letters offer evidence of what Drake's friends believed
would interest him; and he valued their news enough to copy letters into his
commonplace book alongside other 'things of policy'. But – untypically – he
added no comment or marginal gloss, so his own reaction to such developments remains, at least in these pages, silent. We have seen him note the 'inclination of the great ones to advance the authority of arbitrary jurisdictions'.

---

382. Above, p. 98.
383. Ogden MS 7/7 f. 120v.
384. Ogden MS 7/7 ff. 166, 165v, 162v; quotation f. 142; cf. f. 161v.
385. Ogden MSS 7/7 ff. 120v, 145; 7/8 ff. 2v, 6v. Cotton also praised Somerset for not
   selling honours, Sharpe, *Sir Robert Cotton*, p. 129.
386. Ogden MS 7/7 ff. 45, 145, 120v.
387. Ogden MS 7/29 ff. 20–1. Similarly he lists precedents for, but makes no comment
   on, the proclamation ordering the gentry to reside in the country, 7/11 f. 19; but cf.
   below, pp. 145–6.

He appears to have concurred with the views of 'wise men' 'that there hath
bin never a prince since the Conquest that hath pitched upon so many peculiar ways of improvement as our king';[388] but there is no sign in Drake's commonplace books that, for all his breadth of reading and knowledge, he foresaw
the storms that were to break the government coming from within England
– or from Scotland.

When the storm broke in 1638, Drake interpreted the course of events and
the motives of the principal actors in the light of his Machiavellian worldview. Where the Scots were concerned, after the failure of a military campaign, he noted Lord Grey's pessimism about the prospects of lasting peace
and advocacy of a deception that bought time:

> we patch up a peace with them that I cannot for my part repose any assur-
> ance in the contrivance of it, nor for the honour of it highly commend
> it. The best is that by this occasion some time may be won to yield us the
> more liberty to deal with the . . . rebels.[389]

When it came to apportioning blame for what had happened, while he joined
in the condemnation of Laud, against the grain Drake exonerated the Earl of
Strafford, whom he evidently admired as the embodiment of Machiavellian
virtues:

> The Deputy was a man of that wit and spirit that had he not had the Scots
> armies upon his back, or had he been in health, he would have carried
> through his design in spite of all opposition but, to say the truth, the Arch-
> bishop spoiled both the King's work and the Lieutenant's by so extremely
> troubling men's consciences at the same time when there were so many
> pressures upon their fortunes, which made the patriot and puritan join as
> in common cause, which being backed by the Scots made others united
> strength so considerable that what the King and his party opposed against
> it was to little purpose.[390]

Drake evidently shared with Strafford (and Laud) a belief that there was a
radical puritan party that brought in the Scots to advance their ends: and
'there is a very great danger', we recall he wrote, 'in a sect or party if it hath
an aim to supplant or oppose what hath been long established by law and
authority.'[391] He thought the discontented noble leaders of this sect, who had
'great reputation with the people' the principal cause of trouble. Yet rather

---

388. Above p. 116; Ogden MS 7/8 f. 1v.
389. Ogden MS 7/8 f. 38. The notes are followed on ff. 39v–40 by material on Strafford's
     trial.
390. Ogden MS 7/8 f. 39v. Drake blamed Laud for the Scots War, 7/23 f. 49v.
391. Ogden MS 7/8 f. 39v. Above, p. 109. We can now see that these notes apply to 1641.
     Drake discussed Wentworth with Jack Cockshutt, on the Lord Deputy's return to
     England in 1639, H. Lords MS 49 f. 138.

than counselling as others did an accommodation with them (along the lines of the Bedford plan to bring opposition leaders into the king's counsels), he noted that Roman emperors banished men who became too popular to remote parts, where they could do no harm.[392] Certainly, as events unfolded, he saw that the malcontents became bent on revolution:

> All their stirs and motions of the principal actors draw to no other centre but to transfer to some other the government as the principal foundation not only of their particular interests but of their own safety; having so far engaged themselves there is no retreat and they find that the present power stands in their way, that they cannot cast their great designs by that mould they had projected.[393]

Drake felt sure that such incendiaries needed to be snuffed out before they ignited a larger conflagration.[394] But it was not to be. His note of the adage that 'he who can get the militia can erect any structure and introduce any form ecclesiastical or civil' appears to belong to the period of the militia ordinance and to acknowledge the triumph of the rebels.[395] Only a couple of folios later, William reflects on whether a republic could be established in a country where there were many gentlemen.[396]

Though then he appeared to join in the criticism of the king's government in 1640–1, it seems that Drake grew increasingly suspicious of the aims of Pym and his party and opposed to the radical courses that led to civil war. His elevation to a baronetcy may have come in recognition of his moderation. Evidently he doubted whether parliament was best placed to tackle the 'affairs of Ireland' which 'cannot attend such slow remedy as our counsels are like to produce'.[397] The Irish rebellion had broken a vein in the body politic which needed to be stopped before the whole state bled to death. 'Let's take heed', he advised his countrymen, 'how we leave open the wounds of the Commonwealth, too long lest they turn to a gangrene and become incurable.'[398] For all his efforts, the wounds were not cured and the body politic bled.

With the outbreak of war, Drake was named to the county committee established by parliament. But he evidently had no appetite for the cause. William left England in 1643, ostensibly for reasons of his health, and was still abroad in May 1644. After returning, he left again in 1647, perhaps when it

---

392. Ogden MS 7/8 f. 50v. On the Bedford plan, see C. Roberts, 'The Earl of Bedford and the Coming of the English Revolution', *J. Mod. Hist.* 49 (1977), pp. 600–16.
393. Ogden MS 7/8 f. 72. This assessment echoes that of the Venetian ambassador, see *Cal. S.P. Venet. 1640–2*, p. 244. See also 'Notes for a speech', Ogden MS 7/23 f. 49v.
394. Ogden MS 7/8 f. 72v.
395. Ogden MS 7/8 f. 81v.
396. Ogden MS 7/8 f. 83.
397. Ogden MS 7/52 f. 17.
398. Ogden MS 7/8 f. 72v.

became clear that the end of the first civil war had not guaranteed a settlement. Drake was excluded from the Commons in Pride's Purge, and it may be of significance that he was overseas on '2 January 1648', especially if he was still deploying Old Style and Charles I was awaiting his execution.[399] Sadly we know nothing directly of Drake's reaction to this the most momentous event of the century, nor to the erection of a republic which drew on the classical models with which his reading had made him so familiar.

But, as we shall see, though he did not enter the arena of public debate after his speech in 1641, Drake by no means disengaged from reflection on events. Civil war, regicide, republic and Restoration took him back to his books with new questions and concerns and led him to find in them different meanings and lessons.[400] After 1644 or 1645 the notes of Drake's dialogue with his books are no longer in his own hand.[401] He had earlier resolved, we recall, 'to have a scholar to read my ordinary printed books . . . to reserve the strength of my own mind for things material and important' and failing eyesight explains his acting on the resolution.[402] Yet it is worth our remembering that in 1645 Drake was not yet forty and that his eyesight did not prevent him holding legal office, or his serving in parliament after 1660. It is tempting to speculate on whether the decision to use an amanuensis, a decision taken about the time Drake decided to leave England, signalled a need for some psychological as well as geographical distance from what could hardly have been more 'material and important' – the fate of his country torn by civil war. Drake had deployed his learning in the Long Parliament to try to prevent violent conflict.[403] Did the subsequent events of the 1640s shake not only the fabric of society and state but, for a moment, Drake's belief in the capacity of history to teach lessons in wise conduct? We know that for many scholars and statesmen, civil war and regicide destroyed not only the traditional political structure of England but a humanist culture which had been so integrally part of it. We cannot be sure whether Drake was one of them. But as we ponder his decisions to retreat from direct public life, to leave his country and lay aside his own pen, we are drawn to an observation he copied from one of his favourite authors: 'I will not touch upon our late grievances. I have not the heart to handle so fresh and bleeding wounds.'[404]

399. *C.J.* II, p. 956; III, p. 659; IV, p. 41; V, p. 235; Ogden MS 7/10 f. 175. He deployed Old Style in 7/7 f. 102.
400. See below, ch. 4 passim.
401. Though some of the Folger MS can be assigned to these years and Drake's hand appears occasionally in many of the later notebooks.
402. Above, p. 73.
403. For a discussion of his speech, see below, pp. 152–4.
404. Ogden MS 7/23 f. 16v.

3
Reading and Writing Self and Society: Sir William Drake and the English Civil War

The Journal and the Agenda

Sir William Drake's commonplace books in University College London offer extraordinary evidence of the range of reading of a Buckinghamshire gentleman. More important, they enable us to see why and how he read, and how his reading shaped values and attitudes that sat uneasily with the ideals and norms of his age. In terms of contemporary events and personalities they provide fascinating hints about Drake's perception of people and reactions to moments. But because such comments are brief, and usually undated, they do not enable us confidently to chart the development of Drake's political views or satisfactorily to explain his position in 1641–2.

The recent discovery and purchase of his diary is therefore of major historical importance. Historians of the 1630s have often lamented the paucity of good political diaries for that decade, considered vital in the formation of political sympathies and allegiances.[1] Drake's comments on courtiers, projectors, royal finances and proclamations, masques and social policies arising from the Book of Orders add invaluably to the evidence of responses to the 'personal rule' of Charles I, about which historians remain divided.[2] His observations on the controversial religious programmes of these years suggest the need for a revision of scholarship preoccupied with the theological divisions between double predestinarians and Arminians. His comments on Scottish affairs qualify at least the historiography that has recently reinterpreted the English Civil War as a 'British problem'.[3] But, still more valuably, when we turn to Drake's diary, after research in his commonplace books, we see far more clearly how his reading and experience interacted and informed each

1. See C. Russell, 'Issues in the House of Commons 1621–1629: Predictions of Civil War Allegiance', *Albion* 23 (1991), pp. 23–40.
2. See K. Sharpe, *The Personal Rule of Charles I* (1992), ch. 11.
3. See C. Russell, *The Fall of the British Monarchies, 1637–1642* (Oxford, 1991); Russell, *The Causes of the English Civil War* (Oxford, 1990); J. Morrill, *The Nature of the English Revolution* (1993), chs 12, 13; J. Morrill and B. Bradshaw, eds, *The British Problem c.1534–1707* (Houndmills, 1996).

other over the important decade of the 1630s, the period of many entries in
the commonplace books, and the decade during which he travelled, for the
first time, in the Low Countries.

Drake's diary is a folio volume of eighty-four leaves, originally unfoliated
and unpaginated, bound in contemporary calf. Though it carries no title or
inscription, it is undoubtedly in his hand. As with the commonplace books,
the diary is used from both ends with thirteen folios blank in the middle.
Again, as with some of the Ogden manuscripts, the front of the book apper-
tains more to public affairs and reflections; the back is begun with more personal business, though there is no absolute distinction sustained. Unlike the
commonplace books, the diary is clearly dated, beginning in October 1631
and ending with the beginning of civil war in 1642. The entries are regularly
chronological from 1631 to 1637, with a gap between May 1634 and
November 1635 which was evidently the period of Drake's sojourn abroad.[4]
From 1637, the notes are patchier and the diary entries leap over years until
1639/40, though whether because Drake was absent is unclear.[5] The diary,
like the commonplace books, contains (as we shall see) references to books
Drake has read, especially his heroes Machiavelli and Guicciardini; and, as
before, he pens reminders about works he means to acquire or read. But the
emphasis in this case appears to be more immediate and pragmatic, and the
balance of the manuscript leans more to a record of (personal and public)
affairs than notes from reading.

The Phillips sale catalogue describes it as an 'autograph journal', 'covering
Drake's career in London from the early 1630s until the beginning of civil
war', and adds the suggestion that it complements the only volume of personal memoranda in the commonplace book (Ogden MS volume 7): 'however
most of the entries in the University College volume relate to Drake's travels
in the Low Countries in the 1630s, making it in a sense Drake's foreign
journal: as opposed to ours, which can be thought of as his home journal.'[6]
If this remains more suggestive than convincing, it does raise the question of
the relationship of the diary to the commonplace books and opens the possibility that there may be other Drake journals in private hands, which may
still emerge to illuminate his activities and feelings during the 1640s and
1650s.[7] Meanwhile, though the picture may not be complete, the new-found
diary containing drafts and notes for Sir William's speeches to the Long Parliament enables us better to comprehend the formation of his beliefs and pur-

4. Hunt. MS ff. *25–26 (the Huntington Library has foliated the manuscript from each
   end, with asterisked numbers from the back). Cf. Ogden MS 7/29 f. 20.
5. Hunt. MS ff. *35ff.; see Ogden MS 7/8 f. 198v for notes from 1638.
6. Phillips sale catalogue, 18 Mar. 1993.
7. It seems unlikely that such an assiduous note-taker as Drake would have suspended the
   habit of keeping a journal. His travels after 1647 may, of course, mean these were lost
   or are hidden in foreign archives.

poses in speaking, and to assess the importance of his 'quiet Machiavellianism' in the political discourse of 1641.[8]

On the flyleaf at the front of Drake's diary we find a list of authors, in whom we know, from the commonplace books, he was well read. Aristotle, Plutarch, Xenophon and Cicero are listed as approved 'ancient writers'. The roll of humanist works includes the *History of the Council of Trent*, books of policy such as Duccius's *Ars Aulica*, Refuge's *Courtier* and Balzac's *De Principe*, and most of all, Cardan (both *De Sapientia* and *De Prudentia Civili*), Comines, Machiavelli and Guicciardini.[9] Of these, only Guicciardini and Machiavelli are cited throughout the diary and taken as a principal source of wisdom and counsel.[10] Drake copies out Machiavelli's maxims, notes Guicciardini's cynical observations about justice and government, and praises him as 'the most judicious of modern authors to take rules and grounds of direction for the guiding of a man's course'.[11] In accordance with the practice revealed in his commonplace books, he observes that "'tis more profitable for a civil life to read the discourses that attend upon history than any philosophy whatsoever, as those of Machiavel, Polybius, Comines, Guicciardini and the rest.'[12] But here he makes it even more explicit than in his notebooks that such readings should be supplemented by experience and always directed to action. The 'moralists' Drake suspected as making the mind too 'restive, precise and incompatible of converse': too, we might say, contemplative and retiring.[13] It was the politic writers who 'joined with an exact observation in the course of things and acquaintance with the ablest men of all sorts will much conduce to wisdom'.[14] Drake recorded that his friend Mr Potts (either Charles Potts of the Middle Temple or Sir John Potts) seemed to censure Mr Cotton for having many books and making little use thereof, likening him to a man that had many weapons but never fought.[15] It was a simile that elicited Drake's sympathy. Reading, as we have seen, was to equip a man for action and contest in a hostile world: one in which 'vita nostra est militia.'[16]

Even more than the commonplace books, Drake's diary shows him

---

8. See M. Mendle, 'A Machiavellian in the Long Parliament before the Civil War', *Parl. Hist.* 8 (1989), pp. 116–24; see appendix below, pp. 158–63.
9. These refer to Paolo Sarpi, *The Historie of the Council of Trent* (1620); Lorenzo Ducci, *Arte Aulica . . . nelle quale s'insegna il modo che deve tenere il Cortigiano per devenir possessore della gratia del suo Principe* (Ferrara, 1601); Eustache Du Refuge, *Traicté de la Cour* (1622), translated into English by John Reynolds (1622); Jean Louis Guez, Sieur de Balzac, *Discours sur le livre du Balzac, intitulé le Prince* (1631). *The Prince* was not translated into English until 1648; Girolamo Cardano, *De Sapientia* (Auresopili, 1624); *Heironymi Cardani . . . Proxenata seu de Prudentia Civili Liber* (Antwerp, 1627).
10. See, for example, Hunt. MS ff. *3, *11v, *15, *16v, *25, *30v.
11. Hunt. MS ff. *16v.
12. Hunt. MS front flyleaf.
13. Ibid.
14. Ibid.
15. Hunt. MS f. *4.
16. Folger MS f. 2v; see above, p. 106.

studying for a purpose. He cites contemporary English writers – Francis
Quarles, author of epigrams, poems and emblems, and Robert Burton's
Anatomy of Melancholy[17] – and it is also clear that he is collecting and studying works of direct relevance to contemporary affairs, his own and those of
the commonweal. William lends books of proclamations to Mr Earle, possibly Sir Walter Earle, or Thomas his son, MP for Wareham in 1640.[18] He made
a gift to Laud of a manuscript of orders for the government of Corpus Christi
College, at a time when as Chancellor Laud was revising the statutes of
Oxford University.[19] And Drake took full notes from 'a manuscript written
by Sir Robert Cotton' on how 'the kings of England have supported and
repaired their estates' during a period when we know Charles I's government
was searching for ways to reduce expenditure and raise revenues.[20] To assist
with his own management of his estates and to advance his legal learning and
business William borrowed from Mr Stratton a work on the nature of manors
and manorial courts, and studied Sir Edward Coke and Aaron Rathborne's
Surveyor on the office of steward and bailiff and on copyhold tenures and suits
in courts baron.[21]

Drake's most detailed notes, however, came from Thomas Powell's *The Plain
Pathway to Preferment*, which he read in November 1632.[22] Powell was a figure
to whom Drake was likely to be drawn. The author of a repertory of records,
he was well versed in English history and institutions and believed in the
utilitarian value of knowledge of the past. From his *Pathway to Preferment*,
Drake extracted advice on the best schools and scholarships to university, on
the means to preferment in the ministry, and, most of all, on the ways to rise
through the law. He noted that though a career in civil law was more expensive and 'more painful', the 'way of advancement is more certain' because the
competition was less and posts such as chancellor, archdeacon, commissary,
Master of Chancery and Requests and other positions were open only to
civilians.[23] Where the common law was concerned, he copied Powell's advice
that it was best first to be admitted to an inn of Chancery, and obtain practice as a clerk to a protonotary of the Common Pleas. Thereafter the favour

17. Perhaps F. Quarles, *Divine Fancies Digested into Epigrams* (1632), though Drake also read
    Quarles's *Emblemes* (1634). Robert Burton's *Anatomy of Melancholy* was published in
    Oxford in 1621.
18. Hunt. MS f. 1v. See M. F. Keeler, *The Long Parliament, 1640–1641* (Philadelphia, 1954),
    p. 165.
19. Hunt. MS f. *27v; K. Sharpe, 'Archbishop Laud and the University of Oxford', in H.
    Lloyd Jones, V. Pearl and B. Worden, eds, *History and Imagination* (1981), pp. 146–64.
20. Hunt. MS f. 11. See R. Cotton, 'The Manner and Means How the Kings of England
    have from time to time Supported and Repaired their Estates', printed in J. Howell,
    Cottoni Posthuma (1657), pp. 163–200; see too K. Sharpe, *Sir Robert Cotton,1586–1631*
    (Oxford, 1979), pp. 120–5; Sharpe, *Personal Rule*, ch. 3.
21. Hunt. MS f. 5; A. Rathborne, *The Surveyor in Four Bookes* (1616). I have not identi-
    fied 'Mr Stratton'.
22. Drake probably refers to *Tom of All Trades or the Plaine Pathway to Preferment* (1631).
    Powell, a graduate of Drake's old Inn, Gray's, was known to Cotton and D'Ewes.
23. Hunt. MS ff. 13–15. See B. Levack, *Civil Lawyers in England, 1603–1641* (Oxford, 1973).

of a judge led barristers to advance via positions like feodary of a county or town recorder to judgeships or king's remembrancer or higher honours still. William made a note of the fees of various major office-holders, such as chancellor of the duchy of Lancaster and master of the Court of Wards, as well as lesser officials such as the surveyor of the liveries, clerk of the hanaper, master of the subpoena office, or clerks of the crown in King's Bench.[24] The likelihood is that his unusual preoccupation with such details relates to his own campaign to secure an office and evidences his careful study and planning about the means to achieve his ends and the fruits of success.[25] But such reading, of course, also gave him broader knowledge of the patronage system and the ways to, and rewards of, advancement in Caroline England.

Drake's memoranda of things to buy and read also seem to reflect more contemporary concerns and pragmatic purposes than those in the commonplace books. His admonition to himself on the opening leaf of his diary is clear: 'Be sure not to study much books of learning for they divert business, take up the memory too much and keep one from more useful things.'[26] Drake set out to buy or obtain all the manuscripts he could of law, business or policy, in order to lay foundations of learning that could improve his estate in future times.[27] Those from whom he hoped to borrow books and manuscripts were very much men of affairs: Sir Thomas Cotton, Sir Simonds D'Ewes, Mr (presumably Oliver) St John, and a Mr Sadler.[28] And what they lent was of obvious contemporary import: as well as Campanella's discourse of the Spanish monarchy (which Drake borrowed in 1632), books on the jurisdiction of various courts, books of projects, Star Chamber reports and the journals of parliaments.[29] Drake went to his friend St John to obtain details of the Earl of Bedford's project to build townhouses in Covent Garden, and to Mr Barrell for information about the draining of the Fens in Lincolnshire, one of the lucrative projects of the 1630s.[30] As well as reading Coke and Dyer and the *Doctor and Student*, he sought manuscripts on the courts of Exchequer and Star Chamber from Barrell and Cotton.[31] Mr Potts and John Hampden, the famous defendant in the ship money case, advised him to read

24. Hunt. MS f. 16v.
25. Drake obtained a reversion to an office in 1636 or 1637. See above, p. 70.
26. Hunt. MS f. *1v.
27. See Hunt. MS f. 1v where he describes youth and single life as a time for laying seeds for the future.
28. Hunt. MS f. *1v. There are no clues to the identity of Sadler though one Humphrey Sadler was a stationer of Aldersgate (*Cal. S. P. Dom. 1635–6*, p. 504).
29. Hunt. MS ff. *1v, *5v, 1, flyleaf.
30. Hunt. MS ff. *8v, 1. St John was Bedford's agent and lawyer. One Gilbert Barrell was charged along with Cotton and Selden in 1629 for 'publishing and divulging' the libel against the state (*Cal. S. P. Dom. 1629–31*, p. 96). He evidently had a substantial library (ibid., p. 456) and may be the same Gilbert Barrell who was counsel for Eliot, Holles and Valentine after the parliament of 1629. See J. Reeve, *Charles I and the Road to Personal Rule* (Cambridge, 1989), pp. 150 and 148.
31. Hunt. MS f. *1.

statutes belonging to the practice of a JP and then the works of Lambard, Dalton and West pertaining to the office; Drake resolved to supplement these with the advice of men who frequented King's Bench and Star Chamber and to observe how things were carried on there.[32]

It seems likely that books of projects and legal manuscripts were intended to help Drake to the fortune and post he pursued. Other books and manuscripts he sought – some at the booksellers 'hard by Bedlam' – suggest engagement with more public matters.[33] His endeavour, for example, in 1631 to borrow from Barrell notes on Tyndale's arraignment for buggery must surely have been prompted by the infamous trial of the Earl of Castlehaven that year.[34] And it is likely that his desire to obtain Owen's manuscript treatise on impositions and 'the journal of parliament when the Petition of Right was granted' belongs to the discussion of the demise of the 1628 parliament and the prospects for summoning another in 1631–2.[35] More generally, having read his commonplace books, we can understand Drake's interest in a work he had heard of in the hands of Mr Fletcher, son of Dr Fletcher, which he described as 'a book of all the policies in Scripture paralleled with other policies'.[36] His pursuing 'Walton' (?Izaak Walton) for 'some passages of King Charles and King James latter time writ by Ben Jonson' points not only to Drake's interest in recent and contemporary history and literature, but also intriguingly to a work which has evidently not survived.[37] Like the books annotated, those Drake sought were chosen for their elucidation of the 'passages of our time'.[38] And, while he says little in his diary about how he read, we know from the commonplace books that he returned again and again to his texts. As he put it on the first folio at the back of his journal: 'Be not discouraged if I understand not in reading or discoursing, for that which is not understood at one time may at another.'[39]

Among his memoranda of things to do, Drake writes 'likewise modern histories . . . get and study.'[40] From his commonplace books we know that he was indeed well read in virtually all the civic historians of the Renaissance, as well as Machiavelli and Guicciardini, Spanish, German, Dutch, French and

32. Hunt. MS f. *19; and front flyleaf. The works referred to are evidently W. Lambard, *Archion or a Commentary upon the High Courts of Justice in England* (1568); M. Dalton, *The Countrey Justice* (1618); W. West, *Symbolaeographia* (1590).

33. Hunt. MS f. 1.

34. Ibid. See J. Rushworth, *Historical Collections*, vol. 2 (1680), pp. 93–103.

35. Hunt. MS ff. *1, 1; Sharpe, *Personal Rule*, p. 703. See H. Lords MS 49 for Drake's notes from the 1628 parliament.

36. This may be J. Saltmarsh, *The Practice of Policies in a Christian Life Taught from the Scriptures* (1639) to which Drake refers in Ogden MS 7/19. The references are probably to Giles Fletcher, son of the civil lawyer Giles Fletcher.

37. Hunt. MS f. *7v. Aubrey relates that Walton was friendly with Jonson. I have found no other reference to such a work by Jonson.

38. Hunt. MS f. *1v.

39. Ibid.

40. Ibid.

English historians.[41] What distinguishes the diary is the relative absence of these figures and works, and a preoccupation with the English past, and the recent English past at that. Here we find Drake copying or recording anecdotes principally of the Elizabethan and Jacobean period, many of which must have been heard rather than read. Some indeed appear to belong to legend. The story that Henry VII was so exact in overseeing and signing his accounts that he left £10 million to his successor tells more perhaps about the yearning for fiscal rectitude in early Stuart England than about the legacy of the first Tudor.[42] It is clear that Drake shared the admiration of his age for Queen Elizabeth, praising her (as we shall see) for her handling of church papists and her shrewdness in preserving Dunkirk for reasons of security – both issues again of concern in the 1630s.[43] The reign and character of James I obviously fascinated him. He noted Prince Henry's advice to Dr Richard Milbourne, when the latter was in quest for a deanery, 'to take heed how he came near his father's conscience', and recorded Sadler's observation applied to James that 'there is no weapon to rob a Scot like flattery.'[44]

As a man who collected maxims, however, Drake was especially drawn to James I's witticisms and adages, many of which were published in 1627 in *Flores Regii*.[45] When for example the Archbishop of Spalato, Marc Antonio De Dominis, told James that the souls of men went to Ahibub, the king quipped that he had heard of three places (heaven, hell and purgatory) but not four![46] Drake was evidently amused too by the story that when James needed to ascertain whether a maid told the truth against her master, he asked her to swear on the Bible that she was a maid.[47] There are hints here that, whatever historians may have argued, James's jocular and irreverent style, his facility with words and quips, may well have appealed to some of his subjects. And it is more than probable that Drake, who did not think religious positions worth contesting, admired the king's ecumenical disposition and learning rather than those who pursued controversy.[48]

As a man who took Francis Bacon as a model commentator, it is not surprising that Drake took a close interest in what Bacon titled in his essay the 'rising to great place' in the reign of the first Stuart. He noted down what Mr Deane told him of Archbishop Abbot's rise: how he 'lived in the house

41. Above pp. 78–9; see too below, pp. 174–5.
42. Hunt. MS f. *11.
43. Hunt. MS f. 31v; Sharpe, *Personal Rule*, pp. 87–90.
44. Hunt. MS f. *5v. Milbourne was Prince Henry's chaplain; he became Dean of Rochester in 1611 and Bishop of St David's in 1615 (*Cal. S. P. Dom. 1611–18*, pp. 91, 280, 294).
45. James I, *Flores Regii: or Proverbs and Aphorisms as Spoken by his Majestie* (1627).
46. Hunt. MS f. *13v. De Dominis visited England in 1616. A convert from Catholicism, he appealed to James I as a polemicist for national churches against Rome and was made Dean of Windsor.
47. Hunt. MS f. *24.
48. See above, pp. 110–11; below, pp. 140–3; W. B. Patterson, *King James VI and the Reunion of Christendom* (Cambridge, 1997).

with Bishop Bancroft and was his favourite', how 'he likewise kept an inward friendship with the Lord of Dunbar, so that by his means, after Bancroft's death, he came to be Archbishop.'[49] Planning perhaps his own advancement, he learned that when Sir Sackville Crow and Sir Robert Pye were vying for the Duke of Buckingham's favour, Crow won out by lending the duke money, which Pye had denied.[50] But, perhaps recalling Bacon on the rapid descent that could easily follow painful rise, Drake also noted his friend Sir William Slingsby's conversation with Sir Richard Weston at the time of Buckingham's death, when 'having speech of the Duke the Treasurer told him that he was an uncertain man and that they had their heats and cools.'[51] To the Drake who was then immersing himself in the histories and dicta of Machiavelli and Guicciardini, the reign of James I and the era of Buckingham (the period of young William's early adulthood) must have appeared the English proof of the Florentines' teaching.

Though unusually not attributed in the diary, we find in its pages some of the maxims and observations that Drake copied into his commonplace books.[52] But in a journal much more concerned with business than reading, we sense that those selected here are drawn up for his immediately pressing purposes in the 1630s: the increase of his estate and the attainment of place. Throughout the tone is cynical and cautious. With regard to the professions, Drake recalled the Spanish observation that men commended their souls to priests who cared little what became of them, their bodies to physicians who never took their own physic, and their estates to lawyers who, following only their own interest, 'counsel law but never go to law'.[53] The world he lived in, Drake perceived, was one in which there was 'little love or religion . . . they have their being but in terms' – that is words only.[54] The good words men uttered, he noted on the flyleaf of his newly purchased notebook, lest he should ever forget it, were but baits to catch foxes.[55] It was therefore an essential 'part of a sound judgement to receive with a very suspicion whatever is propounded'.[56] And the best policy at all times was to retain a discreet silence, divulging nothing of one's own intent. 'A man at meals and

49. Hunt. MS f. *7. On the importance of Dunbar's patronage, see N. Cuddy, 'The Revival of the Entourage: The Bedchamber of James I, 1603–1625', in D. Starkey, ed., *The English Court from the Wars of the Roses to the Civil War* (1987), pp. 173–225.

50. Hunt. MS f. *12v.

51. Hunt. MS f. *23v. Slingsby was a commissioner for enquiry into fees (*Cal. S. P. Dom. 1629–31*, p. 236) and JP (*Cal. S. P. Dom. 1635*, p. 567). Cf. Clarendon's comment on Weston's relationship with Buckingham, E. Hyde, Earl of Clarendon, *The History of the Rebellion and Civil Wars in England*, ed. W. D. Macray (6 vols, Oxford, 1888), vol. 1, p. 61.

52. e.g. Hunt. MS f. *2 'Acquisito fine cessat motus'; and ff. *20, *25, 31. See below, p. 191.

53. Hunt. MS f. *20; cf. Ogden MS 7/26 f. 23v for the same adage.

54. Hunt. MS f. *25; cf. Ogden MSS 7/7 f. 52; 7/26 f. 26.

55. Hunt. MS f. *1.

56. Hunt. MS f. *3v; cf. f. *7v: 'It is wisdom to suspect all shows and appearances of friendship.'

many meetings', Drake noted, 'should never produce his opinion and judgement of men but jest and talk merrily.'[57] What was called friendship consisted in the 'mutuality of good offices', in exchanging favour for favour.[58] But in a world in which the restless pursuit of acquisition never ceased, even such mutual support could not be relied upon: men feigned respect but betrayed their fellows. 'The names of friendship and religion', he concluded, 'are the two names which the corrupt world borrows to deceive by.'[59]

Any idea that the commonwealth could, in Aristotelian terms, elevate man, or erect a moral community which subordinated private interest to public justice, Drake dismissed as a deception. 'The most crafty, faithless and audacious men', he observed, 'are those that rule the world; the rest are poor dejected people that live under oppression'.[60] Rather than models of virtue, statesmen epitomised the relentless pursuit of ambition by whatever means, or as Drake put it: ' the ordinary foundations of worldly greatness and correspondency: bribery, flattery, prostitution of bodies.'[61] In his own country, Drake saw that might swayed more than right, concurring with his friend Sadler that

> the times were now such that peradventure a couple of mean fellows might have the benefit of law and justice, but if it came between a mean man and a courtier or a great man, the law was but pro forma, to rob a man with the fairer pretence.[62]

Far from advancing the good of their subjects, Machiavellian princes saw that keeping them poor and passive was the best way to secure their obedience.[63] Rather than condemning such behaviour, however, Drake takes it as a given, as the state of nature in which all men, rulers as well as subjects, lived.[64] Nor did he expect things imminently to improve, believing that with bodies politic, as natural bodies, 'things seldom mend till they come to the worst.'[65] For though all princes and states 'labour[ed] for a unity both in church and commonwealth' and sought to suppress those who opposed them, Drake believed that in the end the internal struggles for supremacy were part of the natural course of history.[66] In a startling passage which blends a Florentine cyclical theory of history with observations on the dislocation of rigid hierarchy and the rapid flux of social change in early modern England, he wrote:

57. Hunt. MS f. *16v.
58. Hunt. MS f. *21v.
59. Hunt. MS f. *6.
60. Hunt. MS f. *25.
61. Hunt. MS f. *29v.
62. Hunt. MS f. *6.
63. Hunt. MS f. *36v.
64. Hunt. MS f. *3. He cites Guicciardini: 'there is the rule of justice and there is the practice of princes.'
65. Hunt. MS f. *2.
66. Hunt. MS f. *5.

Citizens denounce country gentlemen and settle in their seats. After two or three descents they consume all in riot. A lawyer buys out his poor client, after a while his client's posterity buys out him and his, so things go round, ebb and flow, and as Machiavelli in his Florentine History observes virtue [and] industry beget prosperity, prosperity begets rest, rest idleness, idleness riot, riot destruction . . .

Such a nadir, however, marked not the death but the rebirth of the state. From destruction, he continued paraphrasing Machiavelli, 'we come to good laws, good laws engender virtuous actions, glory and prosperity, and no dishonour then (as Guicciardini observes . . .) for a flourishing man, city or state to come to ruin nor infelicity to be subject to the law of nature.'[67]

Drake's anglicised Machiavellianism also points to Hobbes's assertion that 'nothing can be immortal which mortals make.'[68] How far Drake had gone down the road to a Hobbesian view of the state by 1636, when he copied the passage quoted, is not certain, though we have suggested that by 1640 he was articulating a Hobbesian philosophy.[69] What is clear is that when he writes of 'virtuous actions', Drake has in mind not the ethics of Aristotle or the Christian commentators, but those qualities of action, determination, sagacity and aggression that Machiavelli meant by 'virtu', the only force with which man could combat the capricious vagaries of fortune.[70]

Fashioning the Self

Drake's was not, then, the worldview of a scholar or intellectual, abstractly musing on men and affairs. As well as 'contemplation' he knew a man must devote himself to 'the life of action and business'.[71] In all aspects of his life, from the most intimate to the most public, he resolved both to follow rules that his reading and observation had taught him and to continue to be 'thoroughly instructed in the secrets of experience'.[72] As a first principle he took it that in a world that consisted of 'nothing but deceit, lying and vanity', the wisest man was he 'that can make most advantage of an occasion offered'.[73]

---

67. Hunt. MS f. *30v.
68. T. Hobbes, *Leviathan*, ed. R. Tuck (Cambridge, 1991), p. 221.
69. See above, pp. 107–8; and below, pp. 237–8.
70. See Machiavelli, *The Prince*, ed. Q. Skinner (Cambridge, 1988), ch. 6. See E. Garver, *Machiavelli and the History of Prudence* (Madison, 1982), esp. chs 5, 6; J. G. A. Pocock, *The Machiavellian Moment: Florentine Political Thought and the Atlantic Republican Tradition* (Princeton, 1975), pp. 166–81, 104–5, 199–203; R. Price, 'The Senses of "Virtu" in Machiavelli', *Europ. Studies Rev.* 3 (1974), pp. 315–45.
71. Hunt. MS f. *1v.
72. Hunt. MS f. *8.
73. Hunt. MS f. *7v.

To take that advantage, it was necessary to be ever wary and suspicious, distrusting all shows of friendship in others, and to treat all interaction with men as an engagement requiring skilful preparation and manoeuvre.[74] Reading (the distillation of past experience) and his own experience taught that in company it was best to say little and note what others said, to disguise one's true intents and feign other ends, sometimes to give way to an adversary to make him more negligent in future.[75] Drake reminded himself that in public life it was best to 'keep an outward correspondency to all', attaching oneself to no faction, and to avoid making comment on religion or great men.[76]

Friends confirmed his view of the world and added valuable counsel. Sadler, with whom he discoursed much about contemporary politics, advised him that 'it was impossible for a man to raise himself out of nothing unless he joined falsehood and plain dealing together.'[77] Mr Andrews offered the observation that in the great, extraordinary courtesy was 'a certain sign of weakness' to be exploited, 'for wanting real sufficiency they are feigned to allure men's good wills with kindness'.[78] Courtesy and retiring modesty were not, Drake himself knew from experience, as well as from Machiavelli, the way to get on in the world: 'I observe that boldness takes with all men and makes men of ordinary parts much respected and hearkened unto.'[79]

William tried to mould his own personality so as to act according to the rules laid down by the Florentines and confirmed by friends and observation. In a brief passage of extraordinary psychological self-analysis, he catalogued the 'weaknesses I observe in myself'.[80] Here we find no spiritual self-examination, no angst at the human failure to attain the Christian ideals of faith, love and charity, but Drake's regret that he was imprudently too free in revealing his views and too inclined to censure the times when 'excusing' (feigning his true opinions and perhaps the truth itself) would better serve his ends.[81] In a world where "tis not depth but pertinacy and an ingenious simplicity and freedom that takes with men', it was better, he felt, to tell them what they wanted to hear.[82] As much as a comment on the times and his peers, Drake's diary was an exercise in fashioning himself (the word is his) as the man of virtue who could triumph over fortune and his fellows.

Securing his own fortune was Drake's predominant goal in the late 1620s and the 1630s, and he evidently approached it boldly and strategically. Disputes arose over his father's intentions as to his estates, and Drake appears to have played a cunning hand even with members of his own family. When he

---

74. Ibid: 'It is wisdom to suspect all shows and appearances of friendship.' Cf. ff. *14v, 31.
75. Hunt. MS ff. *16v, *7v, *15v, *20v, *23v.
76. Hunt. MS ff. *8, *20v.
77. Hunt. MS f. *5v. The two men obviously had similar values. See below, pp. 137–8.
78. Hunt. MS f. *7.
79. Ibid.
80. Hunt. MS f. 27v.
81. Hunt. MS f. 27.
82. Ibid.

learned that his tenure of his estate stood 'very ticklish', he endeavoured to divert potential challenge by replying to those who pressed him to increase his sister's portion that he would do so at his death.[83] And he discussed with Mr Henley devices for settling his estate so that, should he die without issue, his brother would not get possession of it.[84] Drake considered all ways to improve his holdings. He resolved before taking a fine for lands to let them for some years at the commercial value.[85] He was rigorous in pursuing his rights in the manorial court and in fining tenants who failed in their services.[86] He was canny about the sale and purchase of land.[87] As we know from the commonplace books, he also took an active interest in schemes for improvement.[88] Here in his diary, he enters a decision to investigate 'throughout my woods where ground might be turned to pasture', and notes that improved (probably drained) land not worth three shillings an acre rose to twenty shillings when improved.[89] Perhaps too Drake considered that potentially lucrative course for the enhancement of his estate – marriage; for we find, scattered all over his diary, observations about marriage and women, which, to say the least, imply a utilitarian approach to the holy union. Drake did not think that an active man needed to place much importance on a woman's conversation or companionship, as long as she provided the heir to the estate.[90] He heeded the warning of his friend Potts that women who were too clever either overawed or cozened their husband.[91] Like all other matters, a wife had to be assessed as a means to advance Drake's fortune.

By the mid-1630s, though he had considered money-lending and the purchase of an annuity, Drake had concluded that the quickest route to advancement lay through office.[92] The heading in his diary 'Concerning Office' appears between notes dated 1635 and 1636, and in November 1635 he was discussing with Mr Henley the purchase of a place assigned by Sir William Blake to Mr Rolfe in settlement of a debt.[93] As ever he proceeded carefully, noting for example that no office could be held securely without the king's pardon according to a statute of Edward VI.[94] And he considered a wide range of possible purchases. He heard on the grapevine that the clerk of the crown

83. Hunt. MS ff. *24v, *27, 21v.
84. Hunt. MS f. *27. This may be the merchant George Henley; cf. above, p. 93.
85. Hunt. MS f. *4.
86. Hunt. MS f. *36.
87. See, for example, Hunt. MS ff. *25v, *27, *28,*36.
88. Above, pp. 83–4, 89–91.
89. Hunt. MS ff. *9, *27v.
90. Hunt. MS f. *4v.
91. Hunt. MS f. *7v; cf. above, p. 92. Drake also noted in 1634, from Sir Thomas More's *Life*, that 'he would compare the multitude of women . . . unto a bag full of snakes', H. Lords MS 49 f. 27.
92. Hunt. MS f. *9.
93. Hunt. MS f. *29. This does not square with Blake's still holding the office, of Chirographer of the Common Pleas, in 1636. See *Cal. S. P. Dom 1635–6*, p. 226.
94. Hunt. MS f. *12v; see 5 & 6 Edward VI cap. 16, *Statutes of the Realm*, vol. IV, p. 151.

was willing to part with his office and endeavoured to find out more.[95] Mr Potts informed him that the Clerk of Warrants place was to be sold.[96] He bargained with one Sanders over the two lives held in the subpoena office of the Star Chamber, but Sanders held out for £400, which Drake evidently considered too much.[97] He therefore embarked on a long and involved negotiation with Mr Rolfe, and subsequently Sir William Blake, over the place they had bartered, but these dealings too must have ended in stalemate.[98] For eventually in 1636 William Drake purchased from Sir David Cunningham (to whom Charles I had granted it) the reversion of a post in the Fine Office of the Court of Common Pleas.[99] In June 1636 he confided to his diary an unusual prayer: 'please God that I shall come in possession of the reversion of the office I have lately purchased.'[100] In his commonplace books he made, in anticipation, notes of the fees due to the office.[101] Whether or how it contributed to Drake's fortunes, however, we cannot say. During the Commonwealth and Protectorate an interloper took possession of the place and Drake's interest in the reversion was not secured until the Restoration.[102]

As an avid reader of Bacon, Drake also knew that the best way to rise higher was through contacts. And, like the commonplace books, the diary gives a strong impression that he weighed people in terms of their value to him. A frank but chilling page heading, 'The several uses I may make of men', lists various of Drake's acquaintances with his view of the service they could perform for him.[103] Mr Henley was the man to consult about all matters of profit; from Oliver St John he knew he could learn about the Earl of Bedford's profitable improvements and projects; Sir William Slingsby was the one not only 'to acquaint me with the passages of court and state' but also to 'bring me acquainted with the Countess of Exeter and the Duchess or Lord Privy Seal'.[104] Indeed, Drake appears to have used all men with whom he came into contact, either for their knowledge and advice, or for their own contacts in higher places. On the flyleaf of his diary he listed as men from whom to borrow legal manuscripts Mr Cotton (presumably Sir Robert or Sir Thomas), Oliver St John, Mr Hale (perhaps Matthew, later Chief Justice

95. Hunt. MS f. *28.
96. Ibid.
97. Ibid.
98. Hunt. MS ff. *28v, *30.
99. Above, p. 132 n93; G. E. Aylmer, *The King's Servants* (1971), p. 97. See too W. D. Macray, H. D. Coxe and F. J. Routledge, *Calendar of the Clarendon State Papers* (5 vols, Oxford, 1869–1970), vol. 5, pp. 43–4.
100. Hunt. MS f. *31.
101. Ogden MS 7/7 f. 135.
102. Clark, 'Wisdom Literature of the Seventeenth Century: A Guide to the Contents of the "Bacon–Tottel" Commonplace Books. part I', *Trans. Camb. Bibliog. Soc.* 6 (1976), p. 295; *Clarendon State Papers*, vol. 5 pp. 43–4; G. E. Aylmer, *The State's Servants* (1973), p. 98.
103. Hunt. MS f. 27. There is a sublist: 'Persons to be ware of'.
104. Ibid.; see above, pp. 93–4; 128 n51.

of the King's Bench), Misters Barrell, Stevens, Fountaine, Garthon, Smith and Henley, many of whom he may have met at the Inns of Court or through Sir Simonds D'Ewes, his Chamber mate.[105] Drake consulted his Buckinghamshire neighbour John Hampden about estate matters and discussed with him his 'project' – perhaps the Connecticut project of 1632.[106] In London, on Potts's advice, he endeavoured to befriend the aldermen, as a better means even than bribes to advance his ends, and kept notes of the marriages with the gentry they arranged for their daughters.[107] He got to know the Recorder well enough to discuss with him personal financial matters pertaining to his London estates.[108]

But it is clear that Drake's social aspirations were aimed higher than county or metropolitan society. He resolved early in the 1630s to become most 'inward' with those that 'have a general acquaintance and look most into the world'; and through such men as Barrell, St John, Mr Chute (perhaps Richard Shute of Barking Hall) and Mr Fleetwood (possibly the future Recorder) to obtain an entrée to the circles of the court.[109] Certainly Drake took notes in his diary of courtiers such as the Earls of Bridgewater and Worcester and of society marriages like that of Sir John Holland to Lady Sandys.[110] He was keen to learn of court behaviour – Bedford's 'singular way of speaking in a metaphorical way', for example – perhaps in the optimistic expectation that he might need to know how to conduct himself there.[111] Weighing the best patrons to court he noted that Endymion Porter was held to be true to his friends and followers.[112]

It would seem that Drake also took more direct action to bring himself to the notice of the great. In December 1635, while he was still negotiating for office, he gained access to the Archbishop of Canterbury, William Laud, and

105. Hunt. MS front flyleaf. There are no other mentions of several of these. Fountaine could well be John Fountaine of Lincoln's Inn, later sergeant at law; and 'Stevens', Jeremiah Stephens who collaborated with Sir Henry Spelman in historical research (*DNB*).
106. Hunt. MS f. *1. Hampden owned land in Connecticut and may (*pace* Adair) have planned to emigrate. See J. Adair, *A Life of John Hampden the Patriot* (1976), pp. 101–3.
107. Hunt. MS ff. *19v, *26, 4v.
108. Hunt. MS f. *16v.
109. Hunt. MS f. *8v. Mr Chute could be Richard Shute of Barking Hall, with whom Charles I played bowls (Starkey, *English Court*, p. 247), or perhaps Challoner Chute who served on a royal commission (*Cal. S. P. Dom. 1635*, p. 514; *Cal. S. P. Dom. 1635–6*, pp. 240–50). Fleetwood could be Sir Miles Fleetwood, Receiver-General of the Court of Wards, or possibly George Fleetwood, a Buckinghamshire contemporary of Drake (*DNB*).
110. Hunt. MS ff. *13, *16v.
111. Hunt. MS f. *23. Drake's source for this was 'Dr. Burgess', that is John Burgess who was the Countess of Bedford's physician (*DNB*).
112. Hunt. MS f. *31v. Porter was a gentleman of the bedchamber, one of those whom Drake regarded as an entrée to court, and was also involved in drainage projects in 1632. See D. Townshend, *Life and Letters of Mr. Endymion Porter* (1897), p. 160 and passim.

made a present to him of a copy of Bishop Fox's statutes for Corpus Christi College, Oxford, where Laud was chancellor of the university.[113] It may be that such a clever and appropriate gift eased Drake's way into the circles of court and government. We know that the next year he was in touch with Justice Long, one of the commissioners for buildings, and apparently hoping to use Long for his own purposes.[114] Astutely he singled out Edward Hyde as a man influential with the powerful and destined to rise.[115] He evidently entertained at his home Sir Edward Littleton, who became the king's Solicitor-General in 1634.[116] And he discoursed in familiar terms with Sir Humphrey May, Chancellor of the Duchy of Lancaster.[117] Such contacts eventually brought Drake to the notice of the king and to the honour of a baronetcy, which he had sought since at least the mid-1630s.[118] A Buckinghamshire gentleman, he had made good use of those who looked most to the world to raise himself in it.

But it is worth observing that while he sought out councillors and courtiers, Drake was also in frequent contact with men who fell foul of the government during the 1620s and 1630s – with Walter Long, one of the MPs imprisoned after 1629, with William Strode, another of those MPs who also questioned the ship money writs, and with whom Drake tells us he discussed the 'subjects liberty', with Sir Walter Earle who had denounced the Arminians in 1629, with John Hampden 'the patriot' and with Mr 'Pim', future leader of the Long Parliament who in 1632 discussed with him the situation in Europe.[119] Such an eclectic range of acquaintances underlines the point that, despite the suggestions of some recent historiography to the contrary, concerns about government had not hardened into opposition and party lines were not yet drawn during the 1630s. But it also makes it clear that, in addition to his extensive reading in history and politics, Drake's friendships and conversations undoubtedly equipped him to weigh the views of those affiliated with both 'court' and 'country'.[120]

That capacity was further enhanced by a considerable knowledge of the

113. Hunt. MS f. *27v. See above, p. 124 n19.
114. Hunt. MS f. 4. This was George Long, JP for Middlesex, who was a commissioner for buildings (*Cal. S. P. Dom. 1631–3*, p. 58). It seems that some lands Drake inherited from his grandfather ran foul of the commission (Hunt. MS f. *14).
115. Hunt. MS f. 36.
116. Ibid.
117. Hunt. MS f. *16. May confirmed Drake's worldview by advising him to regard every man as a knave until he had experience to the contrary. Drake's scattered notes offer a nice insight into the quest for minor office. He also took advice from 'Mr Dunkum', perhaps a native near neighbour, John Duncombe of Aylesbury, attorney of the King's Bench (*Cal. S. P. Dom 1636–7*, p. 190) or George Duncombe, clerk of the Treasury of the Common Pleas.
118. Hunt. MS f. *31v. Drake noted in June 1636 that the Earl of Stirling had the making of baronetcies.
119. Hunt. MS ff. *4v, *9, *24, 4v. Pym told him that the Duke of Bavaria had entered into an alliance with France.
120. See Hunt. MS f. *23v.

law and legal cases of the 1630s. We do not know why Drake paid such attention to the trials of the decade. As a landowner, it was not surprising that he
should seek to attain some understanding of the land law and manorial courts.
His 'legal business' obviously demanded a general knowledge of the law. It
may have been his quest for an office that prompted his study of the jurisdictions and courts of Chancery, King's Bench, Common Pleas, Exchequer,
Wards and Requests. His interest, however, went far beyond that, for his diary,
like his commonplace books, suggests that he not only annotated from reports
but may also have attended a myriad of trials – in Star Chamber, High Commission and King's Bench.[121] For the most part, the Star Chamber cases Drake
here recorded were not the most contentious or the causes célèbres of the
decade. He read reports or attended the trials of John Reies for imbracery
(corruption) of a juror, of Sir Henry Anderson for oppression of Browne and
others for destroying an enclosure, of Sandford for the illegal export of wool,
of More and others for erecting buildings in St Martin's-in-the-Fields in defiance of the proclamation, and of some who had coined farthing tokens against
the law.[122] In the main, Drake confined his comments on such cases to points
of law: accordingly he recorded the size of the fine imposed on the
Countess of Shrewsbury for refusing to answer on oath;[123] noted that when
a man was served a subpoena from Star Chamber he needed an attorney from
that court to secure a copy of the bill;[124] and observed the fine distinctions
made in coming to judgment.[125]

While he appears to have disapproved of the disadvantage that coming *ore
tenus* presented a defendant, even when he spoke 'much and well for himself'
in general, Drake confides to his diary none of the criticisms of Star Chamber
which some historians might expect.[126] On the contrary, rather than dwelling
on its peculiar jurisdiction or harsh penalties, he appears to have admired both
the court and its judges and to have respected its justice and mercy. In the
case, for example, of a minister 'charged with many foul and enormous
crimes', he was struck by Cottington's 'inclining to favour him' and argument
that 'there wanted particular proof to the several points of the bill'.[127] When

---

121. On f. *1 he instructed himself to attend these courts and noted (ff. *9v-10) their
jurisdictions.
122. Hunt. MS ff. *2, 18, 20, 21, 26. On Anderson's case (25 Jan. 1632), see Huntington
Library Ellesmere MSS 7889, 7891; J. Rushworth, *Historical Collections* (7 vols,
1659–1701), vol. 3, app. 53; *Cal. S. P. Dom. 1631–3*, pp. 442, 519, 536. On Browne
(June 1632) see S. R. Gardiner, ed., *Reports of Cases in the Courts of Star Chamber and
High Commission*, Camden Soc. 39 (1886), p. 148. For Sandford's case (July 1633) see
Rushworth, *Historical Collections*, vol. 3, app. 62. On More (1634) see Ellesmere MS
7909, BL Harleian 7002 f. 1; BL Add. MS 11764 f. 1; Rushworth, *Historical Collections*, vol. 3, app. 66. Cf. H. Lords MS 49; above, pp. 112–13.
123. Hunt. MS f. *8.
124. Hunt. MS f. *15.
125. Hunt. MS ff. *2, 26.
126. Hunt. MS f. 26. This was the case against John More for erecting houses in St
Martin's-in-the-Fields in defiance of the proclamation (*Cal. S. P. Dom. 1633–4*, p. 431).
On the Caroline Star Chamber, see Sharpe, *Personal Rule*, pp. 665–82.
127. Hunt. MS f. *6.

Alexander Gill came before the court for scandalous words against Coventry, Drake thought it remarkable that he got off, with the Lord Keeper himself among the most favourably inclined to leniency.[128] Similarly in the trial in 1633 of Peter Apsley for a libel and challenge to the Earl of Northumberland, Drake was impressed by Northumberland's 'steady, composed temper', 'not to be moved by the rash, exorbitant and base carriage of Apsley'.[129] After reading or attending several such trials, he wrote: 'I observe extraordinary temper and wisdom in the Lord Keeper, Cottington and Heath . . .'[130] Whatever else may have caused him concern during the decade of Charles I's personal rule, his diary gives us little reason to believe that he was alienated by the Star Chamber or the course of royal justice.[131] If we are to understand Drake's joining the critics of royal government in 1641, we must clearly look elsewhere.

Reading Politics

To some of his critics, it was Charles I's foreign policy which had failed the nation. Many, not all of them the godly, felt a sense of shame at England's reluctance to support the champion of Protestantism, Gustavus Adolphus, and the king's failure to secure the restoration to his sister Elizabeth and brother-in-law Frederick of their lands in the Rhenish Palatinate. Some were indeed suspicious of diplomatic negotiations with Spain, which was widely seen as the secular arm of the popish triumph in Europe.[132] William Drake, who travelled in the Low Countries during the 1630s, clearly came into contact with those who articulated such criticisms. He appreciated that Spanish wealth from the Indies had given them overweening power over the 'affairs of Christendom', such that the Conclave of Rome and the Council of Spain were the places 'where all the great actions of Europe are hammered'.[133] In 1632, at a crucial time of debate about foreign policy, Drake's friend Sadler drew his attention to Campanella's advice to the king of Spain to divide France, England and the Low Countries, and to bring in Arminianism as a means of

128. Hunt. MS f. *25. Alexander Gill had been tried for scandalous words against Buckingham (*Cal. S. P. Dom. 1628–9*, p. 319). He was pardoned in November 1630 (*Cal. S. P. Dom. 1629–31*, p. 393). I have found no record of his scandalous words against Coventry.

129. Hunt. MS f. 26v. See *Cal. S. P. Dom. 1633–4*, pp. 442, 464; BL Add. MS 11704 f. 4v; Rushworth, *Historical Collections*, vol. 3, app. 67.

130. Hunt. MS f. 26v.

131. Though cf. below, p. 145.

132. For a recent interesting study of Milton's views, see S. Achinstein 'Milton and King Charles', in T. Corns, ed., *The Royal Image: Representations of Charles I* (Cambridge, 1999), pp. 141–61.

133. Hunt. MS f. *10. Cf H. Lords MS 49 f. 165 where Drake underlines a speech about Spain cozening England and assisting the number of papists.

taking an England the Spanish had always desired to conquer.[134] Sadler denounced both England and France for encouraging the Swedes to enter Germany and then failing to support them. Drake's own view at that time is not expressed. Rather than seeing the conflict in simplistic terms of Catholics versus Protestants, he had an early understanding of the complex alliances and political manoeuvres that cut across denominational lines. Pym discussed with him in 1631 or 1632 the alliance between France and the Duke of Bavaria, an erstwhile ally of the Habsburgs; and Drake does not appear to have been suspicious of Walter Montagu's secret embassy to Rome to treat for the restoration of the Palatinate.[135] But it would seem that Drake was supportive of the Dutch and critical of an English royal policy that, under the guise of neutrality, aided Spain not least in order to check the Netherlanders. On 6 November 1635, amid talk of peace between the Habsburgs and the French and Dutch, he condemned an English policy that had weakened the allies' position. 'Indeed,' he wrote, 'the cause of the Hollanders' miscarriage is in Brabant . . . the not falling on of the French king upon Artois, which was hindered by the strong guard of the frontiers by the Spaniard which they would have been enforced to have withdrawn if our fleet had not stayed the besieging of Dunkirk as the design was . . .'[136] If he admired the strength of the new navy funded by ship money, Drake did not think it put to proper use.[137] And while he appreciated that in the past Queen Elizabeth had insisted on the need to keep Dunkirk open, he did not support a Caroline policy devised, as it has been argued, to prevent a Franco-Dutch dominance of Flanders.[138] Though his diary yields only hints, it may be that Drake shared Sadler's view that Charles dallied too much with the Habsburgs and failed to pursue the vigorous policy that would have secured the Palatinate, along with England's reputation and interests.[139]

In many cases, dissatisfaction with Charles I's foreign policy went hand in hand with a concern about religious developments at home. Some historians have argued that nothing alienated the people of England more from the regime during the 1630s than an emphasis on ceremony and an alleged attack on doctrinal Calvinism by Arminian clerics led by William Laud, Archbishop of Canterbury.[140] Recently, scholars like Peter White have criticised such an analysis of and concentration on doctrine, and argued rather for a broad spectrum of belief and widespread devotion to an Anglican church, independent

134. Hunt. MS f. *10. Drake refers himself to Campanella, see Ogden MS 7/29 f. 35.
135. Hunt. MS ff. *4v, *26.
136. Hunt. MS f. *26. S. R. Gardiner, *History of England from the Accession of James I to the Outbreak of the Civil War* (10 vols, 1884), vol. 8, pp. 100–1; *Cal. S. P. Venet. 1632–6*, pp. xxiii–xxvi.
137. See Hunt. MS f. *24.
138. Hunt. MS f. 36v. See Sharpe, *Personal Rule*, pp. 88–90.
139. Hunt. MS f. *10.
140. See N. Tyacke, *Anti-Calvinists: The Rise of English Arminianism, c.1590–1640* (Oxford, 1987); P. Collinson, *The Religion of Protestants* (Oxford, 1982).

of Geneva as of Rome.[141] Others have suggested that it was an enhancement of clerical wealth and authority, rather than doctrine, that most caused offence and gave rise to discontent with the church.[142] From his commonplace books, we learn in general that Drake was little interested in doctrinal dispute and inclined to value the church most as the cement of the commonweal.[143] In the diary, we are offered far more insight into his response to the Laudian era and the religious divisions of the 1630s. Though he was the child of godly parents, what we do not learn is anything about his personal piety. Drake's diary is quite unusual in its silence about matters of conscience or faith: his only recorded prayer is to succeed to the office the reversion of which he purchased![144] It is tempting, therefore, to conclude that William's reading in the classical and politic histories favoured a secular, Erastian spirit, that humanist learning shaped him more than did Scripture or the teachings of the church. By the end of his life he may even have become a deist.[145] But, whatever the nature of his private faith, Drake and his friends discussed the religious issues of the decade and Drake held a clear view of what the Church of England was and should be.

By the end of the 1630s there can be no doubt that there was a mounting paranoia about popery and even the beginning of a suspicion that papists infected the court and royal counsels.[146] Drake's diary makes it clear that, like most of his contemporaries, he remained ever suspicious of Rome and her plots, and wary too of the Catholics in England. He noted the intolerance of Catholic countries which never permitted Englishmen dying abroad to have a 'Christian' (that is Protestant) burial.[147] He believed that the Conclave of Rome plotted to introduce the Inquisition into all countries in order to advance papal power.[148] Unlike James I himself, Drake was convinced that many English Catholics were in some way implicated in the Gunpowder Plot: 'for there was not one great papist in England but knew of it and had either his head for projecting or his heart for praying for the success thereof.'[149] In 1633 he attended the arraignment in King's Bench of a Dominican friar

---

141. P. White, *Predestination, Policy and Polemic: Conflict and Consensus in the English Church from the Reformation to the Civil War* (Cambridge, 1992); cf. Sharpe, *Personal Rule*, ch. 6. There has been no full response to these accounts. Tyacke repeats his case with no further evidence in 'Anglican Attitudes: Some Recent Writings on English Religious History from the Reformation to the Civil War', *J. Brit. Studies* 25 (1996), pp. 139–67.

142. A. Foster, 'The Clerical Estates Revitalised', in K. Fincham, ed., *The Early Stuart Church 1603–1642* (Houndmills, 1993), pp. 139–60; cf. Sharpe, *Personal Rule*, pp. 392–402.

143. Above, pp. 110–11.

144. Hunt. MS f. *31. Cf. E. Boucier, *Les Journaux privés en Angleterre de 1600 à 1660* (Paris, 1976), ch. 6.

145. See below, pp. 230–1.

146. See C. Hibbard, *Charles I and the Popish Plot* (Chapel Hill, 1983).

147. Hunt. MS f. 20v.

148. Hunt. MS f. *2.

149. Hunt. MS f. *5v; cf. above, p. 109.

charged with telling Englishmen in Lisbon that, if he could get the chance, he would kill King Charles.[150] Yet for all this, Drake's suspicion of the Catholics never developed into hysteria. At the trial of the priest he noted, with approval, that 'both the Chief Justice and Attorney laboured to satisfy all that he suffered not for his conscience or for any point of the Romish religion but merely for treason.'[151] And he applauded the skill of Queen Elizabeth in appointing secret Catholics to high office and even to her Privy Council so that she could diminish their reputation and bring others to conform.[152] Drake disliked and distrusted the loyalty of the Catholics, but there is no evidence in his journal that he feared that they were gaining the ascendancy or that England was 'going to Rome'.

Nor does he appear at least initially to have been greatly troubled in his conscience by the renewed emphasis on ceremony and ritual in the Caroline church. At a High Commission trial of a nonconformist lecturer, for example, he noted that Laud, then Bishop of London, argued 'that the Eastern and Western church, ever since the primitive church . . . had used *mensa* and *altare* promiscuously'; and added: 'and so our own statutes and canons have ever since Edward VI times'.[153] As for the controversy over kneeling, he could not understand the fuss: 'the superstition of kneeling at the communion being taken away by a public declaration of the state, I see not why men should refuse it.'[154] As we shall see, William held it right for the state to rule in such matters and was inclined to disfavour any who disobeyed. In general, he tended to associate the trend to greater ceremonialism not with a design to move towards Rome but with the clergy's ambitious desire for aggrandisement, under a new monarch. 'In King James' time', he recalled in 1633, 'the court preachers chose texts for peace, as follow peace etc. . . . but now they see that the times incline to superstition they preach for the outward pomp and glory of the church, the splendour and outward beauty of the church they much advance.'[155]

Drake's use of the term 'superstition' expresses a distaste which may have increased as the decade wore on. In 1641, he was to record an incident reported to the Commons of a wooden image being brought into a country church where the congregation fell down in worship before it.[156] However, the campaign for conformity in matters ceremonial he attributed not to an Arminian plot to lead the church to Rome but to the clergy's desire for power:

---

150. Hunt. MS f. 25. The friar was Anthony Geoghagen, not Arthur as Drake writes. For his examination see *Cal. S. P. Dom. 1633–4*, p. 28.
151. Hunt. MS f. 25.
152. Hunt. MS f. ★2; cf. Ogden MS 7/45 f. 182; above, p. 110.
153. Hunt. MS f. 20v.
154. Hunt. MS f. ★2v.
155. Hunt. MS f. ★22.
156. Hunt. MS f. 36v; see too appendix below, p. 162.

The bishops press things of indifferency with so much eagerness because it is a means to uphold their courts, and because they think the preciser sort of men are the greatest enemies to the riches and glory of the clergy who still call for the imitation of Christ and his Apostles in their humility and poverty . . .[157]

That call may have struck a chord with Drake who had little time for clerical pretensions. He thought ambitious divines preached their 'superiors' humours' rather than their 'own conscience'.[158] Rather than sharing Abbot's and Laud's sense that it was the 'poverty and beggary of ministers' that caused problems, Drake probably shared his friend's view that when ploughing, weeding, reaping, and servants' wages were factored in, the parson's tithe was more like a fifth of every man's property.[159] Despite his obvious respect for ambition and the vigorous pursuit of wealth and power, Drake did not value such qualities or behaviour in the clergy, whose enhancement, he felt, weakened the church and therefore the state.

Yet if Drake shared with the puritans a disdain for clerical pomp, in no other respect was he in sympathy with them. From the commonplace books we sensed Drake's disdain for puritan hypocrisy.[160] Here in his diary, in a rare comment of a doctrinal nature, he observed that some claimed foresight for themselves as if to appropriate God's judgement − a coded criticism of those who claimed providential direction or inspiration over the authority of the church.[161] When he attended the trial of Nathaniel Barnard in High Commission, Drake noted that the defendant had heretically distinguished the substance of God's ordinance and the purity. But it was the charge of sedition, of Barnard's threat to the stability of church and state, that most commanded his attention. Drake noted Laud's fear that such a man preaching at St Dunstan's might 'corrupt those fountains' of the Inns of Court nearby. He copied the speech of one of the doctors who said 'that there was none of Barnard's faction but carries a democracy in his belly.'[162] Whether he went all the way with such a view is not clear. Other extracts are suggestive of Drake's views at the time. He annotated the trial of the feoffees for impropriations without comment;[163] though he probably shared Secretary Coke's dislike for images in windows, he appears to have disapproved of Henry Sherfield's acting 'out of his own private humour and fancy';[164] Prynne, he believed, was

157. Hunt. MS f. ★4.
158. Hunt. MS f. ★5.
159. Drake reports Abbot's speech in High Commission (f. 22v). See f. ★32.
160. Above, pp. 109–10.
161. Hunt. MS f. ★23v.
162. Hunt. MS ff. 20–20v. *Cal. S. P. Dom. 1631–3*, p. 335; *Cal. S. P. Dom. 1633–4*, p. 480; appendix below, p. 159.
163. Hunt. MS f. ★14, except to note the Attorney's charge that they endeavoured to control 'the disposing of most burgesses' places'. Cf. Ogden MS 7/7 f. 145v; above, p. 109.
164. Hunt. MS f. 21. Cf above, p. 109.

pilloried for 'writing a scandalous book', but noted – perhaps sympathetically
– 'he took his punishment patiently.'[165] Drake may have shared his friend
Potts's view that the puritan was 'a weak, busy, angry creature but not dangerous'.[166] For Potts told him of his chamber fellow who had joined the puritans 'to be part of a party and so maintain his credit'. Yet, as Drake noted, a
puritan could not maintain his credit with his fellows and comply with
the law; and in that sense they were rightly held to be enemies to the
commonwealth.[167]

In recent years, Professor Collinson and others have suggested that Laud
created the very problem of seditious puritanism he feared, that had he left
the godly unmolested they would have continued as loyal members of the
church, not become the fifth column he believed them to be.[168] Here a
passage from Drake's diary at the end of 1631 is of particular interest as evidence that a man little in sympathy with Laud or ceremonialism was at one
with him in the threat presented to the church by a party – papist or puritan
– manoeuvring from within:

> The church papist and the church puritan are the most dangerous of all,
> the one to the church government and ceremonies, and the other to the
> whole frame of the religion established, for their conformity to the laws
> adds strength to either whereas those that are professed opposites either to
> the religion itself or to the discipline established, the stream and tide of the
> laws running against them, they are still subject to them [laws] and are
> bruited to be turbulent and schismatical and seditious which doth some-
> what diminish that reputation which might be useful in the instilling of
> their opinions into others, whereas the other [i.e. the church puritans and
> papists] may do their work boldly.[169]

For all his disinclination to superstition, therefore, Drake believed in obedience – obedience to a Church of England which he conceived was as best
constructed as was possible to sustain the stability of government. For him,
this was the principal role of religion:

> In all states, religion hath still been made a great art of government, and
> surely the form of our discipline in the English church is framed with as
> much policy of any other whatsoever, for 'tis framed *of such a middle temper*

165. Hunt. MS f. *25. This was Prynne's trial for publishing *Histriomastix*. See J. Bruce and
     S. R. Gardiner, eds, *Documents Relating to the Proceedings Against William Prynne in 1634
     and 1637*, Camden Soc. (1877).
166. Hunt. MS f. *12. John Potts was a moderate, elevated to the baronetcy with Drake
     in 1641. See D. Brunton and D. H. Pennington, *Members of the Long Parliament* (1954),
     p. 75.
167. Hunt. MS f. *12. The Chamber fellow was Edward 'Ipelway'. Potts (or Drake) added
     'and so Sir Francis Barrington . . .'
168. Collinson, *Religion of Protestants*, passim.
169. Hunt. MS f. *2.

that it is not so directly opposite to the discipline of the Roman Church so that there is the better correspondency kept with foreign states . . .[170]

Drake's portrait of the Church of England not only underlines the large measure of realpolitik in his attitude to religious policy, domestic and foreign. It is also a sketch of the very nature of an Anglicanism the existence of which Professor Collinson and Dr Tyacke have denied. If, as we have seen from the commonplace books, Drake disliked Laud, it was because, against the spirit of the church, the archbishop upset the peace it was intended to preserve.[171] But it is unlikely that Drake felt the Caroline church in need of radical reformation, let alone a lopping of root and branch. In 1640, at the end of Hilary term, he attended the address given by Lord Keeper Finch to the justices about to go on assize. After reflections on the foreign situation and the threats to English security, Finch turned to religion. Identifying two threats to the church and state, Finch exhorted the judges to use their authority against both papists and separatists. For England, he continued, had enjoyed peace and prosperity thanks to the flourishing of the gospel. He recalled the statute I Eliz. cap. 2 that compelled all to come to church and urged its enforcement. How could any be reluctant to attend the services of the church and Common Prayer, he asked, 'when that book was penned by the care of such as shed their blood as martyrs and sealed their religion with their lives'.[172] If the language was more passionate than Drake's, the call to unity and obedience to the Anglican church reassuringly echoed his own beliefs.

While, apart from the occasional, undated, remark, Drake's commonplace books are largely silent about the politics of the 1630s, his diary, by contrast, is vocal on a number of matters. In general we will not be surprised to discern in his comments a general cynicism about the court and the government. Drake recorded the purchase and sale of office at court, and expressed his suspicion that the custom of presenting great men with New Year gifts was another form of bribery in a milieu where everything was for sale.[173] Courtiers he regarded as grasping and rapacious, ever ready to exploit the law for their personal gain. Presumably with purveyance in mind, he urged the importance of exact accounts at a time when 'King's servants are apt to take advantage of the rising and falling of commodities and to cozen.'[174] The king's programme for reform of abuses did not dispel his doubts about official dishonesty. Rather he suspected initiatives like the commission to inquire

---

170. Hunt. MS f. *9. My italics.
171. Above, pp. 108–11.
172. Hunt. MS f. 33. This is evidently Finch's first charge to the Assize judges as Lord Keeper. See Bodleian Rawlinson MS D720 f. 51. J. Nalson, *An Impartial Collection of the Great Affairs of State from the Beginnings of the Scotch Rebellion in 1639 to the Murder of Charles I* (2 vols, 1682–3), vol. 1, pp. 286–9.
173. Hunt. MS ff. *13, *26v. He described the presentation of New Year gifts as 'a thing of course for offices'.
174. Hunt. MS f. *22v. On Caroline purveyance, see Sharpe, *Personal Rule*, pp. 109–11.

into fees were truly intended, as so many government reforms, to distract attention from the real culprits at the top: 'the commission that sit about fees no doubt aim not at reformation, only they think that questioning the officers will be a thing very plausible to the people, for if their aims were reformation they would begin at home'![175]

As for court masques and such entertainments, which Charles I saw as a principal medium for the dissemination of his ideals of order and harmony, Drake disparaged them as expensive shows ill fitting the times. When in 1633, the Inns of Court were preparing a grand masque, *The Triumph of Peace*, in order to reingratiate themselves with the king after Prynne's injudicious attack on such entertainments, Drake doubted the wisdom of the gesture. Though, he acknowledged, 'the vulgar did much rejoice, saying that it showed the honour of the kingdom, and that it would much ingratiate the Inns of Court with the king and court', he concurred with those 'men of judgement' who were afraid that if the masque disappointed them, 'the courtiers would be apt to scoff at the gentlemen, of which scoffs may be bred ill blood.'[176] If, on the other hand, it were a splendid success, the Inns would only attract envy at their wealth and talent. *The Triumph of Peace* was in fact so well received that Charles and Henrietta asked for a 'double view' of the procession and a second performance of the whole entertainment the next week.[177] But the vast cost – at £20,000 ten times the average for a masque – recruited William Drake to the ranks of those 'wise men' who 'wished a greater gravity and moderation in them than to give way to the spending of so great sums of money which might have been reserved for better uses'. And he added, 'neither did the condition of the present time befit such shows of magnificence, our neighbour countries being all in combustion about us and his Majesty's only sister and her children wanting money to keep and preserve their country from the spoil of their enemies.'[178] Against the king's philosophy of neo-Platonism, Drake clearly distinguished image from reality, indeed saw representation as a distraction from action. Moreover, he had little faith in the capacity of masque, as some hoped of the *Triumph*, to counsel the king about the abuses of his policies by corrupt servants.[179] 'The king is very fast to his servants and settled to what he undertakes,' he entered in 1631, 'therefore there is no way but compliance.'[180]

That term 'compliance' indicates an unease not only with royal policies, but with the authority that enforced them. And it is unease that echoes

175. Hunt. MS f. *3v. See G. E. Aylmer, 'Charles I's Commission on Fees 1627–1640', *Bull. Inst. Hist. Res.* 31 (1958), pp. 58–67.

176. Hunt. MS f. *22v. On *The Triumph of Peace* see K. Sharpe, *Criticism and Compliment: The Politics of Literature in the England of Charles I* (Cambridge, 1987), pp. 214–23. It is worth noting Drake's observation that the common people took delight in what is usually regarded as an elite spectacle.

177. Sharpe, *Criticism and Compliment*, p. 221.

178. Hunt. MS f. *22v. Princess Elizabeth had recently been widowed.

179. Sharpe, *Criticism and Compliment*, pp. 219–20.

180. Hunt. MS f. *3.

through several other entries in Drake's journal, over matters small and large. Drake recorded, for example, a conversation with Oliver St John in which the latter observed that Castlehaven's crime was wrongly made buggery when no penetration had occurred.[181] He noted that undersheriffs were being punished for not returning more names of those liable to knighthood fines, and copied Hyde's opinion that the statute that compelled men to take on apprentices was invalid.[182] Drake himself observed the disadvantage that befell a defendant, who had erected houses against the king's proclamation, when he appeared in Star Chamber on an *ore tenus*.[183] And he suspected, after attending another case, against the Bishop of Durham's registrar for extortion, that 'they will make the court of Star Chamber supply the king's wants by executing the penal statutes.'[184] Overall, Drake felt that the royal prerogative was being stretched by Charles I in order to enhance the king's revenues. Noting the new royal instructions for wards, he commented:

> the King having passed away so many lands he is feign to relieve his servants out of the Court of Wards, which makes wardships to be enhanced, and now if they set a high rent upon the land, if you complain and tell them tis against the king's instructions, they say King James his instructions do not bind our King, *but he may do as he pleases*.[185]

In the case against the soapboilers, whom Cottington, he noted, compared to 'mutineers', Drake observed too how proclamations, the device for the introduction of so many fiscal expedients in the 1630s, were being termed by the judges themselves 'leges temporis', the laws of the time.[186]

Such developments led Drake to listen sympathetically to those who argued that there was a dangerous tendency in Caroline government to extol the prerogative at the expense of the subjects' liberty and property. After a conversation with Oliver St John, about one proclamation ordering the nobility to return to their rural estates, Drake copied out his friend's sinister reading of an apparently innocuous proposal:

> the pretence of the proclamation is to compel the gentlemen of quality to live in their countries that the poor may be relieved and justice duly administered, but the secret of state is conceived to be under so fair a colour to punish the breach of a proclamation and so induce them by degrees to be as laws and to govern by them. Furthermore by meeting at London,

181. Hunt. MS f. *11.
182. Hunt. MS f. *3, 23. See Sharpe, *Personal Rule*, pp. 112–16, 467–70.
183. Hunt. MS f. 26. More claimed he had sued out a pardon.
184. Hunt. MS f. *17. For the case John Richardson v. Richard Newhouse, registrar of the consistory court of the Bishop of Durham, see *Cal. S. P. Dom 1633–4*, p. 280.
185. Hunt. MS f. *19v, my italics. On wardships, see Sharpe, *Personal Rule*, p. 108.
186. Hunt. MS f. *17.

gentlemen of quality are made more active, and by counselling one another grow more resolute to understand any projects that might be set on foot.[187]

Mr 'Strode' – if this was William they were utterances from prison – was even stronger in his denunciations of assaults on liberty. 'The authority of all arbitrary jurisdictions', Drake records him declaiming, 'strengthened and increased daily' and 'invasions [were] made upon the common law by commitment from the forementioned jurisdictions, so that men [being] chosen by the king to those places, the whole power of all is like to rest with the king.'[188] Such sentiments from two such champions of popular liberties and parliaments are only to be expected. But Drake began to share their concern. The appointment of William Noy as Attorney seemed to confirm the view of those who feared that defenders of the subject's liberty 'might be taken off and made for the king's prerogative'.[189] His own experience further bore out such forebodings. When houses inherited from his grandfather fell foul of the commission for buildings, Drake placed it in a larger constitutional context: 'it is of dangerous consequence in a state when men's persons and estates are drawn under arbitrary jurisdictions and not suffered to have a free trial by law.'[190] Doubtless it was to correct the abuses of such unaccountable commissions that he took the view that by the common law of England the king should call a parliament once a year.[191]

Before, however, we align Drake with those opponents of the personal rule who awaited their opportunity to force the king to call another parliament, we should recall not only his sense of the necessity of 'compliance'. For despite some obvious misgivings, he retained, as we have seen, some respect for Star Chamber jurisdiction and judges, which distances him from those who opposed it on principle. Moreover, whatever his regard for the law and the privileges of parliament, Drake retained a conviction about the need for a prerogative power in the crown. 'A prince', he argued, almost in anticipation of the king's judges in the ship money case in 1638, 'cannot be tied and bound by such strict rules by his positive laws, but you must leave somewhat to his discretion, as if an army should suddenly land, would you have him stay to assemble the three estates to levy money to pay the soldiers?'[192] And

---

187. Hunt. MS f. *20. D'Ewes thought the proclamation compelling the gentry to leave London 'took away men's liberties at one blow', *The Autobiography and Correspondence of Sir Simonds D'Ewes*, ed. J. D. Halliwell (2 vols, 1845), vol. 1, p. 79.

188. Hunt. MS ff. *9v–10. Drake's entry can be dated to 1632; Strode was imprisoned after the 1629 session of parliament and remained confined until 1640.

189. Hunt. MS f. *2. Noy, who was an ardent defender of the royal prerogative, had been a leading spokesman for the liberty of the subject in the parliament of 1628. He was appointed Attorney on 27 Oct. 1631. Another anonymous correspondent reported that Noy had come 'on our side' (*Cal. S. P. Dom. 1631–3*, p. 193).

190. Hunt. MS f. *14; above, p. 135.

191. Hunt. MS f. *12v.

192. Ibid. See T. Hargrave, *A Complete Collection of State Trials* (11 vols, 1776–81), vol. 1, pp. 544–62. Drake's entry was written before 1633.

in contrast to Professor Cogswell, Drake had a less optimistic and more real-istic sense of a parliament's willingness to pay for war or defence:

> Our people in this kingdom make great brag about what charge they would be at in a parliamentary way either in defence of our own land by main-taining a navy, or by maintaining an army in foreign parts, but if the king and parliament should comply and the parliament give liberally and con-stantly in pursuance of their own projects, they would no doubt in a short time grow weary of the charge and be . . . stark cold.[193]

When in 1634, he praised the royal navy and the king's resolve to increase it, Drake may already have known that it was to be financed by ship money.[194] His love of liberty, law and parliaments, and his sense of the need for strong government at home and abroad, made William Drake not the obvious future Parliamentarian, let alone a champion of revolution, but a typical gentleman of the 1630s, concerned at some developments and policies, yet committed to conservative and moderate courses – in the state as well as the church.[195]

The Scottish troubles therefore came to Drake as a shock rather than an opportunity. His first recorded reaction to events in the north came late, in the spring of 1639, as the English armies were marching north and the pam-phlet war was still raging. Drake then 'heard by certain intelligence that the Scotch published a Remonstrance March the 22nd 1638 [1639] in answer to the proclamation published with us February 27th . . .'[196] In response to the king's *Declaration* informing his subjects of 'the seditious practices of some in Scotland, seeking to overthrow our regal power under false pretences of reli-gion', the Scots published a vindication, *The Remonstrance of the Nobility, Barons, Burgesses, Ministers and Commons within the Kingdom of Scotland* which was 'industriously spread by their friends all over England'.[197] Drake obviously obtained a copy and read it carefully.[198] Far, however, from being swayed by Scotch propaganda, he thought the *Remonstrance* full of 'foul' passages, which he copied into his journal. Drake noted the Scots' charge that the prelates had sought 'cunningly to insert the image of their hierarchies into the king's

---

193. Hunt. MS f. ★4; cf. T. Cogswell, *The Blessed Revolution: English Politics and the Coming of War, 1621–1624* (Cambridge, 1989).

194. Hunt. MS f. ★24: 'The king's navy was never in better plight than at this present and the king is resolved to build two new ships every year . . .' The entry precedes notes dated May 1634; the ship money writ was issued in October but debated over the winter and spring of 1633–4. See Sharpe, *Personal Rule*, pp. 545–52.

195. Cf. Sharpe, *Personal Rule*, pp. 690–702.

196. Hunt. MS f. 30. See *The Remonstrance of the Nobility, Barons, Burgesses, Ministers, and Commons within the Kingdom of Scotland* (1639).

197. J. Larkin, ed., *Stuart Royal Proclamations II: Royal Proclamations of King Charles I, 1625–1646* (Oxford, 1983), pp. 662–7, at p. 665.

198. He does not state his source but Oliver St John with whom he was in contact had much Scottish material (see Bedfordshire R. O., St John of Bletsoe MSS). However, the pamphlet was widely available and several copies survive.

image' and the Covenanters' claim to have 'learned to honour the king without acknowledging their [the bishops'] abjured tyranny'.[199] He transcribed their boast that, aside from the prelates and atheists, 'the whole kingdom stands in defence of this cause . . . men of religion, wisdom, and power.'[200] And he copied out their charge that the Archbishop of Canterbury had plotted to make 'Romish' the religion of first Scotland, then England. *The Remonstrance*, the longest text written into Drake's journal, closed with a vindication of liberty and religion, and with a radical distinction drawn between obedience to a just and to an ill-counselled king:

> And where 'tis asked in the proclamation what we will defend we answer not our disobedience but our religion, liberties and lives and where 'tis asked against whom we will defend, we desire this distinction may be made and difference put between the king resident in the kingdom and by opening his ears to both parties rightly informed and the king far from us in another kingdom hearing one party and misinformed by our adversaries . . .[201]

Such a distinction was not to be made in England until the eve of the Civil War and the defence of the militia ordinance.[202] Whatever his own disdain for some of the prelates, Drake was evidently stunned by the treasonous separation of church and state in the Scots' vindication. But it would appear that – typically of his assiduous appetite for knowledge – he endeavoured to learn more. For also early in 1639 he borrowed from 'John' – almost certainly Oliver St John – another pamphlet on the 'pretended causes used in King James his time for introduction of bishops in Scotland'.[203] The author depicted James VI manoeuvring cunningly to instil bishops in Scotland so as to augment his authority over the Kirk and parliament and to ingratiate himself with the English. Thereafter, the tract claimed, the king by degrees succeeded in instituting the High Commission and rigged the assembly in order to pass the Five Articles of Perth which were 'pressed violently', enforced through High Commission and ratified in parliament. Drake makes no comment on the text he summarises. From it, however, he learned – unlike some modern historians – that the policies of Charles I in Scotland differed little from those of his father, who had attempted to secure his authority through control of the Kirk.[204] We do not know whether Drake, with some modern commentators, blamed Charles for not proceeding by 'steps and

199. Hunt. MS f. 30.
200. Ibid.
201. Hunt. MS f. 31. Drake paraphrases the first part of the passage and quotes the second half accurately. See *Remonstrance*, p. 24.
202. See S. R. Gardiner, *Constitutional Documents of the Puritan Revolution* (Oxford, 1889), pp. 175–8.
203. Hunt. MS f. 32v; see above, p. 147 n198.
204. John Morrill makes this point in 'A British Patriarchy? Ecclesiastical Imperialism under the Early Stuarts', in A. Fletcher and P. Roberts, eds, *Religion, Culture and Society in Early Modern Britain* (Cambridge, 1994), pp. 209–37.

degrees'.[205] But it is clear that he admired the Machiavellian tactics deployed by James to secure his ends – 'the fair face . . . put on things . . . to allure consent and keep off opposing' – and was out of sympathy with the Scots' 'foul' railings against an authority which James had established.[206]

There are no entries in Drake's diary concerning the campaign waged against the Scots and the failure of arms in 1639. However, when Charles summoned the Short Parliament in the spring of 1640 to appeal for assistance against the rebels, Drake, taking his seat as MP for the first time, paid careful heed to the king's case. Speaking for Charles, on 13 April, Lord Keeper Finch dwelt on the benefit of union to the Scots and their treasonable dealings with the King of France.[207] Evidently Drake was not in the Upper House when the letter penned by the Covenanters to Louis XIII was read by order of the king; for a few days later, on 17 April, Drake noted Windebank's reading the letter with Lord Loudun's excuse that he had not understood the French when he agreed to be one of the signatories – a defence which Drake dismissed because 'it was very unlikely considering the wisdom of the man.'[208] Besides his recording the king's desire to have tonnage and poundage in a legal way, William took no other notes of proceedings in that brief and abortive parliament (ill. 6).

During the following weeks, cryptic entries give only a glimpse of how he reacted to events in a heady period when many moderate men like himself pondered their position. He probably sympathised with the views he noted of a friend who criticised the clergy for lapsing from their primitive sanctity and integrity.[209] But Mr Henley's caution that it was dangerous to draw together a discontented multitude confirmed Drake's own fears, and reinforced his determination to find a course towards settlement when parliament was resummoned in November.[210]

During the Long Parliament, Drake kept a record of speeches and discussions covering the period from January to June 1641.[211] His diary, like those months, is dominated by the proceedings against the Earl of Strafford – from trial for treason to Act of Attainder. But Drake was also privy to the deliberations of the committees for vintners, lords lieutenant, monopolies and the relief of the north.[212] The only direct evidence in the diary of his own activity is of his speech on taking the Protestation on 3 May, when he pressed

---

205. Hunt. MS f. 32v. Drake did, however, copy the Duke of Lennox's speech to Charles I, reminding him that kings of profound judgement, such as Drake's own heroes Henry VII and Louis XI, had considered it no derogation of their greatness to yield to subjects' demands even when they were unreasonable. H. Lords MS 49 f. 38.
206. Hunt. MS f. 31v. Drake uses adjectives like 'warily', and describes James as 'concealing his design'.
207. See L. J. IV, pp. 45–9.
208. Hunt. MS f. *35; see C. J. II, pp. 4–5.
209. See Hunt. MS f. *36; below, p. 162.
210. Hunt. MS f. *36.
211. J. Jansson, ed., Two Diaries of the Long Parliament (Gloucester, 1984), pp. 1–73; see appendix below, pp. 158–63.
212. Jansson, Two Diaries, pp. xv, 1, 4, 6, 8, 14, 15, 16.

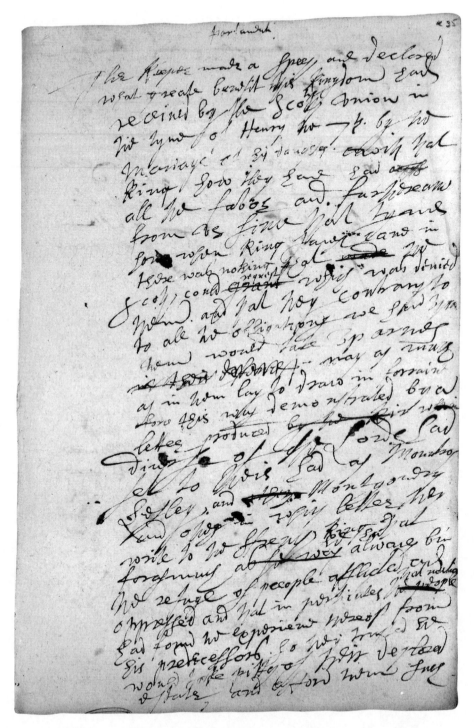

6. From Drake's diary during the Short Parliament, spring 1640.

the need for money and urged that the preamble denounce, as well as popish recusants, all other 'innovators . . . without an authority of parliament'.[213] By May 1641, William had become concerned about the 'illegal taxations' and 'superstitions' in the church listed in the Protestation, and committed to a course to reform them.[214] Drake sat on the Committee for Privileges and the committee for an act to remove the clergy from temporal office.[215] They confirm his sense of the importance of parliament and his anti-clericalism. In his journal in the Huntington Library, which must be read alongside his parliamentary diary, we find him annotating Pym's recollection that Archbishop Abbot had warned the clergy not to overstretch their power: 'for they already had many enemies and few friends and seeking to grasp more they should make all their enemies'.[216] Still wedded, however, to the church, Drake spurned a group of Brownists examined by the house as 'silly tradesmen transported with an irregular humour and fancy'.[217] Besides religion, the journal shows William taking a close interest in the investigation of abuses in trade and corruption in the courts: 'frequent these committees,' he instructed himself in his usual fashion, 'and take notes as also and especially where the report is made to the whole house . . .'; and he reminded himself to observe the circumstances of all offences where the 'ground is profit'.[218]

During the late spring and summer, Drake appears to have been most interested in the negotiations for paying off the Scots and disbanding their army. He noted Secretary Vane's warning that it would be an 'extreme disadvantage to let them get inch by inch upon us' and the need hastily to secure from the Scots a date for their withdrawal.[219] But at a time when settlement was in prospect, and moderate members were praising 'the wisdom of the king and parliament in reducing the kingdom from that forlorn estate [to] which the counsels of some ill ministers had brought it to some tolerable condition again', another disaster struck.[220] On 9 June Drake entered into his journal the details of 'a great plot against the state' – a scheme to land French forces and engage the army against parliament, known to history as the Army Plot.[221] As with his parliamentary diary, the notes in Drake's journal break off in June, and it may be that he drifted away, as MPs increasingly did during that summer, leaving the House by August barely quorate. We are left to guess in what frame of mind he left the first long session of parliament he had

---

213. Ibid., pp. 40–1.
214. Ibid., p. 41; see appendix below, p. 162.
215. C. J. II, pp. 21, 99. These are the only committees to which the *Commons Journal* shows Drake officially appointed.
216. Hunt. MS f. *37.
217. Hunt. MS f. *38v. Drake dated this note 10 June but the *Commons Journal* indicates no such examination in the House.
218. Hunt. MS f. *38. The note supports other indications that Drake was attending committees to which he was not officially appointed.
219. Hunt. MS ff. *39–*39v.
220. Hunt. MS f. *40.
221. Jansson, *Two Diaries*, p. 43; see Russell, *Fall of the British Monarchies*, ch. 7.

attended. Clearly, along with most MPs, he felt that there were abuses in church and state which parliament should correct and reform. But, also along with a growing number, he may have begun to feel some frustration at the slow progress in passing bills and the tardiness in dealing with the Scots. 'If we observe the parliamentary proceedings,' he wrote, 'how slowly they go on in business of weight, and when they make a law they make it in the way of probation as till the next parliament.'[222]

Along with his frustration, we sense too a suspicion of some leaders of the Commons. Ever the cynical observer of political manoeuvre and posture, Drake observed in the House that 'the ablest men showed a contrary affection to their natural inclination.'[223] When Strafford requested that his petition to the House be read, Drake noted that Vane 'though fiercely against him was much for the reading of it, meaning thereby to show his own moderation'.[224] Such suspicions were to grow in the second session, as Drake came to see clearly that no less than the court, parliament itself was another stage for personal vendetta, factional division and ambitious striving, described in the Florentines he had studied.

Soon after the second session convened, on 20 October, news was delivered to the House of the outbreak of the rebellion in Ireland. It was to be the event that hardened divisions, as the issue of trust in the king was thrown into sharp focus by the need to raise an army to suppress the rebels. Could Charles be trusted to adhere to the reforming statutes he had passed, or were more fundamental constitutional changes required to secure liberty, property and Protestantism? Where Sir Edward Hyde was inclined to believe that at home 'all particulars were in a good condition', Pym was (necessarily) determined on further reformation.[225] On 8 November, to win public support, he brought into the House his Grand Remonstrance, a polemical catalogue of all the ills of the Caroline government and a demand that the king substitute for his evil counsellors such as 'the parliament may have cause to confide in'.[226]

A speech that Drake printed and claimed to have delivered on 10 November belongs to this context.[227] Sir William, as he had become in July, began with a recognition of the ills that had beset church and state in the absence of parliaments – 'superstition and innovation', 'illegal taxations, imprisonments, monopolies'. He accepted that such disturbances arose from the

---

222. Hunt. MS f. *36v.
223. Hunt. MS f. *38v.
224. Jansson, *Two Diaries*, p. 25.
225. Russell, *Fall of the British Monarchies*, p. 413. Drake noted that Pym proposed Clotworthy, who had been a vital witness against Strafford, for a command in the army, Hunt. MS f. *40.
226. The text is in Gardiner, *Constitutional Documents*, pp. 127–53; see Russell, *Fall of the British Monarchies*, p. 426.
227. *Sir William Drake, His Speech in Parliament Concerning the Present Distempers and Putting the Kingdom in a State of Defence* (10 Nov. 1641).

'violent counsels of some late ministers of state'.[228] Yet, despite his call for 'frequent parliaments', the thrust of his speech did not follow Pym's prescriptions.[229] Drawing on his knowledge of the history of Rome – 'a pattern of
best government' – Drake emphasised with Machiavelli the need for a strong
and stable state founded on sound 'religion, laws and military discipline'.[230]
In the first case, he praised Queen Elizabeth's religious settlement for uniting
the kingdom at home and pressed the House again to 'settle religion to some
rule and uniformity'. What he meant became clear as he continued: the
church was 'not to be thus suffered in an uncertain condition, between illegal
innovations and superstition on the one side, and I know not what lawless
and irregular confusion on the other . . .'[231] Where others were seeking
to hack at the church root and branch, Drake reasserted his belief in a
moderate religious settlement as the essence of political unity. Turning to the
laws, he moved quickly to the point that without 'provident care' for the
defence of the realm, they were mere 'glorious structures without roof or
covering'.[232] England needed to look to its militia, to see the musters kept
up and powder supplied before foreign states moved to take advantage of
England's weaknesses.[233] Here was a call to unity, at a time when the Grand
Remonstrance was about to divide the Commons almost in two. Beyond that,
Drake hints at criticism of Pym's tactics as he appealed outside the House to
a wider political nation:

> There is one thing more with which I shall conclude; and I shall humbly
> represent it as, in my weak opinion, a great cause of our growing dis-
> temper: this is the abundance of humours we have stirred, and not purged
> away, which are but fit fuel for fresh fire to take hold of, if it should
> burst forth; therefore as there be great numbers in this state, 'Qui paene, a
> calamitate publica, impunitatem sibi spondent', I shall make it my humble
> notion and desire that we make severe examples of some few of the most
> capital offenders; and either pardon the meaner delinquents, if justice will
> admit thereof, or at least to let them know what they may trust to;
> otherwise, as many as look desperately upon their own fortunes will be
> too ready to give their vote for troubles and seek their peace in the public
> disturbance . . .'[234]

It was an appeal to unity that fell upon deaf ears. But it may not have been
Drake's last endeavour to save his country. As the Irish rebellion raged and

228. Ibid., pp. 3–4.
229. Ibid., p. 2: 'had we had frequent parliaments, we should have given a timely stop to
    mischiefs.'
230. Ibid., pp. 3, 4; see appendix below, p. 160.
231. Drake, *Speech in Parliament*, p. 3.
232. Ibid., p. 4.
233. Ibid., pp. 4–5.
234. Ibid., p. 5.

the quarrels at home intensified, he evidently prepared another impassioned plea for cooperation and unity. Undated notes in Drake's journal headed 'For speech in Parliament' show him constructing a speech around a set of adages and observations drawn from history. 'By wisdom peace,' he proposed to begin, 'by peace plenty.'[235] Drake went on to point out the dangers of soldiers, the decay of trade which threatened popular insurrections at home, and the opportunity presented to foreign enemies by 'intestine divisions'. 'Let us', he argued, 'consider how by calmness we may extinguish these flames that are broken out among us.'[236] William proceeded to propose an act of association that might reunite the body politic: 'a way of securing us . . . whereby our religion, liberty and property might be secured and this proposed by the parliament as his Majesty may have the less cause to stick at it'. In order to achieve that end, he suggested a covenant binding king, Lords and Commons 'according to the protestation', but this time 'to be included that we will defend likewise his Majesty's just prerogative as we have often promised'.[237] And he called upon his fellow MPs to 'consider the bleeding condition of Ireland not unlikely to be totally lost' if civil war raged in England.[238]

There is no evidence that Drake delivered his speech. Notes in his journal suggest there may have been more than one version prepared, or that he worked on it as the kingdom divided.[239] On the last folio of his journal, humbly moving that a select committee might be nominated to hear the king's terms, he once again warned of the 'opportunity' the foreigners 'hath . . . by our divisions . . . to attempt upon us'.[240] Prophetically he closed: 'Let us take heed how we engage ourselves in a long and lasting civil war which we may not see an end of in our days.'[241]

When civil war broke out, Sir William Drake was named to the Committee for the Associated Counties. We might therefore easily be led to an assumption about whom he blamed for the outbreak of the conflict. We know that he condemned bad counsellors, and notably William Laud, for disturbances in the church and state. He appears to have accepted, during debates on raising troops for Ireland, that 'an absolute tyranny' might be established 'if a potent and prudent prince had the managing of them'.[242] But in none of his speeches or entries does Drake point directly to Charles I, and in so far as Pym and his junto left the safe course of blaming evil counsel and came closer to

235. Hunt. MS f. *42. These notes follow material from Dec. 1641 and Jan. 1642. See too Ogden MS 7/52 ff. 17–18.
236. Hunt. MS f. *42.
237. Hunt. MS ff. *42v–*43.
238. Hunt. MS ff. *43–43v.
239. Cf. ff. *42–*43v, *41v, 37v, 38–38v. See too Ogden MSS 7/52 ff. 17–18; 7/8 ff. 72–72v; 7/23 f. 49v.
240. Hunt. MS f. *44.
241. Ibid.
242. Hunt. MS f. 38.

attacking the king, Drake may have begun to part company with them, and even to see them as part of the distemper rather than the cure. In December 1641, Drake copied into his journal the speech of the moderate Sir Benjamin Rudyard expressing frustration at the situation in parliament: 'when the parliament first sat we did we know not what and now we know not what we do.'[243] The next month, we find him noting Sandys' criticism that 'the affecting an extreme and sudden innovation of all things instead of a moderate reformation of what was justly blamable hath brought us to the pass we are come to.'[244] Whatever his earlier doubts about Charles I's exercise of authority, as government broke down Drake saw the rights of the crown as essential to order and stability. He regarded the act against the dissolution of parliament without its consent a mortal wound to royal power.[245] Taking from Machiavelli's *Discourses* the point that a republic could never be established unless the nobles and gentry were eliminated, Drake concluded:

> hence let all men of quality in time consider that not only their oaths of allegiance and supremacy and their profession oblige them to defend the king and just and legal powers but all other own personal interest, and those advantages which the frame and constitution of this government hath afforded them.[246]

Increasingly it became clear, however, that some desired not the reformation but the destruction of that constitution.[247] At some point early in 1642, Drake confided to his journal, with rare prophetic insight:

> the p[arliament] by their long sitting have come to know their own strength so well that they have learned that damnable secret of making and unmaking a king at pleasure whereby the foundation of all monarchy, which is due reverence to the loin royal, is so irreparably shaken that like the lost state of innocency can never be restored, so that we are like to grow to such a military anarchy as did the Praetorian bands in Rome . . .[248]

This was not the end for which most MPs had come up to Westminster and Drake offers the important perspective of the backbencher largely ignored in Russell's account of the session. As Drake complained, 'our proceedings and orders are too much framed to the ambitious aims of a few partial men than

243. Hunt. MS f. 36v.
244. Hunt. MS f. *41.
245. Hunt. MS f. 37v. He may have felt the same about the Triennial Act. He speaks of two acts which damaged royal authority but leaves the second blank.
246. Hunt. MS f. 38v. The defence of royal authority in the language of interest in 1642 is striking. Drake refers to Machiavelli's *Discourses*, Book I, ch. 20.
247. Drake returns to history: 'Romani avide ruendo ad libertatem in servitudinem elapsi sunt' (Hunt. MS f. 38).
248. Hunt. MS f. 36v.

to the general good or liking of the wisest of the kingdom, for a few contriving in their chambers how to carry things in public not for the common commodity but for their own ambition . . .'[249] Such, he feared, 'by keeping the preachers their dependants and their power and reputation in parliament, in a very short time will have it in their power to bestow all the honours and rewards of the kingdom, so that both peace and war, arms and laws will depend upon the will and pleasure of these few'.[250] Among them, Drake listed J.H. – perhaps that John Hampden, his Buckinghamshire neighbour, with whom he had once discussed the Connecticut project – a man 'of an ambitious and factious nature and a spirit busy and turbulent, favoured under the authority of parliament where his reputation bears great sway much more than was convenient, all such humours that might serve his ambition though otherwise disposed to set fire on the state.'[251]

These were the men to whom, perhaps more than the king, Drake attributed the blame for the failure to quieten Ireland, settle the peace at home and secure the realm from foreign invasion. As he looked back, rather like Edward Hyde, Drake began to discern a clever conspiracy – not now that of popish counsellors, but one of ambitious MPs. The causes of war, he recognised, were 'various and uncertain'. Yet he felt sure that they proceeded 'not from the general peace and inclination of the kingdom of England', but 'from the secret influences of these Northern planets'.[252] Some, he went on, had taken advantage of the ignorance about these affairs of the vulgar, 'blinded with every appearance of religion or liberty', to advance their own 'ambitious spirit' and to undermine 'the quiet and settled estate of the kingdom'. And in an analysis that Clarendon was to echo, Drake concluded:

> In great mutinies and insurrections of this nature, pretences specious and conscionable were never wanting and indeed are necessary for the disturbers of the peace and happiness of kingdoms, for their own gain or ambition. If they would appear unmasked they would seem so ugly without a vizard they would fright rather than draw people to them . . . let us look to the original of this fantastic disturbance we shall surely find upon said enquiry the service book sent into Scotland but a lapswing flight to draw man's eyes from prying into the centre of the main design, and that the prime authors of the disturbances rather employed conscience than conscience them.[253]

Where he had once held Laud to be the man who had disturbed the peace of the church, Drake now condemned those who 'ran with as violent a course' to the other 'extreme' – 'to irreverence and contempt of God's public

249. Hunt. MS f. 37; cf. appendix below, p. 161.
250. Hunt. MS f. 37v.
251. Ibid.
252. Hunt. MS f. 39.
253. Ibid.

worship and ordinances'.[254] In analysing the causes of distemper and civil war, he evidently returned to his favourite writers, Machiavelli, Guicciardini and Bacon. In Bacon, he read again that the worst course for religion was to 'nourish seditions' and that tyranny was preferable to civil war.[255] And whatever his concerns about Caroline government, he doubtless called to mind Machiavelli's citation from Tacitus: 'that men should honour the past and obey the present; and whilst they should desire good princes, they should bear with those they have, such as they are', the Florentine adding 'and surely whoever acts otherwise will generally involve . . . his country in ruin.'[256]

By 1642, Sir William Drake had no doubt that, as he quoted Guicciardini, 'fury and rashness more governs than wisdom or counsel.'[257] What he had hoped for in 1640–1, the reformation of church and state, was dashed, as the country teetered towards civil war. In the last entry in his journal, William copied a letter which expressed his own despair. Honest men, he wrote,

> conceive the parliaments of England are the happiest constitutions that any nation or kingdom can live under and the most hopeful of human means to make king and people happy, but they think that as the best things are in the corruption the worst, so this Great Council which at the first sitting was looked [upon] by all men as a teeming mother like to produce much fruit for the good of this kingdom . . .[258]

And there, as his mental and political world collapsed around him, Drake stopped. As words gave way to arms, the man who had written so much ended his diary in mid-sentence.

254. Drake, *Speech in Parliament*, p. 3.
255. Cf. Ogden MS 7/7 f. 12 at p. 78; F. Bacon, *The Essays*, ed. J. Pitcher (Harmondsworth, 1987), pp. 70, 230.
256. Machiavelli, *Discourses*, Book III, ch. 6.
257. Hunt. MS f. 39v.
258. Hunt. MS f. 40.

Appendix
William Drake's Parliamentary Notebook

Among the Ogden manuscripts in William Drake's hand listed by Stuart Clark as group 1 is volume 51, a 16° in an old vellum binding. Clark identified it as an 'extremely untidily written diary of proceedings in the House of Commons in the early months of the Long Parliament', and noted that it included a report of one of Drake's own speeches.[1] In 1984, Maija Jansson of the Yale Center for Parliamentary History edited the diary along with an anonymous diary from the Beinecke Library, to supplement the published diaries and journals of the proceedings of the Long Parliament. Jansson drew attention to the hurried and spontaneous nature of the entries, the sparsity of dates, the erratic pagination, and the use of the notebook from both ends. She suggested that since there was no evidence of an effort to make a clean copy, Drake had kept the notes not as any official record but for his personal purposes.[2] Indeed, he interspersed summaries of speeches and proceedings with 'philosophical observations' of his own, which connect the diary to the commonplace books we have begun to examine. Jansson endeavoured to order and date Drake's entries, using the *Commons Journals* and D'Ewes's journals, and identified most of the speeches even where Drake did not name them.[3] Some speeches which could not be so traced she left as 'anonymous'.

Five years after Jansson's valuable edition, Drake's notebook drew the attention of Professor Michael Mendle. In an article in *Parliamentary History* for 1989, Mendle re-examined the diary as a text of political ideas.[4] He argued that the extended speeches that Drake did not attribute, and that Jansson left as anonymous, were written by William himself – albeit, doubtless in most

---

1. S. Clark, 'Wisdom Literature of the Seventeenth Century: A Guide to the Contents of the "Bacon–Tottel" Commonplace Books. Part II', *Trans. Camb. Bibliog. Soc.* 7 (1977), p. 56.
2. M. Jansson, ed., *Two Diaries of the Long Parliament* (Gloucester, 1984), pp. xiii–xvi.
3. W. Notestein, ed., *The Journal of Sir Simonds D'Ewes from the Beginning of the Long Parliament to the Opening of the Trial of the Earl of Strafford* (New Haven, 1923); and BL Harleian MSS 163, 164.
4. M. Mendle, 'A Machiavellian in the Long Parliament before the Civil War', *Parl. Hist.* 8 (1989), pp. 116–24.

cases, not delivered. Pointing to the untypical traits of the anonymous speeches – their full prose, their use of vocatives, 'Sir' and 'Mr. Speaker' – Mendle argued for stylistic comparison between the anonymous speeches in the notebook and Drake's printed speech of 10 November 1641.[5] Having made a case for Drake's authorship, Mendle went on to underline the Machiavellian nature of the speeches: their debt to the *Discourses*, as translated by Edward Dacres,[6] and the 'Machiavellian political prudence' of their message. Demonstrating too Drake's debt in these speeches to Francis Bacon, Mendle stressed that there was in them 'nothing extrinsic to the native agenda as it was generally understood in 1641'.[7] Nor did they exhibit 'even a whiff of the antimonarchical . . . republicanism of the later 1640s and 1650s'. Rather they were concerned with reform, centrist and articulated ideas 'less aggressive than that of the parliamentary leadership'.[8]

Re-examining Drake's parliamentary notebook in the light of his reading notes and political diary enables us to confirm and extend Jansson and Mendle's suggestions. For one, several passages echo and summarise the observations Drake copied from his reading, 'Time and place are servants to occasion' exactly capturing the philosophy of Machiavelli and his disciples whom Drake so much admired.[9] Moreover, the passages from the *Discorsi* which Mendle identified – regarding the need for states to return to first principles, and describing Rome as 'a pattern of best government' – are directly quoted in Drake's commonplace books.[10] But what, I would argue, clinches the case for Drake's authorship of the anonymous speeches is a reference in one (on the Protestation) to a case, 'I observed being once at the High Commission where there was one Mr. Barnard at that time.'[11] The reference is to the case of Nathaniel Barnard fined for seditious preaching at Cambridge – a case Drake attended and annotated in 1633–4.[12] We may safely conclude that, far beyond a bare summary of the speeches of others at committee and in the full House, the parliamentary notebook documents Drake's own perceptions of events, views which he doubtless expressed, even if not in official speech.

As Mendle observes, on the evidence we have, Drake was 'not a prominent member of the Long Parliament'. Jansson suggests that he confirms the inverse relationship between note-keepers and leading speakers in the

5. *Sir William Drake, His Speech in Parliament Concerning the Present Distempers and Putting the Kingdom in a State of Defence* (10 Nov. 1641).
6. E. Dacres, *Machiavels Discourses upon the First Decade of T. Livius* (1636).
7. Mendle, 'A Machiavellian', p. 122.
8. Ibid., and passim.
9. Jansson, *Two Diaries*, p. 19; Ogden MSS 7/8 ff. 5v, 91v; 7/15 ff. 99, 104; 7/25 f. 88v; 7/28 f. 35; 7/32 ff. 8, 23; Folger MS ff. 134, 33, 43.
10. Jansson, *Two Diaries*, p. 74. Cf. Machiavelli, *Discourses*, Book III, ch. 1; and see Ogden MS 7/17 f. 112; Drake, *Speech in Parliament*, p. 2 describes Rome as a 'pattern of best government'.
11. Jansson, *Two Diaries*, p. 43; cf. above, p. 136.
12. Hunt. MS f. 20; above, p. 141.

House.[13] Yet Drake may have been more involved with business than we have recognised. As far as the official record of the *Commons Journal* goes, he was appointed to two committees: the Committee for Privileges and that for the act to disable the clergy from temporal office. The notebook, however, indicates that he may have been a member of – or certainly was privy to the proceedings of – more. On 4 March, for example, his notes commence, 'at the committee for lieutenants' and Drake speaks of what he 'observed', as if present rather than hearing report. And other references to the 'Fen business', and 'at the committee for gunpowder' appear to be to business not discussed in the full House. Drake was evidently either a member of, or permitted to attend, other committees.[14]

What the parliamentary notebook also reveals is something which will not surprise the readers of the commonplace books: that Drake was no passive auditor of speech and debate. Rather the maxims, observations and glosses on speeches he notes indicate that he was always placing what he heard in the broader context of his studies, especially of history and the lessons that it taught. A speech often led him to general reflections: so after the Lord Treasurer's speech for supply on 10 February, he writes: 'What men cannot carry it is wisdom to secure for and to promote it.'[15] Following Hampden's speech on 20 May regarding the disbanding of the Scots' armies, Drake observed: 'Money has a magnetical virtue in it; draws men's hearts and our hands after.'[16] On two occasions of debate on very different subjects – the removal of the bishops from the Lords and the Queen's household – he repeats his favourite lesson from the Florentine: 'the timing of things might be governed by occasion.'[17]

The glosses on speeches Drake recorded evidence not only a critical alertness that we have witnessed in his reading, but often too a cynical interpretation of men's words and motives. Clearly after each speech he weighed what was said in the light of his own knowledge and experience. Following the king's speech of 23 January concerning the difficulties he and the realm faced with 'two armies in a great charge lying upon the land', Drake penned (upside down) his own thoughts: 'No increase nor improvement of his reserve within these last 7 years; cast up and aground upon that.'[18] References to Cicero's counsel to Catiline (not to bring in more woe than he could handle) at a discussion of Sir John Corbet's charge against the Earl of Bridgewater appear to be Drake's rather than a speaker's.[19] More particularly, William paid close attention to the politics of the debates and the strategies deployed by speakers. At the debate on Sir William Russell's 'business' (he was suspected

13. Mendle, 'A Machiavellian', p. 116; Jansson, *Two Diaries*, p. xvi.
14. Jansson, *Two Diaries*, pp. xv, 14, 15, 16.
15. Ibid., p. 4.
16. Ibid., p. 46.
17. Ibid., pp. 18, 21.
18. Ibid., p. 1.
19. Ibid., p. 8. For Corbet, see Sharpe, *Personal Rule*, pp. 496–7.

of popery), Drake 'observed much . . .' and added: 'There was much skill used to frame the questions so as to make it a common case with other deputy lieutenants thereby to engage them for him.'[20]

Throughout the trial of the Earl of Strafford, Drake sensed behind the rhetoric of charge and justice complex and devious manoeuvres and interests. So when Strafford petitioned the House, he noted (in a manner that recalls his account of Coventry's behaviour at Sherfield's case in Star Chamber), 'I observed Treasurer Vane though fiercely against him was much for the reading of it, meaning thereby to show his own moderation.'[21] Vane's ruse he compared to Sir Nathaniel Brent who 'being examined upon what concerned the archbishop's case, knowing there was weight enough upon him, he chose wise on the moderating himself and yet advantaged the bishop nothing thereby.'[22] As the trial proceeded and Strafford defended himself, Drake recorded Wilmott speaking 'with great respect to his judge' and Bristol's seeming 'to speak as much to my lord's advantage as the words would leave'.[23] But he sensed there were those personally antagonistic to the earl who were determined to hound him to death. As well as Vane, who later produced notes that charged Strafford with planning military force in England, Lord Cork had come over from Ireland to witness against his old enemy. Interestingly Drake underlined Cork's denial that he had come over out of malice, or 'had . . . the least thought' to accuse the earl, and Strafford's counter-assertion: 'how *prone he is* to *witness* against me.'[24] Drake discerned, as did others increasingly, that not all were devoted to the elucidation of the facts and a full and fair trial.[25] Amidst charge and defence, he raised the fundamental issue: 'the question is whether matter of truth or not truth in the preamble of his [Strafford's] answer.'[26] Uncertainties remained. And, for all his suspicions of Cork and Vane, Drake could not finally decide whether Strafford himself was an innocent or a schemer. At the end of the earl's speech defending himself, Drake noted he 'then either wept' – 'or made show of doing it'.[27]

Those speeches Mendle identifies as Drake's echo and extend sentiments we have heard him express in his notebooks. So the Drake who counselled himself not to spend too long in contemplative study spoke against the breeding of too many scholars in the kingdom.[28] His dislike and suspicion of Catholics was also, as it was with many, heightened by the political tensions

20. Jansson, *Two Diaries*, pp. 14–15.
21. Ibid., p. 25; see above, pp. 113–14.
22. Jansson, *Two Diaries*, p. 25.
23. Ibid., pp. 32, 36.
24. Ibid., pp. 28–30. See J. Timmis, *Thine is the Kingdom: The Trial for Treason of Thomas Wentworth* (Alabama, 1974).
25. See Digby's speech in Cobbett's *Parliamentary History*, vol. 2, p. 752. John Coke, son of Sir John Coke, spoke of 'private practice for private men to work out their own ends', *Hist. MSS Comm., Cowper*, II, pp. 278–9.
26. Jansson, *Two Diaries*, p. 27.
27. Ibid., p. 37.
28. Ibid., p. 48; cf. Hunt. MS f. *1; Ogden MS 7/7 f. 103.

in 1641. On 15 March, for example, Drake feared that a town had been 'fired by papists' and that 'you will find the disorders arising most frequently from that ground'.[29] Evidently too Drake now joined with those who felt that Laudian ceremonialism had also corrupted the church. Debating the Protestation and its preamble for repressing and punishing popish recusants, Drake urged the House: 'We have suffered no less of late times by superstitious innovators that professed themselves Protestants and therefore I desire it may be added "superstitious innovation" and "introducers of illegal ceremonies."'[30]

We may note that, though the son of puritan parents, Drake appears to have nothing to say about Arminianism or doctrine. Indeed what most exercised him, even over ceremonies, was the overblown pomp of the clergy. At the committee on the secular employments of the clergy, Drake dismissed their suitability for office: 'they understand not the commonwealth in relation to foreign states,' he argued, adding (perhaps from disappointment that his own learning and foreign experience had not been more highly valued) 'so well as others that have seen and travelled in foreign parts.'[31] Calling up precedents from history – the bishop of Ross's bringing the French into Scotland, the bishops inviting the Turks into Hungary – Drake declaimed 'those examples together with our own experience is sufficient to exclude [the clergy] forever from being counsel in this kingdom.' On 1 April he returned to his theme, now blaming the prelates for all the ills that had befallen the realm: 'For if we look to the spring and wellshed of the present sad distempers this kingdom groans under they cannot . . . be more properly be assigned [sic] to any one cause more than to some ambitious churchmen's busy meddling.'[32] And regretting that more had not been done to check them earlier, Drake pressed the bill to limit the clergy now.

In the spring of 1641, then, Drake, as so many MPs, held high hopes of a reforming parliament. 'Had we had frequent parliaments', he believed, 'we shall long before this have prevented the prejudice that the commonwealth now suffers by.'[33] Again like so many other backbenchers, he looked for legislation to reform abuses, and for action not just words. 'Let us not, I beseech you, Sir,' he addressed the Speaker in March, 'rest longer in generals, particularity must bring things to speedy execution.'[34] However, much of the time of the first session of the Long Parliament was taken up in proceedings against persons and especially the trial of Strafford. As the months passed with bills dormant, several MPs began to air their discontents – and even their concerns about the parliament's leader, Pym. As we have seen, Drake appears to

29. Jansson, *Two Diaries*, pp. 19–20.
30. Ibid., p. 41. It seems that in the context of 1641 Drake's dislike of ceremony had escalated into a fear that it might pave the way to popery.
31. Ibid., pp. 18–19.
32. Ibid., p. 34; cf. above, p. 141.
33. Jansson, *Two Diaries*, p. 34; cf. Hunt. MS f. *12v.
34. Jansson, *Two Diaries*, p. 20.

have admired Strafford and to have begun to suspect the witnesses and proceedings against him. We have no evidence of his reaction to Strafford's
attainder and execution in May. But we have seen Drake's disenchantment
with both Pym and later with the parliament in general which, failing its
promise, had lost its way.[35] There may be a hint in his parliamentary notebook that some concern about radical courses had set in as early as the
summer of 1641, before the recess in September. On 12 June, the anonymous
speaker, whom Mendle argues is Drake, is reported as saying in close committee: 'We cannot conceive how the peace can be durable in Scotland unless
episcopacy is abolished in England. It were to be wished that there were a
uniformity, but the alteration would be so great.'[36]

Did Drake begin to foresee the dangers of imminent revolution? Was
Charles I astute in elevating him, in July, to a baronetcy in an effort to win
him? By the second session Drake appears less enthusiastic about the parliament; the end of his parliamentary journal itself may signal some disengage-
ment. But if Drake began to have second thoughts, they did not stem, as did
those of other moderates and constitutional royalists, from a traditional sense
of law, justice and religion as much as from − we will not be surprised to
learn − political calculation. As William said about abolishing episcopacy, what
was right was not always the best course. In a perfect summary of his hero
Machiavelli he told the House: 'You might differ [in] what is just and what
is prudentially and politically fit.'[37]

35. See above, pp. 118–19.
36. Jansson, *Two Diaries*, p. 49. See below, pp. 228–9.
37. Jansson, *Two Diaries*, p. 49.

Part Three
READING AND REVOLUTION

4
Reading Revolutions

Reading in Conflict

Over the summer of 1642, the country drifted into the civil war that Drake had dreaded and predicted. When the Long Parliament convened, he had, along with many, sought and advocated reform of abuses in church and state. But Charles I evidently regarded him as a moderate figure who might be won over by elevation to a knighthood and baronetcy in the summer of 1641. It was not an entirely inappropriate assessment. As we have seen, over the winter of 1641–2 Drake began to have doubts about the increasingly radical course of affairs in parliament and, even more importantly, to suspect the motives of its leaders. It seems likely that, at least at that time, Drake, other than confiding them to his diary, kept these doubts to himself. He was named by parliament to the Committee for Associated Counties and was probably expected to play an active local role in the war effort in Buckinghamshire. In 1642, however, when he subscribed his £200 for the maintenance of two horses, Drake specified (as did others) that they were for the use of king and parliament 'conjunctively'.[1] In the provinces, some gentlemen, genuinely confused by the rival calls for military aid by the parliamentary ordinance and the Royal Commission of Array, expressed bewilderment that each claimed to raise troops for king and parliament, or replied that in serving one they believed they served both.[2] In many cases, however, such respondents were making a point: or rather a last ditch effort to prevent the recruitment of two rival armies that would end any hope of the peaceful settlement they still desperately sought.[3]

1. M. F. Keeler, *The Long Parliament 1640–1641* (Philadelphia, 1954), p. 160; F. K. Lenthall, 'List of the Names of the Members of the House of Commons that Advanced Horse, Money and Plate for the Defence of the Parliament . . . 1642', *Notes & Queries* 12 (1855), pp. 358–60. Interestingly Sir John Holland also offered horse for 'defence of the king's person, his royal authority and dignity, our laws, liberties and privileges conjunctively'.
2. See J. Morrill, *The Revolt of the Provinces* (1976), pp. 36–8.
3. Edward Montagu offered his money 'for the defence of the king and parliament conjunctively, and not divided' (*Notes & Queries* 12 (1855), p. 359).

Drake was certainly not ignorant of the likely course of events. His gesture, therefore, and especially the force of that 'conjunctively', expressed either his last endeavour at peace, or, if it was not to be, a refusal to support in military action either side. Even once war became an apparent inevitability, many – royalists, parliamentarians, and still more uncommitted – hoped that a single battle might end the conflict. Instead the first exchanges, at Edgehill and Turnham Green, ended in stalemate, with the royalists superior in assets and expertise but foiled in their early bid to take London. It then began to dawn on many that the nation faced a protracted civil conflict; and as Pym pushed through the ordinances for sequestration of delinquent property, forced loan, and assessments, not only were the resources for a long war in place, it became clear that it was to be costly to purses as well as in lives. The failure of any side to secure a quick victory also placed new pressure on the moderate and uncommitted. In a long drawn out war, neutrality would be hard to sustain; those who had subscribed to king *and* parliament would be forced to make a hard choice. Drake elected to pursue a different course. On 4 February 1642, he secured from the Commons the warrant of the House to travel to the Low Countries, 'for recovery of his health'. The warrant stipulated that he should, notwithstanding his absence, 'continue a member of this house without any prejudice in regard of this his absence', and he was permitted to leave with his servants and trunk.[4]

We know little about Drake's health – though the entries in his diary and notebooks to remedies indicate minor rather than serious ailments.[5] The Low Countries had attracted him in the 1630s, so a desire to renew old acquaintances and continue his travels may be all that lay behind his decision to leave London and Buckinghamshire. The support from the Commons for his journey suggests no suspicion among MPs about his leaving. Yet we know that in other cases withdrawal or travel signified a reluctance to make hard choices or remain in an England at war: Thomas Howard, Earl of Arundel left for Italy; George Potter the merchant left Exeter for France on account of the 'growing troubles'.[6] And, in Drake's case, a request to leave only weeks after being placed on the committee for the county seems curious. There is too a hint that there had been some differences in Buckinghamshire between Drake and Lieutenant-Colonel Richard Browne, against whom Drake complained to the Speaker and Lord General, Essex.[7] But whether the differences were political – the expression of a growing distance between Sir William and the local parliamentary forces – or merely personal, we cannot say.

4. *C.J.* II, p. 956.
5. See below, pp. 205–6.
6. For Arundel, see D. Howarth, *Lord Arundel and his Circle* (1985), ch. 9; M. Stoyle, *From Deliverance to Destruction: Rebellion and Civil War in an English City* (Exeter, 1996), p. 106.
7. *C.J.* II, pp. 920–1. Browne was an ardent Parliamentarian general who, as commander-in-chief of the forces of the associated counties, was accused of plundering the county. See *DNB* and *V.C.H. Bucks*, vol. 3 (1925), p. 46.

Drake stayed away for nearly two years, until October 1644. Licensing him again to be 'forthwith admitted into this house', the Commons committee noted that he had been 'long absent' – longer perhaps than had been anticipated for his 'health'.[8] Once he was back, however, the House clearly intended to make use of his services again. In January, Sir William was added to the committee for Buckinghamshire, together with Thomas Chaloner, a recruiter member, violently opposed to the king.[9] The alliance with the Scots the previous winter had escalated the military efforts, rendered the conflict avowedly a war for religion, and greatly diminished the prospects of early settlement with the king.[10] Whatever his attitude to the Solemn League or its provisos for a Presbyterian discipline, Drake, as he was bound to do, subscribed the Covenant, on 29 January 1645, along with 'Mr Potts', presumably Sir John Potts, MP for Norfolk, a moderate who like Drake had been created a baronet in 1641 (and who, again like Sir William, was to be excluded in 1648).[11] Four days later, however, Drake again requested and was granted leave to travel – less than four months after his return to the House.[12]

It appears that Drake spent the rest of the 1640s overseas. He evidently returned briefly but in July 1647 he was again granted permission to go abroad, and was excused later in the year when parliament began to take action against absentees as still 'in partibus transmarin . . .'[13] When a call of members was taken the following April, Sir William was not excused by name, but was evidently still absent.[14] So, when on 6 December 1648 Colonel Pride placed his guards to prevent MPs sitting so as to purge the Commons of unreliable members, Drake, though appearing on lists of the excluded, was not there to be forcibly debarred from the House.[15] It seems likely that he was still abroad at the time of the regicide, for we have his record of 'Notes wrote me from England concerning my private affairs' dated January 1648[?9], and a record of bills of exchange between London and Rotterdam, dated a month later.[16] Thereafter, with his parliamentary career over, Drake fades from the public historical record. Though a JP for Buckinghamshire from 1647 to 1653, he clearly took no part in local government. He does not turn up again

---

8. *C.J.* III, p. 659.

9. *C.J.* IV, p. 20. On Chaloner, see D. Underdown, *Pride's Purge: Politics in the Puritan Revolution* (Oxford, 1971), pp. 48, 265.

10. See S. R. Gardiner, *History of the Great Civil War 1642–1649* (4 vols, 1904), vol. 1, ch. 11; D. Hirst, *Authority and Conflict: England 1603–1658* (1986), pp. 236–42.

11. *C.J.* IV, p. 35; on Potts, see Keeler, *The Long Parliament*, pp. 312–13; Underdown, *Pride's Purge*, pp. 59–60, 104.

12. *C.J.* IV, p. 41.

13. *C.J.* V, pp. 235, 329. There is no record in the journal of when Drake had returned; on 19 May 1647 he was granted leave to go to 'the Bath for recovery of his health' and on 6 July to pass overseas, *C.J.* V, p. 177.

14. *C.J.* V, p. 543. Drake was definitely at Breda in December 1647, Ogden MS 7/21 f. 180v.

15. Underdown, *Pride's Purge*, pp. 209–10.

16. Ogden MS 7/10 ff. 175v, 176.

until he was appointed in 1652 Chirographer or Custos Brevium of the Court of the Common Pleas under his old friend Oliver, now Chief Justice St John. Despite having at last obtained office which he had sought since the 1630s, Drake almost certainly left the performance of his duties to a deputy, while he continued to travel and to study. His name does not once appear in the state papers for the 1650s.[17]

Were we to be dependent on the traditional evidence of biography or political history, we could discern little of Drake's attitude to the most dramatic events in English history: civil war, regicide and revolution, followed by the restoration not only of the monarchy but of Charles Stuart in 1660. What we do have, however, is an unusually large collection of some twenty-two volumes of notebooks from the later 1640s and the 1650s.[18] At first sight these would appear to be unpromising materials for the historian of the interregnum. Unlike the political diary now in the Huntington Library, but like the volumes which we examined in chapter 2, they consist almost entirely of reading notes, extracts from a huge range of classical and humanist texts, principally histories, moral treatises, collections of adages, but also philosophical and political treatises, sermons, commentaries and letters. Though the number and range of works cited and which we can identify are extraordinary, some of the books most often mentioned, Aristotle, Plutarch, Cicero, Livy, were the standard reading of any educated gentleman; many we have seen Drake read and annotate before. But although he refers to little contemporary pamphlet literature, some topical works, most famously Hobbes's *Leviathan*, engage Drake's attention, and are read alongside his old favourites – Machiavelli and Guicciardini, Comines and Bacon.[19]

Herein lies the point that will be central to the argument of this chapter: that while Drake read and annotated several works published during the interregnum, the condition, the circumstances of his reading, and *rereading*, of everything was new. Whether in England or overseas, civil war and commonwealth were perforce the spaces in which Drake studied; during the 1650s he was (chronologically and literally) a revolutionary reader, a man who read at and in a revolutionary moment.[20] He was also a revolutionary reader in another sense. Because he now read the classics and Scriptures alongside the texts and experiences of a revolutionary age, he was also a reader *of* revolution. For now, as he turned back to Greek and Roman history, to proverbs

17. With the exception of a Committee for Compounding order that he be left alone in possession of an estate in Herefordshire mortgaged to him by Lord Wilmot, *Calendar of the Proceedings of the Committee for Compounding 1643–1660*, part 3, p. 2236. Drake's steward evidently lived at Shardeloes, and his brother Francis continued to be active in local government. See G. Eland, *Shardeloes Papers* (Oxford, 1947), p. 55, and F. P. Verney, *Memoirs of the Verney Family during the Civil War* (4 vols, 1892–9).

18. These are listed as group 2 in S. Clark, 'Wisdom Literature of the Seventeenth Century: A Guide to the Contents of the "Bacon-Tottell" Commonplace Books. Part II', *Trans. Camb. Bibliog. Soc.*, 7 (1977), pp. 46–73.

19. See Ogden MSS 7/17 f. 151v; 7/22 f. 186; Folger MS f. 42; see below, p. 237.

20. On the concept of 'revolutionary reader', see below, pp. 291–2.

and fables, it was the questions and problems born of civil conflict and republic that filled his mind. To some extent, then, the classical and human-ist texts became, no less than topical political treatises, texts of revolution, or texts that Drake read for his meditation on and negotiation with the revolu-tionary times. If we turn to read his notebooks with that in mind, we may begin to discern how a seemingly unpromising collection of extracts and commonplaces may document the shifting values and politics of a learned and moderate gentleman for whom the world had turned upside down.

Before we attempt to analyse the strategies of Drake's reading or his reading of politics, however, we need to consider the notebooks themselves and the problems they present. The twenty-two volumes forming the collection (seventeen 8°, five 16°) are almost all in contemporary bindings, of leather or vellum, at times deploying old parchment as an internal binding material.[21] None is foliated continuously, though particular sections are paginated, and most are written from both ends.[22] There are blank folios in some volumes, but the overall impression is of crowded pages and margins rather than space – a characteristic consistent perhaps with a scholar who was peripatetic, rather than based in a manor house study.[23] Overall the notebooks all contain an eclectic gathering of extracts and sentences, but sections of books, and even some entire volumes, do appear loosely related to some theme or type of text. Volumes 9, 15, 25 and 37, for example, are almost entirely collections of proverbs, whereas volume 19 is more concerned with the nature of man, and volume 17 (and volume 31) with religious questions and texts.[24] There is no reason to believe that the collection is complete, and some grounds for sus-pecting that it is not. The Drake archive was clearly not complete when C. K. Ogden purchased the Shardeloes material in the 1940s; the recent dis-covery of Drake's journal in private hands and the identification of other commonplace books confirms that important volumes had strayed from the family; most of Drake's printed books have still to be found.[25] More par-ticularly, Drake refers in his notebooks to other volumes of his own which do not obviously correspond to any item now in the collection.[26] His own travels as well as the passage of time may have caused notebooks to go astray. But whatever may be missing, the thousands of pages that survive offer a

21. Volumes 18 and 19 were rebound.
22. As noted earlier, I have foliated all the volumes continuously through, so entries from the back will appear in my citations in reverse order.
23. Different ink suggests that glosses and marginal comments were in some cases added later. See for example volumes 24, 27; and Folger MS f. 22.
24. Similarly much of volume 20 is taken from Gruter's commentary on Tacitus, presum-ably J. Gruteri, *Varii Discursus sive Prolixiores Commentarii ad Aliquot Insignioria Loca Taciti* . . . (Heidelberg, 1604).
25. We recall the volumes in the House of Lords (Historical Collections MS 49), the Huntington Library (HM 55603) and the Folger (v. a. 263), as well as the fragments in Buckinghamshire. On Drake's printed books see below, pp. 260–6.
26. See, for example, Ogden MSS 7/14 f. 161; 7/16 f. 117; 7/17 f. 99; 7/22 ff. 20, 117v; Folger MS f. 85.

unique insight into Drake's reading practices and reflection on politics during the 1640s and 1650s.

None of the volumes is clearly dated, which may be one reason why they have attracted almost no interest from historians of the Commonwealth and Protectorate since they were identified and catalogued in 1976. Even when we have a date, on a board, flyleaf or folio, we cannot be sure that all the entries pertain to the same time. As we have seen, Drake wrote from both ends in his notebooks, and may have used some in tandem rather than sequentially, returning to the same volume over a period of time. That difficulty acknowledged, there are both general and specific indications in several of the manuscripts that enable us to assign them to a period of years, if not to a specific year; and references that clearly point to a book read or extract taken at a particular moment. Indeed volumes such as 21 which appears to have been commenced in the 1630s, and to have been in continual use until 1646 or 1647 (1648 appears on the inside cover), are more the exception than the norm. Volume 22 seems to have been a notebook used in the 1640s, and has as its latest topical reference 'Mr Hobs his book on Human Nature', published in 1650.[27] Most of the volumes have references to texts or events that suggest compilation at some point in the later 1640s to late 1650s. Volume 24, for example, refers to Malvezzi's history of the Catalan Revolt, lives of Alcibiades and Coriolanus, and Henry Wotton's *Reliquiae* published in 1649 and 1650;[28] volumes 12 and 13 refer to works by Matthew Wren and John Gauden published in 1659;[29] volume 53 annotates books by Famianus Strada, Thomas Hobbes and Sir Dudley Digges published over the period 1650–5.[30] One volume opens with notes about the rent of a chamber dated November 1647 and cites a letter dated October 1651.[31] Another contains records of financial transactions from 1648–9 and refers to books published no later than 1655.[32] Volume 30 has the date 2 Jan 1661 faintly on the verso of the first folio; while volume 32 can be clearly dated to the years 1660–3, between Drake's references to his patent of office of 12 June 1660 at the beginning of the manuscript, and a note about Dr Laney, Bishop of Lincoln (elevated to his see on 29 January 1663) at the end.[33]

The composition of many of the volumes, then, can be tied reasonably

27. Ogden MS 7/22 f. 186.
28. Clark, 'Wisdom Literature II', pp. 65–6; Ogden MS 7/24 f. 1v, 153v, 156v, 198v; see V. Malvezzi, *The Chief Events of the Monarchy of Spain* (1647); Malvezzi, *Considerations upon the Lives of Alcibiades and Coriolanus* (1650); H. Wotton, *Reliquiae Wottonianae* (1651).
29. Ogden MSS 7/12 f. 22; 7/13 f. 30; M. Wren, *Monarchy Asserted* (1659); J. Gauden, *Ecclesiae Anglicanae Suspira* (1659).
30. Ogden MS 7/53 ff. 3v, 4v, 91v; Clark, 'Wisdom Literature II', p. 70; F. Strada, *De Bello Belgico: The History of the Low Country Wars* (1650); T. Hobbes, *Leviathan* (1651); D. Digges, *The Compleat Ambassador* (1655).
31. Ogden MS 7/9 flyleaf, f. 5; Clark, 'Wisdom Literature II', p. 57.
32. Ogden MS 7/10 f. 176; see too f. 175.
33. Ogden MS 7/32 ff. 1, 81v, 102v.

closely to a period of a few years. And while some may have been used in tandem, for different purposes – collections of maxims, for example – we can tentatively discern a chronological sequence for certain of the manuscripts and therefore an impression of change in what and how Drake read and thought.

The phrase how Drake read, however, is neither entirely accurate nor unproblematic. For the Ogden notebooks covering the 1640s and 1650s are not, for the most part, in Drake's hand. They are predominantly in the hand of another. Is it then appropriate to consider the notes as Drake's? We recall that in an earlier volume written entirely in his own hand and dating from the 1630s, Drake had contemplated hiring assistants with his legal business and also 'to have a scholar to read my ordinary printed books and still to be discoursing at meals with him or walking in [the] garden to reserve the strength of my own mind for things material and most important'.[34] There was nothing unusual about such a plan. Being read to was the normal experience of reading for the aristocracy and gentry, as well as for the illiterate common folk. Francis Bacon, whom Drake so much admired, had in his essay 'Of Studies' allowed that 'some books also may be read by deputy and extracts made of them by others' but had cautioned that such practices were appropriate only to the 'meaner sort of books'.[35] In Drake's case, the use of a scribe became a necessity rather than a convenience, as his sight failed. Soon after 1645 it would seem that he employed a scribe full-time to 'gather' notes from all his books, not just the 'meaner' or less important. The question is what was the secretary's role and what remained Drake's in the subsequent readings and annotations?

Despite his poor sight, and the reference in his epitaph to Drake becoming an auditor while he was read to,[36] there is evidence that he continued to take his own notes on occasions: some notebooks contain his own hand on pages and in margins that date from the 1640s and 1650s, and the commonplace book in the Folger Library, which extends into the 1650s, is entirely in his hand.[37] But even when the notes are not in his holograph, the evidence strongly suggests that it was Drake who selected the passages to be extracted and copied. In the first place, the proverbs, passages from histories, the illustrations and cross-references frequently repeat those noted in Drake's own hand in earlier or other books.[38] So specific are the references to chapters and pages in some cases that it could only have been Drake's familiarity with

34. Ogden MS 7/7 f. 164. Drake may have used a scribe for some purposes earlier, for he reminds himself when reading Tacitus, Machiavelli and Guicciardini to 'note them with my own hand', Ogden MS 7/7 f. 148.
35. Francis Bacon, *The Essays*, ed. J. Pitcher (Harmondsworth, 1985), p. 209.
36. Clark, 'Wisdom Literature I', p. 297; above, p. 73.
37. For example volumes 10, 16, 21, 27, 32, 37. The Folger notebook appears to run from the late 1630s or early 1640s to the late 1650s.
38. There is a very high correlation of both proverbs and historical illustrations between the Ogden manuscripts and the Folger holograph notebook.

his collections that provided them. Moreover, the language and tone of the comment on passages extracted remain the same, suggesting that whoever's hand is on the page it is Drake's voice we still hear. Indeed, phrases of comment such as 'I like this comparison . . .' indicate that Drake dictated his thoughts to a secretary who literally copied his master's personal pronoun, erasing his own ego, so as to leave the reading and writing still his master's own.[39] Because it seems that Drake still read over, and may have added in his own hand to these notebooks, a sense that he was glossing his own comments and reflections would have remained essential.[40] Drake's secretary doubtless became a learned man in his own right; perhaps, 'discoursing at meals' or on travels in the Low Countries he debated with his employer the meaning and significance of sentences from the classical and humanist books they acquired.[41] All our readings, even those in the 'privacy' of our studies, are a part of such 'conversations'.[42] In Drake's case, his scribe was not the only man with whom converse about books was one of the conditions of reading: discussions with friends and fellow scholars, as well as the reading of commentaries on texts, must complicate the idea of one's 'own' reading.[43] But with that caveat, there is no need to doubt that the readings of the 1640s and 1650s, when he employed his secretary, were (no less than those of the 1630s) Drake's own.

What then did Drake read during the years of civil war, Commonwealth and Protectorate? Many of the references are to authors we have seen Drake reading before. Among the standard classical texts, we find frequent extracts from Plutarch, Lucian, Thucydides, Pindar, Polybius, Euripides, Xenophon, Strabo, Aelian, Aristotle, Cicero, Tacitus, Terence, Sallust and Dion. But now too he adds to his reading some of the Fathers, St Augustine, St Gregory and St Jerome, Gregory of Nyssen,[44] Byzantine histories of Nicephorus, Gregoras and Joannes Zonaras,[45] more of the works of Aquinas, and notably Richard Hooker.[46] Together with more frequent citation of the Scriptures, the additions convey an impression of a greater attention to issues pertaining to religion and the church. As well as returning to the familiar editions and commentaries on the classics he read earlier – Michael Piccarto on

39. See, for example, Ogden MSS 7/20 f. 61v; 7/21 f. 21; 7/25 f. 2v; 7/31 f. 179. A Manguel, who read for the blind Jorge Luis Borges, describes himself as 'simply his notebook', *A History of Reading* (1996), p. 19.
40. For example Ogden MSS 7/21 f. 41; 7/16 f. 14; 7/18 f. 110; 7/21, 24 passim; 7/23 ff. 43, 181; 7/32 ff. 8, 11v; 7/37 ff. 2, 89, 158, 184v. The Folger notebook suggests that Drake reviewed and added to his notes.
41. He is most probably the man to whom Drake bequeathed his foreign books, which would suggest a close intellectual affinity (see below, pp. 270–4).
42. See below, pp. 312–13.
43. Below, pp. 281–2.
44. Ogden MSS 7/13 f. 31; 7/15 f. 90; 7/17 f. 35; 7/27 f. 42; 7/30 f. 62; 7/32 f. 77.
45. Ogden MS 7/37 ff. 8, 13v.
46. Ogden MSS 7/12 ff. 24, 142; 7/55 f. 1v.

Aristotle,[47] Lipsius, Malvezzi and Savile on Tacitus[48] – Drake extended his studies through a wide reading of Renaissance commentators. He read, for example, on Aristotle's *Ethics* commentaries by Archbishop Eustratius, Andronicus of Rhodes, Ludovico Settala and Victorin Strigel;[49] on the *Politics*, Piettro Vettori and Hubert Van Giffen.[50] For the history of Polybius, Drake turned to Girolamo Frachetta, for Dion Cassius to Henry Stephens;[51] and he furthered his reading of Tacitus with commentaries by Scipio Ammirato, Clapmarius, Gruter, Pio Muzio, Carlo Pasquale and Saavedra Fajardo.[52] Drake read again in the humanist works of Petrarch, Vives, Erasmus, Ascham and More, Justus Lipsius, Johannes Loccenius, Tobias Magirus, Jovius Pontanus and Joseph Scaliger;[53] and he extracted passages from the histories of Andrea Morosini, Paolo Paruta, Famianus Strada and the Duc de Rohan.[54]

As well as the texts of continental humanists, Drake also improved his knowledge of English literature by reading Chaucer, Spenser, Sidney's *Apology for Poetry*, Jonson's *Sejanus*, Heywood's *Epigrams*, John Suckling's and Abraham Cowley's poems and Thomas Browne's *Pseudodoxia*.[55] And he furthered his study of English history by reading Polydore Vergil, Thomas More's *History of Richard III*, Thomas Herbert's *History of Henry VIII*, Camden's *Annals* of Queen Elizabeth's reign, Michael Sparke's *History of King James* (1651) and Ralegh's

47. Ogden MS 7/22 f. 35v.
48. Ogden MSS 7/9 f. 120; 7/10 f. 24v; 7/14 f. 151; 7/15 f. 42; 7/21 ff. 79, 181.
49. Ogden MSS 7/14 ff. 53, 56; 7/15 f. 9; 7/18 f. 73; 7/22 ff. 41, 67; 7/53 f. 115. The references are to Eustratius, *Aristotelis . . . Moralia Nicomachia cum Eustrati . . . Explanationibus* (Paris, 1543); *Aristotelis Ethicorum Nicomachorum Paraphrasis Incerto Auctore* (Leyden, 1607); L. Settala, *L. Septali Commentariorum in Aristotelis Problemata* (1602); I have not found to which work of Strigel Drake refers.
50. P. Vettori edited the *Ethics* in 1577 and published *Aristotelis Politicorum libri octo* in 1582; H. Van Giffen (Giphanius), *O. Giphanii Commentarii in Politicorum Opus Aristotelis* (1608).
51. Ogden MSS 7/31 f. 9; 7/9 f. 2. The references are to G. Frachetta, *Il Seminario di'-Governi di Stato et di Guerra* (Venice, 1617); and to H. Stephens [= H. Stephanus], *Dionis Cassii Romanorum Historiarum Libri XXV* (Geneva, 1592).
52. Ogden MSS 7/9 f. 125v; 7/15 f. 73; 7/14 ff. 25, 52, 152v, 198; 7/20 f. 42; 7/21 f. 181; 7/31 f. 134; Clark 'Wisdom Literature II'. See Scipio Ammirato, *Discorsi . . . sopra Cornelio Tacito* (Florence, 1594); A. Clapmarius, *De Arcanis Rerumpublicarum Libri Sex* (Amsterdam, 1641); Gruter, *Varii Discursus*; P. Muzio, *Considerationi sopra Cornelio Tacito* (Brescia, 1623); C. Paschalius, *C. C. Taciti . . . ab Excessu Divi Augusti Annalium Libri Quattuor Priores et in Hos Observationes* (Paris, 1581); Saavedra Fajardo, *Idea Principis Christiano-Politici* (Brussels, 1649).
53. Ogden MSS 7/9 f. 43v; 7/10 ff. 24v, 127, 75v; 7/13 ff. 64, 147; 7/14 ff. 1v, 112v; 7/15 f. 1; 7/16 f. 126; 7/18 ff. 5,135; 7/21 ff. 45–7; 7/27 f. 49.
54. Ogden MSS 7/13 f. 64; 7/15 f. 91; 7/16 f. 48; 7/17 f. 27; 7/21 f. 39v; 7/22 f. 149; 7/53 f. 91v. The histories are A. Morosini, *Historia Veneta* (Venice, 1623); P. Paruta, *The History of Venice* (1658); Strada, *De Bello Belgico*; Henri, Duc de Rohan, *A Treatise of the Interest of the Princes and States of Christendom* (1641). We have Drake's fully annotated copy of this, see below, pp. 262–6.
55. Ogden MSS 7/10 f. 62; 7/13 flyleaf, f. 33; 7/16 f. 1; 7/17 f. 30; 7/19 f. 192; 7/21 f. 27; 7/32 f. 63; 7/29 f. 143; Folger MS ff. 15–23v; on *Sejanus* see below, pp. 259–60.

History of the World.[56] Drake now took special interest in Henrician times, reading the letters of Stephen Gardiner and the correspondence of Henry VIII with Vives and Sir Thomas Wyatt.[57] Evidently while in exile from the wars that raged at home, William read deeply in the letters and histories of Tudor and Jacobean England.

Some of Drake's new readings were of works newly edited or published since the 1630s: Clapmarius's *De Arcanis Rerum Publicarum* and Rohan's *Treatise of the Interest of Princes* from 1641, Fajardo's *Idea of a Christian Prince* (1649), or Sparke's *Narrative History of King James* (1651).[58] During these years Drake appears to have developed some taste for a topical read: John Goodwin's *Right and Might Well Met* (1648), Sir Henry Vane's *The Retired Man's Meditation* (1655), John Gauden's *Ecclesiae Anglia Suspira* and Matthew Wren's *Monarchy Asserted* (1659), Matthew Griffith's *The Fear of God and the King*, and, most interestingly, Hobbes's treatise *Of Human Nature* and *Leviathan* (1650, 1651).[59] Such works reveal Drake engaging with important contemporary political and philosophical positions. But there is little here to suggest that he was well read in the pamphlet polemics that poured from the press during the English Revolution and were collected by the London bookseller George Thomason. Drake's absence from England for most of the 1640s and 1650s may have been a factor, but the book market by the mid-seventeenth century was international and the Dutch, among whom he spent most of his time, were well informed of events in England. Whether he paid no attention to the pamphlets, or perused but did not annotate them, we are led to the conclusion that it was not in the polemical treatises that Drake sought counsel for the conduct of affairs or lessons of state.

Indeed, just as in the 1630s, the authors most often cited in his notebooks from the civil war years are the civic humanists and advocates of realpolitik – Machiavelli and Guicciardini, Justus Lipsius, Comines and Cardan, Pierre Charron and Montaigne, Davila and Botero, Ralegh and Bacon. Not only did Drake read and reread their works, Machiavelli's *History of War* and *History of Florence*, as well as *The Prince* and *Discourses*,[60] he read them through and with a host of translations and commentaries: for example, Frachetta, Remigio Nannini Fiorentino, Francesco Sansovino and Robert Dallington on Guicciardini;[61] 'Bellarmontano', 'Claremontius', Frachetta, Gentillet and Edward

---

56. Ogden MSS 7/10 f. 30v; 7/14 f. 94; 7/15 f. 34; 7/18 ff. 5, 10, 65; 7/19 f. 192; 7/32 f. 74; 7/37 f. 184v.
57. See, for example, Ogden MSS 7/10 f. 30v; 7/21 ff. 12, 16, 45.
58. Ogden MSS 7/9 f. 125v; 7/14 ff. 25, 94; 7/16 f. 48; 7/17 f. 151v; 7/22 ff. 149, 186.
59. Ogden MSS 7/10 f. 174; 7/12 f. 22; 7/17 f. 151v; 7/22 f. 186; 7/30 f. 1v; 7/17 f. 136v; Clark, 'Wisdom Literature II', p. 59.
60. Ogden MSS 7/9 f. 152; 7/18 f. 73. Extracts from *The Prince*, the *Discourses* and Guicciardini are found in almost every volume.
61. Ogden MSS 7/10 f. 180v; 7/16 f. 113; 7/21 f. 26; 7/24 ff. 4, 24. The references are to Frachetta, *Il Seminario*; R. Nannini, *La Historia d'Italia con le Annotationi . . . fatte dal Padre Remigio Fiorentino* (Florence, 1563); F. Sansovino, *Propositioni overo Considerationi in Materia di Cose di Stato, sotto Titolo di Avertimenti . . . di M. F. Guicciardini* (Venice,

Dacres on Machiavelli.[62] Not only do the 'Machiavellians' appear most often in Drake's notebooks, they shaped the reading of other works and the reader's values.

For again, as in the 1630s, it is these works that constitute the key sources for Drake's collection of adages and sentences: that is his rules for behaviour in private and public life. Still more than before, Drake's studies in the 1640s and 1650s involved reflecting again on proverbs, pondering their meanings and applications, and extending lists of adages as an arsenal of prudence. Volumes 9, 13, 15, 18, 20, 24, 25, 28, 37 and the Folger commonplace book consist largely of proverbs – from the Book of Proverbs, Seneca and Polybius, and from the well-known Renaissance collections by Erasmus, Gruter, Magirus, Del Rio, Charles de Bouelles and Jean van de Driesche.[63] In these volumes, to a greater extent than before, Drake's proverbs are also extracted from, and glossed and illustrated by, the fables of Aesop with explication by Grégoire Tholossain, and the emblem books of Joachim Camerarius, Jacob Cats, Saavedra Fajardo, Silvestro Pietrasanta, Cesare Ripa, Joannes Sambucus and Geoffrey Whitney.[64] Yet, for all the greater interest in fables and emblems, in almost every volume, Drake copied and illustrated adages from the works of Machiavelli and Guicciardini, who remained for him the principal sources of wisdom.

Drake's lists and reminders of books to read and things to do tell the same story. The best of the ancient writers he held to be Aristotle, Plutarch, Polybius, Seneca, Xenophon and Tacitus.[65] In an age of frenetic publication

1583); R. Dallington, *Aphorismes Civil and Military . . . out of the first Quarterne of F. Guicciardini* (1613).

62. Ogden MSS 7/22 f. 8v, 37; 7/19 f. 22; 7/30 ff. 67, 74, and ff. 1–110 passim. The references are evidently to Girolamo Frachetta, *Il Principe* (Venice, 1599), I. Gentillet's *Commentarium de Regno* (1577) and Edward Dacre's English editions of the *Discourses* (1636) and *The Prince* (1640). Claremontius is uncertain but appears to be a reference to Scipio Clareamontos who, as well as writing commentaries on Aristotle, published *Della Ragion di Stato* in 1635. 'Bellarmontano' remains unidentified but might possibly be a reference to Cardinal Bellarmine's treatise on the Christian prince.

63. See, for example, Ogden MSS 7/9 f. 25v; 7/10 f. 127; 7/13 passim; 7/15 f. 29; 7/18 ff. 17v, 169v, 170v; 7/20 f. 42; 7/53 f. 49. See J. Gruter, *Florilegium Ethico-Politicum* (Frankfurt, 1610–12); T. Magirus, *Polymnemon sive Florilegium Locorum Communium* (Frankfurt, 1629); M. Del Rio, *Adagialia Sacra Veteris et Novi Testamenti Collectore ac Interprete* (Lyons, 1612); C. Bouillus, *Proverbiorum Vulgarium Libri Tres* (Paris, 1531); J. Van Drusius, *Apophthegmata* (Frankfurt, 1612).

64. Ogden MSS 7/10 ff. 9, 50, 67, 75v; 7/14 f. 136; 7/16 f. 18; 7/18 ff. 13v, 65; 7/20 f. 179; 7/21 f. 181; 7/22 f. 176; Folger MS ff. 128v, 24v. The references are evidently to P. G. Tholossain, *De Republica Libri Sex et Viginti* (Frankfurt, 1609); J. Camerarius, *Fabellae Aesopicae* (1590); J. Cats, *Maechden-plicht, ofte Ampt Der Iconckvrouwen* (Amsterdam, 1618) (Clark 'Wisdom Literature II', p. 62) – there is no other evidence that Drake read Dutch; S. Fajardo, *Idea Principis Christiano-Politici 101 Symbolis Expressa* (Amsterdam, 1659); S. Pietrasanta, *De Symbolis Heroicis Lib IX* (Amsterdam, 1634); C. Ripa, *Iconologia* (Rome, 1593); J. Sambucus, *Emblemata cum Aliquot Nummis Antiqui Operis* (Antwerp, 1564); G. Whitney, *A Choice of Emblemes and Other Devises* (Leyden, 1586).

65. Ogden MS 7/15 f. 3v.

his list of the best moderns was starkly concise: Guicciardini, Machiavelli, Comines and Davila.[66] Sir William turned to other authors for specific purposes, of course: to Balzac on the nature of man, to Frachetta, Bernegerus and Conestaggio for an understanding of proverbs.[67] But on all aspects of wisdom he returned time and again to his favourites. The most prudential sentences and precepts from history, he noted, were to be found in Polybius, Tacitus and the Florentines.[68] So, he observed, the actions of and conspiracies against tyrants were studied to best effect in Tacitus, Guicciardini and Machiavelli.[69] 'To furnish arcana vitae civilis', he reminded himself at the start of volume 12 to read Polybius and Tacitus and extract wise aphorisms from Machiavelli's *Art of War* and Guicciardini's *History of Italy*.[70] 'Well weigh', he added in volume 19, 'and consider the judgements of Guicciardini, Machiavelli and Comines, being all men of action and experience.'[71] It is noteworthy that at the very time he was reading new authors and texts, even works that we would regard as seminal in the study of politics, such as Hobbes, Drake had not fundamentally changed his mind about the books that mattered. His reminders of books to read, were − principally − lists of works to *reread*. It was in the light of those rereadings that he read the English revolution.

Drake's scribe was not his only company as he read. While all those with whom we come into contact influence the ways in which we interpret the world, how we 'read', those with whom we directly exchange and discuss texts become living commentaries on those texts, members of an interpretive community that shares habits of thought, even if not the same views. We have little information about where Drake purchased his books or with whom he came into contact in obtaining them. When he reminds himself that 'the best edition of Thucydides' was that 'printed at Frankfurt 1594: ask for it', we do not know whom he is planning to ask.[72] But we do know the names of some from whom he borrowed books and manuscripts during this period: one Stansby lent him a discourse on the state of Christendom and other things; Mr Mountagu loaned law reports; Mr Ashley lent an unknown discourse.[73] It would be surprising if men who had gone to the trouble of obtaining copies of manuscripts in particular did not discuss them, and the evidence suggests that they did. With regard to the address of Francis Bacon on the postnati, Drake recorded that 'Mr Hall hath the original', apparently as a reminder of the source of his own copy.[74]

66. Ogden MS 7/15 f. 3v; cf. 7/16 f. 81v.
67. Ogden MSS 7/9 f. 9v; 7/19 f. 188v.
68. Ogden MS 7/17 f. 1.
69. Ogden MS 7/16 f. 187.
70. Ogden MS 7/12 f. 4v.
71. Ogden MS 7/19 f. 198.
72. Ogden MS 7/9, note on back board.
73. Ogden MS 7/21 ff. 4, 186v.
74. Ogden MS 7/21 f. 15. The case of the post nati concerned subjects born in Scotland after the dynastic union with England in 1603.

There is evidence of other influences on Drake's reading. In the Nether-
lands, Mr Poignier urged him to read French writers, Cardinals Perron and
'Dorcet', and Paolo Sarpi on the Council of Trent; he also 'commended to
me much Mac[hiavelli] his Florentine History and told me that he had read
it more than twelve times and had found more than at the former reading'.[75]
Drake also discusssed at length with the leading philologian and historian
Gerard Vossius the books most fitting he should read. Vossius recommended
Dion, Quintus Curtius, Paterculus, Polybius, Tacitus and Justus Lipsius. In particular he 'commended Machiavelli his discourses on Livy as a most prudential piece'.[76] Vossius shared more than his views on books with Sir William.
They discussed the situation in Europe, Queen Elizabeth's policy towards the
bishops, the execution of Strafford and the French stirring of the troubles in
England.[77] Conversation, in other words, moved naturally between texts and
events. It is Drake's many discussions about both texts and events that we have
to imagine if we are to understand his reading and his politics.

We do not have to imagine in all cases. There are hints in the notebooks
of the types of discussion that helped form Drake's reading and values. In
what appears to have been a conversation, Dr Hammond warned him to
beware wolves in sheep's clothing, reinforcing the importance of a proverb in
a specific context, and doubtless at the expense of the puritans.[78] Dr Ames's
opinion on imposters proved Drake's own observations that 'universus mundus
exercet histrionem.'[79] With 'Mr. P.' he conversed often of books, the nature of
men and politics: 'he much condemned Mr Hobbes for not delivering his
opinions seasonably nor warily in his book.'[80] 'Dr. J' often talked with Drake
about the nature and education of a prince, and about Machiavelli's prince as
a composite of vice and virtue.[81] Such conversations fed Sir William with
gossip or reported anecdotes about the Duke of Buckingham, Richard
Weston, Charles I's Lord Treasurer, and the Earl of Strafford.[82] With Mr
Sedgewick he discussed army pay; Mr Rive delighted in recounting his memories of meeting James I.[83] 'J.R.' informed him of some affair in England, and

75. Ogden MS 7/21 f. 144. 'Dorset' may be Cardinal Arnaud Dossat.
76. Ogden MS 7/21 f. 145. Vossius went through each author with Drake, pointing out
    their use.
77. Ogden MS 7/21 ff. 145–144v. This is the only direct hint we have of the influence
    of Vossius on Drake's historical and political thinking. See N. Wickenden, *G. J.
    Vossius and the Humanist Concept of History* (Assen, Netherlands, 1993), and below, pp.
    314–15.
78. Ogden MS 7/15 f. 14v. If this was Henry Hammond, one of Charles I's chaplains,
    evicted and imprisoned during the Commonwealth, Drake was evidently in contact
    with staunchly Royalist figures.
79. Ogden MS 7/16 f. 37. 'Everyone plays a part.' William Ames, the Calvinist opponent
    of Arminianism, died in Rotterdam in 1633.
80. Ogden MS 7/21 f. 151v. The identity of Mr P. remains unknown, though the math-
    ematician John Pell was in Breda, and Drake evidently knew him (f. 167v).
81. Ogden MS 7/21 ff. 150, 169v–169, 164, 162v, 158.
82. Ogden MS 7/16 ff. 124, 143, 165.
83. Ogden MSS 7/13 f. 2; 7/21 f. 150.

aired his view that governments in all ages were 'shot at' by crafty and violent men.[84] These snippets of conversation are found between notes from classical histories and proverbs,[85] presumably because in reading Drake remembered a recent encounter or paused in his studies to receive a visitor or walk abroad. In either case, as he turned back to his books, the conversations of the world remained in the study with him.

Strategies of Reading

The manuscript notebooks in the Ogden collection permit rare insight into habits of reading in the Renaissance, and graphically underline how different they were to our own material and intellectual practices. The ways in which we annotate a book or books express our purposes in reading but also our mode of ordering our thoughts and consciousness of the world. Even the seemingly dry details of pagination, reference and indexing are ideological practices which relate to, express and help determine broader values and perceptions. So we shall need to look closely at how, in the 1640s and 1650s, Drake took and organised notes, how he moved to and from books, bringing information together, how his organisation of reading and mode of annotation determined the way he read and interpreted what he read. Only then may we consider what for him was the purpose of reading and analyse the relationship of the texts he studied to his 'own' views – by which we mean his personal synthesis of that reading and his experience.

   Though he neither foliated nor paginated consistently through his notebooks, Drake did at times give page, as well as chapter, references to books, possibly in cases where he had more than one edition. His notes from Tacitus' *Histories* and *Annals* in volume 12, for example, and from Erasmus and Machiavelli's *Discourses* have page numbers.[86] This method of reading sequentially through a book, noting points of interest as the pages turn, is the mode of working most familiar to a modern scholar. In Drake's case it is his least common method. More frequently he organised what he read under topic headings. Accordingly notes from Magirus, Cicero and Pliny and other authors are arranged under 'Beneficiam' (favour), 'Eloquentia', 'Prudentia';[87] passages from Tacitus are sorted into groups of references on anarchy, sedition, fame, prudence, modesty and dissimulation;[88] extracts from Thucydides, Cardan and

84. Ogden MS 7/27 f. 2.
85. Drake also conversed with a 'Mr Pet' and 'Mr Jons'. For other examples, see 7/29 ff. 131, 134.
86. Ogden MSS 7/12 f. 99; 7/9 f. 127; 7/19 ff. 36ff.
87. Ogden MS 7/10 f. 127.
88. Ogden MS 7/14 ff. 7ff.

Guicciardini fill out sections on the populace and the prince;[89] and a variety of texts and historical examples is used to explore flattery and artifice, and the nature of man.[90]

The organisation by topic headings was of course the typical practice for Renaissance commonplace books, recommended by Erasmus and Bacon. But its familiarity should not lead us to lose sight of its importance. Our modern reading habit, of annotating as we proceed through a whole book, privileges the text: to a great extent what we annotate is prompted and conditioned by the text. Because we have not laid out headings (at least explicitly) in advance, the book itself gives rise to thoughts about how to arrange its observations. By contrast, the commonplace method places the reader in a more dominant position and forces the text into categories he has conceived – albeit as a consequence of earlier readings, as well as experience. The topical arrangement of notes may also help to explain the Renaissance reader's custom of frequent rereadings. Since the topics being explored often relate to a present question or event, and because the student does not have continuous notes from the text, a shift of interest compels a rereading, so as to effect a rearrangement. And this is clearly what Drake did. The same texts appear extracted under different headings and when passages are summarised and indexed as a mode of recall, it is the topic – 'contra torrentem', 'hypocrisy', for example – not the author or text that is most often summarised and indexed.[91] Unlike our own indices of the subjects in a single text, Drake's were usually to subjects which derived from a variety of texts: history, proverb, emblem, Scripture, etc. Return to a topic on a later occasion led him at times to a different shuffling of the pack, that is to another way of figuring a question.

Despite, or perhaps it was because of, his wide reading, Drake reminded himself that it was better to read and comprehend a few things carefully than have a superficial knowledge of many. Under the topic 'Lectio' he copied the advice 'qui quo destinavit pervenire vult unam sequatur viam et non per multa vagetur.'[92] He developed the point in taking notes on Seneca's counsel to Lucillius:

> the multitude of books distracteth and distempereth the judgement; when as therefore thou canst not read as much as thou hast, it sufficeth thee to have as much as thou canst read. Read therefore always the most approved, and though for vanity's sake you sometimes change, let the others be unto thee as thy harbour, these as thy ordinary habitation.[93]

89. Ogden MS 7/19 f. 186.
90. Ogden MS 7/20 ff. 1 onwards.
91. See, for example, Ogden MSS 7/12 f. 99; 7/19 f. 186; 7/21 f. 21; 7/20 f. 40.
92. Ogden MS 7/22 f. 96. 'Whoever seeks to arrive at his destination should pursue one path, not many.'
93. Ogden MS 7/14 f. 131.

Reminding himself on another occasion of the importance of 'fixing upon certain choice authors', he listed his selection as Polybius and Tacitus, Machiavelli, Guicciardini and Comines. These he would 'chew and digest' again and again.[94] The simile of digestion, taken from Seneca, was more than mere rhetoric; it describes a process by which the reader appropriates, consumes and reconstitutes the text:

> The meat which we have taken, so long as it swimmeth whole in our stomachs, is a burden, but when it changeth from that which it was, then at length it turns into strength and nourishment. The same let us do in our reading books. Let us not suffer these things to remain entire which we have gathered from various authors *for they will not then be ours*, but let us endeavour to digest and concoct them – otherwise they will fill the memory and leave the understanding void and empty.[95]

Drake did not discount the importance of memory as the first step to understanding. 'For memory's sake' he instructed himself to write out again passages concerning the nature of man from Polybius, Aristotle and Tacitus, Machiavelli, Guicciardini and Cardan, Lipsius, Magirus and Bacon.[96] We find, similarly, in volume 27, a list of 'similes to be continually remembered'.[97] But the memory was merely a means to an end: the possession of a databank of adages, sentences, historical examples, speeches, fables and lives that illustrated qualities and instructed in behaviour. To the memory the reader needed to bring judgement: 'certainly to attain wisdom and learning there is required not only much reading but likewise a memory to retain what is read [and] *most of all* a sound judgement to apply things read or heard to the right use.'[98] Such judgement was sharpened by comparison: by cross-referring passages to other texts, to 'some proverb, apothegm or sentence of gravest historians'.[99] As Guicciardini put it, the more a reader meditated on passages, the better he understood and knew how to act.[100] Drake concurred: 'For the gaining wisdom there is nothing more effectual than frequent reading apothegms, proverbs, prudent fables, wisest speeches . . . emblems, strategems, judgements and sentences raised upon various occasions in history.'[101] In our age of the soundbite and an infinity of text, the habit of close reading and exegesis

---

94. Ogden MS 7/14 f. 108; cf. 7/27 f. 140v.
95. Ogden MS 7/13 f. 73v, my italics. Interestingly Ben Jonson deployed the same metaphor, urging that the poet be 'not as a creature that swallows what it takes in crude, raw or undigested; but that feeds with an appetite and hath a stomach to concoct, divide and turn all into nourishment', *Ben Jonson Works*, ed. C. H. Herford and P. Simpson (12 vols, Oxford, 1925–52), vol. 8, p. 638.
96. Ogden MS 7/14 f. 221v.
97. Ogden MS 7/27 f. 195.
98. Ogden MS 7/37 f. 170v, my italics.
99. Ogden MS 7/31 f. 2; cf. 7/25 f. 197; 7/30 f. 183; 7/37 f. 1v.
100. Ogden MS 7/53 f. 167.
101. Ogden MS 7/25 f. 197.

threatens to fade into history. What we are beginning to see is that habits of thought – processes of critical judgement and the ways we formulate values – will almost certainly pass with it. Drake's usual method of the frequent meditation and ingestion of a few favoured works was intrinsically an ideological practice. The list of the books he selected made it the practice of a particular ideology.

A casual reading of Drake's notebooks gives the impression that he did not practise what he advocated. There are hundreds of references in these pages, not just the few select ones he enjoined; and appended to many extracts we find several cross-references and citations. In our own literary culture the cross-reference is usually given to support a passage, or sometimes to counter it and point up a contrary argument. In Drake's case, references to other works, in different languages, or to examples from various historical periods, or to different genres – say an emblem book or fable – were intended to explain and amplify a passage rather than to support or contradict it. At the simplest level, cross-referring Machiavelli's *History of Florence* to his *Discorsi* helps him to explicate an adage.[102] Similarly he moves from Tacitus' dealing with Rhescuporis, King of Thrace to Machiavelli's counsel, from his chapter of the *Discorsi* on conspiracies, 'to leave still somewhat as an obstacle between men's desires and a kingdom'.[103] For more context to Machiavelli's passage about Severus' dealing with the Emperor Julian, he refers to Herodian's history.[104] Similarly Guicciardini's advice not to give men the power to hurt us is extended by Drake from the observation of Comines that nothing restrains men from violence when they have power.[105]

Such cross-references not only amplify and explain, they render a passage more familiar and more personal by bringing it within circles of already well-known texts or observations. John Earle's character of a detractor was rendered all the more familiar when Drake recalled, without quoting, Hooker's observation that those who criticised governments seldom wanted for an audience.[106] Such familiarising, however, could subtly shift the meaning. The passage from Earle, for instance – 'a detractor passeth the more plausibly because all men have a snatch of his humour' – does not explicitly refer to political calumny, as does Hooker. The explication of one text by another or others, of a different genre or period, helps give meaning to the original, and at the same time shifts meaning, each time the passage is differently contextualised. This is particularly true when an adage or general observation is glossed and 'explained' by a specific historical example or event. For example, Drake's observation on the proverb 'responsio mollis frangit iram' – that had

102. Ogden MS 7/21 f. 81. Bacon advised: 'read not to contradict or confute', quoted in E. R. Kintgen, *Reading in Tudor England* (Pittsburgh, 1996), p. 186.
103. Ogden MS 7/9 f. 39.
104. Ogden MS 7/24 f. 179.
105. Ogden MS 7/18 f. 10v.
106. Ogden MS 7/25 f. 44. Drake refers to this observation of Hooker's in several other volumes.

Rehoboam remembered his father's advice he would have kept his kingdom – quite explicitly politicises a general adage.[107] Cross-references and historical illustrations were devices for extracting meaning and wisdom from proverbs or passages of a text.[108] Sometimes when he returned to that text, the same example or reference recurs. But as in different circumstances other historical illustrations or glosses sprang to mind, so the 'meaning' for Drake of the original text was subtly, or indeed more radically, transformed. Cross-referencing, in other words, was not a process that fixed interpretation but one that rendered the same original extract or text fit for different uses through changing times.

The detail and extent of cross-referencing raises the question of *how* Drake (and his circle) worked. A good memory allows a scholar to recall a passage in a book, even a chapter; but seldom a specific page – or indeed an exact quotation. The many cross-references, then, in Drake's notebooks to particular editions and pages point to his using several books at once. This was a not uncommon Renaissance practice, as we know from the case of Gabriel Harvey; there were even machines called book wheels that enabled the scholar to move more easily from one text to another – we might think of them as Windows 1498.[109] What has not been adequately discussed is the significance of this practice. While the modern scholar may move across and between books for information, we seldom fragment the reading of a book to turn to another before pursuing the original text. In Drake's case, however, this appears to have been his usual method of reading. He takes for instance, a volume such as Janus Gruter's *Tacitus*, and, as he reads through it, moves across to other works, including Comines and Guicciardini.[110] In volume 14, he interposes between notes on Seneca extracts from Michael Sparke's history of James I;[111] in volume 21 notes on Laud's life are found between extracts from Guicciardini;[112] and references to Hugh Peter's *God's Doings and Man's Duty* (1646) are found in the middle of a section of notes on Machiavelli's *Discourses* and *History of Florence*![113]

This practice of fragmenting texts, opening them to other works, detaches them from their own historical context and from the 'meaning' they had and performed in it. Drake seldom read his classical authors without their many Renaissance humanist commentators. In the case of Tacitus he praised as the most 'acute interpreters' Lipsius, Clapmarius, Saavedra Fajardo, Botero, Lopez, Bacon, Malvezzi, Scipio Ammirato, Cats, Gruter, Piccarto, Locconius, Magirus,

107. Ogden MS 7/25 f. 103. 'A gentle response subdues anger.'
108. See below, pp. 217–18.
109. See A. Grafton and L. Jardine, '"Studied for Action": How Gabriel Harvey Read his Livy', *Past & Present* 129 (1990), pp. 30–78.
110. See Ogden MS 7/20.
111. Ogden MS 7/14 f. 94.
112. Ogden MS 7/21 ff. 101–101v, 105.
113. Ogden MS 7/21 f. 126.

Refuge and Hannibal Scotus.[114] In this company Tacitus inevitably becomes an exponent of the school of modern realpolitik. And the process of recruiting him is furthered when, pursuing Tacitus through Barriento's edition and commentary of 1618, Drake dwells on Catherine de Medici's subtle dealings with the Duc d' Anjou.[115]

The fragmentation of texts was by no means an equal practice. A few selected authors were those that dominate the pages and the margins of Drake's notebooks, and the number of his cross-references. These are the texts that are most frequently allowed to permeate other works and interpret them. When, as Drake instructed himself, he 'put things of Polybius, Tacitus, Aristotle and Seneca together', regarding the first two as 'choice authors', Aristotle and Seneca are read rather differently than they are by those who take them as the principal source of traditional moral and political values in a Christian commonweal.[116] When Seneca's words are read through other modern 'various authors', including Montaigne, the figure, who along with Machiavelli, was demonised as the greatest threat to those values, a very radical rereading is taking place.[117]

In part this reinterpretation was a matter of language. John Pocock and Quentin Skinner have argued that changes in political thought are effected through linguistic shifts; and Pocock has posited that a vocabulary of *ius*, grace and custom slowly gave way to one of rights and interests.[118] The early modern period is of especial importance, not least because for some time both vocabularies were in play, as indeed were Christian Aristotelianism and Machiavellian notions of political life, or faith in eternal verities and scepticism. To a large extent the clashes of values revolved around the status and interpretation of particular texts: Machiavelli, after all, claimed to be only glossing Livy. What he did in fact was, in several senses, translate Livy: not only from Latin into Italian, but from the last century BC to the Cinquecento, and from the idioms of Ciceronian Latin to those of *ragione di stato*. In Drake's case his admiration for Tacitus, as read through Renaissance commentators, and for the 'Florentines' – Machiavelli, Guicciardini and Botero – inflected his own language. The influence can seem trivial: in one instance, he refers to Psalm 55 and its lesson that 'David judged the treachery of a familiar friend much more dangerous than the violence of an open enemy.'[119] In the Authorised Version David's lament was that it was 'thou . . . mine acquaintance' that

114. Ogden MS 7/21 f. 181. As well as the texts we have already cited, Drake apparently refers to G. Botero, *Della Ragion di Stato* (Venice, 1589); J. Marianae, *De Rege et Regis Institutione* (Toledo, 1599); E. Du Refuge, *Traité de la Cour* (1619, English trans. 1652); A. Scotus, *A. Scotti in P. C. Taciti Annales et Historias Commentarii* (1589).
115. See Ogden MS 7/16 ff. 22–6.
116. Ogden MS 7/19 f. 195.
117. Ogden MS 7/14 f. 153.
118. See J. G. A. Pocock, *The Machiavellian Moment: Florentine Political Thought and the Atlantic Republican Tradition* (Princeton, 1976); above, pp. 18–19.
119. Ogden MS 7/15 f. 71v.

reproached him. The Scriptural text (as we shall see in detail) is translated into the language of adages, and into sententiae of a Machiavellian stripe. A more extreme example is Sir William noting that 'Plato says ragione di stato transforms a man into a wolf.'[120] Here the language of cinquecento humanism is placed in the mouth of the father of philosophy, leading Plato to speak the words of the Italians. Drake himself wrote, as well as read, Latin and Italian (and French) well. That is to say that he could think in those various cultural idioms. Indeed he often copies an adage, from Polybius or Thucydides, in Italian either because he was working from an Italian edition or commentary, or because the axiom had now become most familiar to him in its Italian rendition.[121] To sense a natural inclination to frame a proverb in Italian, often one whose sentiments can be pithily captured in English, is to discern not just familiarity with the Italian language, but an immersion in the values it encoded.[122]

To put it bluntly, Drake read his ancient authors at times as though they were quattrocento and cinquecento texts. And in the process he made them so. Take Plutarch's *Morals*, one of the central texts of Renaissance education in virtue. In Drake's notes it becomes a source of advice concerning the use of force to suppress dissension and the effectiveness of deceit in obtaining one's ends.[123] Seneca, too, glossed through other authors, becomes virtually the 'author' of a Machiavellian injunction to seize 'occasion'.[124] But the best illustration comes from Drake's annotations and interpretation of Aristotle. Not only the father of scholastic philosophy and an important source of Thomism, Aristotle through the *Ethics* and *Politics* defined the moral life and the state as a community established to make possible the good life. In the *Ethics* Aristotle described moral excellence as the feeling which makes men ashamed to do wrong. Man had the capacity to attain to that condition: 'what the statesman is most anxious to produce is a certain moral character in his fellow citizens, namely a disposition to virtue and the performance of virtuous actions.'[125] The state, Aristotle argued, exists 'for the good life'; rule must be by the best man or men.[126] When we turn to Drake's Aristotle, he becomes virtually unrecognisable. Drake evidently read widely in the works of Aristotle: the *Metaphysics* and *Physics* as well as the *Ethics*, *Politics* and the *Rhetoric*.[127] But he chops up Aristotle under his headings ('Prudentia' and

120. Ogden 7/15 f. 58v.
121. See, for example, Ogden MS 7/24 ff. 63, 75v.
122. Ogden MS 7/24 f. 81v, and passim; cf. below, pp. 313–15. Manguel reminds us that 'translation proposes a sort of parallel universe, another space and time in which the text reveals other . . . possible meanings', *A History of Reading*, p. 276. Drake may have travelled to Italy but there are no direct references to such a journey in the notebooks.
123. Ogden MSS 7/21 f. 80; 7/19 f. 43.
124. Ogden MS 7/15 f. 97v.
125. Aristotle, *Ethics*, ed. J. A. K. Thomson (Harmondsworth, 1953), p. 44.
126. Aristotle, *The Politics*, ed. T. A. Sinclair (Harmondsworth, 1962), p. 114 and Book III passim.
127. See Ogden MSS 7/22 f. 44v; 7/9 f. 170v.

'Artifice' as well as 'Iustitia') and he reads him through commentaries by Settala, Strigel, van Giffen, Piccarto, Laertius, Vettori;[128] and alongside extracts from Magirus, Grotius, Heinsius, and Malvezzi, Guicciardini and Comines, Machiavelli and Cardan.[129]

As a result, Aristotle takes on some of the flavour of other authors with very different views. Drake has Aristotle arguing that one should regard what men do not what they say and be wary of dissimulation; stating that cunning is an essential attribute of prudence; defending artifice; counselling tyrants to make a show of religion to advance their goals; advising them how to support their regime, how to rule men by sophistry and fear; and advocating expediency, hypocrisy and perjury in an uncertan moral universe.[130] To realise just how far these summaries take us from Aristotle's meaning, we need to place Drake's claim that 'Aristotle saith that a man cannot be well honest without prudence Ethics' alongside what the *Ethics* says on this point. 'What do we need prudence for?' Aristotle asks in the twelfth chapter of Book VI: 'What it studies is the just and the noble and what is good for man, things which a virtuous person does by the very law of his being.'[131] This is a rather different notion from, say, Machiavelli's sense – that 'a prudent ruler cannot keep his word' – which corresponds closely to Drake's own understanding of the word, as the pursuit of interest by whatever means.[132] While it is true, as Drake writes, that Aristotle acknowledged that 'the question of the morally fine' admits of divergence and 'variation of opinion', the philosopher did not say that 'the least circumstance vary the matter', nor did he intend in any sense to detach morality from politics.[133] Finally, to list in his index of lessons from Aristotle the sentence that 'fear is a powerful means to preserve states' is to subvert Aristotle's principal argument that it would be 'completely unreasonable' if the statesman 'were to be reduced to seeing how he could rule and dominate others with or without their consent'.[134] No less, the claim that Aristotle would have princes taught 'to purge their minds from compassion that they might not stick at cruelty where their interest required it' grossly misrepresents Aristotle's passages about the qualities of a ruler.[135] 'The

128. Ogden MSS 7/15 f. 9; 7/18 f. 73; 7/22 ff. 22, 41, 67; Clark 'Wisdom Literature II'. The references are to L. Settala, *Septali Commentariorum in Aristotelis Problemata* (Frankfurt, 1602–7); O. *Giphanii Commentarii in Politicorum Opus Aristotelis* (1608); M. Piccartus, *In Politicos Libros Aristotelis* (Leipzig, 1645); Laertius Diogenes wrote a life of Aristotle (1552); Pietro Vettori edited and commented on Aristotle's *Ethics, Politics* and *Rhetoric*. These differ from the late antique commentators Drake was using earlier.
129. Ogden MSS 7/15 ff. 4vff.; 7/18 ff. 47, 105; 7/22 passim.
130. See Ogden MSS 7/15 f. 4v; 7/16 f. 171; 7/18 ff. 47, 105v; 7/19 f. 43; 7/20 ff. 60–1; 7/22 ff. 4, 61, 62, 74, 80, and passim; 7/37 f. 78v; 7/53 f. 79.
131. Ogden MS 7/22 f. 74. Aristotle, *Ethics*, p. 187.
132. N. Machiavelli, *The Prince*, ed. Q. Skinner (Cambridge, 1988), p. 61.
133. Aristotle, *Ethics*, Book I, ch. 3, p. 27; Ogden MS 7/22 f. 62v.
134. Aristotle, *Politics*, Book VII, ch. 2, p. 260.
135. Ogden MS 7/53 f. 79.

friendship of a king for his subjects', Aristotle put it in Book VIII of the *Ethics*, expresses itself in benevolence.[136]

One cannot escape the conclusion that, though Aristotle is the apparent main text in volume 22, it is the Aristotle of the later commentators, still more a Machiavellian Aristotle, that Drake extracts: the Aristotle who falls into line with the Florentines in illustrating those qualities of self-help, artifice and expediency which formed Drake's own values. In fact at times Drake appears not only to render Machiavellian the morality of Plutarch, Seneca and Aristotle, but even to outdo the advocates of realpolitik by claiming they departed further from conventional morality than they did.[137] One example may be taken from a section of Drake's notes from Bacon's *Essays*, in particular the essay 'Of Goodness and Goodness of Nature'. Drake cites Bacon's reference to Machiavelli's observation (from the *Discourses*, Book II) that Christianity had given up good men as prey to the tyrannical and unjust. (It is a point he makes in different words, often without attribution, throughout the volumes.) What, however, is not cited here is Bacon's clear statement that 'the inclination to goodness is imprinted deeply in the nature of man.'[138] Bacon epitomises the ambiguities of Jacobean England about social and political morality: he was a Christian who knew what men should be, but also a realist who, knowing what they were, saw the need for pragmatism and expediency. Drake picks up Bacon the Machiavel and silences the Bacon who had a more conventional and optimistic perception of human nature and the state.

It is worth noting that even Machiavelli qualifies the argument here extracted. For the tendency of Christianity to render men weak, he goes on to say, is the fault, not of the faith itself, but of those 'who have interpreted our religion according to the promptings of indolence rather than those of virtue': the result of a 'false interpretation of our religion'.[139] It is not an isolated instance of the less than faithful representation of perhaps Drake's favourite writer. In volume 16, Drake summarises Machiavelli's *The Prince* chapter 18 as 'bad man makes best king', and illustrates the adage from the example in the *Discourses* of Cyrus who attained greatness through practising fraud and deception.[140] While he does defend princes who break faith to preserve their interest, however, Machiavelli still urges that they 'not deviate from right conduct *if possible*', albeit they be able to do evil if constrained.[141] Machiavelli's important caveat, his general recognition that if men were good the

---

136. Aristotle, *Ethics*, p. 248.
137. On Seneca see, for example, Ogden MSS 7/15 f. 97; 7/22 f. 126v; on Plutarch 7/19 f. 43.
138. Ogden MSS 7/22 ff. 146–7; Bacon, *Essays*, 'Of Goodness and Goodness of Nature', p. 96; N. Machiavelli, *Discourses*, ed. B. Crick (Harmondsworth, 1970), Book II, ch. 2.
139. Machiavelli, *Discourses*, Book II, ch. 2.
140. Machiavelli, *The Prince*, p. 62; *Discourses*, Book II, ch. 13.
141. Machiavelli, *The Prince*, p. 62.

ruler could and should be virtuous too, is elided. In reducing him to adages, Drake out-machiavels even Old Nick.

Drake's reading practices – the arrangement by topic, the digestion of a few books amplified by commentary and observation, the way notes were organised and authors simplified into axioms – were part and parcel of the purpose, the goal of his reading. This is another area in which, if we are to understand Renaissance readers, we must again lay aside our own post-Romantic assumptions. The scholar today reads for the furtherance of knowledge and understanding of an academic subject, for intellectual advancement. The common reader most often reads for entertainment, diversion or escapism, or perhaps to learn a craft. Such readers existed in early modern Europe. But it was more common for the Renaissance scholar to 'study for *action*' rather than contemplation, and for the literate to read for use rather than for recreation. Time and again Drake asserts as the central purpose of his reading its use and application. 'The chief use of studies', he wrote, as he took notes on Bacon's essay, 'is for ability and disposition of business'. (Bacon had opened his essay with 'ability' as the last of a list: 'Studies serve for delight, for ornament and for ability'.)[142]

It was this utilitarian approach to learning that dictated the careful rereading and reordering of information and arguments from the best sources, rather than the reading of more new titles. 'He that would read to make profit and form his judgement ought to make election of certain choice authors which he ought to chew and digest . . . multitude of books breed but inconstancy of mind.'[143] Recalling Demetrius Cynicus's advice that it was better to have a few precepts of wisdom in use than many not applied, he added: 'The profit rests not in reading many men's books but remembering the choicest things therein contained and knowing dexterously to apply them as occasion serves.'[144] In a conversation about books and learning with Drake, Gerard Vossius, the Dutch humanist, reiterated the need for the prudent to instruct themselves in the manners of men and of courts.[145] In his notebooks we see Drake endlessly rearranging his authors under the headings that rendered them most useful in teaching prudent behaviour in a hostile world. Volume 30 for example contains extracts from Cicero, Aristotle, Polybius, Tacitus, Livy, Guicciardini and Bacon – on the Nature of Man – all '*ad usum* applicata'.[146] It was adages and axioms that encapsulated the prudent counsel of these authors and not just reading their precepts 'but . . . fixing upon few of the most excellent and putting them in execution upon occasion' that fostered 'prudence'.[147] No less than Gabriel Harvey, Drake studied not for scholarly

142. Ogden MS 7/30 ff. 140v–141; Bacon, *Essays*, p. 209.
143. Ogden MS 7/13 f. 77.
144. Ogden MS 7/25 f. 2v.
145. Ogden MS 7/21 f. 145. Vossius recommended Tacitus, Guicciardini and Machiavelli.
146. Ogden MS 7/30 f. 149 and passim.
147. Ogden MS 7/21 f. 158v.

contemplation but for action, preparing a self-help manual of prudential instruction for engagement with the world.

Axioms, adages, proverbs dominate Drake's Civil War notes. Sometimes they are quotations in the original language, or translations of sentences in a classical or humanist text. However, Drake not only copied (and paraphrased), he was also ever formulating new adages as he distilled from his reading the lessons for life that he read to learn. Drake's usual source is history, and time and again he makes a general rule out of a specific historial event: from Clapmarius's commentary on Tacitus he observes of page 63: 'dangerous to leave succession uncertain'; from Livy he draws the lesson that 'sudden surprises most effectual'.[148] Even when the notes taken are on specific historical figures or events – Augustus, Junius Brutus, Varro's errors at the battle of Lima, the Florentines' tactical mistake at Pisa – the lesson is made universal: 'Caesar's wisdom in observing his passions', 'Junius Brutus feigning folly', 'Clement 7 error in not obliging men'.[149] History becomes for Drake not only a source of lessons but of new proverbs that gloss existing adages and add to their number. As he took notes on the *Discourses* and Livy's account of the Romans dealing with Philip at Antiochus, Drake frames an axiom: 'prudent eye excells potent hand.'[150] It was a deliberate and conscious, not merely instinctive, way of working. Reading Walsingham's correspondence with Cecil, Leicester and others, Sir William makes of Leicester's advice about burning letters the axiom 'ill effects of not secreting weighty affairs', and as a new proverb comes to mind he even writes 'Pro' in the margin – perhaps as a reminder to cross-reference it to his collection of adages.[151] Drake's notebooks become a data-bank of sententious adages, some familiar, copied and glossed, some distilled from a history, some constructed from Drake's own chewing over a passage.

The familiarity of so much of the material in Drake's commonplace books would seem to discourage any attempt to read them as evidence of his own views. What is 'commonplace' in our culture is trite and platitudinous. We value original thought and observation and are most interested in those figures who exhibit it. Our sense of self is tied into notions of 'possessing' ideas some at least of which are not 'common', a term which is derogatory as well as descriptive. Such assumptions and judgements, themselves undermined by critics in recent years, were not those of the Renaissance. Those who read sought to partake of a common wisdom, to come to an understanding of God's world and works by working through the obfuscations and misinter-pretations by which fallen men had obscured them. This is not to argue that there was a naive belief in one shared worldview. Men knew that even the Scriptures, that light of God's truth, had always been the subject of conflict-

148. Ogden MS 7/14 f. 52.
149. Ogden MS 7/19 f. 36.
150. Ibid.; the reference is to *Discourses*, Book II, ch. 1.
151. Ogden MSS 7/53 ff. 185ff.; 7/19 ff. 36ff.

ing interpretations, and recently religious war. But where we regard different interpretations as natural and positive, to the early modern world they were cause for regret. The philologians' pursuit of the perfect text, of Scripture or Aristotle, the linguists' quest for the lost language of Adam expressed *desire* for a shared interpretation. The commonplace, that on which most could agree, rendered the understanding closer to that of man before the fall. Such ideals were being undermined while they were still strongly held, not least by the Protestant emphasis on personal faith through reading of Scripture and the sceptical relativism of scholars such as Montaigne. Perhaps the central faultline in the early modern age was that between belief in a common hermeneutic and a growing emphasis on individual judgement.[152]

If so, the Renaissance commonplace book is an example and site of that fissure. Here, as the note-taker copies the important passages of the most learned authors, he shares in the wisdom of all literate humanity. Yet as he selects, paraphrases, arranges, glosses, cross-references and indexes, he performs a very individual reading and interpretation, and an act of power 'over' the text, an act which makes what he writes and thinks his own. In several ways Drake makes very much his own the works of those he reads, and it would appear that he was quite aware of doing so. In a discussion with Drake about ancient writers of authority, 'Mr. P.' observed that Aristotle was so ambiguous that none could be certain exactly what he believed.[153] Commentary and gloss, any 'reading' therefore, was seen as an act of interpretation, of giving 'meaning', an act that blurred the distinction between author and reader. All of Drake's notebooks evidence the permeability of the author/reader boundary. We have noticed how the fragmentation of the texts, reading along-side other works, could refashion their meaning; we have argued that language translated – sometimes wrenched – meaning into quite a different realm of values. In other ways, Drake made the texts he read his own. When, for example, he annotated Bacon's essay 'Of Studies', Drake titles his notes 'Of Studies and Books'.[154] The change may appear trivial, but it also reflects Drake's approach to his reading. Books he valued, but 'studies', as a scholarly pursuit, he suspected as too concerned with contemplation rather than use and action. To take another illustration from Bacon, in his essay on vicissitude the Lord Chancellor wrote of 'speculative heresies, such as the Arians and *now* the Arminians'. When Drake quoted the passage, evidently in the 1660s, he omitted the 'now': Arminianism was no longer novel, nor indeed the political issue that it had been for him in the 1630s.[155] The subtle shift reveals how Bacon was updated for new circumstances, in which different 'speculative heresies' were still a cause for concern. Drake's frequent discussions about books, his own 'observations from converse with men', always

152. See also below, pp. 277–83.
153. Ogden MS 7/21 f. 151v.
154. Ogden MS 7/30 f. 140v.
155. Ogden MS 7/30 f. 135v; see Bacon, *Essays*, p. 230. The notebook has a memorandum dated 1661 on f. 1v.

brought onto the pages he read the experiences of the world outside.[156] As England moved from the halcyon days of personal rule through civil war and revolution to Restoration, Drake not only reread and reannotated his books, to some extent he also rewrote them, to make them texts for his purposes and times.

It was principally through the reading, formulation and interpretation of proverbs that Drake worked out his personal values, his view of men (and women) and his perception of politics. Proverbs distilled all the texts and experience of ancient wisdom. Aristotle himself had argued that 'proverbs were but the relics of philosophy', and philosophy the fount of all wisdom.[157] Drake himself put it slightly differently when he described proverbs as 'the oracles of time and experience'.[158] For he did not value them as the dead remains of scholastic philosophy but as the lessons of experience that might form guides to conduct in the present. Seneca had advised men to govern themselves by maxims 'which is like laying a solid foundation of our life and course'.[159] Drake had an even more utilitarian view: 'a sentence', he wrote, 'is a universal proposition concerning those things which are to be desired or avoided in the actions or passions of common life.'[160] Though of an age proverbs were for all time because 'occasions run round in a ring and what was once profitable may again be practised and again [be] effectual whether a man speak them as ancient or *make them his own.*'[161]

If, however, the benefits of their ancient wisdom were to be fruitfully imbibed, they had first to be understood. And if they were, as Bacon put it, to cut to the knot of a business, they had to be skilfully applied.[162] Though most of the humanist scholars applauded and collected *sententiae* and proverbs, they acknowledged that they did not yield their meanings easily. Erasmus, whose *Adagia* was perhaps the most influential collection of proverbs in Renaissance Europe, spoke of their lessons needing to be drawn from obscurity ('moderata quadam obscuritate') and lying in their deeper rather than surface meaning.[163] Drake indeed copied a similar passage from Erasmus's letters: 'apothegmata habent plus philosophiae in recessu quam in prima fronte prae se ferunt . . .'[164] Proverbs that is, though the distillation of reading, had themselves to be read. If they were to serve as a foundation for life they required careful exegesis of their ancient wisdom, and if a man were to 'make them his own' he needed always to *re*consider their meaning in changed and changing times.

156. Ogden MS 7/21 f. 180v.
157. Ogden MS 7/18 f. 42.
158. Ogden MS 7/37 f. 19.
159. Ogden MS 7/53 f. 143v.
160. Ogden MS 7/22 f. 32v.
161. Ogden MS 7/27 f. 31, my italics.
162. Drake twice refers to this Bacon comment, Ogden MSS 7/25 f. 3v; 7/27 f. 31.
163. Ogden MS 7/24 f. 216.
164. Ogden MS 7/21 f. 46.

There was plenty of ancient wisdom in the sources Drake combed for proverbs and sentences. Among the lists of those he cites and recommends we find Aristotle, Xenophon, Thucydides, Plato, Polybius, Seneca, Demosthenes, Isocrates, Euripides, Lucian, Plutarch, Apollonius, Quintilian, Livy, Tacitus, Plautus, Pliny, Martial, Petronius, Valerius Maximus, Ovid, Curtius, Epictetus, Jugurtha, Terence, Aeneas, Cato, Horace, Dion, Virgil and others.[165]

But mingled in with such lists of 'sententiae promiscue collectae', we find the names of the great humanist collectors of and commentators on proverbs: Petrarch, Peter Martyr, Justus Lipsius, Erasmus, Bodin, Scaliger, Bacon, Cardano, Bouelles, Botero, Machiavelli and Guicciardini.[166] Italian proverbs are the most commonly annotated and Guicciardini and Machiavelli the most cited of the modern authors. But Drake kept up with the latest collections, all published in the early seventeenth century, by Tobias Magirus, Paolo Manuzio, Del Rio, Janus Gruter, Michael Jermin and others.[167] Nor was this all. There is evidence that Drake may have read collections he does not mention by name, such as James I's *Flores Regii: or Proverbs and Aphorismes*. (If not he had certainly heard reports of King James's table talk, including the famous quip 'No bishop, no king'.)[168] And he had evidently acquired a collection of the apothegms of Albert Wallenstein, the commander of the Habsburg imperial forces during the 1620s and 1630s.[169] Other axioms in current use came from report of the conversation of Drake's contemporaries. The Earl of Strafford was quoted as saying that Lord Coventry could 'pull a goose and never make her cry'; friends such as 'Mr. P.' passed on the bon mots of others.[170] As their deployment of proverbs in learned conversation, and the fashion for collections of modern axioms as well as ancient adages, remind us, Drake was not alone in believing that sententiae, ancient and modern, were a prevailing currency of wisdom.

Yet, however eclectic the sources of his adages, Drake had his own rigorous methods of working with them so that they served his particular turn. At the start of one collection of hundreds of proverbs, he signals his

---

165. See, for example, Drake's lists of his sources in Ogden MSS 7/9 f. 21; 7/14 f. 207.
166. Ogden MS 7/14 f. 207.
167. See especially Ogden MSS 7/9 and 7/53. See Gruter, *Florilegium Ethico Politicum*; Gruter, *Florilegii Magni* (Strasbourg, 1624); Magirus, *Polymnemon*; Del Rio, *Adagialia Sacra Veteris*; M. Jermin, *Paraphrasticall Meditations upon the Proverbs of Solomon* (1638); P. Manuzio's, *Adagia* (Venice, 1591) was an edition of Erasmus's proverbs.
168. Ogden MS 7/9 f. 130; cf. 7/12 f. 191v; James I, *Flores Regii: or Proverbs and Aphorismes Divine and Morall as Spoken by His Majestie* (1627). This collection deserves more attention. See K. Sharpe, 'The King's Writ: Royal Authors and Royal Authority in Early Modern England', in K. Sharpe and P. Lake, eds, *Culture and Politics in Early Stuart England* (Houndmills, 1994), pp. 117–38.
169. Ogden MS 7/19 f. 143: 'See Wallenstein's Apophth . . .' I have found no collection, but Drake's source could be P. Gaudenzio's *Fortuna Pentita Ottave nella Morte del Gia Generalissimo Valestein* (Pisa, 1634), translated into English anonymously the same year. Pagnini Gaudenzio, a theologian and classical scholar, also published on Tacitus.
170. Ogden MS 7/12 ff. 67v–66v; see too f. 63; 7/16 f. 143; 7/21 ff. 177v–162 passim.

7. From Drake's notes of
proverbs illustrated from history.

plan: 'Method. Proverbs in this order: first such as are confirmed with reasons; 2ly such as are proved by fables; 3rdly such as are backed with examples or illustrated by emblems; after these historical precepts what we can add discourses to.'[171] He amplified his approach in volume 16 (ill.7):

> Study proverbs most illustrated by history or examples, choose sentences out of Guicciardini, Tacitus, Polybius, Comines and other choicest historians that are illustrated by examples or places of the same nature in them, comments upon them or authors any way enlightening them to a further degree of understanding.[172]

To the list he added in other volumes Bentivoglio and Conestaggio, but the method of reading remained consistent and clear.[173] In order to be under-

171. Ogden MS 7/13 f. 1.
172. Ogden MS 7/16 f. 81v.
173. Ogden MS 7/19 f. 188v; cf. 7/17 f. 1.

stood and appreciated, proverbs had to be arranged, explained, illustrated and expanded. Only then could he 'mark the proverbs that are grounded upon soundest reason', and enter them in a separate volume.[174]

The first step in Drake's method was to rearrange proverbs often promiscuously collected from different sources and periods by topic. He prepares, in traditional commonplace fashion, his headings – 'Amor', 'Odium', 'Lex', 'Pax', 'Senectus'; he groups them by type – 'Adagia ad prudentiam spectanda', 'things relating to wisdom', 'oeconomical proverbs', 'proverbs conducing to government'.[175] As he progresses with his reading and thinking, he expands his 'files': 'proverbs to be added to those relating to wisdom'; but he begins also to select and refine the list, delineating, for example, 'the choicest of the oeconomical proverbs'.[176] Under the subject headings, the individual proverbs are illustrated and cross-referenced and the collections at various points have one-line summaries and an index, which perhaps facilitated finding the original by topic, or source.[177] Other than their thoroughness there appears to be nothing remarkable about these arrangements. What we need to see more clearly is how these material practices interpret and reinterpret as well as arrange the adages collected. First we should note the arrangement itself. To list a proverb such as 'put a good face on an ill game' as conducing to government places a particular interpretation on a proverb that could, like many, be read a number of ways; and it affirms a view of government as the art of deception.[178] Secondly the repetition of proverbs is worthy of remark. Old favourites appear time and again, often within a few folios in the same volume; some, such as 'make an enemy a golden bridge to fly over' crop up in almost every notebook.[179] In part, this reflects Drake's searching for the deepest significance in the wisest adages, as in this example: 'Paruta notes that to be ['grounded on soundest reason'] which gives in precept to make an enemy that flies a golden bridge.'[180]

But the repetition of a proverb under different heads also shifts its meaning in its new context. So the familar proverb 'concordia res parvae crescunt' has a message which is different when read as an 'economical proverb' than as political counsel.[181] And the self-advice 'semper tibi propone pessima' carries

174. Ogden MS 7/53 f. 74v. See too Folger MS f. 6.
175. For example, Ogden MSS 7/12 ff. 141–102; 7/14 f. 161; 7/15 ff. 16, 106, 119; 7/16 ff. 75, 78; 7/19 f. 142v; 7/22 f. 120; 7/52 f. 113.
176. Ogden MS 7/22 ff. 110, 120v.
177. See, for example, 7/15 ff. 117 onwards; 7/16 ff. 38ff.; 7/18 ff. 59, 182, and passim; 7/22 f. 117v; 7/25 passim; 7/37 ff. 45 onwards (see f. 142); 7/53 (see f. 113); Folger MS f. 131.
178. Ogden MS 7/16 f. 78v.
179. 'Put a good face on an ill game' occurs three times in the first forty-four folios of volume 13. See too the repetition in the lists of proverbs in 7/19, 7/37 and the Folger commonplace book.
180. Ogden MS 7/53 f. 74v.
181. Ogden MS 7/18 ff. 41v, 49. 'Through concord small things grow.'

very different freight as good counsel when glossed on different occasions for lovers or for statesmen.[182] Cross-references to the same proverb, identified by different numbers in different places, make it clear that Drake knew that he had 'read' it differently on another occasion and was reinterpreting now.[183] A similar shift of meaning took place when the 'same' adage was cited in different languages. There are detectable differences between the Latin adage 'rem res parit', the Italian rendition 'di cosa nasce cosa e il tempo la governa', and the English 'make a colt first and a horse afterwards' – and they are differences greater than the significant shift of idiom.[184] Similarly 'melius est videre quod cupias quam desiderare quod nescias' is only approximately rendered by the English 'a bird in the hand is worth two in the bush.'[185] Quoting Spanish proverbs in Italian (Drake appears not to read Spanish) or Dutch and Arabian adages in English reconstituted them as part of an Italian and English culture, and as we shall see, of a specific reading of Renaissance Italy and early modern England that was very much Drake's own.[186]

This process of interpretation and reinterpretation was furthered by Drake's method of reading proverbs in connection with histories. Nearly all the proverbs Drake cites are 'illustrated' by histories: some have 'Hist.' penned alongside them and Drake linked them, believing that 'proverbs and history preserve both men and states.'[187] But historical examples did not merely 'illustrate' proverbs, they often determined their meaning. Sometimes the reading is contemporary. The French proverb, 'il perd le jeu qui laisse la partie', Drake notes as one applied at the time to Queen Elizabeth for her inconstancy to the faction she had first supported in Scotland.[188] Elsewhere the historical gloss is his own. Accordingly he 'illustrates' the proverb 'in vain is the net spread in sight of the bird' by Philip II's astuteness in sending to Portugal not the Duke of Alva but the Duke of Osuna.[189] And he explains the meaning of the Italian proverb 'chi troppo abraccia poco stringe' by reference to Louis XI's dealings with the Duke of Burgundy.[190]

It may not be insignificant that the historical glosses tend to be drawn from either ancient times or the relatively recent history of sixteenth- and seventeenth-century Europe, when classical histories became manuals of statecraft. For historical readings of proverbs not only made specific what was

182. Ogden MS 7/53 f. 123v; Folger MS ff. 69, 75, 84. 'Always prepare for the worst.'
183. For example, Odgen MS 7/18 f. 59. The proverb 'Chi si misura gli dura' is here listed as number 42; on f. 43 it is 22. Cf. 7/22 passim, esp. ff. 110–25.
184. Ogden MS 7/37 f. 25; cf. 7/19 f. 122. 'One thing leads to another and time rules all.'
185. Ogden MS 7/25 f. 113v. The Latin is literally translated as 'It is better to have in sight what you desire than to desire what you do not know.'
186. Ogden MSS 7/25 ff. 68, 76v; 7/37 f. 42v.
187. See Ogden MS 7/18 ff. 182ff.; 7/30 f. 41; 7/17 f. 132v; cf. 7/13 f. 9 where Drake makes the heading: 'History applied in proverb.'
188. Ogden MS 7/14 f. 161.
189. Ogden MS 7/17 f. 126.
190. Ogden MS 7/15 f. 23v: 'He who tears off too much holds on to little.'

more open and general, they often stamped on proverbs the values of real-politik which do not appear intrinsic to the adage. Take the proverb 'media consilia periculosa' – which itself questions the accepted wisdom about the virtue of the mean or middle way, and of moderate courses. Drake interprets it as a counsel of war and as a warning about the dangers of mercy, recalling the opinion of Pontius on capturing 4,000 Romans: that, if they were not to be freed, it would be better to put all to the sword rather than some.[191] Because the historians Drake most frequently used to gloss a proverb, or because the historians he most often 'applied in proverb', were his favourites, Tacitus, Polybius and Machiavelli, Guicciardini and Comines, history rendered even those proverbs that seemed to encapsulate traditional moral values as axioms of self-interest, ambition and advancement.

Drake's deployment of recent history to gloss familiar proverbs, like his rearrangement of them under topics, was directly related to how he saw their purpose. Proverbs, he took it from Erasmus, 'multum in sese continens utilitatem'. Yet to exploit fully their usefulness, precepts had 'to be always at hand in order to several occasions'.[192] They were to be used as guides to conduct, in conversation to support arguments, even as a weapon. To counter the adversary who used proverbs against one, he knew that the best response was a witty payback in the same currency – 'physician heal thyself.'[193] Acquaintance with proverbs, the ability to summon the adage appropriate to an argument or moment, was an act of power. The wise man kept the best to himself.[194]

What use, then, did Drake make of them? What may we learn of his attitudes and values by the way he used the axioms he had gathered? While we have no record of Drake's conversations or, after 1641, any speeches in parliament, his notebooks offer fascinating insight into how he drew lessons from adages and how they helped to form and confirm his views of society and state. Familiar proverbs evidently led him to a pessimistic view of the world, and the precariousness of his own place in it. The proverb 'homines magis reguntur opinione quam re' he believed had led corrupt minds 'to say that there is no difference between truth and falsehood but by the advantage that can be drawn out of them'.[195] The world he perceived as so ruled by deception that he knew that the proverb 'when you hear cry a wolf there is certainly a wolf or a fox' 'instructs us . . . not to trust in words . . . and to look beyond the pretences'.[196] When others were out to cozen, Drake believed that proverbs warned him not to be deceived, not to trust men and to look to oneself. The Italian adage 'spero poco e tene assai' he knew to be good advice 'because hope makes us embrace more than we can hold, and lose the right

191. Ogden MS 7/15 f. 94v.
192. Ogden MSS 7/24 f. 216; 7/14 f. 98, the latter quotation from Seneca.
193. Ogden MS 7/24 f. 218v.
194. Ogden MS 7/25 f. 190: 'Reveal the best adages to few.'
195. Ogden MS 7/9 f. 158: 'Men are led more by opinion than truth.'
196. Ogden MS 7/12 f. 159.

measure of ourselves'.[197] The man who understood the point of not disposing of the bear's skin before taking the bear, knew not to trust in what was
future and contingent, rather to take opportunity as it arose.[198] As he pondered what exactly should be learned from the axiom 'he that handles a matter
wisely shall find good', he felt sure that to have a good intelligence of adver-
saries' intentions and 'to help ourselves with the advantage of occasion' were
very much part of what it meant to be wise.[199]

Often the language of his exegesis reveals how Drake politicises personal
relations and views human life as a battle or war. Many of the proverbs he
annotated applied directly to politics – for instance, 'qui nescit adulare nescit
regnare' (he who knows not how to fawn knows not how to rule). But
more generally he felt too that the most mundane of adages, when probed,
offered political as well as domestic counsel – that prudent maxims held 'not
only for men but likewise for states'.[200] The Italian proverb 'Padrone
improvente fa servitor negligente' seems to belong obviously under Drake's
heading of 'economical' or household proverbs; but he had no doubt that 'it
holds with same proportion with princes and people, for ministers are ordinarily either active or negligent as they find the prince able to judge of their
industry and endeavours.'[201] He was doubtless encouraged in his political exegesis by the use that contemporary statesmen made of proverbs to make their
own point. We have heard him quote Strafford on Coventry's ability to pluck
the goose without making it cry; he notes too that the proverb 'the subtle
ape pulled the chestnut out of the fire with the cats claw' 'King James applied
. . . to Bohemian lords who subtly sought to engage him in the Bohemian
cause.'[202]

Proverbs, today usually deployed as political cliché, were an important part
of early modern political discourse. By the late 1650s, Drake could even have
seen the collections gathered of Charles I's as well as James I's adages and
proverbs.[203] We cannot be surprised that as Drake read and reread during the
Commonwealth and Protectorate it was the political meanings of adages that
often sprang to mind. Maxims extracted from Tacitus, Machiavelli and others,
evidently in the 1650s – adages such as 'rigid reformations rather ruin than
reform' – are cited now in language that evokes contemporary politics.[204]
When Drake recalled the familiar caveat 'beware those that come in sheep's

197. Ogden MS 7/53 f. 80v. The adage is repeated frequently (e.g. Folger MS ff. 25v, 29,
    68v) and means 'Hope for little and hold on to much.'
198. See Ogden MS 7/53 f. 83v: 'Polybius says wisely we should not reckon on things
    future and contingent as present and certain.'
199. Ogden MS 7/18 f. 68.
200. Ogden MS 7/53 f. 143v.
201. Ogden MS 7/18 f. 176. The Italian reads literally 'an unwatchful master creates a
    negligent servant.'
202. Ogden MS 7/12 ff. 67v, 157.
203. *Effata Regalia: Aphorisms Divine, Moral, Politick . . . of Charles I* (1661); *Witty Apothegms
    Delivered by King James, King Charles* (1658).
204. Ogden MS 7/17 f. 150. The end of the volume contains notes from 1660.

clothing' he read it now as aimed against those who 'do specious acts of piety'.[205] The proverb 'falsa sub specie veri decipiunt' he now explained in his margin: 'care would [*sic*] be had that under the specious name of religion and liberty ambition slyly and closely creeps not in.'[206] This is now the language less of the ancients or cinquecento Italy than of Cromwell's England. Drake had organised, examined, glossed and illustrated his proverbs – for their use. And during the 1640s and 1650s he used them to read and make sense of the politics of a revolutionary time.

Before we turn to a full study of Drake's personal values and political perceptions, we must dwell on aspects of his reading we have hitherto ignored. When he set out his 'method' for reading proverbs Drake listed in addition to those supported by historical examples 'such as are proved by fables' 'or illustrated by examples'.[207] Throughout he cross-refers adages to fables: 'media consilia periculosa' led him immediately to remember the fable of the bear with the beehive.[208] Quintilian, he records, had argued that proverbs were but fables in brief.[209] In that spirit Drake unpacks the Latin axiom 'fronti nulla fides' – put no faith in appearances – by a reading of Aesop's fable of the cat turned into a virgin which reverted to its true nature only when a mouse ran across the room.[210] Just as with his proverbs, Drake arranged his fables under the topics they illustrated, 'Sagacitas', 'Circumspectus', and cross-referenced them to each other, to adages and to historical events and lives which illustrated them.[211]

Fables are familiar to us principally as children's tales; their significance for early modern readers was for long lost to us. More recently critics and historians have begun to recover them (along with other texts such as *Gulliver's Travels* or *Robinson Crusoe* curiously confined to the shelves of children's literature) and to reread them as texts of political import in early modern England. Annabel Patterson in *Fables of Power* has argued for the political and subversive origin of the collection of fables published as Aesop's and has demonstrated the political and polemical purposes of the editions, interpretations and citations of fables in seventeenth-century England.[212] Most recently, in a brilliant brief essay, Mark Kishlansky showed how one fable in

205. Ogden MS 7/17 f. 115v.
206. Ogden MS 7/18 f. 57; literally 'falsehood deceives under the appearance of truth.' The gloss is in the margin. Cf. Folger MS f. 98 on the fable of the fowler and the blackbird: 'take care of empiricks in state and imposters in religion.'
207. Ogden MSS 7/13 f. 1; 7/16 f. 38.
208. Ogden MS 7/15 f. 94. Fable 44 in John Ogilby's edition of *The Fables of Aesop* (1668).
209. Ogden MS 7/24 f. 216.
210. Ogden MS 7/28 f. 20v; *Fables of Aesop*, no. 73. Drake interprets it: 'her tale shows that nature will be buried and obscured till provoked by *occasion and opportunity*' (my italics).
211. See, for example, Ogden MS 7/31 ff. 114 onwards.
212. A. Patterson, *Fables of Power: Aesopian Writing and Political History* (Durham, N.C., 1991). See, too, Patterson, 'Fables of Power', in K. Sharpe and S. Zwicker, eds, *Politics of Discourse* (Berkeley, 1987), pp. 271–96.

particular – that of the frogs asking Jupiter for a king – was reinterpreted over two hundred years, from the Caxton edition of Aesop, published in 1484, to that of Sir Roger L'Estrange, the Tory polemicist and licenser of the press, printed in 1692.[213] What we begin to discern is how each edition and reading of the 'timeless' fable, like the proverb, was an act of exact historical and often polemical appropriation – appropriation for a moment and a cause. Fables were read and taken seriously because still in the early modern period (and not for the last time) it was held that nature and the natural world were texts of instruction, part of God's created universe. Sir William Drake quotes the words of the twelfth book of Job: 'Ask the beasts and they shall teach thee', and paraphrases Proverbs 30: 'we are sent in Scripture for providence to the ant, for knowing the time to the stork, for wisdom to the serpent, to laying our foundation well to the conies.'[214] Aristotle had written *De Animalibus* not least out of a conviction that 'opus naturae opus intelligentiae';[215] Aquinas ascertained that man was composed of the qualities of all creatures.[216] Drake read them both along with Gesner's treatise on quadrupeds, with its studies of the characteristics of the monkey, dog, sheep, camel, cat, bear and so on.[217] Observation of creatures could be, as Drake reports Sir Henry Wotton saying, the best school of instruction.[218]

When Machiavelli wrote famously of the need for the prince to imitate the lion and the fox, his animal imagery was not in itself new; here as so often, it was the uses to which he put conventional texts that were revolutionary. Drake himself believed that 'to travel safely through the world it behoveth to have a falcon's eye, an ass's ears, an ape's face, courtier's words, a camel's back, a hog's mouth and a deer's feet.'[219] He made lists of all the animals and the qualities that could be learned from them: the dog teaching sagacity, the ape the art of flattery.[220] Drake read the standard fables in Aesop, Plutarch's moral fables, Aristophanes, and commentaries and applications of them by Aulus Gellius, Cardano, Tholossain and others.[221] In some cases Drake's readings are in tune with conventional morality. The fable of the bear and wolf he interpreted as teaching that 'partiality to ourselves makes us not

---

213. M. Kishlansky, 'Turning Frogs into Princes: Aesop's *Fables* and the Political Culture of Early Modern England', in S. Amussen and M. Kishlansky, eds, *Political Culture and Cultural Politics in Early Modern England* (Manchester, 1995), pp. 338–60.

214. Ogden MS 7/19 f. 79, repeated in 7/32 f. 94; 7/18 f. 73.

215. Ogden MS 7/18 f. 73. 'Nature's work is the work of wisdom.'

216. Ogden MS 7/37 f. 129.

217. Ogden MS 7/16 f. 62. See Conrad Gesner, *De Quadrupedibus* (Frankfurt, 1586), translated into English in 1607; and *De Avium Natura* (Frankfurt, 1585). See also E. Topsell, *Gesner's Beasts* (1607). Gesner also wrote commentaries on Aristotle and Homer.

218. Ogden MS 7/18 f. 74.

219. Ogden MS 7/53 f. 53v.

220. For example, Ogden MS 7/30 f. 179v.

221. Ogden MSS 7/16 f. 74; 7/9 f. 144; 7/10 f. 75v; 7/31 ff. 1v, 14; f. 109v. Folger MS f. 101. See A. Gellius, *Fabularum Quae Hoc Libero Continentur Interpres atque Authores Sunt* (1515). The cross-references to G. Tholossain's *De Republica* (Frankfurt, 1609) show how Drake worked and thought politically.

see our own faults'; in the case of the ass and the horse 'the moral teacheth us to bear one another's burdens.'[222] But overall what fables taught him was that the world was a dangerous jungle and that to survive in it men needed to imitate the circumspection and guile of the most cunning beasts. From the lion inviting the bull to supper he was warned about simulated friendships; the fable of the fowler and the blackbird 'instructs us to be wary of ... promises'; the fox and the cat were 'models of subtlety and wisdom'.[223] Aristotle, he noted, 'terms a fable the ape of action respecting what is done and suffered in human life'. Drake read them to avoid suffering and to become more adept in negotiating his way in the world, a world of 'many savage creatures'.[224]

When he listed the qualities it behoved the prudent man to have, he included with those exhibited by animals 'courtier's words'.[225] Because the exchange between bestial and courtly creatures, fable and politics, came naturally to him, he inevitably read fables as political allegory. The ants, he noted from Aristotle, symbolised democratic states, the bees monarchical;[226] the fable of the lion and the wolf, he believed, instructed how it was dangerous for a prince to suffer ill habits to grow in a state;[227] the fable of the wolf and the sheep showed how 'subtle tyrants suffer subjects to grow fat before they devour them.'[228] Most interestingly, Drake returned in several volumes to that most political of all fables, the frogs and the prince. In volume 15, after citing the proverb 'ut habeas quietum tempus perde aliquid', he cross-refers to the fable of the frogs, both 'teaching subjects to let go some part of their own rights [rather] than contending with *our* prince and hazard all'.[229] In volume 17, which we may date to the early 1650s, Drake, annotating Tacitus' grave observation that all changes in government 'do chafe . . . them most who at first did most desire them', recalls: 'the mythologist aptly illustrates this ill affection of change in a fable of frogs who petition Jupiter to grant them a king.'[230] The fullest reference is found in volume 31, where Drake is reading and reflecting on Malvezzi's argument that an excess of love or fear destabilised states:

> this the ancients covertly taught us in the fable of Jupiter and the frogs who desiring a king . . . he gave them a block, and he being quiet and not stirring, the frogs contemned him whereupon Jupiter changed their king

222. Ogden MS 7/31 ff. 118v, 125. See *Fables of Aesop*, no. 47.
223. Ogden MSS 7/25 ff. 107, 179 (see 7/25 passim); 7/37 f. 194. See *Fables of Aesop*, no. 57.
224. Ogden MSS 7/31 f. 113v; 7/7 f. 87.
225. Ogden MS 7/9 f. 94.
226. Ogden MS 7/32 f. 94.
227. Ogden MS 7/31 f. 122v.
228. Ogden MS 7/31 f. 125; cf. *Fables of Aesop*, no. 31.
229. Ogden MS 7/15 f. 42, my italics. Again we note the political reading of the Latin adage that means only 'be prepared to give up something for a quiet life.'
230. Ogden MS 7/17 f. 135v. See Clark, 'Wisdom Literature II', pp. 61–2.

and gave them a stork but he eating them up, they hated him more than they despised the other. By this they would show two things: first that a prince should not be so gentle to have more of the block than of the man, nor yet so cruel to resemble a beast in sucking the blood of his subjects. *The fable further penetrated* declares likewise that men generally are of restless and unquiet natures and are prone to grow weary of rest and quietness itself . . .

In a marvellous demonstration of how he read across genres, Drake continues:

This fickleness the Italian proverb seems to tax, and instructs us that che vuol ben del popolo lo tenga magro a quasso for either the passion of love . . . grows suddenly unto the wane and is apt to faint and fail or else to produce dangerous effects . . . men like wanton beasts are sometimes prouder [?] prickt and grow skittish or like full fed oxen throw the hay upon their horns.[231]

Drake clearly reads his Aesop through the medium of Latin and Italian proverbs. But few can doubt that the reference to the fickleness of a nation in peace and plenty and the dangers of trusting in the people reveal the traces of contemporary English events and Drake's perception of them. If so, in his reading of the fable as demonstrating the 'ill affection of change' we may chart not just his own, but perhaps a perceived shift to a broader reaction against revolution.

Though they have lost their significance, fables remain with us. The other genre Drake read as a source of and commentary on proverbial learning has all but passed from our culture. The emblem was central to the culture of the Renaissance. The combination of an image and a motto was how aristocratic families portrayed themselves on impressa, how guilds and corporations portrayed their craft and values on pendants, how regiments identified themselves on standards and banners in the field. In Elizabethan England the emblem was the principal representation of identity, not least the queen's own as the phoenix rising from the ashes. Emblems were a currency of social and political intercourse. When worn on dress and jewels (like Elizabeth's phoenix jewel), embroidered on tapestries and cushions, or carved onto panelling they conveyed messages – of assertion and authority, of love and desire for union, of flattery and the quest for favour. They could be direct political statements: when Mary Queen of Scots, imprisoned in England, sent the Duke of Norfolk a cushion she had embroidered figuring a pruning knife lopping the unfruitful branch of a vine, with the motto 'virtue flourishes by wounding',

---

231. Ogden MS 7/31 f. 176 (my italics). The Italian phrase means 'he who would wish well of the people keeps them poor and weak.'

the injunction to assassinate the heretic queen Elizabeth was thinly veiled. Emblems were ubiquitous not only in the portraits of the Elizabethans but throughout the material culture of clothes, utensils, painted cloths, ceilings and printers' devices. The fashion generated an interest in the literature of the emblem and its meaning. By 1700 some fifty emblem books had been published in England and the educated English were familiar with many more that appeared on the continent. By the early seventeenth century sections on emblems were incorporated into the best-selling courtesy books, such as those by Henry Peacham. Emblems exemplify a culture in which the image and the word were still held as integral rather than distinct: and it is our loss of that integrity which has impoverished our understanding not only of the emblem itself, but of the art of portraiture which the emblem tradition helped to shape.[232]

Drake read the standard emblem books – of Ripa and Cats, Sambucus and Camerarius, Alciati and Saavedra Fajardo, Quarles and Whitney.[233] He regarded these emblems principally as another source of proverbial learning and cross-refers his emblem books to other sententiae and proverbs.[234] As with proverbs he also illustrates them by historical examples. The emblem 'spes chymica', for example, is illustrated by reference to Louis XII shipwrecked on the rock of vain hope at Blois; 'Divide et impera' – divide and rule – reminded him of Louis XI's conduct with Edward IV.[235] But emblems were more than just proverbial *words* to Drake. He pays attention to the image and often associates images with other proverbs. So the adage 'a disarmed peace is weak' leads him to recall the emblem of the hedgehog; the moral 'qui captat saepe capitur' he thought captured in the emblem of the bird with the shellfish, and illustrated by Guicciardini's comments on the French.[236] Just as with his proverbs,

232. We owe our recent understanding of the emblem to Peter Daly and Michael Bath. See P. Daly, ed., *The English Emblem Tradition* (Toronto, 1988); Daly, ed., *The English Emblem and the Continental Tradition* (New York, 1980); Daly, *Literature in the Light of the Emblem* (Toronto, 1979); P. Daly and M. V. Silcox, *The Modern Critical Reception of the English Emblem* (Munich, 1991); M. Bath, *Speaking Pictures: English Emblem Books and Renaissance Culture* (1994). See also Janet Arnold, *Queen Elizabeth's Wardrobe Unlock'd* (Leeds, 1988), and R. Freeman, *English Emblem Books* (1948); P. Mario, *Studies in Seventeenth-Century Imagery* (Rome, 1974) for lists of emblem books.
233. Ogden MSS 7/10 ff. 9, 50, 67, 146; 7/14 f. 136; 7/16 f. 18; 7/20 f. 179; Folger MS ff. 128v, 24v. C. Ripa, *Iconologia* (Padua, 1611); J. Cats, *Silenus Alciabadis . . . Vitae Humanae Ideam Emblemata Trifariam Variato* (Middleburg, 1618); Sambucus, *Emblemata*; J. Camerarius, *Symbolorum & Emblematum . . . Una Collecta* (Nuremburg, 1590); A. Alciatus, *Omnia . . . Alciati . . . Emblemata* (Antwerp, 1577, and many editions); Saavedra Fajardo, *De Principe Politico-Christiano Representada en Cien Empresas* (Munich, 1640); F. Quarles, *Emblemes* (1634); Whitney, *A Choice of Emblemes*.
234. See, for example, Ogden MSS 7/17 f. 107v; 7/19 f. 83v onwards; 7/22 ff. 88v–9; Folger MS passim. Drake may have kept a book of his own collection of emblems (see Folger MS f. 128v).
235. Ogden MS 7/19 ff. 39v, 83v.
236. Ogden MSS 7/12 f. 155; 7/19 f. 39v. Literally, 'he who captures is often captured'.

Drake arranged emblems under the qualities they represented: 'False Hope', 'Discretion', 'Eloquence', 'Counsel', 'Tyranny'.[237] Some – the coy duck with the motto 'friend in enemies bosom', the mulberry tree standing for 'cunctatio prodest' – he repeats many times, as we have seen he does his favourite axioms.[238] The porcupine he thought one of those emblems that 'taught the most matter'.[239] As with proverbs, Sir William also explicates and glosses the meaning of emblems. The emblem of the whale, he notes, taught how to weaken a powerful enemy;[240] 'caecus amor sobolis' he believed 'an emblem no doubt to show that the fond and indiscreet love of friends prejudices as much or more than the hatred of enemies'.[241] Moving freely between emblem and proverb to explicate both, Drake writes of 'capra lupum': 'this emblem shows that improbitas nullo flectitur obsequio and the truth of the Spanish proverb bring up a carrion crow and she will peck out your eyes.'[242] 'Nec a quo nec ad quem', imaged by the serpent, 'instructs to use agents as instruments without discovering our purpose' and leads Drake to recall Guicciardini's advice that a prince who would deceive his neighbour should first deceive his ambassador.[243]

Here we are offered rare insights into how a contemporary interpreted and learned from emblem books, and are given a glimpse of how images as well as words evoked lessons. The emblem in fact renders visually and succinctly the lesson of the fable and the proverb. In Drake's case his reading of them was often in conjunction with ancient and humanist histories of a particular stripe. Indeed he viewed Cats's emblems as one of the most astute sources for interpretation of Tacitus; and he politicised many emblems by drawing for his illustration of them from the histories of Magirus, and principally Guicciardini.[244] As a consequence the emblems, so often a statement of chivalric values, or conventional Christian morality, become in Drake's hands yet another text of realpolitik.

Our study then has followed what we might now call Drake's strategies of reading. We have seen how, for all the range of his sources, his reading practices privileged particular authors and interpretations of texts. He endlessly returned to, rearranged and cross-referenced them so that they were ready for use in a multiplicity of situations. Rejecting any idea of the disengaged scholar in detached contemplation in his study, we have argued for readings influenced by conversation and experience of the world. By corollary, Drake read in order more effectually to survive and advance himself in the world. Learned

237. See his organised notes from Ripa, Ogden MS 7/14 f. 136 onwards.
238. Ogden MSS 7/16 ff. 18, 180; 7/20 f. 179; Folger MS f. 129. 'Delay may be beneficial.'
239. Ogden MS 7/27 f. 154v.
240. Ogden MS 7/16 f. 18; in Folger MS f. 128v he refers to the whale diverted by pitch barrels as the emblem of Maurice of Saxony.
241. Ogden MS 7/17 f. 100v. Literally, 'the love of offspring is blind'.
242. Ogden MS 7/19 f. 40. 'Wickedness is not directed by allegiance.'
243. Ogden MS 7/19 f. 40v. 'Neither from whom, nor to whom.'
244. Ogden MSS 7/21 f. 181; 7/19 ff. 39v, 40v; see too 7/14 f. 207.

in the grave sententiae and the lessons of history, he believed he might assemble rules for private and public life. It is time for us to turn from how Drake read – to how he wrote himself.

Values for Self and Society

There is surprisingly little evidence of Drake's private life. Though he was bound with Simonds D'Ewes when he entered the Middle Temple, we know nothing of their relations, depite their common delight in books. Drake's name does not surface in the surviving correspondence of scholars or gentlemen; though his epitaph in Amersham church describes him as a 'promoter and patron of letters', there is no indication as to who were the scholarly beneficiaries of his munificence. As for his locality and kin, he was said to have been generous with neighbours and family, but no letters survive between Drake and the brother who sat in Cromwell's parliaments, nor records of his involvement in Buckinghamshire (or London) life. Sir William never married: so his estates passed to his nephew, son of his younger brother Francis.[245]

Do Drake's notebooks provide the missing information? Though principally volumes of reading notes and conversations, many Renaissance commonplace books yield titbits of valuable biographical information: most obviously the names and dates of birth of children, deaths, significant appointments or events in the note-taker's life. We have seen from earlier volumes that Drake often used his notebooks to make jottings of estate business or other financial matters: leases, rentals, the pursuit of an office.[246] There is little of this type of material in the notebooks dating from the 1640s and 1650s other than the odd reference to a room rented, a bill of exchange for money or a reference to his patent of office.[247] The most obvious way in which Drake left traces of his personal life on the pages of his commonplace books was in medical remedies. On the fly of some notebooks there are recipes for laxatives and jottings for herbal remedies for unspecified ailments.[248] The historian of medicine may be more interested in his cure for the pleurisy – a brew of cut green broom, 'ail' (garlic?) and nutmeg, evidently imbibed or inhaled to create a sweat.[249] Other recommendations for a home-made purgative were passed on to him by a Dr Wurthurst, along with probably traditional remedies by the less obviously qualified Mrs Hill's headwoman in Cheapside.[250]

245. See Keeler, *The Long Parliament*, pp. 159–63; for Drake's will, see below, p. 273.
246. See above, pp. 89–91, 131–4.
247. See Ogden MSS 7/9, 7/10, 7/32.
248. See 7/37 cover (a laxative of stewed prunes); 7/15 flyleaf.
249. Ogden MS 7/25 f. 1v.
250. Ogden MS 7/24 back board.

For our purposes, these odd notes lead us to imagine a conversation on a walk as a break from reading, a letter or prescription received and read amidst a pile of books. They also return us to the natural body of the reader with all the reminders seventeenth-century living imparted of the frailty of the human constitution and the proximity of death.[251] The absence of prayers for health or any deep personal spirituality is one of the most striking features of Drake's notebooks. By far the most poignant of such references is an entry 'For the eyes': 'Tis conceived that euphregia [euphorbia?] is the best herb, only somewhat drying and to temper that quality tis conceived best to boil the herb of borage or bugle therewith . . .'[252] In the midst of reading Thucydides, Drake perhaps had trouble with his failing eyesight. It is only the most explicit connection between his bodily person and his reading.

For though Drake records few direct facts of his biography, his notes give clues to the most personal and private aspects of his life. The still unmarried Sir William turns at several points in annotating books and conversations to the subject of marriage. 'The most important actions', he wrote, 'are friendship, marriage, calling and education of children.'[253] And he notes that in the New Atlantis Bacon criticised those Europeans who sought in marriage only a fair portion or good bargain 'and not the faithful nuptial union of man and wife'.[254] This is hardly the language of a cynic, and suggests that Drake, a bachelor in his forties, may have held high ideals about the institution of marriage. But because of its importance marriage had to be approached with great circumspection. The Italian proverb – 'Bisogno star si [r]egliato accorto attento chi di un disordina non nascon[de] conti' – he believed 'instructs us that in all our actions, especially those of most importance, as marriage, friendship and the like, to be deliberate, foreseeing and considerate' (that is considering).[255] Marriage, though an ideal state, had its pitfalls: children were 'certain cares but uncertain comforts' and a huge expense – Drake seemed attracted by the Dutch habit of never lodging their offspring once they had married.[256] Moreover, the choice of a partner was fraught with risk: 'many men fall into a snare whilst they think to find a treasure'; as Seneca wrote in his letter to Lucillius, 'our marriage bed often proves suddenly our death bed.'[257] Whatever Drake believed constituted 'the faithful nuptial union of man and wife', it was not sexual love. Frequently he records adages warning against the heat of passion. 'Love doth often much mischief in human life' is how he rather unfairly paraphrased Bacon's essay, and 'fond love disposes men to credulity.'[258]

251. See too A. Johns, The Nature of the Book (Chicago, 1998), ch. 6.
252. Ogden MS 7/10 f. 182v. On Drake's eye trouble, see above, p. 173.
253. Ogden MS 7/12 f. 62.
254. Ogden MS 7/31 f. 204.
255. Ogden MS 7/16 f. 43. The sense of the proverb is that he who does not organise so as to conceal his affairs needs be very attentive and wary.
256. Ogden MSS 7/19 f. 151; 7/21 f. 163.
257. Ogden MSS 7/12 f. 69; 7/14 f. 131.
258. Ogden MSS 7/30 f. 127v; 7/37 f. 112v. Bacon's argument is that love needs

As a foundation for a stable marriage it was unstable: an ardent love like a straw fire burned out quickly.[259] And 'he that marries for love merely hath pleasure in the night but sorrow in the day.'[260] Rather than the expression of passion, marriage assisted men, especially young men, to regulate passion and live by the dictates of reason. 'Indiscrete' love, by contrast, made young lovers 'slaves' to their mistresses.[261]

Modern pyschological and feminist criticism might seek to detect here a circumspection about sex and women, a misogyny founded on personal fear as well as social convention. In Drake's case such a reading may not be entirely fanciful. Certainly he has little good to say of women: with Aristotle he concurred that, if more pious, they were also more malicious than men; and even their piety was often sinful weakness.[262] In his own day, he felt, the puritan preachers appealed to women as 'the serpent applied himself to the woman at the beginning.'[263] Annotating Jacques de Bosc's treatise translated in 1639 into English as *The Compleat Woman*, Drake listed all the female's failings: they were light and insubstantial, and never spoke but ill of others.[264] Most of all 'mulier est animal imperfectum' because dominated by passion not reason, 'animal . . . indomitum, infidum, mutabile, crudele, mille passionibus deditum.'[265] There was a sexual dimension to this barrage of criticism: Drake's fear that only religion fostered in women a sense of shame and checked their natural libertinism may speak to a personal as well as cultural anxiety.[266] But there is a hint too that poor William may have been jilted in love. For the term 'crudele', cruel or wounding, resonates oddly in the list of adjectives. And the man who wrote of women who love you today and another tomorrow may have been recalling painful experience.[267] Whatever the explanation, for all his foreseeing and deliberation, the bachelor Drake failed to secure the 'faithful nuptial union' that together with friendship he regarded as one of the most important things in life.

Drake's failure to realise his ideal, in this and other departments of life, may become explicable when we consider the advice he gave himself. His basic principles of behaviour were conventional enough. Just as he warned against

regulation, but he also writes: 'There is in man's nature a secret inclination and motion towards the love of others', *Essays*, p. 89. Drake is more in this spirit in 7/53 f. 136.
259. Ogden MS 7/9 f. 86v.
260. Ogden MS 7/53 f. 53.
261. Ogden MSS 7/53 f. 136; 7/17 f. 113v.
262. Ogden MSS 7/30 f. 162.
263. Ogden MS 7/17 f. 8v. This stereotype, of course, informs *Bartholomew Fair*.
264. Ogden MS 7/31 ff. 178–9.
265. Ogden MS 7/53 f. 151. 'The woman is an imperfect creature . . . a creature ungovernable, unfaithful, changeable, cruel, and the slave to a thousand passions.'
266. Ogden MS 7/31 f. 178.
267. Ogden MS 7/53 f. 151. 'Non enim est in muliere ulla stabilitas quae nunc te amat, cras alium amabit'. ('For there is no stability in a woman who loves you today, but will love another tomorrow.')

reading too much and understanding too little, so he regarded it as 'an error of most men's minds to desire to embrace and comprehend all things and not to reserve the strength of their minds for those which are essentially in order to their main end of life'.[268] What Sir William resolved was to pursue some few precepts of wisdom, through 'reading, conversation, and meditation', and apply their lessons to the regulation of himself.[269] If it was 'good to govern our lives by the most solid maxims', one of the first rules to be learned was the need to 'bridle passions and be . . . a free man'.[270] The self-government of passion by reason was the first rule of prudence: 'Wise men hold one steady and constant temper.'[271] Having come to know himself, Drake believed the next principle of wisdom was to come to an understanding of the nature of men.[272] But here his tone shifts from that of conventional moral self-teaching to precepts for a world of very different values. It was on the flyleaf of a volume of proverbs that Drake instructed himself 'to have a deep understanding of the nature of man' because 'it gives us great light both in our conversation and negotiation with them, what to hope and fear from them.'[273] 'Negotiation' and 'fear' are the vocabulary of circumspection and it is circumspection that pervades the adages that he copies or glosses as if to himself, reminding himself, 'expect not a golden life in an iron age.'[274] Drake warned himself: 'let us bethink ourselves what may happen going through the wilderness of the world'; 'consider that thou walkes in the midst of snares.'[275] The man whom we have seen valuing friendship highly may have failed in this, as in marriage, if he literally applied his self-counsel of circumspection: 'never make thyself too inwardly familiar with any, and though thou mightest have less joy thou shall be sure to have less sorrow.'[276] Being circumspect and foreseeing meant not trusting. It meant taking advantage of any situation as it arose: 'of all take heed, of them most that seem truth and honesty and are not,'[277] and it necessitated disguising one's own true self so as not to give others advantage. While it was 'good to have a thorough knowledge of the world', it was best 'to seem not to know it', for in a bad world candour was dangerous.[278] With Sir John Potts, Drake discussed those who showed a face of great plainness while remaining 'close and reserved in the bottom'; it seems likely he held them as a model.[279]

268. Ogden MS 7/9 f. 128v.
269. Ogden MS 7/31 f. 180. He added: 'By reading we discourse with the dead, by conversation with the living and by meditation with ourselves.'
270. Ogden MSS 7/18 f. 171v; 7/19 f. 134v.
271. Ogden MSS 7/13 f. 1; 7/18 f. 64v.
272. Ogden MS 7/13 f. 57.
273. Ogden MS 7/13 fly leaf.
274. Ogden MS 7/37 f. 88.
275. Ogden MSS 7/22 f. 177; 7/25 f. 54.
276. Ogden MS 7/15 f. 19v.
277. Ogden MS 7/53 f. 176v.
278. Ogden MSS 7/9 f. 129; 7/12 f. 60.
279. Ogden MS 7/31 f. 1.

Learning from reading the wisest authors and conversing with the wisest men, Drake set out to write himself as the man of self-knowledge, who controlled his own passions, probed the nature of men, trusted none, approached all with circumspection, kept his counsel, but took advantage of all occasions. It may not have been his 'nature'. But the man who viewed the world as a theatre believed he could script a role, a 'persona' for himself that would secure him in it. From the same principles and perspectives he also wrote a script for society and state that might even be called a political philosophy.

Drake's commonplace books are full of notes on the nature of man and society. He filed under that heading extracts from Aristotle, Polybius, Tacitus, Bodin, Cardan, Claremontius, Barclay, Bacon, Frachetta, Lipsius and Magirus, Machiavelli and Guicciardini.[280] Because he believed that the same passions, humours and desires recurred throughout generations, what each author had written about the characteristics and manners of men in his age formed one picture of mankind. They were, of course, authors not only writing in different periods but from very different values. There is some recognition of this in the notes Drake took. Reading Aristotle in volume 14, he notes the observation that man is by nature a social animal and 'cui hoc natura innata est ut libenter cum aliis vivat.'[281] From Bacon he copied the similar sentiment: 'there is in man's nature a secret inclination and motion towards the love of others.'[282] A Christian dimension is clearly evident too in his noting the force of conscience in men: 'so that we may conceive that men cannot be wholly wicked because they cannot quench all sparks of conscience.'[283] He even went so far as to accept that 'a man in his perfection is the best of creatures.'[284]

But, overall, his view of men was far less positive. Fallen man was a wild beast, more dangerous than any other creature because possessed of depraved reason: 'in the generation and birth of man there is a kind of wild nature', 'a depraved and malignant nature'.[285] Beneath the veneer of social institutions and politeness walked the human savage: 'man's nature is more discovered in brute creatures than in themselves, for human nature is much disguised and concealed by doctrine and discourses of men . . .'[286] If any doubted it, as Dr J. and Drake discussed it at Breda, they only needed to go to the Indies where they might see, stripped of the artifice of European society, 'man in his pure nature' – wild and unregulated.[287]

The depraved and malignant nature of man was characterised above all by deceitfulness and self-interest. As cunning animals deceived their prey, so men

280. See Ogden MS 7/14 f. 221v.
281. Ogden MS 7/14 f. 62v: 'and it is in his nature to live willingly with others'.
282. Ogden MS 7/30 f. 128v; cf. f. 167.
283. Ogden MS 7/18 f. 53v.
284. Ogden MS 7/53 f. 179.
285. Ogden MSS 7/12 f. 80v; 7/19 f. 174v; 7/25 f. 138.
286. Ogden MS 7/9 f. 1v.
287. Ogden MS 7/21 f. 162v.

deceived each other. After the fall there was 'so much inconstancy and hypocrisy in [man's] nature'; men became naturally 'inconstant dissemblers' deriving pleasure from cozening.[288] Deception and lies were such a pleasure to man that they constituted 'the serpentine and viperous disposition of the generality of the world'.[289] Whatever men said, then, it was to be assumed that they always acted out of self-interest not the common good. 'Men speak according to their duty but they act according to their interest.'[290] Self-interest was what drove men, the foundation of their being. By nature man 'never looks with an equal and indifferent mind between his own and another's good but is *passionately* partial [that is partial by course of his natural passions] to his proper interest'.[291] This pursuit of self-interest fostered in all men an ambition for advancement that led to violence and unrestrained power. Even Seneca, despite his belief in the essential morality of human nature, had held that every man carried in his heart 'somewhat of a tyrant', some innate desire to dominate others.[292] Along with Comines, Drake appears more direct and pessimistic: 'tis manifest that neither natural reason nor fear of God, nor love to our neighbour is sufficient to help us from using violence against others when we have power.'[293] Tacitus, he thought, captured the natural human drive for power in the character of Tiberius, the living demonstration of the axiom that 'the more power men get the worse they use it.'[294] As each struggled for the same dominance over all, the inevitable outcome was conflict: 'such is the inconstant and unquiet nature of man . . . that as soon as they are freed from fighting for necessity they presently fall a quarrelling out of ambition.'[295]

Far, then, from society being a natural condition, social life became a warfare. Men's desires being infinite, always dissatisfied with what they had, they fought to obtain what belonged to others.[296] As the Spanish proverb put it, two sparrows sitting on an ear of corn were bound to fight before they left it.[297] No man could stand outside the conflict – not only because his nature compelled him to fight too, but also because 'he that fights not or stands not in a posture of defence either lives not or lives unhappily saith Malvezzi.'[298] What then was the fate of society? Drake's answer to the problem

288. Ogden MSS 7/18 f. 87v; 7/37 f. 96.
289. Ogden MSS 7/53 f. 159; 7/19 f. 195v.
290. Ogden MS 7/9 f. 130v. Drake refers to Guicciardini.
291. Ogden MS 7/13 ff. 62, 141.
292. Ogden MS 7/19 f. 107. Drake is evidently here reading his Seneca between taking notes on Machiavelli's *Discourses*.
293. Ogden MS 7/19 f. 12v.
294. Ogden MSS 7/15 f. 31v ('Tacitus excellently describes the nature of man in the character of Tiberius'); 7/19 f. 25v. Drake glosses this by a remark of Sir Benjamin Rudyard that a servant, once given power, becomes more tyrannical than a master.
295. Ogden MS 7/15 f. 44v. See above, p. 107.
296. Ogden MS 7/16 f. 97. Drake is reading Machiavelli.
297. Ogden MS 7/37 f. 120.
298. Ogden MS 7/15 f. 107v. Drake adds 'our life is a warfare'; cf. above, p. 106.

of anarchy partly lay in education and the law. He speaks of man's nature being 'tamed and mollified by education', as we have seen him determined to subject his own passions to reason. Custom and education might form men's deeds and manners; however their thoughts remained determined by their natural inclination.[299] Good laws and good magistrates could also do much. As long as men 'gave ear to . . . the persuasion of religion, laws and magistrates eloquently and sweetly couched in books, to sermons and harangues, so long is society in peace maintained'.[300] In the end, however, as Dr Sheldon was to put it after the Restoration in a sermon that struck a chord with Drake, men remained 'by nature . . . proud and querulous, impatient of government, greedy of liberty [i.e. licence], always displeased with the present'.[301] Even when they flew to good rulers in difficult times, 'so soon as the storm is gone they become unthankful creatures.'[302] The moment Orpheus' harp was laid aside, 'all things dissolve and fall back into anarchy and confusion.'[303] The successful ruler, therefore, had to 'personate the passions of the people', pretend to serve their interest, deceive them, in the end rule them not through love but through hope and fear.[304]

This leads us to a distinctly atomistic view of society that was famously the basis for the theory of the state of nature outlined in Hobbes's *Leviathan*. Drake read Hobbes – *On the Nature of Man* as well as *Leviathan*.[305] He extracted passages that come as no surprise given what we have seen of his views. 'Mr Hobbes would say that man was more wicked than other creatures because he was more capable of lying'; 'Mr Hobbes sayeth that man is not animum politicum naturam for if so he would direct all his actions to the common good, but it is found that men generally . . . aim at their own interest.'[306] Yet men could be drawn to believe anything 'from such . . . as have gotten credit with them', so the ruler might use hope as well as fear to trick them into obedience.[307] We shall have occasion to return to the influence of Hobbes on Drake's political thought. What is striking here is that Drake's views on the nature of man – based on his reading – were almost certainly formed before Hobbes published *On the Nature of Man* in 1650. Hobbes, that is, confirmed a 'Hobbesian' view that Drake had constructed through his reading of Aristotle, Tacitus, Machiavelli and Guicciardini, in the light of his own observation and experience. It was not the only area in which Sir William Drake read himself into revolutionary conceptions of society and state.

299. Ogden MS 7/19 f. 190v. He goes on to praise the education of heathen states as inculcating qualities of magnanimity and heroism.
300. Ogden MS 7/27 f. 28v.
301. Ogden MS 7/32 f. 81v.
302. Ogden MS 7/25 f. 138.
303. Ogden MS 7/27 f. 28v.
304. Ogden MSS 7/20 f. 78v; 7/9 f. 149; 7/19 f. 192v.
305. Ogden MS 7/22 f. 186: 'Mr Hobs his books of Human Nature.'
306. Ogden MSS 7/17 f. 151v; 7/21 f. 172v.
307. Ogden MS 7/30 f. 169.

In early modern England, traditional and prevailing social values were premised on a perception of men as moral beings. The language of 'commonweal' encapsulated the values of a Christian community in which all advanced the common good. Despite the many demonstrations that the ideal was not practised we should not underestimate its force as an ideal or ideology of state: Machiavelli, after all, was so loudly condemned because he dared to discount those values. Given his ideas on the nature of man, Drake could not subscribe to the traditional values of community, mutual assistance and public good taught in school, church and household. In Christian charity he knew he ought to think the best of men, but in worldly dealing he felt it was necessary to think the worst. In a polity in which 'magna pisces edunt minores', subjects had to be taught the arts of survival.[308]

This led Drake to a different view of education and the values it should teach. Drake regarded education as fundamental to society: education determined the degree of virtue in a society and had 'great influence upon the very form of government'.[309] 'Corrupt books produced corrupt manners'; the strength of the Roman state, he believed, rested on its manners and 'their manners from their education differ[ed] totally from the modern.'[310] Polybius had argued that disorder stemmed from the ill education of youth; citing him, Drake stressed how the right education in boyhood was crucial in making the man.[311] But education, as he conceived it, was a process that continued through life: 'it requires a long time to know the world's pulse for our life is half spent before we know what it is to live.'[312] 'To know the world': for Drake the purpose of education was a practical guide for life. Like Lord Keepers Egerton and Bacon, he thought that the traditional grammar school placed too much emphasis on the contemplative rather than the active life.[313] 'Tis not', he noted from Montaigne, 'the knowledge but the application of learning that makes a wise man.'[314] Since the Romans' education had inculcated the right values, they were still to be taken as guides for action. And in the modern age, those such as Guicciardini were to be studied for their 'civil and moral antidotes against the venom of the world'.[315]

What men most needed to learn was what Drake most endeavoured to teach himself: control of the passions. 'Most of the disorders of our lives proceed from the darkness of our understanding or from the command or sway that our passions have over our reason.'[316] The English were especially

308. Ogden MS 7/28 f. 150. 'The big fish eat the smaller.'
309. Ogden MSS 7/13 f. 128v; 7/31 f. 179.
310. Ogden MS 7/13 f. 47v.
311. Ogden MSS 7/25 f. 105v; 7/37 f. 46v.
312. Ogden MS 7/37 f. 41v.
313. See Ogden MS 7/10 f. 2v.
314. Ogden MS 7/10 f. 41.
315. Ogden MS 7/24 f. 4.
316. Ogden MS 7/28 f. 32. This emphasis probably owed something to Drake's reading of Justus Lipsius and the neostoics. See G. Oestreich, *Neostoicism and the Early Modern State* (Cambridge, 1982), and below, pp. 314–15.

prone to passions and needed to study to control them, 'moderate passions'
being 'the certain signs of a strong and well composed mind'.[317] Traditional
Aristotelian and Christian teaching pressed the same message: the need for
reason, the soul, to regulate the lower appetites; but Drake's stress on the need
for self-regulation, on order, rule and measure, owed little to the dictates of
conventional philosophy or piety. Reason and control of the passions for him
were necessary for effecting one's ends: 'where reason precedes our actions,
fortune ordinarily follows them but where passions, then fortune ordinarily
commands them.'[318] The man dominated by passions failed to seize the opportunities to advance his ends in the world: 'he that cannot bridle and suppress
his passions tis impossible he should comply with persons, times and occasions as his interest require. He can never take the true measure of himself
nor others with whom he is to negotiate.'[319] Reason for Drake was not what
brought man close to the perfection of his prelapsarian state: it was the instrument of interest, for the advance of business.[320] For Drake self-regulation
meant men should govern themselves by rules and maxims, learned from
reading and experience. These instructed in the qualities needed for living
in society – caution, secrecy, dexterity, audacity, prudence. Education and
experience tutored men first in the perennial need for circumspection. 'Since
men's life is full of deceit wise men's minds should be full of mistrust', for
'so infinite is the malice and envy of the world that to him that is fallen there
are few that will lend their hands to help him up again.'[321]

In a radical rewriting of the code of honour and shame, Drake maintained
that there was no shame in being suspicious but 'it is a great shame to be
deceived.'[322] The cautious man therefore warily observed his fellows but never
trusted, nor did he ever reveal his true self. Plain dealing, the proverb had it,
was a jewel but those who used it often died beggars.[323] As Sir Walter Ralegh
observed, the person who 'makes himself a body of crystal' (interestingly the
metaphor James I used to demonstrate his sincerity) that all may look through
him, was a fool.[324] For survival men needed to learn to live in the half-light,
conceal their affections and dissimulate with respect to their intentions: 'He
that cannot feign a friend never proves a dangerous enemy.'[325] Having learned

---

317. Ogden MSS 7/19 f. 5; 7/9 f. 157v.
318. Ogden MS 7/16 f. 188.
319. Ogden MS 7/15 f. 113v; cf. f. 104.
320. See Folger MS f. 115.
321. Ogden MSS 7/25 f. 54v; 7/30 f. 170; the last quotation is from Guicciardini.
322. Ogden MS 7/19 f. 8v.
323. Ogden MS 7/53 f. 124; the proverb is annotated under the heading 'Astutia'.
324. Ogden MS 7/15 f. 34; James I spoke of 'a crystal window in my breast wherein all
     my people might see the secretest thought of my heart', W. Notestein, F. H. Relf and
     H. Simpson, eds, Commons Debates 1621 (7 vols, New Haven, 1935), vol. 2, p. 2. See
     too K. Sharpe, 'Private Conscience and Public Duty in the Writings of James VI
     and I', in J. Morrill, P. Slack and D. Woolf, Public Duty and Private Conscience in
     Seventeenth-Century England (Oxford, 1993), pp. 77–100.
325. Ogden MSS 7/16 f. 152; 7/19 f. 141v.

caution and the need to feign, men had to grasp the crucial importance of seizing occasion and opportunity. Wise men 'cognoscer il tempo'; they learned to know when to carry out a plan and when it was necessary to change course.[326] The importance of 'occasio' recurs time and again in the proverbs Drake copies and in his observations from history.[327] A sense of the moment was the vital ingredient of the social value he stressed most of all: that of prudence. At the most basic level 'our own prudent actions are our strongest security' against the malice of men.[328] Prudence instructed men to 'look upon all as enemies' and to take preventative action against them: 'The prudent conduct of a man's life consists chiefly in this: to have such a tie and obligation upon men that they may not have the power or will to hurt us . . . to keep the interest of things in our own power.'[329] Beyond mere self-defence, prudence was the art of living that enabled men to secure their ends: the prudent man was he who knew 'everything to his purpose and advantage', who knew the point of the adage 'con poco cervello se governo il mondo.'[330] For in the end one's reputation was built not upon virtue but upon success. 'All human actions', Drake noted, 'are measured by utility'; the corrupt world favoured the successful even when they were unjust.[331]

If we are here a long way from traditional social values, the point would not have been lost on Drake. He knew that the clergy like the renowned Dr Preston continued to preach that honesty was the best policy and cunning the device of weak men.[332] He knew that Christian charity taught that one should think the best of men.[333] Yet experience taught that it was dangerous to follow them in a corrupt society when 'all the things in the world have two faces . . .'[334] In such a world he that *departed* from evil was the one who made himself a prey.[335] And in such a society 'too much goodness and conscientiousness [that is adherence to conscience] made a man some what less fit for . . . business.'[336] Drake saw his society not as a moral commonwealth but as a theatre in which all feigned and took on parts.[337] The man therefore who read and annotated hundreds of books distrusted words, rhetoric, as crafty posturing. What he held was that men should learn the practical arts of

---

326. Ogden MS 7/28 ff. 35–35v.
327. See Ogden MSS 7/18 f. 125; 7/25 f. 88v; 7/32 passim; Folger MS passim.
328. Ogden MS 7/18 f. 135.
329. Ogden MSS 7/22 f. 11v; 7/24 f. 122v.
330. Ogden MSS 7/19 f. 81: 'prudentia est ars vivendi'; 7/37 f. 163v; 7/28 f. 94v ('with a little wit or cunning he governs the world').
331. Ogden MSS 7/15 f. 58; 7/16 f. 185.
332. Ogden MS 7/15 f. 2.
333. Ogden MS 7/37 f. 177. He immediately added that, in the world, it was necessary to think the worst of people; cf. 7/20 f. 25.
334. Ogden MS 7/18 f. 143. He adds: 'what seems friendly, feigned and unfriendly, what holy, hypocritical.'
335. Ogden MS 7/25 f. 159.
336. Ogden MS 7/53 f. 163v.
337. See, for example, Ogden MSS 7/18 ff. 143ff.; 7/37 f. 111v ('Universus mundus exercet histrionem' is one of Drake's favourite adages).

prudence not from the schools or Christian morality but from 'judgement' derived from experience. And the best record of experience, of what men did rather than what they said, was history.

One of the key features of the age of the Renaissance was a revived interest in history, especially the histories of Greece and Rome, as a font of wisdom. In late sixteenth-century England, a fashion for Roman history, especially Livy and Tacitus, took hold in the universities and at court.[338] And the revived study of the ancients led to a vogue for so-called 'politic histories' – written very much to point up lessons of more recent times – by the likes of Bacon, Hayward and Speed.[339] In his general belief that history offered counsel, Drake therefore exemplified those interests and developments, and stated the philosophy that lay behind them with clarity and eloquence. 'All our wisdom', he wrote, 'consists in our experience or memory . . . and our own time cannot afford us observations enough for so many cases as we need direction in. Needs must we then . . . interrogare generationem pristinam, what they did in like case.'[340] And he went on to explain why:

> there is nothing under the sun that may be said is new but that it hath been already in former generations, so that it is but turning the globe and setting before us some case of antiquity which may sample ours and either remembering to follow it if it fell out well, or to eschew it if the success were ill.[341]

Not to know what had gone before was to live in the world like a child, whereas 'he that is well read in history seems to be of every country, to have lived in all ages, to have assisted at all the councils and public assemblies . . .'[342]

Along with many of his contemporaries Drake adhered to a view of the past as cyclical, so that as states rose and fell, 'the same causes and events arrive under divers shapes and appearances.'[343] Men did not change but were 'subject to the same desires and passions in all ages'; there was almost the same proportion of virtue and vice in all past as present societies.[344] Whilst, then, it was necessary carefully to consider 'all the circumstances concerning the parallels', the astute student of the past could plot his course by the lessons of history.[345] 'It is evident that in all cities and all people there are the same desires and the same humours that were always so that . . . for him that

338. Henry Savile's edition of Tacitus' *Histories* was published in 1591. See too M. Smuts, 'Court-Centred Politics and the Uses of Roman Historians, 1590–1630', in Sharpe and Lake, *Culture and Politics*, pp. 21–43.
339. See D. Woolf, *The Idea of History in Early Stuart England* (Toronto, 1990).
340. Ogden MS 7/21 f. 59: 'We must interrogate the earlier age.'
341. Ogden MS 7/21 f. 59v. Drake is glossing Ecclesiastes 1: 9.
342. Ogden MS 7/31 ff. 192, 193v.
343. Ogden MS 7/20 f. 36.
344. Ogden MS 7/16 ff. 96–96v.
345. Ogden MS 7/16 f. 113.

examines with diligence the things that are past to foresee the future in any commonweal' there was the opportunity 'to serve himself of those remedies which were used to devise new . . .'; otherwise 'it follows that continually in all ages the same errors happen.'[346] If then, as Comines put it, histories were the greatest guides for a man to 'steer and govern his actions by', how did Drake read history and what 'excellent lessons', to use Davila's phrase, did Drake derive from the past?[347]

Drake drew on modern as well as ancient historians, and even on the histories of recent events for instruction. From Tacitus he observed the craft of rulers, from Machiavelli's *History of Florence* the folly of building on the false ground of popular support.[348] Comparing ancient and modern histories showed that when it came to the art of disguising, Ferdinand of Spain and Tiberius had much in common, and for that matter that Machiavelli prescribed what Tiberius practised.[349] Essex and Ralegh found, just as had Sejanus, that friends forsook them when most needed; and Rutilius's policy to break a conspiracy had 'some resemblance . . . with that of Louis XI to get out of Burgundy's power'.[350] In the case of the Low Countries, he felt that

> the readers of the modern histories . . . must set before them and consider the images and pictures of now Arminius now Civilis the two whirlwinds of ancient Belgia, . . . the like springs and principles of each man's motion will present themselves . . . shaking off obedience to Tiberius and Vespasian, courting the people with hope of liberty . . . so much the same that unless you knew the difference by particular names you would think yourself present in the old Belgick tumults and troubles . . .[351]

Histories, ancient and modern, were full of lessons for citizens and for governors – examples of virtue and valour, the dangers of credulity, the tendency of men to follow a rising star, the stratagems of cunning, colloquies and corrupt ministers.[352]

Often lessons came from the lives of those who had stamped their mark on history. So Scipio taught men how to make use even of adversity, Appius the danger of sudden changes of custom, Pompey the futility of struggling against the inevitable, Henry VIII the inefficacy of good words and the need for force in difficult cases.[353] Drake gathered under a heading collections of

---

346. Ogden MS 7/13 f. 129.
347. Ogden MSS 7/12 f. 31; 7/10 f. 110v.
348. Ogden MSS 7/13 f. 128; 7/53 f. 160v; 7/16 f. 93v.
349. Ogden MSS 7/16 f. 79; 7/53 f. 164.
350. Ogden MSS 7/18 f. 10; 7/19 f. 92.
351. Ogden MS 7/31 f. 193v
352. For examples, see Ogden MSS 7/16 f. 86 onwards; 7/18 f. 89v; 7/19 f. 27v; 7/24 f. 89 onwards; 7/30 ff. 188, 189 onwards; 7/53 f. 90v.
353. Ogden MSS 7/16 f. 86; 7/25 f. 4v.

'Civil Characters out of Ancient and Modern Historians', with the lessons to be drawn from their lives. Pompey III showed 'the ill effects of rigid reformations', Galba the need for intrepidity, Pope Alexander VI the successes of sharp wit, Ferdinand, King of Naples, the benefits of industry and wisdom, Cosimo de Medici the importance of sagacity in public affairs, and so on.[354] As we earlier saw Drake illustrating proverbs from history, here we find him turning particular examples into adages – 'severity tends more to union than clemency' – and past lessons into rules. From Ferdinand of Naples' efforts to secure papal aid against France he concluded: 'We often see that no less easily is the timorous man carried by despair into deliberation headlong and hurtful than the rash man by credulity.'[355] The lessons and rules from history were especially 'most necessary for governors'; and Drake's heroes among rulers, ancient and modern, were those like Tiberius and Louis XI or Ferdinand of Spain who observed, as a prince should when reading history, the 'arts and errors of others' in the past.[356] So William of Nassau's astute advice to the Duc d'Alençon about religion it was thought 'he learned out of Machiavelli whose book he diligently studied.'[357] By contrast, when he reflected on 'Revolutions caused by *not* remembering and considering history and why', Sir William had the less sagacious rulers, perhaps his own king, in mind.[358] 'Proverbs and history', Drake noted, 'preserve both men and states.'[359] The past not only taught citizens how to negotiate a hostile world but counselled princes in the arts of statecraft.[360] The man most familiar with histories then could reasonably claim to be the best counsellor of kings.

Though the records indicate only an occasional involvement in public affairs, Drake was immersed in the politics of his age. Contemporary politics shaped his reading of history, and recent and current political events and actors sprang to his mind as he read and annotated his texts. He knew, too, that how one read was often a political act: that, for example, Erasmus's name had been used 'variously according to the difference of persons'.[361] He knew that interpretation was intimately bound up with power and authority. Words used to rulers met with the danger that they 'not be taken as the party means but as it pleaseth the prince to construe'.[362] Drake therefore appreciated that his own

354. Ogden MS 7/24 ff. 89–122; cf. 7/16 f. 86.
355. Ogden MS 7/24 f. 100.
356. Ogden MSS 7/16 f. 96; 7/19 f. 11 Cf. Drake's own 'examples of art and error drawn from the best historians', 7/16 f. 86. On Louis XI, see, for example, 7/15 passim; Folger MS f. 31 and passim.
357. Ogden MS 7/53 f. 94.
358. Ogden MS 7/30 ff. 108–10.
359. Ogden MS 7/30 f. 41.
360. Ogden MSS 7/10 f. 110v: 'past occurrences teach excellent lessons to govern the future'; 7/14 f. 3: 'things of counsel . . . more than ordinary in history'. See too 7/19 f. 27v; and 7/31 f. 193 on the value to government of precepts drawn from history. See too 7/53 f. iv on the need for men in public life to read histories.
361. Ogden MS 7/16 f. 140v.
362. Ogden MS 7/18 f. 152.

reading was a political act, and one in divided times not without its dangers. Yet, as Bacon had argued, 'rough times and full of mutations and accidents are most instructive to the reader.'[363] Drake's notebooks are the product not only of reading but reading in 'rough times'.

We have observed Drake's tendency to politicise a familiar proverb. We should also note how often his historical examples and illustrations come from recent English politics, on which he was clearly well informed. The tendency of factions to flatter themselves, for instance, he felt well illustrated by the Hampton Court conference, which itself took on historical significance as the puritans came to the fore in the 1640s.[364] Apelles' lesson about the need to know when to give up brought to his mind and margin the note 'Duke of Buck[ingham's] error at Ile de Rhé', in 1628.[365] An Italian adage about deceiving an enemy again led him to Buckingham – and his feeding the Earl of Bristol with false hopes of a reconciliation.[366] As important as these particular instances is Drake's habit of translating what he reads from the past into the languages and images of his own experience. So when he takes notes on the religion of the Muscovites, he writes of their reading of the 'homilies' of the 'Ancient Fathers' in churches to keep people in unity.[367] Similarly when he reflects on the religious divisions of Rome or quattrocento Italy he uses the term 'conventicles' to describe them.[368]

Such a domestication of vocabulary is not only an Anglicisation of the account; it is also a politicisation: the proliferation of conventicles is a major fact of the reader's experience in the 1640s and 1650s. Throughout the notebooks the worlds of ancient Rome and Renaissance Italy are read through the experience of England during civil war and interregnum. As he notes how Italy, having cast off Roman imperial rule, fell into faction and disorder, Drake observes that 'the king and the church are the two anchors which hold any kingdom steady and quiet under God.'[369] Similarly he took the message of the proverb 'we cannot brush our garments without losing wool' to be that states could not be reformed without expense and loss.[370] When he read Abraham Cowley's poem about a land that in twenty years had scarce enjoyed a calm day, Drake immediately knew that it 'applied to the British troubles'.[371] Both the writer's and the reader's imagination were inevitably seeped in civil war and revolution, even though both were in exile from England. The very act of writing, always bound up with authority in early modern England, had

363. Ogden MS 7/27 f. 10.
364. Ogden MS 7/22 f. 141v.
365. Ogden MS 7/25 f. 34.
366. Ogden MS 7/24 f. 156. Significantly the adage concerned the treatment of an enemy in war.
367. Ogden MS 7/12 f. 60.
368. Ogden MS 7/24 f. 210v.
369. Ogden MS 7/16 f. 107.
370. Ogden MS 7/53 f. 80. He reads the proverb 'he who breaks up a hedge will find a snake bites him' as counsel against disturbing religion and law.
371. Ogden MS 7/17 f. 30. See A. Cowley, *The Works* (1668), p. 17, and below, pp. 228–30.

become still more intensely politicised during the Civil War and Revolution. So entwined in Drake's consciousness were the events of those decades with his own reading and annotations that he used the language of the annotator as an axiom for government, warning that 'seeking to reform faults [is] like to wiping off a blot, which if not done by a dexterous hand makes a greater.'[372] As careful reader and dexterous annotator, William Drake constructed on the page not only his own values and social codes but a blueprint for good government.

Scripts for State

'Rules of government ought to be drawn from the nature of people and not from spectacular [that is speculative] forms or ideas.' In writing this sentence from de Bellagarde as he read, Sir William Drake laid down the foundation of his own political thought – in experience rather than philosophy.[373] All the experience of history indicated that the fortunes of states were bound to rise and fall, that they were destined to enjoy virtue and quiet, descend to corrupt luxury and destruction, and be reinvigorated again by good laws that fostered greatness.[374] This, however, did not mean that the nature of the state or the qualities and actions of governors were immaterial. Though it fragmented at last, the Roman Empire for long held sway over the world; and rulers such as Cesare Borgia and Louis XI demonstrated what an effective prince could do to revive an ailing state. From the histories of classical Rome to the narratives of his own day, therefore, Drake formed views on law, order and statecraft.

One of the constant themes of his annotations on politics during the 1640s and 1650s was the necessity of order: 'All things in the world have an end of their life,' he observed, 'and they enjoy it longest that keep closest to orders.'[375] What good there was in the world resided in order, without which all descended to chaos.[376] Anarchy Drake held with Polybius to be the most pernicious of all conditions, and anarchy loomed when ambitious men endeavoured to subvert order and degree.[377] 'A servant that reigneth' was among 'the things that disquieteth the earth'.[378] Given the dangers of disorder, obedience

---

372. Ogden MS 7/18 f. 13.
373. Ogden MS 7/37 f. 178v. Roger de St Lary, Sieur de Bellagarde was either the favourite of the Duc d'Anjou, or his son Roger, a Gentleman of the Chamber and intimate of Henri IV and Louis XIII.
374. Ogden MS 7/30 f. 72v; cf. 7/16 f. 95.
375. Ogden MS 7/16 f. 48.
376. Ogden MS 7/18 f. 7v: 'bonum universum consistit in ordine'; cf. 7/20 f. 14v.
377. Ogden MS 7/9 f. 148v.
378. Ogden MS 7/16 f. 46.

to authority Drake considered as much the interest of subjects as of rulers; it was, he put it, 'the father . . . of felicity'.[379] The history of Rome demonstrated the rule that 'order begets union and union strength' and so brought benefits to all.[380] By corollary the greatest threat to happiness and order, Drake judged, lay in division: 'All good things in the world are overthrown by division . . .'.[381] Where a united state was like the faggot that could not easily be broken, disunity left all subjects to be broken like twigs.[382] Division led to factions, which impoverished states, and ultimately 'from factions springs civil wars.'[383] In all ages divisions among the nobles or between the nobility and the people had been the grounds of disorder.[384] In all states, therefore, some 'sovereign power' was essential to 'give rule to the disagreeing judgements and interests of many' and to unite them in concord.[385]

Order and stability were also put at risk by any change in the nature of states. This presented a problem because Drake acknowledged that since commonwealths grew corrupt it was sometimes beneficial to restore them to their primitive institution.[386] However, history demonstrated that change of the form of government proved often 'sufficient to ruin any state or kingdom'.[387] Reformers then had to proceed with subtlety and patience. 'Statists in their changes and mutations of commonweals', Drake noted, 'should imitate nature . . . who in all things proceeds gently and by little and little.'[388] Sudden reform, remedies too weak or too strong, did more damage than good.[389] Sudden courses were not the only danger. 'Reformation of states' was 'seldom successful because commonly they are begun by men transported with ambition and vainglory'.[390] And change, once embarked upon, was not easily checked from more radical and destructive courses: 'no man stirs any change or alteration in a state that knows how to work it at his will or stop it at his pleasure.'[391] The best course therefore was to build upon good laws and customs, remaining vigilant that, even in the 'most happy and halcyon days', the seeds of corruption were not sown.[392] It was by an adherence to old ways that Rome had sustained its stability and strength; and 'stare super antiquas vias' was the best counsel to rulers.[393]

If order and stability were to Drake the principal ends of the state, what

379. Ogden MSS 7/16 f. 83v; 7/20 f. 14v.
380. Ogden MS 7/18 f. 7.
381. Ogden MS 7/19 f. 17.
382. Ogden MS 7/20 f. 81v.
383. Ogden MSS 7/9 f. 3; 7/13 ff. 53–4; 7/15 f. 59.
384. Ogden MS 7/20 f. 85v.
385. Ogden MS 7/13 f. 151.
386. Ogden MS 7/13 ff. 138–138v.
387. Ogden MS 7/10 f. 171v.
388. Ogden MS 7/10 f. 153.
389. Ogden MS 7/13 f. 146. Cf. Folger MS f. 134: 'sudden changes savour too much of violence and seldom produce either happy or durable effects.'
390. Ogden MS 7/15 f. 97.
391. Ogden MS 7/19 f. 1v.
392. Ogden MS 7/15 f. 32.
393. Ogden MSS 7/25 f. 165 ('moribus antiquis stat res Romana viresque'); 7/32 f. 49.

form of government did he believe best secured them? The history of republican and imperial Rome offered examples of the strengths and weaknesses of commonwealths and kingdoms. Machiavelli and Guicciardini, the moderns whom Drake most admired, praised those rulers who exhibited virtu and arrested the decline of their states, but they lauded more highly the rule of many in a republic as the best of all political constitutions. Drake occasionally echoes such sentiments: in republics, he noted from Machiavelli's *Art of War*, there 'arise commonly more excellent men than in kingdoms, because in commonwealths . . . virtue is honoured'.[394] He was also prepared to see the ideal that 'when men are in perfect freedom, there it is that countries make large progresses.'[395] Yet, in the main, Drake rejects apologia for republics. None, he writes, 'endure heavier servitude than such as become subjects to a republic'.[396] For whatever the ideal of a citizenry of virtue, what Machiavelli believed to be the best state, Drake, taking his rules of government from 'the nature of men' not ideal forms, knew that good popular government was a dangerous fantasy.

Drake was unequivocal about the multitude. He that grounds himself upon the people, he put it bluntly, 'lays his foundation in the dirt'.[397] He believed that nothing was more dreadful than a multitude without a head.[398] For the people spoke of liberty but desired to live licentiously and 'licentia non est libertas.'[399] Ever restless, they were easily persuaded that they were ill governed and stirred to commotion.[400] Because they followed their passions rather than reason, often preferring tyrants to good rulers, multitudes were 'not to be managed . . . otherwise than by fear and hope'.[401] 'Men', Drake had determined, 'are seldom good unless either forced or deluded', so the multitude, for their own good, had to be either compelled or deceived into following the dictates of authority.[402] With anarchy always looming as the worst of evils and the people, once stirred, unstoppable, what was most needed was a ruler who knew how to deceive and compel: to 'stroke his people but keep the bridle in his hand'.[403]

An unconventional thinker in many ways, Drake nevertheless believed strongly in monarchy. The end of the state was stability and only 'monarchia pacem conducet'.[404] Kings, he wrote, had been created as a shelter from the

---

The adage from Scripture – 'Stick to the old ways' – was a favourite of the Earl of Strafford (*The Earl of Strafford's Letters and Despatches*, ed. W. Knowler (2 vols, 1739), vol. 1, p. 269).

394. Ogden MS 7/30 f. 78v.
395. Ogden MS 7/13 f. 136.
396. Ogden MS 7/13 f. 139.
397. Ogden MS 7/9 f. 107v.
398. Ogden MS 7/19 f. 30.
399. Ogden MSS 7/16 f. 95; 7/25 f. 196.
400. Ogden MS 7/12 f. 142.
401. Ogden MSS 7/9 f. 30; 7/19 f. 32.
402. Ogden MS 7/13 f. 140.
403. Ogden MS 7/17 f. 89v.
404. Ogden MS 7/10 f. 134.

rage of multitudes; they were owed obedience because obedience alone earned security for all.[405] It was in order to secure that obedience, rather than from any intrinsic divinity in kings, that, Drake argued, 'there is good *reason* that the prince's person should be sacred':[406] for 'the reverence towards the government and governor is the shelter and protection to each man's particular safety'.[407] Sanctity and ceremony were devices that lulled the people into compliance. If crowns were revered as sacred, even when worn by idolators, their authority remained unchallenged.[408] Indeed Drake recognised that the very substance of authority was 'maintained and preserved by ceremony'.[409] As Lord Treasurer Weston put it, ceremony was the fence of the substance, protecting authority from contempt.[410] For 'a prince . . . whose glorious pomp doth so dazzle you in public, view him but behind the curtain and you see him but an ordinary man.'[411] Extending the striking image, Drake viewed the exercise of rule as a play, in which all were complicit in the illusion performed:

> in a stage play all men know that he that plays the greatest man's part may be the meanest, yet if a man should . . . call him by his own name while he stands in his majesty, one that acts his part with him may chance to break his head [for] marring the play. And so they said that these matters be king's games, as it were stage plays upon scaffolds, in which poor men are but the lookers on and they that be wise meddle no further.[412]

Drake made the same point in another metaphor graphically revealing of both his sexual anxieties and the relationship of political to sexual transgression: 'the showing of arcana imperii is like the showing naked the pudenda of a curious woman.'[413] Power was best preserved when veiled from the onlooker who bowed to its mystery.[414]

405. Ogden MSS 7/15 f. 7; 7/30 f. 85. 'Monarchy leads to peace.'
406. Ogden MS 7/37 f. 77v, my italics. The combination of the languages of divinity and interest is striking.
407. Ogden MS 7/53 f. 184.
408. Ogden MS 7/10 f. 116v, citing Balzac: 'crowns are to me sacred even upon idolators' heads.'
409. Ogden MS 7/9 f. 130; cf. 7/19 f. 189: 'majesty is the very life and soul of monarchy.'
410. Ogden MS 7/16 f. 124.
411. Ogden MS 7/30 f. 174. Another striking mixed metaphor appears in Folger MS f. 121: 'Majesty without ceremony looked like a peacock without a tail, ceremony being like a slight glass that preserves precious liquor that would be lost without it.'
412. Ogden MS 7/18 f. 153. This is a highly original interpretation of the familiar trope of the king on the stage, underpinning metaphorically the complicity of the subject in the exercise of authority. See below, p. 333.
413. Ogden MS 7/22 f. 20. This opens up the relationship, awaiting exploration, between the demystification of both authority and female sexuality evident in Restoration culture. I will be exploring this subject in a study of representations of authority in early modern England.
414. Ogden MS 7/15 f. 3v: 'magestate major ex longinquo reverentia'; cf. 7/20 f. 181.

Ceremony and mystery, however, could not alone sustain authority. Some substance of power was needed to support the illusion, or as Drake put it: 'it is a vain thing to seek the pomp of things without having a real power of upholding that pomp.'[415] In part, power rested on force, on armies, but, still more, Drake believed it rested on the skills of the prince. While the people ought to obey their ruler, it was for the prince to secure his authority; rulers had 'no reason to complain of the fault of their subjects, for all their disorders proceed[ed] from the prince's own negligence or ignorance'.[416] In the first place, then, the ruler was to study the nature of his subjects and build his power 'either upon the love or fear of his people'.[417] The prudent prince was he who so tied his people to him that they had neither the power nor the desire to remove him.[418] Such prudence in part consisted in the conventional virtues of a good ruler – knowing who and when to reward, 'how to do graces', how to 'give rule to the disagreeing judgements and interests of many'.[419] But it also involved stratagem. In several places Drake returned to the need for kings to 'hide affections', to practise dissimulation, for 'qui nescit dissimulare nescit regnare.'[420] Moreover it was often necessary for a ruler to lay aside conscience, and to pursue expediency: 'to prefer', as Guicciardini put it, 'utile before honeste'.[421] Against all the conventional literature on kingship, therefore, Drake accepted that the good man did not always make the best ruler – 'difficile est bonum virum ad bonum principem agere.'[422] He even went so far as to quote Bodin that 'sometimes the worst man makes the best king.'[423] While the subjects' judgement was not 'formed with due maturity nor measured by just and convenient proportion', the prince could not limit himself by conscience and virtue; he had to secure compliance by whatever means he could.[424] Whatever his cunning, the bad prince was preferable to a weak one, the weak prince being one of the 'greatest judgements' on a land: the cause of division and civil war.[425]

At times Drake's annotations may appear to amount to a cynical endorsement of any ruler, however evil or tyrannical. But this may be the reductio ad absurdum of his position. Whilst rulers at times had to act against

---

415. Ogden MS 7/21 f. 156. The notes belong to the late 1640s.
416. Ogden MS 7/15 f. 55v.
417. Ogden MSS 7/16 f. 92v; 7/27 f. 138.
418. Ogden MSS 7/16 f. 101v; 7/15 f. 92.
419. Ogden MSS 7/9 ff. 9, 129v; 7/13 f. 151.
420. Ogden MSS 7/9 f. 9; 7/18 f. 129v. 'He who does not know how to dissimulate knows not how to govern'; cf. 7/24 f. 171v.
421. Ogden MSS 7/28 f. 82; 7/25 f. 52; 'What is useful before what is honest'.
422. Ogden MS 7/18 f. 113: 'It is difficult for a good man to become a good prince.'
423. Ogden MS 7/9 f. 130v; cf. 7/16 f. 83v.
424. Ogden MS 7/9 f. 140 (from Guicciardini).
425. Ogden MS 7/15 f. 59. Cf. 7/13 f. 133: 'Guicciardini gravely notes that men may lawfully pray for good princes but ought to bear with the bad, for if every man that is subject should aspire to equality or sovereignty, it would shake and confound all the empires and kingdoms of the world.'

conventional morality, while subjects were bound to tolerate a bad prince for fear of the worse evil of anarchy, the prudent prince was he who secured consent and won the trust of his people, for in their love lay his security.[426] Prudent princes, therefore, should keep their subjects well affected, by not straining obedience through excessive exactions or measures. When it came to taxes, 'money drawn from the bowels of the people by a prudent prince is like moisture drawn from the earth which gathers into a cloud and falls back upon the earth again, princes being but stewards for the public.'[427] And the wise prince was he who devised good laws and himself ruled in accordance with them.[428] Next to kings it was laws that secured the state. 'Law no doubt is the greatest organ by which the sovereign power doth move', but it was not at the mercy of that power.[429] Drake notes Caenarus's reference to Moses ordering the magistrates not to lord it over the laws but to keep them, since 'the laws alone are they that always speak with all persons in one and the same impartial voice.'[430] While he reserved to the ruler authority 'in operationibus suis', Drake followed Aquinas in urging the prince to do 'per legem quam oportet legem dominari'.[431] For rather than a competition between regality and law, he maintained, 'it is the law that unites the king and the people.'[432] And he quotes an important passage from Ralegh's *History of the World* (one echoed by James I in his speech of 1610) on the change in government from kingship 'regal absolute to regal tempered with laws': where once the will of the king had made law, in order to restrain kings from tyranny laws were instituted; only that government which was qualified with laws was termed the truly regal.[433] 'Law', the quotation concludes, was 'a right rule prescribing a necessary mean for the good of a commonwealth or civil community'. It was for princes, and for subjects, to observe it.

In Drake's notes on order and rule, on the dangers of democracy and on the rule of law, we clearly sense a tension between the ideals and reality of government. It was a tension exposed ever since Machiavelli defended realpolitik, and one acknowledged, even in an England that officially anathematised Machiavelli, by Ralegh, Bacon and others. Behind passages about the menace of the people and the dangers of division and change, and the need for sovereignty, we may also begin to discern the experiences of the 1640s and 1650s. As we continue to explore Drake's views of politics, we shall see them become more specific and more distinct.

426. See, for example, Ogden MS 7/13 f. 71.
427. Ogden MSS 7/27 f. 185; 7/16 f. 101v.
428. Ogden MS 7/16 ff. 101v–102.
429. Ogden MS 7/21 f. 15v.
430. Ogden MS 7/13 f. 62. The reference may be to Antoninus de Caenario.
431. Ogden MS 7/31 f. 159; that is while the prince had power 'in his own matters', or arcana imperii, he should follow the law in matters determined by the law.
432. Ogden MS 7/16 f. 102.
433. Ogden MS 7/37 f. 181v. For James I, see C. H. McIlwain, *The Political Works of James I* (Cambridge Mass., 1918), pp. 307–25. For a good discussion of this speech, see G. Burgess, *The Politics of the Ancient Constitution* (Houndmills, 1992), pp. 152–6.

At the head of a list of the 'signs of a prudent government' – 'justice in the tribunal, plenty in the market, security in the high ways' – Drake placed what he deemed to be one of the pillars of state: 'devotion in the temple'.[434] The conjunction of the two concepts – prudence and devotion – was no slip of the pen. Of all the political reflections and ideas scattered throughout Drake's notebooks none is more striking, even shocking, than his attitude to religion. In order to understand how those attitudes were formed, we need to return to an aspect of Drake's reading that hitherto we have passed over: his reading of Scripture.

The Bible was the central text of early modern England, the source for private faith, social values and public affairs. For the illiterate it was quite probably the only book they heard read or expounded; for all, it represented the font of truth in a world of opinion, misrepresentation and false witness. Ever since the Reformation, however, the Bible had been plunged into the arena of contest; none questioned its truth but increasingly Catholic and Protestant, Lutheran and Calvinist read it differently – even in different editions – and anathematised any reading but their own. In England James I's sponsorship of an Authorised Version had endeavoured to secure unity, and to displace the Geneva Bible with its subversive marginalia. The contest over Scripture, for scriptural validation, however, did not abate. The logic of Protestantism's emphasis on the individual's reading of God's word led to a multiplicity of interpretations, to a proliferation of sects.[435] William Drake was born shortly after the Hampton Court conference agreed to a new edition of Scripture. As civil war approached, he saw clearly how the different interpretations of the Bible related to other disagreements and contests. He experienced violent demonstrations of how, as he put it, 'Scripture doth . . . service to the right hand and left at once.'[436] His own reading was a negotiation with that problem of interpretation as much as with Scripture itself.

Drake, of course, would have been familiar with the Bible in childhood, and his capacity for recall and cross-reference would have enabled him easily to call up the contradictions and ambiguities that fuelled the theological wrangles between Catholics and Protestants, Anglicans and puritans. It is, however, in these later notebooks dating from the 1640s and 1650s that we find him fully annotating Scripture; volumes 21 and 32 for example contain substantial sections of comment on biblical books. Where he paraphrases, we cannot be certain in all cases which edition of the Bible Drake had to hand. But the frequency of citation from Ecclesiasticus, the book of the Apocrypha, rejected by the godly and absent from the Geneva Bible, indicates that for most of the time he was using the Authorised Version. Though the offspring of puritan parents, Drake neither favoured the Geneva Bible, nor, as we shall see, the theology of the hotter Protestants. Despite all his annotation on the Bible,

434. Ogden MS 7/22 f. 114.
435. See C. Hill, *The English Bible and the Seventeenth-Century Revolution* (1993).
436. Ogden MS 7/24 f. 225.

Drake displays little interest in passages that lay at the heart of doctrinal or theological wrangles. Rather he went back to the Bible for the counsel it might offer men and states in troubled times. And he went most often to those books in which scriptural wisdom was pithily stated in adages: the books of Psalms, Proverbs, and chiefly Ecclesiasticus.[437]

As with his classical texts, Drake read the Scriptures alongside and through the medium of commentaries: the Fathers St Augustine and St Jerome, and Aquinas,[438] the theologians Melanchthon, Hooker and Andrewes,[439] the humanist commentators – Michael Jermin on Proverbs, Del Rio's adages taken from the Old and New Testaments, Saavedra Fajardo's treatise on the Christian prince and politics.[440] More generally Drake cross-referenced his annotated passages of Scripture to works of a distinctly secular colour. Accordingly we find him connecting the Book of Ecclesiastes to the counsel of Polybius, St Matthew's gospel with Aesop's fables, the Book of Job with Comines, and Ecclesiasticus with the adages of Sir Henry Wotton, Francis Bacon and others.[441] 'Places of Scripture' occur 'illustrated by Saavedra, Malvezzi and others', some of the others being Seneca, Tacitus, Comines, Bacon and, most often, Guicciardini and Machiavelli.[442] Drake was principally interested in the proverbs and sententiae to be found in Scripture. As he quoted Ecclesiasticus 39: 3: 'He will seek out the secrets of grave sentences and be conversant in dark parables.' These he cross-referred to his other collections of proverbs and illustrated by examples from classical and humanist histories.[443] And so Ferdinand of Spain appears in the margin to illustrate the axiom from Ecclesiasticus: 'separate thyself from thine enemies', and Lorenzo de Medici is deployed as an example of Proverbs 4: 11: 'I have taught thee in the way of wisdom.'[444]

We have seen enough of Drake at work to know that such practices of cross-reference involved a process of interpretation. At the most obvious level they demote Scripture to one of a group of texts read alongside each other – alongside not only pagan, but in some cases forbidden books. Few conventional students of the Bible would have read Ecclesiasticus with Tacitus and Machiavelli alongside on the desk, or the Book of Proverbs with

---

437. As the prologue indicates, the Book of Ecclesiasticus contained 'wise sayings, dark sentences, and parables' of Jesus, son of Sirach, 'a man of great learning', 'no less famous for wisdom' than Solomon.
438. Ogden MSS 7/13 ff. 31, 101; 7/15 f. 90v; 7/18 f. 39v.
439. Ogden MSS 7/12 ff. 5, 142; 7/15 f. 1v; 7/18 f. 65.
440. Ogden MSS 7/32 ff. 63, 85v, 99; 7/16 f. 160. See M. Jermin, *An Exposition Upon the Two Doctrinal Books of King Solomon: the Proverbs and Ecclesiastes* (1639); Del Rio, *Adagialia Sacra Veteris*; Saavedra Fajardo, *De Principe Politico-Christiano*.
441. Ogden MSS 7/16 f. 163 (Ecclesiastes 8: 6); 7/32 ff. 21–21v (Matthew 7: 15); 7/18 f. 39v (Job 29); 7/19 f. 80 (Ecclesiasticus 33).
442. Ogden MSS 7/16 f. 160; 7/17 f. 136v; 7/18 f. 49v; 7/19 f. 80; 7/32 begins with proverbs from Scripture read alongside Italian adages and Guicciardini.
443. Ogden MS 7/24 f. 3v.
444. Ogden MS 7/32 f. 9 (Ecclesiasticus 6: 13); f. 43v.

8. From Drake's notes on the Bible.

Guicciardini's history. The person who did was likely to take from Scripture rather different lessons from those of the dictates of Christian piety. Indeed, Drake not only 'raided' the Bible for adages, he organised the 'places of Scripture' he extracted under headings already chosen as the topics under which he arranged extracts from more secular texts (ill. 8).[445] 'Silence', 'Hypocrisy', 'Riches' were therefore the headings for passages from the Books of Amos and Proverbs;[446] under 'Against Rigid Reformations' Drake collected references from Exodus, Proverbs and Corinthians.[447] And the biblical notes collected, like Drake's other lists, were to be 'applied', put to use.

In some cases, the relationship of the scriptural reference to the heading appears strained, or the reading of the biblical passage as a gloss on the theme tendentious. The reference to Psalm 5: 5 in the context of feigned friendship stretches the meaning of 'thou hatest all workers of iniquity.'[448] As he read the

445. Ogden MS 7/16 f. 160.
446. Ogden MS 7/21 f. 25.
447. Ibid.
448. Ogden MS 7/20 f. 20.

Bible with other texts and organised his notes under headings, Drake was consistently to rewrite the meaning of Scripture. In some instances the alteration is one of tone occasioned by selection and omission of words. The adage from Proverbs 'He that handleth a matter wisely shall find good' reads rather differently when completed in the Bible by 'and who so trusteth in the Lord, happy is he.'[449] To take another case, the use of the second chapter of St John's gospel, relating to Christ's overturning the tables of the money lenders, is deployed to show that, like Guicciardini, the Lord himself counselled against trusting men.[450] The sense of Proverbs 18: 1 ('Through desire a man, having separated himself, seeketh and intermeddleth with all wisdom') is quite altered by juxtaposition with the adage 'occasiones quaesit qui vult recedere ab amico', especially when the latter adage is illustrated by Comines' passage on prudent princes always finding colour for their actions.[451] Similarly Psalm 32: 9 with its reference to the horse and bridle is pressed into serving one of Drake's favourite adages that fear is more effective than love as an instrument of rule.[452]

What we begin to discern is Scripture being deployed to support adages that Drake admired, even when to us such a reading seems strained or inappropriate. To illustrate 'divide et impera' by the example of St Paul's handling of the Pharisees and Sadducees may not be entirely unreasonable, but to take Genesis 6 (the story of God's mercy to Noah) as an example of God himself dividing tyrants distorts Scripture.[453] In Drake's hands Scripture becomes a text of realpolitik, yet another source of illustration of the arguments and values advocated by Machiavelli and Guicciardini. So the passage from Ecclesiastes – 'because to every purpose there is a time' – immediately leads him to that central message of the Florentines: 'force of occasion'.[454] Even Christ – 'Jehu feigning himself to be of the opinion of the false prophets in order to destroy them' – emerges in Drake's notebooks as a master of the art of dissimulation.[455] A reader who interpreted Scripture in these terms was likely to arrive at a very unconventional attitude to religion.

At first sight there is nothing unconventional about Drake's passionate belief in the importance of religion for social and political order. Religion, he believed, was an essential 'anchor to stay the fluctuating minds of men'.[456] Without it there was little prospect of order in society or state for 'there was

449. Ogden MS 7/18 f. 78. See Proverbs 16: 20.
450. Ogden MS 7/18 f. 131v.
451. Ogden MS 7/25 f. 103. 'He who wishes to distance himself from a friend seeks for his opportunity.'
452. Ogden MS 7/21 f. 65. The scriptural verse reads: 'Be ye not as the horse, or as the mule, which have no understanding: whose mouth must be held in with bit and bridle . . .' Drake gives the passage a Machiavellian slant.
453. See Ogden MS 7/28 f. 24. See Acts 23.
454. Ogden MS 7/32 f. 8; Ecclesiastes 8: 6.
455. Ogden MS 7/37 f. 82. Christ is used to illustrate the Latin adage 'tell a lie to dig out the truth'!
456. Ogden MS 7/25 f. 112.

never any legislator to make his laws take impression but had been forced to have recourse to some deity.'[457] Those who laid the right grounds of worship deserved to be esteemed in the commonwealth for they laid the foundation of the manners and customs of its citizens; the 'principals of religion rightly taught to children' had 'a great influence upon all the future actions of life'.[458] Few would have departed from these truisms; what divided men was the nature of right religion. For Drake what had now come to seem essential was an element of mystery and mystification. Mankind, he held, was naturally superstitiously inclined and prone to reverence what was remote and least understood.[459] Illustrating the adage 'Populus adeo religione gaudet et etiam favet superstitionem', Drake recalled in the margin how at the siege of Haarlem the townspeople had set up saints' images on the walls to frighten Alva's troops.[460] Mysteries and ceremonies – 'pleasing and sensual rites', as he was *now* prepared to describe them – could foster devotion; and the 'due reverence' paid to sacred places had often restrained men from 'fucinorous', wild and depraved, acts.[461]

But if right religion, with some element of mystery and ceremony, helped secure order, Drake believed by corollary that the corruption of religion soon brought ruin on the state: 'as the observance of divine worship occasions the greatness of a commonwealth, so the contempt of it destroys it.'[462] Writing from the experience of the 1640s, Drake saw divine worship corrupted by innovation and division. Changes in religion, 'the great anchor that keeps the commonwealth steady', had cast the ship adrift in turbulent waters.[463] Nothing more threatened to erode established customs and laws than innovations in faith; therefore

Maecenas in Dion gravely advises Augustus thou oughtest to show thyself highly offended and to punish those who do innovate anything in matter of religion . . . [for] those that seek to innovate in matter of religion do stir up many to desire a change and alteration of things, whence conventicles which doubtless are most dangerous in any state.[464]

The wise ruler, Drake concluded, did not lightly meddle with things 'che dependano immediate del Dio', knowing they 'ha troppe forza nille menti

457. Ogden MS 7/13 f. 140. Drake's utilitarian views echo both Machiavelli and Livy.
458. Ogden MSS 7/19 f. 32; 7/25 f. 106v.
459. See Ogden MS 7/9 f. 53: 'libenter obscura credunt': 'men readily believe obscure things'.
460. Ogden MS 7/24 f. 183. The quotation, from Cardano, means 'people take delight in religion and are even inclined to superstition.'
461. See Ogden MSS 7/24 f. 226v; 7/30 f. 123 (from Bacon); 7/57 f. 134v. Ogden MS 7/16 f. 111: 'superstition seems a light thing but produces solid effects.'
462. Ogden MS 7/30 f. 80; cf. 7/16 f. 94v: 'when religion begins to be corrupted . . . tis a certain sign of a country's approaching ruin.'
463. Ogden MS 7/12 f. 154.
464. Ogden MS 7/25 f. 165v; cf. 7/16 f. 181.

de gli huomini'.[465] Like innnovation, religious divisions sounded the death knell for order in the commonweal. Surveying history, Drake saw that divisions among Christians had brought about the downfall of Jerusalem and, recently, the collapse of the German empire.[466] Religious divisions fostered factions that then rent the state, and 'a factious churchman', Drake now knew, 'makes a seditious commonwealthsman.'[467] When heresies and divisions fragmented 'the truth of religion' into 'vain and fantastic opinions', when 'the understanding of God's law' was determined 'by women and children', all authority was 'brought into their hands', and all order collapsed.[468]

Drake therefore believed strongly in the need for an authority in the church to secure unity. 'Of this we are right sure,' he wrote, 'that nature, Scripture and experience itself have all taught the world to seek for the ending of contentions by submitting itself unto some judicial and definitive sentence.'[469] And that authority, Drake believed, had to reside in the ruler. Returning to Hooker, Drake dismissed any argument for a separation of church and state: 'a horse never goes quickly unless the bridle and riding rod be in one hand, the state and the church in the power of the magistrate.'[470] It was for the 'princes of a republic or kingdom' to 'maintain the grounds of religion . . . this being done they shall easily keep the commonweal religious', and return the state 'to the ancient bonds of unity in the church'.[471] 'A set liturgy' and prescribed ceremonies were the necessary checks against schism and the passions of misguided men who 'give themselves to imagine prayers'.[472] Just as government needed the support of religion, so religion itself needed regulation. For religion, 'if not limited by laws tis prone to run men into vain opinions and frenzy or to turn into faction.'[473] The teachings 'published by some Christians, sometimes for interest . . . sometimes out of passion' had 'infused a kind of madness into men's minds and disobedience into all government'.[474] To protect the state, therefore, the magistrate had to establish unity within and control over the church.

When he wrote of the support that religion gave the ruler, Drake spoke of all legislators' recourse to 'some deity'.[475] It is an unusual phrase for an early seventeenth-century Christian gentleman, born of godly parents, but one

---

465. Ogden MS 7/24 f. 20; things 'directly concerned with God' which 'had great force in men's minds'.
466. Ogden MSS 7/21 f. 105v; 7/27 f. 14v.
467. Ogden MSS 7/12 f. 146v; 7/17 f. 134v.
468. Ogden MSS 7/24 f. 225; 7/53 f. 158.
469. Ogden MS 7/17 f. 9v.
470. Ogden MS 7/21 f. 156. The notes date from the later 1640s.
471. Ogden MSS 7/10 f. 111v; 7/30 f. 42. The phrase 'princes of a republic or kingdom' may be significant, as notes in this volume are from the 1650s.
472. Ogden MS 7/21 f. 62.
473. Ogden MS 7/12 f. 146v.
474. Ogden MS 7/31 f. 8.
475. Above, p. 229.

that offers a clue to Drake's complex personal views on faith and the influences on his thinking. In places William writes of God traditionally as the beginning and end of all, directing the course of all affairs including man's relationship with him. 'God', he observes, 'hath put an incertainty in all worldly things' and God bestowed and withdrew his favour from nations, giving them wise and foolish princes.[476] Created man, beyond those abilities infused into him by God, had 'no other self ability than a clock after it is wound up by a man's hand hath'.[477] And Drake condemns those hypocrites who pretend a familiarity with God but have no 'awful sense of his greatness'.[478] Yet in other passages the conception of the divine and the language of the annotations appear strikingly unusual and even radical. 'Nature working by instinct', he posits, 'and that guided by the supremest intellect ought to be a secret school of instructions to men.'[479] Here God equates with the Platonic higher reason, or the supreme being of the Deists rather than the Old Testament judge or the divine monarch of the Revelation.

Indeed Drake questions the power of God to check men's tendency to use violence and abuse power, and appears to place more trust in wisdom and reason than in religion.[480] Prayers at times may be more efficacious than force but as Polybius had 'wisely' observed: 'had the world been composed all of wise men there would have been no need of . . . superstitious stratagems.'[481] Where most of his contemporaries regarded atheism as the solvent of moral order, Drake took from Bacon's essay the argument that it presented a lesser threat than 'superstition': 'for atheism leaves a man to sense, to philosophy, to natural piety, to laws, to reputation, all which may be guides to an outward moral virtue though religion were not . . .'[482] Times inclined to atheism, such as the age of Augustus Caesar, had been, after all, 'civil times'.[483] While neither Bacon nor Drake defended atheism, there is an emphasis in these passages on human reason and wisdom which, to say the least, jars with the prevailing Calvinist teaching on the corrupted reason and absolute depravity of fallen man.

Doctrinal differences have been prominent in recent historiography and were undoubtedly important issues in the early Stuart church.[484] Sir William Drake, we know, was brought up in a godly household and in an earlier

476. See, for instance, Ogden MSS 7/16 f. 167; 7/19 f. 10.
477. Ogden MS 7/37 f. 184, from Ralegh's *History of the World*.
478. Ogden MS 7/53 f. 134v.
479. Ogden MS 7/19 f. 78v.
480. See Ogden MS 7/21 f. 74v.
481. Ogden MS 7/24 f. 220v.
482. Ogden MS 7/30 f. 122v; see Bacon, 'Of Superstition', *Essays*, pp. 111–13.
483. Bacon, 'Of Superstition', p. 111.
484. Compare, for example, N. Tyacke, *Anti-Calvinists: The Rise of English Arminianism c.1590–1640* (Oxford, 1987) and P. White, *Predestination, Policy and Polemic: Conflict and Consensus in the English Church from the Reformation to the Civil War* (Cambridge, 1992).

chapter we detected his lack of sympathy for the Arminians who, Tyacke and others have argued, disrupted the Calvinist consensus in the Jacobean church.[485] However, in those notes taken during the 1640s and 1650s, there are indications of some shift in his sympathies and opinion. Drake seems very seldom to extract passages that do not resonate with his overall view at any given time, and during these decades such annotations as he makes on doctrine are far removed from a Calvinist conception of grace. Reading Montaigne's *Essays* in volume 10, for example, Drake notes that 'he censures the presumption of men who [were] seeking into the secrets of God's will and decrees, the incomprehensible springs of his works.'[486] From Balzac, Drake copies a sentence that directly challenges predestinarianism and implies free will: 'God saves none but such as contribute themselves to their salvation.'[487] Against the prevailing providentialism of puritan polemics in the 1640s, Drake, appropriating Montaigne, criticised religions that took prosperity and success as evidence of divine favour 'as in our civil wars wherein we are now for religion's sake, that party which got the victory made the success an assured sign of God's approbation of their faction; when they came afterward to excuse their disaster they call them scourges and fatherly chastisements.'[488]

As for the more exotic cults that flourished during the revolution, as well as condemning them as threats to political order Drake regarded them as 'delirious', the hallucinations of men of disordered minds.[489] Drake appears impatient with all parties, recalling Lipsius's view that if the papists were superstitious, the Lutherans were proud and drunken and the Calvinists turbulent.[490] While 'the substance of doctrine', basic belief, was maintained, their emphasis on differences served only to fracture the unity that was as essential to the church as to the state.[491] If religious divisions were unknown in heathen times, he noted as he read Bacon, 'the reason was because the re-

---

485. See above, pp. 109–11, 140–4.

486. Ogden MS 7/10 f. 42; See Montaigne, 'Judgements on God's Ordinances Must be Embarked upon with Prudence', in *Michel de Montaigne: The Complete Essays*, ed. M. Screech (Harmondsworth, 1987), pp. 242–4.

487. Ogden MS 7/10 f. 120. Drake is reading Balzac's letters, published in English in 1654.

488. Ogden MS 7/10 f. 42. The original, from Montaigne's essay on 'Judgements on God's Ordinances', reads: 'As in the religious wars which we are now fighting, after those who had prevailed at the battle of La Rochelabeille had had a great feast day over the outcome, exploiting their good fortune as a sure sign of God's approval for their faction, they then had to justify their misfortune at Montcontour and Jarnac as being fatherly scourges and chastisements' (*Essays*, p. 243). Drake's rendering of this passage brilliantly demonstrates his generalising a text into an adage, and then his rescripting it into a comment on his own time.

489. Ogden MS 7/25 f. 194v; cf. the words 'fantastic' (7/53 f. 158) and 'frenzy' (7/12 f. 146v).

490. Ogden MS 7/21 f. 179 (the date is c.1647–8). Lipsius stressed the need for religious unity. See Oestreich, *Neostoicism*, ch. 3.

491. Ogden MS 7/10 f. 111v.

ligion of heathens consisted rather in rites and ceremonies than in any constant belief.'[492]

Drake expressed rare admiration for the pagan religion of the ancients. The
religion introduced to Rome by Numa Pompilius, the successor to Romulus,
though invented and feigned for his ends, proved the foundation of good laws
and of good order; no less than their departure from it abetted their ruin.[493]
For ancient religion glorified great deeds and men of action, where Christianity lauded passivity and humility.[494] When Scipio Africanus persuaded his
men that Neptune favoured them, they were emboldened to victory;[495] most
of all the religion of the Romans fostered those qualities that Drake valued
so highly – prudence, sagacity and virtu. 'Religion', he noted, 'is a good
husband of all opportunities', and he clarifies his meaning for us by attaching a favourite adage: 'Sappi cognoscere il tempo.'[496] Religion could help men
secure their ends ('ubi utilitas ibi pietas') for even when false it 'put an exceed-
ing boldness in men's minds'.[497] The right religion could enrich a people and
advance the interests of the state.[498] In particular 'the advantages of religion
are for princes' as an aid to the art of statecraft, to draw men to duty.[499] Against
all the prevailing ideals, Drake defended a blend of religion and 'policy' for
the pursuit of interest.[500] He defended princes who feigned piety or cor-
roborated false miracles to advance their ends.[501] Where James I and Charles
I powerfully reiterated the need to subordinate politics to conscience, Drake
recalled the advice of Machiavelli: 'a prince not absolutely to disavow conscience but to manage it with such a prudent neglect as is scarce discernible
from a tenderness'.[502] On Drake's pages, a traditional perception of religion
as the basis of social and political order transmutes into a utilitarian attitude
to faith as a device by which greater men fulfil their ambitions and rulers
kept a credulous people in subordination.

The place of religion in the polity, the relationship of conscience to politics, the deployment of religion to advance designs, these were not issues
that Drake by chance found in his texts; they were central concerns of the
1640s and 1650s when the godly claimed to build a new Jerusalem in England.
From the bare facts of biography – his upbringing and Parliamentarian
allegiance – we might have expected Drake to have greeted the religious

492. Ogden MS 7/30 f. 119v. See Bacon, 'Of Unity in Religion', *Essays*, p. 67.
493. Ogden MSS 7/16 f. 109; 7/10 f. 158. Drake refers to Machiavelli, *Discourses*, Book I,
     ch. 11. See Pocock, *Machiavellian Moment*, p. 192.
494. Ogden MS 7/13 f. 138v.
495. Ogden MS 7/28 f. 66v.
496. Ogden MS 7/16 f. 73: 'wise men recognise opportunity.'
497. Ogden MS 7/20 f. 62. 'Where there is utility there is piety.'
498. Ogden MSS 7/9 f. 105v: 'chi dice religione dice ricchezze'; 7/19 f. 138v; 7/22 ff.
     110, 150.
499. Ogden MSS 7/27 f. 1; 7/24 f. 220v.
500. Ogden MS 7/31 f. 115v.
501. Ogden MS 7/30 ff. 74–74v.
502. Ogden MS 7/30 f. 76v. Machiavelli, *Discourses*, Book I, ch. 12.

changes of those decades as the sign at last of God's favour to his chosen. But, whatever his earlier sympathies, it is clear that revolution led him to think again and to condemn outright the puritan party and all they stood for.

The superstition of the Catholics might have eroded reason and erected 'an absolute monarchy in the minds of men', heresies such as the Arminians' might have infected men's wits; but these, he now believed, did not 'produce any great alterations in state'.[503] Civil war, however, far from advancing religion, 'sogliono guastar il buon governo della cotta e de culta divina'.[504] And as he looked back now while the sects proliferated, Drake little doubted who was to blame. As authority in church and state crumbled, William returned to his Hooker and read how the puritans had gained a stronghold in Elizabeth's reign through a reputation for holiness. First they imputed all faults to the established ecclesiastical government, proposed their own model as a remedy, and then taught men to read Scripture so that 'everything resoundeth towards the advancement of that discipline and to the disgrace of the contrary.' In consequence they fostered 'separation' between 'the one sort . . . named the brethren, the godly, and the worldlings' and divided the state as well as the church.[505] Looking back, Drake now saw they had been the serpent in the garden: the proverb 'Erat in oblectamentes serpens' he thought should be 'applied to church of England's destruction from weak schismatics'.[506] And he concluded now too that it had been and was 'ridiculous to propose Geneva discipline as a pattern for England'.[507]

Drake still retained his low regard for an episcopacy or clergy who by quarrelling among themselves, by their 'superfluities and excesses', had eroded support.[508] But as it disintegrated around him, the importance of the established church, and its hierarchy and liturgy, seemed never clearer. He now regarded those who destroyed images as out for social as well as religious change, to 'subvert religion and the state . . . and especially the nobility who by images . . . spread abroad to be read of all people their lineage'.[509] Those who advocated 'imagined prayers' and left the interpretation of scripture to women and children sought to bring a parity in the state as well as the church.[510] In such circumstances Drake undoubtedly shifted his view of religion and authority. We might say that he became more 'conservative'. But in the circumstances of civil war and revolution, a conservative regard

503. Ogden MSS 7/30 ff. 122v, 135v; 7/17 f. 15.
504. Ogden MS 7/28 f. 70: long civil conflict 'tends to ruin the government of the surplice and divine worship'.
505. Ogden MS 7/17 ff. 5v–8.
506. Ogden MS 7/13 f. 30; literally 'there was a snake amid all the delights', or, as we would say, a serpent in the garden.
507. Ogden MS 7/28 f. 5v.
508. Ogden MS 7/30 f. 61; cf. above, pp. 108–9.
509. Ogden MS 7/24 f. 225.
510. Ogden MS 7/24 f. 225; 7/21 f. 62v.

for authority, as we know from Hobbes, could result in a radical rewriting of politics.

We have deduced Drake's own politics from his readings and rereadings of and his notes and observations on proverbs, *sententiae*, classical and humanist histories. Our whole argument has been that reading them in, and interpreting them in relation to, his contemporary circumstances, he worked out his attitudes through a conversation between past and present. Drake, however, was well read in the recent and current affairs of Europe as well as of England. Interestingly, but not surprisingly, during the 1640s and 1650s he took great interest in the French Wars of Religion and especially the reign of Henri IV, and in William of Orange and the Dutch Revolt. And as we have seen, he read widely in original letters of the Reformation era in England, particularly those of Henry VIII. Queen Elizabeth and James I were monarchs whom he admired for their skills in government. Concerning events in his own lifetime, he returned in the 1640s to reflect on events and characters of the 1620s and 1630s, the York House conference and the trial of the feoffees for impropriations, Weston and Bristol, Buckingham and Laud. His knowledge of and interest in contemporary figures and events should not surprise us; what is remarkable is how Drake read his own age as another text that taught the values of interest, prudence and policy and the need for rulers to practise the Machiavellian art of statecraft.

Where some still conceived the long battles of the Thirty Years' War as a confessional conflict, with the survival of Protestantism at stake, Drake viewed Europe as a stage on which, by force and dissimulation, a series of actors manoeuvred for advance and control. Though, for example, he concurred with most of his English contemporaries that 'the main cause of the ruin of the Prince Palatine's affairs may be ascribed to the subtle practices of the Spaniard', Drake did not regard Spain as principally motivated by religion nor view the conflict as a struggle between the forces of Christ and Antichrist.[511] In a conversation in the Low Countries, Drake and a companion observed how Gustavus Adolphus, to many the champion of Protestantism, treated the Elector Palatine with scant respect, and calculated that 'if we consider the present posture and scheme of Christendom, the estate of the Prince Palatine's affairs are but one eighth or tenth consideration, the interests of England, Scotland, Ireland, Sweden, Catalonia, Portugal and Naples needing to be weighed as well as those of the major protagonists.'[512] Reading the Duc de Rohan's treatise on the *Interests of the Princes and States of Christendom*, Drake weighed the strategic options for each country. It was a dispassionate analysis founded on the premise that princes had to pursue their interests.[513]

511. Ogden MS 7/24 f. 181.
512. Ogden MS 7/21 f. 169.
513. Ogden MS 7/22 ff. 149–68; see below, pp. 262–6.

Similarly when Drake regretted that Queen Elizabeth had not followed
Burghley's advice to ally with France and the Netherlands, there is no hint
that he lamented her failure to champion the Protestant cause but rather
regretted the rejection of 'prudent counsel' that might have led England to
'security and glory'.[514]

Like several of his contemporaries who experienced the 1640s and 1650s,
Drake took particular interest in the politics and personalities of Queen
Elizabeth's and James I's reigns. He read avidly the correspondence of Sir
Francis Walsingham and his negotiations over the Anjou marriage; Archbishop
Whitgift he observed as a skilful politician, adept in manipulating the rudders
of fear and hope in order to steer men to his ends.[515] But most of all the
queen herself seemed to embody many of the attributes required of governors. She proceeded with skilful moderation in the case of Mary Queen of
Scots; she was frugal and cautious, not least in the naming of a successor; she
ruled so that 'all the passions of the people' were reduced to 'a simple and
humble obedience in her time'.[516] Only perhaps in pitching the bishops
against the Calvinists did she enflame rather than extinguish the fire of faction
that was to burn so destructively.[517] If not her equal, James I too exhibited
some skills in the art of government. Though he felt that his passion could
sometimes override his interest, Drake praised the first Stuart for securing a
peaceful succession to the throne and a long, moderate and tranquil reign.[518]

It may be that in the midst of revolution, Drake, as others, looked back to
Elizabeth's and James's reigns either as a halcyon age or as a means of understanding the roots of the later breakdown of government. But there were
additional reasons for an interest in late sixteenth- and early seventeenth-
century history. It was the age of the revolt of the Netherlands, and the 'religious' wars in France and Scotland that witnessed a shift in political values
on the continent, signalled by a revived interest in Tacitus and even a respect
in avant-garde circles for Machiavelli. Despite the official language of confessional allegiance and religious security, contemporary political discourse
echoes with terms such as 'interest', 'sagacity' and 'prudence'. In England those
great Elizabethan and Jacobean figures, Bacon and Ralegh, exemplify these
changes, as does the fashion for Tacitus, Machiavelli and the emergence of
satirical literature that interrogated and criticised the exercise of power. Drake
clearly was interested in how rulers and courtiers furthered their interests by
sagacious and subtle arts. He noted the prudence of Queen Elizabeth in
dealing with disputes, the skill of James I in detecting his servants' pursuit of
'sinister courses'.[519] He admired the political arts of the favourite, the Duke
of Buckingham, who conferred favours in such a way that the manner of his

514. Ogden MS 7/10 f. 2.
515. Ogden MSS 7/20 f. 177; 7/53 f. 9.
516. Ogden MSS 7/19 f. 130v; 7/21 f. 159v; 7/22 f. 102v.
517. Ogden MS 7/21 f. 142v. Drake was discussing this with Vossius.
518. Ogden MS 7/21 f. 101. These notes were taken in late 1641.
519. Ogden MSS 7/18 f. 107; 7/19 f. 9v.

patronage pleased as much as the grant itself.[520] He remarked on the need for great figures to have servants of different dispositions able to give satisfaction to various parties.[521] Reviewing the recent history of his own country, as well as that of ancient Rome and quattrocento and cinquecento Italy, Drake discerned and explored government and politics – not as the godly rule of a Christian commonwealth but as the art of statecraft in a world of interest and intrigue.

During the first half of the seventeenth century, such views – though held by a few and recognised by many – were still unorthodox. Still in the 1640s the state was held to exist for the common weal and all, including rulers, were expected to subordinate private interest to the public good. In this respect the Civil War was not fought between those with fundamentally different political philosophies, but between men and women who disagreed about the interpretation of the public good, still more about the means to secure it. The facts of civil war, however, of bloody battle, divided families, factional divisions and regicide transformed the fundamentals of political thinking. As experience palpably demonstrated, the ideals – of one faith, one Christian community – were dissolving and their dissolution brought fundamental political change in its wake. It is one of the ironies of the English Revolution that the triumph of the saints, the era of the rule of the Puritans during the 1650s, was to sound the death knell to godly politics. As radicals defended regicide and republic in the name of providence, and the church fragmented into sects, contemporaries were forced to acknowledge that Scripture could no longer function as a unifying discourse of state. Rather we begin to discern – on all parts – a more utilitarian language of politics, a recognition that once unity, authority and obedience could not be assumed as natural, some symbiosis of private and public interest had to be constructed and argued.[522] It was in these circumstances that English political pamphleteers and thinkers reread and embraced Machiavelli. If the influence of the Machiavelli of the *Discorsi* on Harrington's *Oceana* has been well argued, the importance of the Machiavelli of *The Prince* for an understanding of Hobbes's rewriting of politics as interest awaits full exploration.[523] More generally, others less philosophically or speculatively inclined, former Royalists and Parliamentarians, whether commenting on diplomatic or domestic affairs, began to

520. Ogden MS 7/18 f. 173.
521. Ogden MS 7/21 f. 22.
522. De facto arguments for allegiance to the republic fostered a more pragmatic and utilitarian ideology and language. See Q. Skinner, 'Conquest and Consent: Thomas Hobbes and the Engagement Controversy', in G. E. Aylmer, ed., *The Interregnum: The Quest for Settlement 1646–1660* (1973), pp. 79–98; Pocock, *Machiavellian Moment*, pp. 377–80. See too J. A. W. Gunn, *Politics and the Public Interest in the Seventeenth Century* (1969).
523. See Pocock, *Machiavellian Moment*, pp. 380–400. After I wrote this chapter I read D. Wootton, 'Thomas Hobbes's Machiavellian Moments', in D. R. Kelley and D. H. Sacks, eds, *The Historical Imagination in Early Modern Britain: History, Rhetoric and Fiction, 1500–1800* (Cambridge, 1997), pp. 210–42.

deploy the language of interest as common currency, ensuring that, even though Hobbes might be condemned, a new discourse would write a new script for the English state.[524] As far as we know, Sir William Drake did not contribute anything to the pamphlet debate. What makes him important in this context is that he had already himself 'read' much of what Hobbes and others were to write.

In a volume that can be tentatively dated to the later 1640s, Drake noted in reflecting on a proverb, 'when men's authority is equal and their opinions different, things are seldom or never well resolved.'[525] He expanded on the idea in two other notebooks:

> God hath created man in such a sort that they can desire everything but not attain to it, so that the desire of getting being greater than the power to get, thence grows the dislike of what a man enjoys; hereupon arises the change of states, for some men desiring to have more and others fearing to lose what they have already, they proceed to war and destroying one another.[526]

It is a distinctly Hobbesian passage and in a volume that was clearly compiled over the 1650s we might reasonably take it as Drake's paraphrase of Hobbes.[527] Drake, however, does not, as he does elsewhere, cite Hobbes.[528] Indeed in volume 30 he cites what appears to be the source for the passage or idea – 'Dis 157'.[529] It may well be that a reading of Hobbes sent him back to Machiavelli – though if this were so the absence of a cross-reference or marginal gloss is untypical in his note-taking. What needs to be remarked is that Drake could in particular circumstances read in other sources, in this case (as often) Machiavelli, one of the fundamental tenets of the Hobbesian revolution in political thought. Hobbes defended any authority that could secure order and security, and Harrington, writing at the time of the offer of the crown to Cromwell, read Machiavelli as the advocate of civic virtues in a free republic. The new language of interest and utility did not in itself favour any particular constitution. As even a staunch royalist like Matthew Wren acknowledged in his answer to Harrington, the case for monarchy had to be asserted. Interestingly Drake annotates the passage in which Wren accepts that 'every particular man thinks government was instituted for his particular advantage' and argues:

524. Gunn, *Politics and Public Interest*, chs 1–3; S. Pincus, *Protestantism and Patriotism: Ideologies and the Making of English Foreign Policy 1650–1668* (Cambridge, 1996); and J. G. A. Pocock, *Virtue, Commerce and History* (Cambridge, 1985).
525. Ogden MS 7/9 f. 148v.
526. Ogden MS 7/13 f. 139v. Drake cross-refers to Machiavell, *Discourses*, Book II, ch. 12.
527. See T. Hobbes, *Leviathan*, ed. R. Tuck (Cambridge, 1991), part 1, ch. 13.
528. For example, Ogden MSS 7/27 f. 180v; Folger MS f. 42.
529. Ogden MS 7/30 f. 50v. The page number does not correspond to the 1636 English edition of the *Discourses*. See *Discourses*, Book I, ch. 46. The passage also appears in Ogden MS 7/8 f. 46v, a volume that predates 1650.

Government is nothing else but an art by which one part of mankind disposes of the other for attaining the common utility of both; which consists in arriving at such a degree of plenty and security as mankind is capable of by society . . . this art is not obliged to one solitary method for attaining the end and design proposed to it, but has sometimes made use of a monarch, sometimes of an aristocracy, sometimes of a democracy and in all these of several frames and models.[530]

Wren, of course, went on to argue for monarchy. And we have seen Drake, as he glossed his proverbs and read his classical histories, while he acknowledged the virtue to be found in commonwealths, favoured the prudent prince who 'by his sovereign power may give rule to the disagreeing judgements and interests of many'.[531] If, as seems possible, Drake doubted in the 1630s whether England had such a prudent ruler, he never questioned monarchy itself. And the experience of the 1640s and 1650s confirmed to him that a democracy was 'the worst and basest of all governments', a 'chiamare'; and perhaps even led him to regard resistance to 'god's viceregent' as 'not only the guilt of treason but theomachie', sacrilege.[532]

Drake had never been in the usual sense 'conservative'. Already by 1642 it would seem that he had formulated a fully Machiavellian theory of society and state, in which religion was important principally for its civil function as a prop to order, and the most important qualities in a ruler were prudence and cunning. In some ways the events of the 1640s reinforced his views. But with the collapse of order, the need for a powerful authority argued by Machiavelli in *The Prince*, as by Hobbes in *Leviathan*, appeared more pressing. For Drake the only locus of that authority was the monarchy. As, therefore, he reread classical and humanist histories, Drake dwelt more on the texts and passages that stressed obedience to rulers and the disastrous ills of treason and civil war.[533]

There was always a dialogue between Drake's reading and the circumstances in which he read. Current issues helped to determine how he read general axioms or past events; in turn he applied familiar adages and observations on history to specific occurrences in his own experience. The notebooks we have pursued in this chapter all span the decades of the 1640s and 1650s. Behind so many of the sententiae he collected and histories he annotated we have glimpsed a mind pondering an analogy, perhaps hoping to find a lesson or a solution to the ills besetting England. We are tempted, that is, to read Drake's

530. Ogden MS 7/12 f. 22. See M. Wren, *Monarchy Asserted* (1659). Drake's notes are headed 'Out of Mr Wren's appendix in answer to Harrington.'
531. Above, p. 223; Ogden MS 7/13 f. 151v.
532. Ogden MSS 7/13 f. 2; 7/27 f. 22v (Drake is reading Bacon's *Advancement of Learning*).
533. See, for example, Ogden MS 7/21 ff. 60v, 106, 108v, 110, 112, 123, 126v, 162v, 176.

general political reflections as his reading of the English Civil War. His interest during the 1640s in conspiracy, in the Wars of the Roses and the civil
wars of sixteenth-century France and the Netherlands seems more than coin-
cidental. Drake translates his Latin and Italian into English terms that fit the
circumstances in which he writes, deploys the pronoun 'us' ('what government soever is enforced upon us . . .')[534] and directly applies some texts to
current events. Moreover, in some volumes, the dates of notes enable us to
pinpoint quite closely when and in what current circumstances a book
is being read. We know, for example, that since they appear after notes
on Strada's *De Bello Belgico* published in 1650, Drake's annotations on
Bishop Andrewes' sermons and Nathaniel Carpenter's *Achitophell* (1629), as
well as on Tacitus and Plutarch, show that they were read or reread in the
shadow of the regicide.[535] In such cases we are not left to guess at the connections between past and present Drake made in his mind; their material
traces appear clearly on the page.

During the sixteenth and seventeenth centuries, histories and plays set in
other times and locations often enabled a discussion of current English
politics without attracting censorship and punishment.[536] Such coded writing
only functioned in a culture in which readers knew how to decipher the
codes. In Renaissance England political debate through the media of history
and fiction became a habit of mind. At one level civil war put an end to the
habits of argument by allusion: censorship collapsed, at least for a time, and
in the thousands of pamphlets that poured from the press almost every
political position could be argued directly and unequivocally. There was
undoubtedly a new freedom for the committed to air their views. Yet there
were still dangers. While the outcome of battle remained uncertain, the bold
public expression of sympathies involved risks. As Royalists from the king
downwards found to their cost, papers and correspondence could be intercepted.[537] Just as importantly, to those who wavered and agonised over the
right course in an unnatural war, the pressure to declare support, on paper as
in the field, was unwelcome. For those who experienced defeat − of their
values as well as their armies − meditation on events through the media of
romance or epic offered perhaps a psychological as well as a political outlet.[538]

534. Ogden MS 7/17 f. 1.
535. See Ogden MS 7/21 ff. 40v, 54, 60v and passim. Strada had written: 'It is now my
     purpose clearly to explain those causes to you that such as read my history may learn
     by the example of the Low Country men, what it is that commonly embroils a state
     or kingdom.' *De Bello Belgico*, p. 36.
536. See A. Patterson, *Censorship and Interpretation: The Conditions of Writing and Reading in
     Early Modern England* (Madison, 1984).
537. Charles I's private letters captured at Naseby were published as *The King's Cabinet
     Opened* (1645).
538. See L. Potter, *Secret Rites and Secret Writing: Royalist Literature 1641–1660* (Cambridge,
     1989); see too T. Corns, *Uncloistered Virtue: English Political Literature 1640–1660* (Oxford,
     1992), esp. chs 4, 7; and N. Smith, *Literature and Revolution in England* (New Haven,
     1994), ch. 7.

Drake appears not to have been outspoken or rigid in his political sympathies and allegiance. Though he supported the critics of the king in 1640 and 1641, he began to have reservations about the leadership of parliament and left England with the onset of civil war. With property and family in England, however, as well as his own future to consider, it is not surprising that he did not publicly declare his view on events at home. Drake recorded Gerard Vossius saying that he would remain neutral so as to avoid offending either party, and himself knew 'there is a time when a wise man is to hold his peace.'[539] Even his notebooks, that might be thought of as a private space, he knew not to be safe when, as Mr Barrell informed him, studies were searched and 'nothing convicts [a man] sooner than his own hand.'[540] But beyond fear, or healthy caution, about expressing views in difficult times, the notebooks reveal glimpses of Drake still working out his responses. He took interest in Sir Henry Worsley, who in 1642 had wanted to resign his seat 'by reason of some scruples that he hath in his conscience' which led him to 'great dispute with himself'.[541] Later, reading Sir Thomas Browne's *Pseudodoxia* (published in 1646), he underlined a passage he copied in his own hand: 'we are often constrained to stand alone against the strength of opinion.'[542] Perhaps Drake, increasingly disenchanted with the course of events and with those leading the Parliamentary party, felt alone. Yet whatever his sense of the need for caution, as he discussed with friends in the Netherlands, and as he reread and annotated his books, William worked out his own clear views on the origins, course and consequences of the civil wars in England.

Though Drake knew from his study of history that the fall as well as the rise of states was part of a natural cyclical process, and that the English, naturally choleric, were given to settle quarrels by the sword, he had not foreseen civil war until his country stood on the brink of it.[543] 'For a foreign war,' he notes, 'that cloud is seen long before the tempest falls, not so a civil.'[544] History taught that in periods of too much luxury states had sowed the seeds of their destruction, and looking back to what others were already calling the halcyon days of the 1630s, Drake saw that England was no exception.

England's luxury in the turning the grace of God into wantonness, the long continuance of their peace, the increase of their trade, riches and plenty begot in them a general insolency and pride, so that when they waxed fat . . . they kicked against God, in the authority and due regard in the principal officers, the prince and the priest.[545]

539. Ogden MSS 7/21 f. 150; 7/17 f. 114.
540. Ogden MSS 7/29 f. 30; 7/30 f. 4.
541. Ogden MS 7/37 cover; see Underdown, *Pride's Purge*, p. 56.
542. Ogden MS 7/21 f. 27.
543. Ogden MSS 7/16 f. 95v; 7/21 f. 69v.
544. Ogden MS 7/10 f. 112.
545. Ogden MS 7/13 f. 1v. Drake evokes here almost the halcyon days of Royalist nostalgia.

With Hobbes, Drake blamed the bad education of youth for undermining authority:

> certainly it was a great error that rhetoric and modern divinity were chiefly studied with a little logic in our universities without seasoning the young students in the grounds of morality and the ethics, for want thereof every light brain was but too prone to turn religion into ambition and to make his sermon . . . but satires against the government.[546]

More immediately, Drake recalled the events of the Long Parliament in which he had participated and pondered why what had appeared a promising beginning had led to a bloody end. In retrospect, as he noted from a sermon, the Protestation could be compared 'to a viper that had its teeth so buried in its gums that it seemed at first sight a harmless beast though the bite thereof was deadly'.[547]

Who, then, was to blame for the destruction of peace and plenty? Drake recalled Peter de Medici's advice concerning troubles at Florence: 'he that took up arms was not to be termed properly the cause but he that gave the first occasion of provocation for so doing.'[548] The question, then, was which of the protagonists bore most blame for that provocation. Study of history revealed that 'the causes of war most ordinarily . . . may be assigned to the ambition of princes who cannot endure any limitation of power [and] . . . to their ignorance or negligence in matter of government.'[549] And in a discussion with a friend in the Netherlands Drake was frank in criticising Charles I:

> The King of E[ngland] though he had been a great opinionator and tenacious to his opinion, yet no man had been more unconstant to his principles and the reason hath been because he hath always strove to hold that which was not tenable and not complied with necessities, whereas in prudently letting go a little in time he might have saved much of that which had been forced from him afterward.[550]

For all the criticism of his tactics, Drake did not hold the king principally responsible for civil war, but rather blamed his detractors and those who plotted against him. It was 'the indiscrete publishing and disseminating' of criticisms of government that caused 'so many discussions and confusions

---

546. Ogden MS 7/18 f. 159v. cf. Hobbes, *Leviathan*, pp. 225–6.
547. Ogden MS 7/17 f. 135; cf. 7/13 f. 30.
548. Ogden MS 7/25 f. 91.
549. Ogden MS 7/21 f. 139.
550. Ogden MS 7/21 f. 158. We recall he annotated similar advice given to Charles I by Lennox, above, p. 149 n. 205. And we note that the statement is a particular application of several of Drake's favoured axioms.

in states'.[551] For sovereign authority only held sway when it was venerated, 'not when it was propounded by public harangues and questions, as what is the latitude, whence the original, what is the bounds . . .'[552] Those, then, who at first had seemed loyal critics of the king in the end had proved to be seditious conspirators.[553] In the 1650s, Drake was reading Nathaniel Carpenter's account of the conspiracy against King David by the 'wicked politician' Achitophel and ambitious prince Absalom; in particular he noted how Absalom had deployed imposture, especially a pretence of religion, as a mask for his treasonous designs.[554] So, he now discerned, schismatics in England had flattered the people with pretences and, promising they would 'never let loose the golden reins of government', had opened the floodgates of revolution.[555] Drake did not name the Achitophel of England. But in condemning the 'chief rulers in their Remonstrance' he surely pointed to Pym, whose leadership of the Commons had begun to cause Drake concern while he was still in England.[556] In this context we may have an insight into Drake's innermost thoughts as he took notes from Book VII of the *History of Florence* about how princes needed to ensure that none could hurt them and how 'private persons' needed to learn 'how vain it is to think that the multitude . . . will in their perils follow or accompany them.'[557] For in the margin he writes – simply – a capital 'P'.

Whether this stands for Pym or not, Drake was clearly thinking of those who 'turn religion into ambition', who 'out of an ambitious aim seek to disturb the repose of princes and states'.[558] Looking back with hindsight at the beginnings of the conflict, Drake now saw that those who had used the language of religion and liberty had sought ambitiously to advance themselves. The 'great design' of imposters in religion was to secure dominion over men's consciences in order to command their persons and property; 'great attempts for liberty' had 'frequently their beginning from ambition'.[559] In all ages, he read, the 'ambition of a few joined with the ignorance of the multitude hath been that which . . . hath disquieted states'.[560] The ambitious conspirators, believing that they could control the multitude, set them on only to find that, once released, the 'heady and headstrong animal', the people, could not be restrained, but stormed forward

551. Ogden MS 7/32 f. 50v.
552. Ogden MS 7/25 f. 21.
553. Ogden MS 7/32 f. 23v.
554. Ogden MS 7/21 ff. 54–56v; cf. 7/53 f. 161.
555. Ogden MS 7/13 ff. 30v–31.
556. Ibid. See above, pp. 119, 153–5.
557. Ogden MS 7/21 f. 91v. The reference is to Machiavelli's *History of Florence*, Book VII, ch. 6 where Montano taught the people the faults of the prince to lead them to desire his destruction.
558. Ogden MSS 7/18 f. 159v; 7/21 f. 139.
559. Ogden MSS 7/32 f. 47; 7/53 f. 5.
560. Ogden MS 7/24 f. 2. Drake cross-refers to Machiavelli.

'in all their wild humours' to destroy the state and turn conspiracy into revolution.[561]

From its origins in ambition, Drake traced the course of civil war and revolution in England. The 1640s bore out the general rule that 'it is ordinary in civil dissensions for men to be transported beyond their first intentions.'[562] From the experience of France as related by Comines he knew that 'though at the beginning of civil wars all men hope quickly to see them at an end' yet 'the contrary is feared.'[563] The fires of civil war spread especially rapidly when 'they are near that feed the flames, they far off that should extinguish it.'[564] Drake copied from the Digby–Jermyn correspondence passages about a general war weariness and desire for peace and quiet 'at any price'.[565] As we have seen, he interpreted the proverb 'ut habeas quietum tempus perde aliquid' as 'teaching subjects rather to let go some part of their own rights than contending with *our* prince and hazard all'.[566] But the negotiations for peace came to nought and the Civil War ended in regicide and republic.

Drake is silent on the subject of regicide – unless we take his comment that nothing more pointed to Tiberius' responsibility for Augustus' death than his distance from Rome as an oblique reference to Cromwell, who had delayed coming south to press the trial of Charles I.[567] His notebooks, however, are littered with references and allusions to the Commonwealth established in 1649. For one – and this is an important contemporary perspective often ignored – he appears to have doubted its survival. Rereading Guicciardini, most probably in 1650, he took as personal counsel the advice that 'it is a great indiscretion to oblige ourselves to a perpetual peril upon foundation not perpetual.'[568] Taking an oath to the new republic demanded a dangerous commitment at a time when Prince Charles claimed his father's throne and was soon to be crowned King of Scotland. Drake recalled his Roman history that 'by killing Caesar they only cut down the tree but left the root standing from which sprung up Augustus' – an image which indeed formed the motif of royalist engravings on behalf of Charles II.[569]

His doubts about the new regime, however, went further. Reflecting on

---

561. Ogden MS 7/13 ff. 30v–31; cf. 7/10 f. 24v.
562. Ogden MS 7/21 f. 147v.
563. Ogden MS 7/19 f. 12.
564. Ogden MS 7/21 f. 41v. The extract is from Strada's *De Bello Belgico* (1650), Book 6, p. 23. See below, p. 259.
565. Ogden MS 7/19 f. 159v.
566. Ogden MS 7/15 f. 42. 'Be prepared to surrender something for a quiet time.'
567. Ogden MS 7/21 f. 167 (from Malvezzi's *Tacitus*). Cromwell was absent from London at the time of Pride's Purge and disclaimed any knowledge of it.
568. Ogden MS 7/21 f. 93.
569. Ogden MS 7/27 f. 157. Cf. 7/21 f. 198 on Augustus turning a free state into a monarchy. For an engraving of a new shoot branching from a felled oak, see Huntington Library Richard Bull Granger, vol. 10, no. 26.

the origins of commonwealths, Drake dwelt on the need for some safeguard
for liberty, fearing that 'none endure heavier servitude than such as become
subjects to a republic.'[570] Not least from the fable of the frogs desiring a king,
Drake knew that 'all changes in governments commonly do chafe them most
at last who at first did most desire them', that the people might soon discover that they had changed for a worse tyranny and again desire a king.[571]
Moreover there was seldom success with the counsels of many, the absence
of a king bringing only disorder and confusion.[572]It would appear that Drake
therefore concluded that in the aftermath of regicide the best course was to
establish a new prince:

> In a troublesome time tis good to suffer no interregnum but in one and
> the same time to make known the death of one prince and the assump-
> tion of the other. The reason is because as wax is more apt to take a form
> or impression when tis without any than when it hath a form before, seeing
> in the first case there need but one action to imprint a new form, where
> in the second case there needs two, first to take away the old form and
> then to bring in a new, which certainly is double as difficult.[573]

The complex metaphor, written most probably in 1650, urged the immediate assumption of a new prince before the republic became established.[574]
Though events did not turn out that way for some time, the life of the
Commonwealth, as we know, was short, Cromwell succeeding as Protector
in December 1653. To his contemporaries Cromwell was a figure larger than
life, military hero, godly ruler, or, to Royalists, Machiavellian schemer. Those
who opposed his principles and policies still exhibited grudging respect for
his forceful determination and political skills. It would then be invaluable to
know how Drake viewed such a man who exhibited some of the qualities
he lauded in past princes – Louis XI, the Medicis and others. Cromwell,
however, never appears by name in Drake's notebooks, and Drake appears not
to have sat in any Protectorate parliament and evidently remained overseas.
It is tempting to imagine him personalising as he quoted Bishop Morton's
remark to the Duke of Buckingham of Richard III: 'that he would not kick
against the prick . . . but saith the Protector was now king. I purpose not to
dispute his title but to lay my hand upon my mouth.'[575] Certainly Drake,
reflecting on the action of Augustus refusing the crown, observed that those
who took the government of a free state under their 'protection' but with a
desire to rule tyrannically usually proceeded gradually, managing their ends
with care; and he had read Lentillius on Augustus' eventual 'turning a free

570. Ogden MS 7/21 f. 112.
571. Ogden MSS 7/21 f. 136; see 7/25 f. 197v; 7/27 f. 176v.
572. Ogden MS 7/21 f. 56v.
573. Ogden MS 7/27 f. 168.
574. The notes appear in a couple of folios, before notes from Strada's *De Bello Belgico*.
575. Ogden MS 7/18 f. 151v.

state into a monarchy'.[576] Such were the accusations levelled against Cromwell after his assumption of the Protectorate. As we shall see, whatever Drake thought of Cromwell, far from opposing monarchy, he believed even more in the need for a strong king.

Drake spoke so powerfully to secure a settlement in 1641 because he had learned from ancient and recent history that 'a civil war gives a kingdom a terrible wound which will bleed many years after.'[577] In a country at war, he read in Lamentations, 'they that did feed delicately are desolate in the streets'; 'princes are hanged up by their hand.'[578] From Guicciardini's history he read what was to be England's experience: 'imprisonment of great men, desolation of family, dearth of victuals'.[579] Throughout the 1640s Drake doubtless heard from England of 'the miserable effects of civil discord, that the law and equity of things are measured by the wills of soldiers and nothing judged unreasonable against him that is able to allege authority, might or will'.[580] At any point he feared, too, what he had predicted in 1642, that 'in a short time all the neighbouring princes will be bid to the banquet' and that England would fall in servitude to strangers.[581] As the battles continued, negotiations failed and conflict was renewed, Drake was led to ask what Abner asked of Joab: 'Shall the sword devour for ever? Knowest thou not that it will be bitterness in the latter end? How long shall it be then, ere thou bid the people return from following their brethren?'[582] As the rule of soldiers marked the end of battles, all seemed a 'universal face of troubles and confusion' that would 'end in disorder and confusion'.[583]

Those historians who have argued recently that the English Revolution was limited and contained risk obscuring the extent to which for men like Drake the 1640s threatened total anarchy, 'rem omnium perniciossimam'.[584] In Bishop Andrewes he read that 'without order every body falls to be doing with everything so nothing is done.'[585] 'Without an established government we should have no commonwealth but a wild forest where Nimrod and his crew would hurt and chafe all others.'[586] Drake aired his anxieties about the collapse of order at home in a number of conversations in the Netherlands. He and Mr P. agreed that 'if it were not for government every man aiming at his particular interest would overthrow the commonweal', P. adding that those outside of government were destined 'to live all their days like

576. Ogden MSS 7/24 f. 163v; 7/21 f. 198.
577. Ogden MS 7/10 f. 112, repeated in 7/27 f. 156.
578. Ogden MS 7/13 f. 1v; cf. 7/21 f. 60v.
579. Ogden MS 7/21 f. 110.
580. Ogden MS 7/21 f. 108v. Drake is reading and annotating Guicciardini's *History of Italy*.
581. Ogden MS 7/19 f. 12; cf. f. 28.
582. Ogden MS 7/21 f. 60v; 2 Samuel 2: 26.
583. Ogden MSS 7/21 f. 110; 7/54 f. 5.
584. Ogden MS 7/9 f. 148v.
585. Ogden MS 7/21 f. 60v.
586. Ogden MS 7/21 f. 65.

Nehemiah's builders, sword in one hand, trowel in the other'.[587] Even before he read *Leviathan*, Drake voiced the spirit of what he paraphrases Hobbes as saying: 'without a power to keep them all in awe [men] are in that condition which is called war and such a war as is every man against every man.'[588] For want of a king, 'Israel . . . was fair onward to be no longer Israel but even Babel.'[589]

Whatever then his official Parliamentarian leanings, it appears that Drake was opposed to civil war in 1642 and, as anarchy loomed, hostile to the regimes of the 1640s, the regicide and the Protectorate. 'He that ariseth against his prince', he notes in volume 16, 'ruins both himself and his country.'[590] Subjects were obliged to obey bad kings and even a heretic or heathen remained as much a monarch 'as if he were the best Christian living'.[591] Though as war began he may have believed, as well as hoped, with Abraham Cowley that 'the king and truth have greatest strength', the trial of battle proved otherwise.[592] To Drake the experience of civil war demonstrated that soldiers, fleets, magazines of arms and stores of treasure had been 'of strength to oppose truth and an unarmed king'.[593] As events took a more radical turn, and the voice of the lowly soldier was heard in politics, Drake, reading Sir Thomas Browne's *Pseudodoxia* (1646), noted that the more things receded from unity, the more they approached imperfection, and went on to stress the danger of any trust placed in the vulgus, especially when they too were deceived by 'subtle devisers'.[594] Perhaps against those who advocated a republic, Drake deployed the advice from Bacon's essay 'Of Innovation': 'It is good not to try experiments in states'; for, as Bacon put it, 'what is settled by custom, though it be not good, yet at least it is fit.'[595]

The country did not follow that counsel. And in volume 32 we can hear Drake reflecting as he read on the recent regicide and new regime. 'See how one disorder fell upon another for want of a king,' he read in the Book of Judges; what a 'mass of mischief' ensued – rapes and robberies, murder and idolatry.[596] Against those who would read the passage as referring to the absence of *all* government, not just monarchy, Drake noted Andrewes's exposition of the text: 'there was no king. He doth not charge them with an absolute anarchy that there was no estates nor kind of government amongst them but this only, there was no king . . .'[597] As a commonwealth was

587. Ogden MS 7/21 ff. 176, 162v.
588. Ogden MS 7/54 ff. 1–3.
589. Ogden MS 7/21 f. 56, quoting Judges 17.
590. Ogden MS 7/16 f. 111v.
591. Ogden MSS 7/21 f. 95; 7/37 f. 1. The quotation is from John Robinson's *Observations Divine and Morall* (1625), p. 48.
592. Ogden MS 7/17 f. 30.
593. Ogden MS 7/17 f. 30v.
594. Ogden MS 7/21 ff. 27, 30v.
595. Ogden MS 7/30 f. 110v; Bacon, *Essays*, p. 132.
596. Ogden MS 7/32 f. 23.
597. Ibid.

established in England ending a thousand years of monarchy, Drake asserted the rule of one, certain that it was 'requisite there be one over all that is none of all but a common father to all that may prize and keep them in equilibrium . . .'[598] A kingdom was the best government 'for strength, steadiness and duration'; any other government amounted to confusion.[599] Whatever his earlier doubts about Charles I, civil war and commonwealth confirmed Drake as an ardent monarchist who awaited the return of a king.

The later 1650s were uncertain times of rapid change and shifting hopes. Would Cromwell become king, as many in the nation hoped? If not, in what course would a long-term constitutional settlement lie? Would the critics of Protectorate re-establish a free commonwealth after Cromwell's death? Because his notes are not dated precisely we cannot clearly determine Drake's own thoughts on all these questions. Yet there are clues in his notebooks, reflections on and between books that we can date that allow us some insight into his attitudes. As always his guiding principle was order: 'though we differ in our opinion yet we shall not in our ends which is the like to us all, to endeavour the order and stability of the commonweal.'[600] And he looked for order in a peaceful constitutional settlement, knowing that 'what is got by arms must be kept by arms.'[601] Whether or not he would have accepted Cromwell as king, Drake must have viewed the chaos that ensued on his death and his son Richard's fall with horror. Perhaps he feared that the leader of one party would emerge as a tyrant, or worse that the mob would rule, for he observed from history that such were the outcomes of civil conflict.[602] Perhaps, however, he drew hope from a passage he annotated from Bentivoglio's history of the Low Countries in the 1630s: 'factions are the very pest of states yet out of their evil grows oftentimes this good, that seeking to overthrow each other they make way for the lawful prince to recover his power.'[603]

If so, as is more likely from what we have seen of his views, Drake would have been encouraged in his hopes by a growing tide of opinion in the late 1650s that only a restored monarchy could resettle the nation. Nor were such beliefs confined to the gentry classes and men of property. During 1659 and 1660, as republican sympathisers like Milton divined, the common people were committed to a king.[604] In such circumstances it may be that Drake revised his views about the role of a 'vulgus' whom he had earlier feared and condemned. Notes in volume 17, which contains material relating to 1660,

598. Ogden MS 7/21 f. 56v: the quotation ends 'so that all the estates may be evenly balanced'.
599. Ibid.
600. Ogden MS 7/17 f. 1v.
601. Ibid.
602. Ogden MS 7/24 ff. 38v, 49v.
603. Ogden MS 7/18 f. 86v. Cardinal Guido Bentivoglio's *L'Historia della Guerra di Fiandra* was published in 1644 and was translated by Henry, Earl of Monmouth as *The Compleat History of the Wars of Flanders*, in 1654.
604. See J. Milton, *A Readie and Easie Way to Establish a Free Commonweal* (1660).

reflect on the need for any government to be based on 'the general consent of the people'.[605] A clue to the circumstances in which the notes were taken is offered by apparent references to the army grandees and Commonwealthsmen of 1659–60. Are not these, Drake writes, the same men who made promises before to the people, who promised to make the last king glorious, then, having abused him, set up another 'single person' in his place?[606] Further notes, on the privileges of an MP to speak freely, may point to the last weeks of the Rump between 21 February and March 16 1660.[607] At that time Drake returned to England and, with the other MPs, to a parliament which outvoted the republicans and, in declaring itself dissolved and preparing elections, paved the road to Restoration.

Reading Restoration

Drake learned as much from his reading of events in England during the 1640s and 1650s as he learned from his books. As he put it, 'the reading of rough and rugged times wherein great revolutions and changes have happened, where there is commonly much of conspiracy and plots are . . . exceedingly instructive.'[608] One thing the nation had learned was to value stability and government, learned that 'tis not good to learn to do by undoing nor never to see order till disorder shows it.'[609] In 1660, as in the 1630s, there was again the prospect, after years of turmoil and destruction, of riches, learning, justice and order. 'These are the triumphs of peace,' Drake annotated an earlier sermon, probably in 1660, 'and the God of peace continue this our peace that the fury of war may never turn this paradise into a wilderness nor make England which is now a map of majesty to other nations a map of confusion.'[610]

'Princeps est vinculum per quod respublica cohaeret.'[611] A monarch offered again the prospect of drawing the state together into concord. And, as a text he copied argued, the monarch-to-be had been 'bred from infancy in the school of affliction and having travelled in diverse countries hath had the

605. Ogden MS 7/17 f. 1. Drake notes: 'the voice of the people is the declaratory voice of providence'.
606. Ibid.: 'What government so ever that is forced upon us must certainly expire with [the] force that imposed . . .'
607. Ogden MS 7/17 f. 1v.
608. Ogden MS 7/12 f. 32v. His list of Tacitus, Guicciardini, Machiavelli and Davila following this observation may help to explain why he returned to reread them amidst civil war.
609. Ogden MS 7/18 f. 134.
610. Ogden MS 7/12 f. 28. These were 'Notes taken out of Dr. Stoughton's sermon before K. James', but the same volume contains notes from 1659.
611. Ogden MS 7/32 f. 30: 'A prince is the chain that binds together the commonweal.'

opportunity of studying men and manners'.[612] Having studied past revolutions, Drake had counsel for the new king and the times. 'Shall we retain the memory of former unkindnesses?' Bishop Sheldon asked in a sermon Drake read and noted.[613] Some called for revenge and Drake recalled how Brutus had even sat in judgement on his own sons, any change of state necessitating 'some memorable execution be made on enemies of the present condition'.[614] But if a few hardline republican opponents of the king merited death, long-term stability required peace and concord. 'A wound', Drake noted from a sermon of Dr Hacket delivered in March 1660, 'will never be healed but by drawing the parts together that were dissolved.'[615] In the process of healing and settling Drake now saw that the king's court, which he had earlier criticised, had a vital role to play. His much admired Machiavelli had observed 'that after the civil wars occasioned by the Guelph and Gebellian factions, the statists of the time chose to introduce masks and interludes and comedies and Davila noteth that dancing and the like sports were enjoined at weddings to qualify the rancour and animosities which civil broils had engendered.'[616] Most of all the prince had to rule with vigilance, prudence and foresight to maintain his own position and the peace of the kingdom.

In the pages of his notebooks, Drake wrote wise counsel to the new monarch. He recalled Cicero's advice to Atticus about changing a republic into a monarchy.[617] The new king needed to remember Rehoboam's dictum that a prince should not use severity at the start of his reign, the advice of Scripture to pursue traditional courses, and Bacon's argument that power was always most effective when held in tacit veneration rather than subjected to dispute.[618] Moderate rule, however, did not imply handing the reins of sovereignty to parliaments. The Civil War had confirmed Sir Henry Wotton's belief that parliament had disturbed the peace by probing into the secrets of kings.[619] Accordingly, while 'principalities are wont to be on the point of falling when they go about to slip from the civil order to the absolute', monarchs still needed to exercise control.[620] 'Princes either command of themselves or by their magistrates or parliaments.' In this last case their state is more weak and dangerous,

> for that they stand at the will and pleasure of those chief citizens who in
> adverse times by the help of the people are able to take the state from

612. Ogden MS 7/13 f. 70.
613. Ogden MS 7/32 f. 82.
614. Ogden MS 7/30 f. 13. The notes follow a memo of 1661.
615. Ogden MS 7/32 f. 85.
616. Ogden MS 7/20 f. 13v; cf. above, p. 144.
617. Ogden MS 7/30 f. 8.
618. Ogden MSS 7/32 ff. 35v, 47v, 49v.
619. Ogden MS 7/20 f. 55.
620. Ogden MS 7/30 f. 65. Drake urges the placing of trust in the king and not standing upon terms, Ogden MS 7/13 f. 70v.

them, either by rising up against them, and then the prince is not at hand in those dangers to take the absolute authority upon him for the citizens and subjects that are accustomed to receive the commands from the magistrates are not like in those factious times to obey him.[621]

After the destruction of civil war, a man like Drake was more than ever prepared to see the benefits of strong monarchical rule.

Yet the Civil War and republic had changed things in a manner that meant the clock could not simply be set back. Drake had often noted Machiavelli's point that there was frequently more virtue in commonwealths than in kingdoms, even his argument that against mischievous princes there may be no 'other remedy but the sword'.[622] It was therefore incumbent on the new king to learn the lesson of historical experience: that 'a prudent government is nothing else but to have such tie and hold upon the people as either they cannot or may not have a desire to hurt the prince, which they will not when they find a common interest for their own good.'[623] That concept of common interest was to become more familiar in Restoration political discourse. Now, at the height of the king's happiness and of public celebration of his Restoration, Drake penned a caution to him:

> whosoever sits at the helm of a state . . . should consider beforehand what contrary times may come upon them and what men in their trouble they may stand in need of, and therefore should live with them always in such a manner that upon any accident chancing they may find them ready and willing to serve their occasion.[624]

During the early years of Restoration, Charles II, a skilful and prudent king, seemed almost to follow Drake's counsel. Apart from the execution of a few regicides he was merciful, even magnanimous, to former enemies. He neither ruled absolutely nor abnegated government to ministers and parliaments. He sought to reconcile differences – in church, as well as state. And he never forgot the experiences of civil war and exile, or those ordinary folk who had helped him in adversity. Charles was a new monarch who discussed and learned the arts of political management, of manipulating interest, in a changed political world. Over the next few years, however, the euphoria over Restoration faded. Sexual scandals, disagreements about finance and the settlement of the church, the king's attempt in 1662 to pass a Declaration of Indulgence, created political tension and evoked memories of earlier disputes. Sir William Drake, having not attended the Convention, was returned for Amersham to the so-called Cavalier Parliament in 1661. He was immediately

---

621. Ibid. Drake is writing this while reading Machiavelli's *Prince*. See *The Prince*, ch. 9.
622. Ogden MS 7/30 ff. 50, 78v onwards, 83.
623. Ogden MS 7/30 f. 57.
624. Ogden MS 7/30 f. 9v.

appointed to the Committee for Privileges and Elections, on which he served until at least 1666.[625] There is no evidence that he spoke in parliament. In 1661 he was included as a 'friend' by Philip Lord Wharton among a list of 135 members, but whether this was on account of shared sympathies or Buckinghamshire connections it is hard to say.[626]

Drake had been a critic of the government in church and state before the Civil War. He blamed the bishops and clergy for many of the ills that befell them, and perhaps the king for imprudent courses. He had in 1641 desired and supported reform of abuses. But he had never wished reform to run to revolution. With the Civil War he feared the greatest of all ills – anarchy and democracy. Returning to his favourite histories – and to Machiavelli and Guicciardini – during the 1640s and 1650s, Drake condemned the republic and stressed the need for one sovereign to suppress sects and factions and to unite the realm in peace and concord. It seems clear that he supported Restoration, returning to England and to positions as MP and JP, Commissioner for the Militia and Assessment in his county. Whether, as old quarrels between king and parliament, factional divisions at court and religious differences revived, he became disenchanted with the restored monarchy we cannot say. We have no notebooks for the last six years of Drake's life – either because in his last years he was too weak to continue his studies or possibly because they have not survived. Sir William died in 1669 before the worst political crises again threatened the government of the realm. All readers of his notebooks must be tempted to speculate on how he might have reacted – to the fiasco of the Dutch wars, to the fall of Danby, to the Exclusion crisis and Popish Plot. What we can be sure of is that with each turn of the wheel of political fortune, he would have returned for counsel to his books, knowing that 'all our wisdom consists in our experience of memory.'[627]

625. *C.J.* VIII, pp. 246, 437 (18 Feb. 1663), 567 (24 Nov. 1664), 615 (11 Oct. 1665), 627 (Sept. 1666).
626. See G. F. T. Jones, *Saw-Pit Wharton: The Political Career from 1640 to 1691 of Philip, Fourth Lord Wharton* (Sydney, 1967), p. 187; B. D. Henning, *The Commons 1660–1690* (3 vols, 1983), vol. 1, p. 236.
627. Ogden MS 7/32 f. 24.

Appendix
Sir William Drake and
The Long Parliament Revived

In 1661 there was published in London a tract entitled *The Long Parliament Revived, or an Act for the Continuation and the not Dissolving the Long Parliament . . . but by an Act of Parliament with Undeniable Reason . . . to prove that the Parliament is not yet dissolved.* The pamphlet praises Charles I 'of blessed memory' and offers 'humble respects of due allegiance' to Charles II. But it also asserts the importance and independence of parliaments, and denies that the death of a king dissolved them. Because the Long Parliament had not been properly dissolved, the pamphlet argues, the Convention, for all the wise courses it had pursued, could not constitute a legal assembly or lay the foundations for a peaceful settlement.

To avert any fears evoked by the prospect of the Long Parliament's recall the author claims that by far the largest number of surviving MPs were those who had been excluded at Pride's Purge – 'thrust and forced out of the house for their loyalty to the king'; rather than a threat these men had been 'the chief instruments of his present Majesty's happy restoration' (p. 17). The king could therefore recall them with confidence, and urge them to confirm the acts of the Convention and legally dissolve themselves to make way for a new parliament: 'so things may sweetly return again without violence or injury done either to his Majesty's prerogative or his people's liberties into a regular and legal way of proceeding to the general security and satisfaction of the whole' (p. 17). As the postscript made clear, the author's design was to heal the nation's wounds: to secure 'lawful powers' so that all might enjoy stable peace and security (p. 21).

The author of the pamphlet is one 'Thomas Philips', a gentleman who describes himself as 'a sincere lover of his king and country'. However, in the Wing Catalogue, and all subsequent library catalogues presumably on the basis of it, 'Philips' is described as a pseudonym for Sir William Drake. It is tempting to concur. The moderation of tone, the desire for peace and stability, the respect for royal prerogative and the people's liberties, the harsh reflections on the recent Commonwealth all echo views we have argued Drake held. Moreover, the author's concern to reassert the legality and standing of the Long Parliament, especially of the full assembly that predated Pride's Purge, might fit with Drake's initial admiration for the assembly. Similarly his absence from the Convention could be explained with reference to the arguments outlined here that it lacked proper legal standing. We might then want to go further and study *The Long Parliament Revived* as an important contribution by Drake to the debates that produced the Restoration settlement.

It would seem, however, that the attribution to Sir William Drake is an error. In one of the Bodleian Library copies of Thomas Philips's *The Long Parliament Revived*, part of the pamphlet collection made by Anthony Wood, we find a manuscript note:

> Nov 15 an[no] 1660. The printer and dispenser of the book called The Long Parliament Revived being secured by such as His Majesty hath appointed for preventing scandalous and seditious books and pamphlets, on Friday night (9th November) Mr. Will[iam] Drake was apprehended who, contrary to expectation, being examineth hath since confessed himself to be the author of that book, which being reported to the House of Commons Mr. Secretary Morrice on Sunday morning, the House ordered him to be taken into custody and the particulars of the book to be examined by the committee for privileges who have found this book to be scandalous and seditious, and ordered a charge to be drawn up against the author, and the book to be burnt by the hand of the common hangman.

The note continues:

> November 20, 1660. The offensive passages in this book called The Long Parliament Revived were by the committee to whom it was referred reported to the House of Commons whereupon it was resolved that the said book entitled The Long Parliament Revived is a seditious pamphlet and it was referred to a committee to draw up an impeachment against William Drake of London merchant which being reported and agreed upon . . .[1]

Mr William Drake of London, merchant, was clearly not our Sir William Drake MP who a few months later sat on that same Committee for Privileges which impeached his namesake. Whatever Sir William's view about the Long Parliament or the mood in the Commons in 1660, *The Long Parliament Revived* was not his.

---

1. Thomas Philips, *The Long Parliament Revived* (Bodleian Wood 620), manuscript note at end. I am grateful to Professor Michael Mendle for drawing this copy to my attention.

Part Four

READING AND POLITICS

5

The Politics of Reading and the Reading of Politics in Early Modern England

Reviewing the Case: Sir William Drake as Reader and Annotator

As we review the huge list of authors and titles annotated or cited in Drake's notes, we cannot but be immediately struck by the extent of his reading. Though all the classical texts familiar to any gentleman with a grammar school and university education are here, though the most popular Renaissance humanists recur throughout, Sir William Drake clearly read far more widely than his peers, in the classical texts, and in Renaissance editions, commentaries, histories, books of adages and manuals of statecraft. If for most 'a few hundred pages of Cicero and Demosthenes, a few hundred lines of Virgil and Homer . . . came to represent the sum total of the Graeco-Roman legacy', Drake was clearly one of the exceptional few classical scholars described by the historian of the classical heritage.[1] Indeed Drake fulfilled the ideals for a student of the classics, as outlined in 1655 by an English scholar priest who prescribed the purchase and reading of hundreds of classical texts and commentaries, and humanist works on ethics, chronology, history, volumes of rhetoric and epistles, grammar, divinity and proverbs.[2]

But perhaps just as striking are the books absent from Drake's notebooks. Though he was well read in the law and was acquainted with contemporary drama and verse, with Chaucer, Spenser, Jonson and Cowley, Drake's reading was not that of a typical English gentleman. If Sir William read the courtesy literature popular with the gentry of his day, Henry Peacham's *Complete Gentleman*, Anthony Stafford's *Guide to Honour*, Brathwait's *English Gentleman* and the like, works on heraldry, or husbandry and horticulture, they leave no traces in his notes. The absence of such ephemeral contemporary literature might confirm a sense we derive from the huge corpus of his reading that Drake

1. R. Bolgar, *The Classical Heritage and its Beneficiaries* (New York, 1964), p. 365.
2. A. De Jordy, ed., *'A Library for Younger Scholars', Compiled by an English Scholar Priest about 1655* (Urbana, 1961).

was, as his funeral monument proclaimed, a devoted scholar of the classical rather than vernacular literature.

He was not, however, a scholar in our usual sense – one preoccupied with a dispassionate academic study of texts – or even in one contemporary Renaissance sense of concern with philology and textual provenance. As we have seen, Drake disdained reading and study that was not directed to practical ends – to the attainment of wisdom for survival in a selfish and competitive world. Like many of the humanists he admired, Cardano, Lipsius and Vossius, he studied for action and the ends of his reading dictated the way in which he read.[3] Because he sought advice and counsel from his books, Drake did not read and annotate whole texts at once; he pursued the values and lessons of a passage from book to book, classical text to modern history, and garnered illustrations from antiquity to his own times. Extensive as was his range of reading, even more remarkable are his rereadings, his return, sometimes after years, sometimes perhaps the same day or week, to a work or passage, as another text – be it history, proverb or fable – took him back to reconsider its meaning and (what amounted to the same thing for him) its use.

As he moved between his texts, juxtaposing them differently, Drake was led at times to read a new lesson from a historical moment or to interpret a proverb somewhat differently. But though such moves may appear at first sight serendipitous, there was nothing random or unstructured about Drake's approach to study. Rather, his self-instructions on how to read proverbs and histories make it clear that he devised an intellectual system in which different genres (adages, histories, fables and emblems) were read together and texts approached in defined sequences so as to draw out their richest treasures of wisdom. No less, Scripture and works of divinity were read, unorthodoxly, alongside secular and Machiavellian treatises to assist him in the weighing of counsels and the moral ambiguities of his own age. When Drake annotated passages on prudence from Aristotle and Aquinas, Machiavelli, Guicciardini and Davila, his interest was not in the changing meaning of the term 'prudence' but in what prudential counsel could be extracted from all those authors for his own purpose and time.[4]

Across all his notebooks we have remarked the characteristic strategies of Drake's reading: his habits of explication, cross-reference to other texts and moments, the reading of one work through the perspective and values of another, the constant dialogue between texts and other negotiations – with friends, with circumstances, with personal matters of money, lands and health. Only occasionally do we have extended, unbroken notes on a single text, and

3. We should recall that, though famous as a philological scholar, Lipsius wrote on the military aspects of the Dutch revolt, as well as the *Six Books of Politics*. See G. Oestreich, *Neostoicism and the Early Modern State* (Cambridge, 1982).

4. The Pocock/Skinner study of paradigmatic shifts in language has been less helpful in understanding how texts were received than in explicating what authors intended.

they offer further insight into how Drake read and how his mind worked. We know, from his reference to Ammianus Marcellinus' *Roman Histories*, for example, that when, rarely, Drake quoted at length, he copied and cited his texts accurately.[5] Notes from Nathaniel Carpenter's *Achitophel or the Picture of a Wicked Politician* (1629), most probably taken in the 1650s, confirm that the circumstances – here the events of civil war and regicide – directed both what Drake read and what he selected from his reading. Accordingly, as he read through Carpenter's account of the conspiracy of Absalom and Achitophel, Drake dwelt on the conspirators' pretence of religion, copied the prophetic axiom 'treason and usurpation cannot support themselves but by the sword of tyranny' and repondered a favourite adage (from Richard Hooker) that 'he that goes to persuade a multitude that they are not well governed will sooner want argument than attention.'[6]

To take another example, as we compare Drake's notes with the English text he used of Famianus Strada's *De Bello Belgico* (1650), we discern what he took away from Strada's invitation to his readers to 'learn by the example of the Low Country men what it is that commonly embroils a state or kingdom'.[7] Licentiousness, he noted, copying Alva, 'more easily increases than begins'; and civil war, he annotated from the Duke of Ebora's speech, 'can never be extinguished without the conqueror's loss'.[8] Other adages, some carefully collected in an appended 'Alphabetical Table of the Most Remarkable Passages and Sentences', passed into Drake's collection, including Ebora's advice that the flames of civil conflict were carefully to be watched, 'especially in such a place where they are near that feed the flame'.[9] As he read Strada, Drake extracted his own general lessons from the particular events – of Margaret of Parma's handling of religious dissent for example – and selected and applied them in accordance with his other reading – of texts and the times.[10]

Drake's notes on Ben Jonson's *Sejanus* offer a good example of the relation of Drake's reading to his circumstances. Evidently taken in the 1650s, the extracts dwelling on the need for a prince to act at times tyrannically, the volubility of the vulgar and the fragility of virtue may point to Drake's reflection on the reign of Charles I (compared to Tiberius), or more likely to the rise of a new favourite who, like Sejanus, came to strength by reducing all

5. I have checked Ogden MS 7/14 f. 201 against P. Holland (translator), *The Roman Histories . . . Digested into Eighteen Books by Ammianus Marcellinus* (1609), p. 193, to which Drake refers.

6. Ogden MS 7/21 f. 54; [N. Carpenter], *Achitophel or the Picture of a Wicked Politician* (1629), pp. 10, 19.

7. Ogden MS 7/21 f. 41v; Famianus Strada, *De Bello Belgico: The History of the Low Country Wars*, trans. Robert Stapylton (1650), p. 36.

8. Strada, *De Bello Belgico*, pp. 23–4.

9. Ibid.: 'Alphabetical Table', under 'C'; p. 23. Cf. above, p. 244.

10. Ibid., pp. 117 (cf. Ogden MS 7/21 f. 40), 32. The dedication of the book described its 'very prudent observations summed up in brief sentences'.

the Praetorian guards into one camp, as Cromwell did the New Model Army.[11] A decade later, as he read Matthew Griffiths's appeal to Monck in a sermon to effect a restoration of the Stuarts, Drake paraphrased Griffiths into adages, annotated sections on schismatics and sedition, but passed over the most specific and topical references to the government of Charles I and the restoration of his son.[12] Similarly, as he read Cowley's 'Ode upon the Blessed Restoration and Return of His Sacred Majesty', Drake paid more attention to the early question posed by the poet: 'Will Peace Her Halcyon nest venture to build / Upon a Shore with Shipwracks fill'd?' than to the denigration of Cromwell or celebration of Charles II.[13] Whether Drake's failure to annotate the most polemical and celebratory passages owed more to disapproval or to caution in 1660 we are left to guess.

Drake's notes, cross-references and returns to books and passages indicate that he owned perhaps the bulk of the books he read. Were his library to survive, we could doubtless move from the annotations to the original texts, obtaining fuller knowledge of the editions Drake sought, and discover how he selected, marked or glossed the printed passages that were then extracted by him or his amanuensis into his commonplace books. Unfortunately his library has not survived, and while a catalogue of books at Shardeloes almost certainly contains some of Sir William's books, it is not complete, and we are not able to distinguish from the mere list books acquired in the sixteenth and seventeenth centuries from later acquisitions.[14] Evidently the library of printed books, like the manuscript notebooks, was dispersed or sold.

On the hunch that some may have come into the hands of C. K. Ogden along with the commonplace books, I ordered at University College London all the printed books dated before 1669 in its Ogden collection. The Ogden deposits include works frequently cited by Drake – works by Aristotle, Alciati, Bacon, Camden, Erasmus, Selden, Ammianus Marcellinus, Machiavelli and Guicciardini, Botero, Cicero, Charron, Pliny, Tacitus and Virgil – but several remain unannotated, or are marked by other identified owners. In a few cases, John Hayward's *Answer* to R. Dolman's tract on the succession, or Bacon's *Wisdom of the Ancients*, there is a hand that appears to be that of Drake or his scribe, but with only little marginal annotation, the ascription to Drake on the basis of handwriting must remain tentative rather than conclusive.[15] One volume elicits more confidence. The 1657 edition of *Resuscitatio or Bringing Into Public Light Several Pieces of the Work . . . of the Rt. Hon. Francis Bacon* is

11. Folger MS ff. 15–21.
12. Ogden MS 7/17 f. 136v; compare M. Griffiths, *The Fear of God and the King, Preached in a Sermon . . . on 25th March 1660.*
13. See Ogden MS 7/17 f. 30 and A. Cowley, *Poems . . . and Davideis* (1656); *The Works of Mr Abraham Cowley* (1668), pp. 16–25. Drake probably read this poem in manuscript.
14. See Bucks R.O., D/DR/10/50, a library catalogue (n.d.).
15. See Sir J. Hayward, *An Answer to the First Part of a Certain Conference Concerning Succession* (1603, Ogden A603); F. Bacon, *The Wisdom of the Ancients* (1619, Ogden A305). See too the marginalia in N. Machiavelli, *Discorsi* (1532, Ogden 257).

scattered through with marginalia in English, Latin and Italian, in a manner characteristic of Drake's commonplace books. The annotator explicates passages, identifies quotations, cross-refers to proverbs, notes similes as does Drake with the abbreviation 'sim', and draws out general axioms from specific references or events in the text.[16] Not only do the range and type of reference point to Drake, the tone of the marginalia – 'time past is a pattern for time to come', 'the wisest princes . . . have sought to limit their passions' – is his;[17] and the political observations, on treason, the condemnation of 'schismatical controversies' and separatists, echo views we have heard Drake air in his notes from the 1650s.[18] The repetition of one of his favourite Italian proverbs – 'vento al visaggio fa l'huomo saggio' – greatly strengthens the link to Drake.[19] If we can take the book as his, we begin to see more clearly both how he reread in 1657 his favourite English author, and how the other texts and experiences shaped that reading. By 1657, Drake brought to the page of *Resuscitatio* forty years of study and the experience of civil war, republic and sectarian division. Yet, ever collecting new sources of wisdom, he marks passages that point to sententiae, and lists on the back flyleaf the important observations he has underlined or annotated in the text: 'Tis good advice', he writes next to '107', 'in dealing with cautelous and malicious persons non quod dixerunt sed quo spectarint videndum' – to regard not what they have said but to whom they are inclined. By summaries and cross-references, noted similes and adages, invented axioms and indexed observations, Drake makes his text serve his turn and renders it ready to annotate into a commonplace book organised under heads and compiled for use.

If the *Resuscitatio* offers our only good example of Drake's annotating books donated by C. K. Ogden, it is fortunately neither our only nor our best evidence of Drake's use of his books. Among the manuscripts catalogued by Stuart Clark as part of the 'Bacon–Tottel' collection is a printed edition of Guicciardini's *Hypomneses Politicae* published in 1597, which he lists as annotated in Drake's hand.[20] We know that Drake had read the work and his holograph is here unmistakable. And on the title page he pens one of his favourite passages from Ecclesiasticus 39 ('He will seek out the secrets of grave sentences') – perhaps a reminder of how to use the text.[21] The annotations offer revealing insights into how he used it. Given what we know from his commonplace books, we will not be surprised to see Drake cross-referring – to Machiavelli and Tacitus, for example.[22] For his purpose in reading was, as with

16. *Resuscitatio or Bringing Into Publick Light Several Pieces of the Work . . . of the Right Hon. Francis Bacon* (1657, Ogden A329), e.g. pp. 2, 3, 5, 7, 10, 11, 12, 16, 51, 52, 103, 115, 116, 118, 154, 159, 222, 223, 224.
17. Ibid., pp. 12, 103.
18. Ibid., pp. 117, 151.
19. Ibid., p. 222. Literally, 'the wind in the face makes a man wise'; that is, adversity and experience produce wisdom.
20. Ogden MS 7/39. Drake cites the work in Ogden MS 7/7 ff. 121v, 158.
21. See above, p. 221.
22. Ogden MS 7/39 p. 22 (at foot); 'Sententiae' (at back of book).

the commonplace books, the extraction of lessons in axioms and adages. He underlines in Guicciardini passages that distil lessons and the 'Sententiae' gathered at the end. And, in his usual process of personalising and appropriating his texts, Drake summarises, glosses and translates.[23] At the foot of the preface, for example, he writes, 'A prince should not only deceive his enemy but . . . deceive his own instrument'; Guicciardini's section on 'Vana Hominum', he glosses 'ambitious luxurious men though opinion and rapacity be mixed with it'.[24] The lessons Drake extracts (not surprisingly from Guicciardini) are the need for prudent foresight, for care to distinguish substance from appearance and for caution about excessive optimism.[25] In politics, the passages he annotates stress, rulers required eloquence, an eye for occasion and the art of manipulating the people's hopes and fears.[26] As he marks up and glosses such extracts, cross-references and garners maxims as he reads, we can glimpse William Drake in his first encounter with a text that was later to be distilled in his commonplace notes.

A more heavily annotated text will enable us to observe him at work more closely. In the Folger Shakespeare Library in Washington DC, as well as another of Drake's commonplace books, I found a copy of the 1641 edition of the Duc de Rohan's *Treatise of the Interest of the Princes and States of Christendom*, annotated on every page in Drake's hand.[27] The book, frequently referred to throughout Drake's commonplace notes, is a text that clearly influenced or confirmed his perceptions of politics; and his notes and comments on every page enable us to witness him in his first engagement with a book before the extracted passages poured into his notebooks unidentified and fragmented under headings and adages. In this text we see how Drake underlines key passages, marking those that deserve the status of general axiom with 'sentence' or 'maxim' in the margin (ill. 9).[28] Accordingly, Rohan's passage about the huge frame of many parts that was Germany moving by several springs is marked as a 'sentence' and generalised into one in Drake's own words: 'the frame of kingdoms moves by several springs.'[29] Drake read closely – altering here and there a word: on page 44, for example, he changed 'disabuse' to 'undeceive'.[30] He may have read through the whole text and then reread for annotation, or more likely he annotated and reannotated (cross-referring to

---

23. On Ogden MS 7/39 p. 18 in the margin to Guicciardini's section on Beneficentia Commendata, he writes the Italian adage: 'Qui briu donne caro vende' – 'he who gives readily sells at a high price.'
24. Ogden MS 7/39 p. 44.
25. For example, Ogden MS 7/39, pp. 50, 58, 60, 63.
26. For example, Ogden MS 7/39, pp. 45, 48, 57, 'Sententiae'.
27. Duc de Rohan, *A Treatise of the Interest of the Princes and States of Christendom* (1641, Folger Library R1868). The Folger catalogue does not identify the annotations.
28. See for example p. 142: 'after so many storms past one seems upon the point to suffer shipwreck in the haven.' Drake underlines this passage and writes 'Sen' in the margin. See also pp. 2v, 3, 4, 15, 22, 28, 42.
29. Ibid., p. 15.
30. Similarly in the preface to *The Second Part* he changes the word 'recital' to 'narration'.

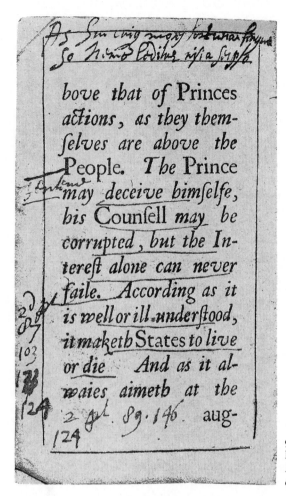

9. From Drake's own copy of
Henri de Rohan's *Treatise of the
Interests of the Princes and States
of Christendom*, 1646.

later passages which he could only have known from an earlier reading) as
he read again and again.[31] By a number of means he made Rohan's text into
his own. As well as extensive underlining, sometimes of whole pages, Drake
itemised points and summarised arguments in the margin in his own words.[32]
On the front and back flyleaves he indexed the various rulers and countries
discussed in the text, focused on events that interested him – the Jülich Cleves
Succession, the Mantuan crisis – and noted the 'particular interests' of the participants.[33] His personal index included, as well as Rohan's own topics, twenty
or more sentences he had drawn from the work.[34]

As he read through the text, as well as internal cross-references, Drake refers

31. See, for example, pp. 3, 9, 15, 23.
32. See *First Part*, pp. 10–11, 28; Part 2, pp. 28–9. For a summary of points by Drake see
the margin notes to *Second Part*, pp. 42, 79. For 'Points of Interest', see *First Part*, p. 32.
33. The back flyleaf notes are entitled by Drake 'Particular Interests Examined'.
34. The 'Sentences' are indexed by pages where they are also marked up, ready perhaps
for copying into a commonplace book.

to other works that explicate a point – to Polybius and Sallust,[35] to Paruta,[36] to Bacon and Sir Robert Cotton,[37] most of all to Guicciardini and Machiavelli.[38] Rohan's treatise leads him to other observations entered on to blank pages as well as the margins of the text – observations on 'Barneveldt's cunning', Henri III's misguided actions against his own interest, Gustavus Adolfus's entry into Germany.[39] Noting the Venetians' refusal of Turkish aid for fear that the remedy might compound the ill, he commends their 'admirable prudence'.[40] Observing, amidst Rohan's discourse on the war in Savoy, that excessive desire for an end prevents the pursuit of interest, Drake is led to think of recent events in England – 'so King James'.[41]

As with his commonplace books, particular historical episodes and actors are studied for what they teach more generally about the ways of the world. Drake reminds himself on the title page of the book that 'tis good to observe the arts and errors in great states and to consider what were the events of each.'[42] He prompts himself to read of great changes and to 'note the causes of the advantages of the world'.[43] And at the end of Rohan's *Treatise* he redirects himself to Bacon's *Advancement of Learning*, Apollolloque's 'Discourse of War with Spain', Malvezzi, Tacitus and Brucioli's *Del Capitano* to further such observations.[44]

Rohan's *Treatise* then helps to shape Drake's worldview but is also read through and in the context of values already formulated. Not only does Drake draw maxims and adages from Rohan, he imports them to Rohan's pages, and so anglicises, rewrites and personalises the passages of the *Treatise*.[45] Manuscript proverbs and adages in English, Latin and Italian recur throughout the text, some familiar to us from the notebooks. 'The shrewdest mischief wrought by friends', Drake writes alongside an account of Spain's assistance to Odenbarneveldt;[46] of the Duke of Savoy's naivety in believing that he might share Montserrat with the Habsburgs, he observes: 'he that divides honey with a bear is like to have least share.'[47] Philip II, was, he observed, like Narcissus, 'ad occasiones intentus'.[48] At times Drake cross-references these proverbs to other works or his own collection of adages: the need for a prince

35. *Second Part*, preface (Polybius); title page (Sallust).
36. *Second Part*, preface.
37. Ibid., *First Part*, p. 10 (Bacon); p. 3 (Cotton).
38. Ibid., *First Part*, pp. 10, 27; *Second Part*, 144, 146 (Guicciardini); *First Part*, pp. 4, 5, 10, 12, 28, 33; *Second Part*, 38, 54, 67, 116, 124 (Machiavelli).
39. Ibid., *Second Part*, pp. 14, 47, 76.
40. Ibid., *Second Part*, p. 64.
41. Ibid., *Second Part*, p. 35; see also *First Part*, p. 26: 'So England'.
42. We see how Drake's writings on the title pages act as reminders and self-counsel on how to read the work to best use.
43. *Treatise*, sig B6v; *Second Part*, p. 104.
44. The reference is to Antonio Brucioli, *Dialogo del Capitano* (Poitiers, 1551).
45. See, for example, *Second Part*, pp. 39, 67, 132, for manuscript proverbs added to the text.
46. *Second Part*, p. 86.
47. Ibid., p. 144.
48. Ibid., p. 26.

to manifest desire for peace, he notes, 'Mac. Dis. 396 gives in precept';[49] the rule to 'watch where an enemy lies most open' he draws from Polybius.[50] The axiom familiar from his notebooks, 'he that handleth a matter wisely shall find good', Drake references to a book of proverbs, perhaps his own – 'l.16 20';[51] similarly the adage that often a private interest prejudices a public bears a margin note: '113 Sent.'[52] as though to a personal collection of Sententiae.[53] The observations Drake makes on and the lessons he draws from Rohan's text emerge from a dialogue audible on every page he reads: a conversation between this text, Drake's other books and notes, and the values he has formed and continues to form.

Rohan's *Treatise*, as it announces, examines interest and realpolitik for all the major powers of Christendom. In valorising and applauding princes who acted with prudence, cunning and dissimulation to advance their interest, it ran counter to Christian ideals but very much echoed the qualities Drake admired in ancient and modern rulers. From his notebooks we have seen how for Drake the values of prudence and interest both emerged from observation of men's behaviour and in turn offered guidance to subjects as well as sovereigns. As he read in Rohan, he did not confine his observations to the conduct of princes but extended the lessons statecraft taught into a social universe, no less characterised by deceit and intrigue. 'All things in the world', he observed on the very first page, 'have their motion from interest', so there was much for all to learn in observing the 'arts and errors' of states and princes. In society at large, because 'everyone seeks his own advancement . . . which depends ordinarily on the destruction of another', it was imperative to learn how to protect oneself.[54] 'Men', he added, 'do not only not gain but lose their estates by neglect of their interest.'[55] As he took personally on board the lessons taught by statecraft, Drake moved to the personal pronoun: 'when *we* come to consult of serious affairs', he took from Sallust, 'we should put off all . . . affection.'[56] Without intelligence, he reminded himself, '*we* cannot make use of occasions.'[57] To Drake the rules of politics, the principles of prudence and interest, were the rules for all who lived in society; they were manuals for the self. In the most literal sense, his reading personalised Rohan's treatise on interest; like astute rulers such as Pope Urban, Drake read that he should not conduct himself by passion.[58] 'Take heed', he reminded himself on the last page, 'of a faint and sluggish mind, a passionate mind.'

49. *Treatise, First Part*, p. 10.
50. *Second Part*, preface.
51. Ibid., p. 49.
52. Ibid., p. 51.
53. See too *Second Part*, preface, with the reference to 'Sentence 119'.
54. *Treatise*, sig [B1ᵛ].
55. Ibid., *Second Part*, p. 124.
56. *Second Part*, title page (top).
57. *Treatise, First Part*, p. 21.
58. *Second Part*, p. 123; 'pope's wisdom above his passions'. Cf. *Treatise, First Part*, p. 16; *Second Part*, p. 61, back flyleaf.

What the Duc de Rohan showed for the successful princes of Christendom, such as Philip II or Ferdinand Duke of Florence, applied to himself: '*our* lives should be ex preceptis acta.'[59] We will not be surprised that they were the now familiar precepts of seizing occasions, deploying guile, 'profound dissimulation'.[60]

Drake read the Duc de Rohan's *Treatise* in 1645, as delegates gathered at Münster to settle a peace.[61] With nearly two hundred rulers represented and 'so many conflicting interests' around the table, with, as he noted, the Habsburgs scheming to make the Duke of Bavaria an elector, it is not surprising that Drake was preoccupied with intrigue and interest.[62] Though in this case they leave no direct traces in his marginalia, events and machinations in his own country also fostered Drake's view that men acted from ambition and interest, whatever else they claimed or feigned. Yet, as we have seen from Drake's diary and those notebooks which we can date to the 1630s, already by his twenties or thirties Drake had come to a cynical view of his fellow men and women, and of the society and polity in which he lived. The question we must ask therefore is to what extent from quite early on Drake read only to confirm his prejudices, and to what extent reading changed his mind or at least refined his perception.

Our own experience may suggest that the contrast in the question is drawn too sharply. Though we read our daily newspaper or favourite authors for information and to learn their views, we bring to them – and choose them to some extent because they have affinity with – our own values and prejudices. Because he returned time and again to his favourite authors and read others with them always in his mind or on his desk, there are clear echoes, of tone as well as substance, of passages extracted and explicated in the notebooks. The preoccupation with interest and self-protection may become more insistent but it is evident from the beginning, when the young William had all the promise of the future before him. More positively, his commitment to and belief in the law and parliaments appear to have survived the violence of army rule and the constitutional revolution of regicide and republic.[63] In many areas, however, we have seen Drake altering his views. We have discerned the man critical of courts and kings become the figure who lauded sovereignty and defended the ceremonies of state (which he had earlier

59. *Treatise, First Part*, sig B5.
60. See, for example, ibid., pp. 3, 10, 26; *Second Part*, pp. 26, 34, 67, 86, 96.
61. See *Treatise, Second Part*, foot p. 91: 'They this instant year 1645 in their treaty at Munster endeavour to make the Duke of Bavaria an Elector.' See G. Parker, *The Thirty Years' War* (1984), p. 178. Blair Worden argues that it was about this time that Marchamont Needham invoked the Duc de Rohan to defend 'interest' politics. See B. Worden, 'Journalism and Politics in Cromwellian England: the Case of Marchamont Needham' *Pub. Hist.* 29 (1991), pp. 87–9; cf. Worden, 'Wit in a Roundhead: The Dilemma of Marchamont Needham', in S. Amussen and M. Kishlansky, eds, *Political Culture and Cultural Politics in Early Modern England* (Manchester, 1995), pp. 317–18.
62. Parker, *Thirty Years' War*, p. 178.
63. See above, pp. 249–52.

dismissed as trivial) as necessary props to majesty. And we have observed the critic of Archbishop Laud, and the castigator of an overambitious clergy, come to attach more importance to the authority of the church, and to set forms of liturgy as integral to social order. He even adds the Christian injunction to abide in the place God assigns to Guicciardini's counsel of non-resistance.[64] If the former scion of a puritan family became the Restoration MP, it was not least through a process of reading and rereading through changing experience.

Though Drake was powerfully influenced by those he read, he never perhaps absorbed the views of any writer whole, and, in the process of weighing them all, formulated a very personal worldview. He took much from Charron on wisdom and prudence but not that author's injunction that 'God, nature and all reason urges us to do good and merit the gratitude of our fellows.'[65] He follows Lipsius and Vossius in their preoccupation with order and discipline, religious unity and prudence, but not in their commitment to a 'characteristically humanist concern for morality'.[66] Bacon was the English writer who most influenced him from youth, yet Drake did not share Bacon's optimism that men's natures 'carry ever an appetite to good', nor his views on religion.[67] If, as the historian of the proverb argues, 'the most striking trait in the ethics of proverbs is the adherence to the middle way', that was not Drake's reading.[68] And, as we have argued, at times he went beyond his favourite Machiavelli in advocacy of realpolitik. Because he brought together different combinations of texts at different times, Drake's readings led to changing views.

Indeed, though his view of the world remained shaped by his favourite authors – especially Machiavelli – even Drake's Machiavellianism undergoes subtle transformation. With the threat of the mob looming in the 1640s and 1650s, Drake exhibits little sympathy with that faith in the people that underpins Machiavelli's *Discorsi*.[69] And yet as Restoration again promised renewed stability, Drake retreated from the extravagant claims for princes made in *The Prince*, urging rather such moderate government as the people may not have a desire to hurt the prince.[70] As we have seen, after 1660 Drake began to speak of a 'common interest' between the prince and people as the foundation of stability.[71] Though the language of 'interest' continued over the nearly four decades that he took notes, what it meant for individuals,

---

64. Ogden MS 7/21 f. 95v.
65. E. F. Rice, *The Renaissance Idea of Wisdom* (Cambridge, Mass., 1958), p. 199.
66. See Oestreich, *Neostoicism*, ch. 3, and N. Wickenden, *G. J. Vossius and the Humanist Concept of History* (Assen, Netherlands, 1993).
67. F. Bacon, *The Advancement of Learning and New Atlantis*, ed. A. Johnston (Oxford, 1974), p. 141.
68. A. Taylor, *The Proverb and an Index to the Proverb* (Copenhagen, 1962), p. 168.
69. In Ogden MS 7/18 f. 15 he refers to Heinsius describing Machiavelli as a force for disorder.
70. Ogden MS 7/30 f. 57.
71. Ibid. See above, p. 251.

society and government had altered. As Drake selected, glossed and reinterpreted his favourite proverbs, passages and texts, his political thought, though
still rooted in the classical and Renaissance commentaries and histories, altered
too.

Some might argue that 'political thought' is an inappropriate term for the
readings and reflections of Drake's notebooks. John Pocock, in *The Machiavellian Moment*, argued that before James Harrington in *Oceana* (1656) anglicised classical and Machiavellian ideas of citizenship, the Englishman had no
'awareness of himself as a political actor in a public realm'.[72] What I would
like to suggest is that in a number of ways Drake questions that argument.
In the first place, he developed a clear classical humanist approach to politics
and conceived of himself as a political actor in the broadest sense. Just as significant, Drake formulated and reformulated his views so as to fashion an
'interest' view of politics, and a Hobbesian view of the world before Hobbes
had published. If, as Pocock has argued in an important methodological essay,
even a text seen by none but the writer reveals how 'at a particular time the
state of language permitted the articulation of particular states of consciousness',[73] then Drake stands as an important admonition that studies in the
history of political thought, or even of shifts in the discursive paradigms,
should not be confined (as in Pocock's and Skinner's work they still are) to
canonical authors.

Drake too requires us to rethink what politics and political ideas meant to
early modern England. For we have argued that Drake viewed all social intercourse, the act of being in the world, as political acts: acts of negotiation and
diplomacy, power and persuasion; and that he regarded the self no less than
the prince as a being requiring training and advice in wisdom and prudence
to survive and thrive in the world. Politics for Drake was not something discrete, or separate from the personal, the business of others; it was the human
condition. And because to him the personal, the social and the political were
all one, he read fables and proverbs and emblems as texts of politics. If as historians we are to understand the early modern age, we will need to dispense
with our anachronistically attenuated and segregated concept of the 'political'
and also learn to read as 'documents' of Renaissance politics those genres
which we have not privileged as texts of politics.

Finally, of course, our whole argument is that Drake's own politics is not
simply the outcome of a set of authored texts, but the product of a process
which historians have not been inclined to regard as political: the process of
reading. For as we read through Aristotle or Polybius, Livy or Tacitus, Bacon
and Charron, Machiavelli and Guicciardini, let alone the volumes of axioms
and proverbs, we become fully aware that it was Drake's method of reading
that produced the political values and ideas he found in them – sometimes

---

72. See G. Burgess, 'Renaissance Texts and Renaissance Republicanism', *Ren. Forum* 1
    (1996), p. 7; J. G. A. Pocock, *The Machiavellian Moment: Florentine Political Thought and
    the Atlantic Republican Tradition* (Princeton, 1975), ch. 12 and p. 335.
73. J. G. A. Pocock, *Virtue, Commerce and History* (Cambridge, 1985), p. 25.

ideas that we or other contemporaries would consider against the grain of the text, let alone authorial intention. To recognise that is to acknowledge that the history of reading may question our understanding of all Renaissance texts, and discursive and rhetorical practices. That is also to recognise that the history of reading is central not only to the history of political thought, but to political history itself.

Contextualising the Case: William Drake and Early Modern Readers

Sir William Drake's papers, commonplace books, journal, parliamentary diary and annotated books together constitute the richest archival source we have for the study of reading in early modern England. Their very richness also, of course, presents us with a problem, the problem of any case study: how typical was Sir William Drake, and what may we learn more generally from our study of him? There is a broad methodological issue here as well as a specific question. The old conventional history, concerned with an overarching narrative, had little time for case study. As our suspicion of the master narrative as ideological construct has grown, and our awareness of what it also excluded has sharpened, historians have turned to case studies or micro histories — to Martin Guerre and Montaillou, to Justice Fleming and Sister Bernadette.[74] A historical version of the Geertzian method of 'thick description', such case studies offered entry to the wider cultural and ideological contexts of specific situations or individuals. Most pertinent to our purposes, of course, is Carlo Ginzburg's study of the Friulese miller, Domenico Scandella, called Menocchio. In *The Cheese and the Worms*, Ginzburg showed how Menocchio read himself to a heretical and radical view of the world.[75] As Ginzburg acknowledged, he was clearly not typical. But once we have his story, his views expounded, our view of his age — of popular culture, religion and heresy, authority and resistance — is transformed, transformed both by our knowledge that such views were held by him and by the possibility that they,

74. See N. Z. Davis, *The Return of Martin Guerre* (Cambridge, Mass., 1983); E. Le Roy Ladurie, *Montaillou* (Harmondsworth, 1980); A. Macfarlane, *The Justice and the Mare's Ale: Law and Disorder in Seventeenth-Century England* (Cambridge, 1981); J. Brown, *Immodest Acts: The Life of a Lesbian Nun in Renaissance Italy* (Oxford, 1986).

75. C. Ginzburg, *The Cheese and the Worms: The Cosmos of a Sixteenth-Century Miller* (Baltimore, 1980). Ginzburg's use of sources has been criticised and his arguments modified in A. Del Col, *Domenico Scandella Known as Menocchio: His Trials Before the Inquisition* (Binghamton, N.Y., 1996), a transcript of the trials. In an excellent critical introduction Del Col demonstrates how 'Ginzburg's analysis of Mennochio's culture has . . . limited itself to and strangely enough accepted and credited the explanations and frame of reference adopted by the judges' (p. lvi).

or other radical thoughts, could be entertained by others. His case in other words offers an entry to a wider cultural world.

The scholars of the linguistic turn, Pocock and Skinner, have argued that study of language usage and shifts opens onto the history of ideas and consciousness: that analysis of any text offers insight into how 'at a particular time the state of language permitted the articulation of particular states of consciousness.'[76] Language is both social and individual, both general and particular. And the same is as true of reading as of speaking or writing; all are acts of translating and using language. When we read we, albeit silently, translate, interpret into our 'own' language, one that our culture allows us to deploy but one we deploy too in our individual way.[77] As Pocock argued, a figure like Machiavelli could take the language of civic humanism to rewrite a whole different set of meanings and values. No less Menocchio's heretical worldview owed less to the books he read, most of them conventional enough, than to the 'aggresive originality' of his reading.[78] Though, as far as we know, Menocchio is exceptional, there is no such thing as *a* typical reader.

Sir William Drake was certainly not typical, even of the educated gentry class to which he belonged. His case, however, may enable us, indeed it should impel us, to reconsider other Renaissance books and readers. And, beyond that, it invites us to think again about early modern education, the performance of texts (the classics, proverbs, fables and emblems) in Renaissance culture, in fine the ways values were constructed and revised, how political ideas were formulated and reformulated in that culture. Exceptional though he may turn out to be, if we follow Drake's example, we may not only fruitfully reread early modern history, but better comprehend how early modern Englishmen read as well as wrote their world.[79]

Returning to the Reader

Much of the work in the history of reading has been characterised by unsupported assumptions drawn from the authors and publishers of works and the texts themselves; alternatively scholars have endeavoured to piece together the reading habits of an individual from incomplete or fragmentary evidence. For

76. See above, p. 268.
77. Manguel writes that reading is 'a common and yet personal process of reconstruction', *A History of Reading* (1996), p. 39; Adrian Johns points out that 'no reader was an island', *The Nature of the Book* (Chicago, 1998), p. 626.
78. Ginzburg, *The Cheese and the Worms*, pp. 33–4.
79. Compare the remarks of James Raven, 'Du qui au comment: à la recherche d'une histoire de la lecture en Angleterre', in R. Chartier, ed., *Histoires de la lecture* (Paris, 1995); cf. Manguel: 'Ultimately, perhaps, the history of reading is the history of each of its readers', *A History of Reading*, p. 22.

several famous readers who were also established authors – Shakespeare or Montaigne – we have their writings but no reading notes, marginalia or diaries as evidence of how a text was first encountered, or the processes of digestion and bricolage that underlay the acts of rewriting. In the case of Jonson, Milton or Clarendon, we are fortunate also to have some common-place books, which have yet to be fully studied as documents of reading. More generally, scores of diaries kept by early modern English men and women contain occasional references to books or pamphlets read, and in the case of figures like Sir Simonds D'Ewes and John Rous, they provide invaluable insights into the acquisition and circulation of books and reactions to them. However, the case of Sir William Drake is exceptional in offering us most of the pieces of the jigsaw: we know what he read, crucially *how* he went about reading, how his views were formulated and changed, how he deployed his reading. As a consequence, what he prompts us to do is to return to theories and generalisations, and reconsider other individuals, both to place our detailed study in context, and to fill in and refine the sketchier large picture of Renaissance reading that scholars have begun to draw.

One of the characteristics of the early modern period was the tendency for men and women to be read *to*. This was true at both ends of the social spectrum: the illiterate poor heard the Bible read in church, a proclamation read aloud or reported at the market cross, a ballad or squib recited or sung in an alehouse; the aristocracy and gentry were served by those who read to them, as they were by those – doubtless often the same men or boys – who attended to their other domestic needs, or played a lute to soothe them. Reading did not always take place as the quiet activity of leisure: Rubens had 'some good historian or poet' read to him while he painted;[80] there was probably bustle in the more modest household of the London turner Nehemiah Wallington while members of the family read aloud.[81] The experience of hearing a reading was common to both genders, despite the identification of women with leisure and the private sphere: the diary of Lady Anne Clifford, who was portrayed surrounded by her books, contains numerous references to being read to.[82] The less privileged Elizabeth Isham of Northamptonshire took pleasure in hearing her sister read.[83] The practice continued to the end of the seventeenth century and beyond – Pepys was read asleep by his boy Tom; it was the rise of the novel, it has been argued, that reflected and fostered a culture of 'private reading'.[84] Though scholars are familiar with the practice of hearing a book read, none has adequately considered its

---

80. H. Peacham, *The Complete Gentleman* (1634), p. 110.
81. P. Seaver, *Wallington's World: A Puritan Artisan in Seventeenth-Century London* (1985), p. 40.
82. See below, pp. 299–300.
83. E. Boucier, *Les Journaux privés en Angleterre de 1600 à 1660* (Paris, 1976), p. 290.
84. R. Chartier, 'Leisure and Sociability: Reading Aloud in Early Modern Europe', in S. Zimmerman and R. F. E. Wiseman, eds, *Urban Life in the Renaissance* (Newark, N.J., 1989), pp. 115, 103–20.

importance, or the relationship of 'readers' and auditors for the processes of the absorption and comprehension of, and the reaction to, texts. Listening to books on tape as we negotiate the morning traffic on the school run and relaxing with a few pages late in bed should also be enough to indicate that the moment and place of Rubens's workshop and Pepys's boudoir affected their relations – with 'readers' and books.[85] What seems clear is that *listening* to texts in no way diluted their impact on early modern auditors. Pepys and Lady Anne Clifford learned lengthy quotations, an important reminder that print did not replace the skills or habits of an oral culture.[86]

In Lady Anne Clifford's case, she not only heard her servants read extracts but caused them 'to write them in papers'.[87] To us, writing, if anything, is an even more personal and private act than reading, but as we have recently begun to appreciate, early modern England retained many of the features of an earlier pre-print scribal culture; not least gentlemen and scholars employed amanuenses, not only to take letters, but to write out passages from books. Fulke Greville, Lord Brook employed research assistants to gather material and epitomise books for him; the exact antiquary Sir Simonds D'Ewes had an industrious servant extract material from the Tower records and 'out of some printed books'.[88] Francis Bacon even employed assistants in keeping his commonplace books, as he makes clear in one: 'the principal use of this book is to receive such parts and passages of authors as I shall note and underline in the books themselves *to be written forth by a servant* and so collected into this book.'[89] Bacon, however, was cautious about the use of assistants or scribes: 'I would have you', he advised the young Greville on the keeping of a commonplace book, 'gather the chiefest things and out of the chiefest books yourself, and to use your other collectors in gathering arguments and examples to prove or illustrate any particular position or question.'[90] Whatever the use of assistants, Greville, he insisted, should be the 'master workman'.[91] For all Bacon's attempts at distinction, the practice of using scribes raises a number of questions about 'authorship'. The 'master workman' may have underlined a passage, but did the scribe copy it accurately? Where in the commonplace book did he place it? Did he leave space for later addition or gloss? In what order were a variety of extracts copied? And when he was left to 'gather arguments' did not the scribe help to form the very views of the master, or at

---

85. Cf. P. Sainger, 'Silent Reading: Its Impact on Late Medieval Script and Society', *Viator* 13 (1982), pp. 367–414.

86. M. E. Lamb, 'The Agency of the Split Subject: Lady Anne Clifford and the Uses of Reading', *Eng. Lit. Ren.* 22 (1992), pp. 347–68; F. Yates, *The Art of Memory* (1966).

87. Lamb, 'Agency of the Split Subject', p. 367.

88. V. Snow, 'Francis Bacon's Advice to Fulke Greville on Research Techniques', *Hunt. Lib. Quart.* 5 (1960), p. 378; H. Love, *Scribal Publication in Seventeenth-Century England* (Oxford, 1993), p. 136.

89. P. Beal, '"Notions in Garrison": The Seventeenth-Century Commonplace Book', in W. Speed Hill, ed., *New Ways of Looking at Old Texts* (Binghamton, N.Y., 1993), p. 139.

90. Snow, 'Bacon's Advice to Greville', p. 374.

91. Ibid.

least set the discursive parameters within which his judgement could be exercised? What was the nature of the relationship, intellectual and personal, between master and amanuensis?

Drake's notebooks are an invaluable example of the role of scribes. Because we have volumes entirely in Drake's own hand, followed after the mid-1640s by volumes penned by a scribe, we are able to review the extent of change. And what immediately strikes us is how little material change there was. The pages of some of the later books are more crowded and cramped but this may owe more to circumstance than a scribe. The continuity of content and tone suggests that Drake's amanuensis faithfully copied the passages his master marked or dictated, and *his* observations on those passages. Despite his weakening sight, Drake closely read the Duc de Rohan's *Treatise* in 1645, continued to keep notebooks in his own hand, and evidently went back over other scribal notebooks later, adding occasional extra comment. If a dialogue went on in his study about the texts, it would seem that Drake remained very much the 'master workman', for all that his assistant was learned in Latin, Italian and French as well as English. Indeed, it may be that Drake's scribe became something of a pupil, replicating the close relationship Drake sustained with his own schoolmaster, Dr Charles Croke, whom he consulted in 1640 about the establishment of a workhouse and stock for the poor at Amersham.[92]

We cannot be certain of the identity of Drake's scribe. But on 25 June 1670 one Thomas Ken deposed that he had been a servant 'of the said Sir William Drake deceased for many years together'.[93] Indeed, Drake's will was 'written by this deponent according to the particular directions of the said Sir William Drake', and subsequently read over to him.[94] The relationship between the two men was obviously one of intimacy and trust. During his lifetime Drake granted to Ken manors in Shardeloes and Amersham, in Lincolnshire and Fleet Street, London on very favourable terms.[95] In his will he extended his generosity, bequeathing an annuity and £200 capital to Ken 'of whose fidelity, care and diligence I have had much experience'.[96] The conjecture that Ken was Drake's amanuensis is strengthened when to all this we add Drake's grant to him of 'all such French and Italian books that are noted and written upon together with all my manuscripts and dictionaries'.[97] All the other books passed to Sir William's nephew and namesake. It seems almost certain that Thomas Ken inherited the texts that he and his master had

92. Bucks R.O., D/DR/12/1, decretal order about the workhouse at Amersham, 14 Charles I; see too D/DR/12/3, A Plan of the Alms House in Amersham, built by Drake in 1657.
93. Bucks R.O., D/DR/1/68, 25 June 1670; depositions in connection with the will of Sir William Drake.
94. Ibid., will of Drake, f. 5.
95. Bucks R.O., D/DR/1/68, pp. 39, 50, 61, 113. Several grants were for peppercorn rent.
96. Bucks R.O., D/DR/1/68, p. 81 (will of Drake, 17 Dec. 1667).
97. Ibid.

worked on together, though whether the 'manuscripts' included Drake's own notebooks is not clear. It would appear from the writing of Drake's will that, close to his master as he was, Ken copied Drake's words and executed his instructions with 'care and diligence'. Over the many years of his service, a scribe had become an intimate family friend, scholarly disciple and heir. If such relationships were common in early modern England, and other fragments of evidence suggest they were, then the acts of reading and being read to may deserve a place in the social history of family and property, as well as the history of ideas.

One of the important recent approaches to the history of reading has returned scholars' attention to the material signs and marks of readers on the page – to flynotes and marginalia. For years, archivists and librarians have been careless of marginal marks or endnotes, cropping or covering them with rebindings, a practice that itself reflected a New Critical privileging of the text and an ideological elevating of the author over and above the contemporary, or later, reader. Much evidence therefore of important readers and readings has been lost, but a vast resource remains in the variant copies of early modern books. Some of the most obvious are almost unknown: James I's annotated copy of Selden's *History of Tithes* or Charles I's own Shakespeare read in prison on the eve of his death remain unexamined in the Royal Library.[98] Many others emerge only from systematic trawls of research libraries and smaller collections, a process for which work on microfilms can never substitute. Even when the marginal hand remains anonymous, annotations offer invaluable evidence of how a text performed at moments of publication and circulation.[99] When scholars are able to identify the readers, we can begin to evaluate the place of those readings in the formulation of attitudes – to give a much needed specificity to theories about how texts circulated their 'social energy'.[100]

As with the modern student's highlighter pen, underlinings and marginal marks usually announce a passage to which the annotator accorded, or felt he should accord, especial importance. Often simple pointers or asterisks indicate a passage that the reader copies, or intends to copy, into a commonplace book, in the fashion Bacon recommended.[101] In other cases, marked passages were committed to memory. When during Queen Elizabeth's visit to Cambridge in 1564, the Dean of Ely, Andrew Perne, quoted from twelve volumes,

98. Both are in the Royal Library at Windsor.
99. W. E. Slights writes of a 'conversation with the larger cultural discourse'. See Slights, 'The Edifying Margins of Renaissance English Books', *Ren. Quart.* 42 (1989), pp. 682–716, at p. 687.
100. The Marquis of Halifax, for example. See S. Zwicker 'Reading the Margins: Politics and the Habits of Appropriation', in K. Sharpe and S. Zwicker, eds, *Refiguring Revolutions: Aesthetics and Politics from the English Revolution to the Romantic Revolution* (Berkeley, 1998), pp. 101–15.
101. See Slights, 'Edifying Margins', pp. 685–6.

he recalled the very passages underlined or annotated in the books in his library, and may indeed have marked them with the visit in mind.[102] Marginal marks, however, indicate far more than passages committed to notes or memory. Both John Dee and Gabriel Harvey developed elaborate systems of symbols and signs to demarcate subjects, approval or disagreement, turning the margin into a dialogue with the text.[103] Harvey also dated his notes, enabling us to follow his readings and rereadings over different times and circumstances, a habit that confirms the importance attached to the record of his own readings, and the pleasure he derived from a remembered encounter with the book: 'enjoy', he counselled himself, 'sovereign repetition of your most excellent notes.'[104]

That use of the word 'sovereign' for an act of reading and Harvey's choice of marginal symbols, the sun to represent the king for example, suggest that marginalia were ideological, indeed political sites in Renaissance books and culture. 'Just as there are no politically innocent texts,' writes a scholar of Scriptural annotation, 'so too there are no politically neutral marginalia.'[105] This is true in the narrowest and broadest understanding of politics, and of authors as well as readers. For authors' printed marginal notes could distract from, conceal or point up political allusions and topical references. Where in More's *Utopia* they disguised its political relevance, in 1605 Ben Jonson, it is suggested, was able to plant criticism of the English monarchy amidst 'the dense thicket of his marginal quotations from Tacitus, Suetonius and others in the quarto editions of *Sejanus*'.[106] Readers, however, valued margins for their own political commentary: in a 1625 edition of Barclay's *Argenis* marginal notes point up its concern with 'tribute and impositions of kings upon their subjects'.[107] And the Earl of Pembroke systematically annotated his copy of Chapman's *Conspiracy . . . of Charles Duke of Byron* with references to topical events and contemporary figures.[108] Not all applauded such habits. We have remarked the efforts by authority from Henry VIII to James I to prevent marginalia in Bibles, not least because Scripture was a key text of authority. In 1658, the editor of Lucius Annaeus Florus's epitome of Roman history condemned the notes in an earlier translation which had criticised James I's

---

102. See W. Sherman, *John Dee: The Politics of Reading and Writing in the English Renaissance* (Amherst, Mass., 1995), p. 67.

103. Ibid., p. 77; V. F. Stern, *Gabriel Harvey: His Life, Marginalia and Library* (Oxford, 1979), pp. 140–1.

104. Stern, *Gabriel Harvey*, pp. 139, 190. Cf. A. Grafton and L. Jardine, '"Studied for Action": How Gabriel Harvey Read his Livy', *Past & Present* 129 (1990), pp. 30–78.

105. W. E. Slights, '"Marginal Notes that Spoile the Text": Scriptural Annotation in the English Renaissance', *Hunt. Lib. Quart.* 55 (1992), pp. 255–78, at p. 258.

106. Ibid.

107. See L. Potter, *Secret Rites and Secret Writing: Royalist Literature, 1641–1660* (Cambridge, 1989), p. 75.

108. A. H. Tricomi, 'Philip, Earl of Pembroke and the Analogical Way of Reading Political Tragedy', *J. Eng. & Germ. Philol.* 85 (1986), pp. 332–45.

dealings with Spain, and went on to make a larger objection: 'I do not think the margins of books very proper for such politic discourses and speculations . . .'[109]

The reader could not, however, so easily be erased. With the heightening of political controversy in the early Stuart years and the outpouring of pamphlet propaganda in the 1640s, the habit of readers' marginalia not only grew but changed. As the author of what will be the definitive work on this subject puts it: 'it is in these years that the practice of marginal annotation was transformed from a humanist concern with exemplarity and ethics to a battlefield of correction, denial and repudiation.'[110] In the margins, Steven Zwicker argues, readers not only responded to the fact of armed conflict, they helped to translate it from the battlefield to the page. In so doing, they not only further politicised writing and reading, making way for the battle of the books, they also scripted a new political culture in which dispute and engagement were normalised – the culture of coffeehouse and club, the politics of party. In Professor Zwicker's account, the study of readers' marks and margins becomes a political narrative, part of the master narrative of politics.[111]

Only a few of Sir William Drake's printed books have turned up as yet, and unlike Gabriel Harvey, he did not sign or date his marginalia. The works in which we can reasonably confidently detect his hand, works dated 1645 and 1657, bear few direct or obvious political pointers to contemporary events – the battles or manoeuvres of civil war, the collapse of the republic or rise of Cromwell to be Lord Protector. What instead we have argued is that the endless cross-references, the shift from English text to marginal Italian adage, represent not just reading as interpreting and personalising but the process of reading as politicising – constructing a set of values from the intertextual play that goes on in the margins. Nor was it just a play between books. Marginalia involved, it has been stated, 'complex strands of conversation with the larger cultural discourse'.[112] And in particular, Drake's habit of making sentences and similes has been characterised as a dialogue with all social constructions of meaning: 'The simile provided a convenient place for the reader to move out of the text with his nugget of quotable truth to find other similitudes with the world beyond the text.'[113] Drake did not, as did many, dispute directly with his texts. Rather he plundered them, escaped with the spoils and gathered them with the booty of other textual raids to stockpile an arsenal of wisdom. He spans both the humanist concern with exemplarity *and* the

109. *The History of the Romans by Lucius Florus* (1658, Thomason E1849/1).
110. S. Zwicker, 'Passions and Occasions: The Politics of Reading *c.*1649', paper, International Conference on History and Literature, Reading 1996. Steven Zwicker is currently completing a major study of the politics of marginalia (see his 'Reading the Margins'). I am extremely grateful to him for his encouragement and advice.
111. See Zwicker, 'Reading the Margins', passim.
112. Slights, 'Edifying Margins', p. 687.
113. Ibid., p. 691.

later habit of writing politics in the margins.[114] If he is at all representative of other readers, we shall need to recognise that the politicisation of the reader was not just a freeing of the reader to dispute and contest authority, but a broader freedom to construct a personal identity, a personal politics, a political self.[115]

Both typically, and it would seem in Drake's case, underlinings and marginal marks and annotations often indicated passages that were to be entered into commonplace books. During the Renaissance period, indeed perhaps from the twelfth century to the eighteenth century, the keeping of a commonplace book was a normal habit of reading. The leading Renaissance theorists of education, Erasmus and Vives, advocated and gave directions for the keeping of commonplace books. And under their influence in the grammar schools of Tudor England, 'commonplace books in which could be written down words and idiomatic phrases from "authoritative" sources to be used in various written and oral exercises formed the background to the main business of writing and speaking Latin.'[116] The experience of reading for most boys was, it is not too much to say, the practice of commonplacing. Like all pedagogic methods, of course, the practice was ideological, directed to an end. As early as the twelfth century, Peter of Blois had defended the habit of excerpting and compiling 'from a repeated reading of books' as fostering 'the stuff of virtue and the exercise of prudence'.[117] Erasmus and his disciples undoubtedly considered the commonplace book an effective means in training young men in virtue, that is in the values of the Christian humanism that he taught. As the historian of the commonplace book has argued, 'the virtue and vice function of the commonplace remained constant and sharp through the Renaissance.'[118] As Richard Rainolde, the cleric and doctor, defined it in *The Foundation of Rhetoric*: the commonplace 'is an oration dilating and amplifying good or evil'.[119]

The name 'commonplace' of course announces that the virtue the books were believed to promote was a *common* good — in both senses: that virtue which was shared by all and exercised for all. Educationalists and rhetoricians recommended the collection of adages or proverbs that had been 'approved by the judgement and consent of all men', making commonplace books collections of 'moral platitudes'.[120] Indeed, like all educational devices, the commonplace book was intended to underpin not only shared values but also the

114. See T. Hampton, *Writing from History: The Rhetoric of Exemplarity in Renaissance Literature* (Ithaca, 1990).
115. See below, pp. 330–40.
116. K. Charlton, *Education in Renaissance England* (1965), p. 110; and J. M. Lechner, *Renaissance Concepts of the Commonplaces* (Westport, Conn., 1962).
117. N. Hathaway, 'Compilatio: From Plagiarism to Compiling', *Viator* 20 (1989), pp. 19–44.
118. Lechner, *Renaissance Concepts*, p. 104.
119. Ibid., p. 17.
120. Ibid., p. 191; M. T. Crane, *Framing Authority: Sayings, Self and Society in Sixteenth-Century England* (Princeton, 1993), pp. 50–1, quoting Peacham.

commonweal, both the Christian commonwealth and the polity.[121] As Margo
Todd concluded, after examining scores of notebooks from sixteenth- and
seventeenth-century Cambridge, 'the authors used most frequently and consistently by all of the students – Seneca, Cicero, Quintilian, Ovid, Virgil,
Plutarch, Pythagoras and Isocrates – guarantee that most of the conclusions
drawn about the social order are in line with Christian humanist thought.'[122]
Evidencing the crucial role of education in the construction of the Tudor
polity, commonplaces were 'building blocks of common knowledge and *thus*
basic elements of social cohesion'.[123]

Yet while this was universally true in theory and often the case in practice, there was an ambiguity at the heart of commonplacing, to which some
scholars have paid too little attention. For though what the compiler copied
was extracted from a common storehouse of wisdom, the manner in which
extracts were copied, arranged, juxtaposed, cross-referenced or indexed was
personal and individual. Certainly the advocates of commonplace books
instructed keepers about method. In *De Copia*, Erasmus advised the collecting of epithets and idioms in a book 'verborum', and the extracting of histories in another 'rerum' (of things); and he showed how collections of lives,
by Plutarch or Epiphanus, could become rich sources for commonplaces.[124]
Similarly Vives suggested separate notebooks for idioms, proverbs and sentences.[125] Bacon, summarising a whole English literature on the subject, gave
Fulke Greville advice on the sorts of headings to establish in notebooks, and
the questions and topics to order under them.[126] And it is clear from the practice of Richard Holdsworth at Cambridge that tutors often gave detailed
advice to students about annotating commonplaces right down to instructions about the size of notebooks to be used.[127]

Yet, when all that is said, it remains the case that commonplacing was, and
was seen to be, personal. The compiler essentially rewrote, fashioned a new
text, which was anything but common, indeed was unique.[128] As Terence Cave
has brilliantly demonstrated, the very idea of 'imitatio' made the Renaissance
writer into a rewriter, writing being 'the dismembering and reconstruction

---

121. See A. Moss, *Printed Commonplace Books and the Structuring of Renaissance Thought*
    (Oxford, 1996), p. 164.
122. M. Todd, *Christian Humanism and the Puritan Social Order* (Cambridge, 1987), p. 85.
123. Crane, *Framing Authority*, p. 18, my italics.
124. R. R. Bolgar, ed., *Classical Influences on European Culture, 1500–1700* (Cambridge, 1976),
    pp. 8, 94.
125. Bolgar, *Classical Heritage*, p. 273.
126. Snow, 'Bacon's Advice to Greville', pp. 372–4.
127. Todd, *Christian Humanism*, p. 81. Similarly, the late Sir Geoffrey Elton specified the
    size of record cards to be used by his graduate students.
128. On the contemporary concern that the act of writing itself was regarded as danger-
    ously individual and in need of standardisation and control, see the fascinating study
    by Jonathan Goldberg, *Writing Matter: From the Hands of the English Renaissance*
    (Stanford, 1990).

of what has already been written'.[129] Similarly the commonplace book keeper became an author, the perpetrator of what Harold Love would call 'user publication', the creation of a text for the use of one.[130] Individual practices of selection, transcription and organisation, and still more personal notions of 'use', made the commonplace book not only an individual act of writing but a personal construction of meaning. In a commonplace book the 'platitudes' were taken out of the textual contexts that had endowed them with meaning and reconstituted in a new environment: 'No individual text within a commonplace book can safely be viewed as an independent entity divorced from the collection in which it occurs and considered without regard to the habits of the compiler himself.'[131] Francis Bacon, in his preface to his *Apothegms*, urged readers to 'take out the kernel of them and make them your own.'[132] In consequence he recognised that: 'one man's notes will little profit another because one man's conceit doth so much differ from another's.'[133]

As even Sister Lechner, whose study tends to the idealist, acknowledged, once on the page of an individual's commonplace book 'thoughts were manipulated like objects.'[134] Erasmus himself discussed the ways in which a single instance could be used to 'illustrate several morals'.[135] And as he sorted the materials he entered, every keeper of a commonplace book faced 'a new critical confrontation of his material'.[136] Far, then, from simply circulating a common repository of wisdom and reinforcing shared Christian humanist values, the act of commonplacing led to a questioning of that wisdom and those values. Though Bacon was unusual in setting up in his notebooks one adage against another 'to conceive of the opposition as thesis and antithesis',[137] the space provided by disagreement or ambiguity between lines of passages extracted was a space in which the early modern reader exercised his own mind and wrote his own identity. From their beginning in collecting familiar knowledge, the commonplace books served 'to furnish argument to dispute . . . likewise to minister unto our judgement to conclude aright within ourselves'.[138]

---

129. T. Cave, *The Cornucopian Text: Problems of Writing in the French Renaissance* (Oxford, 1979), ch. 2, esp. pp. 35, 76; Cave, 'The Mimesis of Reading in the Renaissance', in J. D. Lyons and S. G. Nichols, eds, *Mimesis: From Mirror to Method, Augustine to Descartes* (1982).

130. Love, *Scribal Publication*, p. 79.

131. Beal, '"Notions in Garrison"', p. 133.

132. H. O. White, *Plagiarism and Imitation during the English Renaissance* (New York, 1965), p. 196.

133. Snow, 'Bacon's Advice to Greville', p. 374.

134. Lechner, *Renaissance Concepts*, p. 236.

135. Bolgar, *Classical Heritage*, p. 273.

136. A. Blair, 'Humanist Methods in Natural Philosophy: The Commonplace Book', *J. Hist. Ideas* 53 (1992), pp. 541–52.

137. Francis Bacon, *The Essays*, ed. J. Pitcher (Harmondsworth, 1985), p. 22.

138. Bacon, *Advancement of Learning*, p. 123.

The habits of dispute, criticism and opposition that commonplacing could foster were not always easily confined within its pages. When, writing in 1642, Thomas Fuller described a commonplace book as 'notions in garrison whence the owner may draw out an army into the field', his military vocabulary recognised a world of violent contest, far removed from the old ideals of commonwealth.[139] Did then the habit of commonplacing change with altered times? And if so did those changes reflect or effect the onset of division and finally conflict in society and state? The theories and models remained constant: the antiquary and scholar Sir Simonds D'Ewes in the 1620s and 1630s copied pages of Erasmus's adages.[140] As late as 1675 the author of the *Lusus Poeticus Latino-Anglicanus*, a book for schoolboys, was still recommending the annotation of Virgil, Ovid, Martial and Seneca, and the collecting of 'excellent precepts of morality'.[141] Indeed, amidst the violence of the French Revolution, the Thermidoreans dreamed of a family book of exempla, a commonplace book that might inculcate virtue in citizens.[142]

But, as such a dream reminds us, traditional practices can over time be differently configured and appropriated for different purposes and causes. And there can be no denying that change took place within the pages of both printed and manuscript commonplace books. One scholar has noted a tendency for secular adages to be replaced by biblical citations in seventeenth-century England.[143] More generally we might fruitfully reconsider the decline of commonplacing – at least as the standard pedagogic method. Perhaps the gradual recognition of the 'author', the vogue for experiment and discovery exemplified by the Royal Society, a stronger sense of change and of narrative eroded the humanist programme of gathering from a timeless store of wisdom.[144] But there can be little doubt that politics played a key role too. As religious division sharpened and civil war erupted, the ideal notion of a common storehouse of virtue, always an ideal under strain, broke. In 1654, Thomas Blount's *Academie of Eloquence* published, under the guise of a commonplace book, 'what is virtually an anthology of royalist writers'.[145] Similarly John Gibson, incarcerated in Durham Castle, having begun a commonplace book with entries from St Paul and John of Chrysostom, 'to pass away my melancholy', ended up writing a memoir of civil war and a collage of emblems, poems and extracts from Royalist favourites.[146] Gibson

---

139. Beal, '"Notions in Garrison"', p. 131.
140. Todd, *Christian Humanism*, p. 88. D'Ewes filled thirty-six folios with notes from Erasmus's *Adages*.
141. J. Langston, *Lusus Poeticus Latino-Anglicanus in Usum Scholarum* (1675), preface to reader.
142. F. Furet and J. Ozouf, *Reading and Writing: Literacy in France from Calvin to Jules Ferry* (Cambridge, 1982), pp. 316–17.
143. Crane, *Framing Authority*, p. 198. This adds to a sense that seventeenth-century culture was more engaged with religious issues than was that of the sixteenth century.
144. Ibid., p. 162; Moss, *Printed Commonplace Books*, ch. 9.
145. Potter, *Secret Rites*, p. 115.
146. Ibid., p. 136.

structured his experience, his Royalist commitments, as he chose what to include and as he mingled extracts with personal and domestic material. The commonplace had for him become the source of personal commitment in a contested world. Always a mediation between the common and the individual, past and present, public and private, the commonplace book was fundamentally altered by political change.

Blount and Gibson remind us that the act of keeping a commonplace book was neither cut off from other social practices, nor private in any simple sense. The printed commonplace books, of course, which were public and published, both influenced and were influenced by personal and manuscript collections, in a way that makes drawing a clear differentiation between print and manuscript problematic.[147] Moreover, though 'originally designed for notes from reading, the commonplace book easily accommodated material from non bookish sources.'[148] As Erasmus made clear in De Copia, commonplace books were intended to marshal rhetorical arguments and topics for conversation, and conversations in turn re-entered the pages of the commonplace book along with the other annotations of domestic and social experience: family dates of birth, encounters with friends, the record of exceptional events.[149] Commonplace books were also read, and reread, albeit most commonly by the keeper, who returned, as it were, from a different outside world to the text with each rereading. As was said of Francis North, 'looking over' his commonplace books 'on any occasion gave him a sort of survey of what he had read about matters not then inquisited'.[150] Far from a retreat into private space, the commonplace book is the site of successive conversations between text and reader, between readers and society.

Indeed we might usefully think of commonplace books in the context of Stanley Fish's model for a study of reading, the idea of interpretive communities. 'It is interpretive communities', Fish argued in influential essays and a book, 'rather than either the text or the reader that produce meanings.'[151] As we applied the thesis to early modern England, the reading circles that grew up around court factions and figures like Sir Philip Sidney or Sir Walter Ralegh came to mind, as do gatherings of puritans to hear or discuss a sermon, or less godly folk in an alehouse to sing a ballad.[152] Fish argued that

---

147. A. Moss, 'Printed Commonplace Books in the Renaissance', *J. Inst. Romance Studies* 2 (1993), pp. 203–14; Moss, *Printed Commonplace Books*, passim.

148. Blair, 'Humanist Methods', p. 547.

149. Erasmus, *De Copia* in *Collected Works of Erasmus*, ed. C. R. Thompson, vol. 24 (Toronto, 1978), esp. pp. 605–6, 635–48.

150. Love, *Scribal Publication*, p. 223.

151. S. Fish, *Is There a Text in this Class? The Authority of Interpretive Communities* (Cambridge, Mass., 1980), p. 14.

152. See M. Tribble, *Margins and Marginality: The Printed Page in Early Modern England* (Charlottesville, 1993), p. 72; J. E. Phillips, 'George Buchanan and the Sidney Circle', *Hunt. Lib. Quart.* 12 (1948), pp. 23–56; M. C. Bradbrook, *The School of Night: A Study in the Literary Relationships of Sir Walter Raleigh* (Cambridge, 1936); J. Shapiro, 'The

interpretive communities were also made up of those who shared strategies for writing texts. And in an important development, Harold Love has extended that notion to scribal texts, to open up 'the idea of a group or network in which manuscripts circulate'.[153] Among early seventeenth-century antiquaries and scholars, Sir Robert Cotton and Sir Simonds D'Ewes for example, we know that manuscripts were lent, exchanged and copied.[154] We know too from commonplace books that poems and other manuscript texts, libels or letters for example, circulated.[155] Love argues persuasively that such circulations 'helped to confirm friendships', and in some cases led to the 'bonding groups of like-minded individuals into a community, sect or political faction with the exchange of text in manuscript seeming to nourish a set of shared values'.[156] Extracting manuscripts that circulated among a small group, and recording the reflections of others as well as the authors, commonplace books may give us some insight into how small groups of educated men and women formed not only personal judgements but communities of friends: associates who read not only books but even their world in a similar way.

Because they are many and full, Drake's notebooks may help us to develop and refine our understanding of the importance of commonplace books in early modern culture. In many respects he is conventional enough: Erasmus, Vives and Bacon appear to be the major influences on his 'commonplacing'; but, as we have seen, personal reminders, often on the flyleaves of books, indicate that Drake moved across his texts with a very personal agenda. While the headings he sets up are often familiar, 'Eloquentia', 'Beneficiam', Drake is also fond of topics such as 'dissimulation', or 'artifice' that were unconventional in this genre. And while the usual sources of moral precepts are annotated, we have seen that Drake read them alongside the advocates of realpolitik, Tacitus and Machiavelli, whose ideas impart their force to the whole. Certainly in Drake's hands, the commonplace book is no exercise in learning Christian morality. The language of virtue and vice is absent from his pages, as actions are weighed according to prudence, a quality largely measured by the criterion of success. Drake's bricolage of annotations from his reading was a very personal script, penned for his use as a manual for living in a self-interested and competitive world. But as the record of books borrowed and discussions of men and events make clear, Drake was part of a community of men reading and reflecting on events, many of whom

Mermaid Club', *Mod. Lang. Rev.* 45 (1950), pp. 6–17; A. Marotti, *Manuscript, Print and the English Renaissance* (Ithaca, 1995).

153. Love, *Scribal Publication*, p. 52.

154. K. Sharpe, *Sir Robert Cotton: History and Politics in Early Modern England* (Oxford, 1979), chs 3, 6; R. J. Fehrenbach and E. S. Leedham-Green, eds, *Private Libraries in Renaissance England*, vol. 1 (Marlborough, 1992), p. 139.

155. See Marotti, *Manuscript, Print*, passim; and for the case of John Rous see below, pp. 296–7.

156. Love, *Scribal Publication*, p. 177.

shared his admiration for particular writers and therefore no doubt aspects of his worldview.[157] In all these respects, Drake appears far removed from the figure imagined by the educationalists and moralists who advocated the gathering of commonplaces. He compels us to rethink the distance between the theory or prescription and the practice when it came to reading, and the room that even the authorised educational practice, commonplacing, a device for uniform thought and social cohesion, left for not only personal idiosyncracy and judgement but also for radical politics.[158] To perceive more clearly the freedom that such prescribed educational and cultural practices left to readers and writers, and to appreciate the radicalism of Drake's politics, we may fruitfully turn to other early modern commonplace annotators and readers about whom we have some knowledge.

In a fascinating study of 'les journaux privés', a term that embraces both diaries proper and some commonplace books, Elizabeth Boucier examined over seventy journals in print and manuscript as evidence of political, religious and social history, documents of the self, and, most interestingly for our purposes, evidence of reading.[159] Most of those who kept diaries or commonplace books, she discovered, were avid readers. They bought books locally, and where necessary travelled to London to obtain them, putting money aside for a trip to a bookshop.[160] Borrowing was common, and reciprocally even a fairly modest farmer like Adam Eyre lent books, keeping a record of loans so as to preserve his collection.[161] The classics were predictably widely read and so familiar to some that they knew them by heart: Roger Manningham, for example, records his cousin reciting the *Aeneid* in 1635.[162] Histories too were popular, notably the classical histories of Pliny, Livy and Sallust, and among the moderns, Holinshed, Comines, Camden and Justus Lipsius, Speed and Ralegh. Books of chivalry, romances, newsbooks and ballads were all annotated, even by serious scholars like Sir Simonds D'Ewes, though Boucier found little evidence of reading plays.[163] Above all, the Bible and religious writings predominate in the notebooks. The diarists had eclectic tastes in their reading of religious works: Latin and French Bibles and editions from Douai are found alongside the Authorised Version or Geneva Bible.[164] Adam Winthrop, one of the family that emigrated to Massachusetts, read Spanish mystical theology.[165] Godly ministers such as Ralph Joscelyn acquired Catholic

---

157. Cf. E. Long, 'Textual Interpretation as Collective Action', in J. Boyarin, ed., *The Ethnography of Reading* (Berkeley, 1992), pp. 181–94.

158. For an example of a recent study that places too much emphasis on prescriptive writings or reading, see E. R. Kintgen, *Reading in Tudor England* (Pittsburgh, 1996).

159. Boucier, *Les Journaux privés*.

160. Ibid., pp. 277–9, and ch. 5 passim.

161. Ibid., p. 278.

162. Ibid., p. 285.

163. Ibid., pp. 284–6.

164. Ibid., p. 279.

165. Ibid., p. 281.

theology, even praising a work by Bellarmine on raising the spirit closer to God as a 'pretty discourse'.[166]

As Boucier discovered, reading was neither idle nor recreational: 'Ce qui frappe chez les diaristes c'est leur sérieux du moins en matière de livres, leur désir de s'améliorer et de s'instruire.'[167] In line with the conventional teaching of Erasmus, the diarists appear to have believed that reading led them to wisdom and virtue – and to God. While we are familiar with the soul-searching and spiritual self-examination of the puritan diarist, Boucier found most journal keepers, whatever their religious sympathies, preoccupied with the hereafter.[168] The Anglican Lady Mordaunt organised her notebooks under columns of prayers 'to return thanks for', 'to ask pardon for'.[169] In the context of this research, the absence of any reference to prayer or the fate of his own soul in Drake's commonplace books is striking.[170]

But if the values and ends of the diarists were conventional, they were by no means unthinking or uncritical disciples of authority. Those, laity included, who were well read in religious controversies were able to weigh contemporary disputes; more generally questioning our stereotypes about the ignorant provincial squire, Adam Eyre claimed that reading made him acquainted on his farm with all the variety of human opinions.[171] Moreover, the diarists not only borrowed but discussed books, and, though often silent about the events of the Civil War, also exchanged political news and gossip. Their sympathies cover the spectrum from ardent royalist to republican. Given that the diarists read a large number of books in common, we can only deduce that it was the influence of those books that differed in each case. The edition of Sir John Newdigate's notebooks poses the crucial question: given that 'the influences to which he was exposed were available to a large number of his literate contemporaries, why not therefore the potent sense of social and political responsibilities which they engendered in him'?[172] In large part the question directs us from what was read to how people read. We have glimpses in many of the diaries about how material extracted and copied was organised, how different hands sometimes distinguished different subjects. But in

166. Ibid.
167. Ibid., p. 289.
168. William Prynne described 'an exact diary' as 'a window into the heart that maketh it', ibid., p. 350.
169. Ibid., p. 368.
170. Cf. above, p. 139. The best parallel is Sir Thomas Mainwaring's diary (Boucier, *Les Journaux privés*, p. 57).
171. H. O. Morehouse, *The Diurnall of Adam Eyre, 1646–1649*, in *Yorkshire Diaries*, Surtees Society 65 (Durham, 1875), p. 8. Cf. J. S. Morrill, 'William Davenport and the "Silent Majority" of Early Stuart England', *J. Chester Arch. Soc.* 58 (1974), pp. 115–30, which exaggerates provincial isolation. A study of reading compels a reconsideration of the political consciousness of the provincial squire.
172. V. Larminie, ed., *The Godly Magistrate: The Private Philosophy and Public Life of Sir John Newdigate, 1571–1610*, Dugdale Society (Oxford, 1982), p. 19, cf. pp. 10–11; and Larminie, *Wealth, Kinship and Culture; The Seventeenth-Century Newdigates of Arbury and their World* (Woodbridge, 1992).

most cases we know too little about how reading shaped the diarists' perceptions, about how they studied or read. We need therefore to turn to richer examples of readers who have left traces not only of what they read, but of the process of their encounters with books and the relationship of their reading to their worldview.

Where literary figures are concerned, long before the history of reading became an established field of enquiry, critics investigated their negotiations with other books under the concept of 'influence'. To take the most obvious case, almost every scholarly edition of Shakespeare contains a discussion of the sources of Shakespeare's plays and the dramatist's reworking of chronicle or classical text. And in a study written over fifty years ago (yet curiously neglected by historians) T. W. Baldwin set out to trace Shakespeare's education and reading and to assess the influence of school and books on his plays.[173] Baldwin analysed the Tudor grammar school curriculum, stressing the tendency over the sixteenth century for the system to 'harden into uniformity', as the cathedral schools and Edwardian foundations aped Canterbury, Eton and Winchester.[174] He argued for Shakespeare pursuing a course that included Cicero and Quintilian, Virgil and Horace, Caesar and Livy, Mantuan and Erasmus. Following such a course led the playwright, Baldwin maintained, to proverbs and sententiae 'typical of the Christian view of his age', and, in his Bible reading, to 'conventional patterns' of belief.[175] And yet, for all Shakespeare's reading was familiar enough, Baldwin was led to conclude, what any reading of the plays bears out, 'that Shakespeare had usually taken from those authors things which are inevitably characteristic of himself rather than of them'.[176] Baldwin's study is in danger of being circular: because we neither have evidence that Shakespeare attended grammar school, nor any commonplace notes of his readings, his writings are here studied as both the sources and product of his reading. Nevertheless both in detail (the brilliant examination of his use of Aesop)[177] and generally, Baldwin lays out important information concerning how Shakespeare's dramatic genius was both based in the standard texts of his day and on a highly individual imagination that not only re-presented but often interrogated conventional wisdom.[178]

In the case of Shakespeare's contemporary and rival we have vastly more information about what and how he read – not least because he also chose to display his learning. For Ben Jonson, in fact, we have a list of his library, copies of classical texts annotated by him, and what amounts to one of what

173. T. W. Baldwin, *William Shakespeare's Petty School* (Urbana, 1943); Baldwin, *William Shakespeare's Small Latin and Lesse Greek* (2 vols, Urbana, 1944). These volumes contain valuable material on the reading of Edward VI, Elizabeth I and James I.

174. Baldwin, *Shakespeare's Small Latin*, vol. 1, pp. 164, 179; Kintgen talks of a method of reading that was 'monolithic', *Reading in Tudor England*, p. 99.

175. Baldwin, *Shakespeares's Small Latin*, vol. 2, pp. 616, 647.

176. Ibid., vol. 2, p. 678.

177. Ibid., vol. 1, ch. 27.

178. Ibid., vol. 2, pp. 377, 673.

were probably numerous commonplace books, his *Timber or Discoveries*, as well as Jonson's published works, themselves heavily annotated with authorities and the sources of his learning.[179] Scholars are beginning to piece together Jonson's library, aided by his habit of signing books or marking them with his motto 'tanquam explorator': though chance findings are never likely to present us with the full picture, and we will never know what printed books as well as manuscripts were consumed by the fire that broke out in his study in 1623.[180] What are invaluable are the copies of Jonson's texts found with his markings and marginal notes. In Jonson's copy of Chaucer, underlinings and marginalia reveal a close reader who responded to passages that most accorded with his values.[181] To take another example, a recent study of Jonson's copy of Seneca has revealed the expected pattern of markings to note summary arguments, memorable phrases and sound counsel. But more revealing is the flagging of passages in the text on the public responsibilities of the scholar, the rewards of heroism and immortality for the writer, the ideal qualities of kings and the celebration of liberty.[182] For all the difficulties in interpreting what lay behind marginal marks (difficulties exacerbated by the possible presence of another annotator), as R. C. Evans has argued, 'the markings provide new data about his [Jonson's] responsiveness to the Roman frame of mind.'[183] They offer an insight into how Jonson interpreted from the large and ambiguous corpus of the classics 'Roman values' and translated them for his own time – and purpose.

In *Timber*, we encounter another stage of that interpretation and translation, as Jonson takes into his notebooks extracts from Plato and Seneca, Cicero, Perseus and Plotinus to formulate his views on nature, virtue, the art of poetry and the nature of government. Jonson subtitled *Timber* 'Discoveries Made upon Men and Matter as they Have Flowed out of His Daily Readings, or Had their Refluxe to his Peculiar Notion of the Times', a title that announces the drive of the present in selecting what to extract from the past.[184] And for all his proclamations of imitating the classics, Jonson

179. See *Timber: Or Discoveries*, in *Ben Jonson*, ed. C. H. Herford and P. Simpson (11 vols, Oxford, 1925–52), vol. 8, pp. 557–649.
180. See D. C. McPherson, 'Ben Jonson's Library and Marginalia: An Annotated Catalogue', *Studies in Philology* 71 (1974), pp. 1–106; for the fire and some hints of what Jonson lost see 'Execration upon Vulcan', in *Ben Jonson*, ed. Herford and Simpson, vol. 8, pp. 202–12.
181. R. C. Evans, 'Ben Jonson's Chaucer', *Eng. Lit. Ren.* 19 (1989), pp. 324–45; see too Evans, 'Ben Jonson Reads *Daphnis and Chloe*', *Eng. Lang. Notes* 27 (1990), pp. 28–32; and Evans, *Habits of Mind: Evidence and Effects of Ben Jonson's Reading* (Lewisburg, 1995).
182. R. C. Evans, 'Jonson's Copy of Seneca', *Comparative Drama* 25 (1991), pp. 257–92; cf. Evans, 'Ben Jonson's Library and Marginalia: New Evidence from the Folger Collection', *Philol. Quart.* 66 (1987), pp. 521–8; Evans, *Habits of Mind*, ch. 2, cf. ch. 5.
183. Evans, 'Jonson's Copy of Seneca', p. 290.
184. *Timber*, passim. See esp. pp. 591–2. Curiously, *Timber* awaits a full critical exegesis as a dialogue between Jonson's reading and contemporary values. Though he read several of the same texts as Drake, their values could hardly have been more different.

rewrote his classical sources to address contemporary issues and questions. Accordingly the tragedy *Catiline His Conspiracy*, written in 1611, takes the story of the planned assassination of Cicero to point up parallels to the Powder Plot.[185] More generally, as David Riggs has persuasively argued, Jonson represents Cicero not as the epitome of humanist ideals, but as an unrelenting pragmatist, a figure at home in the world of realpolitik.[186] This is a reworking both of classical legacy and humanist readings, and, of course, an accommodation with Machiavellian politics.

Earlier, in *Sejanus*, Jonson had taken on the overtly political subject: the suppression of liberty under the tyrannical regime of the Emperor Tiberius and his favourite Lucius Aelius Sejanus. As well as his core source in Tacitus, Jonson 'wove literally hundreds of allusions to . . . Suetonius, Dion Cassius, Pliny, Juvenal and Seneca into the text of *Sejanus*, and he inserted citations to nearly all of them on the margins of the 1605 quarto'.[187] The references appear to claim a simple rehearsal of classical text, and discourage another notion of authorial interpretation or application. Indeed Jonson directly stated that his marginal notes were 'forty fold proof', cited 'to show my integrity in the story, and save myself from those common torturers that bring all wit to the rack'.[188] It was an understandable claim from a man who had two years earlier been imprisoned awaiting punishment of mutilation for indiscreet passages in his play *Eastward Ho!* But it was disingenuous. For all the accuracy of detail, in several senses Jonson's 'integrity', that is his whole self, was 'in the story'. David Riggs has suggested that on a psychological level Tiberius' favouring of patronage over parentage spoke to Jonson at a time when he deserted his own family.[189] And recently Blair Worden has argued persuasively that Jonson took the story of Tiberius and Sejanus to articulate very personal and topical concerns: about excessive authority, court corruption, the decline of aristocratic virtue, the constraints on writers. To point up those concerns, Jonson both ventriloquised and reworked his classical sources: 'Where the evils of Jonson's time correspond to those in Tacitus, *Sejanus His Fall* follows Tacitus. Where they do not, Jonson adjusts Tacitus or adds to him.'[190]

In Ben Jonson, we have perhaps the best example – and he is yet to be studied fully as such – of a reading of the classics in early Stuart England: an example of how classical sources gave language and shape to contemporary values and were simultaneously reread in the light of them.[191] Jonson

185. *Catiline*, in *Ben Jonson*, ed. Herford and Simpson, vol. 5, pp. 409–549; cf. B. Worden, 'Ben Jonson among the Historians', in K. Sharpe and P. Lake, eds, *Culture and Politics in Early Stuart England* (Houndmills, 1994), pp. 67–90.

186. D. Riggs, *Ben Jonson: A Life* (Cambridge, Mass., 1989), p. 177.

187. Ibid., p. 102. See *Sejanus His Fall*, in *Ben Jonson*, ed. Herford and Simpson, vol. 4, pp. 329–485.

188. Worden, 'Ben Jonson', p. 79.

189. Riggs, *Ben Jonson*, p. 102.

190. Worden , 'Ben Jonson', p. 85.

191. See D. Norbrook, 'Lucan, Thomas May, and the Creation of a Republican Literary

dramatised and published that dialogue, and, while claiming to foreclose topical readings, clearly expected and desired that his contemporaries would perform them. The commonplace books of Sir William Drake (with, we recall, extensive notes from *Sejanus*) not only reveal that such expectations and hopes were not misplaced; they provide clear evidence that, away from the stage, other readers of the classics brought their 'integrity', their self and moment, to those texts and reread them as a commentary on their own society and state.[192]

Ben Jonson rose to the height of a dramatist's career, devising the court masques for the king and queen from James I's accession to the early 1630s. We might then expect his literary works, indeed his imagination, to be engaged with politics and power. Another early modern literary figure, whose 'reading' has recently been studied, was far removed from that world. George Herbert, the incumbent of Bemerton, Wiltshire, appears the archetype of the rural clergyman. One of his most famous works, *The Country Parson*, proclaims that identity. And yet a recent study entitled *Prayer and Power* conjoins, as its subtitle has it, 'George Herbert and Renaissance Courtship'.[193] Michael Schoenfeldt's brilliant study is not specifically a book about Herbert's reading. But Schoenfeldt argues powerfully for Herbert not only refiguring Scripture for himself but translating Holy Writ into the language of his social experience: the discourse of patronage and courtesy. Herbert's devotional poetry, like all devotional verse, is a personalising, a rewriting of scriptural text. Individual poems and lines become virtual exegesis of biblical text, 'Sinnes round', for example, developing Isaiah 59: 5.[194] But, as with Jonson's reworking of his classical texts, Herbert was willing to wrench and even subvert what seem to be the most obvious interpretations of biblical verse in his quest for his own personal faith and values. He takes the biblical injunction against hewn stone (Exodus 20: 25) as an 'occasion for investigating the problems of composing devotional poetry'; 'Joseph's coat' presents God not as the paternal lover of his children but as the unpredictable and incomprehensible force he appeared to Herbert's troubled psyche.[195] More strikingly in a rendering of Job 1:21, 'God is not "blessed" but accused as an afflictor of mankind, as Herbert agonises over his own relationship with the Almighty.'[196]

In Herbert's verse Scripture is not only recast by personal spiritual struggle and psychology; Schoenfeldt's central thesis is that Herbert prays in the language of feudal relations and courtesy literature. The poet views God

---

Culture', in Sharpe and Lake, *Culture and Politics*, pp. 45–66; and now see Norbrook, *Writing the English Republic: Poetry, Rhetoric and Politics 1627–1660* (Cambridge, 1999).

192. Folger MS ff. 15–21; above, p. 259.

193. M. C. Schoenfeldt, *Prayer and Power: George Herbert and Renaissance Courtship* (Chicago, 1991). For my review see 'Religion, Rhetoric and Revolution in Seventeenth Century England', *Hunt. Lib. Quart.* 57 (1994), pp. 269–71.

194. Schoenfeldt, *Prayer and Power*, p. 242.

195. Ibid., pp. 118, 163.

196. Ibid., p. 145.

as a feudal overlord, the eucharist as a feast at the (land)lord's table, the relationship of sinner with God as that of a subject prostrate before the power and violence of sovereign authority. Through the deployment of prevailing social idiom, Scripture is made contemporary and local: literally in a breathtaking comparison between the man who sought mediation to God and he who lived at Windsor but went to London Bridge for his water.[197] The reverse is also the case. As Scripture is read through social experience and discourse, so it becomes a social and political text through which feudal discourse and relations can be reread and interrogated. In Herbert the blend of courtesy books and manuals of devotion opens the space for social and political criticism, as Christ's injunction to humility is read alongside prescriptions of social hierarchy. Herbert can deploy the language of courtesy itself to critique the authorities it legitimises. In the end *The Temple* and *Country Parson* pass beyond personal devotion and rural retreat to criticisms of the Renaissance court and its structures of power.[198]

Both Jonson and Herbert point up the ways in which texts that possessed authority were read, appropriated and interpreted in early modern England. They also remind us of the differences between the classics and Scripture, and the variant ways of reading promoted by humanism and biblical hermeneutics. For many early modern Englishmen it was those tensions and differences, the textual and interpretive dissonance that Erasmus and his disciples endeavoured to erase through a Christian humanism, that facilitated, or even compelled, personal interpretation and judgement. To put it another way, in constructing meaning for himself, each reader had to work out the relation between pagan and Christian texts and their different modes of exegesis.

The fourth of our literary readers, John Milton, presents an excellent case study in the reading of secular and sacred texts in early modern England. We do not have Milton's library, or books annotated by him. But we do have his commonplace book, though it remains curiously neglected even by a study of Milton as a 'revolutionary reader'.[199] The manuscript commonplace book originally contained 126 leaves paginated to page 250, some of which have been torn or cut away. Some entries are in hands of amanuenses. However, the holograph table indicates that nothing Milton singled out to index is lost and that the principal entries were written or selected by him.[200] The organisation of the notebook is interesting. Milton returns to subjects – 'Rex' for example – on different pages, suggesting that space was not left, and that the book was composed over time.[201] Indeed the headings reveal how Milton

197. Ibid., p. 69.
198. Ibid., part 2.
199. *Milton's Commonplace Book*, ed. J. H. Hanford in *The Works of John Milton*, vol. 18 (New York, 1938), pp. 128–227; S. Achinstein, *Milton and the Revolutionary Reader* (Princeton, 1994).
200. *Works of Milton*, vol. 18, pp. 505–6.
201. *Milton's Commonplace Book*, pp. 173, 196.

began to structure his reading and experience, and may suggest how changing circumstances influenced his thinking.[202] What strikes us about the notebook is the range and type of texts extracted. Surprisingly there are almost no references to Scripture – though it may well be that Milton kept a separate notebook for this purpose. We do find extracts from the Fathers – Basil, Chrysostom, Cyprian and Constantine[203] – and from ecclesiastical histories – Bede, Theodoritus and Eusebius.[204] However, by far the majority of works cited and annotated is secular literature: classical texts – Tertullian, Lactantius, Aristotle and Tacitus;[205] poetry – Chaucer, Sidney, Dante and Tasso;[206] chronicle – Holinshed, Malmesbury, Asser, Stow and Paris;[207] and in particular history – Camden, De Thou, Speed, Girard, Du Chesne and Comines.[208]

But still more important than the notes on what Milton read is his organisation of very different – sacred and pagan, 'conservative' and 'radical' – texts under his chosen headings. Under the topic of 'marriage', for example, Milton copies extracts from Eusebius, Cyprian and Justin Martyr, together with Chaucer, Selden and, as he moves to ponder dynastic marriage, Camden and Girard, historian of France.[209] Under 'Rex', along with references to Sigonius, Severus Sulpicius and Justinian, we find passages from Holinshed and Sir Thomas Smith, author of *De Republica Anglorum*, Dante, Guicciardini and Machiavelli.[210]

Milton assembled an eclectic range of texts and passages as he reflected on politics and political developments in the later pages of his notebooks. Under the topics of 'Rex', 'Different Forms of Government', 'Property and Taxes', 'Civil War', 'Sedition' and 'Tyrant', Milton brought together his reading in sacred history, chronicle, law, Roman history, English history from Saxon times to the reign of James I, and the recent history of France and Italy into a set of political ideas that move from limited kingship to the advocacy of republic. Milton's selection from his texts was very much his own. He had read Bodin's *Republic* – but significantly he cites it not under any of his political headings but with reference to Bodin's views on divorce.[211] He excerpts from Sir Thomas Smith sentences not about the prerogatives and power but the duties of kings and the rights of subjects to resist them.[212] Comines may have been the intimate of Louis XI, one of the most Machiavellian of princes, yet Milton cites him to reinforce the limited powers of kings to tax their sub-

202. Most obviously, note the heading 'De Bello Civili', ibid., p. 212.
203. Ibid., pp. 139, 148, 138, 161.
204. Ibid., pp. 139, 136, 146, 163.
205. Ibid., pp. 128, 134, 164, 165, 177, 180.
206. Ibid., pp. 151, 161, 133, 195, 192.
207. Ibid., pp. 132, 135, 144, 152, 143, 148.
208. Ibid., pp. 203, 130, 163, 171, 133, 137, 152, 156, 157, 140, 155, 150.
209. Ibid., pp. 147–52; Milton cross-references: 'vide de Divortio.'
210. Ibid., pp. 173–7.
211. Ibid., pp. 136, 156.
212. Ibid., pp. 175, 182.

jects.[213] Reflecting on 'The King of England', Milton marshals ecclesiastical history to show that even the King of the Hebrews was not exempt from the law,[214] and cites Buchanan's *History of Scotland* and Jean Hotman's *Franco Gallia*, two of the most radical Calvinist treatises of the sixteenth century, to support the right to elect and depose princes.[215]

Most interesting of all, in the context of our study of Sir William Drake, is Milton's extensive reading and citation of Machiavelli. Not, however, the Machiavelli of *The Prince*. Rather, from the *Art of War* Milton takes the adage that 'well constituted kingdoms do not give absolute power to their rulers.'[216] And he quotes the Florentine's claim that 'a commonwealth is to be preferred to a monarchy . . . because in the former virtue is honoured while in the latter it is feared.'[217] The *Discorsi* provides him with the argument – perhaps one needed at the moment he took his notes – that 'Against a bad ruler there is no remedy but the sword.'[218] Finally the discourses on Livy lent weight to the view that 'it is often of advantage to bring back a republican form to the actual beginnings of government . . . by restoring the full control of affairs to the will of the people.'[219] Though Milton cites few classical histories, Machiavelli and Guicciardini led him back to an understanding of the lesson of Roman history: that mature people 'were ripe for a more free government' than a 'lordly and dreadful monarchy' that reduced citizens to slaves.[220]

Milton read himself into a republican. His reading 'freed him from the conceptual limitations of contemporary political debate', a debate still focused on English law and history in which no models of republic were found.[221] Moreover, Milton recognised the radical politics of his own reading and the need to refashion the reader in order to secure revolution and republic. He understood, what is our whole argument, that ways of reading were implicated with the exercise of power. As Sharon Achinstein, Tom Corns, Elizabeth Skerpan and Steve Zwicker have argued, Milton endeavoured in his own works to educate the reader to become a participant in politics, a critic of polemic, and a judge.[222] Accordingly in *Areopagitica*, he set out 'his theory of capable

213. Ibid., p. 202.
214. Ibid,. p. 182.
215. Ibid., pp. 186, 200.
216. Ibid., p. 177.
217. Ibid., p. 164; cf. Drake above, p. 221.
218. Ibid., p. 183 citing *Discorsi*, Book 1, ch. 58.
219. Ibid., p. 200, cf. p. 217.
220. Ibid., p. 163. Milton offers a starkly different emphasis to Drake's in his reading of Machiavelli.
221. See B. Worden, 'Milton's Republicanism and the Tyranny of Heaven', in G. Bock, Q. Skinner and M. Viroli, eds, *Machiavelli and Republicanism* (Cambridge, 1990), p. 231. Milton himself wrote in *The History of Britain* of the need for civil virtues to be 'imported into our minds from foreign writings'. See K. Sharpe, '"An Image Doting Rabble": The Failure of Republican Culture in Seventeenth Century England', in Sharpe and Zwicker, *Refiguring Revolutions*, p. 30 and pp. 25–56 passim.
222. Achinstein, *Milton*; T. Corns, *Uncloistered Virtue: English Political Literature 1640–1660*

readers who were to exercise their choice'.[223] During the 1640s, he strove to constitute a new subject, capable of reading and resisting the blandishments of royal propaganda. Most dramatically, in 1649, in *Eikonoklastes*, Milton tried to wrench open to reading and to readers the brilliant propaganda of the king's last testament, the *Eikon Basilike*. To Milton reading *was* politics: a process of demystifying royal authority that was constituted both through royal words and silent royal spectacles; an opening of arcana imperii to critical public scrutiny and debate. No less than his Royalist enemies, of course, Milton expected and desired that, once they had learned to read, readers would share his interpretation and so follow him on the road to republic. No less than the *Eikon Basilike*, his treatise against the king's book is deeply and cleverly polemical, directing the reader at the very moment it calls upon him to exercise his freedom.[224] But in his argument for the reader's own judgement – 'in words which admit of various sense that liberty is ours to choose that interpretation' – Milton politicised reading and democratised the reader and, for all the defeat of his cause, created a new political consciousness.[225] During the 1640s, it is argued, the readers of revolution were reconstructed as revolutionary readers and so as self-conscious political actors.[226]

While the argument is excitingly suggestive in outline, it must be qualified. While for most the experience of civil war, pamphlet debate, and charge and countercharge opened up a new space for reading, and the exercise of personal judgement and political consciousness, Milton's own ideas were formed more by classical and foreign texts than by English broadsides or polemical treatises. The case of Sir William Drake makes it clear that he was by no means unique. Long before civil war broke out in England, men like Drake and Milton, from their very different perspectives (and that is the point), were formulating values and political ideas from their personal synthesis of classical texts, commentaries, histories and – as vital – experience and observation. That Shakespeare, Jonson and Herbert, for all their criticism of kings and courts, remained conservative in their views while Milton became an architect of revolution may be explained by changed times. It may, however, also be a powerful testament to the ability of each reader, especially those educated readers who were also writers, to exercise 'that liberty . . . to choose . . . interpretation' that they all, no less than Milton, cherished.

Milton's commonplace book (like Jonson's *Timber*) awaits full study as a document of reading: study of how he extracted passages, and how they fash-

(Oxford, 1992), ch. 6; E. Skerpan, *The Rhetoric of Politics in the English Revolution* (Columbia, Miss., 1992), ch. 5; S. Zwicker, *Lines of Authority: Politics and English Literary Culture, 1649–1689* (Ithaca, 1993), ch. 2.
223. Achinstein, *Milton*, p. 124.
224. Cf. ibid., pp. 66, 155.
225. Milton, *Eikonoklastes*, ed. W. H. Haller, in *The Works of John Milton*, vol. 5 (New York, 1932), p. 68.
226. Achinstein, *Milton*, passim.

ioned his own writings and thought. Poets and dramatists, though clearly engaged with contemporary issues, we often regard as exceptional figures in the history of reading, people with a special sensitivity to language and form, to rhetoric and genre, who read texts differently, more responsively than less 'creative minds'. Whether this is the case or a post-Romantic reconstruction of the 'writer' is too complex a matter to discuss here. What is apparent is that during the Renaissance the generic distinctions between writers – poets, historians, dramatists – were far less rigid than our own. Different reading practices therefore probably owed little to 'disciplines' (an inappropriately anachronistic concept), and more to the individuals' ends and goals and the circumstances of their reading.

Fortunately scholars have begun to investigate the reading of a few other important early modern figures, and a wealth of material, some untouched, remains for others. Recently the Elizabethan magus, astrologer, scientist and antiquary John Dee has been the subject of a case study in 'the politics of reading and writing in the English Renaissance'.[227] Dee, who amassed a very large library of some three to four thousand volumes, may appear the epitome of the bibliophile scholar, devoted to the *vita contemplativa*. But in reality Dee read, and organised his library and reading, for use, and for participation in public life. As well as his large collection at Mortlake, Dee had a travelling library, which served like a laptop computer to this busy man on the move.[228] Dee marked up the books themselves with symbols and pictures which facilitated easy return to subjects, as well as marginalia. As Bill Sherman has argued, he read closely and to an end: 'Dee's marginalia in books of ancient history were highly selective and indicate not a general reading but a systematic plundering of particular precedents.'[229] Knowledge for Dee was a political commodity, and he deployed his own stock in writings arguing for ship money and jurisdiction over Scotland for Queen Elizabeth.[230] Dee, argue Lisa Jardine and Bill Sherman, was a 'pragmatic reader', one of those active scholars in early modern England who parlayed their knowledge of books into political service and influence.[231]

Perhaps the best example of this breed is Gabriel Harvey, Doctor of Civil Law and Fellow of Trinity Hall Cambridge, who became the Earl of Leicester's secretary in 1580. Harvey, a friend of Spenser, wrote educational treatises and popular pamphlets. He collected a sizeable library of nearly two hundred volumes, many of which bear his marginal annotations. Harvey's marginalia first attracted scholarly interest over eighty years ago when, obviously drawn by the fact that he was Shakespeare's contemporary, G. C. Moore Smith

227. Sherman, *John Dee*.
228. Ibid., pp. 31, 41.
229. Ibid., p. 94.
230. Ibid., pp. 158–9, 193–7.
231. L. Jardine and W. Sherman, 'Pragmatic Readers: Knowledge Transactions and Scholarly Services in Late Elizabethan England', in A. Fletcher and P. Roberts, eds, *Religion, Culture and Society in Early Modern Britain* (Cambridge, 1994), pp. 102–24.

published an edition of the annotations.[232] In 1979 a biographer, bringing the library and marginalia into a larger study of the man, re-examined Harvey's notes for the attitudes and values they disclosed. V. F. Stern found that Harvey's habits of recording marginalia remained amazingly constant over a span of at least forty years, but that his personality and attitudes changed.[233] Harvey reread his books, sometimes signing and dating each reading, and he reread his own earlier notes, the traces of earlier readings.[234] His marginalia signalled points he wanted to commit to memory, intimate reflections (on the duplicity of women and the folly of love, for instance) and self-counsel.[235] They express his admiration for Livy, Guicciardini and Machiavelli, and for those he considered astute politicians, Wolsey and Cromwell, Gardiner and Cecil.[236] Revealingly in his copy of Guicciardini's *History* he wrote: 'It is not books that make the skilful man but the knowledge of books and the memory of knowledge and the practice of memory both in words and in deeds. He deserves to be esteemed the most cunning man that can best negotiate his learning viva voce e viva opere.'[237] Harvey in other words read 'to negotiate his learning', to deploy it for his advancement and influence at court.

His biographer in 1979 did not examine precisely how he effected that negotiation, how, at his desk, surrounded by his books, he 'studied for action'. Such an examination awaited the questions and approaches only later formulated by theorists and critics of reading and historians of the book. Accordingly, in 1990, in the locus classicus of those new approaches, the leading scholars of Renaissance humanism, Anthony Grafton and Lisa Jardine, undertook close investigation of how Harvey studied for action through analysis of his readings of the 1555 Basle edition of Titus Livy's *Romanae Historiae Principis, Decades Tres.*[238] Harvey's notes span the period 1568–90. He records the time he spent on passages, the books he read alongside the text, those with whom he discussed them, the meanings extracted and lessons learned, and his doubts about or disagreements with episodes of Livy's history.[239] Each reading, Grafton and Jardine demonstrated, was conducted for a particular person and for a specific purpose – Colonel Thomas Smith's expedition to Ireland in 1571, a diplomatic embassy by 'Dr. Dale' in 1584, or Harvey's own career as

---

232. G. C. Moore Smith, *Gabriel Harvey's Marginalia* (Stratford, 1913). See too H. S. Wilson, 'Gabriel Harvey's Method of Annotating his Books', *Harvard Lib. Bull.* 2 (1948), pp. 344–65.
233. Stern, *Gabriel Harvey*, p. 137.
234. Ibid., pp. 139, 190.
235. Ibid., p. 189.
236. Ibid., pp. 152, 154, 190.
237. Ibid., p. 190.
238. Grafton and Jardine, '"Studied for Action"'. See too A. Grafton, 'Discitur ut Agitur: How Gabriel Harvey Read his Livy', in S. A. Barney, ed., *Annotation and its Texts* (Oxford, 1991), pp. 108–29.
239. Grafton and Jardine, '"Studied for Action"', pp. 41–3.

a lawyer in the Court of Arches in the 1590s. And each reading, they argue, was not merely a political act – an act of service to secure patronage and influence – but an act of political thought. More importantly, with each act, each reading, Harvey interpreted differently and learned new lessons from his text, as he reread in conjunction with other works and with altered purposes and needs. 'Harvey read the Carthaginian and Roman past above all in terms of the English present' – a shifting present in which at all times Harvey sought to offer counsel or argument to serve a moment or a courtier's ends and ambitions.[240] He defies those historians who strictly differentiate intellectual and political history, or exclude the history of reading from the 'master narrative' of politics.

Gabriel Harvey was a man of very obvious, albeit unfulfilled, ambition.[241] Grafton, Jardine and Sherman suggest, however, that he might lead us to consider others who read as a form of service in early modern England – men such as Henry Wotton, or even Francis Bacon.[242] And this indeed may be a helpful way of thinking again about some of the famous antiquaries of the period, not least Sir Robert Cotton. I have argued recently that, for all the work on Cotton's manuscripts and occasional writings, scholars have largely neglected his reading practices – the ways in which he read, and the use he made of passages and precedents, either in performing service, writing position papers for the king or MPs, or in supporting an argument that was very much his own. Though we do not have Cotton's printed books and marginalia, nor commonplace books of reading notes, Cotton's hand and marks of reading are found throughout his collection. Moreover, the ways he extracted leaves, bound items together or chose a more or less expensive binding all give insights into how he valued manuscripts, and indeed how he arranged them in volumes organised around topics.[243] More valuable still are Cotton's loan lists. Though these have been used by scholars to identify the wide circle of contemporaries borrowing from Cotton's library, they also provide invaluable information about how Cotton saw items he had acquired and studied. When, for example, Cotton described his 'book of St. Albans, having the history in pictures', this may have been a mental device for recalling items, but it may, too, indicate Cotton's sense of the importance of the illustrations. His large book of precedents in ecclesiastical courts he described directly as 'of good use'. We know from his published and unpublished writings that Cotton was highly selective in his use of precedents, that at times he plundered the past to push a case in the present. The closing of his library by Charles I is evidence that Cotton was seen to read 'selectively' and in a manner that the government found dangerous. By the late 1620s, at least in

---

240. Ibid., p. 72.
241. Stern, *Gabriel Harvey*, p. 255.
242. Jardine and Sherman, 'Pragmatic Readers'.
243. K. Sharpe, 'Rewriting Sir Robert Cotton', in C. E. Wright, ed., *Sir Robert Cotton as Collector* (1997), pp. 1–42.

the eyes of authority, he had become a scholar who, far from deploying his reading and knowledge for 'service', manifested a critical independence of authorised interpretations and a readiness to question government itself.[244] Over the period from his days as a pupil under Camden at Westminster to the events surrounding the abrupt dissolution of the 1629 parliament, Cotton's political attitudes and ideas changed as he became concerned at developments in church and state. We have only begun to touch on how his reading of civic histories and of Machiavelli, Guicciardini and Botero, as well as his rereading of modern state papers and ancient records, shaped those ideas. But looking at him again, with the case of Sir William Drake in mind, we can have little doubt that, through all his experience in government and parliament, Cotton returned to reread in his library and there to rewrite his own values.

Dee, Harvey and Cotton, along with others such as Sir Simonds D'Ewes, were London scholars, connected with court circles and powerful patrons. They read and wrote in the environment of influence, power and intrigue. We should not assume, however, that only metropolitan readers will be worthy of the attention of political historians. In the diary cum commonplace book of John Rous, indeed, we begin to see how not only texts but readings of texts, discussion and gossip about them, were themselves reread and circulated in the provinces.[245] Rous, the incumbent of Santon Downham, Suffolk, was certainly no provincial hick starved of information. As well as making a point of reading proclamations, he was a regular at the booksellers, was up to date on the latest publications and was sent a wide range of material, including scurrilous and satirical songs and verses.[246] Moreover, though the range of texts he perused was eclectic, Rous exercised judgement and discrimination in his reading. His favourite aside – 'ut dicitur' – often implies his scepticism about the veracity of what was hearsay; sometimes he dismisses a 'foolish rime' or rejects news outright: 'it is not true.'[247] Much of what Rous read and heard was political news – of continental affairs, court manoeuvres, the unpopularity of favourites, the fate of parliaments, events in Scotland. Though there is need for caution about the effect of his reading in moulding his Parliamentarian sympathies, what we can say is that he was very well acquainted with literature unsympathetic to the king and government: libels against the Duke of Buckingham, the Commons Protestation, the declaration of puritans leaving for America, ballads in praise of the Scots.[248] Perhaps even more importantly, what his notebook manifests is the opportu-

---

244. See Sharpe, *Sir Robert Cotton*.
245. *The Diary of John Rous . . . from 1625 to 1642*, ed. M. A. E. Green, Camden Soc. (1856).
246. Ibid., pp. 10, 35, 37, 54.
247. For example, ibid., pp. 26, 33, 36, 38.
248. Ibid., pp. 20–1, 40, 54, 110. R. Cust, 'News and Politics in Early Seventeenth-Century England', *Past & Present* 112 (1986), pp. 60–90. Cf. K. Sharpe, *The Personal Rule of Charles I* (1992), pp. 683–90, and on Rous, ibid., pp. 695–6.

nity, indeed the need, for Rous to make up his own mind, and the extent to which public news and texts melded on his page with personal observations and preoccupations. Between the official proclamation or direction and the corantos and ballads, between the rhymes 'some against the orthodox, others against the "new churchmen"', Rous was left to make his own choice as to which carried authority.[249] And as is evidenced by his recording of heavy rain and violent winds, tragic accidental death and freak curiosities, the impact of any item of news on him vied with other personal concerns and experiences.[250] Though we cannot clearly observe Rous forming his political values in his study, we can undoubtedly conclude that he read his own world.

Our argument for the interconnections between reading and the exercise of power is reinforced when we consider the question of gender. Nearly all the readers about whom we have information are male. Educated women read but in a patriarchal culture that valued female silence as well as obedience, women's responses to books were seldom articulated or recorded publicly.[251] It may be that the cultural acquiescence to male authority permeated to the innermost spaces of the private sphere. No marks of reading are found in the Countess of Bridgewater's large collection of books, or in most other collections owned by women – perhaps a sign of a larger female occlusion from public participation and engagement.[252] Any such suggestion awaits further research on women readers and meets with exceptions. However, the best known exception may support the generalisation, if not prove the rule. No scholar interested in the history of women and books can fail to take notice of the 'Great Picture' of Lady Anne Clifford, now hanging in Appleby Castle (ill. 10). The large canvas is a triptych: the fifteen-year-old Lady Anne is depicted in the left panel surrounded by books; the centrepiece is a family composition of her parents and siblings; and the right panel has Anne as a mature fifty-six-year-old, with books on her table and untidy shelves of volumes behind her. The books are clearly identifiable: among the titles on the left we find St Augustine, Epictetus and Boethius, Eusebius's *History of the Church*, Ortelius's book of maps and Camden's *Britannia*, Ovid, Castiglione

---

249. *Diary of Rous*, p. 79.
250. Ibid., pp. 44, 81. For Rous's interest in tragic death see p. 66; for the disabled man who span with his mouth, p. 85, and the toad eater, p. 45.
251. See S. Hull, *Chaste, Silent and Obedient: English Books for Women 1475–1640* (San Marino, 1982).
252. H. Brayman, 'Impressions from a Scribbling Age: Recovering the Reading Practices of Renaissance England', Ph.D. diss., Columbia University, 1995, ch. 4. We await the publication of this important thesis. I am most grateful to Heidi Brayman for stimulating discussions at the Huntington Library in 1993. The absence of marks of reading may usefully be considered in the light of contemporary women students' disproportionately low percentage of first class degrees – which is often explained in terms of women's reticence about adversarial engagement with examination questions.

10. *The Great Picture of the Clifford Family* (1646). Appleby Castle, Cumbria.

and Montaigne, Chaucer, Spenser and Sidney. On the right panel, Anne is represented with her right hand touching a Bible and Charron's book of wisdom; on her shelves, as well as the works of Herbert, Greville, Jonson and Donne, and the histories of Comines and Guicciardini, are volumes of sermons by Donne and Henry King, Henry Cuffe's *Age of Man's Life* and George Hakewill's *Apology*.[253]

We can supplement our knowledge of Lady Clifford's reading from the sermon preached at her funeral and from her diary, in which she records 'reading' or hearing read the Bible, and St Augustine, Ovid's *Metamorphoses*, Chaucer, Sidney and Montaigne, and the histories of the Low Countries and the Turks.[254] Other references suggest that she had, or had access to, an extensive library – possibly as large as the Countess of Bridgewater's two hundred volumes.[255] Lady Clifford, however, did not annotate her books and 'she does not comment on the books she read': we are left to deduce by other means the place of reading in her life and self-fashioning.[256] Both the triptych and

253. For a complete list of the titles, see B. Lewalski, *Writing Women in Jacobean England* (Cambridge, Mass., 1993), ch. 5. For a reading of the painting see G. Parry, 'The Great Picture of Lady Anne Clifford', in D. Howarth, ed., *Art and Patronage at the Caroline Court* (Cambridge, 1993), pp. 202–19.

254. See E. Rainbow, *A Sermon Preached at the Funeral of the Right Honourable Anne Countess of Pembroke, Dorset and Montgomery* (1677); *The Diaries of Lady Anne Clifford*, ed. D. J. H. Clifford (Stroud, 1992), pp. 41, 45, 48, 54, 61, 68, 70, 76.

255. *Diaries of Clifford*, p. 56; Brayman, 'Impressions from a Scribbling Age', pp. 209–10.

256. Lewalski, *Writing Women*, p. 140.

the diaries are important texts of Clifford's self-presentation, and it is equally apparent that books were an essential part of that representation. Anne Clifford was most famous in her age for the long running battle she waged (against the wishes of her husbands, the Earls of Dorset and Pembroke) to secure the inheritance of the Clifford estates, willed by her father to her uncle. The case attracted royal intervention and wide publicity, not least on account of the unusual courses pursued by a woman to assert property rights which a patriarchal legal system assigned to men.[257]

The 'Great Picture', commissioned by Anne in 1646, was another assertion of her right to that claim, painted just three years before she succeeded in taking possession of the last of her father's estates. Like Anne's campaign, the painting is untypical. The dynastic family portrait, that familiar genre representing lineage and landed inheritance, was traditionally a male genre, with the paterfamilias taking centre place in the composition. Here Clifford focuses on her own lineage, a narrative of self, with even in the centrepiece her mother (then pregnant with Anne) as the prominent figure.[258] The elder Lady Clifford holds a book of psalms – which returns us to the place of books in the polemics of the canvas. Anne's self-presentation with books (as well as with family portraits) serves to assert her place in a conventionally masculine public sphere. As Mary Lamb has pointed out, the books (on the right especially) are disordered, portrayed as for use, not decoration.[259] Books, the portrait appears to suggest, were what structured this woman's independent and public identity, and what enabled her to question the conventions of the age, just as Guicciardini, Montaigne and Charron questioned conventional knowledge and values.[260]

Clifford's diary supports such a reading. It records not only 'the emergence of a female self able to resist existing social norms', but the role played by books in fostering that 'self-realisation and resistance'.[261] Reading enabled Lady Clifford to determine her own meaning and rewrite herself. There may be a hint of nervousness in her husband's order that 'I must leave off reading the Old Testament till I can get somebody to read it with me' – somebody perhaps who would direct understanding and interpretation.[262] Most of the time Anne was indeed read to by other men – Mr Dumbell, Mr Rivers and Mr Marsh, Mr Ran and Wat Coniston.[263] But sometimes she read with other women – the Arcadia with Moll Neville, even the Bible with Kate

257. See G. C. Williamson, *Lady Anne Clifford* (Kendal, 1922); M. Holmes, *Proud Northern Lady: Lady Anne Clifford, 1590–1676* (1975); and now R. T. Spence, *Lady Anne Clifford, Countess of Pembroke, Dorset and Montgomery* (Stroud, 1997).
258. Parry, 'Great Picture of Lady Anne Clifford', pp. 207–9.
259. Lamb, 'Agency of the Split Subject'.
260. Ibid., p. 365.
261. Lewalski, *Writing Women*, pp. 150–1.
262. *Diaries of Clifford*, p. 52.
263. Ibid., pp. 41, 50, 51, 68, 70.

Buchin.[264] And it was Anne Clifford who selected her favourite adages and had them written out and pinned up on walls, and embroidered on furnishings.[265] Not only did she read texts of history and politics – *Leicester's Commonwealth*, for example; she discussed with other women religion and 'a great deal of newes'.[266] We can only begin to imagine the importance of such dialogues in the formation of women's political consciousness. But what may have been even more important in shaping Lady Clifford's defiant spirit was her conversation with books, religious and secular, whether read by others or 'in my lord's closet', alone.[267]

The Clifford triptych was painted in 1646, and there is little evidence of Lady Anne's later reading. By the outbreak of civil war, Dee, Harvey and Cotton were long dead. Curiously few studies have been undertaken of Civil War readers or reading – of how the new genres of pamphlet polemic and the culture of contest affected habits of reading or engagement with books. In many cases, no doubt, the evidence is too fragmentary to explore the interactions for individual cases. Hitherto we have found no collection to equal the twenty-three volumes of Sir William Drake's that we can date to the 1640s and 1650s. One rich source, however, has been inexplicably neglected, the commonplace books of a figure who strove to avert civil war, reflected in exile on revolution and successfully engineered Restoration: Edward Hyde, Earl of Clarendon. Two bound volumes among the Clarendon manuscripts in the Bodleian Library are what remain of Hyde's reading notes.[268] One is dated from March 1646 to October 1647, with a single reference to 1673.[269] The other contains notes dated June 1636, but continues into the 1640s and contains specific references to the Civil War.[270] The volumes have annotations in different hands, suggesting that, like Drake, Clarendon used a scribe, or scribes. The leaves are not in chronological order and may be loose sheets from other books now lost.

Clarendon takes his notes both under the authors and titles of books and under his own commonplace headings – 'De pace futura constituenda', 'De armis et classibus' – and extracts passages in English and Latin.[271] He annotates passages from and refers to classical texts (Pliny, Pericles, Livy, Plutarch);[272] historians ancient and modern (Josephus, Thucydides, Sarpi and Camden);[273]

264. Ibid., pp. 54, 61, cf. p. 76.
265. Lamb, 'Agency of the Split Subject', p. 367.
266. *Diaries of Clifford*, pp. 81, 67.
267. Ibid., p. 54. The perceived 'danger' of private female reading as female self-pleasuring awaits investigation.
268. Bodleian Clarendon MSS 126, 127. I am very grateful to Hugh Trevor-Roper for urging me to read these volumes, and for all his help and encouragement.
269. Clarendon MS 126 f. 204.
270. Clarendon MS 127 f. 66.
271. Clarendon MS 126 ff. 136–7.
272. Ibid. ff. 55v, 62v, 61v, 74, 86.
273. Ibid. ff. 56, 64, 156, 167.

lawyers such as Alberico Gentili and Grotius;[274] and writers on statecraft –
Cardano, Comines, Bacon and Machiavelli.[275] There are also occasional references to contemporary material: to Donne's 'Pseudo Martyr', Archbishop
William Laud's *Conference with Fisher the Jesuit*, and Thomas Fuller's *Holy War*.[276]
Evidently, like Drake, Clarendon read for use. He indexed his notes and placed
markers in the margin to facilitate the location of subjects.[277] And he paused
in the midst of taking notes to review the 'courses and occasional considerations', the lessons that passages taught 'to be used upon occasion'.[278]
Throughout the notebooks we witness Clarendon reading his sources in the
circumstances of civil war. His applications of ancient texts to contemporary
occasions are persistent and explicit. Relating, for example, Aelian's account
of the sheep bringing forth a lion, Hyde compared it to sober parliaments
giving way to those that devoured the kingdom.[279] The debate over whether
Turks or Tartars were more conformable to Christianity he paralleled with
those modern infidels, the Presbyterians and Independents.[280] The story of the
temptation of Athanasius over four years led him directly to the experience
of his own king.[281] Clarendon noted that Athanasius set them to work on
building a monastery and he found hope in the story: having resisted the
hundred devils who tempted him.

> it is not impossible but his Majesty who hath endured the vexation
> and temptation of a greater number a longer term may in the end by
> his greatness of mind and magnanimity so tame and humble them that
> he may employ them and use them to the undoing of the ill they have
> done.[282]

Similarly Plutarch's account (in the life of Timoleon) of the two captains who,
on the pretence of setting Sicily at liberty, did greater harm than any tyrant
immediately prompted a reflection on the times: 'What those pretences and
discourses of liberty and reformation have commonly brought forth besides
the experience of former times . . . I see have been sufficiently instructed by
the woeful tragedies of our own country . . .'[283] Better, he concluded from
ancient texts and his own experience, to suffer straining of power than unbri-
dled licence.[284]

274. Ibid. ff. 99, 141, 143v.
275. Ibid. ff. 56v, 57v, 62, 59.
276. Ibid. f. 176.
277. Ibid. ff. 51v, 150.
278. Ibid. ff. 53, 85.
279. Ibid. f. 53.
280. Ibid. f. 55.
281. Ibid. f. 53v.
282. Ibid.
283. Ibid. f. 77.
284. Ibid. ff. 127, 144; though see Clarendon MS 127 f. 60.

Explicitly and obliquely the Civil War conditioned Clarendon's reading during the 1640s. Amidst notes on his texts, he often refers to specific episodes of the Civil Wars. So, while reading Plutarch, he recalls the costly loss of life at the battle of Newbury;[285] Bacon's passages in *The Advancement of Learning* on wisdom and virtue lead him to praise Charles I's constancy to his principles, even under the hardship of restraint;[286] reading Comines it occurred to him that no generals were selected for the New Model Army who exhibited the qualities or ambition to take the rein of government.[287] More subtly and generally, we can detect how the course of events led Clarendon to reread his texts and times, and to change, if not his fundamental beliefs, then the tenets and values he emphasised. Perhaps it was still in the 1630s, when traditional beliefs about prerogative and law still held, that Hyde wrote in his notebook: 'Kings rule by their laws . . . and ought as rarely to put in use the supreme prerogative as God doth his power of working miracles . . .'[288] By 1646, in exile in Jersey, he had come to a different conclusion: mixed government he now rejected, regarding sovereignty as indispensable and indivisible. 'It is a very vulgar error to believe that subjection to authority and government takes away or diminishes our liberty when in truth our liberty can no other way be preserved but by subjection . . .'[289] And 'this sovereign authority to protect must be absolute against which no appeal can be.'[290] As anarchy loomed, Clarendon read even the jurist and natural rights theorist Hugo Grotius as an apologist for sovereign power.[291] It was not the most obvious reading of Grotius, but one the text permitted and Clarendon's circumstances favoured (ill. 11).

The dialogue between his texts and his and the country's circumstances – that is to say his reading – shaped the development of Clarendon's religious, social and political thought. It was, as his philosophy was, a blend of traditional ethics and politics, a pragmatic sense of realities that fell short of ideals, and of the experiences of displacement and defeat. Hyde placed more faith than his contemporary Drake in traditional virtues, private and public. He believed that wise conversation could convert men to good causes and that, whatever their temporary subjugation by violent conflict, reason and logic would ultimately hold sway.[292] He held that good rulers should also be virtuous men, and so disdained figures like Comines's (and Drake's) hero, Louis XI, for all his success in advancing the territory and power of the French

285. Clarendon MS 126 f. 77v.
286. Ibid. ff. 57–57v.
287. Ibid. f. 59v.
288. Clarendon MS 127 f. 60v; see above, p. 224 and the speech of James I in 1610, p. 234 n 433.
289. Clarendon MS 126 f. 144, cf. f. 127.
290. Ibid. f. 144.
291. See, for example, ff. 143v onwards. See Richard Tuck, *Natural Rights Theories: Their Origin and Development* (Cambridge, 1979), ch. 3, esp. pp. 68–70, 79. Tuck describes Grotius's *De Iure* as 'janus faced'.
292. Clarendon MS 126 ff. 57–57v.

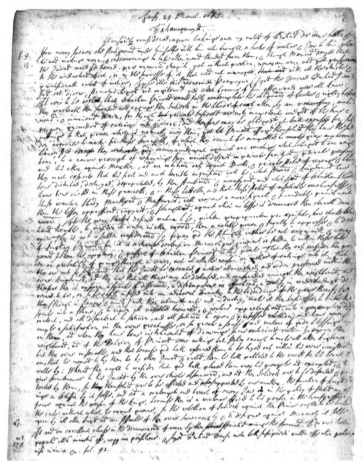

11.
Clarendon's
notes on
Grotius.

crown. 'How politic a prince soever', Clarendon regarded him as 'certainly the most unkingly pattern and example for others to follow'.[293] As he read in ancient histories and lives, Hyde found his own conservative beliefs confirmed and reinforced. Princes, he read, needed to keep state in a comely fashion, 'the state and splendour of a prince [being] necessary to procure such an awe and reverence from the people that he may be able to protect and execute the laws'.[294] Religion, he believed the reign of Numa Pompilius demonstrated, laid the foundations for a peaceful commonwealth.[295] However, as we have seen, Clarendon had also read the advocates of realpolitik – Comines, Bacon, most notoriously Machiavelli.[296] He embraced the Florentine's counsel that all men needed to seize the opportunity of the times; he

293. Ibid. f. 58v; in contrast to Drake, see above, p. 97.
294. Clarendon MS 126 f. 87, cf. f. 85.
295. Ibid. ff. 87, 91v.
296. Ibid. ff. 56v, 57v, 59v.

endorsed his faith in history as a guide, and he weighed his advice to the
prince on war and government.[297]

Traditional political values and Machiavellian pragmatism coexisted in
tension in Clarendon's worldview; which ideas and values predominated was
the outcome of time and circumstance. As the Civil War threatened the end
of all the values he had held dear, Clarendon came close to a more ruthlessly
pragmatic, Hobbesian vision of society and politics in which conscience was
subordinate to sovereign will, and even fear constituted a legitimate basis for
contracts.[298] Like all readers, Clarendon took what made sense to him from
what he read; and what made sense in the midst of civil conflict was quite
different from that in the halcyon days of peace.

Clarendon's commonplace books are often explicit in revealing how, as well
as what, he read. He informs us that, with regard to ancient texts, his approach
was selective and critical. The reader owed to antiquity careful hearing and
consideration but not the resignation of his own judgement.[299] Mankind, he
argued, echoing Bacon, progressed by taking advantage of what their prede-
cessors taught, but also by their own 'wits'.[300] Similarly, though the lives of
great men were held as models to be emulated, Clarendon noted that 'he that
thinks the great actions of great men or the wise sayings of wise men to be
always fit for his imitation . . . will find himself much mistaken.'[301] The reader
of ancient texts had to exercise his own judgement about the lessons to be
learned from the past, the 'fragments to be used upon occasion'. Practising
that method, Clarendon read selectively and critically. He praised Machiavelli,
for example, as a 'wise man', a writer of 'excellent judgement' in his view of
the past and historical insights; he admired many of his 'true observations' and
'wise resolutions'.[302] But he rejected, on the basis of experience, Machiavelli's
argument that money was not the sinews of war; and he was completely at
odds with the faith the Florentine (especially in the *Discorsi*) placed in the
people.[303] Rereading Livy himself, Clarendon concluded against his cinquecento commentator, that 'it is a very difficult matter for a commonwealth to
subsist under a popular government' because the people lacked judgement
and were 'wild' and 'incorrigible'.[304]

At times Clarendon appears to have read more critically than Sir William
Drake. As well as from Machiavelli, he took extensive notes from Plutarch
and Grotius, weighing their judgements carefully. 'I cannot but exceedingly
differ from the learned Grotius,' he writes, condemning the latitude the jurist

297. Ibid. f. 59v. Clarendon writes of Machiavelli's 'excellent judgement and insight'.
298. See Clarendon MS 126 ff. 133, 144. He cites Hobbes's Thucydides (f. 56; Clarendon
    MS 127 ff. 50, 53v) and Grotius 'Against Mr Hobbes' (Clarendon MS 126 f. 150).
299. Clarendon MS 126 f. 57v.
300. Ibid. f. 61v.
301. Ibid. f. 80.
302. Ibid. ff. 59v–60.
303. Ibid. ff. 60, 151v.
304. Ibid. ff. 90v–91.

allowed to promises in a passage of his *De Iure Belli et Pacis*.[305] What prompted Clarendon's criticism, however, was not so much the consideration of, or cross-referencing to, alternative writings but the unsuitability of Grotius's argument to the times. Clarendon read while civil war raged and the fortunes of his master waned; and he extracted the passages that offered practical help or reinforced Royalist values. Passages about the conduct of war, about soldiers and garrisons, Clarendon doubtless copied while the battles were still being won and lost and the lessons of the past might be of use. In exile, news came to his study daily and he paused amid his reading to pen letters to Sir John Berkeley, commander in Devon, to Edward Brinton, to Mr Hardinge, commissioner for the Navy and to Prince Charles's attorney.[306] As battle gave way to the politics of treaty and negotiation, as some perhaps began to think of a government without a king, he reread the past of the Roman commonwealth as the best argument for monarchy. 'There cannot be a better argument for monarchical government and the incomparable benefits received thereby than the city of Rome.'[307] No less than his unceasing activities on Charles I's behalf, his reading was a committed political act. Whether he was conscious of the politics of his reading we cannot say. He knew that others read the past differently; he believed that sectaries did not apply Scripture 'according to the true and genuine sense of it', but were guilty of 'wresting and distorting it to unnatural significations' for their 'own weak purposes'.[308] Perhaps like most he still believed in some truth, some common interpretation, that all could be brought to share. Increasingly, however, the pamphlet war made it manifest that truth itself would be fought over and that reading would become part of the political contest.

As a consequence, the adages and sentences Clarendon collected from his reading were no longer the 'commonplaces' of a shared humanist culture; they were the weapons of a party.[309] 'Take the kings away,' he copied from Scripture, 'every man out of his place, and put captains in their rooms.'[310] No man, he noted, ought to be condemned without answer.[311] 'Novelty and innovations to be prevented,' he asserted.[312] Those that had the power to compel, he realised, could overweigh the law. But the learned man, Clarendon consoled himself in exile, was never alone: his thoughts were always company.[313] 'The strength of mind', he perhaps felt as defeat loomed, 'to be preferred before that of the body.'[314] It was a familiar precept; but in Clarendon's case

---

305. Ibid. f. 145.
306. Ibid. ff. 129 and passim.
307. Ibid. f. 88. We need to be reminded that many read the history of Rome as a defence of monarchy.
308. Ibid. f. 53v.
309. See, for example, ibid. ff. 150–4.
310. Ibid. f. 154; see 1 Kings 20: 24.
311. Clarendon MS 126 f. 154v.
312. Ibid. f. 151v, cf. f. 76.
313. Ibid. f. 56v.
314. Clarendon MS 127 f. 47v.

it announces no retreat from public affairs, rather a shift from armed engagement to the battle for minds.

Immersed in the intrigue of high politics, the treaties between king and parliament and the factional fighting within the Royalist camps and counsels, Clarendon's readings were, unsurprisingly, explicitly political and partisan. 'Neutrality' he rejected as 'dangerous'.[315] Sir William Drake was more ambivalent in his commitments and less obviously a man of party in his reading. Yet, in many ways, the two readers have much in common. Clarendon read many of the authors favoured by Drake. Like Sir William he copied passages about beauty, love and marriage, as well as lessons of statecraft.[316]

Both would have concurred that 'there seems to have been in the foundation and institution of the Roman commonwealth so great a disposition of all the faculties to the public service.'[317] The two even copied English and Latin axioms in common.[318] As one, however, championed the king and church, the other, at least initially, was recruited to the Parliamentary cause. And where Clarendon, for all his experience, still more or less held to traditional notions of social and political morality, Drake accepted as given a society of self-interest and contest. For all the texts they had in common, their reading led them to very different understandings, and to a very different politics.

Historians of reading have posited generalisations about a shift in reading habits from intensive to extensive, public to private, from reading directed by authority to a more democratised hermeneutics. Such arguments have usually been based on anecdotes and fragments, often too on assumptions that habits of reading were part of shared cultural practices – that of, in Bennett's words, for example, 'the Jacobean reader'.[319] Our case study of Drake has questioned or moderated many of these generalisations. Considering him alongside other readers, literary figures and men of affairs, may help us to gauge just how far his case should take us in reevaluating early modern reading. What strikes us is the extent to which, for all our cases, private reading was inflected by the concerns and issues of public life, of politics. The Civil War may have rendered the act of reading as overtly partisan, but even before, none of our readers read, as did the merchant Jean Ranson a century later, for an aesthetic or emotional response, or for an intimacy with the writer.[320] They all read for action in the public realm; they all read politically. The fact that their values, political attitudes and allegiances differed and altered graphically under-

315. Clarendon MS 126 f. 150.
316. Ibid. f. 151v; Clarendon MS 127 f. 47v.
317. Clarendon MS 126 f. 88.
318. See, for example, ibid. f. 60v; Clarendon MS 127 ff. 66v, 71.
319. H. S. Bennett, *English Books and Readers, 1603–1640* (Cambridge, 1970), p. 78.
320. See R. Darnton, 'Readers Respond to Rousseau: The Fabrication of Romantic Sensitivity', in Darnton, *The Great Cat Massacre and Other Episodes in French Cultural History* (Harmondsworth, 1985), pp. 209–49.

pins what post-revisionist historians have begun to appreciate: that the culture of early modern England, for all its rhetoric of common codes, was multivalent.[321] Despite a common education, the homilies on obedience and the prescriptions of authority, people were able to construct meanings for themselves, and constitute themselves as political agents. We shall need to turn from the politics of reading to how politics itself was reinterpreted and reconstituted by those citizens, not least through their reading. But first, we need to re-examine the common educational practices and texts of early modern England, to assess how a study of reading transforms our sense of their performance in the culture.

Reading in the Culture

Scholars of Renaissance texts and education have focused their attention on the institutions of study, universities, schools and libraries; on the directives for study, pedagogic treatises and manuals; and on the editions of texts prescribed, their authors and translators. To look at the questions of reading and reception is to present a different perspective on all these matters, to reconsider the ways in which education shaped the minds and culture of literate early modern English men and women.

Historians of education have differed about the learning imbibed by the young gentlemen of England at Oxford and Cambridge. Mark Curtis argued that the early modern period saw a transition in the ancient universities that transformed Oxford and Cambridge from bastions of scholasticism to centres of the new humanism.[322] Curtis has been criticised, however, for idealising: for taking as the norm the high standards set by some tutors and their directions as the typical reading experience of undergraduates, most of whom never completed a degree. Oxford and Cambridge, Kenneth Charlton has proclaimed, were not the places where the 'heirs of the landed gentry were all bred together in learning'; Curtis's 'examples of the *studia humanitatis* at work failed to become general practice'.[323] Study at the universities, Charlton claims, remained 'largely scholastic' rather than humanist.[324] As Francis Bacon was to argue in *The Advancement of Learning*, 'most of the usages . . . of the universities were derived from more obscure times', and the curriculum required 'amendment and reformation'.[325]

In part the disagreement stems from the evidence one chooses to favour. The official statutes of the universities provided only a bare outline for student

321. See Sharpe and Lake, *Culture and Politics*, introduction.
322. M. Curtis, *Oxford and Cambridge in Transition, 1558–1642* (Oxford, 1959).
323. K. Charlton, *Education in Renaissance England* (1965), pp. 149, 167.
324. Ibid., p. 152.
325. Bacon, *Advancement of Learning*, pp. 64–6.

reading: 'tutors were expected to assign considerable additional readings from the *litterae humaniores*.'[326] The most diligent and demanding of them, like Richard Holdsworth, drew up full directions instructing his pupils to supplement medieval authors by reading Cicero, Ovid, Terence, Horace, Juvenal, Lucan, Plautus, Suetonius, Quintus Curtius, Livy's and Florus's histories, and Erasmus and Lorenzo Valla among the moderns.[327] By studying other tutors' directives and student commonplace books, Margo Todd has helped us to assess how many students experienced tutors like Holdsworth and what was the influence of their studies. She argues that, though students were studying scholastic and increasingly from 1600 new scholastic theology, student reading notes and book inventories reveal that Cicero, Isocrates, Seneca, Plutarch, Euripides and Sophocles were the most popular of the ancients, with Erasmus predominant among the modern authors. Moreover tutors and students both made critical comments on the scholastics, expressing their preferences for 'new writers', Petrarch, More and Vives, as well as Erasmus.[328] The reading of early modern students was not still fundamentally scholastic; it was humanist, and, in particular, Erasmian.

The preoccupation of tutors and students alike, Todd argues, was with the active life of virtue: 'The concern of seventeenth-century tutors was that their students should learn to live virtuously.'[329] And in that spirit their 'students read the classics as Christian humanists . . . for instruction in virtuous and godly living, for answers to practical ethical questions and for political precepts and directions on civic involvement.'[330] In the university notebooks of Sir Simonds D'Ewes, Todd found a student who had read widely in logic and metaphysics, classical and humanist writings and who regarded Erasmus as his guide to the virtuous life.[331] As the courtesy literature and guidebooks for gentlemen all insisted, virtue was the symbol of a gentleman, and the purpose of education was 'by reading moral precepts' to make men 'absolute commanders of their own affections', and to bring them closer to God.[332]

We know almost nothing about Drake's education. He matriculated at Christ Church, Oxford and at the Middle Temple was bound with Sir Simonds D'Ewes and the puritan John White. But no evidence survives of his studies there. The figures who most influenced him were evidently his old tutor at Amersham, Dr Charles Croke, to whom he remained close, and George Morley, Bishop of Winchester, 'my kinsman and tutor', to whom he

---

326. Todd, *Christian Humanism*, p. 63.
327. Charlton, *Education*, pp. 146–7.
328. Todd, *Christian Humanism*, ch. 3; ibid., p. 66.
329. Ibid., p. 86.
330. Ibid., p. 64.
331. Ibid., p. 88.
332. See R. Brathwait, *The English Gentleman* (1630), epistle dedicatory, and 'To the reader', and pp. 357, 382; quotation p. 97; and Peacham, *The Complete Gentleman*, e.g. pp. 5, 18–22.

left £100 'to buy him a ring or plate'.[333] What is clear, however, is that a university education did not instil in Drake an inclination to scholasticism. Though he read Aquinas and the Fathers, he paid the greatest attention to the classics and the humanist editions and commentaries. But if in this he supports Todd's arguments about the pervasiveness of humanist texts and approaches, Drake clearly did not read 'for instruction in virtuous and godly living'. Nor, though he shared a chamber as well as a devotion to historical and legal studies with Sir Simonds D'Ewes, did Drake emulate his Erasmian prescriptions regarding the good life.[334] Neither official pedagogic counsel nor prescribed texts moulded Drake's worldview. We do not know at what age he first read Guicciardini and Machiavelli, though his good Italian meant that he had no need to await the English editions; and he may early on have had a manuscript translation. Drake therefore cautions us not to frame conclusions about what students read based on official statutes, or even tutors' guides. He reminds us that the risqué literature circulating among the intellectual avant garde, Machiavelli in particular, was, at least for some, more than a mere fashion.[335] Most of all he demonstrates that humanist texts and approaches could be deployed by a reader to very different uses from that of the Christian and commonwealth ideology celebrated by Erasmus and his English disciples.

Theorists of education, and indeed of the early modern state, have often depicted educational programmes and policies as the means by which authority endeavoured to inscribe itself on the subject by, as Foucault would put it, a process that led the student to interiorise the systems of order, ending the need for violent agencies of control.[336] With a reader like Drake we are ourselves forced again to recognise that the humanist assault on scholasticism, the texts it made available and its critical practices enabled a self-education and permitted an independence of judgement that began to constitute a subjectivity that was anything but passive or uncritical.[337] The influence of official curricula has been usefully considered alongside the inventories and lists of student libraries, in which Professor Todd found a predominance of classical and humanist works. We are only just beginning, however, to investigate the private collections of gentlemen after they left university, or of those below the gentry, or who did not attend university but were literate and in some cases autodidacts. While work has advanced further on the continent, as was argued in 1992, 'scholarship that examines the reading of the various social levels of Renaissance England . . . is virtually non-existent.'[338] Other

333. M. F. Keeler, *The Long Parliament, 1640–1641* (Philadelphia, 1954), p. 159; Bucks R.O., D/DR/1/68. Morley went into exile after 1648, see *DNB*.
334. Todd, *Christian Humanism*, pp. 88–9.
335. See Curtis, *Oxford and Cambridge*, pp. 119, 137.
336. See M. Foucault, *Discipline and Punish* (Harmondsworth, 1991), esp. part 2, ch. 2.
337. Contrast E. R. Kintgen, 'Readers read . . . as they were taught to read', *Reading in Tudor England*, p. 97; see below, pp. 333ff.
338. Fehrenbach and Leedham-Green, *Private Libraries*, vol. 1, p. xv.

than a handful of famous scholars, such as Sir Edward Coke, John Dee, D'Ewes, Selden, Camden, Lancelot Andrewes, Henry Savile and Lord Lumley – little is known about the books people bought or collected.[339] Peter Clark may well be right to suggest 'that almost every country landowner of note had several shelves of books at home', but their number and nature remain unknown.[340] Our ignorance is now being overcome by the project headed by R. J. Fehrenbach and E. S. Leedham-Green to list Tudor and early Stuart private libraries and the first results indicate that such research will transform our understanding of early modern culture and politics.

Sir Edward Stanhope, vicar-general to Archbishop Bancroft, possessed, as his position might lead us to expect, works of canon and civil law, commentaries on the Decretum, and theological treatises; but he was also an avid purchaser of classical texts (Cicero, Dion Cassius, Terence, Livy) and modern histories by Benzoni and Demetrius. In the case of Sir Roger Townshend, of Norfolk, a meticulous servant prepared a full inventory of his extensive library. Townshend had nearly all the classics recommended by Holdsworth and more: Lactantius, Apuleius, Epictetus, Pliny, Ovid and Martial. He also had a good collection of humanist works – Erasmus and Valla, Scaliger and Castiglione – and histories by Polydore Vergil, Camden, De Fonseca, Buchanan, La Popelinière and Goulart's history of the League. Like Drake, Townshend also owned works by Justus Lipsius, Cardan, Charron, Magirus, as well as Dallington, Botero and Machiavelli's *Discourses* in Latin. These he read with an equally impressive holding of contemporary theological works by Bayley, Hall, Denison, Perkins, Ward, Dent, Gataker and Jewel, in a manner that immediately leads us to wonder how he read, and how such eclectic and contrary texts shaped his perceptions and beliefs.[341]

Perhaps the most interesting list for our study is the inventory of Sir Edward Dering's library. Dering like Drake was a bibliophile and private scholar; a Kentish gentleman and JP who travelled on the continent; he was active in the Long Parliament, in which he spoke powerfully. It has been estimated that Dering's library numbered two thousand titles, ranging from divinity to drama, and including engravings as well as books. With a library of this size it goes without saying that Dering owned all the standard classical texts and

339. See W. O. Hassall, *A Catalogue of the Library of Sir Edward Coke* (New Haven, 1950); J. O. Halliwell, ed., *The Diary of John Dee and the Catalogue of his Library of Manuscripts*, Camden Soc. (1842); A. Watson, *The Library of Sir Simonds D'Ewes* (1966); D. M. Barrat, 'The Library of John Selden', *Bodleian Lib. Record* 3 (1950), pp. 128–42, 208–13, 256–74; R. De Molen, 'The Library of William Camden', *Proc. Amer. Philos. Soc.* 128 (1984), pp. 329–409; D. D. C. Chambers, 'A Catalogue of the Library of Bishop Lancelot Andrewes', *Trans. Camb. Bibliog. Soc.* 5 (1970), pp. 97–120; J. P. Gilson, 'The Library of Henry Savile of Bank', *Trans. Bibliog. Soc.* 9 (1906–8), pp. 127–210; S. Jayne and F. Johnson, *The Lumley Library* (1956).
340. P. Clark, 'The Ownership of Books in England, 1560–1640: The Example of Some Kentish Townsfolk', in L. Stone, ed., *Schooling and Society* (Baltimore, 1976), pp. 95–114, at p. 97.
341. Fehrenbach and Leedham-Green, *Private Libraries*, chs 2, 3.

a large number of histories, ancient (Eusebius, Suetonius, Eadmer, Florus) and modern (especially English – Camden, Daniel, Knollys, Stow, Ralegh and Speed). Dering's library has much in common with what we can piece together of Drake's. About half his books were published on the continent; he bought some of Sir William's favourite authors – Charron, Dallington, Botero and Machiavelli's *Prince* in a 1589 Latin edition. But there are also important and interesting differences. Dering purchased titles that were specifically acquired to assist him with his responsibilities and standing as a gentleman or in the exercise of an office: he owned books on gardening, heraldry and honour, instructions for musters, and a treatise on the duty of an MP. More generally, Dering accumulated, especially during the 1630s and 1640s, an excellent library of theology, ranging from Bibles, prayer books and concordances, and the Koran, through the Fathers and devotional works, the major Protestant divines, to recent and contemporary controversy (Parsons, Bellarmine, Kellison, More, St Ignatius, Ames, Hall, Davenant, Mede, De Dominis and Laud).

As well as his phenomenal range of reading in Catholic and Protestant divinity, Dering would have been equipped to evaluate contemporary religious controversies through works such as Davenport on predestination, Chillingworth's *Religion of Protestants* and Fuller's *Holy War*, Hall's *Defence of Episcopacy*, and debates over the Scottish Kirk and Covenant. Indeed what is most striking about Dering's inventory is the high profile of works published in 1641, dealing with the contested religious and political questions that were to lead to civil war. Dering evidently purchased or was given works by Prynne and by Heylyn, a vindication of Bishop Cosins, and treatises against images; as well as Hall's and Thomas Cooke's defences, Parker's and Milton's attacks on episcopacy; and he collected the articles against Strafford as well as Leslie's speech against the Scottish Covenant. The events leading to civil war clearly influenced Dering's library. And by corollary we can comprehend more clearly from the inventory of his books how he weighed the crisis and how, with a sagacity to understand a range of viewpoints, he was neither extreme nor unerringly constant in his political commitment.[342]

Interestingly too, for all that the preachers of realpolitik were represented in the library, Dering developed no Machiavellian view of the world. Dering's adherence (by contrast with Drake) to the godly values of his upbringing is clearly reflected in the library. They may also, in difficult times, have been sustained by his library of divinity to which he 'addicted himself' in the last years of his life.[343]

'Where exactly Dering bought his books', the editors of his inventory write, 'he seldom says.'[344] Yet it would seem that the majority were purchased in London, even continental books, since Dering did not travel overseas after

342. Ibid., ch. 4.
343. Ibid., p. 140.
344. Ibid., p. 143.

1620. He refers to buying fifty-four at a 'Mrs Taylor's', another clue that the book trade, like the beer trade in early modern England, may not have been a male domain. And though he had to lay out significant sums for a collection of this size – Dering regarded 'six hundred pound [as] but a mean expense in books' – he was no ascetic bibliophile.[345] With a true gentleman's priorities, he spent less on books than on clothes. Large libraries like Dering's and Drake's, we begin to see, were not the preserve of those who, devoting their all to the swot's garret, removed themselves from polite society. Rather in Dering's as in Drake's case, books and reading were part of the social milieu. Dering's library was well known in his lifetime, and he, Sir William Dugdale, Sir Christopher Hatton and Sir Thomas Shirley formed a society in which all promised to exchange books and notes.[346] Sir Edward also paid to borrow books, suggesting that collecting and reading were permeated by commerce with a wide variety of men and women, of various stations, with whom, doubtless, books and pamphlets were discussed. Scholars interested in the constitution of a public sphere in early modern England will need to follow carefully the investigations into those 'private libraries' that were semi-public collections, in London and in the provinces.

Libraries, as the controversy over the new British Library made starkly apparent, are more than collections of books. In Professor Sherman's words, the library was an ideological and psychological space which allowed 'the self to meet itself without the distortion of public, social life'.[347] While we might question the extent to which the library was an entirely 'private' domain, the general point about the importance of the place and space in which books were, and are, read is borne out by contemporaries. Sir Edward Dering went to pains not only to acquire books but to furnish his study and to carpet and decorate it. His efforts appear to have been more for himself than to impress others, for he described his library as his 'Utopia', his ideal place in which he most found fulfilment.[348] It is Michel de Montaigne who most famously discussed his library in Sherman's terms, as a solitarium on the top floor of a circular building in which he could find himself – albeit he was accompanied by his scribe.[349] Libraries, in other words, were places both public and private in which men reflected on the outside world, away from its press and bustle, where personal judgement was exercised, away from the immediate influences of friends or patrons. Both Dering's and Montaigne's language points to the political significance of these places: utopia was after all a political (non)place, a site through which More had critically considered the Tudor polity. And Montaigne directly appropriated the language of authority for the activity he pursued in his library: 'Tis there', he wrote, 'that I am in

345. Ibid., p. 145.
346. Ibid., p. 139.
347. Sherman, *John Dee*, p. 46.
348. Fehrenbach and Leedham-Green, *Private Libraries*, p. 145.
349. A. Ophir, 'A Place of Knowledge Recreated: The Library of Michel de Montaigne', *Science in Context* 4 (1991), pp. 163–89.

my kingdom, and there I endeavour to make myself an absolute monarch and to sequester this one corner . . .'[350]

Montaigne describes his library as the place where 'I have my seat', 'my dominion', the only place where he governed his universe.[351] Sir William Drake has left us no such evocative description of his study space. The inventory of his household stuff gives little information about the study with its table, stool, old boxes and 'divers old books and papers'.[352] Yet there, as well as on his travels, Drake, as we know from his notebooks, read, exercised his private judgement, and formulated his own very independent and very unusual attitudes and ideas. No less than the House of Commons or the court, the gentleman's private library could house a political faction or become the place in which was articulated, if often only to the self, important political ideas.

Drake's library and the others we have examined also bring home a simple truth that, despite the work of Charles Schmitt, James Binns and others, English historians of political ideas are inclined to forget. Ordinary literate Englishmen in the seventeenth century were exposed to continental books and ideas, both in the original and in translation; their minds were not formed only by an indigenous discourse on society, politics and state. Individual studies have drawn attention to the circulation of works of resistance theory – Buchanan and Du Plessis Mornay's *Vindiciae Contra Tyrannos* for example – among the Sidney/Essex faction at the court of Queen Elizabeth I.[353] As we have seen, Drake, Townshend, Milton and Dering had Latin texts of Buchanan's *History* and the *Vindiciae*, histories of the French and Low Countries' civil wars, works that provided an important historical and interpretive context for considering the Scots' justifications of their rebellion against the Prayer Book. After the regicide Milton was to insist upon the need to look to foreign books and discourses to write a new republic in England. He was right that in order to eradicate monarchy the texts of majesty had to be erased from the English imagination. But, as the reading notes of Milton's and others evidence, those 'foreign writings' were well represented in English gentlemen's libraries well before the Civil War.

It has been estimated that it was not until the two decades after 1620 that the number of published books in English overtook those in Latin, whether ancient or modern works.[354] Yet the British Library, for reasons of copyright, has only about a fifth of the continental books published before 1800 and so

---

350. W. Sherman, 'The Place of Reading in the English Renaissance: John Dee Revisited', in J. Raven, H. Small and N. Tadmor, *The Practice and Representation of Reading in England* (Cambridge, 1996), pp. 62–76, at p. 70.
351. *Montaigne: The Complete Essays*, ed. M. Screech (Harmondsworth, 1993), p. 933.
352. Bucks. R. O., D/DR/10/1. 'A True and Perfect Inventory of all the Household Stuff in the Mansion House of Sir William Drake . . . called Shardeloes.'
353. Phillips, 'Buchanan and the Sidney Circle'; K. Sharpe, 'A Commonwealth of Meanings', in Sharpe, *Politics and Ideas* (1989), pp. 17–18, 324 nn 107–9.
354. D. Hay, '1500–1700: The Bibliographical Problem', in Bolgar, *Classical Influences*, p. 39.

fails to reflect the importance of Latin texts and continental editions to the
early modern English reader who wrote and thought as easily in Latin as in
his own tongue.[355] In Drake's case, as in many others, Italian came just as
easily: as with his Latin he thought in the language, and was able therefore
to think in the idioms of the quattro- and cinquecento. Indeed we have shown
that it was through Latin and Italian texts that he read the works of his own
country and culture. He should lead us to think again about the core texts
of English political thought.

Of course, even when fluent in other languages, Drake and his peers often
read the classics and continental texts in translation. Of all the books listed
in the Short Title Catalogue, one-eighth are translations, the largest proportion of these translations of the classics. Markku Peltonen has argued recently
for the importance of translated works, especially the classics, in sustaining a
discourse of civic theory in England, at a time when, Pocock maintained, the
language of the common law and the hold of monarchy dominated political
discourse and thought.[356] Certainly translation meant the classics reached a
wider audience than the educated gentry – though how wide is a question
that still awaits exploration. But translations were also important in other ways.
Francis Bacon in his dedication to King James of the *Advancement of Learning* called for 'new editions of authors, with more correct impressions, more
faithful translations, more profitable glosses, more diligent annotations and the
like'.[357] 'Profitable glosses' and 'faithful' translations are, of course, value judgements. But in some cases, such as an early seventeenth-century translation of
Florus's *Epitome of Roman History*, rather than the textual notes of a modern
scholar, the edition pointed to contemporary political parallels, for example
the deluding of James I by the king of Spain.[358] Annotations such as this
localised and politicised classical and continental texts, fostering the habits of
reading for use and in the context of experience. In some measure, all translation involved this transfer to English circumstance; translators were lauded
for such practice: as a poem to the translator of Cornelius Agrippa put it,
'You add correct and so the whole Refine / that tis no more Agrippa's now
but thine.'[359] Whether he read a translation or performed his own, an early
modern reader like Drake added to, corrected, refined the texts he read – and
made them his own.

Whether in Latin or in translation, the importance of these continental
texts in shaping Drake's attitdues to history and political ideas should not be
underestimated. In particular Drake's reading, as well as years of sojourn in

355. Ibid., p. 34.
356. M. Peltonen, *Classical Humanism and Republicanism in English Political Thought,
    1570–1640* (Cambridge, 1995), ch. 1 and passim. See too J. W. Binns, *Intellectual Culture
    in Elizabethan and Jacobean England: The Latin Writings of the Age* (Leeds, 1990). Con-
    trast Pocock, *Machiavellian Moment*, p. 360.
357. Bacon, *Advancement of Learning*, pp. 61–2.
358. See *History of the Romans by Lucius Florus*, preface.
359. C. Agrippa, *Female Preeminence* (1670), prefatory verse.

the Netherlands, appear to have led him to be influenced by the fashionable neostoicist humanist writings of Justus Lipsius and his disciples. In his emphases on the control of the passions, the importance of learning for the active life, the lessons of history for statecraft, and the need for rulers to deploy not only prudence but at times deception, fear and force, Lipsius may have provided an important influence on Drake's thinking. We know too that William met and conversed about history and contemporary affairs with Lipsius's disciples at Leiden, Daniel Heinsius and Gerard Vossius who wrote on the Greek and Roman past and the art of history. But, as always, Drake took from his texts what most spoke to his own circumstances and perceptions. In consequence, though Vossius and Lipsius counted truth and morality as central and denounced the 'sect of Machiavellians', William deployed them as counsellors of realpolitik and modern Machiavels who taught, as had the Florentine, the arts of survival in a vicious social and political world.[360] It is just such conversations and negotiations between continental texts and local circumstances and readers that we need to imagine and explore if we are to understand the political thought of late humanism and early modern England.

Before we leave the early modern library, we should note in scanning the shelves that manuscript treatises appear, undifferentiated, along with print. Drake's translation of Machiavelli's *The Prince* was a manuscript, and he evidently had others. Once scholars tended to pass over manuscript culture, dismissing it as an anachronism in the age of print. More recently we have been made aware of the predominance of manuscript as the medium of lyric verse, political poetry, squib or bawdy poem. Manuscript, it has been suggested, helped define particular communities, and escaped the control of both author and censor. In manuscript, Arthur Marotti puts it, 'the uses and interpretation of texts were more obviously under reader control.'[361] The freedom of reading opened by manuscript as opposed to print must remain a suggestion. However, the circulation of texts – parliamentary speeches as well as poems – in different editions and forms opened not only more materials to the reader but fostered a sense of unauthorised ideas or utterances, of the relations between authorised and unauthorised ideas.[362] The presence of manuscripts and the large numbers of continental books in the original or translation in early modern libraries indicate that future histories of political thought will need to look beyond the printed English treatises from which generalisations about the Englishman's political consciousness are still too often constructed.

It is those scholars who have used the language of 'classical republicanism' in an English context who have begun the move away from an insular Anglocentrism that has characterised the history of ideas. Blair Worden in

360. Oestreich, *Neostoicism*, p. 44 and passim; Wickenden, *G. J. Vossius*.
361. Marotti, *Manuscript, Print*, p. 242.
362. Cf. Love, *Scribal Publication*, p. 17; speeches circulated in manuscript in different versions.

particular has traced the intellectual origins of the republican ideas of the 1650s to Philip Sidney and his brother Robert's reading in the classics in the reigns of Elizabeth and early James I.[363] His argument takes off from Thomas Hobbes's belief that the Civil War had been caused by 'the reading of the books of policy and histories of the ancient Greeks and Romans'. 'From the reading I say, of such books', Hobbes wrote in the twenty-ninth chapter of *Leviathan*, 'men have undertaken to kill their kings because the Greek and Latin writers . . . make it lawful and laudable for any man so to do . . .'[364] And he went on to suggest that even in peaceful times, 'they that live under a monarch conceive an opinion that the subjects in a popular commonwealth enjoy liberty but that in a monarchy they are all slaves . . .' 'I cannot', he concluded, 'imagine how anything can be more prejudicial to monarchy than the allowing of such books to be publicly read without present supplying such correctives of discreet masters as are fit to take away their vermine.'[365] Hobbes was not alone in his analysis. John Aubrey was sure that it was Milton's reading of Livy and other Roman authors that had turned his mind against monarchy; and Bishop Burnet believed that the arch republican Henry Marten had founded his politics 'upon Roman and Greek principles'.[366] David Norbrook has similarly argued that a reading of Lucan's *Pharsalia* drove Thomas May to republican sympathies.[367]

Contemporary comment and recent historical enquiry lead us to the incontestable conclusion that for some key thinkers and politicians, the classics were a source for republican ideas. Yet hitherto we have an inadequate understanding of *how* the process of reading made the classical heritage for some into an apologia for republic. And until we understand it better Jonathan Scott urges caution about generalisations. Classical republicanism, as he says, 'drew principally on classical Greek and Roman and Italian Renaissance sources, combining Aristotelian political forms with the Polybian idea of balance . . . and the republicanism of Machiavelli's *Discourses*'.[368] Yet though the sources were common, 'there [was] within the tradition a wide variation of emphases in the use of sources';[369] not all classical republicans came to their views through the same assembly of texts. Nor did those same texts lead all readers to republican sympathies. Tacitus and Machiavelli were well read in

363. A. B. Worden, 'Classical Republicanism and the Puritan Revolution', in H. Lloyd Jones, V. Pearl and B. Worden, *History and Imagination* (1981), pp. 182–200; Worden, 'The Commonwealth Kidney of Algernon Sidney', *J. Brit. Studies* 24 (1985), pp. 1–40; Worden, *The Sound of Virtue: Philip Sidney's Arcadia and Elizabethan Politics* (New Haven, 1996); Peltonen, *Classical Humanism*.
364. T. Hobbes, *Leviathan*, ed. R. Tuck (Cambridge, 1991), pp. 225–6.
365. Ibid.
366. Worden, 'Milton's Republicanism', p. 232; S. Wiseman, '"Adam the Father of all Flesh": Porno-Political Rhetoric and Political Theory In and After the English Civil War', in J. Holstun, ed., *Pamphlet Wars* (1992), p. 139.
367. Norbrook, 'Lucan, Thomas May'.
368. J. Scott, *Algernon Sidney and the English Republic, 1623–1677* (Cambridge, 1988), p. 15.
369. Ibid.

Royalist circles in the 1640s; and in the case of Sir William Drake, reading of the classics and Machiavelli led him at last to conceive of a republic as oppressive of liberty, as the dissolution of government.[370]

Along with the Bible, the classics were the most important texts of early modern culture. But we have yet to understand fully how they performed, how they were read and interpreted, alongside other texts, in that culture, and how those performances and readings changed over time. Even the most obvious question, the relationship between the classical and Christian heritage, remains inadequately explored. After Aquinas took a softer line to St Augustine's denunciation of all secular wisdom, Christian thinkers endeavoured to accommodate and appropriate classical culture, culminating in Erasmus's brand of Christian humanism.[371] The Protestant Reformation, however, placed strains on the Erasmian synthesis, as Luther and Calvin returned to an Augustinian emphasis on the absolute depravity of fallen humanity. In England, at least initially, those tensions were muted, as the first generation of reformers, Cranmer and Jewel, endeavoured to build solid bridges between the new humanism and Protestantism.[372] But classical texts remained 'potentially dangerous to Christian readers', and both puritans and Laudians reacted sharply to what they perceived as an increasingly secular gentry culture in Elizabethan and early Stuart England.[373] What Drake reveals is the extent to which their concerns were justified, the ways in which for this reader the synthesis of classical and Christian texts could lead not to a Christian humanism but to an Erastian, indeed more secular Christianity, an almost deistic belief, in which religion was valued for its social function. We cannot but be led to wonder, as we think ahead to the deism of the Augustan age, how many had come to read like him.

Clearly, within the heritage of the classics there were very different texts that were likely to lead to different views of the world: Cicero and Seneca articulated a moral position quite divorced from that of Tacitus. Historians have begun to trace the rise and fall in popularity of classical authors as a key to shifting social and political thought, and such a study could helpfully be extended.[374] In the end, however, it may not have been the particular authors favoured that most determined what students took from their reading of the ancients. Professor Todd found puritans and non-puritans in the universities reading essentially the same works.[375] As with Drake, it was why and how the works were read that determined in each case what meanings the reader discerned and what lessons he learned. The classical editor, professor

370. Worden, 'Classical Republicanism', p. 183; F. Raab, *The English Face of Machiavelli* (1964); Ogden MS 7/21 f. 112.
371. Cf. Rice, *Renaissance Idea of Wisdom*.
372. Todd, *Christian Humanism*, pp. 58–65; cf. Hampton, *Writing from History*, p. 61.
373. Crane, *Framing Authority*, p. 15; Sharpe, *Politics and Ideas*, pp. 23–6.
374. See, for example, P. Burke, 'A Survey of the Popularity of Ancient Historians 1450–1700', *History & Theory* 5 (1966), pp. 135–52.
375. Todd, *Christian Humanism*, p. 90.

of history and political theorist Justus Lipsius was clear that it was for modern scholars to take from the ancients those lessons of antiquity that seemed most relevant or useful to their own situation,[376] and in his preface to his edition of Tacitus, he demonstrated how one text could yield a variety of messages to his time. To Lipsius, Tacitus presented 'a theatre of our modern life', a staging of various characters and scenes. 'I see a ruler rising up against the laws in one passage, subjects rising up against a ruler elsewhere. I find the devices that make the destruction of liberty possible and the unhappy effort to regain it . . .'[377]

As they viewed the stage of antiquity from different perspectives, English editors of and commentators on the classics offered very different interpretations and glosses. Where Samuel Daniel described the Roman period of empire as one of corrupt degeneration from republican virtue, Edmund Bolton and later Peter Heylyn interpreted the Tacitean period of Roman history as demonstrating the benefits of monarchy.[378] Though Sir Henry Savile in his translation and additon to Tacitus praised the rebellion of Julius Vindex against Nero, Prince Henry, who praised Tacitus, presumably did not read him as the enemy of kings;[379] while Clement Edmondes, author of *Observations upon Caesar's Commentaries*, cited Tacitus to sustain the argument that civil wars could never be justified.[380] Tacitus, in other words, could be of 'utility' to apologists for absolutism or resistance. In the words of a modern editor, 'he seemed to provide slogans for – and against – every section of political opinion. Everybody saw in him something different.'[381] Such different interpretations were not always the outcome of different readers but of the same reader at different times. As Gabriel Harvey read and reread his Livy to different ends and with different conclusions, and Drake read and reread his favourite authors to become a keen advocate of monarchical authority, so, at each moment, other readers worked out what the legacy of the classics meant for them. Hobbes may have been wrong to fear that the Greek and Roman writers led readers to republicanism, but reading them may have fostered what would have horrified him even more: the formation by readers of their own judgement and politics.

The age of revival of the classical texts also witnessed a historical revolution: a preoccupation with the past, with historical study, and with histories

376. A. Grafton, 'Renaissance Readers and Ancient Texts; Comments on Some Commentaries', *Ren. Quart.* 38 (1985), pp. 615–49, at p. 639.
377. Ibid.
378. M. Smuts, 'Court-Centred Politics and the Uses of Roman Historians c.1590–1640', in Sharpe and Lake, *Culture and Politics*, pp. 21–43, esp. pp. 29, 39; P. Heylyn, *Augustus* (1632). See too A. T. Bradford, 'Stuart Absolutism and the "Utility" of Tacitus', *Hunt. Lib. Quart.* 45 (1983), pp. 127–55.
379. Smuts, 'Court-Centred Politics', pp. 26–7, 34; J. H. Salmon, 'Seneca and Tacitus in Jacobean England', in L. Peck, ed., *The Mental World of the Jacobean Court* (Cambridge, 1991), pp. 169–90.
380. C. Edmondes, *Observations upon Caesar's Commentaries* (1609), p. 2.
381. M. Grant, ed., *Tacitus: The Annals of Imperial Rome* (Harmondsworth, 1971), p. 23.

as guides to present action.[382] For early modern England, scholars have studied the rise of the antiquarian movement, the vogue for chronological local histories, and the civic histories of Bacon, Hayward and Speed.[383] And they have elucidated the role of precedent in legal and political debate, the need to appeal to the past to validate present positions.[384] Once again, however, scholarly emphasis on the writing of history has passed over the audiences for those histories: who read what (chronicle or antiquarian treatise, politic history or local perambulation), and how they read the stories of the past. Prefaces to historical works, like all prefaces, endeavoured to direct readers: 'The principal work of history', Hobbes wrote in the preface to his Thucydides, is 'to instruct and enable men by knowledge of actions past to bear themselves prudently in the present and providently towards the future.'[385] Courtesy books not only urged gentlemen to read histories, they specified authors and directed readers to learn from them 'how to demean or behave ourselves in all our actions'.[386] But beyond such generalised guidance, the question of how histories were to be read remains. Some commentators recognised that the process of reading the past as a guide for the present involved the exercise of personal judgement. Francis Bacon held histories the best storehouse of examples for wisdom, but acknowledged that the lessons drawn by different readers might not be the same. 'It is the true office of history', he wrote in *The Advancement of Learning*, 'to represent the events themselves together with the counsels, and to leave the observations and conclusions thereupon to the liberty and faculty of every man's judgement.'[387] Going further, the author of *The Honest Man* discerned that present circumstances would, and should, determine the ways in which the past was read. 'Whoever is not naturally capable to discern the times and to consider of the variety of experience', the English translator of Nicholas Faret put it in 1632, 'shall never reap much fruit . . . by history.'[388] As Timothy Hampton has argued, such statements reflect the deep ambiguity in Renaissance attitudes to history and its lessons: 'a faith in transcendent models of action' and a historical sense that examples belonged to their 'own cultural moment'.[389]

Political divisions exposed those ambiguities and ultimately fractured the 'common tradition' of exemplary history, and with it humanist ideology. Hampton regards Machiavelli as the turning point in the way histories were read. As he read *his* histories to overturn the prevailing paradigms of

382. F. Smith Fussner, *The Historical Revolution: English Historical Writing and Thought* (1962).
383. See, for example, G. Parry, *The Trophies of Time: English Antiquaries of the Seventeenth Century* (Oxford, 1995); S. G. Mendyck, *Speculum Britanniae: Regional Study, Antiquarianism and Science in Britain to 1700* (Toronto, 1989); D. Woolf, *The Idea of History in Early Stuart England* (Toronto, 1990).
384. See Sharpe, *Sir Robert Cotton*; F. Levy, *Tudor Historical Thought* (San Marino, 1967).
385. T. Hobbes, *Eight Books of the Peloponnesian Warre* (1629), preface to the reader (sig A3).
386. Brathwait, *English Gentleman*, p. 210.
387. Bacon, *Advancement of Learning*, p. 77.
388. N. Faret, *The Honest Man* (1632), p. 95.
389. Hampton, *Writing from History*, pp. 78–9.

virtuous conduct, Machiavelli powerfully demonstrated the possibilities of individual interpretation of the past.[390] And the Reformation explicitly polemicised and politicised readings of the past to sustain denominational claims – even, in some cases, by invention or forgery.[391] As in so many respects, in its attitudes to history early modern England seems divided between the old paradigms of history as example and a pragmatic realisation that histories were written, and read, not just differently but politically. History, that is, became histor*ies*, plural and contested texts, in England (as before on the continent) when political differences were written from and into accounts of the past. Famous instances, Elizabeth I's identification of herself with Richard II, Charles I's fear that he was compared with Tiberius, remind us that contemporaries read their present with the past. What Sir William Drake reveals to us is how a gentleman widely read in British and continental histories of different genres and perspectives, early on rejected the 'moral idealism' of the exemplary history for a ruthless pragmatism, and exactly how his 'discerning' of his own time melded with the lessons, the 'patterns for action' history presented to him.[392] The way histories were read, he reminds us, no less than the way they were written, was shaped by what individuals valued and valorised – that is by ideology.

If experience of modern times (the invocation of Victorian values, for example) makes it easy to comprehend how history can be read as well as written to push a position or support a cause, we have lost a sense of how proverbs, fables, still more emblems, could be the sites of ideological reading or contested interpretation. To us the proverb has lost nearly all its ideological freight and values. For the Renaissance, however, as we have argued, the proverb distilled all wisdom, sacred and divine. Erasmus described proverbs as the 'vestiges of God's shaping presence in history' and as the richest bequest of antiquity.[393] To him the proverb represented a synthesis of the best of Christian and secular notions of wisdom and a common treasury of sage counsel and truths. 'For what is more probable than what no one denies,' he asked, and added: 'who is not to be moved by the *consensus* of so many ages.'[394] Hundreds of volumes of proverbs met the demands of readers to partake of that wisdom,[395] and proverbs were copied from texts and oral memory into commonplace books, and onto ornaments and the very walls of great houses and private studies.[396] Yet though they gathered from and published a common storehouse, each collection of proverbs was a selection, and those the reader

390. Ibid., p. 299.
391. For a recent study of the polemicisation, see E. Jones, *The English Nation: The Great Myth* (Stroud, 1998).
392. Hampton, *Writing from History*, p. 298; Bacon, *Advancement of Learning*, p. 177.
393. D. Kinney, 'Erasmus's *Adagia*: Midwife to the Rebirth of Learning' *J. Med. & Ren. Studies* 7 (1981), pp. 169–92, at p. 191.
394. Ibid., p. 188, my italics.
395. See the list recommended in De Jordy, '*A Library for Younger Scholars*', p. 17.
396. See, for example, E. McCutcheon, *Sir Nicholas Bacon's Great House Sententiae*, *Eng. Lit. Ren.* suppl. 3 (1977).

rewrote or engraved on domestic objects were, in the most obvious sense, personalised. Moreover, the 'meaning' of proverbs was by no means self-evident. As the author of *Paroemiologia*, a 1639 collection of English and Latin proverbs for use in schools, put it in his epistle to the reader: it was difficult to use proverbs skilfully and 'seasonably', and some 'may be applied and used to diverse and sundry senses'.[397]

The meaning of proverbs was of course rendered more indeterminate by their inconsistencies and contradictions: for every adage there was (and is – it is still a party game) an opposing axiom. The reader of proverbs, then, was presented with contraries from which to select those that gave most meaning to his or her life. That the readings in consequence could differ markedly is nowhere better demonstrated than in the case of Sir Nicholas Bacon and his son Francis. Sir Nicholas's selection of sixty proverbs to adorn his walls reflected his own profession in the law, his public aspirations and his 'high ethical ideals', drawn from Cicero and Seneca. Though he presented extreme positions, it appears that he did so to balance and mute antitheses.[398] Though brought up surrounded by his father's adages, Francis by contrast 'frequently tries to remove even an implicitly unitary attitude, wanting to break down traditional philosophical systems'.[399] In his case, personal readings of the proverbs formed the basis of the new genre of essays in which, like Montaigne, Bacon reworked traditional adages into very personal arguments. For both Bacons, the proverb was a political text: Nicholas built the Long Gallery in which his were displayed for Queen Elizabeth's visit; Francis dedicated his *Essays* to the royal favourite, the Duke of Buckingham. When one considers that the superiority of love to fear as the basis of government was one of Sir Nicholas's choices, the political import of proverbs cannot be in doubt.[400]

Much would be learned from a careful study of the collections of proverbs in different languages, their selections, arrangement, and their prefaces and dedications. One popular collection alone, however, may make the point about the political valence of such editions. In 1660 James Howell, Royalist writer of letters, romances and tracts, published his *Lexicon Tetraglotten*, a dictionary together with 'another volume of the choicest proverbs'. His intention, he argued, was to rescue the reputation of England for witty adages, but his project was not merely one of upholding national pride. As well as ancient proverbs, Howell added topical adages ('civil wars like fire in the bed straw') and explicitly partisan axioms: 'From a Long Parliament Lord deliver me.'[401]

397. *Paroemiologia Anglo Latina in Usum Scholarum Concinatta or Proverbs* (1639), sig [B1]. The author left vacant spaces under each heading in his collection.
398. McCutcheon, *Sir Nicholas Bacon's Sententiae*, p. 30.
399. Ibid., p. 55.
400. Ibid., p. 32.
401. J. Howell, *Lexicon Tetraglotten: An English-French-Italian-Spanish Dictionary . . . with Another Volume of the Choicest Proverbs* (1660), pp. 4, 5. On Howell, see D. Woolf, 'Conscience, Constancy and Ambition in the Career and Writings of James Howell', in

And in a dedication to Charles II, he expressed his joy that the sun shone again in England, restoring order to heaven and earth. Howell's 'choicest proverbs' were meant to celebrate and support Restoration, and to rescue language and adages from other than Royalist readings. In the end, however, the 'meaning' of a proverb rested with the reader. As the author of *Paroemiologia* wrote, 'my mind to me a kingdom is', and when the individual mind wrestled with the message of a proverb, it performed a political act.[402] Recognising, for all his desire to arrest change, the altered times, even Howell sensed that 'it is the common people alone that have the privilege of making proverbs.' He may have sensed that such a 'privilege of making' would soon extend to politics too.[403]

Fables were regarded as a form of exposition of proverb, as a parable that conveyed a lesson in a story of animals which symbolised diverse human traits and virtues or vices. 'Many excellent morals', Richard Brathwait advised the young English gentleman, 'are shadowed in these fables which may deserve observation of the . . . maturest conceit.'[404] As Brathwait's language reveals, however, the morals in fables were not always perlucid but 'shadowed'; and the animals – bear, fox or ape – could, and were seen to, represent not just human traits but particular social groups.[405] The identification of courtiers with foxes and apes developed with other satires against courts that fell far short of their ideals. Fables, in other words, left ample room for reading and interpretation, and, as we have seen, the most obviously political of fables was reread, reinterpreted and reappropriated by contending factions, Catholic and Protestant, Royalist and Parliamentarian, Whig and Tory, throughout the early modern period.[406]

Emblems combined the symbolism of fable and concise lesson of proverb in a juxtaposition of word and image – 'intellectual conceptions reduced to sensible images', Bacon called them.[407] They have been neglected by scholars until recently, not least because the emblem cannot easily be accommodated to the modern disciplinary divisions of history, literature, art history and philosophy. In early modern England, they were pervasive in the literature and culture. It is impossible to understand the Renaissance portrait without an understanding of emblems. Emblems are vital to the poetry of Spenser, Sidney and Marvell and formed a subtheme of Herbert's *The Temple*.[408] The leading educational treatise for early Stuart gentlemen included woodcut emblems of

J. Morrill, P. Slack and D. Woolf, *Public Duty and Private Conscience in Seventeenth-Century England* (Oxford, 1993), pp. 243–78. See also Taylor, *Proverb.*

402. *Paroemiologia*, p. 16.

403. 'Divers Catalogues of New Sayings', p. 1 in *Lexicon Tetraglotten.*

404. Brathwait, *English Gentleman*, p. 86.

405. See also R. Braithwait, *A Strange Metamorphosis of Man* (1634) which surveys the traits of all animals.

406. Above, pp. 200–2.

407. Bacon, *Advancement of Learning*, p. 130.

408. R. Colie, *The Resources of Kind: Genre Theory in the Renaissance* (Berkeley, 1973).

Youth, Recreation, Moderation and Education.[409] And they were central to heraldic devises where the gentry displayed those virtuous attributes that emblems signified.[410] It is hard to exaggerate their popularity. Between 1530 and 1600 there were over ninety European editions of Alciati's book of emblems, and an English volume outsold *Paradise Lost* four times over.[411] As well as such textual abundance they were frequently reproduced in wood panellings and decoration as well as household stuff, cushions, tapestries and carpets, dress and jewellery.[412]

As with proverbs and fables, there was a religious and secular dimension to emblems. Francis Quarles (whose book of emblems sold 5,000 copies in its first edition) called them 'silent parables' and informed his readers that 'before the knowledge of letters God was known by hieroglyphicks.'[413] Many of his examples are accompanied by verses from Scripture and biblical stories explicating the moral. Like proverbs, emblems were held to impart rules of moral and civil life. And they were deployed by kings and queens to announce the virtues the ruler embodied, Elizabeth I, as we have seen, adopting the phoenix and the rainbow as emblems of eternal constancy (to complement her motto *Semper Eadem*) and the pelican as symbolic association with Christ. Emblems, we might say, were a, perhaps the, principal mode of signification and representation, and in the Renaissance state that was to make them vehicles of ideology.[414] Not surprisingly therefore the emblems on ensigns and banners became important to both sides in the English Civil War. Where the Royalists deployed emblems to represent divine assistance to the king and the destruction of a pleasant land by the barbarous vulgar, Parliament's forces rode to battle beneath emblems announcing Death or Victory, both sides thereby announcing their beliefs and faith in their causes.[415] The translator of a treatise on emblems published amidst the battles of civil war betrays – perhaps understandably – some uncertainty about their intended audience. Though he felt they should, traditionally, be not 'so plain as the common people may comprehend' them, he cited Ammirato's belief that they 'may give comment to all'.[416] And Blount makes clear his own view that the various elements of an emblem might signify to different audiences; 'if the picture of it be too common, it ought to have a mystical sense'; 'if they be something

409. Brathwait, *English Gentleman*, pp. 39–52.
410. See R. Estienne, *The Art of Making Devices* (1646).
411. R. Altick, *The English Common Reader* (Chicago, 1957), p. 29; P. Daly, *The English Emblem and the Continental Tradition* (New York, 1988); L. Febvre and H. Martin, *The Coming of the Book* (1958), p. 275.
412. Daly argues the influence of Ripa's emblems on Rubens's Whitehall ceiling, *English Emblem*, p. 13.
413. F. Quarles, *Emblems* (1660 edn), 'To the Reader'.
414. See M. Bath, *Speaking Pictures: English Emblem Books and Renaissance Culture* (1994).
415. Several Civil War emblems are engraved in Huntington Library Richard Bull Granger, vol. 8/1.
416. Estienne, *The Art of Making Devices* (1646, E338/8), trans. R. Blount, p. 21.

obscure they must more clearly inform us by the words.'[417] Emblems, then, derived their meanings not only from their devices, but from their readers and viewers who could, to varying degrees, decipher and interpret the 'philosophy', the ways individuals figured their codes for 'moral and civil life'.[418]

Sir William Drake helps us to a fuller understanding of how all three inter-related genres, emblem, fable and proverb, signified not least because, as we have seen, he read them together and against each other. And as his phrases such as 'no doubt' indicate, he formulated his own sense of what an emblem meant, and what lesson *he* felt it taught.[419] In Drake's case the use of Jacob Cats's emblems to interpret Tacitus and of Guicciardini to explicate the emblem of the serpent demonstrates the very individual hermeneutic that the supposedly common storehouse of Renaissance wisdom licensed. When he instructed himself to pursue the emblems that furnished 'most matter', we have seen that what 'mattered' was very much Drake's own values. When he proceeded to apply the moral of a fable after discussion with friends in the late 1640s, we now know that present concerns shaped interpretation of its meaning. And when he explicitly drew from the fable of the master and the maid a parallel to the Presbyterians losing ground to other sects, we have a rare glimpse into how common fables were read to construct personal political perceptions.[420]

In many ways, then, Sir William Drake suggests that we need to qualify some of our assumptions about, and even reorient our approach to, the ped-agogic practices and texts of Renaissance culture. Concentration on the aims and values of the humanist educationalists, notably Erasmus, may distort the reality of what students took from their experiences of learning and reading. And whilst it remains true that generic distinctions were important to the communication of ideas, we should not in our own studies too rigidly sepa-rate those classical texts, modern histories, fables and emblems that Drake read and made sense of together. Most of all, against those critics who, following Foucault, view Renaissance culture as a matrix of hegemonic dis-courses that effectively repressed or policed different values, Drake stands as an excellent demonstration of the possibility of critical and independent judgement.

Indeed, to use their own language we might even suggest that Drake 'deconstructed' those very discourses which modern critics have identified as the instruments of state power, and that he did so through a clear recogni-tion of the gap between the signified and the signifier. For Sir William, who spent much of his life immersed in them, distrusted words, whatever their

417. Ibid., p. 8.
418. Ibid., p. 13. Cf. Bath, *Speaking Pictures*, pp. 29–30; Bath reminds us that there was an ambivalent view of emblems and that all signs involved 'representation and interpre-tation' (p. 4).
419. See Ogden MS 7/17 f. 100v.
420. Ogden MS 7/31 f. 94v; see above, pp. 200–2.

source: 'ne crede omni verbo,' he reminded himself.[421] The language of duty, he discerned, often masked interest; true liberty was often suppressed by those who invoked its name. 'There is', he concluded in revealingly political language, 'a secret tyranny in eloquence . . .'[422]

This, once again, is striking. For eloquence was at the core of the humanist education received by most grammar school boys in early modern England. The Roman rhetoricians, especially Quintilian and Cicero, stressed the moral virtues, and a training in rhetoric was held by Erasmus, Vives and other Renaissance educational theorists to be the foundation for *scientia civilis* and good citizenship.[423] In Elizabethan grammar schools boys were taught the skills of judicial, deliberative and demonstrative oratory, the features of a good style and the declamatory arts. English rhetoricians such as Leonard Cox, Thomas Wilson, Thomas Vicars and Thomas Farnaby stressed that 'the point of studying the *ars rhetorica* was to advance the cause of Christian . . . culture' and Christian virtues.[424] Though we know nothing of Drake's schooling, it is likely that his tutor, Croke, took him through the curriculum in rhetoric; certainly huge numbers of Drake's annotations and many of the headings he adopted in his commonplace books suggest rhetorically inspired readings. But in Drake's case rhetorical training did not foster the conventional virtues of generosity and liberality. Nor did the arts of rhetoric, fundamental in the education of governors, delude him. 'He who speaks best is commonly craftiest,' he reflected, and eloquence was often far removed from wisdom.[425] It was the violent power of authority that made 'the optative mode . . . all one with the imperative', the 'strongest sword' that 'speaks best'.[426]

In his obvious distrust of rhetoric, Drake joins those satirists of the courtly arts of verbal agility and dissimulation who fostered a more cynical view of rhetoric and of politics during the late years of Elizabeth's reign and the early Stuarts.[427] Such critics, it has been argued, 'showed how politics could be understood, not only in terms of abstract, formal principles of law and divinity, but as a product of the hidden goals and concrete actions of rulers and their associates'.[428] And what Drake's case further manifests is that to

---

421. Ogden MS 7/21 f. 64, cf. 7/22 f. 98. Significantly he notes that Machiavelli urged the same distrust in words, 7/30 f. 92v; and note the reference to Montaigne's advice to trust Brutus talking privately in his tent rather than addressing his soldiers, 7/22 f. 140v.

422. Ogden MS 7/9 f. 149.

423. For the most recent and best discussion of Renaissance rhetoric see Q. Skinner, *Reason and Rhetoric in the Philosophy of Hobbes* (Cambridge, 1996), part 1.

424. Ibid., p. 66

425. Ogden MSS 7/37 f. 30; 7/25 f. 142v.

426. Ogden MSS 7/20 f. 80; 7/25 f. 18v; cf. 7/24 f. 79v where he notes that as long as men retain arms one should distrust their words.

427. Skinner discusses the contemporary concern, exemplified by Machiavelli, that the arts of persuasion could be deployed to misrepresent vice as virtue, *Reason and Rhetoric*, ch. 4.

428. Smuts, 'Court-Centred Politics', p. 42.

subject the power of rhetoric and the rhetorics of power to critical scrutiny
was not just to interrogate Renaissance educational practices but to draw
authority itself from shadows of divine mystery into the full glare of utilitarian rationalism.

Reading as Politics

In many respects, historians of politics have always been concerned with texts
and with the conditions of writing. The history of political ideas is focused
on a set of canonical texts, and subjects such as regulation of the press, or
licensing and newsletters and pamphlets are established subjects for the historian of politics. I have argued that more attention to the 'textuality', the
rhetoricity of texts, and broader consideration of the material culture and circumstances of print and manuscript would enrich political history. Here, after
a study of Sir William Drake and his notebooks, I want to return to the question of how politics in the early modern period was read, and to how our
address to habits of reading might not only develop but in some cases refigure our comprehension of traditional subjects hitherto not studied from this
perspective.

    Let us begin with a central and still much debated subject: censorship.
Historians have argued sharply over the extent and effectiveness of censorship in early modern England. At one extreme, Christopher Hill has argued
for wide-ranging and effective control of print and heterodox ideas in
early modern England until the eve of Civil War.[429] At the other, Sheila
Lambert, Blair Worden and Cyndia Clegg suggest that regulation of the press
was neither draconian nor easily enforcible.[430] In part disagreement arises from
the problem of definition. At various stages of print circulation and production, censorship could involve attempts to have a book burned, call in an
edition, refuse a licence or frighten an author from public pronouncements
on forbidden subjects. But at no stage could authority exercise total control:
foreign imports and pirate presses circumvented the need for imprimatur;
a book once published could not be completely suppressed; analogy and

429. C. Hill, 'Censorship and English Literature', in Hill, *Collected Essays I: Writing and
    Revolution in Seventeenth-Century England* (Brighton, 1985), pp. 32–71. All of Hill's
    work is premised on the existence of a pre-revolutionary radicalism silenced by
    censorship.
430. S. Lambert, 'The Printers and the Government, 1604–1637', in R. Myers and M.
    Harris, eds, *Aspects of Printing from 1600* (Oxford, 1987), pp. 1–29; B. Worden, 'Litera-
    ture and Political Censorship in Early Modern England', in A. C. Duke and C. Tamse,
    eds, *Too Mighty to be Free* (Zutfen, 1988), pp. 45–62. See also C. Clegg, *Press Censor-
    ship in Elizabethan England* (Cambridge, 1997). I am grateful to Cyndia Clegg for dis-
    cussions of this subject at the Huntington Library.

coded language enabled authors to escape the censor.[431] In this last case Annabel Patterson has suggested that oblique reference to contemporary politics and indirect criticisms were even tolerated by authority.[432] Pastoral, romance, the staging of a play in another time and location were genres and devices in and by which writers were allowed to encode political commentary and criticism, provided the 'functional ambiguity' of the texts occluded direct statement.

Patterson's argument turns attention to the readers as well as writers of texts. Coded writing, whether literally in cipher or through allusion, is intended to speak to some readers and not (or differently) to others. If early modern governments were willing to tolerate ambiguous or oblique criticisms, it was presumably because they believed that only the learned elites would 'understand' them, and not make the move from textual play to radical politics. We cannot be sure, for all the plausibility of Patterson's argument, whether early modern governments had such a carefully worked out theory of hermeneutics. We can say for certain that they were concerned with the readers as well as writers of texts.[433] Not least of the reasons behind injunctions to compulsory attendance at church was that the Sunday service guaranteed an audience for homilies on obedience and, in theory, the reading and repetition of admonitions to moral behaviour and Christian humility (in whatever station of life one found oneself) and to obedience to God's lieutenant on earth. Books that were licensed in Latin or a foreign language but not for English translation – Machiavelli's *Prince* is an obvious example – evidence the perceived need to police reading as well as writing. In some cases, especially after a book was called in, there were heavy punishments for the possession, as well as the authorship, printing or circulation of defamatory or heterodox works. More subtly, 'official' texts and government writers endeavoured to control and direct meaning and interpretation. As David Womersley writes, 'one of the most striking features of many sixteenth-century books is the subtlety and force with which they actively stifle heterodox thinking amongst their readership.'[434]

Yet if the regulation of publishing was difficult, the control of reading was (and remains) impossible. In an oral culture, with devices for and traditions of memory, 'texts' could be spread far beyond the reader of the material page, and long after a book had been called in. The arguments and ideas in classical Latin and continental texts could also, albeit in simplified

431. Imprimaturs are found in only one-third of books published in the first half of the seventeenth century, see Bennett, *English Books and Readers, 1603–1640*, pp. 45, 57.
432. A. Patterson, *Censorship and Interpretation* (Madison, 1984).
433. See Johns, *Nature of the Book*, p. 159.
434. D. Womersley, 'Sir Henry Savile's Translation of Tacitus and the Political Interpretation of Elizabethan Texts', *J. Eng. Studies* 42 (1991), pp. 313–42. Note Manguel's remark: 'Absolute power requires that all reading be official reading', *History of Reading*, p. 283.

form, permeate from elite to popular culture. Ballads and squibs surprisingly often echo court news and more learned exchanges. Most importantly, no censor could police or even determine what went on in the reader's (or auditor's) mind. We have not hitherto found the equivalent of an English Menocchio. Sir William Drake, a Buckinghamshire gentleman of education and means, able to buy books and read Latin and Italian, cannot stand as an archetype of how politics was read in early modern England. But that he could, even from perfectly common, respectable, orthodox texts, many of them histories, many in translation, construct such unusual and unorthodox political values must at least give us pause for thought. And we might think not only of Drake's friends with whom he exchanged books, and his peers whose reading notes have not survived, but also of his scribe and other servants and attendants who were party to a discussion of interest, civic religion or republic. Moreover, once we see how a gentleman reader like Drake fashioned his own sense of order from texts, adages and emblems that were in themselves commonplace and innocuous, we begin to wonder how a less learned reader, less schooled in humanist values, still more the illiterate, engaged with texts, read, heard or performed. What we begin to suspect is that, whatever the directives of the magistracy or the codes of the village, each subject read authority and constructed his or her own worldview differently – and, in his or her own way, differently on each encounter with those texts in changed circumstances and moments, be they Reformation, Civil War or Commonwealth. The sometimes ambiguous texts of authority, law, custom and memory, we begin to see, opened spaces for 'a broad spectrum of interpretive positions'.[435]

The possibilities for a broad spectrum of interpretations and beliefs are most obviously demonstrable in the realm of faith and conscience. Once the Bible was translated, for any reader the experience of Scripture, of the divinity, was personal, unmediated. Though at one level Protestantism fostered the development of personal faith, religious and secular authorities were from the beginning of the Reformation concerned that Scripture should be read aright. Not only was the Bible the principal text of authority, as Roger Chartier has said, 'the reading of the Bible provided a model for all reading.'[436] For much of the sixteenth century, religious contest revolved around editions and interpretations of the Bible. And, for all the persistent myths about Protestantism and freedom, the reformers were no less anxious than the Catholics about the hermeneutic indeterminacy of Scripture. Indeed the Geneva Bible, the main Protestant edition, it has been argued, far from celebrating the individual reader's solitary communion with Scripture, 'provides the private reader with the guidance of a congregation'.[437] The Geneva Bible divided the text

435. A. Fox, P. Griffiths and S. Hindle, eds, *The Experience of Authority in Early Modern England* (Houndmills, 1996), p. 6. See below, pp. 341–2.
436. R. Chartier, *The Cultural Uses of Print in Early Modern France* (Princeton, 1987), p. 224.
437. Tribble, *Margins and Marginality*, p. 32.

into verses, with headings at the top of each page and notes glossing and interpreting 'difficult' passages – that to Revelations 17: 4 for example explaining that the scarlet woman was the Antichrist.

In England, from the beginning of Reformation, authority exhibited nervousness about the possible consequences of subjects reading Scripture in the vernacular. For a long time Henry VIII refused to sanction an English Bible and insisted that Scripture be expounded by preachers.[438] On 16 November 1538, we recall, he issued a proclamation against marginal notes in Bibles.[439] When at last he gave way to an English edition (not least to supplant the Coverdale translation produced on the continent) Henry endeavoured to exercise control over 'the orderly transmission of the text'. As Greg Walker has recently argued, the title page illustration to the Great Bible of 1539 displays Henry's 'preoccupation with social control and the limits to free discussion of doctrine'.[440] The king hands the text, *his* text, to prelates who pass it on to the laity who intone 'vivat rex' in recognition of the authority of the royal word. As with his own writings on the sacraments, the *Necessary Doctrine* or *The Glass of Truth*, Henry VIII's Great Bible was an attempt to control, not to open, the interpretation of Scripture. Thomas More wanted each person who owned the Bible to be scrutinised by his bishop in a manner reminiscent of modern gunlaw.[441] And in 1543 Parliament forbad reading of the Bible by women, journeymen and apprentices.[442]

For all the mounting evidence of the failure to police reading or determine faith, the history of the Bible in England continues to be one of efforts by authority to prescribe meaning and direct and control readership. The 1568 Bishops Bible, with its centre panel of Queen Elizabeth and portraits of Cecil and Leicester, not only directly associates Scripture with authority: the Bible also had printed marginalia instructing the minister on the teaching of difficult or sensitive passages.[443] James VI and I, as we have seen, was most concerned about the Geneva Bible which continued to be the most popular, believing that at some points its marginal glosses fostered sedition. The Authorised Version of the Bible which he sponsored at Hampton Court was intended to supplant the Geneva edition, and to nurture a still vulnerable Anglican church and faith. The Authorised Version endeavoured to foreclose differences about Scriptural passages, to repel 'the calumniations and hard interpretations' of other exegetes and editions.[444] And in rejecting individual readers who 'give liking unto nothing but what is framed by themselves', it

---

438. See G. Walker, *Persuasive Fictions: Faction, Faith and Political Culture in the Reign of Henry VIII* (Aldershot, 1996), pp. 86ff.
439. See P. L. Hughes and J. F. Larkin, eds, *Tudor Royal Proclamations I: The Early Tudors* (New Haven, 1964), pp. 270–6.
440. Walker, *Persuasive Fictions*, p. 92. See too Kintgen, *Reading in Tudor England*, ch. 4.
441. Brayman, 'Impressions from a Scribbling Age', p. 38.
442. Altick, *English Common Reader*, p. 25. See 34 & 35 Henry VIII cap. 1.
443. Tribble, *Margins and Marginality*, p. 36. See Manguel, *A History of Reading*, pp. 270–5.
444. See the preface to the Authorised Version.

firmly associated the truth of Scripture with the king who had, in his own
writings and actions, declared and defended that truth.[445]

Neither James's exegesis of Scripture nor the Authorised version of the
Bible circumscribed debate and disagreement. His reign saw the claims to
conscience of a militant puritanism and fundamental theological divisions over
salvation and free will among the clergy. Of as great concern to authority
was what was seen as a growth of scepticism among the beau monde, while
at the other end of the social scale popular ignorance of the basic tenets of
Christian faith alarmed preachers of all denominations.[446] Not only in many
areas did Catholic, indeed pelagian, belief in the simple efficacy of good works
persist, there were feared to be many more like the man who had heard of
Christ only that he was a 'a towardly young youth'.[447]

The outpouring of heterodox ideas during the 1640s may then be evidence
of beliefs long held but not expressed, beliefs that men and women had formulated through their own negotiations with Scripture. Thomas Hobbes, following Henry VIII and his successors, regarded this 'anarchy of interpretations'
of the Bible as the principal cause of political anarchy and insisted that the
sovereign should authorise a reading of Scripture, or appoint 'interpreters of
the canonical Scriptures' to prescribe its meaning.[448] Hobbes, concerned with
public obedience to authority, does not discuss the consequences of private
reading and belief: how reading or listening performs in spaces and places
beyond the reach of power.[449] Remarkably, however, even amid the interpretive anarchy and the proliferation of the sects in civil war, some still dreamed
of establishing an agreed meaning for Scripture by means of a definitive text.
The author of *A Design about Disposing the Bible into an Harmony* still believed
in 1647 that a reordering of biblical books into a continuous history (a nice
early recognition of the ideology of narrative) might reduce disagreement. 'It
will serve abundantly', he rather optimistically proclaimed, 'to the clearing of
the genuine historical meaning of the text everywhere.'[450]

We know of course that, like earlier attempts, his failed.[451] Whatever the
material form of the Bible, readers could choose to read as they would. And
ironically some attempts at authorised versions and meanings may have facilitated individual hermeneutic. John Locke famously disdained the arrangement
of Scripture 'crumbled into verses which quickly turn into independent

---

445. We await a full study of James VI and I's exegeses of Scripture. Cf. K. Sharpe 'The
     King's Writ: Royal Authors and Royal Authority in Early Modern England', in Sharpe
     and Lake, *Culture and Politics*, pp. 123–7.
446. See K. Thomas, *Religion and the Decline of Magic* (1971).
447. Ibid., pp. 189–97; cf. P. Collinson, *The Religion of Protestants: The Church in English
     Society, 1559–1625* (Oxford, 1982), ch. 5.
448. G. Shapiro, 'Reading and Writing in the Text of Hobbes' *Leviathan*', *J. Hist. Philos.* 18
     (1980), p. 151. See Hobbes, *Leviathan*, p. 378.
449. Cf. Shapiro, 'Reading and Writing', pp. 152–3.
450. *A Design about Disposing the Bible into an Harmony* (1647, E377/9), p. 15.
451. See, for example, E. Vaughan, *A Method or Brief Instruction . . . for the Reading . . . of the
     Old and New Testament* (1590).

aphorisms'.[452] And his comment leads us nicely back to Drake and how his case develops our understanding of reading Scripture. Most of the examples we have of heterodox readings of the Bible concern theological wrangles or heresy. When church and state were inseparable and the authority of the ruler as monarch and supreme governor was one, heresy was by definition a political threat. But what Drake reveals is how a reader, taking Scripture as 'independent aphorisms', could deconstruct its authority and reconstitute it as an entirely different script for self, society and state. As we have seen, for Drake, Scripture became a source of prudent counsel, reinforcing arguments drawn from secular works about self-preservation, interest and dissimulation. In short, Drake read his Bible almost as a treatise of a new politics of interest rather than as a text of Christian commonweal.[453] Given the survival of the Bible as a central text of state, and the increasingly audible language of interest, we cannot but wonder how many others had also come to such different readings of Scripture, and thence to a new politics.

It is singularly appropriate that the most important texts in Drake's reading of politics were the works of Machiavelli. For the Florentine's own revolutionising of the precepts of political conduct was founded on his own readings. As John Wallace put it in an essay on reading and meaning, 'Machiavelli startled the world with the precepts he found in Livy.'[454] And after him, the classics, indeed the world, could not be read only in the old way again. The historian of Machiavelli's reception in early modern England has argued that though some writers, like Ralegh or Bacon, drew on his writings, and though 'the Machiavellian villain strutted the stage in innumerable disguises', Machiavelli was read by few and denounced by almost all:

> The general tenet of political writing [before 1640] was anti-Machiavellian in the sense that most men could not accept the basic assumptions upon which Machiavelli's statecraft was built. Although they frequently agreed on points of detail . . . there was a point at which his blatant secularism aroused hostility and rejection. For many that point was 'politick' religion, the principle of religion as a political device.[455]

Machiavelli's *Discourses* were not translated into English until 1636, *The Prince* until 1640, and in prefaces to his translations, Edward Dacres criticised the Florentine for impiety and for his 'poison'. As we have seen, for all his different approach to the subject, John Pocock argued that the Machiavellian moment did not come to England until the 1650s.

In reality, Machiavelli was more widely read, and even admired, than such

---

452. R. Chartier, *The Order of Books: Readers, Authors and Libraries between the Fourteenth and Eighteenth Centuries* (Cambridge, 1994), p. 12.

453. See above, pp. 225–8.

454. J. Wallace, 'Examples are Best Precepts: Readers and Meaning in Seventeenth-Century Poetry', *Critical Inquiry* 1 (1974), pp. 273–90, at p. 284.

455. F. Raab, *The English Face of Machiavelli* (1964), p. 90.

studies allow. Long before the published English translations, Machiavelli was read in English in manuscript, and, of course, by the learned in Latin and Italian. Indeed, though she refused a licence for editions of *The Prince* and *Discourses*, Queen Elizabeth permitted publication of English versions of the *History of Florence* and *The Art of War*. And significantly she made no attempt to ban the *reading* of *The Prince* or *Discourses*, which became the cult texts of students in the 1580s and 1590s.[456] From the page, Machiavelli, whatever the official anathema, entered the imagination of Englishmen, and from the stage, the imagination of those below the elite.[457] Doubtless his tenets shocked and disturbed readers, but shock and disturbance can often be the creative catalysts for new thought. Analysing the 'legitimising fictions to which any institutional exercise of power must ultimately appeal', Harold Love suggests that 'Machiavelli provided a recipe book from which new fictions could be generated.'[458]

There are hints even in the denunciation of him that Machiavelli was perceived to have generated such a new fiction, to have altered the script of state. Bacon regarded Livy as the best of historians, and admired Machiavelli's *History*.[459] *The Uncasing of Machiavel's Instructions* (1613) was ambivalent in its critique.[460] In his epistle to the reader of *The Prince*, Dacres acknowledged 'thou shall find him much practised by those that condemn him.'[461] And the author of *Modern Policies Taken from Machiavelli* (1652) concurred: 'wherever I come Machiavell is curs'd and damned, yet practically embraced and asserted.'[462] Loud denunciations are often testimony to the force of new ideas. And it may be that a concentration on the published critiques of Machiavelli underestimates his influence and appeal. What we need to consider is how Machiavelli was read, and what was the effect of reading him on men's interpretation of other texts and their world. Long before scholars had turned attention to Renaissance readers, Felix Raab suggested that what was important in understanding Machiavelli's influence was 'not Machiavelli's purpose but that of the reader relative to the political situation immediately before him'.[463] And from the late sixteenth century across Europe, and at home in England, the political situation of wars fought in the name of religion, deceitful and secret alliances, factional intrigues and court corruption must to many have appeared akin to the politics of the cinquecento city-states that Machiavelli had described.

456. Ibid., p. 52.
457. Marlowe's *Tamburlaine* and *Doctor Faustus* have deeply Machiavellian traits.
458. Love, *Scribal Publication*, pp. 160–1.
459. Bacon, *Advancement of Learning*, pp. 16, 85, 189.
460. On *The Uncasing of Machiavel's Instructions to his Son* (1613) see Sharpe, *Politics and Ideas*, pp. 27–8.
461. E. Dacres, *Nicholas Machiavel's Prince* (1640), epistle to the reader. Cf. Raab, *English Face of Machiavelli*, p. 100.
462. *Modern Policies Taken from Machiavelli* (1652, E1399/3), epistle dedicatory. Contrast *Anti Machiavell or Honesty Against Policy* (1647, E396/16), p. 2.
463. Raab, *English Face of Machiavelli*, p. 127.

Sir William Drake clearly read Machiavelli as an important text for his own times. Though he knew that some held the Florentine responsible for corrupting the world, Drake admired Machiavelli's counsels for personal, social and political behaviour and regarded him as a vital source of precepts.[464] Moreover, far from being most affronted, as Raab argues readers were, by Machiavelli's criticism of Christianity, it is to those passages we have seen Drake returning frequently. He appears sympathetic to Machiavelli's suggestion that Christianity may have fostered cowardice or dulled ambition, and he goes beyond Machiavelli in discussing the civic role of religion as the cement of order. If we study the writings of early modern England, especially if we do not read between the lines for the nervous anxieties they endeavoured to conceal, we might conclude that thinkers like Drake did not exist. A study of his reading, however, reveals an enthusiastic disciple and advocate of Machiavellian ideas. If the history of political thought is to give us a picture of how society and state were conceived, it must take on board not merely the canonical texts and public discourses of political thought – in which perhaps 'conservative' notions tend to predominate. It must address itself, as hitherto it has not, to the histories of reading and reception.

The history of reading offers more to the historian of politics than a better understanding of the influence of texts of political thought. It helps us to discern how contemporaries conceived of the social and began to think of the political domain and their own place in it. Modern critics have stressed the theatrical nature of Renaissance society and the importance of representation in the exercise of rule. And we are familiar with Queen Elizabeth and James I speaking of kings on a stage, performing before an audience of subjects. Francis Bacon saw 'so great an affinity' between 'fiction and belief'; and pamphleteers as well as playwrights frequently described the polity in the language of drama.[465] The author of *The Perfect Politician*, for example, outlined 'the main scope of this discourse', a life of Cromwell, as 'a continued series of tragical scenes with comical interludes'.[466] What Drake's notebooks open to us is a subject's own understanding of the drama of state, and the shifts in what it meant to him. As we have seen, William early on appeared ambivalent about the masks and mysteries of state. But while he saw through the artifice, the play, he also grasped the importance of all, especially rulers, acting roles: 'universus mundus exercet histrionem.' Drake's image of government as like a stage onto which a man might enter and strip the mask from the actor is taken from Erasmus's *Encomium*.[467] But his deployment of the conceit owed much to observation of a world in which he took it for granted that artifice and dissimulation were necessary for survival. We have a sense that after 1649, when the real tragedy of kingship was dramatically brought to its close on

464. Ogden MS 7/18 f. 15.
465. Bacon, *Advancement of Learning*, p. 30. Bacon here cites Tacitus.
466. *The Perfect Politician* (1660, E1869/1).
467. V. Khan, *Rhetoric, Prudence and Scepticism in the Renaissance* (Ithaca, 1985), p. 103; above, p. 222.

the scaffold, Drake was more inclined to *appreciate* the importance of the fictions of rule. Though he grasped, and to some extent shared, the utilitarianism of Hobbes's social and political analysis, Drake still seems to have desired that power be veiled and masked. He was perhaps an unusually incisive observer of his age. But from reading notes like Drake's (as well as diaries such as Whiteway's and Woodforde's) we may sense the subject's seemingly contradictory but simultaneous desire for the rational examination and mystical elevation of authority, and better understand the ambivalence of a Restoration settlement that sought both to humanise and resacralise the king's person.[468] A grasp of the subject's own observance of the theatre of society and state cannot but further enrich our own readings of the drama as representation of social and political practices, and as interrogation of those ambiguities and ambivalences.[469]

Drake's reading teaches us that politics was not just an activity but a type of consciousness. In the realm of European ideas, historians have charted a change in the meaning of 'politics' from 'the art of the founding and preserving just constitutions' to the 'knowledge of the means of preserving and enlarging a state'.[470] Such an argument holds if we pursue the shifts in political thought by moving, as does Professor Viroli, from Aristotle and Cicero and Ficino, to Machiavelli, Guicciardini and Botero. However, as Glenn Burgess rightly counsels, no adequate history of political ideas can be written 'simply on the basis of examining those works that we identify as belonging to the category "political writing"'.[471] Even those works themselves acted on different societies in different circumstances at different moments. In early modern England there was little theorising of constitution or state. But as Drake's notebooks powerfully demonstrate, there was a ferment of ideas – about not just government, kingship and authority, but about society, the individual, personal advancement and survival. Drake wrote no political theory, but his universe was thoroughly political, his imagination, we might say, fully politicised. Once we see that, we must acknowledge that all the texts and experiences that shape the imagination must be studied by historians of political ideas. And, in fine, we must appreciate that the imagination, the psyche, is itself a text of politics whose political history awaits investigation.

Drake's 'reading' of Civil War, republic and Restoration nicely underlines a larger point. We have remarked both that Sir William makes surprisingly few direct references to the events or arguments of the revolutionary years 1640–60, and yet the circumstances of revolution shaped his thoughts, his reading, his figuring of all texts. It may then be that the most important legacy

---

468. I shall explore this ambivalence in *Representing Rule: Images of Authority in Early Modern England*.

469. For one recent study of the drama as a site of cultural and political ambivalence, see N. Maguire, *Regicide and Restoration: English Tragicomedy, 1660–1671* (Cambridge, 1992).

470. M. Viroli, *From Politics to Reason of State: The Acquisition and Transformation of the Language of Politics, 1250–1600* (Cambridge, 1992), pp. 3, 53.

471. Burgess, 'Renaissance Texts', p. 7.

of Civil War to politics lay not only in events – battle and regicide – nor even in political ideas, whether those of Hobbes and Milton, or of Lilburne and Winstanley. What the Civil War did irrevocably was explicitly politicise the imaginations of English men and women in a way that brought politics more directly into social and personal life. Indeed one of the ironies of Civil War polemic (is it finally the irony of all propaganda?) is that, for all the attempts to direct and control the way subjects thought, such writings fostered the exercise of individual imagination and personal judgement. From the beginning of the pamphlet war, many texts staged debates and posed questions, bringing to print culture the dialogic genre and space of drama in which, in the end, the reader or auditor has to choose and perform.[472] More or less happily, the authors of texts invite readers to exercise judgement: as *The Shepherd's Oracle*, a reworking of Virgil's *Eclogues*, put it in a preface to the reader in 1644, 'Whosoever these lines were, Readers they are now yours.'[473]

As we have seen, Sharon Achinstein has argued that the Civil War parliamentary pamphleteers and especially Milton asked readers to 'become hermeneuts', so as to demystify and revolutionise politics.[474] Yet, in another way, the Royalists no less contributed to a politicising of the imagination and all the texts that shaped the imagination. For all its mystifying and brilliant polemic, the *Eikon Basilike* opens – or appears to open – the royal person, the king's conscience and emotions, to the subject's scrutiny and gaze. The text works not least through empathy and intimacy, through an emotional politics that is no less important than the politics of reason.[475] During the 1650s, as Earl Miner and Lois Potter have demonstrated, the Royalists appropriated allegory and romance as both encoded political communication and psychic consolation, explicitly politicising the fictions of self and state in the process.[476] And, Steven Zwicker has brilliantly argued, in a text such as Izaak Walton's *Compleat Angler*, nature and pleasure, relaxation and contemplation become political, indeed partisan, places and practices.[477] During the 1640s and 1650s, many feared that 'every fantasy' was occupied with matters of government and politics; and it was true in a literal as well as pejorative sense.[478] The images in the mind became more overtly politicised, and 'imaginings', fantasies, were more clearly seen, and in conservative quarters suspected, to

---

472. A high percentage of Thomason tracts raise questions, consider cases and stage (often as though a play text) debates.

473. *The Shepherd's Oracle Delivered in an Eclogue* (1644, E52/2), 'to the reader'.

474. Achinstein, *Milton*, p. 172.

475. This suggestion is now developed in E. Skerpan Wheeler's '*Eikon Basilike* and the Rhetoric of Self Representation', in T. Corns, ed., *The Royal Image: Representations of Charles I* (Cambridge, 1999), pp. 122–40.

476. E. Miner, *The Cavalier Mode: Jonson to Cotton* (1971); L. Potter, *Secret Rites and Secret Writing*.

477. Zwicker, *Lines of Authority*, ch. 3.

478. See *A Letter Intercepted* (1660, E1017/36), p. 2: 'every fantasy is occupied in the framing of government.'

be political terrain. Poems, plays, romances and pastorals would now more than ever be read as texts of state.

The initial impulse of those who made the Restoration settlement was to re-establish control – not just of the press and of writing but of interpretation itself. David Lloyd's *Eikon Basilike or The True Portraiture of . . . Charles II* (1660) proposed that four books might be bestowed on each church providing an official explanation of the origins, course and calamaties of Civil War and the glories of Restoration.[479] Arguments that printing had been the downfall of Charles I, turning ordinary subjects into 'statists', and filling 'the brains of the people with so many contrary opinions', led to proposals by Sir Roger L'Estrange for a strict regulation of the press.[480] In 1674, a proclamation to restrain the spreading of false news threatened punishment of those who heard as well as disseminated such news.[481] In addition, the production of an official organ in 1666, *The Current Intelligence*, 'published by authority', attempted to manage the news in a manner favourable to the government. Words, texts and their interpretation were seen to be unstable and destabilising. It was for political as much as intellectual reasons that the Royal Society took as its motto 'nullius in verba', and that one of its leading fellows, John Wilkins, in his *Essay Towards a Real Character and a Philosophical Language* endeavoured 'the clearing of some of our modern differences' by careful control of language.[482]

Such efforts and gestures, of course, bear witness to the fact that interpretation could not be controlled. Despite all the attempts to unify and heal divisions and to elevate and mystify monarchy, some recognised, as did the author of *Speculum Politiae*, that 'we are cast into a war-like world, where the pen itself cannot be exempted from skirmishings.'[483] All genres of writing, politicised during the Civil Wars, continued to be appropriated and contested for partisan ends. And very soon after the initial euphoria over Restoration, the Civil War itself became a contested text, that taught different readers different lessons about the present state and future course of government. Those who had experienced the war had formed their own judgements, read events in the light of their own knowledge and values, and some would not, as the author of *A Brief Chronicle of the Late Intestine War* feared, simply dismiss the revolution as an evil or interlude of darkness.[484]

As the realisation dawned that, whatever Hobbes's desire, there could be no sovereign hermeneutics, no single authorised interpretation of texts and

---

479. D. Lloyd, *Eikon Basilike or The True Portraiture of . . . Charles II* (1660, E1922/2), epistle dedicatory. See also *God Save the King* (1660), 'to the unprejudiced reader'.
480. See R. Atkyns, *The Original and Growth of Printing* (1664); R. L'Estrange, *Considerations and Proposals in Order to the Regulation of the Press* (1664).
481. *A Proclamation to Restrain the Spreading of False News, 2 May 1674.*
482. Achinstein, *Milton*, p. 99; J. Wilkins, *An Essay Towards a Real Character and a Philosophical Language* (1668), epistle dedicatory.
483. *Speculum Politiae or England's Mirror* (1660), 'to the reader'.
484. *A Brief Chronicle of the Late Intestine War* (1663), 'to the reader'.

events, a new intellectual and political culture was born.[485] J. Heath, who reported the *Glories and Magnificent Triumphs of the Blessed Restitution of His Majesty*, knew that it was 'not in the power of reason or force of words to charm . . . subjects into . . . veneration of their princes', but hoped spectacle might still awe them.[486] Others felt, however, that the common people interpreted for themselves images no less than words, and a spate of publications demystifying the 'charms' and arts of painting and emblems appeared to bear him out.[487] Even the texts of high culture were opened to critical debate and evaluation. As the author of *Reflections on Aristotle's De Poetica* put it, once there would have been few critics of such a work, 'but now this privilege, whatever extraordinary talent it requires, is usurped by the most ignorant.'[488] Recognising that the Civil War had opened all authorities, cultural and political, to judgement, the ninth edition of Owen Feltham's popular *Resolves* was presented 'all to every man's just liberty, to approve or dislike as he pleases'.[489]

Indeed some began to maintain that personal judgement and difference – over politics as well as aesthetics – were neither surprising nor destructive. In his powerful argument against Harrington, *Monarchy Asserted*, Matthew Wren informed his readers that different readings of past and present circumstances were no more than different points of view:

That Mr Harrington who undertakes to vindicate the reason of popular government and I who have professed myself a friend to monarchy should from the observation of the same natural causes and of the same actions in history form different judgements is no more a wonder than that two men viewing the same object by various lights should judge it to be of various colours.[490]

Fifteen years later, Matthew Clifford overturned all the conventional wisdom by arguing against 'submitting our judgments to authority' and for the exercise of individual reason: 'There cannot certainly in the world', he posited,

---

485. As Manguel puts it: 'Absolute power requires that all reading be official reading', *A History of Reading*, p. 283.

486. J. Heath, *The Glories and Magnificent Triumphs of the Blessed Restitution of His Majesty Charles II* (1662), 'to the reader'.

487. See, for example, R. F. de Sieur de Chambray, *An Idea of the Perfection of Painting* (1668) which spoke of common people judging art. See too W. Faithorne, *The Art of Graving and Etching* (1662); J. Evelyn, *Sculptura: Or the History and Art of Chalcography* (1662); *The Excellency of the Pen and Pencil* (1668). The relationship of changed attitudes to aesthetics and politics is also manifest in the emergence of the 'Instructions to a Painter' genre. I shall be exploring this subject in *Representing Rule*.

488. R. Rapin, *Reflections on Aristotle's De Poetica* (1674), sig. A3.

489. O. Feltham, *Resolves* (1670), 'to the reader'.

490. M. Wren, *Monarchy Asserted* (1659), 'to the reader'. We recall that Drake annotated this text, Ogden MS 7/12 f. 22.

'be found out so mild and so peaceable a doctrine as that which permits a difference in beliefs; for what occasion can any man take to begin a quarrel when both he himself is suffered . . . to enjoy his own opinion, and his own opinion is this, that he ought to suffer others to do the same.'[491] Hopes of unity, especially in religion, Clifford starkly put it, were gone. God, he came to think, had intended that the Scriptures should be interpreted differently, so it was unsurprising that there were 'diverse receptions of it'.[492] Men constructed their faith and beliefs from their own interpretation and judgement. Truth, he radically concluded, should not be imposed or sought outside of the self: 'we must seek it in the centre and heart of ourselves . . .'[493]

Clifford's language, as well as hermeneutic theory, leads us back to the subject to which Drake's notebooks and the study of reading direct us: the constitution, and politics, of the self. The history of the self is a difficult subject: at times one despairingly suspects that the self emerges in all periods, just as the middle class always rises. Certainly there was a strong self-consciousness in the classical world, but Stephen Greenblatt is right to argue that Christianity 'brought a growing suspicion of man's power to shape identity', a subjugation, if not denial, of self.[494] By contrast, in Greenblatt's famous title, the age of humanism, the sixteenth and seventeenth centuries in England, was a period of conscious self-fashioning, a period of 'an increased self-consciousness about the fashioning of human identity as a manipulable artful process'.[495] Not all Greenblatt's followers have been as sensitive as he to the ambiguities of that self-fashioning: that (as the self always is) it was constituted by and in an intensely social sphere, indeed in a social drama in which 'selves' played roles. The early modern 'self', and the identity of the self in early modern England, was a social and political phenomenon, one that needs to be further studied by social and political history. Francis Bacon conventionally compared the government of the mind to that of the state, and took poetry and history as the best texts for studying the affections.[496] The need for regulation of the appetites by the reason was a persistent theme of educational treatises and courtesy literature. Sir William Drake, as we have seen, was obsessed with ordering and 'fashioning' himself. But what his notebooks reveal is a man for whom regulation of the self was not a subordination of self and self-interest to a wider public order or good, but the means to advance the self, to take advantage of others and occasions, to equip the self as a force, a power, in a competitive world.

491. M. Clifford, *A Treatise of Human Reason* (1675), p. 10.
492. Ibid., pp. 38–9.
493. Ibid., p. 6. Compare A. Roper: 'men were much exercised by the question of whether authors or readers should take responsibility for meanings', 'Drawing Parallels and Making Applications in Restoration Literature', in R. Ashcroft and A. Roper, *Politics as Reflected in Literature* (Los Angeles, 1989), p. 51.
494. S. Greenblatt, *Renaissance Self-Fashioning: From More to Shakespeare* (Chicago, 1980), p. 2.
495. Ibid.
496. Bacon, *Advancement of Learning*, p. 164.

Students of diaries and private journals have argued that the writing of a diary became a site of self-consciousness, helping to forge the self as an independent agent, able to interpret and act on the world.[497] At first it might seem that the keeping of commonplace notebooks worked in quite another way: to subordinate the self to, or constitute the self from, received wisdom. In *Framing Authority*, a study of 'Self and Society in Sixteenth-Century England', Mary Crane writes of 'a subjectivity' that was 'gathered and framed by a common body of aphoristic wisdom'.[498] Yet, we have suggested, no less than the diary, the selection, arrangement and deployment of commonplaces could be, and in Drake's case clearly was, the means for a development of the self as a critical social observer. As Bacon put it, the marking of passages in books and gathering of commonplaces was not just for public debate 'but likewise to minister unto our judgement to conclude *aright within ourselves*'.[499] We need to reconsider the commonplace book as a place where the early modern self emerged from contemplation of the exemplary codes and figures – the place where individuals came to exercise, and ultimately valorise, their 'judgement', and in doing so transformed the culture of politics.

That, of course, is to assert that the self was made through reading, that 'we are what we read.' Theorists of reading have argued that the process of construing meaning from texts 'also entails the possibility that we may formulate ourselves', and to most modern intellectuals the argument is intrinsically persuasive.[500] Moreover there is testimony to such a process from the past. In his *Confessions*, Jean-Jacques Rousseau revealed: 'I don't know how I learned to read. I only remember my first readings and their effect on me; it is from that time that I date my consciousness of self.'[501] In this respect, the Romantic revolution is often seen as the period of transition. As Jane Tompkins put it, Renaissance literature sought a public response, the modern, post-Romantic writer anticipates an individual response.[502] Though there is something to this as a narrative of reading and identity, the argument needs to be refined. The cultivation of sensibility and emotional response in readers may be an eighteenth-century story. But it is not the only story about reading and self-consciousness.[503] As several scholars have observed, for Montaigne

497. Boucier, *Les Journaux privés*, p. 31.
498. Crane, *Framing Authority*, p. 137.
499. Bacon, *Advancement of Learning*, p. 123, my italics.
500. Manguel, *A History of Reading*, p. 173; J. Tompkins, *Reader Response Criticism: From Formalism to Post Structuralism* (Baltimore, 1980), p. xv, citing Iser. See too C. Belsey, *Critical Practice* (1980), p. 89.
501. Quoted in Darnton, *Great Cat Massacre*, p. 221. See too N. Holland, 'Recovering the "Purloined Letter": Reading as a Personal Transaction', in S. R. Suleiman and I. Crosman, eds, *The Reader in the Text* (Princeton, 1980), pp. 350–70.
502. J. Tompkins, 'The Reader in History: The Changing Shape of Literary Response', in Tompkins, *Reader Response Criticism*, p. 210.
503. Cf. M. Ferguson: 'the [Renaissance] reader is not only allowed but encouraged to master any secular, literary authority in order to serve his . . . "self-interest"', *Trials of Desire: Renaissance Defences of Poetry* (New Haven, 1983), p. 158.

writing and reading were 'a progress of self-knowledge';[504] and Montaigne, in his essays, invited the reader 'to constitute himself as a subject through the act of reading'.[505]

Sir William Drake, I have argued, readily took up the invitation to constitute himself as a subject – that is as a political agent with capacity to understand the pyschology of power and to formulate his own political thought. But, I would suggest, he constituted himself too as a 'subject' in another sense, as a thinking and feeling entity, an ego, a 'conscious self', and as an entity to be so conceived; and he did so through writing and reading.[506] Drake's notes may be just one *individual* case study in reading politics. But not least in demonstrating the reader's constitution of self, he urges us to give the history of reading – well, at least a chapter in the history of politics.

---

504. Khan, *Rhetoric, Prudence and Scepticism*, p. 127; cf. Hampton, *Writing from History*, pp. xi, 301; R. L. Regosin, *The Matter of My Book: Montaigne's Essays as the Book of the Self* (Berkeley, 1977), p. 95.

505. Cave, 'Mimesis of Reading', p. 159.

506. See D. R. Olson, *The World on Paper: The Conceptual and Cognitive Implications of Writing and Reading* (Cambridge, 1994), esp. ch. 8.

Afterword: Possibilities

Sir William Drake was a figure of note in his locality but made only a relatively small mark on the history of the nation. It might then seem inappropriate to make too large a claim for his importance in our understanding of early modern England, let alone of history or our approach to history more broadly conceived. Yet I would suggest that his example may both lead to our rethinking the early modern past and offer fruitful possibilities for our historical method.

Traditional political history has often been criticised for its preoccupation with high politics – kings, queens and privileged elites. Social historians, in particular advocates of 'history from below', have ably demonstrated that 'our identity has not been formed purely by monarchs, prime ministers and generals'; but, as Jim Sharpe regretfully acknowledges, such studies have not yet redefined the main narratives.[1] Indeed, too often the histories and historiographies of elites and lower orders remain separate. More recently, a group of scholars has endeavoured to broaden the focus from the exercise to the 'experience of authority', to explore the 'negotiations between dominant ideologies . . . and those subordinate to them'.[2] Authority, the editors of a recent collection of essays posit, consisted of a broad matrix of discourses and practices which were disseminated, negotiated, 'interpreted' and 'reinterpreted'.[3] The written word that lay at the centre of early modern authority, they argue, could be 'a territory of multiple meanings'. Whatever the desires embedded in the governors' scripts, they were 'appropriated and reinterpreted in the acts of reception'.[4] Yet despite this opening recognition of the importance of reception, no essay in the volume takes up directly the question of how authority was read.

Sir William Drake was not one of the lower orders, and notebooks such as his, rare for his own class, are not likely to be found for any below the

---

1. See J. Sharpe, 'History from Below', in P. Burke, ed., *New Perspectives on Historical Writing* (Oxford, 1991), p. 37.
2. A. Fox, P. Griffiths and S. Hindle, eds, *The Experience of Authority in Early Modern England* (Houndmills, 1996).
3. Ibid., pp. 1–3 and passim.
4. Ibid., p. 5.

middling orders. But what his case invites is a recognition that authority is 'experienced', negotiated and critiqued not only in the institutions of mano-rial courts or the cultural practices of the parish, but in the study, on the page and in the mind. The history of reading belongs in the master narrative of the history of politics. It opens what we too narrowly delineate as the 'political' to subjects that early modern historians have marginalised or rejected as political performances: the negotiations with texts, hermeneutics, personal identity and the psychology of power.

For Drake, who spent much of the 1640s overseas, the experience of the English Revolution was predominantly textual: he received letters and infor-mation, and he read contemporary treatises, and reread ancient histories. His experience of authority and his reconstitution of conventional political values was a textual practice; and what we as historians can know about him comes almost entirely from those textual practices. His case may then not only illus-trate what critics, alienating traditional historians, have called the textuality or discursiveness of Renaissance culture; he leads us to see that, without an appreciation of the textuality of early modern culture, we may have a limited grasp of the history of power and politics themselves.[5]

Drake did not regard his texts as truths. While he respected and concurred with some writers more than others, his criteria of value were those writers who spoke most meaningfully, that is most usefully, to him. To some extent, we as readers, and as historians, cannot but do the same. For all the proper and important rules of our discipline, when we return to the past we ask questions prompted by our present concerns – recently questions about family and gender, about race – yes, about reading. And the 'documents' we study, the 'evidence', are open to our questions and our values because they too do not yield 'truths' about the past; because they also offer representations, textual mediations of experience which we must, as Drake did, 'read' if we are to make any sense of them. To recognise the 'textuality of history', of both our documents and our own practices, to be conscious about our own 'reading', and the 'constructed, rhetorical nature of our knowledge of the past', is not to be nihilistic or to 'reduce' what historians do.[6] Rather it is to see that, in theorising our own practice, we might helpfully shift attention from the writing of history to questions about the reading of the texts of history, and to the strategies and experiences we bring to texts – as individuals as well as 'historians'.

Though the rules and conventions of our discipline, like those of Renais-sance pedagogy, direct our studies, though the texts/documents we investigate try to determine what we take from them, our other readings, our experi-ences, our conversations and values shape how we read and interpret them.

---

5. Cf. above, pp. 25–6.
6. H. Kellner, 'Language and Historical Representation', in K. Jenkins, ed., *The Post-modern History Reader* (1997), p. 134.

All texts 'represent situated uses of language';[7] Drake's readings of his texts are early modern situations, just as mine of his is situated in a late twentieth-century moment. If theories of text and reception have helped me to understand the importance of Drake's readings and notebooks, it may be that his 'archive' also makes us less uncomfortable with some textual theorising of our own discipline.[8] If we leave a study of Drake, as we began it, thinking more about questions of text, meaning and reception, in the present and the past, we may be able to escape the methodological wars that have begun to rage around us. We may bring together the historical archive and new critical perspectives, even begin to reconcile 'history' and 'theory', and so rewrite as well as reread our subject.

7. G. Spiegel, 'History, Histories and the Social Logic of the Text in the Middle Ages', *Speculum* (1990), pp. 59–86, at p. 77.
8. Cf. A. Johns' comment that historians 'need to be more aware than hitherto of the historical specificity of their own reading practices', *The Nature of the Book* (Chicago, 1998). This book appeared after mine was written but in a different way adds powerfully to the case for attention to readings in the past and present.

Index

NOTE: Where surnames only have been used by Drake, possible forenames appear preceded by a question mark in parentheses. Page numbers followed by *n* indicate information is to be found in a footnote.